P9-CPY-468

The Netherlands

Neal Bedford
Simon Sellars

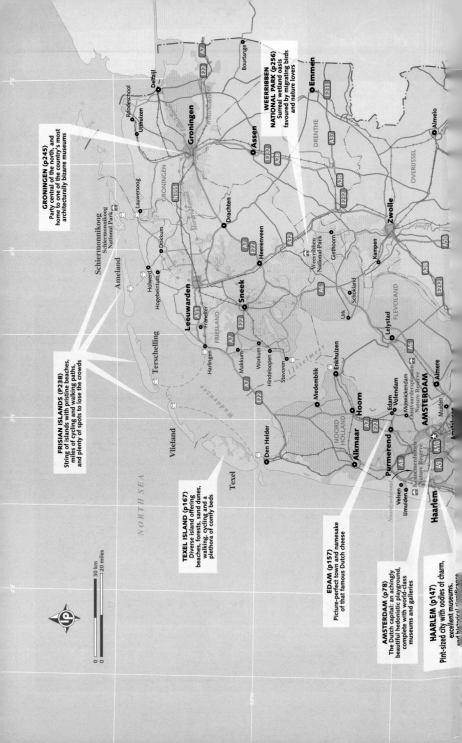

GRONINGEN (p245)
Party central of the north, and home to one of the country's most architecturally bizarre museums

WEERRIBBEN NATIONAL PARK (p256)
Surreal wetland oasis favoured by migrating birds and nature lovers

FRISIAN ISLANDS (P238)
String of islands with pristine beaches, miles of cycling and walking paths, and plenty of spots to lose the crowds

TEXEL ISLAND (p167)
Diverse island offering beaches, forests, sand dunes, walking, cycling and a plethora of comfy beds

EDAM (p157)
Picture-perfect town and namesake of that famous Dutch cheese

AMSTERDAM (p78)
The Dutch capital: an achingly beautiful hedonistic playground, complete with world-class museums and galleries

HAARLEM (p147)
Pint-sized city with oodles of charm, excellent museums,

NORTH SEA

Schiermonnikoog
Schiermonnikoog National Park

Ameland

Terschelling

Vlieland

Texel

Den Helder

Alkmaar

Purmerend

Velsen
IJmuiden

Haarlem

AMSTERDAM

Muiden

Almere

Lelystad

FLEVOLAND

Urk

Schokland

Kampen

Zwolle

OVERIJSSEL

A50

E232

A28

Emmen

Almelo

DRENTHE

A37

Assen

A28
E232

Groningen

GRONINGEN

Drachten

Heerenveen

Sneek

Leeuwarden

FRIESLAND

Franeker

Harlingen

Makkum

Workum

Hindeloopen

Stavoren

Medemblik

Enkhuizen

Hoorn

Edam
Volendam

Monnickendam

Oostvaardersplassen
Nature Reserve

Kennemerduinen
Nature Reserve

Noord-
zeekanaal

NOORD HOLLAND

Giethoorn

Weerribben
National Park

A6

A32

A7
E22

A7

A7
E22

A6

A8

A9

A10

A7

A31

N355

E22
A7

Bourtange

Delfzijl

Roodeschool

Uithuizen

Lauwersoog

Dokkum

Holwerd

Hogebeintum

A7

0   30 km
0   20 miles

5°E   6°E   7°E

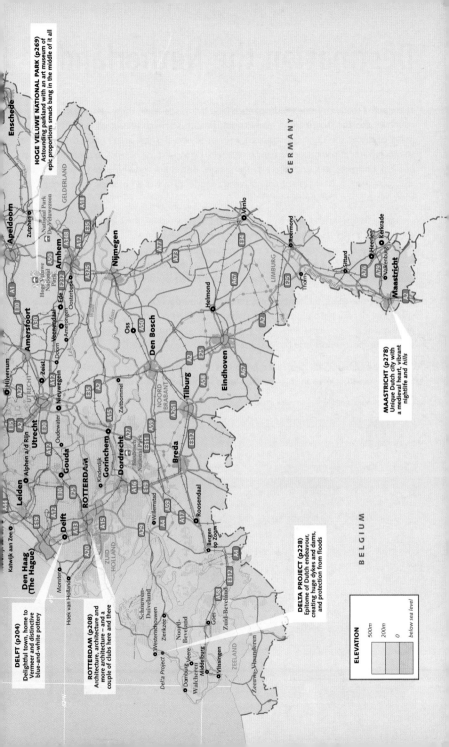

DELFT (p204)
Delightful town, home to
Vermeer and distinctive
blue-and-white pottery

ROTTERDAM (p208)
Architecture, architecture and
more architecture – and a
couple of clubs here and there

DELTA PROJECT (p228)
Epitome of Dutch endeavour,
creating huge dykes and dams,
and protection from floods

HOGE VELUWE NATIONAL PARK (p269)
Astounding parkland with an art museum of
epic proportions smack bang in the middle of it all

MAASTRICHT (p278)
Unique Dutch city with
a medieval heart, vibrant
nightlife and *hills*

GERMANY

BELGIUM

ELEVATION

500m
200m
0
below sea level

Enschede

Apeldoorn

Arnhem

Nijmegen

Zutphen

Hoge Veluwe
National Park

National Park
De Veluwezoom

GELDERLAND

Venlo

Roermond

LIMBURG

Sittard

Thorn

Heerlen

Kerkrade

Valkenburg

Maastricht

Helmond

Oss

Den Bosch

Eindhoven

Tilburg

NOORD
BRABANT

Breda

Roosendaal

Bergen
op Zoom

Goes

Zuid-Beveland

Noord-
Beveland

Middelburg

Vlissingen

Veere

Domburg

Westenschouwen

Schouwen-
Duiveland

Zierikzee

Delta Project

Zeeuws-Vlaanderen

ZEELAND

Willemstad

Dordrecht

Gorinchem

Kinderdijk

Biesbosch
National Park

Zaltbommel

Gouda

Oudewater

Alphen a/d Rijn

Utrecht

UTRECHT

Zeist

Nieuwegein

Leiden

Delft

Den Haag
(The Hague)

Monster

Hoek van Holland

Katwijk aan Zee

ROTTERDAM

Amersfoort

Hilversum

Ede

Veenendaal

Doorn

Amerongen

Oosterbeek

Doorwerth

Naarden

Destination the Netherlands

There aren't many countries with so much land below sea level. There aren't many – if any – countries this flat. There aren't many countries with so much reclaimed land. There aren't many countries this densely populated, and yet so liberal. There aren't many countries with so much water and wind, or so many boats, sails, bikes, birds, dykes, polders, windmills, flowers, fish, bridges, cafés, cheese – and tall people. And there certainly aren't many countries who can claim such a vibrant colour (vivid orange in this case) as their own. Simply put, there is no place like the Netherlands.

Start with the Dutch cities. Who hasn't heard of Amsterdam, the capital of culture, coffeeshops and canals? Its mesmerising beauty is hard to overestimate, and yet a surfeit of stunning metropoles are only hours, or even minutes, away by train. Haarlem, Edam, Groningen, Rotterdam, Utrecht, Den Haag, Leiden, Delft, Deventer, Breda, Maastricht – the list seems endless, a mind-boggling concept considering the size of this small nation.

Outside the cities, the Netherlands once again borders on over-achievement. Its bucolic splendour of national parks and sheep-patrolled polders is perfectly complimented by shimmering lakes, sandy coastlines, and a chain of windswept islands. Best of all, it can all be seen from the comfort of a bicycle seat.

As we've already said, there's no place like the Netherlands. But don't take our word for it; come join the Dutch in their *gezellig* ways – you won't be disappointed.

FRANS LEMM

Highlights

Admire the ingenuity and beauty of traditional gabled buildings (p55) in Amsterdam

Tulips blaze against a gorgeous blue sky at Keukenhof gardens (p195), Zuid Holland

OTHER HIGHLIGHTS

- Explore the glistening lakes and canals near Sneek (p235), Friesland
- Treat yourself to a coffee at a unique below-street-level canalside café in Utrecht City (p179), Utrecht
- Wander the 1000-year-old dunes of Kennemerduinen Nature Reserve (p152), Noord Holland

Multihued farmland stretches to the horizon in Flevoland (p174)

ELLIOT DANIEL

A beverage can be accompanied by an unusual garnish in Amsterdam's coffeshops (p44)

The face of Vincent Van Gogh (p40) adorns a tram in Amsterdam

MARTIN MOOS

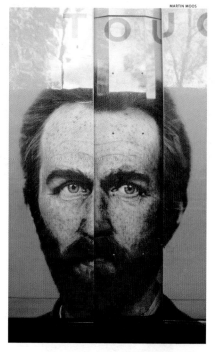

OTHER HIGHLIGHTS

- Stroll the strong defences of fortified Bourtange (p251), Groningen
- Track down prehistoric burial chambers, known as *hunebedden* (p253), in Groningen and Drenthe
- Experience the Netherlands' nautical past at Hindeloopen (p237), Friesland
- Marvel at the cultural charm of Haarlem (p147), Noord Holland

This Art Nouveau newspaper office is but one striking edifice in Groningen City (p245), Groningen

LEANNE LOGAN

A modern-day tulip admirer (p27) photographs fields in bloom near the Keukenhof gardens, Zuid Holland

Go north to verdant Friesland (p230), home to the Frisian dairy cow

Traditional sailing boats race near Volendam (p156), Noord Holland

FRANS LEMMENS

Crisscrossed by canals, reminders of the region's former location on the shore of the Zuiderzee, Overijssel (p256) is best explored by boat

OTHER HIGHLIGHTS

- Experience the splendid isolation of the windswept Frisian Islands (p238), Friesland
- Cycle or stroll around pretty Texel (p167), largest and most popular of Noord Holland's Wadden Islands
- Set sail on the IJsselmeer in a classic Dutch ship, the *botter* (p155)

The gentle hills of Limburg (p278) – a precious rarity in the Netherlands – are a walker's paradise

FRANS LEMMENS

Enjoy some wide-open space along the coast of Zuid Holland (p190)

TAMSIN WILSON

Contents

Regional Map Contents

Friesland p231

Groningen & Drenthe p245

Noord Holland & Flevoland p146

Amsterdam pp86-7

Overijssel & Gelderland p256

Utrecht p179

Zuid Holland & Zeeland p190

Noord Brabant & Limburg p272

The Authors

NEAL BEDFORD
Coordinating Author, Front chapters, Noord Holland & Flevoland, Friesland, Groningen & Drenthe, Directory, Transport

Neal's first memory of the Netherlands occurred early in childhood – a postcard, sent by his father's former work colleague on his return to his native land, showed a middle-aged Dutchman in solid yellow shoes with no laces plugging a leaking dyke with his butt. Neal found the Dutch not only instantly funny but also highly practical. Since then, he's left his homeland of New Zealand and settled in Europe, which has offered ample opportunity to travel to the Netherlands in search of bottom-plugged dykes. He's yet to find one, but hopes to on his future jaunts to this wonderful country.

Neal's Favourite Trip

It's a given but still has to be said – **Amsterdam** (p78) is the place to begin any trip to the Netherlands. After a few days wallowing in culture and hedonism, I'd slowly make my way north through **Edam** (p157) and on to **Alkmaar** (p159; timing it just right for the cheese market), before settling into a bit of island hopping – first **Texel** (p167), then **Vlieland** (p239) and on to **Ameland** (p241). While I'm up north, it would be rude not to stop into **Groningen** (p245) to enjoy all the city has to offer, but then the south would beckon. First **Den Haag** (p195), then **Rotterdam** (p208), and on to Middelburg and the **Delta Project** (p228), after which I'd end my travels in **Maastricht** (p278) with my feet up, enjoying a fine Trappist beer and a bit of *gezelligheid*.

SIMON SELLARS
Amsterdam, Utrecht, Zuid Holland & Zeeland, Overijssel & Gelderland, Noord Brabant & Limburg

A few years ago, when Simon worked in London, he took the opportunity to visit the Netherlands on a number of occasions, for he's been fascinated by the country ever since he was old enough to fashion his own Dutch oven. He can't forgive the Dutch for killing off the dodo, although the phenomenon of Johan Cruyff and Total Football went some way to making up for it. Simon wishes Paul Verhoeven would stop mucking about and make another dystopian sci-fi blockbuster, preferably starring Rutger Hauer.

LONELY PLANET AUTHORS

Why is our travel information the best in the world? It's simple: our authors are independent, dedicated travellers. They don't research using just the internet or phone, and they don't take freebies in exchange for positive coverage. They travel widely, to all the popular spots and off the beaten track. They personally visit thousands of hotels, restaurants, cafés, bars, galleries, palaces, museums and more – and they take pride in getting all the details right, and telling it how it is. For more, see the authors section on www.lonelyplanet.com.

Getting Started

The Netherlands is an exceedingly user-friendly place to visit. Up-to-date information is plentiful, almost every Dutch person speaks decent English, transport links are swift, and there's an abundance of sights and activities. All this means you can add a fair amount of spontaneity to your trip.

That said, a bit of foresight is helpful to pinpoint sights that match your interests, and to get the timing right – the bulb fields aren't much to look at before the blossoms open. It's also advisable to think about accommodation beforehand, as Amsterdam's best (and sometimes worst) hotels book up months in advance, and other towns may have limited sleeping options.

WHEN TO GO

The Netherlands has a typical maritime climate, with cool winters and mild summers, so any time is a good time to visit. Be prepared for blustery and changeable weather, however, and only a handful of sunny days in summer – although global warming may be changing that. Precipitation (79cm a year) is spread rather evenly over the calendar, and spring is marked by short, violent showers.

See Climate, p289, for more information.

Like much of Europe, the high season runs from June to August, which is known for its hot, sticky spells but isn't quite the Riviera shown in some tourist brochures. Hordes of tourists pulse through the Netherlands at this time, but these are the best months to sit on the canals drinking and chatting. Many Dutch take a summer holiday, and the last July weekend is deadly for traffic. You may be surrounded by other foreigners in August, but the month is crammed with events – see p291.

Mid-March to May and September to mid-October are the shoulder seasons. Spring is wonderful, as the bulbs are in bloom – April for daffodils, May for tulips. Easter is busy in Amsterdam, but if you can visit during Koninginnedag (30 April, see p291) it's worth fighting the crowds. Early October with its Indian summer can be an excellent time to come.

As the temperature drops, so does the number of tourists – things are calmest from mid-October to mid-March. Museums are quiet and you can mingle with the 'real' Dutch in cosy pubs around this time. Accommodation is also relatively cheap (except around New Year), though some hotels might be closed. The winter months (December to February) see periods of slushy snow and temperatures close to freezing.

School holidays are staggered according to region but fall around mid-February, early May, July and August, and the end of October (see p292).

HOW MUCH?

1L gas/petrol €1.40

1½L bottled water €0.80

Glass of Heineken €2.50

Souvenir T-shirt €15

Size 37 plain/painted clogs €17.50/20.50

Kibbeling snack €3

Cinema ticket €7.50

One hour of parking (Amsterdam) €3.50

2/15 strip card €1.60/6.70

Day's bike hire €6-10

COSTS & MONEY

The Netherlands really isn't a budget buy, but neither is it the most expensive European destination. If you're happy eating chips, sleeping in hostels and walking around, it's possible to hang in the country for around €35 per day. Those who prefer a couple of solid meals a day, a comfy bed with private facilities and travelling by public transport are looking at €80 per day as a starting point. Things start to feel comfortable on €110 per day. Add between €5 and €10 to each category when in Amsterdam.

There are a lot of free activities to stretch your budget, especially in Amsterdam in summer, and discount passes like the Museumkaart and the Amsterdam Pass (p290) can save loads on admission. The first Sunday of the month is free at many museums, the Concertgebouw holds lunchtime concerts for free and some restaurants have cheaper kiddie meals.

TRAVEL LITERATURE

My 'Dam Life by Sean Condon is a witty and hilarious true-life tale of three years in the Dutch capital, where the Australian and his wife spend much of their time looking for work and trying to define the Dutch character. It's an excellent read for anyone contemplating a trip (or a move) to the Netherlands.

Xenophobe's Guide to the Dutch by Rodney Bolt takes an irreverent look at all things Dutch and strikes a fine balance between humour and truth. A quick, fun read.

The Dutch, I Presume? by Martijn de Rooi, Jurjen Drenth and friends is another book attempting to explain the peculiarities of the Dutch psyche, and their love affair with windmills, wooden shoes and shelf toilets. It has more facts than insights, but it's still an interesting read and the photos are inspired.

Amsterdam: A Traveler's Literary Companion (edited by Manfred Wolf) is a collection of 20 short stories by Amsterdam writers, including Harry Mulisch, Cees Nooteboom, Marga Minco and Bas Heijne. The tales delve into a side of the capital that is rarely seen by tourists. The anthology contains highly readable prose, and it's accessible even for armchair travellers.

The UnDutchables by Colin White and Laurie Boucke takes a humorous look at Dutch life, from language and transport to child-rearing and social habits. Sometimes it's spot-on and sometimes it's so wide of the mark it becomes slapstick.

Amsterdam by Geert Mak interweaves tales of ordinary citizens with the bigger picture of cultural, social and economic history. It also delves into the Dutch psyche: for instance, why the Dutch eschew nationalism for business reasons.

Girl with a Pearl Earring by Tracy Chevalier, made into a major Hollywood film, is a tale of duty and sexuality and offers a peek into life in Delft during the Golden Age, and that of painter Jan Vermeer.

The Acid House by Irvine Welsh is a collection of gritty short stories, some of which are set in Amsterdam's drug underworld. While it's not for everyone, it's a good read and a sample of life beyond the capital's touristy façade.

DON'T LEAVE HOME WITHOUT...

- ▪ Checking the visa situation
- ▪ Travel insurance
- ▪ Passport/EU papers
- ▪ 220V converter for European plugs
- ▪ Ear plugs to counteract fellow hotel guests and street noise
- ▪ Cholesterol meter (*frites!*)
- ▪ Good jacket and scarf
- ▪ Appreciation for flowers
- ▪ Open mind to drugs, sex and Dutch honesty/bluntness
- ▪ Taste for bad '80s music, because you won't be able to escape it
- ▪ Quick reflexes to avoid cyclists and dodge dog doo-doo

TOP TENS

Our Favourite Festivals & Events

The Dutch have a penchant for celebrating, and some of the biggest and best festivals and events are listed below. See p291 for a full list of festivals in the Netherlands.

- Carnaval (Limburg, Noord Brabant, Gelderland) February/March (p291)
- Koninginnedag (Queen's Day) 30 April (p291)
- Nationale Molendag (National Mill Day) May (p291)
- Oerol (Terschelling) June (p240)
- Holland Festival (Amsterdam) June (p116)
- North Sea Jazz Festival (Rotterdam) mid-July (p214)
- Gay Pride Canal Parade (Amsterdam) August (p105)
- Grachtenfestival (Amsterdam) August (p117)
- Cannabis Cup (Amsterdam) November (p118)
- Sinterklaas (National) 5 December (p291)

Must-See Films

Dutch cinema has breached the upper echelons of world film with the following highly recommended releases:

- *Spoorloos* (*The Vanishing*, 1988) Director: George Sluizer
- *Turks Fruit* (*Turkish Delight*, 1973) Director: Paul Verhoeven
- *06* (1994) Director: Theo van Gogh
- *Karakter* (*Character*, 1997) Director: Mike van Diem
- *Antonia* (*Antonia's Line*, 1995) Director: Marleen Gorris
- *Abel* (1986) Director: Alex van Warmerdam
- *De Vierde Man* (*The Fourth Man*, 1983) Director: Paul Verhoeven
- *Amsterdam, Global Village* (1996) Director: Johan van der Keuken
- *Fanfare* (1958) Director: Bert Haanstra
- *Father and Daughter* (2000) Director: Michael Dudok de Wit

Memorable Museums

The Netherlands is peppered with exceptional museums. The following are some of our most beloved:

- Kröller-Müller Museum (p269)
- Rijksmuseum (p106)
- Van Gogh Museum (p106)
- Mauritshuis (p197)
- Frans Hals Museum (p149)
- Nederlands Architectuur Instituut (p211)
- Museum Boijmans van Beuningen (p209)
- Groninger Museum (p246)
- Nederlands Scheepvaartmuseum (p109)
- Zuiderzeemuseum (p164)

INTERNET RESOURCES

British Library (www.bl.uk/collections/wider/dutchinternetres2.html) Authoritative lists of links for Dutch and Flemish history, politics and culture.

Dutch Ministry of Foreign Affairs (www.minbuza.nl) Wealth of background facts and information, but not officious.

Dutch Tourism Board (www.holland.com) Attractions, cultural articles and loads of practical stuff hiding amongst the PR.

Expatica (www.expatica.com/holland) Entertaining all-round guide to life in the Netherlands, with daily news and listings.

Learn Dutch (www.learndutch.org) Online Dutch course for those keen to learn the language.

Lonely Planet (www.lonelyplanet.com) General information on the Netherlands and links to various useful Dutch sites.

Uitburo (www.uitburo.nl) Events site for the Netherlands. It's in Dutch but easy to navigate.

Itineraries

CLASSIC ROUTES

THE LAY OF THE LOWLANDS

Begin in **Amsterdam** (p78). Visit the **Van Gogh Museum** (p106) or **Rijksmuseum** (p106) and rent a bicycle to explore the pretty neighbourhood of **Jordaan** (p100). On the second day board a **canal-boat tour** (p115) and walk the **Red Light District** (p85) before hitting a brown café or coffeeshop.

Move on to **Haarlem** (p147) – stroll the compact old quarter, and view the masterpieces of the **Frans Hals Museum** (p149) and the stained glass of the **Grote Kerk** (p148). In tulip season (April and May) witness the unbelievable colours of the **Keukenhof gardens** (p195), south of town.

Spend one day each in **Leiden** (p190), for its old-world splendour, and **Den Haag** (p195) – don't miss the **Mauritshuis** (p197) collection, with works from Vermeer to Warhol.

In the remaining time take a harbour boat tour in **Rotterdam** (p208) and visit either the **Museum Boijmans van Beuningen** (p209) or the **Maritiem Museum Rotterdam** (p212). The next morning do a walking tour of **modern architecture** (p211) before departing for **Kinderdijk** (p219) and its picturesque windmills.

This popular route from Amsterdam through the historic Dutch cities of Haarlem, Den Haag and Rotterdam is a mere 103km; the sheer variety of charms will make a week flash by.

SOUTHERN SOJOURN

If you've two weeks to spare, start in **Amsterdam** (p78), but extend your stay to three days, and alongside a visit to the city's big museums, take time out to relax in **Vondelpark** (p107), the capital's English-style park. Once again, discover the delights of the **Jordaan district** (p100) by foot or bicycle, then take a load off in a grand café on the **Spui** (p127), and browse the exotic wares in the **Albert Cuypmarkt** (p134). Divide the rest of your time in Amsterdam between viewing the wild kingdom of **Artis Zoo** (p108), learning about the glories of the Dutch East India Company at the **Scheepvaartmuseum** (p109), and escaping the city by bicycle to enjoy the windmills and seascapes of the **Waterland Region** (p154).

Continue as on the one-week tour to Haarlem (Keukenhof in season), Den Haag, Delft and Rotterdam, but add a day for **Leiden** (p190) and its student vibe and old-world splendour. Stop in to see the spinning sails of the windmills at **Kinderdijk** (p219), then head for **Middelburg** (p224), Zeeland's prosperous capital, and the nearby **Delta Project** (p228). Take a train through the Netherlands' southern provinces to **Maastricht** (p278), a city with more panache than most; two days should be enough to sample some great cuisine and meander through the medieval centre. Head north to visit **Hoge Veluwe National Park** (p269) whose lush forests and dunes make an enchanting setting for the excellent **Kröller-Müller Museum** (p269), and polish off your trip in the cosmopolitan city of **Utrecht** (p178).

A two-week tour covering 700km that passes through some of Holland's biggest and boldest cities, and allows an exploration of the country's astounding Delta Project, and its most acclaimed national park.

CIRCUMNAVIGATING THE IJSSELMEER

A practical place to start this tour is **Amsterdam** (p78); three days in the capital will whiz by in a blur of museums, parks, canal tours and nightlife. From here, head north along the IJsselmeer coast through the **Waterland Region** (p154) to the tiny fishing village of **Marken** (p156) where a ferry will transport you across the inland sea to **Volendam** (p156). Enjoy a meal overlooking the harbour, but escape the crowds to **Edam** (p157), which comes second only to Haarlem as the prettiest town in Noord Holland. Overnight here before reaching **Alkmaar** (p159) early to experience its kitsch but fun cheese market, then spend the afternoon wandering through Enkhuizen's enthralling **Zuiderzeemuseum** (p164).

The next morning catch a bus to **Den Helder** (p166), and from there a ferry to **Texel** (p167). Spend two days (or the entire two weeks…) dividing your time between the beach and bike exploration, then take another ferry to **Vlieland** (p239) to appreciate the wilder side of the Frisian Islands. From Vlieland, a ferry will take you back to the mainland and dump you at **Harlingen** (p236), from where **Leeuwarden** (p232) is only a short train ride away. Friesland's capital is not only a good spot to enjoy Frisian hospitality, but it's also a fine base for exploring the surrounding area; the water sports centre of **Sneek** (p235) is close at hand, as are a chain of captivating **coastal towns** (p237) on the IJsselmeer.

The train trip from Leeuwarden to Amsterdam completes the circumnavigation of the IJsselmeer, but it's worth breaking your journey in **Naarden** (p172) and **Muiden** (p171), two of Noord Holland's historical fortress towns.

This two-week trip, covering 570km, provides a taste of Dutch life on the open sea. It passes through historically important nautical towns, holiday islands and watersports centres.

ROADS LESS TRAVELLED

ISLANDS ESCAPES

The necklace of low-lying Wadden Islands (Texel, Vlieland, Terschelling, Ameland and Schiermonnikoog) is just the ticket for a week of island-hopping, preferably with bicycle in tow. Some ferry links require advance planning, but if you've time and energy, it shouldn't prove too big a problem. A full day on **Texel** (p167) is a good starting point; hop on your bike and snake along the western coast from sleepy **Den Hoorn** (p167) through dark copses to the **Ecomare** (p167) seal and bird refuge. Take a catamaran ride near **De Cocksdorp** (p167) before bedding down here for the night. The next day comb the eastern side of the island, admiring pretty thatched houses in **Oosterend** (p167) and visiting the **Maritime & Beachcombers Museum** (p168) in **Oudeschild** (p167).

From De Cocksdorp board the morning ferry to car-free **Vlieland** (p239) to explore its nature and hiking trails before catching the boat to **Terschelling** (p240), Friesland's main tourist island. Hole up in peaceful **Oosterend** (p240) for the night and cycle through untouched **De Boschplaat** (p240), then hightail it by ferry to **Harlingen** (p236), a pretty little port on the Frisian coast, and on to Holwerd, where you ferry across for a stay on **Ameland** (p241). Its four towns are pretty for a brief stroll, and the eastern end is ideal to bike away from it all. Return to the former whaling port of **Nes** (p242) for the night. The next day stay put for a boat tour to the sea lions, and to commune with nature. Your last stop, via the ports of Holwerd and Lauwersoog, is **Schiermonnikoog** (p242), the smallest of the Frisian Islands and a wild national park.

This week-long hop along the Wadden Islands covers just 200km, but you will be tempted to spend longer soaking up their wild, enchanting beauty.

EASTERN EXPERIENCE

The Netherlands' eastern expanse is largely ignored by tourists who settle for the big guns of the Dutch lowlands, but there are some hidden highlights among the polders waiting to be discovered.

Begin your trip in **Groningen** (p245), a vibrant city populated by students, bars, cafés, and a couple of fine museums. Spend the morning roaming the inner city, the afternoon in the first-rate **Groninger Museum** (p246), and the evening enjoying the city's thriving nightlife. If your hangover allows, greet the next day early and bus southeast to **Bourtange** (p251), a perfectly preserved 17th-century fortified town on the border with Germany, before moving on to Borger and its prehistoric **hunebedden** (p253), stone arrangements once used as burial chambers. From nearby **Emmen** (p254), catch a train to **Zwolle** (p260), capital of Overijssel province and a compact, easy-going town. A bike trip through the eerie expanse of nearby **Weerribben National Park** (p256) is a good way to spend the afternoon.

From Zwolle, it's only a short train ride to **Deventer** (p258), an unhurried town that's big on relaxation and small on tourism. Deventer is also a good base for exploring the **Hoge Veluwe National Park** (p269), a natural oasis that's home to one of the finest art museums in the country. After a night in Deventer, head for **Den Bosch** (p272), a city ringed by canals and defensive walls; its quiet back streets are a pleasure to stroll. **Breda** (p275) is your next stop, where a day and a night can easily be spent appreciating the city's compact centre. To round the trip off, it's back to nature at **Biesbosch National Park** (p223).

This seven-day excursion through the Netherlands' eastern provinces covers 530km and touches on the country's less-visited towns, cities and natural attractions.

TAILORED TRIPS

FAMILY FORAYS

The Netherlands is made for family holidays – beaches, parks, cycling (with no hills!), museums, it's all here to entertain parents and their prodigies.

Aside from canal tours and bike rides, **Amsterdam** (p113) is filled with family attractions. The likes of the **Scheepvaartmuseum** (p109), with its tall-ship replicas, and **Tropenmuseum** (p109), featuring a separate children's section, will spark the imagination of both young and old, while excess energy can be spent running wild in **Vondelpark** (p107) or **TunFun** (p99), a large underground playground.

Close to the capital, the windmills and boat rides of **Zaanse Schans** (p154) will surely delight, as will the sand dunes and pristine beaches of the **Kennemerduinen Nature Reserve** (p152).

Gelderland has a legion of zoological parks, including Harderwijk's aquatic park, **Dolfinarium** (p263), Apeldoorn's primarily primate zoo, **Apenheul** (p263), and Arnhem's well laid-out **Burger's Zoo** (p263). The cute seals and interactive nature displays of Texel's **Ecomare** (p167) and Pieter-buren's **Zeehondencreche** (p250) never fail to please.

De Efteling (p275), with scary rides aplenty, is the 'Dutch Disneyland', while a miniaturised Netherlands at **Madurodam** (p199) may be far more sedate, but no less entertaining. Maastricht's **underground caves** (p281) are perfect for the entire family, as is the **Waterland Neeltje Jans** (p227) in the heart of the Delta Project.

ADULT ENTERTAINMENT

There is no denying that the Netherlands is a playground for grown-ups. Breweries, brown cafés, coffeeshops, red light districts, world-class clubbing, and the old masters' art are just waiting to be enjoyed.

There's no better place to start than Amsterdam. Its centre is full to overflowing with **brown cafés** (p127), but if you want to get to the source of the matter, the **Heineken Experience** (p107) is the place to head. If this isn't to your taste, try **Brouwerij 't IJ** (p129), a small brewery with potent beers. With over 250 **coffeeshops** (p129), the capital offers ample opportunity to partake in a spliff or two, and no one, but no one (unless they suffer from erythrophobia) should miss a stroll through Amsterdam's legendary **Red Light District** (p85). **Clubs** (p129) abound, as do museums devoted to the likes of Van Gogh and Rembrandt.

Rotterdam's **clubbing scene** (p217) is world-renowned, as are its **summer festivals** (p214), and Groningen's **nightlife** (p249), fuelled by thousands of students, is a lively hedonistic mix.

Beer is a particular Dutch delight. **Maastricht** (p278), with its close proximity to Belgium and Trappist breweries, should be the first stop for any beer connoisseur, while the best of the Low Countries' amber brew can be sampled at Alkmaar's **Nationaal Biermuseum** (p160). Small, local breweries, like Texel's **Bierbrouwerij** (p169) and Nijmegen's **De Hemel** (p266), dot the country.

Snapshot

The Netherlands is in a state of flux. Recent events have challenged Dutch society and its axiom of 'live and let live', and the Dutch talent for tolerance has been attacked on a number of fronts. Parties on both sides of the political partition are calling for change, and at present it seems as though the pendulum of power is swinging to the right.

The hottest topic on many Dutch lips today is the country's new immigrants, or how to limit their numbers. It seems the assassinations of Theo van Gogh and Pim Fortuyn (p32) were the straws that broke the camel's back; once taboo, public discussions about quotas, dress codes and language requirements are now commonplace. Would-be immigrants must currently sit an entrance exam, in Dutch, covering the language and culture of the Netherlands, and watch a video which includes images of two men kissing and a topless woman bather.

The public debacle over Ayaan Hirsi Ali's right to Dutch nationality hasn't helped matters either. The Somalian-born former MP and outspoken critic of Islam (she co-wrote the short film *Submission: Part 1* with Theo van Gogh and received death threats for her efforts) revealed that she had used a false name and date of birth on her naturalisation decree; the Minister for Immigration and Integration, Rita Verdonk (known as 'Iron Rita'), ruled that Ali was 'deemed not to have received Dutch nationality'. The subsequent public and political outcry forced Verdonk to reconsider her judgment, but by then the damage was done. Within a matter of weeks the ruling coalition collapsed over the issue, a minority government was formed under Prime Minister Jan Peter Balkenende, and early elections were called. At the time of research, Ali was set to move to the US sometime in September 2006 and the next round of national elections were to be held on 22 November 2006.

Without question, the Netherlands is still one of the most liberal countries in the world; a quick run-through of its policies on recreational drugs, euthanasia, same-sex marriage and prostitution is proof alone. However, recent court approval of a political paedophilia party is pushing things too far. The campaign manifesto of the Brotherly Love, Freedom and Diversity party (PNVD) includes a call for a reduction in the age of consent from 16 to 12 (and eventually doing away with it altogether), and the legalisation of child pornography and sex with animals. The court's decision has caused widespread disapproval throughout the country.

Normally avid supporters of the European Union (EU), the Dutch resoundingly rejected the EU constitution in a referendum held in 2006 (almost 62% voted no), the first national referendum in 200 years. Dissatisfaction with recent governments and the economies of key European players, along with concerns over immigration, loss of national identity and EU expansion were all cited as reasons for the rejection.

The Dutch economy is one of the most open and outward looking in the world, and the Netherlands has an enviable track record for such a small country. It experienced a rough patch from 2001 to 2005, however, during which time parliament made deep cuts in the welfare state – the generous health care system went under the knife, and early retirement is no longer a soft option. But, given the fact that the Dutch are some of the sharpest traders on the planet, it's no surprise to learn that the economy is presently rebounding.

Global warming (p52) is a matter of concern for the Dutch populace. Unseasonably high temperatures in summer (and an increasing number

FAST FACTS

Population: 16.3 million

Land in tulip bulbs: 110 sq km

Per capita GDP: €26,500

Unemployment rate: 6.5% (2005)

Inflation: 1.7% (2005 average)

Religion: Catholic 31%, Protestant 21%, Muslim 5.5%, other 1.5%, not religious 41%

Number of mobile phones: 14.8 million

Waterways: 5046km (navigable for ships over 50 tons)

Height of the average male: 185.5cm (6ft 1 in)

Number of windmills: 1180

of heat waves) mean not only that quite a few peat-based dykes dry out but also that some of the country's annual events are severely affected: two heat-related deaths at Nijmegen's Internationale Wandelvierdaagse (p265) forced the race's cancellation, something previously accomplished only by a world war. The effects of global warming are not limited to rising temperatures, however: the spring of 2005 saw record snowfalls and freezing temperatures (minus 21°C in Marknesse, Flevoland).

H5N1 – or its more comprehensible moniker, bird flu – has raised fears in the Netherlands, one of the world's biggest meat exporters. In 2005 there were outbreaks of the deadly virus in a number of European countries, causing sweeping panic in the rest. The Dutch government took pre-emptive steps to stop the spread of the virus by vaccinating chickens and confining them indoors (the outdoor ban was later lifted), a move at odds with the EU's normal policy of culling.

Despite the desire to keep the social peace, the government has made moves to ban smoking in public places. Initially the service industries were allowed to draw up their own plans to protect employees and the public at large from second-hand smoke, but legal action has been threatened by a government tired of feet-dragging in the hotel and catering sector. Coffeeshops are up in arms; as Arjan Roskam, chairman of the Union for Cannabis Retailers, put it, 'The whole point of going to a coffeeshop is to smoke'. All establishments are required to have a non-smoking section by 1 January 2009.

The Netherlands' liberal drugs policy continues to be a reliable source of controversy, in particular rankling with France and the USA. The Dutch, in turn, point to relatively low rates of drug-related crime and argue that decriminalisation is the way to go for soft drugs. But the government has stepped up pressure against trafficking in cannabis, hard drugs and designer drugs (the Netherlands is a major producer of ecstasy), and the Amsterdam council has introduced a temporary ban on cannabis use in the Baarsjes district of the city, citing problems of public disturbances by youths.

Dutch national pride is muted except on the soccer field. The national team habitually participates in European championships and World Cups, and the country rallies behind them with unquestioning support. Otherwise, the Dutch love to downplay their place in the world, and often prefer to speak English with foreign visitors.

History

For centuries the rich and turbulent history of the Netherlands, complete with wave after wave of invaders and invading waves, was inseparable from that of neighbouring Belgium and Luxembourg. This trio was long known as the Low Countries, and the founding of the modern Netherlands only took place in 1579, while its current borders were set as late as 1830.

FOREIGN DOMINATION

The territory that became the Netherlands has been inhabited since prehistoric times; *hunebedden* (p253) – stone structures used as burial mounds – are clear evidence of this. The first invaders to take note of the locals were the Romans, who, under Julius Caesar, conquered a wide region along the Rijn (Rhine) and its tributaries by 59 BC. Fiercely independent by nature, Celtic and Germanic tribes initially bowed to Caesar's rule. Over the next four centuries the Romans built advanced towns, farms and the straight roads that still shape the landscape today. Utrecht became a main outpost of the empire, but the soggy territory of Friesland was left to its own devices, and its early settlers built homes on mounds of mud (called *terpen*) to escape the frequent floods; Hogebeintum (p235) has a surviving example.

As Roman power began to fade, the Franks, an aggressive German tribe to the east, began to muscle in. By the end of the 8th century, the Franks had completed their conquest of the Low Countries and began converting the local populace to Christianity, using force whenever necessary. Charlemagne, the first in a long line of Holy Roman emperors, was by far the most successful Frankish king. He built a palace at Nijmegen (p263), but the empire fell apart after his death in 814.

For the next 200 years Vikings sailed up Dutch rivers to loot and pillage. Local rulers developed their own fortified towns and made up their own government and laws – even though, strictly speaking, they answered to the Pope in Rome.

Over time local lords, who were nominally bound to a German king, began to gain power. When one lord struggled with another for territory, invariably their townsfolk would provide support, but only in return for various freedoms. By the beginning of the 12th century these relationships were laid down in charters – documents that not only spelt out the lord's power but also detailed other bureaucratic matters such as taxation. Around the same time, Dutch towns with sea access, such as Deventer and Zwolle, joined the Hanseatic League (a group of powerful trading cities in present-day Germany, including Hamburg and Rostock). These federal towns grew wealthy through the league's single-minded development of laws, regulations and other policies that promoted trade.

Meanwhile the many little lords met their match in the dukes of Burgundy, who gradually took over the Low Countries. Duke Philip the Good, who ruled from 1419 to 1467, showed the towns of the Low Countries who was boss by essentially telling them to stuff their charters. Although this limited the towns' freedom, it also brought to the region a degree of stability that had been missing during the era of squabbling lords. By this time Utrecht had

'Holland' is a popular term for the Netherlands, yet in reality it refers to the combined provinces of Noord (North) and Zuid (South) Holland.

59 BC	1275
Romans conquer the Netherlands	Credited as the founding of Amsterdam

become the ecclesiastical centre of the Low Countries, whereas Amsterdam was but a modest trading post.

The 15th century ushered in great prosperity for the Low Countries. The Dutch became adept at shipbuilding in support of the Hanseatic trade, and merchants thrived by selling luxury items such as tapestries, fashionable clothing and paintings – but also more mundane commodities such as salted herring and beer.

With their wealth tapped through taxes, the Low Countries were naturally coveted by a succession of rulers. In 1482 Mary of Burgundy, Philip's granddaughter, passed on the Low Countries to her son, Philip the Fair.

The family intrigues that followed are worthy of a costume drama: Philip married Joanna, the daughter of King Ferdinand and Queen Isabella of Spain; Philip then bequeathed the Low Countries to his son Charles, now a member of the powerful Habsburg dynasty, in 1530. Charles V was crowned Holy Roman Emperor, making him monarch of most of Europe.

Fortunately, the rule of Charles V did not stand in the way of the Low Countries' growing wealth. But this all changed in 1555, when Charles handed over Spain and the Low Countries to his son, Philip II.

The site www.history-netherlands.nl gives a detailed history of the Netherlands in a number of languages.

THE FIGHT FOR INDEPENDENCE

Philip II of Spain was a staunch Catholic and suffered under a slight case of theomania. Conflict with the Low Countries was then inevitable; the Protestant reformation had spread throughout the colony, fuelled by the ideas of Erasmus and the actions of Martin Luther. However, before the Spanish arrived the religious landscape of the Low Countries was quite diverse: Lutherans wielded great influence, but smaller churches had their places too. For instance, the Anabaptists were polygamists and communists, and nudity was promoted as a means of equality among their masses (in the warmer seasons). In the end it was Calvinism that emerged in the Low Countries as the main challenger to the Roman Catholic Church, and to Philip's rule.

A big believer in the Inquisition, Philip went after the Protestants with a vengeance. Matters came to a head in 1566 when the puritanical Calvinists went on a rampage, destroying the art and religious icons of Catholic churches in many parts of the Netherlands. Evidence of this is still readily apparent in the barren interiors of Dutch churches today.

This sent Philip into action. The Duke of Alba was chosen to lead a 10,000-strong army to the Netherlands in 1568 to quell the unruly serfs; as the Duke wasn't one to take prisoners, his forces slaughtered 80 thousands, and so began the Dutch war of independence, which lasted 80 years.

The Prince van Oranje, Willem the Silent (thus named for his refusal to argue over religious issues), was one of the few nobles not to side with Philip, and he led the Dutch revolt against Spanish rule. Willem, who had been Philip's lieutenant in Holland, Zeeland and Utrecht, began to rely on the Dutch Calvinists for his chief support. He championed the principle of toleration and this philosophy became part of the foundation of an independent Dutch state. The rebels' cause, however, was hampered by lack of money and patchy support from towns.

Changing tack in 1572, Willem hired a bunch of English pirates to fight for his cause. Known as the Watergeuzen (Sea Beggars), they sailed up the myriad Dutch rivers and seized town after town from the surprised and

The Dutch National Archive (www.nationaalarchief.nl) has almost a thousand years of historical documents, maps, drawings and photos. Access to the site is free.

land-bound Spanish forces. The strategy worked like a charm, and by the end of the year Willem controlled every city except Amsterdam.

The Spanish responded by sacking the Duke of Alba and sending in a new commander, Alessandro Farnese, who was a more able leader. Much of the 1570s saw a constant shift of power as one side or the other gained temporary supremacy.

THE UNION OF UTRECHT

The Low Countries split for good in 1579 when the more Protestant and rebellious provinces in the north formed the Union of Utrecht. This explicitly anti-Spanish alliance became known as the United Provinces, the basis for the Netherlands as we know it today. The southern regions of the Low Countries had always remained Catholic and were much more open to compromise with Spain. They eventually became Belgium.

Although the United Provinces had declared their independence from Spain, the war dragged on. In 1584 they suffered a major blow when their leader, Willem the Silent, was assassinated in Delft. The Dutch once again turned to the English for help, and Elizabeth I lent assistance, but it was the English victory over the Armada in 1588 that proved the most beneficial. In a series of brilliant military campaigns, the Dutch drove the Spanish out of the United Provinces by the turn of the 17th century. Trouble with Spain was far from over, however, and fighting resumed as part of the larger Thirty Years' War throughout Europe. In 1648 the Treaty of Westphalia, which ended the Thirty Years' War, included the proviso that Spain recognise the independence of the United Provinces, ending the 80-year conflict between the Netherlands and Spain.

THE GOLDEN AGE

Throughout the turmoil of the 15th and 16th centuries, Holland's merchant cities (particularly Amsterdam) had managed to keep trading alive; their skill at business and sailing was so great that, even at the peak of the rebellion, the Spanish had no alternative but to use Dutch boats for transporting their grain. With the arrival of peace, however, the cities began to boom. This era of great economic prosperity and cultural fruition came to be known as the Golden Age.

The Dutch soon began to expand their horizons, and the merchant fleet known as the Dutch East India Company was formed in 1602. It quickly monopolised key shipping and trade routes east of Africa's Cape of Good Hope and west of the Strait of Magellan, making it the largest trading company of the 17th century. It became almost as powerful as a sovereign state, with the ability to raise its own armed forces and establish colonies.

Its sister, the Dutch West India Company, traded with Africa and the Americas and was at the very centre of the American slave trade. Seamen working for both companies discovered (in a very Western sense of the word) or conquered lands including Tasmania, New Zealand, Malaysia, Sri Lanka and Mauritius. English explorer Henry Hudson landed on the island of Manhattan in 1609 as he searched for the Northwest Passage, and Dutch settlers named it New Amsterdam.

Culturally the United Provinces flourished in the Golden Age. The wealth of the merchant class supported scores of artists, including Jan Vermeer, Jan

Thomas C Grattan's recently updated *Holland: The History of the Nether-lands* takes a detailed – if somewhat academic – look at the past of the Dutch, from the invasion of the Romans to the beginning of the 20th century.

The *Embarrassment of Riches* by Simon Schama is a thoughtful look at the tensions generated between vast wealth and Calvinist sobriety in the Golden Age, with implications for modern society.

The Dutch *bought* (a concept foreign to North American tribes at the time) the island of Manhattan from the Lenape in 1626 for the equivalent of US$24 worth of beads.

1602	1636–37
Dutch East India Company created	Tulipmania grips the country

TULIPMANIA

A bursting economic bubble is not a modern phenomenon. The first occurred in 1636–37 in the Netherlands, and over a flower everyone associates with the Dutch – the tulip.

Tulips originated as wild flowers in Central Asia. They were first cultivated by the Turks ('tulip' is Turkish for turban) and made their way to Europe via Vienna in the mid-1500s. By the beginning of the 17th century Holland was enthralled by the beautiful flower, which flourished in the country's cool climate and fertile delta soil.

It was not long before trading in tulips started to get out of hand. In late 1636 a tulip-trading mania swept the Netherlands; speculative buying and selling made some individual bulbs more expensive than an Amsterdam house, and even ordinary people sank their life's savings into a few bulbs. Speculators fell over themselves to out-bid each other in taverns. At the height of Tulipmania, in early 1637, a single bulb of the legendary *Semper augustus* fetched more than 10 years' worth of the average worker's wages. An English botanist bisected one of his host's bulbs and landed in jail until he could raise thousands of florins in compensation.

The bonanza couldn't last. When some bulbs failed to fetch their expected prices in Haarlem in February 1637, the bottom fell out of the market. Within a matter of weeks a wave of bankruptcies swept the land, hitting wealthy merchants as well as simple folk. Speculators were stuck with unsold bulbs, or bulbs they'd reserved but hadn't yet paid for (the concept of financial options, incidentally, was invented during Tulipmania). The government refused to get involved with a pursuit they regarded as gambling.

The speculative froth is gone, but passion for the tulip endures. It remains a relatively expensive flower, and cool-headed growers have perfected their craft. To this day the Dutch are the world leaders in tulip cultivation and supply most of the bulbs exported to Europe and North America.

Steen, Frans Hals and Rembrandt (see p38). The sciences were not left out: Dutch physicist and astronomer Christiaan Huygens discovered Saturn's rings and invented the pendulum clock; celebrated philosopher Benedict de Spinoza wrote a brilliant thesis saying that the universe was identical with God; and Frenchman René Descartes, known for his philosophy, 'I think, therefore I am', found intellectual freedom in the Netherlands and stayed for two decades.

The Union of Utrecht's promise of religious tolerance led to a surprising amount of religious diversity that was rare in Europe at the time. Calvinism was the official religion of the government, but various other Protestants, Jews and Catholics were allowed to practise their faith. However, in a legacy of the troubles with Spain, Catholics had to worship in private, which led to the creation of clandestine churches. Many of these unusual buildings have survived to the present day.

Politically, however, the young Dutch Republic was at an all-time low. The House of Oranje-Nassau fought the republicans for control of the country; while the house wanted to centralise power with the Prince van Oranje as *stadhouder* (chief magistrate), the republicans wanted the cities and provinces to run their own affairs. Prince Willem II won the dispute but died suddenly three months later, one week before his son was born. Dutch regional leaders exploited this power vacuum by abolishing the *stadhouder*, and authority was decentralised.

International conflict was never very far away. In 1652 the United Provinces went to war with their old friend England, mainly over the increasing

1700	1795
End of Golden Age	French invade Holland

strength of the Dutch merchant fleet. Both countries entered a hotchpotch of alliances with Spain, France and Sweden in an effort to gain the upper hand. During one round of treaties the Dutch agreed to give New Amsterdam to the English (who promptly renamed it New York) in return for Surinam in South America. In 1672 the French army marched into the Netherlands and, as the Dutch had devoted most of their resources to the navy, found little resistance on land. The country appealed to the House of Oranje, which appointed Willem III as general of the Dutch forces.

Tulipomania: The Story of the World's Most Coveted Flower by Mike Dash is an engaging look at the bizarre bulb fever that swept the nation in the 17th century.

In a single stroke Willem improved relations with the English by marrying his cousin Mary, daughter of the English king James II. Perhaps sensing he was no longer welcome in England – his opponents feared that he would restore the Roman Catholic Church there – James fled to France, and Willem and Mary were named king and queen of England in 1689. Using his strong diplomatic skills, Willem created the Grand Alliance that joined England, the United Provinces, Spain, Sweden and several German states to fight the expansionist ambitions of France's Louis XIV.

The Grand Alliance defeated the French several times. In 1697 Louis XIV agreed to give up most of the territory France had conquered. As if to drive the point home, the Dutch again joined the English to fight the French in the War of the Spanish Succession, ending with the Treaty of Utrecht in 1713.

DUTCH DECLINE & FRENCH RULE

Financially weakened by the ongoing wars with France, the United Provinces began to spiral downwards. Its maritime fleet, left battered and bleeding from the wars, lost valuable trading routes to the British, while domestically the population was decreasing. The dykes were also in a sorry state – there was little money to repair them, and widespread floods swept across the country. Merchants were more likely to spend their profits on luxuries than sensible investments in their businesses, which in turn contributed to the country's overall economic decline.

Politically, the United Provinces were as unstable as the dykes. A series of struggles between the House of Oranje and its democratic opponents led to a civil war in 1785; the dispute was settled three years later when the *stadhouders* agreed to limit their own powers. When the French revolutionary forces invaded in 1795, with the aid of those eager for constitutional reform the United Provinces collapsed and became the Batavian Republic. It survived only until 1806, when Napoleon renamed it the Kingdom of Holland and installed his brother Louis Bonaparte as king.

Louis proved to be not quite the kind of king Napoleon would have liked. He actually seemed to like his subjects and often favoured them over France; soon his position became untenable and in 1810 Napoleon forced Louis out of office. With Napoleon's attention diverted in Russia, though, the House of Oranje supporters invited Prince Willem VI back. He landed at Scheveningen in 1813 and was named prince sovereign of the Netherlands; the following year he was crowned King Willem I.

INDEPENDENT KINGDOM & WWI

With the defeat of Napoleon, Europe celebrated with the Congress of Vienna in 1815. It was here that the Kingdom of the Netherlands – the Netherlands in the north and Belgium in the south – was formed. However, the marriage

1814	1830
Willem I crowned as king	Belgium declares independence

was doomed from the start. The partners had little in common, including their dominant religions (Calvinist and Catholic), languages (Dutch and French) and favoured way of making money (trade and manufacturing). Matters weren't helped by Willem, who generally sided with his fellow northerners.

In 1830 the southern states revolted, and nine years later Willem was forced to let the south go. In a nice historical twist, Willem abdicated one year later so that he could marry – surprise! – a Belgian Catholic. It's not known if he ever spoke French at home.

His son, King Willem II, granted a new and more liberal constitution to the people of the Netherlands in 1848. This included a number of democratic ideals and even made the monarchy the servant of the elected government. This document has remained the foundation of the Dutch government until the present day. Its role on the world stage long over, the Netherlands played only a small part in European affairs and concentrated on liberalism at home.

During WWI the Netherlands remained neutral, although its shipping industry was damaged by both the Allies and the Germans. It did however gain economic and financial ground by trading with both sides.

Following WWI the country, like some of its European counterparts, embarked on innovative social programmes that targeted poverty, the rights of women and children, and education. Industrially, the coal mines of south Limburg were exploited to great success, Rotterdam became one of Europe's most important ports and the scheme to reclaim the Zuiderzee was launched in 1932.

A helpful site for those tracing their Dutch heritage is www.godutch.com.

WWII
The Dutch tried to remain neutral during WWII, but in May 1940 the Germans invaded anyway. The advancing Nazis levelled much of Rotterdam in a raid designed to force the Dutch to surrender; they obliged, and the country's tiny army crumbled quickly.

Queen Wilhelmina issued a proclamation of 'flaming protest' to the nation and escaped with her family to England. The plucky monarch, who had been key in maintaining Dutch neutrality in WWI, now found herself in a much different situation and made encouraging broadcasts to her subjects back home via the BBC and Radio Orange. The Germans put Dutch industry and farms to work for war purposes and there was much deprivation. Dutch resistance was primarily passive and only gained any kind of momentum when thousands of Dutch men were taken to Germany and forced to work in Nazi factories. A far worse fate awaited the country's Jews (p30).

The official website of the Dutch royal family, www.koninklijkhuis.nl features mini-biographies and virtual tours of the palaces.

The 'Winter of Hunger' of 1944–45 was a desperate time in the Netherlands. The British-led Operation Market Garden (p267) had been a huge disaster and the Allies abandoned all efforts to liberate the Dutch. The Germans stripped the country of much of its food and wealth, and mass starvation ensued. Many people were reduced to eating tulip bulbs for their daily subsistence. Canadian troops finally liberated the country in May 1945.

POSTWAR RECONSTRUCTION
The Netherlands faced major concerns in the postwar years both at home and abroad. Domestically, it had to restore its money-making businesses while

1932	1940
Zuiderzee reclamation begins	Germany invades the Netherlands

DUTCH JEWS

The tale of Jews in Europe is often one of repression, persecution and downright hatred. In the Netherlands, it is more a tale of acceptance and prosperity, until the coming of the Nazis.

Amsterdam is the focus of Jewish history in the Netherlands, and Jews played a key role in the city's development over the centuries. The first documented evidence of a Jewish presence in the city dates back to the 12th century, but numbers began to swell with the expulsion of Sephardic Jews from Spain and Portugal in the 1580s.

As was the case in much of Europe, guilds barred the newcomers from most trades. Some of the Sephardim were diamond cutters, however, for whom there was no guild. Others introduced printing and tobacco processing or worked as street retailers, bankers and doctors. The majority eked out a living as labourers and small-time traders on the margins of society. Still, they weren't confined to a ghetto and, with some restrictions, could buy property and exercise their religion – freedoms unheard of elsewhere in Europe.

The 17th century saw another influx of Jewish refugees, this time Ashkenazim fleeing pogroms in Central and Eastern Europe. The two groups didn't always get on well and separate synagogues were established, helping Amsterdam to become one of Europe's major Jewish centres.

The guilds and all restrictions on Jews were abolished during the French occupation, and the Jewish community thrived in the 19th century. Poverty was still considerable, but the economic, social and political emancipation of the Jews helped their middle class move up in society.

All this came to an end with the German occupation of the Netherlands. The Nazis brought about the almost complete annihilation of the Dutch Jewish community. Before WWII the Netherlands counted 140,000 Jews, of whom about two-thirds lived in Amsterdam. Less than 25,000 survived the war, and Amsterdam's Jewish quarter was left a ghost town. Many homes stood derelict until their demolition in the 1970s, and only a handful of synagogues throughout the country are once again operating as houses of worship.

Estimates put the current Jewish population of the Netherlands at anywhere between 32,000 and 45,000. Their history is told in the Nationaal Oorlogs- en Verzetmuseum (National War and Resistance Museum; p284) in Overloon, Limburg, and in Amsterdam's Joods Historisch Museum (Jewish Historical Museum; p99).

rebuilding the battered infrastructure, which it did very well; trade took off once again, new wealth followed the discovery of large natural gas fields in the North Sea off the Dutch coast, and Dutch farmers became some of the most productive in Europe.

Overseas, the colonies began to clamour for independence. The Dutch East Indies declared itself independent in 1945, and after four years of bitter fighting and negotiations the independence of Indonesia was recognised at the end of 1949. Surinam also became independent in 1975. The Kingdom of the Netherlands will shrink even further come July 2007, with the end of the Netherlands Antilles as it currently stands. Curaçao and Sint Maarten will be granted *status aparte* (home rule), Bonaire and Saba will remain part of the kingdom, and Sint Eustatius (Statia) was in two minds at the time of writing.

The same social upheavals that swept the world in the 1960s were also felt in the Netherlands. Students, labour groups, hippies and more took to the streets in protest. Among the more colourful were a group that came to be known as the Provos (opposite). A huge squatters' movement sprung up in Amsterdam, and homeless groups took over empty buildings – many of which had once belonged to Jews – and refused to leave.

Tolerance toward drugs and homosexuals also emerged at the time. The country's drug policy grew out of practical considerations, when a flood of young people populated Amsterdam and made the policing of drug laws impracticable (see p293 for the current drug policy). Official government policy became supportive of homosexuals, who are able to live openly in Dutch cities and, since 2001, legally marry.

Queen Beatrix ascended the throne in 1980 after her mother, Juliana, abdicated. Beatrix hasn't indicated how long she will remain in the job, but in all likelihood she will pass the reins to her son, Prince Willem-Alexander, within the next decade.

All governments since 1945 have been coalitions, with parties differing mainly over economic policies. However, coalitions shift constantly based on the political climate and in recent years there have been winds of change. The most recent election, in January 2003, saw the CDA (Christian Democratic Appeal) return as the largest party, with the boyish Jan Peter Balkenende as Prime Minister in a shaky coalition with the VVD liberals and D66 democrats. The shakes became major tremors in June 2006 due to disagreements over immigration policy, and the fragile coalition collapsed when D66 withdrew; Balkenende resigned soon afterwards but formed a minority government to rule until the next early election, at the time of research set for 22 November 2006.

THE PROVOCATIVE PROVOS

The 1960s were a breeding ground for discontent and anti-establishment activity, and in the Netherlands this underground movement led to the formation of the Provos. This small group of anarchic individuals staged street 'happenings' or creative, playful provocations (hence the name) around the Lieverdje (Little Darling) on Amsterdam's Spui (p97).

In 1962 an Amsterdam window cleaner and self-professed sorcerer, Robert Jasper Grootveld, began to deface cigarette billboards with a huge letter 'K' for *kanker* (cancer) to expose the role of advertising in addictive consumerism. Dressed as a medicine man, he held get-togethers in his garage and chanted mantras against cigarette smoking (but under the influence of pot).

This attracted even more bizarre characters. Poet 'Johnny the Selfkicker' bombarded his audience with frenzied, stream-of-consciousness recitals. Bart Huges drilled a hole in his forehead – a so-called 'third eye' – to relieve pressure on the brain and expand his consciousness.

The group gained international notoriety in March 1966 with its protests at the marriage of Princess (now Queen) Beatrix to ex-Nazi Claus von Amsberg. Protestors jeered the wedding couple as their procession rolled through Amsterdam, and bystanders chanted 'bring my bicycle back' – a reference to the many bikes commandeered by the retreating German soldiers in 1945. This was broadcast live to the world on TV.

In the same year the Provos gained enough support to win a seat on Amsterdam's city council. The group began developing 'White Plans', pro-environment schemes including the famous White Bicycle Plan to ease traffic congestion with a fleet of free white bicycles. The movement dissolved in the 1970s, but it left a lasting legacy: the squatters' movement, which encouraged the poor to occupy uninhabited buildings, in turn forced the government to adopt measures to help underprivileged tenants.

1975	**1980**
The Netherlands decriminalises marijuana	Queen Beatrix ascends throne

MORE THAN TRAGEDIES

The Netherlands has for decades been seen as a land of acceptance, tolerance and liberalism, but the assassination of two public lights – Theo van Gogh and Pim Fortuyn – rocked the country's foundations and caused locals, and the ever-present international community, to take a closer look at the fabric of Dutch society.

Pim Fortuyn (pronounced fore-*town*) spent only five months at the head of the LPF (Lijst Pim Fortuyn) party in 2002, but his legacy may last for years to come. His campaign for parliament is best remembered for his declaration that the Netherlands was 'full' and that the government should put the needs of mainstream Dutch people first.

Fortuyn called for the end of backroom politics and for a government led by business people and visionaries. His dynamism instantly struck a chord in Dutch society, and thousands of white low-income earners in Rotterdam and other cities rallied round the gay, dandyish Pim. For a few fleeting months he was fêted as the next prime minister, even though his opponents accused him of pursuing right-wing, racist policies.

Just days before the general election in May 2002 Fortuyn was assassinated by a white animal-rights activist in Hilversum. Riots erupted in front of parliament, and for an instant the threat of anarchy hung in the air.

The LPF won a number of seats in the election and was included in the next coalition, but without a strong leader it soon lost public support and in the 2003 general election voters all but deserted the party.

Theo van Gogh, a well-known film maker and personality, was often in the limelight for his controversial statements and fine films. His 11-minute documentary *Submission Part 1*, which featured four short stories centred on Koranic verses that could be interpreted as justifying violence against women, was a collaborative effort with Ayaan Hirsi Ali, a Muslim-born woman, outspoken critic of Islamic law, Somalian immigrant and member of parliament.

The documentary aired in 2004 on national television, and in November of the same year Van Gogh was shot and his throat cut when he was attacked while cycling through Amsterdam in rush hour. A letter threatening the nation and its politicians (and naming Hirsi Ali) was pinned to his chest with a knife. The killer, a 27-year-old of Dutch and Moroccan descent, was apprehended close to the scene and later sentenced to life imprisonment. The fact that the killer was born and raised in Amsterdam, and professed that he would do the same again if given the chance, threw a nation already in shock.

The Netherlands now faces questions on how best to move forward. Politicians have made the first move, passing laws which require immigrants to know something about Dutch culture, and imposing an exam on prospective immigrants covering Dutch language and culture. However, it's worth remembering that, while the country may currently be rethinking its attitude towards foreigners, Dutch open-mindedness towards newcomers goes back centuries.

Tension between different colours and creeds has never been a problem in the Netherlands, until recently. The murders of Theo van Gogh and Pim Fortuyn have stirred emotions and struck fear into the hearts of some (see above). Also, the Dutch – usually enthusiastic supporters of the EU – resoundingly rejected the EU constitution in a June 2005 referendum. Several reasons for the result were noted, including fears of increased immigration and loss of self-rule to the dominant parties in the EU.

For more on current history, see p22.

2002	2004
Politician Pim Fortuyn is shot dead	Activist film-maker Theo van Gogh is assassinated

The Culture

THE NATIONAL PSYCHE

In general, the Dutch have a sympathetic psyche. They are passionately liberal and believe people should be free to do whatever they want – as long as it doesn't inconvenience others. The most outrageous conduct in public might go without comment; 'Act normal, that's crazy enough' is a common Dutch saying. This high level of tolerance has, however, been put under considerable pressure as a result of two recent high-profile murders (see opposite).

Calvinist traditions have had an influence on the Dutch character, even among Catholics. The Dutch see themselves as sober, hard-working, level-headed and to a certain extent unable to enjoy themselves without feeling guilty – all traits blamed on their Calvinist background. There may be no trace of this whatsoever in crowded pubs, which can seem downright hedonistic. The Dutch also have a tendency to wag the finger in disapproval, which goes against their normally tolerant demeanour.

The country is crowded and Dutch people tend to be reserved with strangers. They treasure their privacy because it is such a rare commodity. Still, they're far from antisocial – their ingrained *gezelligheid* (conviviality) will come out at the drop of a hat. Expect chummy moments at the supermarket.

The Dutch aren't exactly hot-blooded, but given the chance they will speak their minds and expect to be looked in the eye. This manner may seem blunt or even arrogant to foreigners, but the impulse comes from the desire to be direct and, wherever possible, honest.

Subjects such as sex are discussed openly, and you might overhear a pub chat where Jan tells of making whoopee. Dutch parliament even held a debate on whether to ban a TV show called *How to Screw* (but it decided not to). Prostitution is legal, but promiscuity is the furthest thing from most Dutch minds.

Anyone who's worth their weight in bong water knows that you can easily buy marijuana in the Netherlands. This doesn't mean that every Dutch person is a pothead; on the contrary, only about 5% of the population indulges (less than in France, where drug policy is much stricter). Many Dutch people think that hanging out in coffeeshops is for slackers and tourists.

Dutch people have a great love of detail. Statistics on the most trivial subjects make the paper (eg the number of applications for dog licences, incidence of rubbish being put out early), and somewhere down the line it feeds mountains of bureaucracy. That said, when the system breaks down the Dutch aren't rigid about the rules and are happy to improvise; perhaps this comes from a strong legacy of juggling diverse interests.

Last but not least, the Dutch are famously thrifty with their money. They often don't know themselves what to think of this – they laugh at their bottle-scraping (see p34), while at the same time they don't like being called cheap.

LIFESTYLE

Many Dutch live independent, busy lives, divided into strict schedules. Notice is usually required for everything, including visits to your mother, and it's not done to just 'pop round' anywhere. Socialising is done mainly in the home, through clubs and in circles of old friends, which can make it tough for foreigners to 'break in' at first. However, if you're invited to join a family party, you have crossed a major threshold – the Dutch don't invite

DOS & DON'TS

Do give a firm handshake or triple cheek kiss.

Do take a number at the post office counter.

Do show up five to 15 minutes late on social occasions.

Do dress casually unless it's an overtly formal affair.

Do say *'goedendag'* when you enter a shop.

Don't smoke dope or drink on the streets.

Don't be late for official appointments.

Don't ask about a person's salary.

Don't forget someone's birthday.

GOOD TO THE LAST SCRAPE

Arguably, no household item represents Dutch thrift better than the *flessenlikker* (bottle-scraper). This miracle tool culminates in a disk on the business end and can tempt the last elusive smears from a mayonnaise jar or salad-dressing bottle. The *flessenlikker* is a hit in the Netherlands but not, oddly, in its country of origin – Norway.

Another item you'll find in Dutch supermarkets is the traditional Grolsch beer bottle with the resealable ceramic cap. This design was first introduced in the Calvinist north where the steely-eyed imbibers considered the contents of a bottle far too much to drink in one sitting.

---

just *anybody* into their homes, and chances are you've made a friend for life. Birthdays are celebrated in a big way, with oodles of cake and cries of well-wishing loud enough to wake the dead.

The site www.wooden shoes.nl is devoted to a true pillar of Dutch culture, the clog.

Most Dutch families are small, with two or three children. Rents are high, so Junior might live with his family well into his 20s or share an apartment; however, Dutch housing policies have made it easier in recent years to get a mortgage, and many more *yups* (yuppies) buy homes than even a decade ago.

On average the Dutch are fairly well off – they may not flaunt it, but they now earn more per capita than the Germans. Business is no longer booming, but spending for luxury items, especially furniture and interior décor, is jogging along nicely. New cars abound and, apart from the individualists, fewer people chug around in old bombs.

The gay community is well integrated, and the atmosphere is generally relaxed in the big cities. Leading political figures and businessmen are openly gay or lesbian, and attitudes toward gay or lesbian teachers, clergy, doctors and other professionals, even among the older generation, are good. There has however been a rise in gay-bashing in Amsterdam in recent years, and some homosexuals have moved out of the city, citing concerns over safety.

That old chestnut, the weather, always makes fodder for conversation. Evening weather reports merit a timeslot of their own, with presenters waxing lyrical about the size of hailstones or the icicles on Limburg fruit orchards. Rain can last virtually for weeks on end, so when the sun comes out people hit the streets and sidewalks – often just outside their own door. Sitting on the front steps with a cup of coffee and a paper is popular on bright summer mornings, or even when it's just warm and not raining.

ECONOMY

The Netherlands has an extraordinarily strong economy for its size. It's a leader in service industries such as banking, electronics (Philips) and multimedia (PolyGram), and it has a highly developed horticultural industry dealing in bulbs and cut flowers. Agriculture plays an important role, particularly dairy farming and glasshouse fruits and vegetables. Rotterdam harbour handles the largest shipping tonnage in the world, a vital facility in a country that provides more than one-third of Europe's shipping and trucking. Large supplies of natural gas are tapped and refined on the northeast coasts.

GEZELLIGHEID

Variously translated as snug, friendly, cosy, informal, companionable and convivial, *gezelligheid* is a particular trait of the Dutch, and it's best experienced rather than explained. To do so, grab a table with friends in the sun outside a café, hang out for a few hours (preferably the entire day), and you'll soon understand the concept.

Dutch business is largely dependent on exports and has been caught in a larger downturn in Europe and the USA. The last five years have seen a slowdown in the economy, which is a marked change from the heady '90s when the Dutch economy was the envy of Europe. While the country's unemployment rate (6.5%) is not the best in Europe, it's still lower than those of its closest neighbours, Germany (11.6%), Belgium (8.4%) and France (10%).

POPULATION

The need to love thy neighbour is especially strong in the Netherlands, where the population density is the highest in Europe (475 per sq km). Nearly half of the country's 16 million-plus residents live in the western hoop around Amsterdam, Den Haag and Rotterdam; the provinces of Drenthe, Overijssel and Zeeland in the southwest are sparsely settled, in Dutch terms at least. Since 2002, people living in towns and cities outnumbered those living in rural areas.

Over 80% of the population are of Dutch stock; the rest is mainly made up of people from the former colonies of Indonesia, Surinam and the Dutch Antilles, plus more recent arrivals from Turkey and Morocco.

The Dutch are the tallest people in the world, averaging 185.5cm (6ft 1in) for men and 173cm (5ft 8in) for women.

SPORT

The Netherlands is one sport-happy country. About two-thirds of all Dutch engage in some form of sporty activity, and the average person now spends 20 minutes more a week getting sweaty than in the 1970s. Sport is organised to a fault: about five million people belong to nearly 30,000 clubs and associations in the Netherlands.

For virtual entry into the world of the Netherlands' most famous football team, Ajax, log on to www.ajax.nl.

Football (Soccer)

Football is the Dutch national game, and they're pretty good at it. The national football team competes in virtually every World Cup (2006 saw them knocked out in a steamy match against Portugal), and 'local' teams such as Ajax, Feyenoord and PSV enjoy international renown. The country has produced world-class players, such as Ruud Gullit, Dennis Bergkamp and the legendary Johan Cruyff. The unique Dutch approach to the game – known as Total Football (in which spatial tactics are analysed and carried out with meticulous precision) – fascinates viewers even when the teams aren't at the top of the league.

Passions for football run so high it's almost scary. The national football association counts a million members, and every weekend teams professional and amateur hit pitches across the country. Many pro clubs play in modern, hi-tech stadiums such as the Amsterdam ArenA (p132), assisted by a modern, hi-tech police force to combat hooligans.

Brilliant Orange: the Neurotic Genius of Dutch Football by David Winner has interviews with players about their personal experiences, and ties in Dutch architecture, social structure, sense of humour and even Calvinist history in a highly readable attempt to explain the Dutch psyche.

Cycling

To say the Dutch are avid cyclists is like saying the English don't mind football. In sporting terms there's extensive coverage of races in the media, and you'll see uniformed teams whiz by on practice runs in remote quarters. Joop Zoetemelk pedalled to victory in the 1980 Tour de France after finishing second six times. The biggest Dutch wheel-off is the Amstel Gold Race around hilly Limburg in late April, while the five-day Tour de Nederland, which speeds through the country at the end of August, attracts thousands of fans.

Skating

Ice skating is as Dutch as *kroketten* (croquettes; p59), and thousands of people hit the ice when the country's lakes and ditches freeze over. When the lakes aren't frozen, the Netherlands has dozens of ice rinks with Olympic-sized tracks and areas for hockey and figure skating. The most famous amateur event is Friesland's 220km-long Elfstedentocht (p238).

The Dutch generally perform well in speed skating at the Winter Olympics; in 2006 all of its nine medals (three of which were gold) were won in the discipline. International competitions are held at the Thialf indoor ice stadium in Heerenveen, Friesland. Amsterdam's main ice rink was named after Jaap Eden, a legend whose heyday was around 1900.

Swimming

Swimming is the most popular sport when it comes to the raw numbers of practitioners, edging out even football and cycling. One-third of all Dutch swim in the pools, lakes or sea, and fancy aquatic complexes have sprung up in many cities to meet demand. Today's top amphibian is Olympic gold medallist (in both the 2000 and 2004 Olympics) Inge de Bruin, queen of freestyle and butterfly.

Tennis

Tennis has been incredibly popular since Richard Krajicek fell to his knees after clinching the 1996 Wimbledon final. The national tennis club is the country's second largest after football, and many people book time on courts in all-weather sports halls. Krajicek has hung up his racket, but there's fresh blood on the circuit like Martin Verkerk, a finalist at the 2003 French Open, and Michaella Krajicek, who at only 16 entered the top 100 on the professional tour in 2005.

Burgundian duke Philip the Good most likely invented the tennis racquet in Holland in around 1500.

Other Sports

Golf is the fastest-growing sport, with about 170,000 members out on the links every year, and darts has gained an enthusiastic audience following the victories of Raymond van Barneveld, four times world champion. Also, the Netherlands has long had the world's foremost water polo league.

Over the centuries a number of sporting games have evolved in the Netherlands, some of them quaint and curious. *Kaatsen* is ancient Frisian handball played on a large grass pitch, and it's taken deadly seriously in northern towns such as Franeker. *Polstokspringen* is rural pole vaulting over the canals, a pastime known in Friesland as *fierljeppen*. *Korfbal*, a cross between netball, volleyball and basketball, enjoys a vibrant scene across the country.

MULTICULTURALISM

The Netherlands has a long history of tolerance towards immigration and a reputation for welcoming immigrants with open arms. The largest wave of immigration occurred in the 1960s, when the government recruited migrant workers from Turkey and Morocco to bridge a labour gap. In the mid-1970s, the granting of independence to the Dutch colony of Surinam in South America saw an influx of Surinamese.

In the past few years, however, the country's loose immigration policy has been called into question. Politically, there has been a significant swing towards the right and consequently a move towards shutting the door on immigration. The assassinations of Pim Fortuyn and Theo van Gogh caused tensions between the Dutch and Muslim immigrants to rise, and they made many Dutch consider whether immigrants were upholding the *polder* model or trying to force their native traditions on their newly adopted country.

While the government seems to be backtracking on its immigration policy towards developing countries, it is moving ahead with free movement of labour from the new EU countries. As of January 2007, citizens of Poland,

---

DOUBLE DUTCH

For better or for worse, the Dutch have maintained close ties with the English for centuries, and this intimate relationship has led to a menagerie of 'Dutch' catchphrases in the English language. Here are some of the more well known:

- Double Dutch – nonsense or complete gibberish; a jump-rope game using two skipping ropes. 'Going double Dutch' refers to using two types of contraceptive at the same time.
- Dutch courage – strength or confidence gained from drinking alcohol.
- Dutch oven – large, thick-walled cooking pot with a tight-fitting lid; the act of farting in bed, then trapping your partner – and the stench – under the covers.
- Dutch uncle – person who sternly gives (often benevolent) advice.
- Dutch wife – pillow or frame used for resting the legs on in bed; a prostitute or sex doll.
- Going Dutch – splitting the bill at a restaurant. Also known as Dutch date or Dutch treat.
- Pass the dutchie – not a phrase as such, but the title of a top-10 hit by Musical Youth in 1982. 'Dutchie' refers to an aluminium cooking pot supposedly manufactured in the Netherlands and used throughout the West Indies.

Slovenia, Slovakia, the Czech Republic, Hungary, Estonia, Latvia and Lithuania will have unrestricted work access to the Netherlands. How this will change the multicultural make-up of the country, only time will tell.

MEDIA

The Dutch value freedom of expression, and the media have an independent, pluralistic character which is guaranteed by the constitution. Newspapers, TV and radio are free to decide on the nature and content of their programmes.

The Netherlands first set up a public broadcasting system in the 1920s. In an approach that's all Dutch, the airwaves are divided up in an attempt to give everyone a say, and broadcasts are still linked to social or religious groups (air time is allocated in line with their membership numbers). Currently, the TV market is highly competitive, with public stations facing stiff competition from commercial ones. Unsurprisingly, stations are unafraid to push the boundaries of sensibility; you'll see sex tips and prostate cancer examinations (using live models…) broadcast late in the evening. The current reality-TV craze sweeping the globe was born here with *Big Brother*, and the likes of *Fear Factor*, *Extreme Makeover* and *Ready, Steady, Cook* all come from the Netherlands.

The Radio Netherlands website, www.radio netherlands.nl, has articles in English on topical social issues.

Practically every Dutch household subscribes to a daily newspaper. Some of the biggest among the 32 daily papers are the Amsterdam-based *De Telegraaf*, *Het Parool* and *NRC Handelsblad*. Many commuters also pick up copies of the free *Metro* or *Spits* from train-station racks. There's a striking lack of sensationalist rags like Britain's *Sun;* readers rely more on the pulp society mags to catch up on celebrity gossip and the Dutch royal family.

RELIGION

For centuries, religious preference was split between the two heavyweights of Western society, Catholicism and Protestantism, and if you were Dutch you were one or the other. Today, 41% of the population over the age of 18 claims to have no religious affiliation, and the number of former churches that house offices and art galleries is an obvious sign of today's attitude to religion.

The old faith may have suffered a heavy blow in recent decades (secularisation is on the increase), but it's far from dead; 31% of the population follows

Catholicism, 20% Protestantism. Religious communities still have their say in society, and they control much of Sunday morning TV programming. Vestiges exist of a religious border between Protestants and Catholics; the area north of a line running roughly from the province of Zeeland in the southwest to the province of Groningen is home to the majority of Protestants, while anywhere to the south is predominantly Catholic. Protestants can be divided even further, into the Dutch Reformed Church, various orthodox or liberal denominations, and the Lutheran church. In general, Dutch Catholics disagree with the Pope on church hierarchy, contraception and abortion, and they don't go by the term 'Roman Catholic'.

However, church and state are quite separate. The church has little or no influence on taboo subjects such as same-sex marriage, euthanasia, and prescription of cannabis for medical purposes, all of which are legal in the Netherlands.

The latest religion to have any great impact on Dutch society is Islam. It first reached the country's shores with the arrival of immigrants from the Dutch colonies of Indonesia and Surinam in the 1950s, and a second wave broke across the country in the 1960s when immigrant workers were invited in from Morocco and Turkey. Today, approximately 5.5% of the population classes itself as Muslim. Unfortunately, tension has risen between small factions on both sides of the religious fence, but hopefully the commendable Dutch trait of tolerance will continue to prevail.

WOMEN IN THE NETHERLANDS

Dutch women attained the right to vote in 1919, and by the 1970s abortion on demand was paid for by the national health service. Dutch women are a remarkably confident lot; on a social level, equality is taken for granted and women are almost as likely as men to initiate contact with the opposite sex. It's still a different story in the workplace – fewer women than men are employed full time, and fewer still hold positions in senior management.

ARTS

Take a peek behind the doors of Amsterdam's celebrated Rijksmuseum at www.rijksmuseum.nl.

The arts flourished in the Netherlands long before Rembrandt put brush to canvas. The country takes great pride in its world-class museums, the variety of classical and innovative music, and the many theatre productions staged every season. It always seems as though there's room for another arts festival, and the variety boggles the mind.

Painting
THE EARLY DAYS

The Netherlands has spawned a realm of famous painters, starting with Jan van Eyck (1385–1441), who is generally regarded as the founder of the Flemish School and credited with perfecting the technique of oil painting. Hot on his heels was the wonderfully-named Hieronymus Bosch (1415–1516), whose 15th-century religious works are as fearful as they are fascinating, and are charged with fear, distorted creatures and agonised victims. Pieter Brueghel the Elder (1525–69) is another highly acclaimed painter from Holland's early generation, and his allegorical scenes of Flemish landscapes and peasant life are instantly recognisable even by those with a minimal interest in art.

Easily the greatest of the 17th-century Dutch painters was Rembrandt (see the boxed text, opposite), a man of unearthly talent whose plays of light and shadow created shimmering religious scenes. Another great of the era was Frans Hals (1581–1666), who devoted himself to portraits; his expressive

REMBRANDT

Painting is the grandchild of nature. It is related to God.

Rembrandt van Rijn

The son of a miller, Rembrandt van Rijn (1606–69) was the greatest and most versatile of all 17th-century artists. In some respects Rembrandt was centuries ahead of his time, as shown by the emotive brushwork of his later works.

Rembrandt grew up in Leiden, where he became good at chiaroscuro, the technique of creating depth through light and darkness. In 1631 he moved to Amsterdam to run a painting studio, where he and his staff churned out scores of profitable portraits, such as *Anatomy Lesson of Dr Tulp*. The studio work was also good for his personal life; he married the studio owner's niece, Saskia van Uylenburgh.

After Rembrandt fell out with his boss he bought the house next door, now the Rembrandthuis (p99). Here he set up his own studio, employing staff in a warehouse in Amsterdam's Jordaan to cope with the demand for 'Rembrandts'. His paintings became all the rage and the studio became the largest in the country, despite his gruff manners and open agnosticism.

As one of the city's main art collectors Rembrandt often sketched and painted for himself. Amsterdam's Jewish residents acted as models for dramatic biblical scenes.

Business went downhill after Saskia died in 1642. Rembrandt's innovative group portrait, the *Nightwatch*, may have won over the art critics – but his subjects had all paid good money and some were unhappy to appear in the background. The artist's love affairs and lavish lifestyle marred his reputation, and he eventually went bankrupt. His house and art collection were sold and, with the debtors breathing down his neck, Rembrandt took a modest abode on the Jordaan's Rozengracht.

Rembrandt ended life a broken man and passed away a year after the death of his son Titus, largely forgotten by the society he once served. Yet 400 years after his death, the celebrated painter still manages to make headlines. The Netherlands celebrated his 400th anniversary with gusto; a plethora of museums held exhibitions celebrating the man, and the likes of Leiden and Amsterdam created Rembrandt walking routes.

Both the municipal museum in Faro and an art gallery in Liverpool recently discovered fake Rembrandts adorning their walls, and lost works rediscovered in 2006 in Warsaw caused a stir in the art world. To view some of Rembrandt's most famous works, visit the Rijksmuseum in Amsterdam.

paintings can be seen in the Rijksmuseum (p106) in Amsterdam and the Frans Hals Museum (p149) in Haarlem.

A discussion of 17th-century art would not be complete without a mention of Johannes Vermeer (1632–75) of Delft. He was the master of genre painting, such as *View of Delft* and historical and biblical scenes, and he recently gained celluloid fame through *Girl with a Pearl Earring*, a dramatised account of the painting of his famous work of the same name. Both paintings are on display at the Mauritshuis (p197).

Jan Steen (1626–79) skilfully captured the domestic chaos of ordinary Dutch life. Lively and bold, his paintings are not only artistically eye-catching but also fun; *The Merry Family*, on display at the Rijksmuseum, is a classic example, showing adults enjoying themselves around the dinner table, blissfully unaware of the children pouring themselves a drink in the foreground.

If you were to prompt passers-by to name the first painter to pop into their head, a high majority would probably blurt out Vincent van Gogh. Although he spent much of his life in Belgium and France, he is very much claimed by the Dutch as one of their own (for more, see p40).

VINCENT VAN GOGH

Without a doubt the greatest 19th-century Dutch painter was Vincent van Gogh (1853–90). His striking use of colour, coarse brushwork and layered contours put him in a league all his own, yet, astonishingly, he was self taught and his painting career lasted less than 10 years, from 1881 to 1890. In this time he produced a staggering 900 paintings and 1100 drawings.

Born in Zundert near the Belgian border, the young Van Gogh started off in his uncle's art dealership in 1869, but he found it hard to settle and over the next 10 years tried his hand as a teacher in England and a missionary in Belgium. By 1880 he had found his true calling, however, and threw himself into painting with abandon.

He spent much of his early career in the Low Countries, where he produced dark, heavy paintings, such as his celebrated *Potato Eaters* (1885). In the mid-1800s he moved to Paris to live with his brother Theo, a constant support for the troubled artist; it was here that his contact with impressionists such as Pissarro, Degas and Gauguin transformed the Dutchman's painting into blazing flowers, portraits and the wide-open spaces of Paris.

In 1888 Van Gogh moved to Arles and formed an artists' cooperative with Gauguin, but depression and hallucinations began to haunt him. In an argument with Gauguin, Van Gogh conducted possibly his most famous act by cutting off his left ear lobe in his despair and sending it to a prostitute.

Towards the end of his life mental ill health forced him into a psychiatric hospital, but in his lucid moments he continued to paint. His spiritual anguish and depression became more acute, however, and on 27 July 1890 he shot himself; he survived two more days before succumbing.

It is sad to note that his paintings were only appreciated towards the end of his life (he sold one painting while alive, *Red Vineyard at Arles*) and he lived a life of poverty. Today his paintings fetch millions; his *Portrait of Dr Gachet* is the second most expensive painting ever sold, going for a cool US$82.5 million in 1990 (around US$117 million in 2006 with inflation). His works now hang in galleries from New York to Moscow, but a number can be seen in the Van Gogh Museum (p106) and the Kröller-Müller Museum (p269).

DE STIJL & BEYOND

An Amersfoort-born painter named Piet Mondriaan (1872–1944) changed the direction of 20th-century art when he introduced the cubist De Stijl movement in 1917. De Stijl aimed to harmonise all the arts by returning artistic expression to its essence, and the artist – who changed the spelling of his name to Mondrian after moving to Paris in 1910 – did this by reducing shapes to horizontal and vertical lines. His paintings came to consist of bold rectangular patterns using only the three primary colours (red, yellow and blue), a style known as neoplasticism. The moving ode to the USA entitled *Victory Boogie Woogie* is considered the flagship work of the genre. Amsterdam's Stedelijk Museum (p109) has other examples on display, such as *Composition with Red, Black, Blue, Yellow and Grey*. The movement influenced a generation of sculptors and designers such as Gerrit Rietveld, who planned the Van Gogh Museum and other buildings along De Stijl lines.

The last century also saw the perplexing designs of Maurits Cornelis Escher (1902–72), whose impossible images continue to fascinate to this day. A waterfall feeds itself, people go up and down a staircase that ends where it starts, a pair of hands draw each other. He was also a master of organic tile patterns that feed into one another while subtly changing the picture into something else; his work can be viewed at the Escher in het Paleis (p198) in Den Haag.

After WWII, artists rebelled against artistic conventions and vented their rage in abstract expressionism. Karel Appel (1921–2006) and Constant (1920–2005) drew on styles pioneered by other European artists, exploiting bright colours to produce works that leapt off the canvas. In Paris they met up with Danish Asger Jorn (1914–73) and the Belgian Corneille (1922–), and together these artists formed the CoBrA group (Copenhagen, Brussels and Amsterdam). Much of their work can be seen at the CoBrA Museum (p110).

Contemporary Dutch artists are usually well represented at international events such as the Biennale in Venice and the Documenta in Kassel. The ranks of distinguished contemporary artists include Jan Dibbets (1941–), Ger van Elk (1941–) and Marthe Röling (1939–).

Music

The old, dour Calvinists of the 17th century were never fans of music, dismissing it as frivolous. They only began to allow church organ music because they realised it kept people out of pubs.

Despite this inauspicious start, the music scene in the Netherlands is blisteringly good. Dutch musicians excel in the classics, techno/dance and jazz, and the high level of music appreciation means there's a steady stream of touring talent.

There has, however, been a revival in '80s music in recent years. You'll hear it in restaurants, bars and even clubs ('80s nights are all the rage). While we're not bashing the music of over two decades ago (who doesn't like early Depeche Mode?), after a week or two of listening to '80s pop you'll be ready to listen to *anything* else.

CLASSICAL MUSIC

The Netherlands has many orchestras based in cities throughout the country. Den Haag, Rotterdam and Maastricht have a full calendar of performances by local orchestras and groups, but Amsterdam's Royal Concertgebouw Orchestra towers over them all. It frequently performs abroad, mixing and matching works by famous composers with little-known gems of the modern era.

The Orchestra of the 18th Century and the Amsterdam Baroque Orchestra are well-known smaller ensembles. The classics of Bach, Handel and Vivaldi are always in sensitive hands at the Combattimento Consort Amsterdam.

The Dutch have many fine classical musicians. Among pianists, Wibi Soerjadi (who studied at Amsterdam's prestigious Sweelinck Conservatory) is one of the most successful and specialises in romantic works. Halls are always filled for Ronald Brautigam, a grand master and winner of a host of accolades, including the Dutch national music prize.

Top violinists include Isabelle van Keulen, who often collaborates with Brautigam. An engaging personality of seemingly endless vitality, Van Keulen has founded her own chamber music festival in Delft.

Cellists of note include Quirine Viersen, a powerful, intense soloist who won the International Cello Competition in Paris. The fiery bowing of Pieter Wispelwey from Leiden thrills audiences around the world.

In the voice department there's no diva greater than soprano Charlotte Margiono, who pretty much wrote the book on interpretation in *Le Nozze di Figaro*, the *Magic Flute* and other classics. Mezzo-soprano Jard van Nes has a giant reputation for her solo parts in Mahler's symphonies.

Modern Dutch composers include Louis Andriessen, Theo Loevendie, Klaas de Vries and the late Ton de Leeuw. Many of their works are forays into the uncharted waters of experimental music, and nowhere is the sense of adventure more tangible than in Amsterdam. Look out for the Trio, Asko Ensemble, Nieuw Ensemble and, last but not least, the Schönberg Ensemble, conducted by Reinbert de Leeuw. These performers often appear in Amsterdam's IJsbreker music hall.

The Netherlands Opera stages about 10 world-class performances a year at its home, Amsterdam's Muziektheater (p130). Contemporary opera forms an important part of the repertoire and inevitably stirs up a lot of controversy.

'In the voice department there's no diva greater than soprano Charlotte Margiono...'

JAZZ

In the past the Netherlands hasn't bred oodles of jazz talent. However, the phenomenal success of the North Sea Jazz Festival has sown some powerful seeds, and the Dutch jazz scene can now stand on its own two feet. Europe's largest jazzfest, the festival is held in Den Haag every summer. Amsterdam's leading jazz club, Bimhuis (p130), has a concert agenda that's all quality.

The Netherlands has fostered some gifted jazz singers. Familiar to Dutch audiences for decades, the honeyed voice of Denise Jannah finally caught the attention of Blue Note in the 1990s. Her repertoire is American standards with touches of her Surinamese homeland.

Originally a jazz and cabaret vocalist, Astrid Seriese now captures a wider public with a variety of styles, from lyrical Cole Porter to rock and soundtracks for documentaries. Soulful Carmen Gomez is as comfortable singing Aretha Franklin as Ella Fitzgerald tunes. Fleurine is another gifted young chanteuse.

Dutch saxophone romped onto the international stage thanks to Hans and Candy Dulfer, father and daughter of the reeds. On alto sax, Candy is a known commodity, thanks to her funky performances with Prince, Van Morrison, Dave Stewart, Pink Floyd and many others. Hans blows jazz standards but also incorporates hip-hop and other genres.

A great soloist on flute is Peter Guidi, who set up the jazz programme at the Muziekschool Amsterdam and leads its Jazzmania big band.

Born in Amsterdam's Jordaan district, trumpeter Saskia Laroo mixes jazz with dance and has been able to 'play for the people while still being innovative', as one critic put it. She leads a number of acts including Smoothgroovy BreakBeats with HotLicks.

For top-rate jazz piano, pick up a CD of Michiel Borstlap, a winner of the Thelonius Monk award, who has recorded with Peter Erskine, Toots Thielemans, Ernie Watts and many others. His soul and label mate is bass player Hein van de Geyn.

On guitar, Jesse van Ruller's effortless playing is the stuff of complex refinement, especially on up-tempo pieces. He snagged the Thelonius Monk award in 1996, like Borstlap.

Big-band leaders such as Willem Breuker and Willem van Manen (of Contraband) straddle modern classical and improvised music, an acquired taste for some audiences. The XLJazz Orkest, a new big band with strings conducted by composer-arranger Gerrit Jan Brinkhorst, brings together established pros and hungry young blowers.

'bands and DJs are attracted to the city like moths to the flame.'

POP, ROCK & DANCE

Amsterdam is the pop capital of the Netherlands, and bands and DJs are attracted to the city like moths to the flame. However, Rotterdam gives the capital a run for its money in the dance stakes, with a clubbing scene to rival that of most cities around the world.

In the '60s Amsterdam was the hub of counter-culture, but the epicentre of pop was in Den Haag. The Scheveningse Boulevard was the place to see bands like Shocking Blue in full view of Veronica, the radio station that broadcast tunes from a harbour ship. In 1969 Golden Earring's *Eight Miles High* album went gold in the USA.

The '70s brought a few more Dutch hits internationally. In 1973 Jan Akkerman's progressive rock band Focus conquered the charts with Thijs van Leer as chief yodeller. Herman Brood burst onto the scene with *His Wild Romance* and became a real-life, druggy, self-absorbed rock star, until he threw himself off the top of the Amsterdam Hilton in 2001. After his death, his remake of *My Way* went to number one in the Netherlands.

The squatters' movement spawned a lively punk scene, followed by the manic synthesizers of New Wave. By the mid-1980s Amsterdam was a magnet for guitar-driven rock bands such as Claw Boys Claw, dyed-in-the-wool garage rockers. Most vocalists stuck to lyrics in English, but the pop group Doe Maar broke through in Dutch, inspiring scores of bands such as Tröckener Kecks. Around this time Amsterdam also evolved into a capital of club music – house, techno and R&B, with its spiritual base at the überclub Roxy (which later burnt to a crisp).

Dutch bands were power-boosted by the 1991 introduction of commercial radio. In the early 1990s the best-known Dutch variant of house was gabber, which originated in Rotterdam; it's known for its stripped-back sound and monotonous beat (up to 260 beats per minute). Rotterdam Terror Corps are considered the pioneer of this genre and are still around today.

The hip grooves of Candy Dulfer (see opposite) and the hip-hoppy Urban Dance Squad made America's Top 20 during the decade. Bettie Serveert, a nod to Dutch tennis player Betty Stöve, grew into one of the biggest bands on the club circuit. Amsterdam hip-hop was spearheaded by the Osdorp Posse, who rap in their mother tongue. Following in their footsteps is the immensely popular Moroccan-Dutch rapper Ali-B.

The Netherlands has become a major centre for dance music, particularly trance. Amsterdam and Rotterdam attract top DJs from around the world on an almost weekly basis, but quite often clubs only need to scan the local market for internationally-renowned DJs. Tiësto is the undisputed trancemeister, and other top DJs include Armin van Buuren and Ferry Corsten.

'Pop festivals come out of the woodwork in the warmer months...'

Pop festivals come out of the woodwork in the warmer months: Pinkpop in Landgraaf, Parkpop in Den Haag and Dynamo Open Air at Neunen. Dance Valley near Haarlem pulls over 100 bands and even more DJs to the biggest open-air dancefest in the Benelux region.

WORLD MUSIC

Cosmopolitan Amsterdam offers a wealth of world music. Surinam-born Ronald Snijders, a top jazz flautist, often participates in world music projects. Another jazz flautist heading towards 'world' is the eternal Chris Hinze with his album *Tibet Impressions*, though most of his repertoire falls in the New Age category.

Fra-Fra-Sound plays paramaribop, a unique mixture of traditional Surinamese kaseko and jazz, however the bulk of world repertoire from Amsterdam is Latin, ranging from Cuban salsa to Dominican merengue and Argentine tango. A sparkling Dutch-Brazilian band is Zuco 103, which melds bossa nova and samba with DJ rubs on the turntable. The New Cool Collective is a big band with vocals that serves up a groovy cocktail of Latin, jazz, New Age and '60s go-go. Other bands providing a taste of the Dutch world scene include Nueva Manteca (salsa), Sexteto Canyengue (tango) and Eric Vaarzon Morel (flamenco).

The Amsterdam Roots Music Festival (p117) of world music takes place in Amsterdam's Oosterpark every June.

Literature

The Netherlands has a rich literary heritage, but its gems used to be reserved for Dutch speakers. Most of its best-known contemporary authors were finally translated into English beginning in the mid-1990s.

In the Middle Ages Dutch literature stuck to epic tales of chivalry and allegories. But that changed in the 16th century with Erasmus, a name familiar to school children across the globe. The leading Dutch humanist wrote a satire on the church and society called *His Praise of Folly*.

COFFEESHOPS

Love 'em or hate 'em, it's almost impossible to avoid them, or at least the sweet smell wafting from their direction. This is the humble *koffieshop*, an establishment unique to the Netherlands (but tried in a number of European countries) that sells cannabis and, to a lesser extent, magic mushrooms and coffee.

Every major town (and a few minor) has a handful of coffeeshops, and the touristy joints are easy to spot: just look for the telling hemp leaves, Rastafarian colours (red, yellow and green) or *X-Files* alien adorning the façade. However, the better, more comfortable – and far more appealing – shops can be hard to differentiate from a regular *koffiehuis* (espresso bar or sandwich shop) or café, and usually cater to a discerning local crowd. Very few serve alcohol, which is a blessing in disguise as it's not always wise to mix the two drugs.

The range of marijuana on sale can be quite daunting, so it's best to get the advice of someone behind the bar. Be honest – if you're a novice, don't be afraid to 'fess up; it's better to start with something light (like Thai) than end up getting ill after smoking some Skunk or White Zombie. Pre-rolled joints are available for anything between €2 and €5, and these are handy for sampling various types. Most people buy small bags of dope, though, which go for around €4 to €12 (the better the quality, the less the bag will contain). Price and quality are generally OK – you won't get ripped off in a coffeeshop.

Most cannabis products used to be imported, but these days the country has top-notch home produce, so-called *nederwiet* (*nay*-der-weet), developed by diligent horticulturists and grown in greenhouses with up to five harvests a year. Even the police admit it's a superior product, especially the potent 'superskunk' with up to 13% of the active substance THC (Nigerian grass has 5% and Colombian 7%). According to a government-sponsored poll of coffeeshop owners, *nederwiet* has captured over half the market, and hash is in decline even among tourists.

Space cakes and cookies (and even chocolate!) are sold in a rather low-key fashion, mainly because of their potency and the time it takes for them to kick in; some take an hour to work, in which time you've probably consumed a couple more because you're not feeling anything… ask the staff how much you should take and heed their advice. If you do it right, you'll have a very gentle, pleasant ride for up to six hours. Many coffeeshops sell magic mushrooms, which are quite legal as an untreated, natural product.

For information on how much you can buy and at what age you can smoke, see p293.

The literary lights of the Golden Age included Spinoza, an Amsterdam Jew who wrote deep philosophical treatises. Spinoza rejected the concept of free will, contending that humans acted purely out of self-preservation. Mind and body were made of the same stuff, which he alternately called God and Nature – this got him into all kinds of trouble.

Joost van den Vondel is often regarded as the Dutch Shakespeare. His best tragedy, *Lucifer,* describes the archangel's rebellion against God. Dutch literature flourished in the 17th century under writers such as Bredero, one of the early comic writers, and Hooft, a veritable multitalent who penned poems, plays and history. The bible was also translated into Dutch in the 17th century, and the publication of *De Statenbijbel* in 1637 was a milestone in the evolution of the Dutch language.

Postwar literature was dominated by three eminent novelists, Willem Frederik Hermans, Harry Mulisch and Gerard Reve, and the war featured prominently in many works. In recent years they were joined by distinguished writers such as Jan Wolkers, Maarten 't Hart and Frederik van der Heijden, but these offerings are still tough to find in English. Many of these authors have been awarded the PC Hooftprijs, the Dutch national literary prize.

In the contemporary field, Cees Nooteboom is one of the country's most prolific writers; his novel *The Following Story* won the Aristeion European

Prize for Literature in 1991. Other authors to watch for include Simon Carmiggelt, a regular columnist for *Het Parool*, Jan Wolkers, whose *Turkish Delight* – an intense story of obsessive love – shocked Dutch readers in the late '60s, and Arthur Japin, an actor/writer with a number of novels under his belt (his latest work, *In Lucia's Eyes*, has gained plenty of international adulation).

The growing interest in Dutch literature has been no accident. The Dutch Literary Production and Translation Fund (www.nlpvf.nl) began propagating the nation's literature abroad in 1991 and the efforts have paid off. Many titles now appearing in English were already bestsellers in German and other languages.

RECOMMENDED READS

- *Max Havelaar* by Multatuli. An indictment of colonial forced-labour policy in the Dutch East Indies (present-day Indonesia), written in 1860. Multatuli – Latin for 'I have suffered greatly' – was the pen name of Eduard Dekker, a colonial bureaucrat.

- *Diary of Anne Frank (Het Dagboek van Anne Frank)* by Anne Frank. Possibly the most famous book penned in the Netherlands; a moving account of a young Jewish girl's thoughts while hiding from the occupying Germans.

- *A Dutchman's Slight Adventures (Een Handvol Kronkels)* by Simon Carmiggelt. Comical Amsterdam vignettes by the winner of many literary prizes including the PC Hooftprijs. Many items appeared in the Amsterdam paper *Het Parool*. Tricky to find in English.

- *The Happy Hooker* by Xaviera Hollander. An unapologetic yet upbeat look at the world of the sex worker, based on a true story. This classic 1972 novel came out when 'damn' still elicited gasps from the audience.

- *Parents Worry (Bezorgde Ouders)* by Gerard Reve. Historical novel from one of Holland's first out-and-out homosexuals about one day in the ravaged life of a poet looking for truth and a way out. Hard to find, but well worth the search.

- *In a Dark Wood Wandering (Het Woud der Verwachting)* by Hella Haase. Quirky historical novel set during the Hundred Years' War, with a cast of believable characters based on great figures from mad Charles VI to Joan of Arc.

- *The Following Story (Het Volgende Verhaal)* by Cees Nooteboom. Award-winning contemporary Dutch writer tackles a schoolmaster's journey through memory and imagination in the final seconds of his life.

- *The Discovery of Heaven (De Ontdekking van de Hemel)* by Harry Mulisch. Two friends find they were conceived on the same day, and share love, hate, a women and a child who is destined to return the Ten Commandments to God. Made into a film of the same name in 2001.

- *A Heart of Stone (Een Hart van Steen)* by Renate Dorrestein. A terrifying Gothic-style tale of violence, childhood and madness told from inside the minds of three troubled children of a superficially idyllic family.

- *First Gray, Then White, Then Blue (Eerst Grijs, Dan Wit, Dan Blauw)* by Margriet de Moor. An intense tale of passion and deception in which a woman reappears after a two-year absence from her husband, with no explanation or remorse.

- *The Two Hearts of Kwasi Boachi (De Zwarte met het Witte Hart)* by Arthur Japin. The true story of two West African princes sent to study in Holland in the 1830s, and what becomes of them in the ensuing years.

- *The Vanishing (Het Gouden Ei* – The Golden Egg) by Tim Krabbé. Gripping psychological thriller following a man's hunt for his missing girlfriend, and a study of the banality of evil. Made into the Dutch-French film *Spoorloos* and remade as the American film *The Vanishing*.

Cinema & Television

Dutch cinema hasn't rocked the world, but that's not to say there isn't anything worth seeing. The country's small film industry produces around 20 feature films a year, often in association with other countries. Private funding is on the increase as, unfortunately, government funding was pruned in the last few years.

In recent times Dutch films have won a string of nominations for best foreign film at the Academy Awards. In 2003, it was Paula van der Oest's *Zus & So*; 2004 saw Ben Sombogaart's *Twin Sisters* make the final cut; and in 2006 *Paradise Now*, a film by Hany Abu-Assad, a Dutch-Palestinian, did the same. The latter won the Golden Globe in 2006.

Dutch filmmakers who have made it big in Hollywood include Paul Verhoeven (*Robocop, Basic Instinct, Starship Troopers*) and Jan de Bont (*Speed, Lara Croft II*). The former, however, has produced better work at home, such as the violent erotic thriller *De Vierde Man* (The Fourth Man), and *Turks Fruit* (Turkish Delight), a provocative tale of love and sex. George Sluizer has also made inroads into Hollywood but has yet to reach the astounding heights of his *Spoorloos* (the original *The Vanishing*).

Leading actors Rutger Hauer, Jeroen Krabbé and Famke Janssen are often not recognised as being Dutch – it's those good English skills again.

A website devoted to the latest comings and goings in the contemporary Dutch film arena is www.hollandfilm.nl.

The biggest loss to Dutch cinema in recent years is Theo van Gogh. His greatest box-office success was *06*, a film about a phone-sex relationship, but he will be forever remembered for *Submission: Part 1*, a short piece showing how verses from the Koran could be used to justify violence against women, that was aired not long before his murder. Ironically, he was in the middle of filming *06/05*, a fictional version of the assassination of Pim Fortuyn, when he himself was assassinated.

Film festivals worth noting include the Rotterdam International Film Festival in February, Utrecht's Netherlands Film Festival in September, and Amsterdam's International Documentary Film Festival and Fantastic Film Festival, held in December and April, respectively.

For a snippet of information about Dutch TV, see p37.

Photography

The Netherlands has a tradition of photography committed to social themes. The first World Press Photo exhibition was held in Amsterdam in 1975, and the exhibition still opens in the city before touring 80 countries around the globe.

Documentary photography and portraits seem to be the focus of younger-generation Dutch photographers. The photos of Wubbo de Jong, one of the country's best, can range from disturbing to funny, but are always thought-proving and powerful, while the late Ed van der Elsken had the ability to capture the world in its unguarded moments.

The list of leading lights today seems endless. At the fore is Rineke Dijkstra, with her unglamorous head-on portraits of common folk, and Marie Cecile Thijs, who adds more colour and humour to her portrait shots. The photos of Henk Braam, a top docu-shooter, are an unflinching take on some of the troubled corners of the globe. The inseparable Inez van Lamsweerde and Vinoodh Matadin create slick shots for the advertising world, while the internationally-successful Anton Corbijn has had the privilege to photograph the likes of Johnny Depp, Tom Waits, Miles Davis, Keith Richards, Nick Cave, David Bowie and many more.

Excellent collections of photographs can be viewed at Amsterdam's Rijksmuseum and Stedelijk Museum, and at the Print Room at Leiden University. The Netherlands Photography Institute is in Rotterdam, and private galleries in all the major cities hold exhibitions.

Theatre

The Netherlands has a rich theatrical tradition going back to medieval times. In the Golden Age, when Dutch was the language of trade, companies from the Low Countries toured the theatres of Europe. Some highlights of the era – Vondel's tragedies, Bredero's comedies and Hooft's verses – are still performed today, albeit with a modern voice.

By the end of the 19th century, however, theatre had become downright snobbish.

This trend continued until the 1960s, when disgruntled actors began to throw tomatoes at their older colleagues and engaged the audience in discussion. Avant-garde theatre companies such as Mickery and Shaffy made Amsterdam a centre for experimental theatre, and many smaller companies sprang up in their wake.

There are many professional theatre companies, including traditional repertory companies and smaller companies who are exploring new avenues of theatre, often combining music, mime and new media techniques. The language barrier can prove problematic, depending on the production.

When it's not touring abroad, De Dogtroep (www.dogtroep.nl) stages fancy and unpredictable 'happenings' in quirky venues like an Utrecht archaeological dig or Amsterdam's ship passenger terminal. Each show is supported by flashy multimedia effects and technical gadgetry. A spin-off of Dogtroep, Warner & Consorten (www.warnerenconsorten.nl) is a variation on the same theme; it stages dialogue-free shows with plenty of humour, and music is generated with everyday items.

English-language companies often visit Amsterdam, especially in summer. Glitzy big-budget musicals have won over audiences in recent years, as have English-language outfits like Boom Chicago with its fast-paced comedy.

Highlights of the Dutch theatre season include the Holland Festival (p116) and Over het IJ (www.overhetij.nl) in Amsterdam, and the edgier Robodock (www.robodock.org), held at Rotterdam's shipyards. Shows at the latter are driven by feuding robots, ameobic screen projections and choreographed pyrotechnics.

Those with a particular interest in Dutch theatre should check out the Theatre Museum in the Theater Instituut Nederland (p101).

'In the Golden Age, when Dutch was the language of trade, companies from the Low Countries toured the theatres of Europe.'

Dance

The Netherlands is a world leader in modern dance. The troupe of the Nederlands Dans Theater (www.ndt.nl) in Den Haag leaps and pirouettes to international audiences. There are also many smaller modern dance companies such as Introdans, which can truly be described as poetry in motion.

Originally for youth audiences, Rotterdam's Scapino Ballet (www.scapino ballet.nl) has built up a wide repertoire of contemporary dance in recent years. The city is also home to Dansacadamie (www.hmd.nl), the nation's largest dance school. The National Ballet (www.het-nationale-ballet.nl) in Amsterdam performs mainly classical ballets but also presents 20th-century works by Dutch choreographers such as Rudi van Dantzig or Toer van Schayk. The biennial Holland Dance Festival (hollanddance.plant.nl) in Den Haag draws some of the world's most sophisticated productions.

Environment

There's no arguing with the fact that the Netherlands is a product of human endeavour, and a well-manicured one at that. Everywhere you look, from the neat rows of *polders* (strips of farmland separated by canals) to the omnipresent dykes, everything looks so, well, planned and organised. 'God created the world, but the Dutch created the Netherlands', as the saying goes.

Much of this tinkering with nature has been out of necessity – it's hard to live underwater for any length of time. But all this reorganisation has put a strain on the Dutch environment. Whether it's from pollution, deforestation or flooding, the cumulative dangers to natural and artificial environments are arguably greater than ever. Nearly one-third of the country's surface is devoted to agriculture, while much of the rest serves towns and industry.

In the late 20th century Dutch awareness of the environment grew by leaps and bounds. Citizens now dutifully sort their rubbish, support pro-bicycle schemes, and protest over scores of projects of potential detriment – even the air miles offered at supermarket tills. City-centre congestion has been eased by cutting parking spaces, erecting speed bumps and initiating park-and-ride programmes. Country roads tend to favour bike lanes at the cost of motor vehicles.

But all this progress isn't a given. New EU environmental laws don't go as far as the Dutch would like, and the slowing economy has meant cutbacks to major clean-up schemes. Still, the Dutch now tend to monitor pollution as they do their dykes – with extreme vigilance.

THE LAND

Flanked by Belgium, Germany and the choppy waters of the North Sea, the land mass of the Netherlands is to a great degree artificial, having been reclaimed from the sea over many centuries. Maps from the Middle Ages are a curious sight today, with large chunks of land 'missing' from Noord Holland and Zeeland. The country now encompasses 41,526 sq km, making it roughly half the size of Scotland or a touch bigger than the USA's state of Maryland.

A third of the dairy cattle in the world are Holstein Friesian, a high-yielding variety from the Netherlands.

Twelve provinces make up the Netherlands. Almost all of these are as flat as a Dutch pancake, for want of a better term; the only hills to speak of in the entire country rise from its very southern tip, near Maastricht. The soil in the west and north is relatively young and consists of peat and clay formed less than 10,000 years ago. Much of this area is below sea level, or reclaimed land (half the country lies at or below sea level in the form of *polders*). The sandy, gravelly layer throughout the east and south is much older, having been deposited by rivers and then pushed up into ridges during the last ice age. This part of the country is noticeably different in appearance, with patches of forest and heath.

Polders form 60% of the Netherlands landscape.

The efforts of the Dutch to create new land – which basically equates to reclaiming it from the encroaching sea – are almost super-human. Over the past century alone four vast *polders* have been created through ingenious engineering: Wieringermeer in Noord Holland; the Noordoostpolder (Northeast *polder*) in Flevoland; and the Noordpolder (North *polder*) and Zuidpolder (South *polder*) on the province-island of Flevoland. Much of this, just over 1700 sq km, was drained after a barrier dyke closed off the North Sea in 1932 (see p175). In total, an astounding 20% of the country is reclaimed land.

It's impossible to talk about the Dutch landscape without mentioning water. Of the 41,526 sq km that the Dutch claim as the Netherlands, 7643 sq km is liquid; that amounts to around 20% of the entire country. Most Dutch people shudder at the thought of a leak in the dykes. If the Netherlands were to lose its 2400km of mighty dykes and dunes – some of which are 25m high – the large cities would be inundated by rivers as well as by the sea. Modern pumping stations run around the clock to drain off excess water.

The danger of floods is most acute in the southwest province of Zeeland, a sprawling estuary for the rivers Schelde, Maas, Lek and Waal. The latter two are branches of the Rijn, the final legs of a watery journey that begins in the Swiss Alps. The mighty Rijn itself peters out in a tiny stream called the Oude Rijn (Old Rhine) at the coast near Katwijk. The Maas is another of Europe's major rivers to cross the country. It rises in France and travels through Belgium before depositing its load in the North Sea in the Delta region.

WILDLIFE

Human encroachment has played a huge role in the wildlife of the Netherlands. Few wildlife habitats are left intact in the country, and over 10% of species are imported; since 1900, the number of imported species has doubled.

While Holland's flora and fauna will forever be in constant change, one thing remains the same – birds love the place. A great depth of species can be seen the entire year round, and bird-watching enthusiasts will be all aflutter at the abundance of opportunities to spot our feathered friends.

The site www.dutch birding.nl is the online home of the Dutch Birding Society.

Animals

The Netherlands is a paradise for birds and those who love to follow them around. The wetlands are a major migration stop for European birds, particularly the Wadden Islands' Duinen van Texel National Park (p167), Flevoland's Oostvaardersplassen Nature Reserve (p176) and the Delta (p228). Just take the geese: a dozen varieties, from white-fronted to pink-footed, break their V-formations to winter here. New wind-energy parks along the routes are controversial because thousands of birds get caught in the big blades.

Along urban canals you'll see plenty of mallards, coots and swans as well as the lovely grebe with its regal head plumage. The graceful blue heron spears frogs and tiny fish in the ditches of the *polder* lands but also loiters on canal boats in and out of town. Other frequent guests include the black cormorant, an accomplished diver with a wingspan of nearly 1m. Feral pigeons are rarely in short supply, especially for handouts on town squares.

Where to Watch Birds in Holland, Belgium and Northern France by Arnoud van den Berg and Dominque Lafontaine is a regional guide to the best places to see your favourite species, with the locations of observation hides.

A great variety of fish species dart about the canals and estuaries. One of the most interesting species is the eel, which thrives in both fresh and salt water. These amazing creatures breed in the Sargasso Sea off Bermuda before making the perilous journey to the North Sea (only to land on someone's dinner plate). Freshwater species such as white bream, rudd, pike, perch, stickleback and carp also enjoy the canal environment. You can admire them up close at Amsterdam's Artis Zoo (p108), in an aquarium that simulates a canal environment.

In the coastal waters there are 12 crustacean species including the Chinese mitten crab. This tasty little guy from the Far East has adapted so well to the Dutch estuaries that it's a hazard to river habitats. Further out, the stock of North Sea cod, shrimp and sole has suffered from chronic overfishing, and catches are now limited by EU quotas.

Larger mammals such as the fox, badger and fallow deer have retreated to the national parks and reserves. Some species such as boar, mouflon and red deer have been reintroduced to controlled habitats. Herds of seals can

---

BIRD-WATCHING FOR BEGINNERS

Seen through an amateur bird-watcher's eyes, some of the more interesting sightings might include the following:

- Avocet – common on the Waddenzee and the Delta, with slender upturned bill, and black and white plumage.
- Black woodpecker – drums seldom but loudly. To see it, try woodlands such as Hoge Veluwe National Park.
- Bluethroat – song like a free-wheeling bicycle; seen in Biesbosch National Park, Flevoland and the Delta.
- Great white egret – crane-like species common in marshlands. First bred in Flevoland in the early 1990s.
- Marsh harrier – bird of prey; often hovers over reed beds and arable land.
- Spoonbill – once scarce, this odd-looking fellow has proliferated on coasts in Zeeland and the Wadden Islands.
- White stork – nearly extinct in the 1980s, numbers have since recovered. Enormous nests.

---

be spotted on coastal sandbanks. Introduced muskrats are common in the countryside, while their cousins, the water vole and the brown rat, find shelter in the canalside nooks and crannies of cities. The cricket-like squeak of dwarf bats can be heard on summer nights – the dune reserves are a good place to see them.

Plants

Mention plant life in the Netherlands and most people think of tulips. Indeed, these cultivated bulbs are in many ways representative of much of the country's flora in that they were imported from elsewhere and then commercially exploited. A range of other flowers and fruit and vegetables – such as tomatoes and sweet peppers – fit this profile. Others, like the water pennywort, don't. This introduced water plant grows so fast over a short period of time that it often jeopardises water discharge.

Of course, the flowers of the Netherlands are not limited to exotic types. There are also thousands of wild varieties on display, such as the marsh orchid (pink crown of tiny blooms) or the Zeeland masterwort (bunches of white, compact blooms).

Much of the undeveloped land is covered by grass, which is widely used for grazing. The wet weather means that the grass remains green and grows for much of the year – on coastal dunes and mud flats, and around brackish lakes and river deltas. Marshes, heaths and peatlands are the next most common features. The remnants of oak, beech, ash and pine forests are carefully managed. Wooded areas such as Hoge Veluwe National Park are mostly products of recent forestation, so trees tend to be young and of a similar age. Even the vegetation on islands such as Ameland is monitored to control erosion.

The Netherlands is planted in 228 sq km of flower bulbs, the equivalent of around 32,500 football fields.

NATIONAL PARKS

The site www.nationaal park.nl/english.phtml provides a comprehensive list of national parks in the Netherlands.

With so few corners of the Netherlands left untouched, the Dutch cherish every bit of nature that's left, and that's doubly true for their national parks. But while the first designated natural reserve was born in 1930, it wasn't until 1984 that the first publicly funded park was established.

National parks in the Netherlands tend to be small affairs – for an area to become a park, it must only be bigger than 10 sq km (and of course be important in environmental terms). Most of the 20 national parks in the country average a mere 6400 hectares and are not meant to preserve some natural wonder but are open areas of special interest. A total of 1289 sq km, or just over 3%, of the Netherlands is protected in the form of national parks; the most northerly is the island of Schiermonnikoog, and the most southerly is the terraced landscape of De Meinweg. By 2018 the government plans to extend the network of protected areas to 7000 sq km.

The better national parks are often heavily visited, not only because there's plenty of nature to see but also because of their well-developed visitor centres and excellent displays of contemporary flora and fauna. Hoge Veluwe, established in 1935, is a particular favourite. Once the country retreat of the wealthy Kröller-Müller family, it's now open to the public, who can explore the sandy hills and forests that once were prevalent in this part of the Netherlands.

Of the 19 remaining national parks, Weerribben in Overijssel is one of the most important as it preserves a landscape once heavily scarred by the peat harvest. Here the modern objective is to allow the land to return to nature, as is the case of the island of Schiermonnikoog in Friesland, which occupies a good portion once used by a sect of monks, and Biesbosch near Rotterdam, which formerly was inhabited by reed farmers.

The most interesting national parks (NP) and nature reserves (NR) include the following:

Name	Features	Activities	Best time to visit
Biesbosch NP (p223)	estuarine reed marsh, woodland	canoeing, hiking, bird-watching	Mar-Sep
Duinen van Texel NP (p167)	dunes, heath, forest	hiking, biking, bird-watching	Mar-Sep
Hoge Veluwe NP (p269)	marsh, forests, dunes	hiking, biking, wildlife watching	all year
Oostvaardersplassen NR (p176)	wild reed marsh, grassland	hiking, biking, bird-watching, fishing	all year
Schiermonnikoog NP (p242)	car-free island, dunes, mud flats	hiking, mud-walking, bird-watching	Mar-Sep
Weerribben NP (p256)	peat marsh	boating, canoeing, hiking, bird-watching	all year
Zuid-Kennemerland NP (p152)	dunes, heath, forest	hiking, bird-watching, biking	Mar-Sep

ENVIRONMENTAL ISSUES

As a people, the Dutch are more aware of environmental issues than most. But then again, with high population density, widespread car ownership, heavy industrialisation, extensive farming and more than a quarter of the country below sea level, they need to be.

As early as the 1980s a succession of Dutch governments began to put in motion plans to tighten the standards for industrial and farm pollution, and also made recycling a part of everyday life. Nowadays the Dutch love to debate ways to reconcile the 'triple p's' – planet, people and profit.

While people are happy to recycle, they're not so happy to give up their precious cars. Despite good, reasonably cheap public transportation, private car ownership has risen sharply over the past two decades. Use of vehicles is now about 50% above the levels of the late 1980s, which is due also to burgeoning freight transport. Some critics warn that, unless action is taken, the country's streets and motorways will become gridlocked (or should

Shared Spaces (www .sharedspaces.nl) is an online quarterly magazine in English that covers the Netherlands' and Europe's current environmental issues. It's published by the Netherlands Ministry of Spatial Planning, Housing and the Environment.

HIGHS & LOWS

There's no arguing that the Netherlands is a low, flat country (Netherlands in Dutch means 'low land'), but it does have some dips and bumps. Its lowest point – the small town of Nieuwerkerk aan den IJssel, near Rotterdam – is 6.74m below sea level, while its highest point, the Vaalserberg in Limburg, is a meagre 321m above.

However, if the Kingdom of the Netherlands, which consists of the Netherlands, the Netherlands Antilles and Aruba, is taken into account, the scene swiftly changes. Its lowest point remains the same, but its highest point almost triples to 862m, the top of Mt Scenery on the tiny Caribbean island of Saba.

that read 'stiflingly gridlocked'?) over the next decade. Stiff parking fees, the distinct lack of parking spaces, and outlandish fines have helped curb congestion in the inner cities, however, thankfully shifting a lot of car drivers onto bicycles, trams and buses.

The country's congested motorways have proved harder to regulate. Road tolls – common practice in a number of European countries – have been suggested by various Dutch governments, but as yet nothing has been implemented. Aside from boosting the government's spending pot, tolls would help to reduce traffic jams, vehicle emissions and probably the nation's blood pressure.

The effects of global warming, a topic on the mind of everyone except the leaders of various powerful nations, are obvious in the Netherlands. Over the past century the winters have become shorter and milder, and three of the warmest years on record occurred in the past decade alone. The long-distance ice-skating race known as the Elfstedentocht (p238) may die out because the waterways in the northern province of Friesland rarely freeze hard enough. The Dutch national weather service KNMI predicts that only four to 10 races will be held this century.

The lack of ice over winter is simply annoying; a rise in sea levels is a disaster of epic proportions. If the sea level rises as forecast, the country could theoretically sink beneath the waves, like Atlantis, or at least suffer annual flooding. Extra funds have already been allocated to extend the dykes and storm barriers if necessary.

Even if the sea rises, the tenacity of the Dutch will surely keep it at bay, but this is not the only concern when it comes to the North Sea. Water quality appears to be in decline again, with pesticides, unfiltered runoff from farms and industrial waste considered to be the chief culprits. The Dutch government has put in place certain restrictions on farmers and companies, but waste still flows freely through the country and into the North Sea via the Maas and Rhine rivers, which enter the country from Belgium and Germany respectively. Dutch coastal waters meet EU standards, but the pollution can sometimes be obvious even to the casual observer. The European water-quality watchdog Foundation for Environmental Education (FEE) awarded its coveted 'blue flag' to 40 Dutch beaches in 2006 – but, compared to Mediterranean countries, or even Denmark, that's not a hell of a lot.

A wave of animal diseases has raised questions about farming practices. At one point the Dutch chicken population exceeded 100 million, one of the largest concentrations in the industrialised world. That was before an outbreak of bird flu in 2002 made it necessary to destroy millions of birds to stop the spread of the disease. If the current wave of bird flu to hit Eastern Europe reaches the Netherlands, another massive cull won't be far behind it. Swine flu, foot-and-mouth disease and BSE ('mad cow' disease) have vastly reduced pig and cattle stocks in recent years. Farmers, especially in the provinces of Noord Brabant and Limburg, are still reeling from these epidemics.

Partly to blame for such plagues, critics say, are the great numbers of animals (primarily pigs, cattle and chickens) bred and farmed together in close quarters – intensive farming is a major earner for the Dutch economy. Vaccines and stiffer rules on animal transport have been introduced to stem contagion. The crisis has a silver lining, however: fewer farm animals mean that arable lands have less nitrate-rich manure to absorb (overfertilisation is also chronic in the Netherlands).

More attention is being paid to sustainable development. Bowing to pressure by both the government and green organisations such as Greenpeace, Dutch companies are shouldering more responsibility for the impact of their operations on society and the environment. Energy giants such as Shell, Nuon and Gasunie have invested heavily in developing new sources of clean energy such as hydrogen fuel cells for cars; Amsterdam is now graced with a few hydrogen-powered buses. Wind parks in Flevoland and Noord Holland now generate a significant amount of the country's electricity, though at a cost to passing birds and the natural profile of the landscape. Demand has grown for products that are perceived as environmentally friendly, such as free-trade coffee and organic meats and vegetables. So far, however, these products are relegated to a few supermarket shelves or specialist retailers.

Jump online and check out these conservation organisations: Dutch Friends of the Earth, www.milieudefensie .nl (in Dutch); Society for Nature and Environment, www.snm.nl; and Greenpeace, www .greenpeace.org.

Architecture

The Dutch are masters of architecture and use of space, but this is nothing new. Through the ages, few countries have exerted more influence on the discipline of art and construction than the Netherlands. From the original sober cathedrals to the sleek modern structures, their ideas and designs have spread not only throughout Europe but also to the new world.

The wonderful thing about Dutch architecture is that you can time-travel through a thousand years of beautiful buildings in one city alone. The weird thing about Dutch architecture – with all its influence, cleverness and internationally renowned architects – is that you're not going to find bombastic statements like St Peter's cathedral or the Louvre. But, then again, ostentation was never in keeping with the Dutch character. It's the little surprises that charm most: a subtle joke, a flourish on a 17th-century gable or that unending flight of stairs that seems far too tight to be at all practical but still manages to transport you to the 4th floor…

ROMANESQUE

A World History of Architecture by Marian Moffett, Lawrence Wodehouse and Michael Fazio is an excellent introduction to the world of architecture, with many Dutch examples provided.

Romanesque architecture, which took the country (and Europe) by storm between 900 and 1250, is the earliest architectural style remaining in the country, if you discount the *hunebedden* (p253). Its main characteristics are an uncomplicated form, thick walls, small windows and round arches.

The oldest church of this style in the Netherlands is the Pieterskerk (p180) in Utrecht. Built in 1048, it's one of five churches that form a cross in the city, with the cathedral at its centre. Runner-up is Nijmegen's 16-sided St Nicolaaskapel (p264), which is basically a scaled-down copy of Charlemagne's chapel in Aachen, Germany. Another classic example of Romanesque is the Onze Lieve Vrouwebasiliek (p280) in Maastricht; its fortress-like tower with round turrets evokes images of Umberto Eco's novel of monastic intrigue, *The Name of the Rose*.

Holland's countryside is also privy to this style of architecture. The windy plains of the north are filled with examples of sturdy brick churches erected in the 12th and 13th centuries, such as the lonely church perched on a man-made hill in Hogebeintum (p235) in Friesland.

GOTHIC

By around 1250 the love affair with Romanesque was over, and the Gothic era was ushered in. Pointed arches, ribbed vaulting and dizzying heights were trademarks of this new architectural style, which was to last until 1600. Although the Dutch buildings didn't match the size of the French Gothic cathedrals, a rich style emerged in Catholic Brabant that could compete with anything abroad. Stone churches with soaring vaults and buttresses such as Sint Janskathedraal (p273) in Den Bosch and Breda's Grote Kerk (p275) were erected, both of which are good examples of the Brabant Gothic style, as it was later known. Note the timber vaulting and the widespread use of brick among the stone.

Stone is normally a constant fixture of Gothic, but in the marshy lands of the western Netherlands it was too heavy (and too scarce) to use. The basic ingredients of bricks – clay and sand – were however in abundance. Still, bricks are not exactly light material, and weight limits forced architects to build long or wide to compensate for the lack of height. The Sint Janskerk (p202) in Gouda is the longest church in the country, with a nave of 123m, and it has the delicate, stately feel of a variant called Flamboyant Gothic.

GABLES & HOISTS

Travel the length and breadth of the Netherlands and there is one architectural phenomenon you simply can't escape – the elegant gable. These eye-catching vertical triangular or oblong sections at the top of a façade are as important to Dutch architecture as *gezelligheid* is to the Dutch psyche.

The original purpose of a gable was entirely practical – it not only hid the roof from public view but also helped to identify the house (this changed when the occupying French introduced house numbers in 1795). However, the more ornate the gable, the easier it was to spot. Other distinguishing features included façade decorations, signs and cartouches (wall tablets).

There are four main types of Dutch gable. The simple spout gable – a copy of the earliest wooden gables – is characterised by semicircular windows or shutters and looks not unlike an upturned funnel; it was used mainly for warehouses from the 1580s to the early 1700s. The step gable, which literally looks like steps, was a late-Gothic design favoured by Dutch-Renaissance architects from 1580 to 1660. The neck gable, also known as the bottle gable because it resembled a bottle spout, was introduced in the 1640s and proved most durable, featuring occasionally in designs of the early 19th century. Some neck gables incorporated a step. The graceful slopes of the bell gable first appeared in the 1660s and became popular in the 18th century.

From the 18th century onwards many new houses no longer had gables but rather straight, horizontal cornices that were richly decorated, often with pseudo-balustrades.

If you find yourself wondering whether many canal houses are tipping forward, or you've simply had too much to drink or smoke, don't worry. A lot were built with a slight forward lean to allow goods and furniture to be hoisted into the attic without bumping into the house (and windows). A few houses have huge hoist-wheels in the attic with a rope and hook that run through the hoist beam.

Stone Gothic structures do exist in the western stretches of Holland, though; Haarlem's Grote Kerk van St Bavo (p148) is a wonderful example.

If Gothic tickles your fancy, take a peek at the town halls in Gouda (p202) and Middelburg (p225), both of which are nearly overwhelming in their weightiness and pomp.

MANNERISM

From the middle of the 16th century the Renaissance style that was sweeping through Italy steadily began to filter into the Netherlands. The Dutch naturally put their own spin on this new architectural design, which came to be known as mannerism (c 1550–1650). Also known as Dutch Renaissance, this unique style falls somewhere between Renaissance and baroque; it retained the bold curving forms and rich ornamentation of baroque but merged them with classical Greek and Roman and traditional Dutch styles. Building façades were accentuated with mock columns (pilasters) and the simple spout gables were replaced with step gables (see the boxed text, above) that were richly decorated with sculptures, columns and obelisks. The playful interaction of red brick and horizontal bands of white or yellow sandstone was based on mathematical formulas designed to please the eye.

Hendrik de Keyser (1565–1621) was the champion of mannerism. His Zuiderkerk (p99), Noorderkerk (p100) and Westerkerk (p102) in Amsterdam are standout examples; all three show a major break from the sober, stolid lines of brick churches located out in the sticks. Their steeples are ornate and built with a variety of contrasting materials, while the windows are framed in white stone set off by brown brick. Florid details enliven the walls and roof lines.

GOLDEN AGE

After the Netherlands became a world trading power in the 17th century, its rich merchants were able to splash out on lavish buildings.

More than anything, the new architecture had to impress. The leading lights in the architectural field, such as Jacob van Campen (1595–1657) and the brothers Philips and Justus Vingboons, again turned to ancient Greek and Roman designs for ideas. To make buildings look taller, the step gable was replaced by a neck gable, and pilasters were built to look like imperial columns, complete with pedestals. Decorative scrolls were added as finishing flourishes, and the peak wore a triangle or globe to simulate a temple roof.

A wonderful example of this is the Koninklijk Paleis (Royal Palace; p96) in Amsterdam, originally built as the town hall in 1648. Van Campen, the architect, drew on classical designs and dropped many of De Keyser's playful decorations, and the resulting building exuded gravity with its solid lines and shape.

> The Nederlands Architectuur Instituut (www.nai .nl) is the top authority on the latest developments.

This new form of architecture suited the city's businessmen, who needed to let the world know that they were successful. As sports cars were still centuries away, canal houses became showpieces. Despite the narrow plots, each building from this time makes a statement at gable level through sculpture and myriad shapes and forms. Philips and Justus Vingboons were specialists in these swanky residences; their most famous works include the Bijbels Museum (Biblical Museum; p101), the gorgeous Theater Instituut (p101) and houses scattered throughout Amsterdam's western canal belt.

The capital is not the only city to display such grand architecture. Den Haag has 17th-century showpieces, including the Paleis Noordeinde (p198) and the Mauritshuis (p197), and scores of other examples line the picture-perfect canals of Leiden, Delft and Maastricht, to name but a few.

From the mid-17th century onwards Dutch architecture began to influence France and England, and its colonial styles can still be seen in the Hudson River Valley of New York state.

FRENCH INFLUENCE

By the 18th century the wealthy classes had turned their backs on trade for more staid lives in banking or finance, which meant a lot of time at home. Around the same time, Dutch architects began deferring to all things French; dainty Louis XV furnishings and florid rococo façades became all the rage. It was then a perfect time for new French building trends to sweep the country. Daniel Marot (1661–1752), together with his assistants Jean and Anthony Coulon, was the first to introduce French interior design with matching exteriors. Good examples of their work can be found along the Lange Voorhout in Den Haag, near the British embassy. Rooms were bathed in light, thanks to stuccoed ceilings and tall sash windows, and everything from staircases to furniture was designed in harmony.

NEOCLASSICISM

Architecture took a back seat during the Napoleonic Wars in the late 18th century. Buildings still needed to be built, of course, so designers dug deep into ancient Greek and Roman blueprints once more and eventually came up with neoclassicism (c 1790–1850). Known for its order, symmetry and simplicity, neoclassical design became the mainstay for houses of worship, courtyards and other official buildings. A shining example of neoclassicism is Groningen's town hall (p248); of particular note are the classical pillars, although the use of brick walls is a purely Dutch accent. Many a church was subsidized by the government water ministry and so was named a Waterstaatkerk (state water church), such as the lonely house of worship in Schokland (p177).

CYCLING THROUGH ARCHITECTURE

For a first-hand view of how Dutch cities have developed through the ages and how they effort-lessly merge with the surrounding countryside, hire a bike in Amsterdam and cycle to Haarlem (two hours).

Start in the very heart of the capital amongst its gabled houses and grand buildings, then head west through its spacious, modern suburbs and on to the unhurried outer business parks punctuated by wide roads and glass and steel constructions; before you know it, you'll have smoothly arrived in the countryside. An hour of gentle riding is before you until it all starts again, but in reverse; Haarlem's business parks greet you first, followed by contemporary suburbs, and suddenly you're savouring a beer in the shadow of the glorious Gothic Grote Kerk.

If you can, take a few friends and something to smoke – it'll make the journey all the more interesting…

LATE 19TH CENTURY

From the 1850s onwards, many of the country's large architectural projects siphoned as much as they could from the Gothic era, creating neo-Gothic. Soon afterwards, freedom of religion was declared and Catholics were allowed to build new churches in Protestant areas. Neo-Gothic suited the Catholics just fine, and a boom in church-building took place; Amsterdam's Krijtberg (p103) is one of the most glorious.

Another wave of nostalgia, neo-Renaissance, drew heavily on De Keyser's earlier masterpieces. Neo-Renaissance buildings were erected throughout the country, made to look like well-polished veterans from three centuries earlier. For many observers, these stepped-gable edifices with alternating stone and brick are the epitome of classic Dutch architecture.

One of the leading architects of this period was Pierre Cuypers (1827–1921), who built several neo-Gothic churches but often merged the style with neo-Renaissance, as can be seen in Amsterdam's Centraal Station (p83) and Rijksmuseum (p106). These are predominantly Gothic structures but have touches of Dutch Renaissance brickwork.

Rotterdam's 12-storey Witte Huis (built 1898) was Europe's first 'skyscraper'.

BERLAGE & THE AMSTERDAM SCHOOL

As the 20th century approached, the neo styles and their reliance on the past were strongly criticised by Hendrik Petrus Berlage (1856–1934), the father of modern Dutch architecture. He favoured spartan, practical designs over frivolous ornamentation; the 1902 Beurs van Berlage (p84) displays these ideals to the full. Berlage cooperated with sculptors, painters and tilers to ensure that ornamentation was integrated into the overall design in a supportive role, rather than being tacked on as an embellishment to hide the structure.

Berlage's residential designs approached a block of buildings as a whole, not as a collection of individual houses. In this he influenced the young architects of what became known as the Amsterdam School, though they rejected his stark rationalism and preferred more creative designs. Leading exponents were Michel de Klerk (1884–1923), Piet Kramer (1881–1961) and Johan van der Mey (1878–1949); the latter ushered in the Amsterdam School (c 1916–30) with his extraordinary Scheepvaarthuis (p109).

Brick was the material of choice for such architects, and housing blocks were treated as sculptures, with curved corners, oddly placed windows and ornamental, rocket-shaped towers. Their Amsterdam housing estates, such as De Klerk's 'Ship' in the west, have been described as fairy-tale fortresses rendered in a Dutch version of Art Deco. Their preference for form over function meant their designs were great to look at but not always fantastic to live in, with small windows and inefficient use of space.

Housing subsidies sparked a frenzy of residential building activity in the 1920s. At the time, many architects of the Amsterdam school worked for the Amsterdam city council and designed the buildings for the Oud Zuid (Old South, p105). This large-scale expansion – mapped out by Berlage – called for good-quality housing, wide boulevards and cosy squares; it was instigated by the labour party, but the original designer didn't get much of a chance to design the buildings, as council architects were pushing their own blueprints.

Bart Lootsma's *Super Dutch* is a slick book covering the latest in Dutch design from the country's most influential architects.

FUNCTIONALISM

While Amsterdam School–type buildings were being erected all over their namesake city, a new generation of architects began to rebel against the school's impractical (not to mention expensive) structures. Influenced by the Bauhaus school in Germany, Frank Lloyd Wright in the USA and Le Corbusier in France, they formed a group called 'the 8'. It was the first stirring of functionalism (1927–70).

The website of who's who in Holland's architectural scene is www.dutch architects.com.

Architects such as B Merkelbach and Gerrit Rietveld believed that form should follow function and sang the praises of steel, glass and concrete. Their spacious designs were practical and allowed for plenty of sunlight; the Rietveld-Schröderhuis (p182) is the only house built completely along functionalist De Stijl lines.

After the war, functionalism came to the fore and stamped its authority on new suburbs to the west and south of Amsterdam, as well as war-damaged cities such as Rotterdam. High-rise suburbs were built on a large scale yet weren't sufficient to keep up with the population boom and urbanisation of Dutch life. But functionalism fell from favour as the smart design aspects were watered down in low-cost housing projects for the masses.

MODERNISM & BEYOND

Construction has been booming in the Netherlands since the 1980s, and architects have had been ample opportunity to flirt with numerous 'isms' such as structuralism, neorationalism, postmodernism and supermodernism. Evidence of these styles can be found in Rotterdam, where city planners have encouraged bold designs that range from Piet Blom's startling cube-shaped Boompjestorens (p211) to Ben van Berkel's graceful Erasmusbrug (p211). Striking examples in Amsterdam include the NEMO science centre (p110), which recalls a resurfacing submarine, and the new Eastern Docklands housing estate, where 'blue is green' – ie the surrounding water takes the role of lawns and shrubbery.

The *Guide to Modern Architecture in the Netherlands* by Paul Groenendijk and Piet Vollaard is a comprehensive look at 20th-century architecture, arranged by region, with short explanations and photos.

Food & Drink

Like many other countries in northern Europe, the Netherlands has never had a reputation for outstanding, or even fine, cuisine. Hearty, hefty, filling, stodgy – these are the adjectives with which Dutch cooking is usually tagged. This, however, has a historical context; traditionally, the Dutch never paid that much attention to food, as there was too much work to be done and little time to cook. It is quite revealing that, during the Golden Age, spices such as pepper were more of a currency than a culinary ingredient.

In recent years, however, these attitudes have been transformed by a culinary revolution sweeping the Netherlands. The Dutch have begun to experiment with their own traditional kitchen, breathing new life into centuries-old recipes by giving them a contemporary twist. Smart Dutch chefs now prefer to steam or braise vegetables rather than boil them, and they draw on organic ingredients as well as a generous quantity of fresh herbs and spices.

Julius Caesar was a big fan of Dutch cheese.

STAPLES & SPECIALITIES

The Dutch start the day with a filling yet unexciting breakfast of a few slices of bread accompanied by jam, cheese and a boiled egg. Coffee is always involved. Lunch tends to be more of a snack, especially for the working crowd, taken between noon and 2pm. A half-hour is common for the midday break, just long enough for employees to snag a quick sandwich or empty their lunchbox. Dinner is the main meal of the day and is usually a substantial serving, whether it be traditional Dutch cuisine or something from beyond the Netherlands' borders.

Dutch Delights by Sylvia Pessireron, Jurjen Drenth and friends is a playful look at the eating habits of the Dutch. It's easy to digest and filled with superb photos.

DUTCH

Van Gogh perfectly captured the main ingredient of traditional Dutch cooking in his *Potato Eaters*. Typically boiled to death, these 'earth apples' are accompanied by meat – and more boiled vegetables. Gravy is then added for flavour. It's certainly not fancy, but it is filling.

Few restaurants serve exclusively Dutch cuisine, but many places have several homeland items on the menu, especially in winter. Some time-honoured favourites:

- *stamppot* (mashed pot) – simple dish of potatoes mashed with kale, endive or sauerkraut and served with smoked sausage or strips of pork. Perfect in winter.
- *hutspot* (hotchpotch) – similar to *stamppot*, but with potatoes, carrots, onions, braised meat and more spices.
- *erwtensoep* (pea soup) – Plenty of peas with onions, carrots, smoked sausage and bacon. And the perfect pea soup? A spoon stuck upright in the pot should remain standing.
- *asperge* (asparagus) – usually white and often crunchy; very popular when it's in season (spring); served with ham and butter.
- *kroketten* (croquettes) – dough balls with various fillings that are crumbed and deep-fried; the variety called *bitterballen* are a popular pub snack served with mustard.
- *mosselen* (mussels) – cooked with white wine, chopped leeks and onions, and served in a bowl or cooking pot with a side dish of *frites* or *patat* (French fries); they're popular, and are best eaten from September to April.

DISTINCTLY CHEESY

Some Dutch say it makes them tall; others complain it causes nightmares. Whatever the case, the Netherlands is justifiably famous for its cheeses. The Dutch – known as the original cheeseheads – consume 16.5kg of the stuff every year.

Nearly two-thirds of all cheese sold is Gouda. The tastier varieties have strong, complex flavours and are best enjoyed with a bottle of wine or two. Try some *oud* (old) Gouda, hard and rich in flavour and a popular bar snack with mustard. Oud Amsterdammer is a real delight, deep orange and crumbly with white crystals of ripeness.

Edam is similar to Gouda but slightly drier and less creamy. Leidse or Leiden cheese is another export hit, laced with cumin or caraway seed and light in flavour.

In the shops you'll also find scores of varieties that are virtually unknown outside the country. Frisian Nagelkaas might be made with parsley juice, buttermilk, and 'nails' of caraway seed. Kruidenkaas has a melange of herbs such as fennel, celery, pepper or onions. Graskaas is 'new harvest' Gouda made after cows begin to roam the meadows and munch grass.

Lower-fat cheeses include Milner, Kollumer and Maaslander. One has to start somewhere: the stats show that the Dutch are gaining weight despite all that cycling.

Lamb is prominently featured on menus, but – surprisingly for such a seafaring nation – seafood is not. It is more commonly eaten as a snack, in which form it is everywhere. *Haring* (herring) is a national institution, eaten lightly salted or occasionally pickled but never fried or cooked (see opposite); *paling* (eel) is usually smoked.

Typical Dutch desserts are fruit pie (apple, cherry or other fruit), *vla* (custard) and ice cream. Many snack bars and pubs serve *appeltaart* (apple pie), which is always good. Amazingly, some Dutch eat *hagelslag* (chocolate sprinkles) on their bread for breakfast.

Finally, most towns have at least one place serving *pannenkoeken* (pancakes), which come in a huge array of varieties. The mini-version, covered in caster sugar, is *poffertjes*.

Dutch Cooking: The New Kitchen by Manon Sikkel and Michiel Klonhammer is a fresh perspective on traditional Dutch cuisine, in which age-old recipes are given a modern makeover.

INDONESIAN

Indonesian cooking is a rich and complex blend of many cultures: chilli peppers, peanut sauces and stewed curries from Thailand, lemon grass and fish sauces from Vietnam, intricate Indian spice mixes, and Asian cooking methods. Without a doubt this is the tastiest legacy of the Dutch colonial era.

In the Netherlands, Indonesian food is toned down for sensitive Western palates. If you want it hot (*pedis*, pronounced 'p-*dis*'), say so, but be prepared for watering eyes and burnt taste buds. You might play it safe by asking for *sambal* (chilli paste) and helping yourself. *Sambal oelek* is red and hot; the dark-brown *sambal badjak* is onion-based, mild and sweet.

The most famous Indonesian dish is *rijsttafel* (rice table): an array of spicy savoury dishes such as braised beef, pork satay and ribs served with white rice. *Nasi rames* is a steaming plate of boiled rice covered in several rich condiments, while the same dish with thick noodles is called *bami rames*.

Peanut sauce plays a big part in Indonesian cuisine. Dishes such as *gado-gado*, a meal of crisp, steamed vegetables and a hard-boiled egg, come with lashings of the stuff, and *saté* (satay), which is basically marinated beef, chicken or pork barbecued on small skewers, would be substandard without it.

Other stand-bys include *nasi goreng*, a simple yet extremely popular dish of fried rice with onions, pork, shrimp and spices, often with a fried egg or shredded omelette, and *bami goreng*, which is much the same thing but with noodles.

TRAVEL YOUR TASTEBUDS

Raw fish isn't that bad – sushi and sashimi, for instance, are delectable morsels the world is a better place for. However, the sight of a local slowly sliding a raw herring headfirst (thankfully head*less*) down their gullet looks, well, wrong. But the Dutch love this salted delicacy and are eager for visitors to try it. If an entire fish is too much to stomach, it can be cut into bite-sized pieces and served with onion and pickles. You'll find vendors the length and breadth of the country – look for the words *haring* or *Hollandse niuewe* and dig in.

Another acquired taste in Holland is drop. This so-called sweet is a thick, rubbery liquorice root and Arabic gum concoction the Dutch go crazy for – a reputed 30 million kilos of the stuff is consumed each year. Its bitter taste is reminiscent of childhood medicine and some foreigners have trouble taking a second bite. There's also a liquid version; look for a bottle of Dropshot in supermarkets.

SURINAMESE

Dishes from this former colony have Caribbean roots, blending African and Indian flavours with Indonesian influences introduced by Javanese labourers. Chicken, lamb and beef curries are common menu items. *Roti*, a chickpea-flour pancake filled with potatoes, long beans, bean sprouts and meat (vegetarian versions are available), is by far the favoured choice of the Dutch.

Access a collection of Dutch recipes in English, and online shopping for Canadian and US citizens who absolutely need Dutch products, on www .dutchmarket.com.

DRINKS
Nonalcoholic

More coffee is consumed per capita in the Netherlands than in any other European country bar Denmark. Ordering a *koffie* will get you a sizable cup of the black stuff and a separate package or jug of *koffiemelk*, a slightly sour-tasting cream akin to condensed milk. *Koffie verkeerd* is similar to latte, served in a big mug with plenty of real milk. If you order espresso or cappuccino, you'll be lucky to get a decent Italian version. Don't count on finding decaffeinated coffee, and if you do it may be instant.

Tea is usually served Continental-style: a cup or pot of hot water with a tea bag on the side. Varieties might be presented in a humidor-like box for you to pick and choose. If you want milk, say *met melk, graag*. Many locals prefer to add a slice of lemon.

The Dutch drink on average 140L of coffee each year.

Alcoholic

Lager beer is the staple drink, served cool and topped by a head of froth so big it would start a brawl in an Australian bar. Heineken tells us that these are 'flavour bubbles', and requests for no head will earn a steely response. *Een bier* or *een pils* will get you a normal glass; *een kleintje pils* is a small glass and *een fluitje* is a tall but thin glass – perfect for multiple refills. Some places serve half-litre mugs to please tourists.

Belgian beers are widely available, with strong and crisp flavours that make Dutch pilsners pale. Some good brands include De Koninck, Palm, Duvel and Westmalle (beware of their doubles and triples). The lighter *witbier* (blonde beer) is a good choice in balmy weather, and brands such as Hoegaarden are typically served with a slice of lemon and a swizzle stick.

Dutch *jenever* or gin is made from juniper berries and drunk chilled from a shot glass filled to the brim. Most people prefer *jonge* (young) *jenever*, which is smoother; the strong juniper flavour of *oude* (old) *jenever* can be an acquired taste. The aptly-named *kopstoot* (head butt) is a double-whammy of *jenever* and a beer chaser. The palette of indigenous liqueurs includes *advocaat* (a kind of eggnog) and the herb-based *Beerenburg*, a Frisian schnapps.

The official website of the Dutch can-collectors' association is www .blik-op-blik.nl. Hunt for that rare Dutch beer can here.

A TASTY BREW

The Dutch love beer. It's seen as the perfect companion for time spent with friends in the sun or out partying till the small hours. And they've had plenty of time to cultivate this unquestioning love – beer has been a popular drink since the 14th century, and at one time the Dutch could lay claim to no fewer than 559 brewers. Most Dutch beer is pilsner (or lager), a clear, crisp, golden beer with strong hop flavouring.

Heineken is the Netherlands' (and possibly the world's) best-known beer. However, like Fosters in Australia, it has a poor name at home – 'the beer your cheap father drinks', to quote one wag. Amstel (owned by Heineken) is also well known; Grolsch and Oranjeboom can also claim a certain amount of international fame. Most beers contain around 5% alcohol, and a few of those cute little glasses can pack a strong punch.

While the big names rule the roost, the Netherlands has scores of small brewers worth trying, including Gulpen, Bavaria, Drie Ringen, Leeuw and Utrecht. La Trappe is the only Dutch Trappist beer, brewed close to Tilburg. The potent beers made by Amsterdam's Brouwerij 't IJ (p109) are sold on tap and in some local pubs – try the Columbus brew (9% alcohol). If you're around in spring or autumn, don't pass up the chance to sample Grolsch's seasonal bock beers, such as Lentebok (spring bock) and Herfstbok (autumn bock). Like Brouwerij's brews, they kick like a mule, so, depending on your mood, tread carefully or drink as though you want to spend the next day in bed.

Wine seems to be an afterthought in the Netherlands – but an afterthought that is slowly taking hold. Plenty of European and New World varieties are available, but take a second look at the prices as Dutch import duties normally keep them high.

CELEBRATIONS

The Dutch sweet tooth really comes out during the annual holidays and festivities. Early December is a good time to sample traditional treats such as spicy *speculaas* biscuits or *pepernoten*, the little crunchy ginger nuts that are handed out at Sinterklaas. *Oliebollen* are small spherical donuts filled with raisins or other diced fruit, deep-fried and dusted with powdered sugar; you can buy these calorie bombs from street vendors in the run-up to New Year.

Muisjes (little mice) are sugar-coated aniseed sprinkles served on a round *beschuit* (rusk biscuit) to celebrate the birth of a child – blue and white for a boy; pink and white for a girl.

WHERE TO EAT & DRINK

Restaurants abound and they cater to a wide variety of tastes and budgets. Their biggest competitors are *eetcafés*, affordable pub-like eateries with a huge local following.

When the Dutch say café they're referring to a pub, also known as a *kroeg*, and there are over 1000 of them in Amsterdam alone. Coffee is served but as a sideline. Many cafés and pubs also serve food, but few open before 9am. A fixture in many cafés is an outdoor terrace that may be covered and heated in winter. Here the Dutch soak up the outdoor atmosphere and pass the time chatting, people-watching or simply taking a break from everything.

The most famous type is the *bruin café* (brown café). The true specimen has been in business for a while; expect sandy wooden floors and an atmosphere perfect for deep conversation. The name comes from the smoky stains on the walls, although newer aspirants just slap on some brown paint.

Grand cafés are more spacious than brown cafés or pubs and have comfortable furniture. They're all the rage, and any pub that puts in a few solid

---

DOS & DON'TS

Do round up the bill by 5% to 10% (unless the service is bad).

Do split the costs.

Do reserve ahead, especially at weekends.

Do take children to pubs and restaurants.

Do bring flowers or wine when invited home.

Don't ask to go 'Dutch'.

Don't ask for a doggie bag.

Don't cut off a tip on the cheese cart (always slice).

Don't make loud complaints about the service (usually counter-productive).

tables and chairs might call itself a grand café. Normally opening at 10am, they're marvellous for a lazy lunch or brunch.

Falling within the 'other' category are theatre cafés, which attract a trendy mix of bohemian and chic; *proeflokalen*, or tasting houses, which once were attached to distilleries (good for sampling dozens of *jenevers* and liqueurs); trendy bars with cool designer interiors; and the ubiquitous Irish pubs.

The site www.recepten .nl is an exhaustive archive of Dutch recipes and cooking links. It's in Dutch but easy to decipher.

Quick Eats

Broodjeszaken (sandwich shops) or snack bars proliferate. The latter offer multicoloured treats in a display case, usually based on some sort of meat and spices, and everything is dumped into a deep-fryer when you order. Febo snack bars have long rows of coin-operated windows à la the Jetsons.

The national institution, *Vlaamse frites* (Flemish fries), are French fries made from whole potatoes rather than the potato pulp you will get if the sign only says *frites*. They are supposed to be smothered in mayonnaise (though you can ask for ketchup, curry sauce, garlic sauce or other gloppy toppings).

Seafood is everywhere. The most popular – aside from raw herring (see p61) – is *kibbeling* (deep-fried cod parings), while smoked eel has legions of fans.

At www.dinnersite.nl you can sift through over 9000 restaurants and cafés without leaving your chair.

Lebanese and Turkish snack bars specialise in *shoarma*, a pitta bread filled with sliced lamb from a vertical spit – also known as a *gyros* or doner kebab.

VEGETARIANS & VEGANS

For all their liberalism and openness, it's surprising to note that the Dutch are slow on the vegetarian uptake. Outside the major metropolises you'll be hard-pressed to find a strictly vegetarian-only restaurant in the small town you're visiting; in this case, you'll be relying on the couple of veg options available on most restaurant menus. Check their purity before ordering, though, as often you can't be sure whether they're 100% meat- or fish-free (meat stock is a common culprit).

Once you do track down a vegetarian restaurant, you'll be happy to find that they rely on organic ingredients and often make everything from bread to cakes in-house.

TOP RESTAURANTS IN THE NETHERLANDS

- Mamouche (p126), Amsterdam – top-notch Moroccan fare in stripped-back surroundings, accompanied by a decidedly sexy vibe.

- Blauw aan de Wal (p122), Amsterdam – modern French and Italian cuisine served in a delightful 17th-century warehouse; only a stone's throw from the buzzing Red Light District.

- Blits (p216), Rotterdam – exclusive international menu and cutting-edge architecture in a city famous for its cutting edges; what more can you ask for?

- De Librije (p260), Zwolle – triple-Michelin-star restaurant housed in a beautiful 500-year-old monastery library; contemporary French and Dutch cuisine.

- Parkheuvel (p216), Rotterdam – another restaurant rated by the folk at Michelin (three stars). French/International cuisine and seafood to die for.

- Bazar (p215), Rotterdam – one of the finest Middle Eastern restaurants in the land, serving the best the region has to offer in suitably Arabic surroundings.

- Vispaleis-Rokerij De Ster, Texel (p170) – nothing fancy here, just fish freshly caught and cured, and a warm Texel welcome.

EATING WITH KIDS

The Netherlands is a kid-friendly country for eating out. Most restaurants and pubs will have kiddie meals on offer, if not a children's menu, and high chairs are often available. You might feel out of place taking infants into a drop-dead trendy restaurant – ask ahead when you make reservations. See p288 for more tips and information.

HABITS & CUSTOMS

At first take, it looks as though the Dutch aren't all that fussed about food. Meals tend to be rushed, and quantity appears to win over quality. These habits are slowly fading, however, and restaurant patrons are increasingly likely to linger over a multicourse dinner for a couple of hours, and to expect high standards. Social events are in a class of their own, and diners with something to celebrate might camp out in a restaurant for an entire evening.

Windmills in my Oven by Gaitri Pagrach-Chandraby is a mix of Dutch baking, social commentary and regional customs, and a few tasty recipes are thrown in for good measure.

Dinner usually takes place between 6pm and 9.30pm. Popular places fill up by 7pm because the Dutch eat early; if this doesn't suit, aim for the second sitting from around 8.30pm to 9.30pm, when films, concerts and other performances start. Bear in mind that many kitchens close by 10pm, although full-scale restaurants may still serve after midnight.

Many places list a *dagschotel* (dish of the day) that will be good value, but don't expect a culinary adventure. The trend in some places is to limit the menu to several options that change regularly; in this case the food can be quite exciting.

Coffee breaks are a national institution and occur frequently throughout the day. Restaurants will serve a single cookie or biscuit with coffee, but in homes you'll be offered one per cup.

Many restaurants don't accept credit cards; for tipping advice, see p294.

EAT YOUR WORDS

Dutch restaurants are skilled in serving foreigners, so bilingual or English menus are practically the norm. Refer to the Language chapter (p314) for tips on pronunciation.

Useful Phrases

A beer, please.
ən pils/beer als·tu·*bleeft*   *Een pils/bier, alstublieft.*
A bottle of wine, please.
ən fles wayn   *Een fles wijn, alstublieft.*
Waiter!/Waitress!
o·*bay*/sər-*veer*-stər   *Ober!/Serveerster!*
May I see the menu/wine list?
makh ik het mə·*nu*/də *wayn*-kaart zeen   *Mag ik het menu/de wijnkaart zien?*
Do you have a menu in English?
hebt u ən mə·*nu* in het *eng*·əls   *Hebt u een menu in het Engels?*
Is that dish spicy?
is dit gə-rekht *pit*-təkh   *Is dit gerecht pittig?*
I'm a vegetarian.
ik ben vay-khay-*taa*-ree-yər   *Ik ben vegetariër.*
Bon appétit.
ayt *sma*-kə-leek   *Eet smakelijk.*
It tastes good/bad.
het smakt *le*-kər/neet *le*-kər   *Het smaakt lekker/niet lekker.*
May I have the bill, please?
makh ik də *ray*-kə-ning als·tu·*bleeft*   *Mag ik de rekening, alstublieft?*

Food Glossary

appelmoes	*a·pəl·moos*	apple sauce
beenham	*bayn·ham*	leg ham
belegd broodje	*bə·lekht broa·tye*	filled sandwich
boerenomelet	*boo·rən·oa·mə·let*	omelette with vegetables and ham
dagschotel	*dakh·skhoa·təl*	dish of the day
drop	drop	liquorice
frikandel	*free·kan·del*	deep-fried meat snack, like a sausage
hagelslag	*haa·khəl·slakh*	chocolate sprinkles
Hollandse nieuwe	*hol·land·sə nee·wə*	salted herring, first of the season
hoofdgerecht	*hoaft·khə·rekht*	main course
kroket	kroa·*ket*	meat croquette
nagerecht	*naa·khə·rekht*	dessert
pannekoek	*pa·nə·kook*	pancake
patat	pa·*tat*	chips/French fries
poffertjes	po·*fər·tyəs*	mini pancakes
speculaas	*spay·ku·laas*	spiced biscuit
tosti	*tos·*ti	toasted sandwich
uitsmijter	*əyt·smay·tər*	fried egg, ham and cheese on bread
Vlaamse frites	*vlaam·sə freet*	thick chips/fries made from whole potatoes
vlammetjes	*vla·mə·tyəs*	spicy spring rolls
voorgerecht	*voar·khə·rekht*	starter

COOKING TERMS

gaar	khaar	well done
gebakken	*khə·ba·kən*	baked/fried
gebraden	khe·*braa·dən*	roasted
gefrituurd	*khə·free·tuurt*	deep fried
gegratineerd	khə·khra·tee·*nayrt*	browned on top with cheese
gegrild	kh?·*khrilt*	grilled
gegrild aan 't spit	khə·*khrilt* aant spit	spit-roasted
gekookt	khə·*koakt*	boiled
gepaneerd	*khə·pa·nayrt*	coated in breadcrumbs
gepocheerd	khə·po·*shayrt*	poached
gerookt	*khə·roakt*	smoked
geroosterd	khə·*roas·tərt*	toasted
gesauteerd	khə·soa·*tayrt*	sautéed
gestoofd	khe·*stoaft*	braised
gestoomd	*khə·stoamt*	steamed
gevuld	khə·*vəlt*	stuffed
half doorbakken	half doar·*ba·kən*	medium
peper	*pay·pər*	pepper
rood	roat	rare
suiker	*səy·kər*	sugar
zout	zowt	salt

DESSERTS

amandelbroodje	a·*man·dəl·broa·tyə*	sweet roll with almond filling
appelgebak	*a·pəl·khə·bak*	apple pie
cake	kayk	cake
ijs	ays	ice cream
slagroom	*slakh·*roam	whipped cream
taart	taart	tart, pie, cake
vla	vlaa	custard
wafel	*waa·fəl*	waffle

DRINKS

bier	beer	beer
brandewijn	*bran·də·wayn*	brandy
jenever (or genever)	*yə·nay·vər*	Dutch gin
jus d'orange/sinaasappelsap	*zhu do·ranzh/see·nas·a·pəl·sap*	orange juice
koffie	*ko·fee*	coffee
koffie verkeerd	*ko·fee ver·kayrt*	latte
melk	*melk*	milk
met melk/citroen	*met melk/see·troon*	with milk/lemon
rood/wit	*roat/wit*	red/white
spa blauw (a brand)	*spaa blow*	still mineral water
spa rood (a brand)	*spaa roat*	fizzy mineral water
thee	*tay*	tea
water	*waa·tər*	water
wijn	*wayn*	wine
zoet/droog	*zoot/droakh*	sweet/dry

FRUIT, VEGETABLES, STAPLES & SPICES

aardappel	*aart·a·pəl*	potato
appel	*a·pəl*	apple
artisjok	*ar·tee·shok*	artichoke
asperge	*as·per·zhə*	asparagus
aubergine	*oa·bər·zheen*	eggplant/aubergine
boon	*boan*	bean
champignon	*sham·pee·nyon*	mushroom
courgette	*koor·zhet*	zucchini/courgette
erwt	*ert*	pea
groene paprika	*khroo·nə pa·pree·ka*	green pepper (capsicum)
groente	*khroon·tə*	vegetable
kers	*kers*	cherry
knoflook	*knof·loak*	garlic
komkommer	*kom·komər*	cucumber
kool	*koal*	cabbage
maïs	*maees*	sweet corn
olijf	*o·layf*	olive
peer	*payr*	pear
perzik	*per·zik*	peach
peterselie	*pay·tər·say·lee*	parsley
pompoen	*pom·poon*	pumpkin
prei	*pray*	leek
pruim	*prəym*	plum
rijst	*rayst*	rice
rode paprika	*roa·də pap·ree·ka*	red pepper (capsicum)
selderij	*sel·də·ray*	celery
sinaasappel	*see·nas·a·pəl*	orange
sla	*slaa*	lettuce
spinazie	*spee·naa·zee*	spinach
spruitje	*sprəy·tyə*	Brussels sprout
ui	*əy*	onion
witlof	*wit·lof*	chicory
wortel	*wor·təl*	carrot

MEAT & POULTRY

eend	*aynt*	duck
ei	*ay*	egg

everzwijn	*ay*·vər·zwayn	boar
fazant	fa·*zant*	pheasant
gevogelte	khə·*voa*·khəl·tə	poultry
beenham	*bayn*·ham	ham on the bone
hert	hert	venison
kaas	kaas	cheese
kalfsvlees	*kalfs*·vlays	veal
kalkoen	*kal*·koon	turkey
kip	*kip*	chicken
konijn	ko·*nayn*	rabbit
lamsvlees	*lams*·vlays	lamb
lever	*lay*·vər	liver
paard	paart	horse
parelhoen	*paa*·rəl·hoon	guinea fowl
ribstuk	*rip*·stək	rib steak
rookworst	*roak*·worst	smoked sausage
rundvlees	*rənt*·vlays	beef
schapenvlees	*skhaa*·pə·vlays	mutton
slak	slak	snail
spek	spek	bacon
tong	tong	tongue
varkensvlees	*var*·kəns·vlays	pork
vlees	vlays	meat
vleeswaren	*vlays*·waa·rən	cooked/prepared meats, cold cuts
wild	wilt	game
worst	worst	sausage

SEAFOOD

ansjovis	*an*·shoa·vis	anchovy
baars	baars	bream
forel	foa·*rel*	trout
garnaal	khar·*naal*	shrimp, prawns, scampi
haring	*haa*·ring	herring
inktvis	*ingt*·vis	squid
kabeljauw	kaa·bəl·*jow*	cod
krab	krap	crab
kreeft	krayft	lobster
maatjes	*maa*·tyəs	herring fillets
makreel	ma·*krayl*	mackerel
oester	*oos*·tər	oyster
paling	*paa*·ling	eel
rivierkreeft	ree·*veer*·krayft	crayfish
roodbaars	*roat*·baars	red mullet
St Jacobsschelp	sint·*yaa*·kop·skhelp	scallop
schol	*skhol*	plaice
tong	tong	sole
tonijn	to·*nayn*	tuna
vis	vis	fish
zalm	zalm	salmon
zeebaars	*zay*·baars	bass/sea bream

INDONESIAN DISHES

ayam	*a*·yam	chicken
babi pangang	*baa*·bee *pang*·gang	suckling pig with sweet and sour sauce
bami goreng	*baa*·mee *goa*·reng	stir-fry dish of noodles, veggies, pork and shrimp

daging	*da·ging*	beef
gado–gado	*gaa·*doa *gaa·*doa	vegetables with peanut sauce
goreng	*goa·*reng	fried
kroepoek	*kroo·*pook	deep-fried prawn crackers
loempia	*loom·*pee·ya	spring roll
nasi	*na·*see	rice
nasi goreng	*na·*see *goa·*reng	fried rice with meat and veggies
pedis	*pay·*dis	very spicy
pisang	*pee·*sang	banana
rendang	*ren·dang*	stewed beef in dry hot sauce
rijsttafel	*rayst·*taa·fəl	a selection of spicy meats, fruits, vegetables and sauces served with rice
sambal	*sam·*bal	chilli paste
saté	*sa·tay*	peanut sauce
seroendeng	*sə·roon·*deng	fried coconut
taugé	*tow·gay*	bean sprouts

Cycling in the Netherlands

No matter what shape you're in – or what age you are – the Netherlands is a country to explore by bicycle. Even if it's only a day pedalling along Amsterdam's canals, or a couple of hours rolling through green *polder* landscape, it's more than worth it, and you'll be rewarded with the sense of freedom (and fun) only a bicycle can offer.

With around 20,000km of bike paths and a largely flat landscape, there's even more reason to hop on a bike and do as the locals do. And every local seems to be doing it; the Netherlands has more bicycles than its 16 million citizens. You'll see stockbrokers in tailored suits riding alongside pensioners and teenagers, and mutual tolerance prevails. Many Dutch own at least two bikes, a crunchy beast for everyday use and a nicer model for excursions. No mistake, bikes rule and almost everyone is satisfied with the status quo.

INFORMATION

Your first stop is the ANWB, the Dutch motoring association, with offices in cities across the country. Its website, www.anwb.nl (in Dutch), lists all its national offices; choose Contactformulier from the drop-down menu at the top left of the page, then click on Adressen to locate the one nearest you. Otherwise, call ☎ 08000503 for information.

ANWB has a bewildering selection of route maps as well as camping, recreation and sightseeing guides for cyclists. Its 1:100,000 series of 20 regional maps includes day trips of 30km to 50km, all well signposted (look for six-sided signs with green or red print on a white background). Other maps include *Topografische Atlases*, with scales of 1:25,000 and 1:50,000.

Staff will help once you prove membership of your own motoring association, or you can join the ANWB for €16.50 per year. Many tourist offices also sell ANWB materials and book cycling holidays.

A good starting point online is fiets.startpagina.nl (in Dutch); it lists every conceivable website associated with cycling in the Netherlands (and a handful of other countries too), whether the specific subject be cycle routes, clubs or children's bikes.

Bicycle Touring Holland by Katherine Widing details over 50 bike excursions throughout the country; it's heavy on practical information and very comprehensive.

CLOTHING & EQUIPMENT

Wind and rain are all-too-familiar features of Dutch weather. A lightweight nylon jacket will provide protection, and a breathing variety (Gore-Tex or the like) stops the sweat from gathering. The same thing applies to cycling trousers or shorts.

A standard touring bike is ideal for the Netherlands' flat arena, and for toting a tent and provisions. Gears are useful for riding against the wind, or for tackling a hilly route in Overijssel or Limburg – though the Alps it ain't. Other popular items include a frame bag (for a windcheater and lunch pack), water bottles and a handlebar map-holder so you'll always know where you're going. Few locals wear a helmet, although they're sensible protection, especially for children.

Make sure your set of wheels has a bell: paths can get terribly crowded and it becomes a pain if you have to ask to pass every time. Another necessity is a repair kit. Most rental shops will provide one on request.

HIRE

Rental shops are available in abundance. Many day trippers avail themselves of the train-station hire points, called Rijwiel shops, where you can park and rent bikes and buy bicycle parts from early until late. Bike rental costs anything from €4 to €7 per day and €25 to €30 per week. You'll have to show a passport or national ID card, and leave a credit-card imprint or pay a deposit (usually €25 to €100). The main drawback is you must return the bike to the same station – a problem if you're not returning to the same place. Private shops charge similar rates but may be more flexible on the form of deposit. In summer it's advisable to reserve ahead, as shops regularly rent out their entire stock.

For a full list of Rijwiel shops around the country, go to www.ov-fiets .nl/waarhuur (in Dutch); Getting Around sections under individual towns also list local rental options.

'Dutch trains have special carriages for loading two-wheelers – look for the bicycle logos on the side of the carriage.'

ON THE TRAIN

You can take your bike on the train, but it's often more convenient to rent one wherever you're going. A *dagkaart fiets* (bicycle day ticket) costs €6 regardless of your destination. Collapsible bikes are considered hand luggage and go for free, provided they're folded up.

Dutch trains have special carriages for loading two-wheelers – look for the bicycle logos on the side of the carriage. Remember that you can't take your bike along during rush hour (6.30am to 9am and 4.30pm to 6pm Monday to Friday). The Nederlandse Spoorwegen (NS; Netherlands Railways) publishes a free brochure, *Fiets en Trein* (*Bike and Train*, in Dutch), which provides plenty of information on rental, storage and transport of bicycles around the Netherlands – pick one up at the NS ticket counter.

ROAD RULES & SECURITY

Most major roads have separate bike lanes with their own signs and traffic lights. Generally, the same road rules apply to cyclists as to other vehicles, even if few cyclists seem to observe them (notably in Amsterdam). In theory, you could be fined for running a traffic light or reckless riding, but it rarely happens. Watch out at roundabouts, where right of way may be unclear.

Be sure you have one or two good locks. Hardened chain-link or T-hoop varieties are best for attaching the frame and front wheel to something solid. However, even the toughest lock won't stop a determined thief, so if you have an expensive model it's probably safer to buy or rent a bike locally. Many train-station rental shops also run *fietsenstallingen*, secure storage areas where you can leave your bike for about €1.10 per day and €3.80 per week. In some places you'll also encounter rotating bicycle 'lockers' which can be accessed electronically.

Don't ever leave your bike unlocked, even for an instant. Second-hand bikes are a lucrative trade, and hundreds of thousands are stolen in the Netherlands each year. Even if you report the theft to the police, chances of recovery are virtually nil.

ACCOMMODATION

Apart from the camping grounds listed in this book, there are plenty of nature camp sites along bike paths, often adjoined to a local farm. They tend to be smaller, simpler and cheaper than the regular camping grounds, and many don't allow cars or caravans. The Stichting Natuurkampeerterreinen (Nature Campsites Foundation; www.natuurkampeerterreinen.nl, in Dutch) publishes a map guide to these sites, on sale at the ANWB.

You may also wish to try *trekkershutten*, basic hikers' huts available at many campsites. See p285 for more information.

Many hostels, B&Bs and hotels throughout the country are well geared to cyclists' needs; often those on some of the more popular cycle routes, particularly along the coastline, market directly to tourists on two wheels.

ROUTES

You're spoilt for choice in the Netherlands; a good starting point is the easy day trips found in the *Er-op-Uit* book (€5), available from train station bookshops and tourist information offices. The more detailed *Fietsgids Nederland* (€9.95, in Dutch), produced by the ANWB, is another handy publication; it lists 50 popular cycle routes countrywide.

If you're seeking more of an odyssey, there are droves of cross-country and international routes to harden your calves. Most have a theme – medieval settlements, say, or some natural feature such as rivers or dunes.

The ANWB sells guides to signposted paths. These include the Noordzee-route, a coastal trek from Den Helder along dunes and delta to Boulogne-sur-Mer in France (470km), or the Saksenroute from the Waddenzee coast to Twente in eastern Overijssel (230km).

The site www.fiets platform.nl (in Dutch) has comprehensive information on *landelijke fietsroutes* (LF routes; long-distance routes) through the country.

Listed below are five excursions that provide a taster of what is available in the country; our best advice however is simply to rent a bike and head off in a direction that looks appealing.

Waterland Route   37km, 3½ to five hours

The eastern half of Waterland is culture-shock material: 20 minutes from central Amsterdam you step centuries back in time. This is an area of isolated farming communities and flocks of birds amid ditches, dykes and lakes.

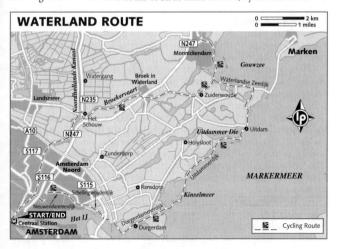

It takes a few minutes to get out of town. First, take your bike onto the free Buiksloterwegveer ferry behind Amsterdam's Centraal Station across the IJ river. Then continue 1km along the west bank of the Noordhollands Kanaal. Cross the second bridge, continue along the east bank for a few hundred metres and turn right, under the freeway and along Nieuwendammerdijk past Vliegenbos camping ground. At the end of Nieuwendammerdijk, do a dogleg and continue along Schellingwouderdijk. Follow this under the two major road bridges, when it becomes Durgerdammerdijk, and you're on your way.

The pretty town of Durgerdam looks out across the water to IJburg, a major land-reclamation project that will eventually house 45,000 people. Further north, the dyke road passes several lakes and former sea inlets – low-lying, drained peatlands that were flooded during storms and now form important bird-breeding areas. Colonies include plovers, godwits, bitterns, golden-eyes, snipes, herons and spoonbills. Climb the dyke at one of the viewing points for uninterrupted views to both sides.

The road – now called Uitdammerdijk – passes the town of Uitdam, after which you turn left (west) towards Monnickendam (p155). Alternatively, you could turn right and proceed along the causeway to the former island of Marken (p156). After visiting Marken, you could take the summer ferry to Volendam (p156) and backtrack along the sea dyke to Monnickendam. Or you could return over the causeway from Marken and pick up our tour again towards Monnickendam. These diversions to Marken and (especially) Volendam would add significantly to the length of your trip (55km, seven to 10 hours).

From Monnickendam, return the way you came (if you came by the first route, not by one of the Marken diversions), but about 1.5km south of town turn right (southwest) towards Zuiderwoude. From there, continue to Broek in Waterland (p154), a pretty town with old wooden houses. Then cycle along the south bank of the Broekervaart canal towards Het Schouw on the Noordhollands Kanaal. Cross the Noordhollands Kanaal (the bridge is slightly to the north); bird-watchers may want to head up the west bank towards Watergang and its bird-breeding areas. Otherwise, follow the west bank back down to Amsterdam Noord. From here it's straight cycling all the way to the ferry to Centraal Station.

'After visiting Marken, you could take the summer ferry to Volendam and back-track along the sea dyke to Monnickendam. '

Mantelingen Route   35km, three hours
Depart from 't Groentje, an eastern suburb of Domburg (p227), a popular beach resort in the southwest coastal province of Zeeland; its tourist office has a list of bicycle-hire shops.

If you're up for the full tour via Westkapelle (making the trip 48km and about 3½ to 4½ hours long), head west along the coastal path past the golf course. Relish a split view of the earth atop the Westkapelse Zeedijk, a protective sea wall erected following the great flood of 1953. Once you're in the former fishing village of Westkapelle, take note of the odd church-lighthouse; the church burnt down in 1831, but the lighthouse was rebuilt on the solitary tower. Head east out of Westkapelle towards Aagtekerke and keep to the path marked Dorpenroute, which follows Prelaatweg. The area suddenly becomes a green and pleasing pastureland, and the tall hawthorn hedges part to reveal the lovely pension De Ark about a third of the way along.

For the shorter tour, turn south from Domburg along the signposted 'Mantelingenroute' path. This region explodes with flowers in season and is rightfully known as 'the garden of Zeeland'. The meadows are typically dotted with *schuren*, tarred farmhouses with green doors. Sticking to the

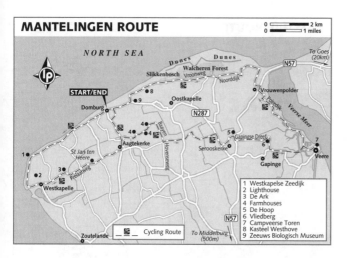

MANTELINGEN ROUTE

Mantelingenroute will lead you to the village of Serooskerke and, just to the east, a cheerily renovated windmill and farmyard tavern, De Hoop. It's a great spot for an afternoon snack of strawberry waffles.

From De Hoop, continue on along Gapingse Dreef towards Veere (p226), and you'll soon stumble across a *vliedberg*, an artificial rise laid in the 12th century as a defence post and refuge in times of floods. Veere itself sits on the south shore of the Veerse Meer, a large lake created when an arm of the North Sea was closed off.

The route swings past the town's enormous Vrouwekerk to the Markt; turn right to glimpse the Campveerse Toren, towers which formed part of the old city fortifications. Continuing west along the quay in Veere, you'll pass a row of handsome 19th-century houses; at the bridge, turn around for an idyllic scene worthy of a snapshot.

From the town head northwest along the Veerse Meer and cross over the N57 road; here begins the chain of dunes that protect the Walcheren Forest from the North Sea. This leafy expanse between the coast and *polders* (drained lands) gives the route its name, Manteling, which roughly translates as mantle or overcoat. The path then turns west (left) along the southern edge of the dunes and becomes dark and leafy in the Slikkenbosch forest.

Near the end of the journey, as you turn left (south) away from the dunes, you'll pass close by Kasteel Westhove (p227), a 16th-century fort that was once the pride of powerful local deacons. Today it houses a youth hostel; in the adjacent orangery there's the Zeeuws Biologisch Museum (Zeeland Biology Museum) and a garden of local flora.

'The route swings past the town's enormous Vrouwekerk to the Markt; turn right to glimpse the Campveerse Toren...'

Baronie Route   52km, four to five hours

The province of Noord Brabant in the south of the country has a definite Flemish-Belgian feel to it, in the cuisine and the ornate architecture. The Baronie is the area around the town of Breda (p275), which belonged to the princedom of Brabant until the 17th century; the counts of Nassau resided here between 1403 and 1567.

The starting point is Breda train station, which has a bicycle-hire shop (p277). The gravel and sand Baronieroute (well signposted) leads alongside the municipal park to Breda's 16th-century *kasteel* (fort), which houses a military academy. It takes a while to get out of town, as you pass through the

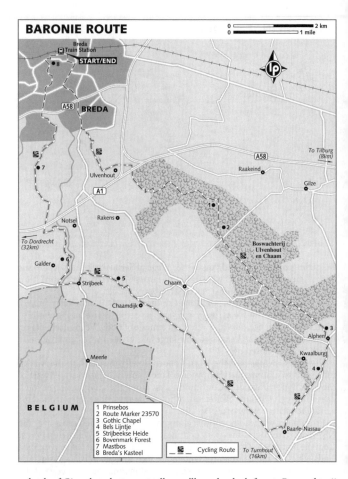

BARONIE ROUTE

1	Prinsebos
2	Route Marker 23570
3	Gothic Chapel
4	Bels Lijntje
5	Strijbeekse Heide
6	Bovenmark Forest
7	Mastbos
8	Breda's Kasteel

Cycling Route

'follow the Maastrichtse Baan (Maastricht Route) towards Alphen, the birthplace of artist Vincent Van Gogh.'

suburb of Ginneken, but eventually you'll reach a lush forest, Boswachterij Ulvenhout en Chaam, which lies southeast of the town. Between Ulvenhout and Alphen you can pedal about 15km on continuous forest paths. In the Prinsebos (Prince's Forest), planted in the early 20th century, you may see sturdy Brabant horses at work hauling timber.

At route marker 23570 you can either turn right to reach Chaam, a Protestant village amid predominantly Catholic Brabant, or follow the Maastrichtse Baan (Maastricht Route) towards Alphen, the birthplace of artist Vincent Van Gogh. Shortly before Alphen you'll pass a Gothic chapel from the 16th century – but the tower was built after WWII. From here a number of routes cross over into Belgium, including the Smokkelaarsroute (Smugglers' Route).

The path here is pretty and follows the old Bels Lijntje (Belgium Line), the train line opened in 1867 to link Tilburg with Turnhout. The last passenger train ran in 1934; the route was converted to a cycle path in 1989.

If you have time, stop off for a look around the town of Baarle-Nassau, which has been the subject of border disputes since the 12th century. The

Belgian and Dutch governments finally settled a 150-year difference in 1995; as a result, Belgian territory grew by 2600 sq metres.

Before you reach Baarle-Nassau, veer right and you'll eventually pass the village of Chaamdijk and a pretty heath, the Strijbeekse Heide. Just beyond, at the village of Galder, you can cross the bridge and turn right into the Bovenmark Forest before doubling back to the main path, the Frieslandroute (LF9). Cross highway A1 to reach the forestry station at Mastbos, but take care with the loose sand and rocks on the final stretch back into Breda.

Plateau Route   35km, three to four hours

The suggestion is it's flat as a Dutch pancake, but make no mistake, this route is the hilliest in our selection. Most ascents are merciful and easily conquered with the aid of gears. Defining features of this trip include windmills, sprawling castles and lovely rolling farmland.

From the bike shop at Maastricht train station, head southeast beneath the underpass and follow the bike route marked 'LF6a' and/or 'Bemelen'. It's a 10-minute ride to the city limits. At the ANWB map board Knooppunt 6 you join the Plateauroute; follow the route north (left), then east (right), to the small town of Bemelen.

At the hamlet St Antoniusbank you leave the paved road behind, passing an abandoned lime kiln on your ascent to the panorama over a limestone quarry. It's no surprise, then, that Limburg is peppered with structures built from the ochre-coloured mineral. A few kilometres on stands the cheery Van Tienhovenmolen windmill (open every second and fourth Saturday of the month).

> 'Defining features of this trip include windmills, sprawling castles and lovely rolling farmland.'

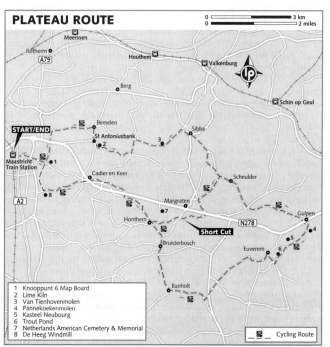

PLATEAU ROUTE

0 —————— 3 km
0 —————— 2 miles

Rötherm • A79
Meerssen
Houthem
Valkenburg
Berg
Schin op Geul
Bemelen   Sibbe
START/END
St Antoniusbank 2   3
Maastricht   1
Train Station
Cadier en Keer   Scheulder
A2   8
Margraten
7
Honthem   Gulpen
Short Cut   4
Bruisterbosch   N278   5
Euverem   6
Banholt

1 Knooppunt 6 Map Board
2 Lime Kiln
3 Van Tienhovenmolen
4 Pannekoekenmolen
5 Kasteel Neubourg
6 Trout Pond
7 Netherlands American Cemetery & Memorial
8 De Heeg Windmill

Cycling Route

'Lunchtime is wisely spent at the Panne-koekemolen, a pancake house in a historic water mill...'

At the roundabout that's watched over by a limestone sculpture about 1km on from the windmill, take a right into Sibbe. The imposing pile on your left is the Sibbehuis, a 14th-century castle that's now a private residence. The route is a bit unclear in the village; follow signs to Gulpen. From Scheulder – where, if desired, you can halve the journey via a short cut labelled 'Route Afkorting' – you whiz through planted fields and finally downhill into the beer-brewing town of Gulpen. Lunchtime is wisely spent at the Pannekoekenmolen, a pancake house in a historic water mill tucked away at Molenweg 2a. To get there, turn left off Rijksweg/N278 at the traffic light onto Molenweg.

Here we suggest a detour to avoid the busy main road. From the pancake house, proceed southeast along cycle path 85, a leafy trail that affords glimpses of the turreted Kasteel Neubourg, a medieval castle (closed to the public). After the trout pond, take the first right towards Euverem, where you turn left to rejoin the Plateauroute.

The home stretch to Maastricht is quite countrified, with memorable views of mixed woodlands and livestock wandering the pastures. Pretty half-timbered houses grace the tidy farm villages where fresh potatoes, apples and strawberries are sold to passers-by. In tiny Banholt sheep graze peacefully in the town square.

Reminders of a grim era lie in Margraten, about 2km northeast of Honthem, at the Netherlands American Cemetery and Memorial (p283).

Onward from the hamlet Cadier en Keer you can coast downhill towards Maastricht, taking care not to miss the sharp right at the windmill in De Heeg. At the Knooppunt 6 map board, bear left on Bemelerweg towards Maastricht train station.

Southern Texel Route　　　　　　　　　　　　30km, three hours

The Wadden islands are a cyclists' paradise. Long stretches of sand dunes are complemented by pockets of woodland and large swaths of fertile farmland, and the North Sea and Waddenzee are never very far away. Of the five islands, Texel (p167) is easily the biggest and far and away the most visited, but it also offers the most diversity.

Begin this tour around the southern reaches of the island in Den Burg, Texel's quiet capital, where you'll find a couple of bike-rental shops. Head west out of the town past the tourist office (p167) and right (north) onto the island's main road, the N501; its bike path is quite separate from what little traffic the island receives. Grazing sheep and fluorescent green *polders* mark the path to your left and right, and at Monnikenweg turn west (left) in the direction of the North Sea. Before you know it you'll enter De Dennen, Texel's peaceful pine forest; it was initially planted for timber but has thankfully been left to run its own course. Not far into the forest turn right onto Ploeglanderweg and make a beeline for Ecomare (p167), an outstanding nature centre and refuge for sick seals found in the surrounding waters. After a mesmerising hour watching the seals' effortless water play, head south towards De Dennen, this time taking Randweg, a little-used road that meanders through the forest. Randweg soon turns into Nattevlakweg, which makes a dogleg and leaves the forest to join Rommelpot. Come springtime along this path, bright fields of tulips on your left are juxtaposed with the expansive heath to the right, which holds back the encroaching sand dunes.

At the junction of Rommelpot and Klif the route turns left into Den Hoorn, arguably the island's prettiest village. This is a good place to recharge the batteries, before following Mokweg south to rising sand dunes; here the path turns left on Molwerk and hugs the dunes until Texel's port, 't Horntje. From 't Horntje, take De Rede northeast along one of the island's protective dykes; when it hits Redoute, turn left and then take the first right to enter

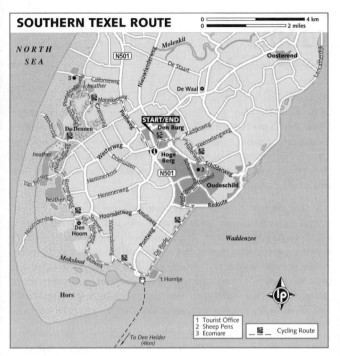

SOUTHERN TEXEL ROUTE

0 ———————— 4 km
0 ———————— 2 miles

1 Tourist Office
2 Sheep Pens
3 Ecomare

Cycling Route

'Of the boulder clay mounds dotting the island, Hoge Berg is the most distinctive...'

the Hoge Berg region. Of the boulder clay mounds dotting the island, Hoge Berg is the most distinctive; it still sports *stolp* farms, garden walls and sheep pens reminiscent of times past. Look for the Texelroute sign and keep to the right – this will lead you up Westergeest, left onto Schansweg, then right into Doolhof. Along Doolhof is one of the few sheep pens (large, A-frame houses which look as though they've been sliced in two) whose front is not facing east.

At the next junction turn left up Skillepaadje and cross Schilderweg into Hallerweg, which will lead you back to Den Burg.

Amsterdam

Amsterdam's always been a liberal place, ever since the Golden Age, when it led European art and trade. Centuries later, in the 1960s, it again led the pack – this time in the principles of tolerance, with broad-minded views on drugs and same-sex relationships taking centre stage. Today the cannabis coffeeshops and the Red Light District are still the city's top drawcards, even if that can sometimes wear thin for the locals. But Amsterdam's more than just an X-rated theme park for weekend warriors.

Quite simply, it's among the most distinctive of all European cities (it's certainly one of the most eccentric). And it may well be the most beautiful, with its breathtakingly scenic, heritage-protected 17th-century housing and ubiquitous canals. Other cities in Europe's premier league are nothing if not monumental, but Amsterdam by contrast is irreverent, intimate and accessible: you can walk across the city centre in around 30 minutes, less by bike, and the place has enough sensory delights to keep the shortest attention spans occupied. All of the major sights are found in or near the city centre: some of the continent's best museums and galleries nestle among attractions that are just plain quirky or silly – but always fun.

Walk or bike around the canal grid, down the historic lanes of the Jordaan district or through the Plantage and bask in the many worlds-within-worlds that make Amsterdam so thoroughly addictive.

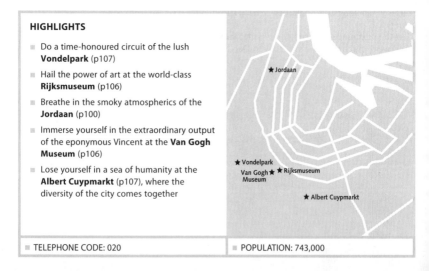

HIGHLIGHTS

- Do a time-honoured circuit of the lush **Vondelpark** (p107)
- Hail the power of art at the world-class **Rijksmuseum** (p106)
- Breathe in the smoky atmospherics of the **Jordaan** (p100)
- Immerse yourself in the extraordinary output of the eponymous Vincent at the **Van Gogh Museum** (p106)
- Lose yourself in a sea of humanity at the **Albert Cuypmarkt** (p107), where the diversity of the city comes together

★ Jordaan

★ Vondelpark
Van Gogh ★ ★ Rijksmuseum
Museum

★ Albert Cuypmarkt

- TELEPHONE CODE: 020
- POPULATION: 743,000

HISTORY

A small fishing town named Aemstelredamme emerged in around 1200. The community was freed by the count of Holland from paying tolls on its locks and bridges, and 'Amsterdam' developed into a major seaport.

Calvinist brigands captured Amsterdam in 1578, and the seven northern provinces, led by Holland and Zeeland, declared themselves a republic. The stage was set for the Golden Age, when merchants and artisans flocked to Amsterdam and a new class of moneyed intellectuals was born.

By the late 17th century Holland couldn't match the might of France and England, but when the country's first railway opened in 1839 the city was revitalised in a stroke.

During the latter part of that century, Amsterdammers were certainly buoyant and in feisty mood – as the Eel Riot of 25 July 1886 proves. At the time, the sport of eel pulling was very popular throughout the city. The rules were very simple: a rope would be suspended over a canal, with a live eel attached to it. Underneath, competitors in boats would try to grab the poor creature, with the ever-present threat of landing in the water adding a frisson to the proceedings.

When the authorities made the game illegal – denouncing it as a 'cruel, popular amusement' – the Jordaan erupted in riots so intense and pitched that 25 people died from gunshot wounds inflicted by the police.

The first part of the 20th century was characterised by more trouble, as unemployment, depression and WWI took their toll. After WWII, growth resumed with US aid (the Marshall Plan).

However, in 1955 the French philosopher Albert Camus wrote, 'Have you noticed that Amsterdam's concentric canals resemble the circles of hell? The middle-class hell, of course, peopled with bad dreams'.

How incredible, then, to see the next few decades unfold.

In the 1960s students occupied the administrative centre of the University of Amsterdam, and the women's movement began a campaign that fuelled the abortion debate throughout the next decade. Meanwhile, pranksters, anarchists and radicals began a systematic programme to derail conservative attitudes – with a peculiarly Amsterdammer dose of absurdism. Nowhere was this more evident than in the antics of the Provos, whose members included poet Johnny the Selfkicker and Bart Huges, an 'open-minded' fellow who drilled a hole in his forehead to achieve enlightenment (see the boxed text, p31).

During that decade, Amsterdam was known as Europe's 'Magic Centre', the crux of a utopian dream where people believed anything could happen. Although the days of excess have been somewhat neutered, much of that famous swagger is still evident (and in some cases, institutionalised and parodied, as in the Red Light District; in fact, if you arrive here on Koninginnedag – see p117 – you might think it never went away).

In the '70s city planners proposed a metro line through the Nieuwmarkt neighbourhood, earmarking a large portion of the derelict district to be razed. When the inhabitants turned to squatting, the area was violently cleared on 24 March 1975, a day fixed in history as 'Blue Monday'.

In the '60s families and small manufacturers dominated inner-city neighbourhoods; by the early '90s they'd been replaced by professionals and a service industry of pubs, coffeeshops, restaurants and hotels. Non-Dutch nationalities made up 45% of the population and the city's success in attracting large foreign businesses resulted in an influx of higher-income expatriates.

ORIENTATION

Centraal Station is the city's hub. From the station the streets radiate outward across the network of canals. The Dam is the heart, a 10-minute walk southwest of the station. Leidseplein is the centre of (mainstream) Amsterdam nightlife, and Nieuwmarkt (southeast of the station) is a vast cobblestone square with open-air markets and popular pubs. The Red Light District (south of the station and east of the Dam) is bounded by Zeedijk, Nieuwmarkt and Kloveniersburgwal in the east; Damstraat, Oude Doelenstraat and Oude Hoogstraat in the south; and Warmoesstraat in the west.

Lush, 17th-century homes occupy the western canals Prinsengracht, Keizersgracht and Herengracht. The Jordaan is filled with quirky shops, bohemian bars and art galleries. Outside the canal belt is ethnic-influenced De Pijp; posh and residential Oud Zuid, east of the Damrak-Rokin axis; and Nieuw Zuid, to the west of the axis, with its 20th-century housing projects. The Eastern Docklands is a showcase of modern Dutch architecture.

AMSTERDAM

AMSTERDAM IN...

Two Days
Begin at the **Anne Frank Huis** (p102), then scoot across town to the **Rijksmuseum** (p106) and the **Van Gogh Museum** (p106). Dive into the **Albert Cuypmarkt** (p107), before coming up for air (and lunch) at **Bazar** (p215). In the afternoon, stop off for a smoke at **Siberië** (p129), then follow the conga line to the **Red Light District** (p85). When the dope's worn off, order a *mojito* at **Café Cuba** (p127), before dining at the sumptuous **Blauw aan de Wal** (p122). On the second day, hire a **bike** (p111) and see where you end up – it's all good, and well you know it.

Four Days
Take in the two-day itinerary, but allow yourself time to explore in greater depth. For example, after the Van Gogh Museum, take a walk around the **Vondelpark** (p107) and indulge in a spot of people-watching. Follow this by enjoying some classical music at the **Concertgebouw** (p107). At night, drink at **Lime** (p127) and eat at **Nomads** (p123).

Maps

The maps in this book will probably be sufficient. Lonely Planet's handy *Amsterdam City Map* has a street index (in rain-proof lamination) that covers most parts of town in detail. The tourist offices also sell maps of the city centre.

INFORMATION
Bookshops

American Book Center (Map pp92-3; ☎ 625 55 37; www.abc.nl; Kalverstraat 185) English-language books, travel guides, newspapers and magazines.

Architectura & Natura (Map pp88-9; ☎ 623 61 86; www.architectura.nl; Leliegracht 22; ☺ Mon-Sat) Charming canalside shop with art, architecture, design, landscape and coffee-table books.

Athenaeum Bookshop & Newsagency (Map pp92-3; ☎ 622 62 48; Spui 14-16) Enormous multilevel store with a vast assortment of unusual titles.

Book Exchange (Map pp88-9; ☎ 626 62 66; Kloveniersburgwal 58) Second-hand books, many in English.

Galerie Lambiek (Map pp92-3; ☎ 626 75 43; www.lambiek.nl; Kerkstraat 78; ☺ daily) Tens of thousands of titles of Dutch and worldwide comic-book art.

Scheltema (Map pp92-3; ☎ 523 14 11; Koningsplein 20) Largest bookshop in town, with many foreign titles.

Waterstone's (Map pp92-3; ☎ 638 38 21; Kalverstraat 152) English-language travel guides, maps and novels.

Cultural Centres

British Council (Map pp92-3; ☎ 550 60 60; www.britishcouncil.nl; Weteringschans 85a) Manages educational and cultural exchanges between the UK and the Netherlands.

De Balie (Map pp92-3; ☎ 553 51 00; www.debalie.nl; Kleine Gartmanplantsoen 10) Theatre, seminars, political debates and lectures.

Maison Descartes (Map pp92-3; ☎ 531 95 00; www.maisondescartes.com; Vijzelgracht 2A; ☺ 9.30am-4pm Mon-Fri, library 1-6pm Tue & Thu) Extension of the French consulate offering films, lectures and exhibitions.

Discount Card

I Amsterdam Card (per 24/36/72hr €33/43/53) Available at VVV offices and some hotels. Includes admission to most museums, canal boat trips, and discounts and freebies at shops, attractions and restaurants. Also includes a GVB transit pass.

Emergency

Emergency (☎ 112) Police, ambulance, fire brigade.
Police headquarters (☎ 09008844; Elandsgracht 117)
Sexual assault (☎ 613 02 45) De Eerste Lijn (The First Line) is a hotline for victims of sexual violence.

Internet Access

Centrale Bibliotheek (Map pp92-3; ☎ 523 09 00; Prinsengracht 587; ☺ 1-9pm Mon, 10am-9pm Tue-Thu, 10am-5pm Fri & Sat, 1-5pm Sun) The main library. Has free Internet.

easyInternetcafé (Map pp88-9; www.easyeverything.com/map/ams; Damrak 33; ☺ 9am-10pm)

Internet City (Map pp88-9; ☎ 620 12 92; Nieuwendijk 76; ☺ 10am-midnight)

Internet Resources

www.amsterdamhotspots.nl Select the hottest spots to eat, drink, smoke, sleep and party down.

www.channels.nl Virtual tour of 'Dam with hotel and restaurant reviews.

www.underwateramsterdam.com The site for *Shark*, the monthly underground events 'zine.

www.visitamsterdam.nl Official Netherlands Board of Tourism site.

Laundry

Clean Brothers (Map pp92-3; ☎ 622 02 73; Kerkstraat 56)

Happy Inn (Map pp92-3; ☎ 624 84 64; Warmoesstraat 30; ⊙ closed Sun)

Wasserette Rozengracht (Map p91; ☎ 638 59 75; Rozengracht 59)

Left Luggage

At Centraal Station there's a left-luggage desk downstairs from track 2, near the southeastern corner of the station. Storage costs €3 for 24 hours.

Libraries

Centrale Bibliotheek (Map pp92-3; ☎ 523 09 00; Prinsengracht 587; ⊙ 1-9pm Mon, 10am-9pm Tue-Thu, 10am-5pm Fri & Sat, 1-5pm Sun) Wide range of English-language newspapers and magazines. Free Internet.

Media

For details of national newspapers and magazines, see p37.

Amsterdam Times Mainstream local news. In English.

Amsterdam Weekly (www.amsterdamweekly.nl) Outstanding English-language paper, free every Wednesday. Offers creative, personal articles on life in Amsterdam plus useful classifieds.

Het Parool (www.parool.nl) The lowdown on the capital's culture and politics.

Medical Services

Centrale Doktersdienst (Central Doctors' Service; ☎ 592 33 33; ⊙ 24hr) Doctor, dentist or pharmacy referrals.

Onze Lieve Vrouwe Gasthuis (Map pp86-7; ☎ 599 91 11; Oosterpark 9) Hospital open 24 hours.

Money

American Express (Map pp88-9; ☎ 504 87 77; Damrak 66; ⊙ 9am-5pm Mon-Fri, to noon Sat)

GWK (Map pp88-9; ☎ 09000566; Centraal Station; ⊙ 8am-10pm Mon-Sat, 9am-10pm Sun) Converts travellers cheques and books hotel reservations; also at Schiphol.

Thomas Cook Dam (Map pp88-9; ☎ 625 09 22; Dam 23-25; ⊙ 9am-7pm); Damrak (Map pp88-9; ☎ 620 32 36; Damrak 1-5; ⊙ 8am-8pm); Leidseplein (Map pp92-3; ☎ 626 70 00; Leidseplein 31A; ⊙ 9am-7.30pm Mon-Sat, 10am-7.30pm Sun)

Post

Main post office (Map pp88-9; ☎ 330 0555; Singel 250; ⊙ 9am-6pm Mon-Wed & Fri, to 8pm Thu, 10am-1.30pm Sat)

Telephone

For information about mobile phones, phone codes, public telephones and phonecards, see p295.

Toilets

There are no public toilets in Amsterdam. Your best bet is to slip into a department store, where you'll pay the toilet attendants around €0.50.

Tourist Information

Tourist Office (VVV; ☎ 09004004040; www.vvv amsterdam.nl); Centraal Station track 2 (Map pp88-9; Centraal Station; ⊙ 8am-8pm Mon-Sat, 9am-5pm Sun); Leidseplein 1 (Map pp92-3; ⊙ 9.15am-5pm Sun-Thu, to 7pm Fri & Sat); Stationsplein 10 (Map pp88-9; ⊙ 9am-5pm Mon-Fri)

Travel Agencies

Kilroy Travels (Map pp92-3; ☎ 524 51 00; www .kilroytravels.com; Singel 413-415; ⊙ noon-6pm Mon, 10am-6pm Tue-Fri, 11.30am-4.30pm Sat).

lastminute.com (☎ 09004050607; www.nl.lastminute .com; per min €0.15)

DANGERS & ANNOYANCES

Theft is rare in hotel rooms, but it's always wise to deposit valuables for safekeeping at the reception desk or, where available, in your in-room safe. Theft is more common at hostels; bring your own lock for your locker.

Watch out for pickpockets in crowded markets and on trams. Violent crime is rare, especially involving foreigners.

Cars with foreign registration are popular targets for smash-and-grab theft. Don't leave valuable items in the car; remove registration and ID papers and the radio/stereo if possible. If something is stolen, get a police report for insurance purposes, but don't expect the police to retrieve your property or apprehend the thief.

There are occasionally some junkie types around the Zeedijk and Gelderskade, and also on the Nieuwendijk near Centraal Station. Generally, they won't bother you if you don't bother them.

DOG SHIT

It's everywhere. The Netherlands doesn't appear to have a 'pooper-scooper' policy, and Amsterdam's streets are full of it.

AN INSIDER'S GUIDE TO AMSTERDAM, PART 1: STEVE KORVER   *Simon Sellars*

Steve Korver is the editor of the super periodical *Amsterdam Weekly* and the irreverent and informative *Time Out Amsterdam*. Who could be better qualified, then, to give me the inside dirt on this wonderful city?

What's your favourite part of Amsterdam?

It varies and stretches further afield day by day as the inner city gets more and more 'organised'. I like those funky bits that were always easy to find in De Pijp and Jordaan and along the waterfront but are now getting scrubbed cleaner than clean. But the stereotypes are still nice: the canal girdle remains one of the planet's most painfully scenic places, especially when the water glows purple just before dawn.

Speaking of stereotypes, what's the least applicable?

The whole sex, drugs and rock'n'roll thang – it's there but mostly for the tourists.

Has Theo van Gogh's assassination (see the boxed text, p32) changed the disposition of Amsterdam and its people as much as we've been led to believe?

It was our September 11 – it only took that one death in this tiny country to have a similar effect. But after the initial hysteria flamed by populist politicians, things have mellowed and people are doing what they've done here forever: gathered as many parties around a table to talk, talk, talk…and, hopefully, hash out solutions.

Do you have a favourite 'Amsterdam experience'?

Talking the shit with friends on a terrace on one of those first sunny days of spring.

What film or book set in Amsterdam would you recommend for first-timers?

Books: *Time Out Amsterdam* (heh heh), *Amsterdam: A Brief Life of the City* by Geert Mak, *The Embarrassment of Riches* by Simon Schama, *The Diary of Anne Frank*, *Blue Mondays* by Arnon Grunberg, *Brilliant Orange: The Neurotic Genius of Dutch Football* by David Winners.

Films: *Diamonds Are Forever*, *Simon* by Eddy Terstall, *The Northerners* by Alex van Warmerdam.

Your favourite nightspot?

I'm not telling. Everyone's got to find their own. But do try to go local rather than endlessly circling around the Red Light District's inner pit. The Melkweg and Paradiso still rule, but there

---

Bicycles are numerous (see p111) and can be dangerous for pedestrians. When crossing the street look for speeding bikes as well as cars; please don't stray into a bike lane without looking both ways. Cyclists, meanwhile, should take care to watch out for unwitting foreign tourists, and to lock up their bikes.

Drugs

Don't light up joints just anywhere without asking permission. In general, stick to coffeeshops. Drugs are technically illegal but tolerated. See p293 for laws relating to hard and soft drugs.

Scams

Beware of thieves masquerading as police in plain clothes. Usually these fraudsters address tourists in English, flash a false ID and demand to see money and credit cards for 'verification' or some other nonsense. They might also go through the victim's pockets and pretend to look for drugs. Dutch police rarely conduct this kind of search. To foil the crooks, ask to see their police identity card (note that Dutch police don't have badges as ID). Then call the real cops at ☎ 09008844.

SIGHTS

The canal belt (p101) is Amsterdam at its most seductive: Golden Age façades, brown cafés, hidden courtyards. The Dam (p96) is the city's heart; throbbing Leidseplein (p102) is a Dutch Times Square; Rembrandtplein (p102) is a brash clubber's mecca; while the ever-popular Nieuwmarkt (p98) hums with markets, cafés and pubs. You don't need us to tell you about the Red Light District (p85).

Outside the canal belt, there's multicultural De Pijp (p107) and the Oud Zuid (p105), posh and residential.

If you want top-line attractions, Amsterdam delivers. The classical art circuit is an obvious route: with the world-class Van Gogh Museum and Rijksmuseum within easy reach, you'll be spoilt for choice. Then there are the theatres, the pubs, the coffeeshops, the cafés, the churches – we could tailor itineraries for you until the cows

are a lot of new, smaller venues like Sugar Factory, Bitterzoet and Nieuwe Anita that are pumping both live music and good ol' fashioned cosiness back into the mix. As for coffeeshops, remember: you can do takeaway, kids!

Any foodie tips?

Fish stalls, for deep-throating herring – the poor, working person's sushi. Perfect for people on the move.

Can you tell me Amsterdam's best-kept secret?

Nope.

What are your favourite local slang or swear words?

Too many to list: just pick a disease, any disease. It's ever evolving, here: today's curse is tomorrow's Ajax football chant.

'Amsterdam equals bicycles' – so says the tourist board. What's the downside?

Tourists on bikes thinking they are in Disneyland, totally oblivious to the fact that basic traffic rules and precautions are just as relevant here as in any other city (see p111). Just because it all looks so cute, it doesn't mean you can't become road pizza. The same goes for pedestrians. And it's not just stoned backpackers – visitors just forget to look both ways before crossing a street. Theories abound as to why, but I haven't figured it out yet.

How has living in Amsterdam changed you?

It's probably slowed me down to enjoy the smaller, more social things in life – doing business over a coffee and a beer instead of over a desk.

Describe Amsterdam Weekly for someone new to it.

We are an English-language alternative weekly but we still use plenty of Dutch – especially when it's funny. We seek to be attached to the city and not detached. Our prime directive is to provide a paper for culturally savvy Amsterdammers to help plan their weekend and go deeper into the cultural workings of this very special city. Oh, and we like to kick city hall's ass on occasion whenever they think they can change things from above and not from the ground up. We are the voice of the grassroots, the subcultures that are always busy bubbling up towards the foreground.

come home. But, ultimately, take our tip and just wander (see the boxed text, p85).

Medieval Centre
DAMRAK & OUDE ZIJDE

Once part of the old harbour, Damrak today is an endless stretch of souvenir shops, beetling bicycles, exchange bureaux and dodgy hotels. East of the Damrak-Rokin axis is the Oude Zijde (Old Side) of the medieval city. It's a misnomer: the Nieuwe Zijde (New Side) to the west is actually older, though the Oude Zijde absorbed the Red Light District in the 14th century. Originally, the city didn't extend further south than Grimburgwal, where the filled-in parts of the Rokin end today.

The gleaming, turreted marvel that is **Centraal Station** (Map pp88–9) dates from 1889 and was the work of AL Ghent and Pierre Cuypers, the master architects who also designed the Rijksmuseum and the Concertgebouw. Centraal's resemblance to the Rijksmuseum is easy to spot: a central section with Gothic towers and wings.

Sint Nicolaaskerk (Map pp88-9; ☎ 624 87 49; Prins Hendrikkade 73; ☼ 11am-4pm Tue-Sat, noon-3pm Mon, services 10.30am & 1pm Sun, 12.30pm Mon-Sat), built in 1887, is the city's main Catholic church. The impressive interior features black marble pillars and an ethereal bluish aura in the soaring dome. The high altar is unusual for its depiction of Maximilian's bulging yellow crown.

The innovative **News Photo** (Map pp88-9; ☎ 330 84 00; www.newsphoto.nl; Prins Hendrikkade 33; admission €5; ☼ 10am-6pm) displays enormous blow-ups (up to 60m long) of headlining photos from around the world. Themed exhibitions (terrorism, the Tour de France etc) change every few weeks, and as news is made the curators use giant printers to print out the latest photos, which are then affixed to the magnetic walls. If you see a photo you like in the main gallery, you can buy it right off the wall (at €100 per sq metre while the exhibition is running, half-price thereafter).

At the **Sexmuseum Amsterdam** (Map pp88-9; ☎ 622 83 76; Damrak 18; admission €2.50; ☼ 10am-11.30pm), which lurks furtively behind a façade

NEIGHBOURHOODS

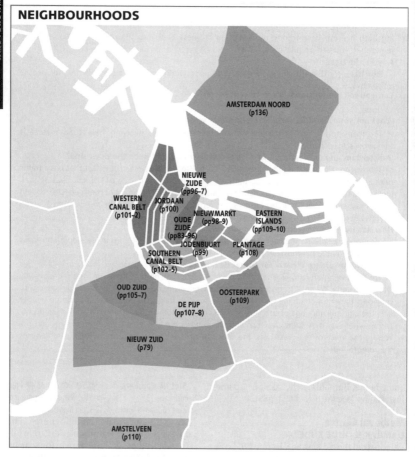

AMSTERDAM NOORD
(p136)

NIEUWE
ZIJDE
(pp96–7)

WESTERN
CANAL BELT
(p101–2)

JORDAAN
(p100)

NIEUWMARKT
(pp98–9)

EASTERN
ISLANDS
(pp109–10)

OUDE
ZIJDE
(pp83–96)

JODENBUURT
(p99)

PLANTAGE
(p108)

SOUTHERN
CANAL BELT
(p102–5)

OUD ZUID
(pp105–7)

DE PIJP
(pp107–8)

OOSTERPARK
(p109)

NIEUW ZUID
(p79)

AMSTELVEEN
(p110)

reminiscent of a sweaty 'swords-and-sandals' film, there are some mildly interesting artefacts: 14th-century Viennese erotica, for example, and Pompeian porn. But with plastic derrieres farting at passers-by and an animatronic flasher, it's more like a tribute to Benny Hill. A sign warns, 'You could be shocked'. Pull the other one.

The **Beurs van Berlage** (Map pp88–9; ☎ 530 41 41; www.beursvanberlage.net; Damrak 243; ⏲ 11am-5pm Tue-Sun) is the old stock and commodities exchange designed by renowned architect HP Berlage. The functional lines and chunky square clock tower are landmarks of Dutch urban architecture, and today the one-time Bourse is a cultural centre and home to the Netherlands Philharmonic Orchestra. Visi-

tors can roam the premises. The large central hall with its steel-and-glass roof was the Victorian-style trading floor for commodities and colonial merchandise. The rich decorations here include three Art Deco tile mosaics by Jan Toorop; stockbrokers distrusted these works because of their anti-capitalist flavour. Be sure to check out the basement vaults, where discreet patrons used to store their stock certificates, money and jewellery. The clock tower affords a view of the old town, and there are more Art Deco features in the café on the Beursplein side.

One of the original dykes on the Amstel river ran along **Warmoesstraat** (Map pp88–9), where the city's wealthiest merchants used to live (it up). Today it's an outgrowth of the Red

---

DIY AMSTERDAM

Follow the canals, the crowds or that deserted side street. Or the colour; that sweet smell in the air. You're bound to trip over something that tickles you pink – a museum devoted to bending light, say, or a guy on his back playing keepy uppy with a football for hours on end. Perhaps you'll see a group of subversives reviving the banned sport of eel pulling (see p79).

You'll more likely find an ancient building tucked away out of sight, redolent with atmosphere and begging to be read as a 'secret history' of the city. Quite possibly, it won't be in this guide. Let us know if it isn't. Or keep it to yourself – we'll understand.

Above all, Amsterdam's a unique template for city life that feels different for each individual – it's a personalised urban 'psychogeography' just waiting to be decoded.

Light District, with rough-edged bars, hotels and sex shops luridly rubbing shoulders with some great old architecture.

East off Warmoesstraat is the city's oldest surviving building (built in 1306), the mighty **Oude Kerk** (Old Church; Map pp88-9; ☎ 625 82 84; www.oudekerk.nl; Oudekerksplein 23; adult/child €4.50/3.50; ⊙ 11am-5pm Mon-Sat, 1-5pm Sun), built to honour the city's patron saint, St Nicholas (the inspiration for red-suited Saint Nick). In one of Europe's great moral contradictions, the tower, arguably Amsterdam's most beautiful, commands a magnificent view – one that includes the Red Light District. Get closer to heaven on a **tower tour** (☎ 689 25 65; admission €40, up to 25 people). But maybe the view's no contradiction at all: some of the 15th-century carvings on the choir stalls are downright naughty. There's also a stunning Müller organ, gilded oak vaults and stained-glass windows from 1555. As in the Nieuwe Kerk, many famous Amsterdammers are buried under worn tombstones, including Rembrandt's first wife, Saskia van Uylenburgh.

The **Allard Pierson Museum** (Map pp92-3; ☎ 525 25 56; www.uba.uva.nl/apm; Oude Turfmarkt 127; adult/child €5/2.50; ⊙ 10am-5pm Tue-Fri, 1-5pm Sat & Sun), run by the University of Amsterdam, has one of the world's richest university-owned archaeological collections, including an actual mummy, ancient Greek and Mesopotamian vases, a wagon from the royal tombs at Salamis (Cyprus), and galleries stuffed to the wainscoting with fascinating items providing real insight into daily life in ancient times.

Red Light District

Amsterdam's famous Red Light District retains the power to bewilder, even if near-naked prostitutes propositioning passers-by from black-lit windows is the oldest Amsterdam cliché. If you feel a twinge of desire, it's around €50 for 20 minutes.

The district, known locally as De Wallen, has for centuries been the undoing of countless sailors with its houses of ill repute and distilleries. The clientele has changed, but the script hasn't, because business never stops: all day and night prostitutes give their come-hither looks from big windows that line the canal. Some sections are in stereo with windows on two floors.

It's seamy for sure, but the ambience is far less threatening than in sex districts elsewhere. Pimps, drunks, weirdos, the fuzz, Salvation Army volunteers, nice girls and boys, and respectable old-age pensioners all rub shoulders and nothing else. Female sightseers are not assumed to be soliciting and tend to be left alone as long as they exercise a modicum of street sense.

Unless you want to end up in a canal along with your camera, don't take photos. And if you hear some guy whispering 'coke, acieeeeed, ecstasy, speed, china white, mother of pearl – what you need', then just walk on by. If want to look but not touch, try the live-sex club **Casa Rosso** (Map pp88-9; ☎ 627 89 54; Oudezijds Achterburgwal 106-108), with its marble penis fountain and rotating balls out front. It's far less threatening than other places: in the audience, grannies might mix with groovers, although more likely it will be like a cheery football crowd. Don't expect to be turned on: the actual show is as mechanical as the English football team.

The **Hash, Marihuana & Hemp Museum** (Map pp88-9; ☎ 623 59 61; admission €5.70; Oudezijds Achterburgwal 148; ⊙ 11am-11pm) features exhibits that cover dope botany; bongs, hookahs and pipes of the world; the relationship between cannabis and religion; and the history of Amsterdam coffeeshops. Queen Victoria used marijuana for menstrual cramps, it says here…

(Continued on page 96)

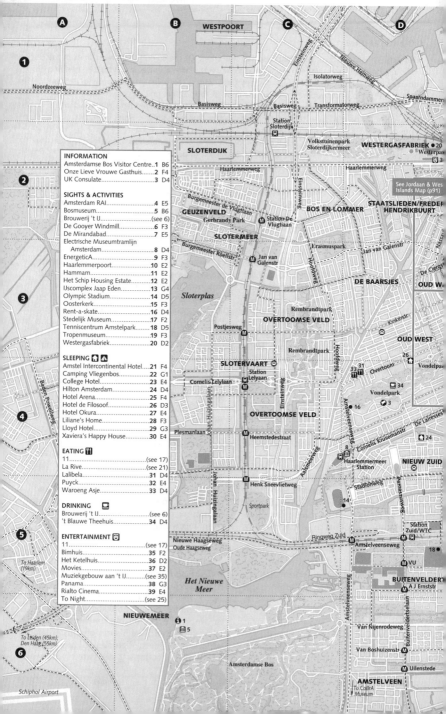

0 ⊏⊐ 1 km
0 ⊏⊐ 0.5 miles

E TUINDORP OOSTZAAN

Het IJ

Klaprozenweg

Distelwegveer

F BUIKSLOOT

Florapark

Johan van Hasseltweg

NIEUWENDAM

Nieuwe Leeuwarderweg

G Oidoornlaan

⊞ 22

IJdoornlaan

Beemsterstr

Hidoornlaan

Ringweg Noord

Zuiderzeeweg

H

IP

①

WESTERN ISLANDS

Houtmankade

2
11

10
⊡ 37

HAARLEMMERBUURT

NOORD

Johan van Hasseltweg

Meeuwenlaan

IJplein

SCHELLINGWOUDE

Zuiderzeeweg

Liergouw

②

See Amsterdam Centre
Map (pp88–9)

...RDAAN

⊟ 3

Centraal
Station

35
⊡

De Ruijterkade

Het IJ

Java Eiland

KNSM Eiland

Zuiderzeeweg

Zeeburg

③

...eng

Damrak

17

⊞

See Eastern Islands
& Plantage Map (p95)

CENTRUM

Rokin

Nieuwmarkt ⓜ

Naval
Dockyards

⊞ 38

Kattenburg

EASTERN
ISLANDS

Oostenburg

⊞ 29

Rietlanden

Sporenburg

Kees Brijdeplantsoen

ZEEBURG

Borneo Eiland

Panamalaan

Zeeburgerdijk

Zuiderzeeweg

Ringweg Oost

See Southern Canal Belt
& De Pijp Map (pp92–3)

PLANTAGE

⊞ 15

ⓜ Waterlooplein

Artis Zoo

⊞
9

6

DAPPERBUURT

Insulindeweg

OUD ZUID

...delpark

⊞ 19

⊞ 28

ⓜ Weesperplein

⊡ 21

OOST

⊞ 25

Oosterpark

ⓜ Muiderpoort

Flevopark

④

Sarphatipark

23
⊡

32
⊡

39
⊡

OOSTERPARKBUURT

Wibautstraat

TRANSVAALBUURT

Amstel

Wibautstraat

Frankendaelpark

Hugo de Vrieslaan

Galileïplantsoen

DE PIJP

NIEUW ZUID

...tionweg

27
⊡

⊡ 30

Vrijheidslaan

ⓜ Amstel

Jaap
Edenhal

13

WATERGRAAFSMEER

Middenweg

Ouderingdijk

Sportpark
Voorland

Diemen ⊟

⑤

Beatrixpark

4

President Kennedylaan

7

ⓜ

RAI

Europaboulevard

Zorgvlied
Cemetery

Amstelpark

OVER
AMSTEL

ⓜ Spaklerweg

Spaklerweg

J Muyskenweg

Nieuwe Utrechtseweg

Ringweg Zuid

Sportpark
Drie Burg

Hartveldseweg

DIEMEN

Eikslotdreef

Diemen-Zuid ⓜ

Verrijn
Stuartweg

Bergwijkdreef

⑥

Amstel

Overamstel

J Muyskenweg

Van der Madeweg

ⓜ Van der Madeweg

DUIVENDRECHT

Venserpolder

Daalwijkdreef

To Gaasper
Camping

ⓜ Duivendrecht

Volkstuinenpark
Dijkzicht
To Amsterdam ArenA Stadium (3km);
Borchland Sportcentrum (3km);
Heineken Music Hall (3km);
Pepsi Stage (3km)

Amsterdamse
Golfclub

ⓜ Strandvliet/Arena

BIJLMERMEER

Bijlmerdreef

See Jordaan & Western
Islands Map (p91)

0
0

300 m
0.2 miles

See Eastern Islands & Plantage Map (p95)

NIEUWMARKT

CENTRUM

See Southern Canal Belt & De Pijp Map (pp92–3)

INFORMATION
COC Amsterdam....................................1 C5
Pink Point..2 D4
Vrouwen in Druk..................................3 D4
Wasserette Rozengracht Laundry.........4 C5

SIGHTS & ACTIVITIES (pp100–1)
Anne Frank Huis...................................5 D4
Felix Meritis Building.............................6 D6
Homomonument....................................7 D4
Houseboat Museum...............................8 C6
Pianola Museum....................................9 D2
Stedelijk Museum Bureau Amsterdam..10 D4
Westerkerk..11 D4

SLEEPING (pp119–20)
Budget Hotel Clemens.........................12 D5
Dylan..13 D6
Hotel Pulitzer.....................................14 D5
Hotel Van Onna..................................15 C4

EATING (p123)
Café Reibach......................................16 D1
Christophe..17 D4
De Bolhoed...18 D3
Koh-I-Noor...19 D4
Local...20 C2
Nielsen...21 D6
Nomads..22 B5
Rakang Thai..23 C6

DRINKING (p128)
Café Nol...24 D3
Café 't Smalle....................................25 D3
De Twee Zwaantjes............................26 D3
Van Puffelen......................................27 D5

ENTERTAINMENT
Felix Meritis..................................(see 6)
Korsakoff...28 B6
La Tertulia...29 C6
Maloe Melo..30 B6
Saarein..31 C6

SHOPPING
Analik...32 D5
Galleria d'Arte Rinascimento..............33 C4
Razzmatazz.......................................34 D6
Vrouwen in Druk...........................(see 3)
Westermarkt......................................35 D4

TRANSPORT
Bike City..36 C4

See Southern Canal Belt & De Pijp Map (pp92–3)

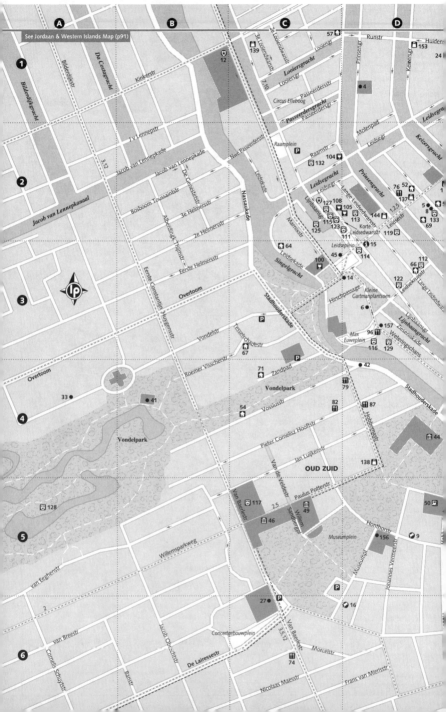

See Jordaan & Western Islands Map (p91)

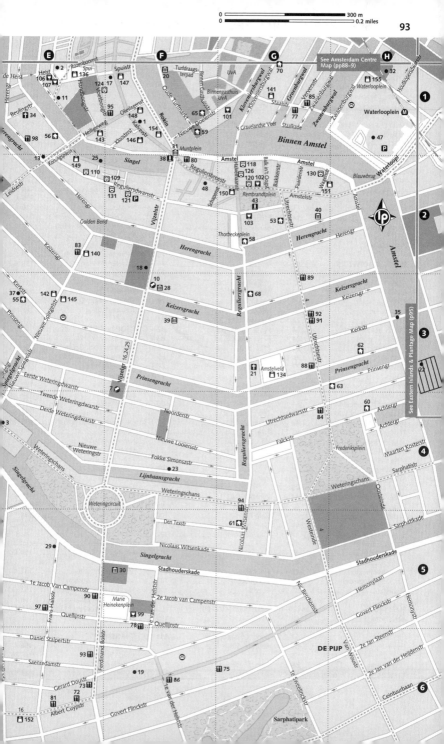

0 — 300 m
0 — 0.2 miles

E F G H

See Amsterdam Centre
Map (pp88–9)

de Heist
Rozenboomst
Spui
Turfdraags-
terpad
UvA
2
106
107
136
124 17
147
Spuistr
20
Binnengasthuis
UvA
70
32
155
Waterlooplein
11
Handboogstr
Voetboogstr
95
Oudezijdse
148
1
141
Staalstr
85
Zwanenburgwal
Waterlooplein M
34
98
56
Heiligeweg
143
Klooststr
Kalverstr
154
146
Roskin
Nieuwe Doelenstr
65
59
101
77
47
P
13
Koningsplein
149
25
Singel
31
Muntplein
38
80
Amstel
Binnen Amstel
110
109
Reguliersbreestr
118
126
120 102
Amstel
130
151
Blauwbrug
Waterloop
131
121
P
Reguliersdwarsstr
48
150
Rembrandtplein
43
103
53
40
58
Amstelstr
Thorbeckeplein
Herengracht
Herengr
83
140
Herengracht
18
10
28
89
Keizersgracht
Keizersgr
37
55
142
145
Keizersgracht
68
Kerkstr
39
92
91
Amstel
35
16,24,25
Prinsengracht
62
21
Amstelveld
134
88
Prinsengracht
Prinsengr
63
Eerste Weteringdwarsstr
Tweede Weteringdwarsstr
Noorderstr
Utrechtsedwarsstr
84
60
Derde Weteringdwarsstr
3
Nieuwe
Weteringstr
Nieuwe Looiersstr
Falckstr
Frederiksplein
Maarten Kosterstr
Weteringschans
Sarphatistr
Lijnbaansgracht
Fokke Simonszstr
23
Weteringschans
Westeinde
Oosteinde
Sarphatikade
Weteringcircuit
Weteringschans
94
Singelgracht
Den Textstr
61
Nicolaas Witsenkade
Sarphatistr
29
30
Stadhouderskade
Stadhouderskade
Stadhouderskade
1e Jacob Van Campenstr
90
Marie
Heinekenplein
Hemonylaan
97
Quellijnstr
99
2e Jacob van Campenstr
Govert Flinckstr
Hemonystr
78
2e Quellijnstr
Daniël Stalpertstr
93
DE PIJP
2e Jan Steenstr
Saenredamstr
19
75
2e Jan van der Heijdenstr
Gerard Doustr
73
86
81
72
Ceintuurbaan
16
152
Albert Cuypstr
Govert Flinckstr
Sarphatipark

1
2
3
4
5
6

See Eastern Islands & Plantage Map (p95)

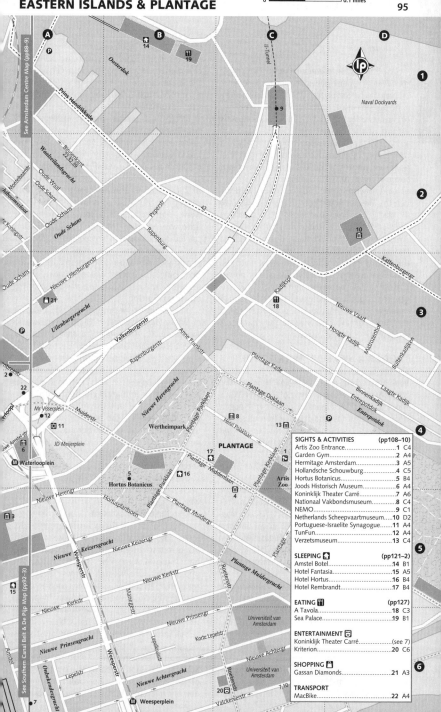

SIGHTS & ACTIVITIES	(pp108–10)
Artis Zoo Entrance	1 C4
Garden Gym	2 A4
Hermitage Amsterdam	3 A5
Hollandsche Schouwburg	4 C5
Hortus Botanicus	5 B4
Joods Historisch Museum	6 A4
Koninklijk Theater Carré	7 A6
Nationaal Vakbondsmuseum	8 C4
NEMO	9 C1
Netherlands Scheepvaartmuseum	10 D2
Portuguese-Israelite Synagogue	11 A4
TunFun	12 A4
Verzetsmuseum	13 C4

SLEEPING 🏠	(pp121–2)
Amstel Botel	14 B1
Hotel Fantasia	15 A5
Hotel Hortus	16 B4
Hotel Rembrandt	17 B4

EATING 🍴	(pp127)
A Tavola	18 C3
Sea Palace	19 B1

ENTERTAINMENT 🎭	
Koninklijk Theater Carré	(see 7)
Kriterion	20 C6

SHOPPING 🛍	
Gassan Diamonds	21 A3

TRANSPORT	
MacBike	22 A4

(Continued from page 85)

The **Prostitution Information Centre** (Map pp88-9; ☎ 420 73 28; www.pic-amsterdam.com; Enge Kerksteeg 3; ☺ noon-7pm Tue-Sat or by appointment), established by a former prostitute and staffed by sex workers, organises evening Red Light walks and sells a map of the district along with 'naughty' souvenirs. For a donation, you can browse a re-creation of a prostitute's working quarters, historical photos of the Red Light District and some enlightening reading material.

And now for something completely different: the **Museum Amstelkring** (Map pp88-9; ☎ 624 66 04; Oudezijds Voorburgwal 40; adult/child €7/1; ☺ 10am-5pm Mon-Sat, 1-5pm Sun), the Red Light District's – and Amsterdam's – holiest place. The highlight is the 'secret' church, Ons' Lieve Heer op Solder (Our Dear Lord in the Attic), a Catholic chapel set up after the Calvinists seized power that remained in use through the 1880s. Curious horizontal steel poles at balcony level provide extra support, unwittingly emphasising the claustrophobic air – as do the chaplain's amazingly cramped quarters.

THE DAM & NEW SIDE (NIEUWE ZIJDE)
On the Singel, tied up at No 40, is the **Poezenboot** (Cat Boat; Map pp88-9; ☎ 625 87 94; www.poezenboot.nl; Singel 40; ☺ 1-3pm), one of Amsterdam's more unusual 'flea markets'. This barge began life as a shelter for hundreds of homeless cats in the 1960s. It's now a registered charity – pat and pet the current feline inhabitants for a small donation.

Further along the Singel is **Torensluis** (Map pp88-9), one of the widest bridges in the city. The big moustachioed bust is of **Multatuli**, the pen name of the brilliant 19th-century author Eduard Douwes Dekker, who exposed colonial narrow-mindedness in a novel about a coffee merchant. The nearby **Multatuli Museum** (Map pp88-9; ☎ 638 19 38; Korsjespoortsteeg 20; admission free; ☺ 10am-5pm Tue, noon-5pm Sat & Sun, closed Sat Jul & Aug) tells the story.

To the east is the **Dam**, the very spot where a barrier giving the city its name was built across the Amstel river. Today it's besieged by thousands of pigeons, tourists and the occasional fun fair.

Facing the Dam, the **Koninklijk Paleis** (Royal Palace; Map pp88-9; ☎ 620 40 60; www.koninklijkhuis.nl; Dam) is the official residence of Queen Beatrix, although she actually lives in Den Haag. Built as a grand city hall in 1665, it later became the palace of Napoleon's fairly incompetent brother, Louis. The interior (particularly the chandeliered Civic Hall) is more lavish than the sober façade suggests, but unfortunately it's closed until 2008. Ring or check the website for updates.

Behind the palace stands the **Nieuwe Kerk** (New Church; Map pp88-9; ☎ 638 69 09; www.nieuwekerk .nl; Dam; adult/6-15yr/under 6yr €5/4/free; ☺ 10am-6pm Fri-Wed, to 10pm Thu), which is the coronation church of Dutch royalty. Crown Prince Willem Alexander and Máxima also took their vows here in 2002. This Gothic basilica from the 15th century is only 'new' in relation to the Oude Kerk. A few monumental items dominate the otherwise spartan interior – a magnificent carved oak chancel, a bronze choir screen, a massive organ and enormous stained-glass windows. Exhibitions and organ concerts are held, but church services are no more. Opening times and admission fees vary, depending on the exhibition.

The magnificent orange-and-white façade of **Magna Plaza** (Map pp88-9; ☎ 626 91 99; Nieuwezijds Voorburgwal 182; ☺ 11am-7pm Mon, 10am-7pm Tue, Wed, Fri & Sat, 10am-9pm Thu, noon-7pm Sun) was built in the late 19th century as the main post office. The complex has since been converted into a multilevel shopping centre, with columned galleries and dozens of upmarket clothing shops.

North of the Dam, the oldest dyke in the city, **Nieuwendijk** (Map pp88-9) used to link up with the road to Haarlem, and its businesses 'served' (read: 'fleeced') travellers on their way to market. Today this pedestrianised shopping street is a mix of souvenir shops, coffeeshops and cheap hostels, although some of the narrow medieval streets leading to the west are pretty.

The **Nationaal Monument** (Map pp88-9) on the eastern side of the Dam commemorates those who died during WWII; the fallen are honoured in a Remembrance Day ceremony here every 4 May. The statues around the phallic white obelisk stand for war, peace and resistance. In the 1960s hippies used to camp out here before being shooed away by police.

South of the Dam is **Kalverstraat**, the shopping mecca where consumers lather themselves into a fever pitch over the latest sales. Beware of pickpockets.

Parallel to Kalversstraat, Damrak becomes **Rokin** and begins to show the business side of Amsterdam with office buildings and art dealers. At Grimburgwal stands a **statue of**

WINDOW SHOPPING

You're not fooling anyone – you know you'll end up here. Everyone does at some stage, even if they think they're too hip, too moral, too conscientious, too prudish, too impotent, too old...the curiosity value is just too strong. But it's not just rubberneckers and pleasure seekers who flock to the Red Light District: Amsterdam's approach to prostitution has generated reams of socio-economic analysis, along with a raft of facts and figures – and some contradictions.

Prostitution was legalised in the Netherlands in 1815 (although brothels were only legalised in 2000). Unsurprisingly, less than 5% of Dutch prostitutes work illegally in the Netherlands. Dutch 'working girls' pay taxes and have their own union. Pimping is technically against the law, but the women are not on their own: their quarters are fitted with panic buttons in case of trouble. Should the button be pressed, it won't be the cops who come running.

An estimated 5% of Amsterdam prostitutes are born in the Netherlands, and around 1000 to 1200 work approximately 380 windows daily, in day, evening and night shifts. The women must rent their window at a cost of between €40 and €100 per day, depending on location. Do the maths: the typical base cost for 'oral favours' or a 'quickie' is €30; the average base cost for both is €50. Encounters typically last 15 minutes.

Dutch customers are most likely to visit on a Monday morning – that's when many businesses and most shops are closed. Of the international clientele, almost half are British – we don't dare speculate why.

A few years back, three chaps installed themselves behind windows as prostitutes, a sociological experiment – and maybe a little bit of performance art – that generated frothing mass debate in the media. In the end, the guys were warned not to give up their day job: no women took the bait (we're not sure if any blokes did). Rubbing salt into the wound, one female prostitute dismissed the whole incident as 'filthy'.

Now that's harsh.

Queen Wilhelmina (Map pp88–9) on horseback, a reminder of the monarch's trots through Amsterdam during official processions.

Rokin ends at Muntplein, a busy intersection dominated by the **Munttoren** (Mint Tower; Map pp92–3). When the French occupied the country in the 19th century the national mint was transferred here from Dordrecht for safekeeping. The French got the mint later anyway when they took Amsterdam.

Here you'll find out why, for many Dutch, football isn't a matter of life or death: it's more important than that. The **Het Oranje Voetbal Museum** (Orange Football Museum; Map pp92-3; ☎ 589 89 89; www.supportersclub-oranje.nl; Kalverstraat 236; ☑ 11am-5pm Sat & Sun) tells the story of orange maestros including Cruyff, Van Basten and Gullit, and the revolution that was Total Football. Hup, Holland, hup!

To the west of the Damrak-Rokin axis is the 'New Side' of the medieval city. It was actually settled earlier than the Oude Zijde – the names date from the construction of the Nieuwe Kerk and the division of the city into two parishes. Amsterdam's first houses were built in this neighbourhood. Some of the first residents were Jewish refugees from Germany and Austria, including writers and artists who settled around Beethovenstraat.

AROUND THE SPUI

The square called Spui (Map pp92–3) was water until 1882. The name means 'sluice' and is pronounced 'spow' (not 'spew' – that's reserved for the effects of Amsterdam hash). The statuette of an Amsterdam street brat, *Het Lieverdje* (Little Darling), was the favoured setting for Provo protests in the 1960s.

The Spui is now a popular meeting spot, with its pubs and bookshops nearby. It holds a book market on Friday, followed by an art market on Sunday.

The extensive **Amsterdams Historisch Museum** (Map pp88-9; ☎ 523 18 22; www.ahm.nl; Kalverstraat 92; adult/child €6/3; ☑ 10am-5pm Mon-Fri, 11am-5pm Sat & Sun) is housed in the former civic orphanage (which was here till 1960). Begin with the large-screen TV depicting an aerial view of Amsterdam's evolution from the tiny settlement on the mouth of the Amstel. Exhibits include models of old homes, religious objects, silver, porcelain, a detailed history of Dutch trading, the popularity of bicycles, WWII, gay rights, civic projects and the city's drug policies.

From the orphanage's courtyard (note the cupboards where the orphans used to store their possessions), walk through to the **Civic Guard Gallery** (Map pp88-9; ☎ 523 18 22; Kalverstraat 92; admission free; ☒ 10am-5pm Mon-Fri, 11am-5pm Sat & Sun), where the static group portraits of medieval guards are in stark contrast to the more dynamic treatment in Rembrandt's *Nightwatch*, the most famous of the group-portrait subgenre of Dutch painting. Combined with the Rijksmuseum's, this is the world's largest collection of its type, and, given the renovations on the former over the next few years, the Civic Guard Gallery should be the best place to view a large number at once.

Hidden behind the walls north of the Spui is the **Begijnhof** (Map pp88-9; ☎ 622 19 18; www .begijnhofamsterdam.nl; admission free; ☒ 8am-5pm), a former convent from the early 14th century. Rows of tiny houses and postage-stamp gardens overlook a well-kept courtyard. The house at No 34 dates from around 1465, giving it claim to being the oldest maintained wooden house in the country. The Beguines who give the Begijnhof its name were a Catholic order of unmarried or widowed women who cared for the elderly. After the Calvinists seized their Gothic church, the Beguines worshipped in the **clandestine church** (Map pp88-9) opposite. The paintings and stained-glass windows here commemorate the Miracle of Amsterdam, and De Stijl artist Piet Mondrian designed some of the pulpit panels. The Gothic church today serves as a **Presbyterian church** (Map pp88-9) and is booked months in advance for weddings.

NIEUWMARKT

Nieuwmarkt (New Market) quarter used to be the heart of Jewish Amsterdam, an industrious community that traded in diamonds, tobacco and clothes. In the 1970s the area was embroiled in a squatters' dispute; hairy activists and long-time residents united in waves of protest against the construction of modern housing estates and a new metro line. The city prevailed and much of the area was razed and rebuilt, with dubious results.

Golden Age ships loaded and unloaded produce at the **Nieuwmarkt** (Map pp88-9) square. The imposing **Waag** (Weigh-house) originally formed part of the city's fortifications but served a variety of functions later, including a spot for public executions. Today it's a café-restaurant with beautifully restored

---

IN A TIGHT SPOT

Amsterdam is chock-full of slender homes because property used to be taxed on frontage – the narrower your façade, the less you paid.

Witness the narrow house at Oude Hoogstraat 22 (Map pp88-9), east of the Dam. It's 2.02m wide, 6m deep and several storeys tall, occupying a mere 12 sq metres per storey. This could well be the tiniest (self-contained) house in Europe.

The Kleine Trippenhuis (Map pp88-9) at Kloveniersburgwal 26 is 2.44m wide. It stands opposite the mansion once owned by the wealthy Trip brothers and, so the story goes, their coachman exclaimed: 'If only I could have a house as wide as my masters' door!'

---

interiors that have a distinctly medieval feel – candles on round chandeliers provide the only source of light.

The **Guan Yin Shrine** (Fo Guang Shan He Hua Temple; Map pp88-9; ☎ 420 23 57; www.ibps.nl; Zeedijk 106-118; admission free; ☒ noon-5pm Tue-Sat, 10am-5pm Sun) is Europe's first Chinese Imperial–style Buddhist temple (completed in 2000). It is dedicated to Guan Yin, the Buddhist goddess of mercy. Some images on the many-armed, long-eared statue include a prayer bell and a lotus flower.

Zeedijk (Map pp88-9) was once the first stop for wine, women and song (in the 1950s the world's best jazz musicians played in pubs such as the Casablanca), but now it's more harmless than the Red Light District to the southwest. Zeedijk's southern end is a little Chinatown with rows of cheap eateries, and the street turns to entertainment with a mixed bag of gay and straight bars further north. Stop briefly at the house at No 1, one of just two half-timbered façades in the city (the other is in the Begijnhof; see left).

East of the Zeedijk is the wide, forlorn and rather stinky Geldersekade. The small brick tower at the tip of this canal is the **Schreierstoren** (Map pp88-9), where English captain Henry Hudson set sail to find a northern passage to the East Indies (and ended up buying Manhattan instead).

South of Nieuwmarkt, the **Pintohuis** (Openbare Bibliotheek; Map pp88-9; ☎ 624 31 84; www.oba .nl; St Antoniesbreestraat 69; admission free; ☒ 2-8pm Mon

& Wed, 2-5pm Fri, 11am-4pm Sat) used to belong to a wealthy Sephardi, Isaac de Pinto, who had it remodelled with Italianate pilasters in the 1680s. Locals used to mutter how someone was 'as rich as Pinto'. It's now a library, so you can peek inside at the beautiful ceilings.

A passageway in the modern housing estate across St Antoniesbreestraat leads to the **Zuiderkerk** (Southern Church; Map pp88-9; ☎ 552 79 87; ☺ 9am-4pm Mon-Fri, noon-4pm Sat). Built in the early 1600s, this was the first custom-built Protestant church in Amsterdam (based on a Catholic design). At the end of WWII it served as a morgue. It now houses the city's planning centre for public housing, as well as Amsterdam's urban blueprints.

The heart of the **Jodenbuurt** (Jewish Quarter) lies in and around the wide Jodenbreestraat, a remnant of a controversial freeway that was never completed. At one time the squares and cramped alleys around here used to echo with the sounds of morning prayer on the Sabbath.

The wonderfully restored **Museum het Rembrandthuis** (Rembrandt House Museum; Map pp88-9; ☎ 520 04 00; www.rembrandthuis.nl; Jodenbreestraat 4-6; adult/child €7.50/1.50; ☺ 10am-5pm Mon-Sat, 11-5pm Sun) is where Rembrandt van Rijn ran the Netherlands' largest painting studio, only to lose the lot when profligacy set in, enemies swooped and bankruptcy came a-knocking. The museum has almost every etching he made (around 250) and holds daily etching demonstrations. Expect to see between 20 and 100 etchings on display at any one time, depending on the exhibit. Shows change a few times per year, often incorporating works by Rembrandt's peers, or contemporary paintings that somehow comment on Rembrandt's own pieces. The collection also includes several drawings and paintings by his pupils and his teacher, Pieter Lastman, and an etching by Albrecht Dürer. There's also an impressive collection of Rembrandt's possessions: seashells, weaponry, musical instruments, a Roman bust and military helmets from as far away as Japan.

Land from the Amstel was reclaimed in the 16th century, creating the island of Vlooienburg. *Vlooien* means 'to flow' or 'fleas', an apt label for the present-day wares hawked at **Waterlooplein** (Map pp92-3). Once lined with the homes of Jewish traders, the square today hosts a daily flea market.

The hulking **Stopera** (Map pp92-3; ☎ 551 81 17; Waterlooplein) complex – the city hall and the music theatre – opened in 1986 after nearly two decades of controversy. One critic remarked that the building 'has all the charm of an Ikea chair' and the theatre has been plagued by logistical problems: the acoustics aren't great, and the ballet practice room has low ceilings. Facing the Amstel is the **muziektheater** (☎ 625 54 55; www.hetmuziektheater.nl; Amstel 3; ☺ advance tickets 10am-6pm Mon-Sat, 11.30am-6pm Sun), while the city hall is closer to Waterlooplein. Opera, music and dance performances take place in the theatre; there are usually free lunchtime concerts on Tuesdays. Tickets for performances are available at the theatre, at tourist information offices and online.

On the eastern side of the Mr Visserplein traffic circle stands the majestic **Portuguese-Israelite Synagogue** (Map p95; ☎ 624 53 51; www.esnoga .com; Mr Visserplein 3; adult/child €6.50/5; ☺ 10am-4pm Sun-Fri Apr-Oct, 10am-4pm Sun-Thu, 10am-3pm Fri Nov-Mar). Built for the Sephardic community in the 17th century, the synagogue was Europe's largest at the time and was based on the Temple of Solomon. The large *chuppah* (Jewish wedding canopy) is made from jacaranda wood, and services are still held beneath large lit candelabra. The Ets Haim seminary contains one of the most important Jewish libraries in Europe.

Under the traffic circle, **TunFun** (Map p95; ☎ 689 43 00; Mr Visserplein 7; adult/under 12 free/€7.50; ☺ 10am-6pm) is a kids' playground built in an old underpass. It has slides, ball pools, trampolines, a mini-cinema, a soccer field and a snack bar – even a children's disco. An adult must accompany children.

South of the synagogue is the **Joods Historisch Museum** (Jewish Historical Museum; Map p95; ☎ 626 99 45; www.jhm.nl; Jonas Daniël Meijerplein 2-4; adult/child €6.50/3; ☺ 11am-5pm), a beautifully restored complex of four Ashkenazic synagogues linked by glass-covered walkways. These synagogues include the Grote Sjoel (Great Synagogue, 1671), the first public synagogue in Western Europe; the Obbene Sjoel (Upstairs Synagogue, 1686); the Dritt Sjoel (Third Synagogue, 1700 with a 19th-century façade); and the Neie Sjoel (New Synagogue, 1752), the largest in the complex.

The Grote Sjoel contains religious objects as well as displays showing the rise of Jewish enterprise and its role in the Dutch economy; displays tend to be on the academic side. The Neie Sjoel focuses on aspects of Jewish identity and the history of Jews in the Netherlands. A kosher café serves Jewish specialities.

AMSTERDAM

Jordaan & Western Islands

JORDAAN

Originally a stronghold of the working class, the Jordaan (Map p91) is now probably the most desirable area to live in Amsterdam. The district is a pastiche of modest old residences and a few modern carbuncles, all squashed together into a skewed grid of tiny lanes and peppered with bite-sized cafés and shops. Its intimacy is contagious, and nowadays the average Jordaan dweller is more likely to be a gallery owner than a blue-collar labourer.

The name Jordaan may be a corruption of the French *jardin* (garden), as many French Huguenots settled here in what used to be the market gardens. But some historians point to *joden*, the Dutch word for Jews, or even a biblical connection to the river Jordan.

Jordaan dwellers have a rebellious streak. Dozens died in the Eel Riot of 1886 (see p79) and 1934 saw unrest over a cut in unemployment benefits.

Many of the Jordaan's narrow canals have been filled in, though the old labels remain: **Lindengracht**, **Rozengracht** and **Palmgracht**. Pretty **Bloemgracht** was spared a similar fate, thanks to lobbying by artisans who owned smart canalside homes.

The Jordaan also has many *hofjes* – private courtyards surrounded by old almshouses. Some have beautiful restored houses and stunning gardens; if the entrance is unlocked, you can usually take a discreet peek.

The **Noorderkerk** (Map pp88–9; ☎ 626 64 36; Noordermarkt 48; admission free; 10.30am-3pm Mon, Wed & Thu, 11am-1pm Sat, 10am-noon & 7-8.30pm Sun) was a Calvinist church for the Jordaan's 'common' people. It's shaped like a Greek cross – four arms of equal length – around a central pulpit. A sculpture near the entrance commemorates the bloody Jordaan riots of July 1934, when five people died in protests over government austerity measures.

The **Noordermarkt** (Map pp88–9) on the edge of the Jordaan hosts a flea market on Monday morning and a *boerenmarkt* (farmers' market) on Saturday morning.

At the **Pianola Museum** (Map p91; ☎ 627 96 24; www.pianola.nl; Westerstraat 106; adult/child €5/3; 2-5pm Sun) you can hear concerts of player pianos from the early 1900s, with rare classical or jazz tunes composed especially for the instrument. The curator gives demonstrations with great zest.

Blink and you might walk right past the unobtrusive **Stedelijk Museum Bureau Amsterdam** (Map p91; ☎ 422 04 71; www.smba.nl; Rozenstraat 59; admission free; 11am-5pm Tue-Sun), a 'project space' of the Stedelijk Museum (p109). Once a clothing workshop, it now holds exhibits that mix contemporary artists who have Amsterdam connections with some 'international context'. The programme is creative and innovative, ranging from painting and sculpture to new media and installation pieces. A recent show displayed visual art inspired by Amsterdam musical duo Arling and Cameron.

WESTERN ISLANDS

The Western Islands were raised from the riverbed to accommodate warehouses for Dutch colonial goods. **Prinseneiland** and **Realeneiland** are the prettiest of this tiny archipelago. A narrow bridge linking the two, the **Drieharingenbrug**, replaced a pontoon bridge that used to be pulled aside to let ships through.

The landmark **Westindisch Huis** (Map pp88–9) on Herenmarkt is the former head office of the West India Company. When Admiral Piet Heyn captured the Spanish silver fleet off Cuba in 1628, the booty was stored here.

The busy road to Haarlem led through the **Haarlemmerpoort** (Haarlem Gate; Map pp86–7) on Haarlemmerplein, where travellers heading into town had to leave their horses and carts. The gateway was built for King Willem II to pass through on the way to his coronation.

Over the past decade the **Haarlemmerbuurt** (Map pp86–7) has evolved into one of Amsterdam's quirkiest districts. New Age shops, wacky boutiques and ethnic gift emporiums line the main **Haarlemmerstraat** (Map pp88–9).

Several minutes' walk northwest of the Haarlemmerbuurt (cross under the railway tracks), the **Het Schip Housing Estate** (Map pp86–7; ☎ 418 28 85; www.hetschip.nl; Spaarndammerplantsoen 140; adult/senior/student €5/2.75/2; 1-5pm Thu-Sun), dating from 1920, is one of the signature buildings of the Amsterdam School of architecture (see p57). This triangular block, loosely resembling a ship, has been very well preserved and it welcomes visitors; Michel de Klerk designed it for a housing corporation of railway employees. There are several other Amsterdam School–designed housing blocks in this area. The complex has just expanded to show workers' apartments, one as it would have been in the workers' days, complete with period furniture.

Outside on the pavement is a small collection of typical Amsterdam School street fixtures (letterbox, fire alarm etc). On the other side of the post office entrance, walk into the attractive courtyard through the arch – the fairy-tale garden house with its sculpted roof was intended as a meeting room.

Along busy Haarlemmerweg, **Westergasfabriek** (Map pp86-7; ☎ 586 07 10; www.westergasfabriek.nl; Haarlemmerweg 8-10), a late-19th-century Dutch Renaissance complex, was the city gasworks until it was all but abandoned in the 1960s, its soil contaminated. Now the soil has been replaced with lawns, a long pool suitable for wading (bring the kids), sports facilities and even child care. As you move west away from town, reedy wilderness, with marshes and shallow waterfalls, begins to take over. The site is surrounded by the long and varied Westerpark; bike on in and stay a while. Inside the main buildings are cinemas, cafés, restaurants, nightclubs and office space.

Canal Belt

WESTERN CANAL BELT

The canals bordered by the Brouwersgracht and Leidsegracht (to the north and south respectively), the Singel to the east and the Prinsengracht to the west are filled with elegant homes, refined museums and cafés, restaurants and speciality shops.

The area was formed in 1613 when the authorities embarked on an ambitious project to expand Amsterdam's area with semicircular and radial canals on the western and southern sides, with bridges and connecting roads. Parcels of land were sold along the way to finance the project, buildings arose gradually, and the western canal belt was completed by 1625.

With its humpback bridges, shiny shutters and tree-lined towpaths, the **Brouwersgracht** is exceedingly picturesque. The dozens of breweries and warehouses that used to operate here have been converted to apartments; houseboats lining the quays add to the lazy residential character.

The **Herengracht** (Gentlemen's Canal) was named after the '17 Gentlemen' of the United East India Company. The first section south from Brouwersgracht shows that these bigwigs sunk some of their profits into show-piece residences.

The **Theater Instituut Nederland** (Map pp88-9; ☎ 551 33 00; www.tin.nl; Herengracht 168; adult/child €4.50/2.25; ☯ 11am-5pm Mon-Fri, 1-5pm Sat & Sun) fea-

tures exhibits that cover the history of Dutch theatre through dioramas, costume displays, sepia-toned 19th-century photos, and film of modern-day productions. Major exhibits change annually, covering such topics as Rembrandt and WWII theatre. The sumptuous interior was completely restyled in the 1730s with intricate plasterwork, extensive wall and ceiling paintings, and a grand spiral staircase. The façade dates back to 1620, and in summer the garden out the back is perfect.

The institute spills over into the **Bartolottihuis** (Map pp88–9) at No 172, one of the most captivating façades in the city – a red brick Renaissance job that follows the bend of the canal. It was built in 1615 for a brewer.

Just beyond, Herengracht is crossed by Raadhuisstraat, which links the Jordaan with the Dam. Note the **shopping arcade** on the far side (west): designed for an insurance company, the façade bears sculptures of vicious animals to stress the dangers of life without insurance.

The **Bijbels Museum** (Biblical Museum; Map pp92-3; ☎ 624 24 36; www.bijbelsmuseum.nl; Herengracht 366-368; adult/child €6/3; ☯ 10am-5pm Mon-Sat, 1-5pm Sun) has a large number of model temples, freshly restored 18th-century ceiling frescos by Jacob de Wit, and several centuries of the good book, including the Delft bible, printed in 1477. There's even a 'scent cabinet', where visitors can smell odours mentioned in the bible. The pretty back garden focuses on a wistful sculpture called *Apocalypse*.

Keizersgracht (the 'Emperor's Canal') was named in honour of Maximilian I, ruler of Habsburg and later the Holy Roman Empire.

The pink granite triangles of the unique **Homomonument** (Map p91; cnr Keizersgracht & Raadhuisstraat), at Westermarkt, commemorate gays and lesbians who were persecuted by the Nazis; flowers are laid out on Liberation Day (4 May).

Further south along Keizersgracht stands the **Felix Meritis building** (Map p91; ☎ 623 13 11; www.felix.meritis.nl; Keizersgracht 324; ☯ box office 9am-7pm), built in 1787 by Jacob Otten Husly for the Felix Meritis organisation (Latin for 'Happy through Merit'), a society of wealthy residents who promoted the ideals of the Enlightenment through the study of science, arts and commerce. Composers such as Brahms, Grieg and Saint-Saëns performed in its oval concert hall, and today the Felix Meritis Foundation stages European performing-arts events.

Prinsengracht, named after Prince Willem van Oranje, is the least showy of the main

ANNE FRANK

The Anne Frank Huis is where the Jewish Frank family hid to escape deportation during WWII. As the German occupiers tightened the noose around the Amsterdam's Jewish inhabitants, Otto Frank – together with his wife, two daughters and several friends – moved into the rear annex in July 1942, and the entrance was concealed behind a revolving bookcase.

The Franks were betrayed to the Gestapo in August 1944 and deported; Anne died in Bergen-Belsen concentration camp in March 1945, just weeks before it was liberated. Her father Otto was the only one of their group to survive. After the war Anne's diary was found among the litter in the annex, and her father published it. The diary, which gives a moving account of wartime horrors seen through a young girl's eyes, has sold 25 million copies and has been translated into 60 languages.

Addressed to the fictitious Kitty, the diary, written in Dutch, traces the teenager's development through puberty and persecution, and displays all the signs of a gifted writer in the making.

canals. It's peppered with cafés and shops rather than stately offices and banks, and the houses are smaller and narrower. Houseboats line the quays.

Although few of its original furnishings remain, the **Anne Frank Huis** (Anne Frank House; Map p91; ☎ 556 71 05; www.annefrank.org; Prinsengracht 267; adult/child/under 10yr €7.50/3.50/free; ☺ 9am-9pm Apr-Aug, 9am-7pm Sep-Mar), where Anne wrote her famous diary, lures almost a million visitors annually. With its reconstruction of Anne's melancholy bedroom and her actual diary – sitting alone in its glass case, filled with sunnily optimistic writing tempered by quiet despair – it's a powerful experience. The focus of the museum is the *achterhuis* (rear house), also known as the secret annexe, a dark and airless space where the Franks and others observed complete silence during the daytimes, outgrew their clothes, pasted photos of Hollywood stars on the walls and read Dickens, before being mysteriously betrayed and sent to their deaths. The modern extension of the museum is for contemporary exhibitions. Queues can be brutally long, so consider going in the early morning or evening, when crowds are lightest.

The **Westerkerk** (☎ 624 77 66; Prinsengracht 281; church/tower free/€5; ☺ 11am-3pm Mon-Fri, Easter–mid-Sep, tower 10am-5pm Mon-Sat Apr-Sep) is the main gathering place for Amsterdam's Dutch Reformed Church community. Rembrandt, who died bankrupt in 1669 at nearby Rozengracht, is buried somewhere in the church – perhaps near the grave of his son Titus, where there's a commemorative plaque. A highlight is the bell tower, Amsterdam's highest church tower at 85m. It's topped by the imperial crown that Habsburg emperor Maximilian I bestowed to the city's coat of arms in 1489. The climb

during the 60-minute tour is steep (186 steps) and claustrophobic, but there are periodic landings where you can rest while the guide describes the bells and other workings of the massive carillon. Of the 50 bells, the largest weighs some 7500kg. You can also see the chamber where the night watchmen slept between keeping a lookout for fires.

The **Houseboat Museum** (Map p91; ☎ 427 07 50; www.houseboatmuseum.nl; Prinsengracht; adult/child under 152cm €3/2.25; ☺ 11am-5pm Tue-Sun Mar-Oct, 11am-5pm Fri-Sun Nov-Feb, closed most of Jan) is south along the canal from Elandsgracht, at Johnny Jordaanplein, opposite No 296 Prinsengracht. The sailing barge (23m long by 4m wide) was built in 1914, and the collection itself is rather minimal, although you can view the iron hull up close, watch a slide show of pretty houseboats, and see sleeping, living, cooking and dining quarters with all mod cons. Fact: houseboat toilets, until this century, could drain directly into the canals, but they now must hook up to the city sewerage system.

SOUTHERN CANAL BELT

If the western canal belt is upscale and refined, the southern canal belt is more diverse and populist, though no less stately. The southern canal belt spans the area from the Leidsegracht in the west to the Amstel in the east, anchored by two key nightlife districts: Leidseplein and Rembrandtplein. In between are the elegant antique and art shops of the Spiegel quarter and the city's gay nightlife centre around Reguliersdwarsstraat.

This wealthy residential area was the soul of discretion, and you'll see that the 17th- and 18th-century façades are less ostentatious than those to the north. The corner of Herengracht and Leidsegracht is a particularly tranquil spot, despite its proximity to the heady action at Leidseplein.

On the southwestern side of Singel are the soaring turrets of the **Krijtberg** (Chalk Mountain; Map pp92–3; Singel 446; ☺ mass 12.30pm & 5.45pm Mon-Fri, 5.15pm Sat, 9am, 11am, 12.30pm & 5.15pm Sun). It's one of the city's most beautiful Gothic churches (built 1883), thanks largely to its colourful interior – a stark contrast to the rather spartan Calvinist churches. A house here belonged to a chalk merchant, hence the name.

Amsterdam has specialised in flower markets since the 17th century, so if they interest you, make your way to the southern side of the Singel between Koningsplein and Vijzelstraat for the **Bloemenmarkt** (Flower Market; Map pp92–3; ☺ 9am-5pm, closed Sun in winter). See p134 for more details.

South down Leidsestraat, at the corner of Keizersgracht, is department store **Metz & Co** (Map pp92–3; ☎ 520 70 36; Keizersgracht 455), built in 1891 for a life insurance company. The functionalist architect Gerrit Rietveld added the top-floor gallery, where you can have lunch with a panoramic view over the canals.

Further southwest along Leidsestraat is **Leidseplein**, one of the liveliest squares in the city. This was once the gateway for travellers heading south towards Leiden; the oil-lamps have given way to screaming neon signs, but street musicians and artists are still drawn to the cobblestone square. There's something for everyone here: cinemas, cafés, pubs and nightclubs, and a smorgasbord of restaurants.

Like so many public buildings, the **Stadsschouwburg** (City Theatre; Map pp92–3; ☎ 624 23 11; Leidseplein 26; ☺ advance ticket sales 10am-6pm Mon-Sat) had a difficult birth. Public criticism of the 1894 edifice stopped funding for the striking façade-cum-arcade, and the architect, Jan Springer, promptly retired. The theatre is used for large-scale plays, operettas and festivals such as Julidans (p117).

South across Marnixstraat, the **American Hotel** (Map pp92–3) is an Art Nouveau landmark from 1902. Have a coffee in its stylish **Café Américain** see (p128).

Leidsestraat's northern end intersects with the southern stretch of the **Herengracht**, where the buildings are noticeably larger than in the western section. By the mid-17th century many Amsterdam merchants had amassed huge fortunes, and they saw to it that restrictions on the size of canalside plots were relaxed.

The Herengracht between Leidsestraat and Vijzelstraat, known as the **Golden Bend** (Map pp92–3), had some of the largest private mansions in the city during the Golden Age. Most of them now belong to bankers, lawyers and financial advisers. French culture was all the rage among the city's wealthy class, so most styles are Gallic with a Dutch twist.

Nieuwe Spiegelstraat, lined with swish antique shops and art galleries, begins at the Herengracht. The extension of this street, the pretty **Spiegelgracht**, leads past more antiques and paintings to the Rijksmuseum.

The corner of Herengracht and Vijzelstraat is dominated by the colossal **ABN-AMRO bank building** (Map pp92–3). It was completed in 1923 as head office for the Netherlands Trading Society, a Dutch overseas bank. Its successor teamed up with a competitor to form ABN-AMRO, the largest bank in the country. This vast edifice continues all the way to Keizersgracht.

Near the bank building's southeast corner is **FOAM** (Fotografie Museum Amsterdam; Map pp92–3; ☎ 551 65 00; www.foam.nl; Keizersgracht 609; adult/child €6/free; ☺ 10am-5pm Sat-Wed, to 9pm Thu & Fri), an impressive museum devoted to photography. Two storeys of changing exhibition feature world-renowned photographers such as Sir Cecil Beaton, Annie Leibovitz and Henri Cartier-Bresson. Simple, functionalist and large galleries, some with skylights or grand windows for natural light, provide the setting for this impressive museum – accessible and inspiring, yet always critical.

Further along the other side of Keizersgracht is **Museum Van Loon** (Map pp92–3; ☎ 624 52 55; www.museumvanloon.nl; Keizersgracht 672; adult/child €5/4; ☺ 11am-5pm Jul & Aug, to 5pm Fri-Mon Sep-Jun), built in 1672 for a wealthy arms dealer. The house recalls canalside living in Amsterdam when money was no object for the wealthy. The rococo rose garden is especially fetching. There are some important paintings, including the *Wedding Portrait* by Jan Miense Molenaer and a collection of some 150 portraits of the Van Loon family.

Northeast of here, at the corner of Herengracht and **Reguliersgracht**, canal tour boats halt for photos at the beautiful 'canal of the seven bridges', cut in 1664. The arches are illuminated at night and reflect dreamily on the rippling water.

Across Herengracht towards the centre of town is **Thorbeckeplein**, with a statue of Jan

GAY & LESBIAN AMSTERDAM

Information

The **Gay & Lesbian Switchboard** (☎ 623 65 65; www.switchboard.nl) is a comprehensive info source, while **COC Amsterdam** (Map p91; ☎ 626 30 87; www.cocamsterdam.nl; Rozenstraat 8) is Amsterdam's gay and lesbian social centre, with a café and a nightclub.

Pick up the *Bent Guide*, published in English, stuffed with gayness, at the **Pink Point** (Map p91; ◷ noon-6pm Mar-Aug, limited hr Sep-Feb), an info kiosk near the Homomonument (p101).

The **Gay News Amsterdam** (www.gayamsterdam.nl) is a free paper and the *Gaymap Amsterdam* is a free map. Gay radio station MVS broadcasts 7pm to 8pm nightly on 106.8FM (cable 88.1FM), with a Sunday English programme.

Mantrav (Map pp88-9; ☎ 638 83 63; Kloveniersburgwal 40) specialises in gay resort and tour travel.

For gay books, try **Intermale** (Map pp88-9; ☎ 625 00 09; www.intermale.nl; Spuistraat 251), with 1½ floors of photo books, sexy mags, videos and porno postcards.

Vrolijk (Map pp88-9; ☎ 623 51 42; www.vrolijk.nu; Paleisstraat 135; ◷ 11am-6pm Mon, 10am-6pm Tue, Wed & Fri, 10am-7pm Thu, 10am-5pm Sat, 1-5pm Sun, closed Sun Oct-Dec) stocks major gay and lesbian magazines, as well as novels, guidebooks, postcards, art, poetry and DVDs.

Vrouwen In Druk (Map p91; Women in Print; ☎ 624 50 03; Westermarkt 5; ◷ Tue-Sat) specialises in secondhand women's titles.

Accommodation

Most hotels in town are lesbian and gay friendly, but some cater specifically to queer clientele:
Aero Hotel (Map pp92-3; ☎ 622 77 28; www.aerohotel.nl; Kerkstraat 45-49; d with/without bathroom from €85/70; 💻) Steps away from Amsterdam's gay action, with cosy rooms. Inevitably, a TV in the café streams *Ab Fab* 24/7.

Amistad (Map pp92-3; ☎ 624 80 74; www.amistad.nl; Kerkstraat 42; s/d from €69/85) Rooms feature designer flourishes such as Philippe Starck chairs, CD players and chic soft furnishings. Take breakfast in the kitchen-dining room with its communal tables and ruby-red walls.

Black Tulip Hotel (Map pp88-9; ☎ 427 09 33; www.blacktulip.nl; Geldersekade 16; s €115, d from €145; 💻) The nine rooms feature full bondage equipment: slings, cages, hooks, chairs, black leather, latex.

Liliane's Home (Map pp86-7; ☎ 627 40 06; l.meisen@zonnet.nl; Sarphatistraat 119; d from €80) Once Amsterdam's sole women-only inn, this place now admits male visitors. Rooms have huge windows (some have balconies too) and personality.

Orfeo Hotel (Map pp92-3; ☎ 623 13 47; www.hotelorfeo.com; Leidsekruisstraat 14; s with bathroom €50, d with/without bathroom €115/75; 💻) Simple wood-panelled rooms and the flirtiest breakfast room˙

Rudolf Thorbecke, the liberal politician who created the Dutch parliamentary system in 1848. A modern art market is held here on Sunday in spring and summer.

Beyond Thorbeckeplein is the raucous (or 'tacky', if you like) **Rembrandtplein**, focused around the statue of the *Nightwatch* artist (Map pp92–3). The grassy square is lined with pubs, grand cafés and restaurants, and is usually buzzing with good-time guys 'n' gals looking for high times and potent toxins.

A night out on Rembrandtplein is best preceded by a meander down **Utrechtsestraat**. It's relaxed, as shopping streets go, with the occasional tram going past cosy restaurants and unique stores.

East of Utrechtsestraat, along the Herengracht, is the **Museum Willet-Holthuysen** (Map pp92-3;

☎ 523 18 22; www.willetholthuysen.nl; Herengracht 605; adult/child €4/2; ◷ 10am-5pm Mon-Fri, 11am-5pm Sat & Sun), a beautiful house museum with a sumptuous interior that was bequeathed to the city a century ago. Highlights include paintings by Jacob de Wit, the *place de milieu* (centrepiece) that was part of the family's Meissen table service, and the intimate garden with sundial. The top-floor galleries hold special exhibitions.

The street running west from Rembrandtplein to Muntplein is **Reguliersbreestraat**, home to strange bedfellows: an art gallery, fast-food joints and a glorious Art Deco cinema, the **Tuschinskitheater** (Map pp92-3; ☎ 626 26 33; Reguliersbreestraat 26-28). Built in the roaring '20s and fully renovated in 2001, this cinema is a tribute to glorious design inside and out – the lobby alone is worth a visit.

Entertainment

Close to 100 gay bars, clubs, hotels and restaurants are dotted all over town. Many popular gay places are along Reguliersdwarsstraat (see Map pp92–3) – it's as camp as a row of tents. Kinky Amsterdam congregates over on Warmoesstraat in the Red Light District.

Some possibilities:

April (Map pp92-3; ☎ 625 95 72; Reguliersdwarsstraat 37) Famous for its happy hour, relaxed atmosphere and flirtatious pretty boys. There's a revolving bar out the back.

ARC (Map pp92-3; ☎ 689 70 70; www.bararc.com; Reguliersdwarsstraat 44) Classy, well-regarded restaurant-bar with minimalist interior and a fashionable crowd (predominantly gay, though also lesbian and straight).

Argos (Map pp88-9; ☎ 622 65 95; www.argosbar.com; Warmoesstraat 95) Amsterdam's oldest leather bar. Dress code for the regular 'SOS' (Sex On Sunday) party: nude or seminude.

Cockring (Map pp88-9; ☎ 623 96 04; www.clubcockring.com; Warmoesstraat 96) Techno and trance downstairs, cruising leather boys upstairs. Occasionally features live strip shows and 'shoes only' nude parties.

Gay Super Bingo (Map pp92-3; ☎ 776 46 00; Ferdinand Bolstraat 10; ☺ 8pm first Wed of month) Yes, bingo. With a theme: all-American rodeo.

Montmartre (Map pp92-3; ☎ 620 76 22; Halvemaansteeg 17) Beneath outrageous ceiling decorations, patrons sing loudly to Dutch ballads and top-40 songs. Like a gay Eurovision – minus the Finnish monster mash.

Saarein (Map p91; ☎ 623 49 01; Elandsstraat 119) Saarein was the focal point of the '70s Dutch feminist movement; today it's a favoured meeting place for lesbians. There's a small menu with tapas and soups. Bar staff can advise on Sapphic nightlife.

Soho (Map pp92-3; ☎ 616 13 12; Reguliersdwarsstraat 36) Kitsch, huge, two-storey bar throbbing with a young, friendly, pretty clientele.

Thermos Day Sauna (Map pp92-3; ☎ 623 91 58; www.thermos.nl; Raamstraat 33; admission €18; ☺ noon-11pm Mon-Fri, noon-10pm Sat, 11am-10pm Sun) Sprawling, popular place for sexual contact: porn movies, darkrooms, roof deck, hair salon, restaurant.

Thermos Night Sauna (Map pp92-3; ☎ 623 49 36; www.thermos.nl; Kerkstraat 58-60; admission €18; ☺ 11pm-8am Sun-Fri, to 10am Sat) Like the day sauna, except no restaurant, roof deck or hair salon.

Festivals

The biggest single party is the **Roze Wester** thrown at the Homomonument on Queen's Day on 30 April, with bands and street dancing. The **Gay Pride Canal Parade** (First Saturday in August; http://www.amsterdamgaypride.nl) is the only water-borne gay parade in the world, with lots of pride showing on the outlandish floats.

South of Rembrandtplein, almost to the intersection of Prinsengracht and Reguliersgracht, stands the wooden **Amstelkerk** (Map pp92-3; ☎ 520 00 70; Amstelveld 10; admission free; ☺ 9am-5pm). The city planners had envisaged four new Protestant churches in the southern canal belt, but the only one that materialised was the **Oosterkerk** (Map pp86–7). The Amstelkerk (built 1670) was meant to be a temporary house of worship, but when funds for a grander structure were lacking it became permanent.

Continue to the Amstel and you'll see the **Amstelsluizen** (Map pp92-3). These sluices allowed the canals to be flushed with fresh river water, and they were still operated by hand until a few years ago. Across the river stands the **Koninklijk Theater Carré** (p131), originally built as a circus but now the city's largest theatre.

To your left is the **Magere Brug** (Map pp92–3), the most photographed drawbridge in the city. Often mistranslated as the 'Skinny Bridge', it was actually named after the Mager sisters, who lived on opposite sides of the canal. As the sweet tale goes, the sisters had a footbridge built so that they could visit with ease.

Old South (Oud Zuid)

This genteel, wedge-shaped neighbourhood features many fine examples of the Amsterdam School of architecture, with porthole windows, mock prows and other maritime motifs gracing the façades of weighty apartment complexes. The area is subdivided into the Museum Quarter, the Concertgebouw area and Vondelpark, names that also appear on street signs.

AMSTERDAM

MUSEUM QUARTER

To paraphrase Arnold Schwarzenegger, 'Get your ass to Rijks'. With a collection valued in the billions, the **Rijksmuseum** (Map pp92-3; ☎ 674 70 00; www.rijksmuseum.nl; Stadhouderskade 42; adult/under 18yr €9/free; ☑ 10am-5pm) is the *ne plus ultra* of Dutch classical art, but until renovations finish in 2008 only 400 masterpieces will be on display.

Previously, there were some 5000 paintings and other artworks displayed in several hundred exhibition galleries. But the mega renovation project (cost: around €300 million) will hopefully create more accessible exhibition halls, as well as the underground gallery that PJ Cuypers, its talented 19th-century architect, laid down in his blueprints. If all goes well, the entire building will be returned to its original 1885 glory.

Never mind the building dust, the much-loved Dutch and Flemish paintings from the Golden Age will remain on display. The museum's crowning glory is here too: Rembrandt's mesmerising *Nightwatch* (1650), the artist's breathtaking group portrait of an Amsterdam civil militia led by Frans Banningh Cocq, a future mayor and apparently not the brightest of lights. The painting only acquired its name in later years after grime darkened the oils, long after Rembrandt painted the scene in a hotel near Muntplein. Warning: at any time, *Nightwatch* will likely be 20 deep with flashbulb-popping, focus-beam-directing rubberneckers.

Other household names still on display include Johannes Vermeer (*The Kitchen Maid* and *Woman in Blue Reading a Letter*), Frans Hals *(The Merry Drinker)* and Jan Steen *(The Merry Family)*. Other must-sees are in Sculpture & Applied Art (Delftware, beautiful doll houses, porcelain, furniture) and Asiatic Art (including the famous 12th-century *Dancing Shiva*), as well as highlights from the museum's store of 800,000 prints and drawings.

Rather than being returned to storage, many other gems will be put on display in grateful venues around the country. Check the schedules for Amsterdam's Nieuwe Kerk (p96), Maastricht's Bonnefantenmuseum (p278), and the Dordrechts Museum (p222). There's also an annexe at Schiphol Airport.

The exterior of the Rijksmuseum remains a feast for the eye, with tiled murals, faux-Gothic towers and glints of gold harking back to the fortunes of the Golden Age. It wasn't popular with everyone: as the finishing touches were being laid, King Willem III dubbed the Rijksmuseum 'the archbishop's palace' because of the Catholic influence on Cuypers' designs. The magnificent underpass with its dreamy acoustics will be closed for the face-lift, to the chagrin of local buskers.

Behind the Rijksmuseum, the sprawling square known as **Museumplein** hosted the World Exhibition of 1883. It has only recently been transformed into a huge park, with an underground Albert Heijn supermarket

---

LUST FOR VINCENT

The outstanding **Van Gogh Museum** (Map pp92-3; ☎ 570 52 00; www.vangoghmuseum.nl; Paulus Potterstraat 7; adult/child €10/2.50; ☑ 10am-6pm Sun-Thu, to 10pm Fri) houses the world's largest Van Gogh collection. Quite simply, it's one of the greatest Impressionist galleries on earth. The museum opened in 1973 to house the collection of Vincent's younger brother Theo, and it consists of about 200 paintings and 500 drawings by Vincent and his friends and contemporaries, including Gauguin, Toulouse-Lautrec, Monet and Bernard.

Trace Van Gogh's life from his tentative start through to his Japanese phase, and on to depression and the black cloud that descended over him and his work: his paintings are shown in chronological order on the 1st floor, from his moody Brabant canvases *(The Potato Eaters)* to the famous works from his French period (*The Yellow House in Arles*, *The Bedroom at Arles* and several self-portraits). Sunflowers and other blossoms display his knack for using Mediterranean light and colour. *Wheatfield with Crows* is an ominous work that he painted shortly before committing suicide.

Designed by Gerrit Rietveld, the exhibition spaces are generous enough to accommodate insane crowds without obscuring the paintings. The sleek rear annex hosts changing exhibitions and is an attraction in its own right, looking very much like an enormous clam (it's nicknamed 'the mussel'). The library opens on weekdays only.

under the slanting 'donkey's ear' near the Concertgebouw.

The neo-Renaissance gem that is the **Concertgebouw** (Concert Building; Map pp92-3; ☎ 671 83 45; www.concertgebouw.nl; Concertgebouwplein 2-6; ☺ box office 10am-7pm) attracts 840,000 visitors a year, making it the busiest concert hall in the world.

Under the 50-year guidance of composer and conductor Willem Mengelberg (1871–1951), the Koninklijk Concertgebouw Orkest (Royal Concert Building Orchestra) developed into one of the world's finest. Dozens of landmark performances have been recorded here; the lure of playing in the venue is so strong that local musicians accept pay that's lower than that in many other countries.

The Grote Zaal has near-perfect acoustics. The layout is surprisingly free of divisions, with a simple flat viewing area and a balcony around the perimeter. Weighty inscriptions show who the world's leading composers were in 1888, the year of its construction. Recitals take place in the Kleine Zaal, a replica of the hall in the Felix Meritis building (p101).

Free lunchtime concerts are held on Wednesday at noon.

VONDELPARK

With its ponds, lawns, thickets and winding footpaths, this **park** (Map pp92-3; www.vondelpark .nl) is indisputably in the English style. Laid out in the 1860s and 1870s for the bourgeoisie, it was named after poet and playwright Joost van den Vondel, whom the Dutch celebrate as their Shakespeare.

During the late 1960s and early 1970s the authorities turned the park into an open-air dormitory to alleviate the lack of accommodation for the hordes of hippies who descended on Amsterdam.

Today, the park is popular with joggers, in-line skaters, buskers, lovers, families, miniature Cruyffs – everyone. Free concerts are held in summer at the open-air theatre, and musicians are always performing throughout the park. There's a charming teahouse as well (see p129). A stand at the Vondeltuin Cafeteria, near the Amstelveenseweg entrance (Map, pp86-7), rents out in-line skates and gear.

The **Nederlands Filmmuseum** (Map pp92-3; ☎ 589 14 00; www.filmmuseum.nl; Vondelpark 3) isn't a museum per se but presides over a priceless archive of films screened in its two theatres, sometimes with live music. One theatre

contains the Art Deco interior of Cinema Parisien, an early Amsterdam cinema. The museum's charming Café Vertigo is a popular meeting place and an ideal spot to people-watch; on summer evenings films are shown on the outdoor terrace. Adjoining the museum is an impressive **information centre** (☎ 589 14 35; Vondelstraat 69-71; ☺ 10am-5pm Tue-Fri, 11am-5pm Sat), with books and videotapes that can be viewed in booths.

Built in 1882, the **Hollandse Manege** (Map pp92-3; ☎ 618 09 42; Vondelstraat 140) is an indoor riding school inspired by the famous Spanish Riding School in Vienna. Through the passage to the rear door and up the stairs is a café where you can sip a beer or coffee while watching the instructor put the horses through their paces. Opening times vary, so ring ahead.

The **Electrische Museumtramlijn Amsterdam** (Tram Museum Amsterdam; Map pp86-7; ☎ 673 75 38; www .museumtram.nl; Amstelveenseweg 264; adult/child return €3.50/1.80; ☺ 11am-5pm Sun mid-Apr–Oct, 1pm & 3pm Wed Jul & Aug) isn't really a museum but a starting point for historic trams that clang from here to the Amsterdamse Bos recreation area – a worthwhile 1¼-hour outing. The museum is just southwest of Vondelpark in the former Haarlemmermeer train station.

De Pijp

This district, lying south of the broad Stadhouderskade, probably got its name from its straight, narrow streets that are said to resemble the stems of old clay pipes. This was the city's first 19th-century slum, but it's now undergoing a determined gentrification. De Pijp is still often called the Quartier Latin, thanks to its lively mix of people: labourers, intellectuals, new immigrants, prostitutes, young urban professionals, gays, lesbians – the whole kit and caboodle, really.

The locals are best viewed at the **Albert Cuypmarkt** (Albert Cuypstraat; Map pp92-3; ☺ 9am-5pm Mon-Sat), Amsterdam's largest and busiest market, which celebrated its 100th birthday in 2005. Here you'll find food, clothes and other general goods of every description and origin, often cheaper than anywhere else, as well as quite a bit of plain junk. This is Amsterdam at its multicultural best. The crowds will be jam-packed, so be wary of pickpockets pressing up close.

The area's other draw is the **Heineken Experience** (Map pp92-3; ☎ 523 96 66; www.heinekenexperience .com; Stadhouderskade 78; admission €10; ☺ 10am-6pm

Tue-Sun), where you can peer inside the malt silos and at Heinie memorabilia. Admission includes three glasses of the brew, after which you might be tempted to follow in Freddie Heineken's footsteps. Freddie was reputed to be a bit of a 'pants man': stationing himself at bars, when he overheard attractive lasses uttering the incantation, 'I'd like a Heineken, please', he'd offer 'I'm right here'. But, then again, he's supposed to have also said that 'death is about becoming a worm cookie', so leave us out of it.

South of Albert Cuypstraat is the **Sarphatipark**, an English-style park named after shrewd 19th-century Jewish doctor, chemist and businessman Samuel Sarphati. With its ponds, fountains and abundant bird life, it's an eminently agreeable spot for a picnic lunch.

Plantage & Oosterpark
PLANTAGE
In the 19th century the Jewish elite began to move from the city's centre into the area called Plantage (Plantation), where they built imposing villas. Until then Plantage had been a district of parks and gardens.

The **Hortus Botanicus** (Botanical Garden; Map p95; ☎ 625 90 21; Plantage Middenlaan 2A; adult/child €6/3; ☼ 9am-5pm Mon-Fri, 10am-5pm Sat & Sun, to 9pm daily Jul & Aug, to 4pm daily Dec & Jan) was founded in 1638 as a herb garden for the city's doctors. It quickly became a repository for tropical seeds and plants brought by Dutch ships from the East and West Indies, and coffee, pineapple, cinnamon and oil palm were distributed from here throughout the world. Guided tours are given on Sunday at 2pm. The wonderful mixture of colonial and modern structures includes a restored octagonal seed house; a modern, three-climate glasshouse with subtropical, tropical and desert plants; and a monumental palm house. The 400-year-old cycad here is the world's oldest potted plant, while the Hortus Medicus is a medicinal herb garden that attracts students from around the globe. The Hortus' café, the Orangery, recently reopened after refurbishment and is deservedly popular, especially for its terrace. Jazz and world music evenings take place here on Friday evening in July and August. Note that a combination admission ticket (€9) is available for the Hortus and the Hermitage Amsterdam, about five minutes' walk away.

St Petersburg's Hermitage collection is so massive it has had to expand abroad, with permanent annexes in London and Las Vegas, and the latest, **Hermitage Amsterdam** (Map p95; ☎ 530 87 51; www.hermitage.nl; Nieuwe Herengracht 14; adult/child €6/free; ☼ 10am-5pm). There are six galleries housing exhibitions twice yearly, and they are as stately and as well curated as you would expect.

The **Nationaal Vakbondsmuseum** (National Trade Union Museum; Map p95; ☎ 624 11 66; Henri Polaklaan 9; adult/child €2.50/1.25; ☼ 11am-5pm Tue-Fri, 1-5pm Sun) used to house a powerful diamond workers' union. Visiting union members will be in their element, but most people come just to see the fanciful design, an Art Deco showcase designed by HP Berlage, who considered it his most successful work. It's a splendid spectacle, from the diamond-shaped pinnacle to the magnificent hall with its brick arches; the murals, ceramics and leadlight windows are by famous artists of the day. The soaring, atrium-style staircase is graced with a three-storey-tall chandelier.

Around the corner, the **Verzetsmuseum** (Resistance Museum; Map p95; ☎ 620 25 35; Plantage Kerklaan 61; adult/child €5/2.75; ☼ 10am-5pm Tue-Fri, noon-5pm Sat-Mon) describes the daily realities of the Dutch resistance during WWII. Fascinating tales of active and passive resistance are told through photos, documents and sound fragments. There's also a library in the Plancius building, built in 1876 as the social club for a Jewish choir.

The **Hollandsche Schouwburg** (Holland Theatre; Map p95; ☎ 626 99 45; www.hollandscheschouwburg.nl; Plantage Middenlaan 24; admission free; ☼ 11am-4pm) played a tragic role during WWII. After 1942 the theatre became a detention centre for Jews awaiting deportation. Little more than the façade is left standing today, and there are a memorial room and an exhibition room with videos and documents on the building's history.

The oldest zoo on the European continent, **Artis** (Map p95; ☎ 523 34 00; www.artis.nl; Plantage Kerklaan 38-40; adult/child €16/12.50; ☼ 9am-5pm, to 6pm summer) has an alphabet soup of wildlife: alligators, birds, chimps and so on up to zebras. The layout is full of delightful ponds, statues, and leafy, winding pathways. Themed habitats such as African savannah and tropical rainforest are pretty convincing. For many, the aquarium complex is the highlight, featuring coral reefs, shark tanks and an Amsterdam canal displayed from a fish's point of view. There are also a planetarium and a kiddie petting zoo.

OOSTERPARK

The Oosterpark district (Map pp86–7), named after the lush park at its core, was built in the 1880s for diamond-industry workers. Many of them were Jewish families who had the means to leave the cramped centre.

A visit to the anthropological **Tropenmuseum** (Tropics Museum; Map pp86-7; ☎ 568 82 15; www.tropen museum.nl; Linnaeusstraat 2; adult/child €7.50/3.75; ☼ 10am-5pm) is a pleasant and easy way to dip your toes into exotic cultures. You can stroll through an African market or a Mexican-style cantina, or listen to recordings of exotic musical instruments. The **children's section** (☎ 568 82 23) offers guides for six- to 12-year-olds if you book ahead. There's an extensive library, a shop selling books, gifts and CDs, and the Ekeko café, serving exotic snacks and meals. The Tropeninstituut Theater screens films and hosts music, dance and plays by visiting international artists. It's a grand place to spend a lazy Monday, when most other museums are closed.

Eastern Islands

East of Centraal Station and north of the medieval centre, Nieuwmarkt and the Plantage area, the islands of **Kattenburg**, **Wittenburg** and **Oostenburg** were constructed in the 1650s to handle the rapidly expanding seaborne trade.

Nowadays the area is all about modern housing, but some splendid façades of old gabled homes remain along Wittenburgergracht, while the ex-islands are seamlessly linked to central Amsterdam. Kattenburg used to be the seat of the Dutch admiralty, and its dockyards here once fitted men-of-war for the royal navy.

East of Artis zoo stands an 18th-century grain mill known as **De Gooyer** (Map pp86–7), the sole survivor of five windmills from this corner of the city. The former public baths alongside now house the **Brouwerij 't IJ** (Map pp86-7; ☎ 622 83 25; Funenkade 7; ☼ 3-7.45pm Wed-Sun), a small brewery producing potent but tasty beers under the distinctive ostrich label. Apart from De Bekeerde Suster (p128), off Nieuwmarkt, it's the only brewery in town. There's a tour on Friday at 4pm.

'Steampunks' will love **EnergeticA** (Map pp86-7; ☎ 422 12 27; Hoogte Kadijk 400; adult/under 12yr €3/free; ☼ 10am-4pm Mon-Fri), one of Amsterdam's more unusual – and appealing – museums. Housed in a former power station, it showcases centuries of technological advances. Galleries are named after groundbreaking scientists, including Marconi, and are filled with steamship engines, antique toasters, early washing machines, electric lights and even gas streetlamps, antique elevators and high-voltage generators.

Once the headquarters of the Dutch navy, the imposing pile on Amsterdam harbour is now home to the **Nederlands Scheepvaartmuseum** (Netherlands Shipping Museum; Map p95; ☎ 523 22 22; www.scheepvaartmuseum.nl; Kattenburgerplein 1; adult/child €9/4.50; ☼ 10am-5pm Tue-Sun mid-Sep–mid-Jun, 10am-5pm daily mid-Jun–mid-Sep). You won't find better displays on the topic, as the heyday of Dutch seafaring comes alive with scores of magnificent paintings: horizons crowded with three-masted merchant schooners, or naval ships engaged in fiery cannon battles. Model ships abound, but there are also a few full-sized vessels, such as the swanky sloop built for King Willem I in the early 1800s. The cinema shows a vivid re-enactment of a voyage to the East Indies.

The *pièce de résistance* is the replica of the *Amsterdam*, a beautiful historic squarerigger moored alongside the museum. The stern bears the three crosses of Amsterdam's emblem as well as the brightly painted statues of Mercurius (god of trade) and Neptune (god of the sea). Apparently the gods weren't watching over the *Amsterdam* on its maiden voyage in 1749: it became stranded off the English coast and was stripped of all valuables, including its iron nails. Climb on board, peruse the captain's quarters and watch actors recreate life at sea.

The **Stedelijk Museum** (Map pp86-7; ☎ 573 29 11; www.stedelijk.nl; 2nd & 3rd fl, Post CS Bldg, Oosterdokskade 5; adult/7-16yr & senior/under 7yr €9/5/free; ☼ 10am-6pm) features around 100,000 pieces including Impressionist works by Monet, Picasso and Chagall; sculptures by Rodin and Moore; De Stijl landmarks by Mondrian; and pop art by Warhol and Lichtenstein. The Post CS building is a temporary home – the original is undergoing renovation until 2008. The 2nd, 3rd and 11th floors at Post CS will be occupied by permanent and temporary exhibitions until 2007. In the meantime the Stedelijk's former home on Museumplein (next to the Van Gogh Museum; Map pp92–3) is undergoing a vigorous face-lift. The responsibility rests heavily on the guardians of Amsterdam's art heritage: 600,000 visitors per year are expected after a spanking new museum is unveiled. Like the

Rijksmuseum, the Stedelijk is presenting some of its works around the country throughout the renovation period.

The green, shiplike building on the eastern harbour is **NEMO** (Map p95; ☎ 09009191000; www .e-nemo.nl; Oosterdok 2; admission €11; ☺ 10am-5pm Tue-Sun, plus Mon Jul & Aug), an interactive science museum with hands-on displays aimed at children and school groups. There are loads of interactive exhibits: drawing with a laser, 'antigravity' trick mirrors, and a 'lab' where you can answer questions such as 'How black is black?' and 'How do you make cheese?'

Normally free, the rooftop plaza is transformed in summer into **Nemo Beach**, (admission €2.50, free with NEMO admission), in reality an elaborate sandbox occupying just a small section of the roof. Further up, DJs spin, and there's a bar, a convivial atmosphere and nice views.

Amstelveen

This quiet dormitory town is next to the **Amsterdamse Bos** (Amsterdam Woods; Map pp86-7; www .amsterdamsebos.nl; Bosbaanweg 5; admission free), the result of a 1930s job-creation scheme. A vast tract of lakes, woods and meadows, the *bos* draws many Amsterdammers looking for a leafy good time. Its only drawback is the background noise from nearby Schiphol Airport. The **visitors centre** (☎ 545 61 00; ☺ 8.30am-5pm) has leaflets on walking and cycling paths.

You'll also find an animal enclosure with bison, a goat farm, and a rowing course with watercraft for hire. The **Bosmuseum** (Forestry Museum; Map pp86-7; ☎ 676 21 52; Koenenkade 56; admission free; ☺ 10am-5pm) has displays about flora and fauna. There's bike hire at the main entrance at Van Nijenrodeweg. Take the historic tram from Haarlemmermeer station (p107) or bus 170, 171 or 172 from Centraal Station.

Nearby is the **CoBrA Museum** (Map pp86-7; ☎ 547 50 50; www.cobra-museum.nl; Sandbergplein 1; adult/senior & student/child 6-16yr/under 6yr €7/4/2.50/free; ☺ 11am-5pm Tue-Sun). Formed by artists from Copenhagen, Brussels and Amsterdam after WWII, the CoBrA movement (p41) vented the fury of abstract expressionism. The modern paintings, ceramics and statues on display here still polarise audiences today. With the temporary relocation of the Stedelijk Museum, this contemporary, two-storey building is your best bet to see the work of this fascinating group. The museum is opposite the Amstelveen bus terminal (bus 170, 171 or 172 from Centraal Station in Amsterdam).

The **Amsterdam RAI** (☎ 549 12 12; www.rai.nl; Europaplein 22), an exhibition and conference centre, is the largest complex of its kind in the country. From boats and caravans to fashion shows, few events are beyond its reach.

ACTIVITIES
Cycling

Pedal power rules in the Netherlands: that's a Dutch truism, simply a fact of life. Bicycles, known in Dutch as *fiets*, are everywhere, and especially in Amsterdam, where they outnumber cars. But visitors are often surprised at the nature of Dutch bikes: it's rare to find fancy mountain bikes in the city's dedicated bike lanes – virtually everyone rides sturdy, heavy two- or three-gear (often no gear) granny rattlers (Gazelle or Sparta brands). There's no need for the fancy stuff in a land that's as flat as a pancake. Also, a 21-speed racer will probably be stolen within an hour of being parked: 150,000 bikes are nicked in Amsterdam per year. See the boxed text, opposite, for more information and tips on hiring a bike.

Gyms

Barry's Health Centre (Map pp92-3; ☎ 626 10 36; www.barryshealthcentre.nl; Lijnbaansgracht 350; day/week pass €15/28; ☺ 7am-11pm Mon-Fri, 8am-8pm Sat & Sun) Latest machines and classes, sauna, steam, tanning beds and a 'cardio theatre'.

Fitness First (Map pp88-9; ☎ 530 03 40; www .fitnessfirst.nl; Nieuwezijds Kolk 15; day pass €16, month pass from €29; ☺ 7am-11pm Mon-Fri, 9am-6pm Sat & Sun) Cardio and weightlifting equipment, group classes, sauna, steam and aroma rooms, sun beds, beauty treatments and free video loans for members.

Garden Gym (Map p95; ☎ 626 87 72; www.the garden.nl; Jodenbreestraat 158; day pass €9-12.50, month pass €40-61; ☺ 9am-11pm Mon, Wed & Fri, noon-11pm Tue, noon-10pm Thu, 9am-4pm Sat, 9am-5pm Sun) Recently rated Amsterdam's best gym for women, with aerobics, sauna, massage, physiotherapy and dietary advice.

Saunas

Saunas are mixed affairs and most saunees like to sweat it out in the raw, so check your modesty at the front desk – or rent a towel. For information about gay saunas, see the boxed text, p104.

Hammam (Map pp86-7; ☎ 681 48 18; www .hammamamsterdam.nl; Zaanstraat 88; adult/2-5yr/6-12yr €15/4/11; ☺ noon-10pm Tue-Fri, to 8pm Sat & Sun, last entry 2½hr before closing) Attractive, women-only, Turkish-style place.

BICYCLES: THE MAN-MACHINE RULES

When researching this book, here are some of the sights we saw on Amsterdam streets:

- A man with one leg in plaster pedalling his bike with the other leg, with crutches strapped to his back.
- A man riding a bike with a blow-up sex doll strapped to his back.
- Four drunks riding one bike.
- A woman riding a bike while wearing stilettos and with her G-string showing.
- A girl riding side-saddle while kissing the boy piloting the bike.
- A customised bicycle modelled after Dennis Hopper's hog in *Easy Rider*.
- A man riding with one hand while holding a plate-glass window with the other, seemingly oblivious to the threat of severed arteries in the event of emergency braking.
- A man who must have been over 100 years old riding a bicycle at about 2km/h.
- A woman riding a bicycle weaving and wobbling all over the place, her vision almost totally obscured by a massive bunch of flowers.
- A group of kids playing football while riding bicycles.
- Numerous mothers riding three-wheelers with toddlers in a barrow attached to the front or in a box towed along behind.
- A bicycle barrelling down a side street with no-one on it.
- An abandoned bicycle that looked as though it had been twisted into a figure 8.
- A bicycle up a tree.
- Bicycles in canals.
- Dutch police riding the same crappy bicycles as everyone else.
- Almost everyone steering their bikes with one hand and talking on a mobile phone or eating a sandwich with the other, while perilously weaving in and out of trams, trucks and cars.

Tips

- When on foot, don't play the dumb tourist and stand in the city's dedicated bike lanes staring at the sights: you'll be knocked over by a speeding bike before you can say *'moederneuker'*, because here you give way to them.
- When riding, watch for cars. Cyclists have the right of way, except when vehicles are entering from the right, although not all motorists respect this. Also watch for dumb tourists (see above).
- Watch out for tram tracks – if your wheel gets get caught in one, you will break your bones.
- By law, after dusk you need to use lights on your bike (front and rear) and have reflectors on both wheels.
- *Always* lock your bike securely. Bike theft is rampant (see opposite).

Fast Facts

- Amsterdam has 400km of bike paths, identified by signage and their reddish colour.
- There are an estimated 600,000 bicycles in Amsterdam at any given time.
- The bike-parking garage at Centraal Station has space for 2500 bicycles.

Find a Bike

- Visit **Frame Fiets Gallery** (Map pp92-3; ☎ 672 75 88; Frans Halsstraat 26A) for custom bicycles.
- Combine two Dutch passions, beer and bicycles: hire a **Fietscafé** (☎ 0653864090; www.fietscafe .nl), a mobile, pedal-powered bar that seats up to 17 people per bike, with a big beer keg attached. One pedals, the other 16 sit at the bar and drink. Then you all swap around.
- See p136 for a list of bike-rental shops.

...; ☎ 555 00 33; www
...nt 321; floating 45/60min €30/38;
... sauna – saltwater flotation tanks
...d.
...pp88-9; ☎ 623 82 15; www
.sau... erengracht 115; noon-3pm Mon-Fri €14,
all other ti... €15; ⏰ noon-11pm Mon-Sat, 1-6pm Sun)

Skating

ICE

When the canals freeze over, Amsterdam resembles an old Dutch painting as skaters cut up tracks, scarves trailing in the headwind, bums and knees frozen solid from falling over. Beware, though: this oil painting bites – drownings happen each year. Stay away from the ice unless you see large groups of people, and be very careful at the edges and under bridges – areas with weak ice.

In winter you can also skate on the pond at Museumplein (Map pp92–3) for a modest fee.

IJscomplex Jaap Eden (Map pp86-7; ☎ 694 96 52; Radioweg 64; adult/child €5.10/3.20; ⏰ Oct–mid-Mar) has indoor and outdoor rinks in the eastern suburb of Watergraafsmeer; ring for hours. Take tram 9 to Kruislaan/Middenweg.

IN-LINE

Amsterdammers are very keen on in-line skating. Check out **Friday Night Skate** (www.friday nightskate.com), a 15km careen through town in the company of hundreds of fellow skeelers. You needn't be a pro, but braking skills and protective gear are essential. Assemble at 8pm near the Nederlands Filmmuseum in the Vondelpark for an 8.30pm departure. The skate is cancelled if the streets are wet.

Vondelpark itself is a good bet for a spot of Rollerblading. For skates and gear, try **Rent-a-Skate** (Map pp86-7; ☎ 664 50 91; Vondelpark 7; skate hire from €5; ⏰ Mar-Oct), near the Amstelveenseweg entrance.

Swimming

Amsterdam has many indoor pools and outdoor pools (in summer). Ring ahead: hours can vary from day to day or season to season, few are open past 7pm, and there are often restricted sessions – nude (of course), Muslim, children, women, seniors, clubs, lap swimming etc.
De Mirandabad (Map pp86-7; ☎ 536 44 44; De Mirandalaan 9; admission €3.30) Indoor and outdoor pools, twisting slides, a beach, a wave machine, squash courts, fitness room. Ring for opening hours.

Zuiderbad (Map pp92-3; ☎ 678 13 90; Hobbemastraat 26; adult/child €3/2.70) Venerable indoor pool (built 1912) restored to original Art Deco splendour; it's a stone's throw from the Rijksmuseum. Ring for opening hours.

Tennis & Squash

Borchland Sportcentrum (☎ 563 33 33; Borchland-weg 8-12; per hr tennis 8am-4pm Mon-Fri €15.50, 4-10pm Mon-Fri, all day Sat & Sun €23, squash to 4pm Mon-Thu €8, after 4pm Mon-Thu €15, after 4pm Fri, all day Sat & Sun €10; ⏰ 8am-11pm) Tennis, squash and badminton courts, bowling alleys, and a restaurant. It's next to the Amsterdam ArenA stadium, well south of town (metro: Strandvliet).

Squash City (Map pp88-9; ☎ 626 78 83; www .squashcity.com; Ketelmakerstraat 6; day pass €7-14, month pass €32-75; ⏰ 8.45am-midnight Mon, 7am-midnight Tue-Thu, 7am-11.30pm Fri, 8.45am-7.30pm Sat & Sun) Closest squash option to the city centre. Also fitness centre and aerobics.

Tenniscentrum Amstelpark (Map pp86-7; ☎ 301 07 00; www.amstelpark.nl; Koenenkade 8; court hire per hr summer €20, per hr winter outdoor/indoor €20/25) Forty-two open and covered courts, plus 12 squash courts, sauna and pool.

WALKING TOUR

WALK FACTS	
Start	The Dam
Finish	Bloemenmarkt (Flower Market)
Duration	Three hours

Begin at the **Nationaal Monument** (**1**; p96) and head northeast along the Damrak past the graceful **Beurs Van Berlage** (**2**; p84). Heading southeast along Oude Brugsteeg, you'll come across **Warmoesstraat** (**3**; p84). The revered **Oude Kerk** (**4**; p85) is the virtual entrance to red light action. Nearby is the **Prostitution Information Centre** (**5**; p96) – pick up a map of the Red Light District here. North is the clean-as-a-whistle **Museum Amstelkring** (**6**; p96). Walk over to the Oudezijds Achterburgwal and whisk past the underwhelming **Erotic Museum** (**7**; ☎ 624 73 03; Oudezijds Achterburgwal 54; admission €3; ⏰ noon-midnight), the **Casa Rosso** (**8**; p85) erotic theatre, and the **Hash, Marihuana & Hemp Museum** (**9**; p85). Near this museum, cross the canal and head north along its opposite bank to Bloedstraat. From here, head east to the Nieuwmarkt, where the historic **Waag** (**10**; p98) commands attention. Heading south from Nieuwmarkt, along

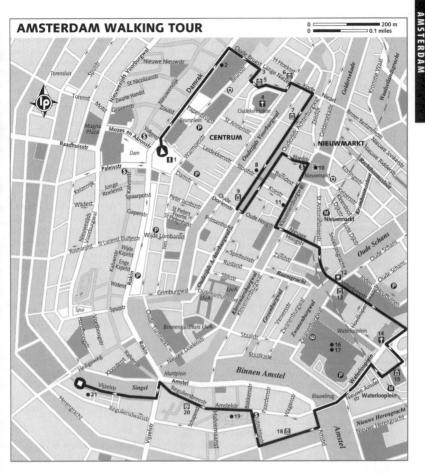

Kloveniersburgwal, note the narrow **Kleine Trippenhuis** (**11**; see the boxed text, p98). Cross the canal and head east along Nieuwe Hoogstraat, then southeast along St Antoniesbreestraat. Across the Oude Schans, have a beer at **Café de Sluyswacht** (**12**; p128); the **Museum het Rembrandthuis** (**13**; p99) is across the street. Walk down Jodenbreestraat past the **Mozes en Aäronkerk** (**14**); 100m southeast is the **Joods (Jewish) Historisch Museum** (**15**; p99). The **Waterlooplein market** (**16**; p134) faces the **Stopera** (**17**; p99); visit the market before crossing the Blauwbrug. Stop at the **Museum Willet-Holthuysen** (**18**; p104) on the Herengracht. Turn right onto Utrechtsestraat toward **Rembrandtplein** (**19**; p104) for cafés galore. Make your way northwest along Reguliersbreestraat, past the sump-

tuous Art Deco stylings of the **Tuschinskitheater** (**20**; p104). The famous floating flower market, the **Bloemenmarkt** (**21**; p134) is on the other side of the Singel; reach it by heading south down Vijzelstraat.

AMSTERDAM FOR CHILDREN

Artis (p108) has a fantastic aquarium, and you can come face-to-face with bison at the children's farm in **Amsterdamse Bos** (p110), in the south of the city. But start with a canal cruise. Then climb the steeple of the **Westerkerk** (p102), with the wacky imperial crown on top.

The **Holland Experience 3D** (Map pp92-3; ☎ 422 22 33; www.holland-experience.nl; Waterlooplein 17; adult/child €8.50/7.25; ☺ 10am-6pm) is truly unbelievably tacky, but the film is interactive: when the dam breaks, your kids will be sprinkled with water.

Science and technology centre **NEMO** (p110) is hands-on, while the **Scheepvaartmuseum** (p109) allows children to clamber on a replica of the *Amsterdam*, the ship that wrecked off the coast of England in 1749. Alternatively, ride a historic tram at the **Electrische Museumtramlijn Amsterdam** (p107).

Your little companions will love **Madame Tussaud's** (Map pp88-9; ☎ 522 10 10; www.madame tussauds.nl; Dam 20; adult/child €20/12; ⏱ 10am-6.30pm Sep-Jun, 9.30am-8.30pm Jul & Aug) and will doubtless be filled with wonderment when they realise there's absolutely no difference between the wax David Beckham and the real thing (if the 2006 World Cup was any guide).

The **Amsterdams Marionetten Theater** (p131) near the Nieuwmarkt gives captivating shows such as Mozart's *The Magic Flute*, and over Christmas there's usually a circus in **Koninklijk Theater Carré** (p131).

Maybe you would like to instil some culture into their tiny brains. **Tropenmuseum** (p109) can deliver, with its separate children's section featuring activities focusing on exotic locations (although shows tend to be in Dutch). The **Joods Historisch Museum** (p99) also has a children's section about Jewish life in Amsterdam.

If the kids are hyper, dunk 'em in the swimming pools at **De Mirandabad** (p112), where there's a beach and a wave machine. The **IJscomplex Jaap Eden** (p112), with indoor and outdoor ice-skating rinks, is another good bet.

The **Oud Zuid** (p105) is a fine neighbourhood for cycling with the kids in tow – wide streets, parks and fine old residential areas. The **Vondelpark** (p107) is great for picnics and has ducks and a children's playground. You can put your kids to work making their own lunch at the park's Kinderkookkafé. The park is also large enough to effectively hide from them when you really need a break.

AN INSIDER'S GUIDE TO AMSTERDAM, PART 2: PETER MOSKOS   *Simon Sellars*

Peter Moskos, along with Toine Rikken, founded the St Nicolaas Boat Club in 1997, a very popular venture that provides an alternative angle on Amsterdam and its waterlogged history. I asked Peter to regale me with his unique perspective.

Favourite area of Amsterdam?

On a boat in the IJ. There's no better place to understand the importance of water and shipping to Amsterdam's history – plus it's beautiful out there.

And your least favourite?

Any big, ugly road with too many cars, although architecturally every place has something interesting and can tell you something about urban planning.

What's the biggest misconception about Amsterdam?

That it's the world's sex capital. It's not – the Dutch just have the sense to put it all out in the open and capitalise on it. And while it may be the world's recreational-drug capital, stop bingeing and enjoy it like you live here year round.

Tell me your favourite 'Amsterdam experience'.

Biking and boating. And Koninginnedag (Queen's Day; p117) – the biggest drunk garage sale in the world.

Least favourite?

The weather – especially the winter weather. Or the winter weather in the summer. And the rain that never stops.

What Amsterdam-specific film or book would you recommend?

The film *Amsterdammed* is fun, with a great high-speed boat chase, but it doesn't depict anything of reality. *Simon* is the best Amsterdam film ever – and maybe the best-ever Dutch movie. Jan-Willem van der Wettering's cop stories are pretty good, but Geert Mak's *Amsterdam* is the single best book about the city.

Your favourite Amsterdam bar and coffeeshop?

Any brown café in the Jordaan is great – get a *jenever* and a beer and talk with the locals. The coffeeshop De Rokerij has a super-cool atmosphere – sort of how I imagine a 19th-century Chinese opium den would have been. And of course my brother's bar at Boom Chicago, because that's the home base for our boats.

Finally, the underground **TunFun** (p99) playground is good for soaking up excess energy.

TOURS
Bicycle Tours

Mike's Bike Tours (Map pp92–3; ☎ 622 79 70; www .mikesbikeamsterdam.com; Kerkstraat 134; bike tour incl bike rental adult/child €22/15, bike & boat tour €29/20; ⊙ bike tour 12.30pm Mar–mid-May & Sep-Nov, 11am & 4pm mid-May–Aug, bike & boat tour noon Tue-Sun Jun-Aug) Highly recommended four-hour tours around the centre of town and into the countryside. Also offers 'bike and boat' tours (about five hours), including drinks on board and a visit to the Vondelpark. Meet at the reflecting pool on Museumplein behind the Rijksmuseum.

Yellow Bike Tours (Map pp88-9; ☎ 620 69 40; www .yellowbike.nl; Nieuwezijds Kolk 29; city/countryside tour per person €18.50/25; ⊙ city tour 9.30am & 1pm Sun-Fri, 9.30am & 2pm Sat Apr–1 Nov, countryside tour 11am daily Apr–1 Nov) Three-hour city tours or six-hour countryside tours through the waterland north of central Amsterdam.

Tours are a little less ~~...~~ limited to 12 tour particip~~...~~ the office. Reservations recomm~~...~~

Canal Tours

Several operators depart from m~~...~~ Centraal Station, Damrak, Rokin and op~~...~~ the Rijksmuseum – just hop on board.

Canal Bus (Map pp92-3; ☎ 623 98 86; www.canal .nl; Weteringschans 26; per adult/child €16/11) Hop-on, hop-off canal boats servicing most of the big destinations. At night, there's a 1½-hour jazz cruise (€43, runs 8pm and 10pm Saturdays from April to November). Pick up the canal bus at one of 14 stops around the city, including one opposite Centraal Station (Map pp88–9).

Holland International (Map pp88-9; ☎ 622 77 88; www.hir.nl; Prins Hendrikkade 33A; 1hr cruise adult/child €8.50/5) The one-hour canal cruise (every 15 minutes 9am to 6pm, every 30 minutes 6pm to 10pm) is very popular. There's also a roster

---

What about restaurants?

Semhar on the Marnixstraat – the only Ethiopian restaurant in town that makes its *enjara* bread with *tef*, the traditional Ethiopian flour. Semhar is distinctive in a city that has a great variety of food but very few truly memorable restaurants. I like the herring stands on bridges. A *broodje haaring* is a very cheap lunch – so Dutch, and you just can't get it anywhere else. Eel is also delicious.

What's Amsterdam's best-kept secret?

Co-ed, naked saunas that aren't sleazy. I like Fenomeen out past Vondelpark – essential when the weather is bad.

Favourite local slang or swear words?

I'm trying to get *spetterend* back into the vocab – it's a very uncool way of saying 'cool'. But the Dutch have a shortage of swear words, so they often resort to English.

I once saw a respectable chap bicycling in Amsterdam with a blow-up sex doll strapped to his back. What's your strangest Amsterdam bike story?

A guy wearing a jockstrap on rollerblades. He used to be everywhere, even in the cold weather. He disappeared a couple of years ago. Perhaps he caught pneumonia and passed on.

What annoys you the most about Amsterdam: the dog shit, the service or something else?

Taxis. Avoid them like dog shit. But the dog-shit problem is basically a thing of the past – if you have a problem with it now, you should have seen how it was before. I really have to say the bad service, without a doubt – it's legendary.

How has living in Amsterdam changed you?

It's made me realise that bikes are the best form of urban transit possible. And that, basically, this is a city that works. There's something to be said for literally living on top of each other and in close-knit surroundings. It's given me the opportunity to see how a large city can allow everyone to do their own thing without getting all bent out of shape about it.

Describe the St Nicolaas Boat Club for someone new to it.

We're a friendly entry point to understanding Amsterdam from the greatest perspective of all: the canals. We offer cosy rides with knowledgeable pilots, and all we ask for is a donation at the end.

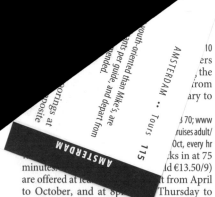

10 ers, the from ary to 70; www ruises adult/ Oct, every hr ks in at 75 minutes. d €13.50/9) are offered at t from April to October, and at Thursday to Sunday throughout the rest of the year.

St Nicolaas Boat Club (Map pp92-3; ☎ 423 01 01; www.petermoskos.com/boat; donation €10) If you blanch at the thought of the foggy windows and stale commentary of the big glassed-in canal boats, do yourself a favour and try this not-for-profit venture (see the boxed text, p114), which takes small, old barges out onto the canals. Patrons are allowed to smoke dope and drink beer on board, while the captains amuse with stories about alternative Amsterdam. The trip will definitely show you a different side of the city – everything from the famous Mohawk Duck to the thinnest house in town. Departure times are according to numbers; inquire at Boom Chicago, Leidseplein 12.

Other Tours

Amsterdam Segway Tours (☎ 0641424344; www.glide.cc; per person €60; 10am & 8pm spring-Christmas) Two daily tours on Dubya's favourite contraption, the Segway. The four-hour daytime tour covers the major sights; the three-hour night tour takes in lesser-known areas such as De Pijp. If you haven't been on a Segway before, they'll train you so you won't get bushwhacked. Up to seven people, by reservation. Meet at the Nieuwmarkt (Map pp88–9) by the metro exit.

Randy Roy's Red Light Tours (☎ 0641853288; www.randyroysredlighttours.com; per person incl a drink €12.50; 8pm Sun-Thu, 8pm & 10pm Fri & Sat) Does exactly what it says on the tin. Over 90 minutes, visit Quentin Tarantino and Iron Mike Tyson's favourite Amsterdam haunts and learn about the business of sex, Amsterdam style. Departs from the Victoria Hotel, across from Centraal Station (Map pp88–9).

Red Light District Tour (☎ 623 63 02; www.zoomamsterdam.com; per person €15; 5pm) This 2½-hour tour covers the history of the Red Light District. All questions answered. Meet at the café inside the Schreierstoren (Map pp88–9), across from Centraal Station.

Urban Home & Garden Tours (☎ 688 12 43; www.uhgt.nl; per person incl a drink €22.50; 10.15am Fri, 11.15am Sat, 12.15pm Sun Apr-Oct) These well-regarded tours (2½ to three hours) look at Amsterdam dwellings from the perspective of home, garden and even gable. Visits include 18th-century, 19th-century and contemporary homes.

FESTIVALS & EVENTS

February

Carnaval A Catholic tradition, best enjoyed in the south of the country, although Amsterdammers also don silly costumes and a party 'tude.

Commemoration of the February Strike (25 February) In memory of the 1941 anti-Nazi general strike.

March

Stille Omgang (Silent Procession; Sunday closest to 15 March) Catholics walk along the Holy Way to commemorate the 1345 Miracle of Amsterdam.

April

Koninginnedag (Queen's Day; 30 April) Celebrated countrywide, but especially in Amsterdam (see the boxed text, opposite).

Amsterdam Fantastic Film Festival (www.afff.nl) European and international fantasy, horror and science-fiction movies.

May

Remembrance Day (4 May) For the fallen of WWII. Queen Beatrix lays a wreath on the Dam and the city observes two minutes' silence at 8pm.

Liberation Day (5 May) The end of German occupation in 1945 is commemorated with street parties, a free market and live music, especially in Vondelpark.

Oosterpark Festival (first week in May; www.oosterparkfestival.nl) Two-day multicultural festival.

Luilak (Lazy Bones) In the early hours on the Saturday before Whit Sunday, children go around ringing door bells, making noise and waking people up. Luilak is a remnant of a pre-Christian festival celebrating the awakening of spring.

Europerve (www.europerve.com) Three-day latex, PVC and rubber S&M party. 'Bring out the gimp…'

Amsterdam Literary Festival (Late May; www.amsterdamliteraryfestival.nl) International and local guests in a three-day wordfest.

June

Holland Festival (virtually all month; www.hollandfestival.nl) The country's biggest extravaganza for theatre, dance, film and pop music, with a justified claim to cutting-edge innovation.

Vondelpark Open-Air Theatre (until late August) Free events held 'for the people'. There's high drama and concerts across the genres from pop and world to classical and jazz.

ORANGE DAY

One Amsterdam event not to miss is Koninginnedag – or Queen's Day, or Orange Day – which is held in celebration of Queen Beatrix's birthday on April 30, when over a million revellers make the city seem like the freakingest place on the planet. People descend from all over the country, clogging and choking the train system to breaking point.

The whole shebang is basically an excuse for a gigantic piss-up and to wear ridiculous outfits, all in orange, the country's national colour. It's quite a sight to see the entire city awash in orange fake afros, orange beer, orange balloon animals, more orange beer, orange dope, yet more orange beer, orange leather boys, orange skater dykes, orange rollercoasters, orange clogs, orange fashion victims, orange grannies and grandpas, even more orange beer, orange Red Bull…Wear something orange.

There's also a free market throughout the city, where anyone can sell anything they like, as well as street parties and live music.

To get you in the mood for Koninginnedag, the website Expatica (www.expatica.com) supplies a helpful 'orange vocabulary', which you can bandy about on April 30 at your leisure. Try this on for size with the nearest reveller: say 'Hey man/woman, I've got…'

- *oranjegekte*: orange madness
- *oranjekoorts*: orange fever
- *oranjestemming*: orange mood
- *oranjeeuforie*: orange euphoria
- *oranjesfeer*: orange atmosphere
- *oranjemania*: orange mania

Most likely they'll look at you with pity, replying, 'Man/woman, you've really got the *oranjeziekte* (orange sickness)'.

Roots Music Festival (last week of June; www.amster damroots.nl) World music and culture with performances, parades, workshops and a market, all in the Oosterpark.
Over het IJ Festival (www.overhetij.nl) From June or July, big performing-arts events (dance, theatre, music) take place for a week and a half around the former NDSM shipyards.

July
Robeco Zomerconcerten (until late August; www .robecozomerconcerten.nl) A quality line-up of 80-odd classical, jazz and world-music concerts at Amsterdam's top concert venue, the Concertgebouw.
5 Days Off (www.5daysoff.nl) Indoor electronica dance parties at various venues, including Paradiso and the Heineken Music Hall. Other events take place at the Netherlands Media Arts Institute.
Julidans (www.julidans.nl) Dance festival that gets some 20,000 visitors, remarkable given that it takes place in small venues.

August
De Parade (first two weeks of the month; www .deparade.nl) Carnivalesque outdoor theatre festival, held in the Martin Luther King Park, with unforgettable ambience.

Hartjesdag (mid-August; www.hartjesdagen.nl) Ancient medieval theatrical celebration involving loads of cross-dressing, revived recently by the city's trannies.
Grachtenfestival (Canal Festival; late August) Five days of free classical concerts in courtyards and private canalside homes, as well as on the canals themselves.
Hartjesdagen Zeedijk (third Monday and weekend leading up to it) Dating back to medieval times, this festival showcases street theatre; there's a parade and all kinds of music along the Zeedijk and in the Nieuwmarkt.
Uitmarkt (late August; www.uitmarkt.nl) The reopening of Amsterdam's cultural season, with three days of free concerts and information booths around the big museums and Leidseplein.

September
Bloemencorso (Flower Parade; first Saturday of the month; www.bloemencorso.com/aalsmeer) Spectacular procession of blossomy floats from Aalsmeer to the Dam and back again.
Jordaan Festival (second week of the month; www .jordaanfestival.nl) This street festival also sees hundreds of small boats take to the canals.
Monumentendag (www.bmz.amsterdam.nl) Registered historical buildings have open days on the second weekend of the month.

Chinese Festival (www.zeedijk.nl/chineesfestival-eng
.html) Along the Zeedijk, Amsterdam's Chinatown, you'll
find food, cultural performances and, of course, the lion
dance.

Dam Tot Dam Loop (www.damloop.nl) A 16km
foot-race between the Dam in Amsterdam and the Dam
in Zaandam, with around 30,000 runners and 200,000
spectators.

Robodock (late September; www.robodock.org) A full-on,
extraordinary festival that blends technology and art. Experience humans and robots interacting and enacting mixed-
media performance art and theatre events, accompanied by
pyrotechnics, explosions, live music, projections –
an audiovisual extravaganza that's sure to blow your mind
(and a lot of machinery).

October

Amsterdam Marathon (mid-month; www.amsterda
marathon.nl) Thousands of runners loop through the
city, starting and finishing at the Olympic Stadium (Map
pp86–7), in a variety of races.

Bock Beer Festival (www.beursvanberlage.nl) Three-
day fest celebrating German 'bock beer' in the Beurs van
Berlage building.

November

Cannabis Cup (last half of the month; www.hightimes
.com) Marijuana festival hosted by *High Times* magazine,
with awards for best grass, biggest spliff and so on, plus
there's a hemp expo and a fashion show.

Zeedijk Jazz & Blues Festival (Last weekend of the
month; www.zeedijk.nl/jazzfestival-eng.html) Amsterdam's biggest jazz festival sees hundreds of jazz and blues
acts out on the street and in the pubs along the Zeedijk, all
free of charge.

SLEEPING

Amsterdam can get crazy with visitors at
any time of year, so book well ahead. It's
worth paying a bit extra for something central so you can enjoy the nightlife without
resorting to night buses or taxis. Many visitors overlook the Museum Quarter and the
Vondelpark area, which both offer quality
digs only a short walk from the action at
Leidseplein.

Amsterdam has no shortage of luxury
accommodation, from intimate boutique
hotels to towering modern complexes.
Historic hotels in the old centre have been
upgraded, but you'll still come across places
without air-con or a lift. Be aware that hotels
with steep staircases and without lifts are
common, so reserve a room on the lower
floors if you can't or won't climb stairs.

The tourist offices and the GWK exchange
office at Centraal Station have hotel-booking
services – see p81 for details. Reviews in this
section are grouped according to the following
price categories for a double room: budget,
less than €70; midrange, €70 to €150; top end,
more than €150.

Medieval Centre

BUDGET

Hotel Winston (Map pp88-9; ☎ 623 13 80; www.winston
.nl; Warmoesstraat 129; dm/s/d from €22/45/56) How
to make a lot out of a little: take some functional rooms and get local artists to theme
them with motifs including Arabian typog-
raphy, jigsaw puzzles and, fittingly for the
red-light location, bizarre sex. There's a jolly
24-hour bar and the Winston's own club
(p129) next door.

Aivengo Youth Hostel (Map pp88-9; ☎ 620 11 55;
Spuistraat 6; dm from €18, d/tr with private bathroom €80/100;
🖳) With friendly management, an inviting,
respectful vibe and funky, Middle Eastern–
style décor, Aivengo is a winner. Party animals
take very careful note: there's a 4am curfew.

Flying Pig Downtown Hostel (Map pp92-9; ☎ 420
68 22; www.flyingpig.nl; Nieuwendijk 100; dm from €14; 🖳)
Multitudinous dope-smoking youngsters
flock to this relaxed backpacker haven. It's
got grungy charm, a throbbing lobby bar with
pool table, cheap booze, DJs and a cushion-
lined basement dubbed the Happy Room.

Other options:

Hotel Groenendael (Map pp88-9; ☎ 624 48 22; www
.hotelgroenendael.com; Nieuwendijk 15; s/d/tr with shared
bathroom €35/50/75) A bargain, although as bare bones as
they come. Central location, friendly owners.

Stadsdoelen Youth Hostel (Map pp92-3; ☎ 624 68
32; www.stayokay.com; Kloveniersburgwal 97; dm from
€24, d €61; 🍴 🖳) Eleven nonsmoking, ultra-clean
dorms, each with up to 17 beds plus free lockers. Single-
sex and co-ed dorms and bathrooms, big TV room, bar
with pool table, laundry.

MIDRANGE

Budget Hotel Clemens (Map p91; ☎ 624 60 89; www
.clemenshotel.com; Raadhuisstraat 39; s €55, d €70-110, d
€125-150; 🖳) The Clemens is a friendly place
with eight warm, cosy rooms, some done up
in creams and yellows, some in gold and red.
Deluxe rooms have antique furniture and
marble fireplaces, and all have mini fridges.
Rooms at the front, though on a noisy street,
make up for it with balconies that overlook
the Westermarkt.

Misc Eat Drink Sleep (Map pp88-9; ☎ 330 62 41; www.hotelmisc.com; Kloveniersburgwal 20; s/d/tr €120/145/167; 🖳) Book the lovely 'baroque' room for romantic times. The 'Africa' room is like its name, while the 'room of wonders' is a modern Moroccan escapade. A fresh-cooked breakfast (included in the rate) is served until noon, and massage services can be arranged. It's just near the Nieuwmarkt.

Hotel Résidence Le Coin (Map pp92-3; ☎ 524 68 00; www.lecoin.nl; Nieuwe Doelenstraat 5; s €110, d from €130, q €248) This shiny new inn, owned by the University of Amsterdam, features 42 high-class apartments spread over seven historical buildings, all equipped with designer furniture and kitchenettes – and all reachable by lift. Breakfast (€9) is served in a nearby café.

Hotel Brouwer (Map pp88-9; ☎ 624 63 58; www .hotelbrouwer.nl; Singel 83; s/d €50/85; ✗) This lovely building dates back to 1652. The eight rooms, named after Dutch painters, are simply furnished but all have canal views and private facilities. The staff are friendly. Note that credit cards are not accepted.

TOP END

Hotel de l'Europe (Map pp92-3; ☎ 531 17 77; www .leurope.nl; Nieuwe Doelenstraat 2-8; s/d €295/365; ✗ 🖳 🖳) Oozing Victorian elegance, l'Europe has welcomed the likes of Arnold Schwarzenegger with its glam chandelier and cavernous marble lobby. The rooms are gloriously large and there's more marble in the bathrooms. The attached Excelsior Restaurant, chi-chi gym and swimming pool are equally impressive.

Jordaan & Western Islands
BUDGET
Hotel Van Onna (Map p91; ☎ 626 58 01; Bloemgracht 102-108; r per person €45; ✗) The rooms won't win any design awards, but they do have private facilities and breakfast is included. Plus you're in a gorgeous section of the Jordaan, within earshot of the Westerkerk bells (rooms out the back are quieter). The attic room, with its old wooden roof beams, has panoramic views over the Jordaan. No phone, TV or credit cards.

Western Canal Belt
MIDRANGE
Hampshire Classic Hotel Toren (Map pp88-9; ☎ 622 60 33; www.toren.nl; Keizersgracht 164; s/d from €125/145; ✗ ✗ 🖳) A title-holder for price, room size and personal service, with communal areas

that are pure 17th century: gilded mirrors, fireplaces and magnificent chandeliers. The guest rooms are elegantly furnished with modern facilities. There's a room with two-person Jacuzzi and garden patio (from €270). Breakfast is €12.

Hotel Amsterdam Wiechmann (Map pp92-3; ☎ 626 33 21; www.hotelwiechmann.nl; Prinsengracht 328; s/d/tr/q from €75/125/175/190; 🖳) This friendly family-run hotel, occupying three houses, has a marvellous canalside location. The cosy but lovingly cared-for rooms are furnished like an antique shop, plus there are country quilts and lobby *tchotchkes* (knick-knacks) that have been there for some 50 years (including a suit of armour and a potbellied stove).

Canal House Hotel (Map pp88-9; ☎ 622 51 82; www .canalhouse.nl; Keizersgracht 148; r from €140) It's hard to know where to spend your time in this splendid boutique hotel. The 17th-century dining room with chandeliers, grand piano and garden views? Or perhaps the plush, burgundy-hued bar? The small but inviting guest rooms are filled with antiques.

't Hotel (Map pp88-9; ☎ 422 27 41; www.thotel .nl; Leliegracht 18; d from €145) Quiet, familiar and understated, 't Hotel is where Dutch modern furnishing meets a 17th-century canal-house setting. Be sure to book room 7, a sun-filled space with a gabled roof and large windows overlooking the canal.

TOP END

Seven One Seven (Map pp92-3; ☎ 427 07 17; www .717hotel.nl; Prinsengracht 717; d from €405; ✗ 🖳) Amsterdam's most wonderful hotel. Its eight hyper-plush, deliciously appointed rooms come with that rare Dutch treat: space. Check into the splashy Picasso suite, with its soaring ceiling, commodious furniture, gorgeous contemporary and antique décor, and a bathroom as big as some European principalities.

Dylan (Map p91; ☎ 530 20 10; www.dylanamsterdam .com; Keizersgracht 384; s/d from €255/405) The Dylan is a true temple of style, from the 17th-century canal house's courtyard entrance, to the staff, to the restaurant, to the black-and-white lobby. The 41 sophisticated, individually decorated rooms might have Japanese or Indonesian motifs; fluffy towels, silk pillows piled high and spacious bathrooms make them serene and sumptuous. Plus, there's free health club access and a lounge par excellence.

ourpick Hotel Pulitzer (Map p91; ☎ 523 52 35; www .pulitzer.nl; Prinsengracht 315-331; d €250; 🅿 ✗ ✗) Occupying a row of 17th-century canal houses, Pulitzer combines big-hotel efficiency with boutique-hotel charm. Beautifully restored rooms feature mod cons galore, and there's a cigar bar, an art gallery, garden courtyards and a wonderful restaurant that's high on elegance and low on pomposity.

Ambassade Hotel (Map pp88-9; ☎ 555 02 22; www.ambassade-hotel.nl; Herengracht 341; s/d/tr from €165/185/195; ✗) Flick through the Ambassade's spiffy little library and you will find signed copies of works by Salman Rushdie and Umberto Eco. The antique furniture and fixtures are traditional without being cloying, but prepare for steep, winding stairwells. Breakfast costs €16.

Southern Canal Belt

BUDGET

Hotel Quentin (Map pp92-3; ☎ 626 21 87; www.quentinhotels.com; Leidsekade 89; s/d from €45/60) This 19th-century mansion has a nice lobby and rooms done up in bright murals and handmade furniture, although singles tend to be small and functional. If you're lucky you might get a balcony and a canal view.

Hotel Prinsenhof (Map pp92-3; ☎ 623 17 72; www.hotelprinsenhof.com; Prinsengracht 810; s/d €45/65, d with shower €85) Dating from the 17th century, the Prinsenhof is wonderfully preserved, with spacious rooms. The attic quarters (slanted ceiling and unbeatable canal views) are booked way in advance by honeymooners. The breakfast policy promises that 'no one's allowed to leave until he or she is completely satiated'.

Hotel Pax (Map pp88-9; ☎ 624 97 35; Raadhuisstraat 37; s/d from €25/35, d with private facilities from €55) The Pax, in hotel-lined Raadhuisstraat, is run by two friendly brothers. All eight rooms have a TV and each is individually decorated. The larger rooms face the busy street with noisy trams, so bring some earplugs. Rates don't include breakfast.

Hans Brinker Budget Hotel (Map pp92-3; ☎ 622 06 87; www.hans-brinker.com; Kerkstraat 136; dm from €21; tw/tr/q per person €35/30/24; 🖳) There's a jacked up *Animal House* feel to the Brinker, with its bouncy bar and disco. Its website takes the art of self-mockery to uniquely Dutch extremes, offering Brinker Wallpaper: 'Your home will soon have the unmistakable feeling of the Hans Brinker Budget Hotel,' it says, 'without the tangy smell, strange gargling noises, and the moaning'. Or is that the Black Tulip?

MIDRANGE

Seven Bridges (Map pp92-3; ☎ 623 13 29; Reguliersgracht 31; s/d from €80/100; ✗) Intimate and sophisticated, Seven Bridges is one of the city's loveliest little hotels on one of its loveliest canals, with eight tastefully decorated rooms, all with lush Oriental rugs and elegant antiques. Breakfast, served on fine china, is delivered to your room.

Hotel Orlando (Map pp92-3; ☎ 638 69 15; www.hotelorlando.nl; Prinsengracht 1099; s/d from €85/100; ✗ ✗ 🖳) The plain entrance hall belies the joys that lie beyond: big canalside rooms and big views. Impeccably chic, boutique-style rooms with custom-made cabinetry and satin curtains. The hospitable host serves brekkie in bed.

Hotel de Munck (Map pp92-3; ☎ 623 62 83; www.hoteldemunck.com; Achtergracht 3; s/d/tr €75/95/145) De Munck is a sane choice in a quiet neighbourhood. The brilliant breakfast room looks like a replica of a 1960s diner with its working jukebox. The 16 spacious, renovated rooms feature comfy contemporary furnishings, and the flower-filled courtyard is as welcoming as the hosts.

Hotel Nicolaas Witsen (Map pp92-3; ☎ 623 61 43; www.hotelnicolaaswitsen.nl; Nicolaas Witsenstraat 4; s/d from €65/89; 🖳) Style aficionados may squirm at the bland pastel décor but there's no quibbling over the amenities. All 29 rooms are neat and come with phone, safe and in some cases even baths. In summer ask for the basement room that's as cool as air-con. There's a lift too.

Other options:

Hotel de Admiraal (Map pp92-3; ☎ 626 21 50; de-admiraal-hotel@planet.nl; Herengracht 563; d with shared/private facilities €70/98) In the thick of the action near Rembrandtplein, with beautiful canal views. Breakfast costs €5.

City Hotel (Map pp92-3; ☎ 627 23 23; www.city-hotel.nl; Utrechtsestraat 2; d with shared/private facilities €70/90; 🖳) Above the Old Bell pub, practically on Rembrandtplein. Clean, neat, well run.

Hotel Agora (Map pp92-3; ☎ 627 22 00; www.hotelagora.nl; Singel 462; s & d/tr/q from €103/158/175; 🖳) Fifteen minutes' walk from everything, with smallish rooms, up-to-date bathrooms and a cheerful garden.

TOP END

Amstel Intercontinental Hotel (Map pp86-7; ☎ 622 60 60; www.amsterdam.intercontinental.com; Professor Tulpplein 1; r from €575; ✗ 🖳 🖳) Everything about this five-star monument is simply spectacular, from its magnificent colonnaded lobby to its hefty room prices and its royalty-and-rock-star clientele. It's a favourite of the Strolling Bones, and the lavishly decorated rooms overlook the Amstel, the river that (according to legend) Mick Jagger nearly fell into when Charlie Watts punched him out perilously close to a window.

Old South (Oud Zuid)
BUDGET
Stayokay Amsterdam Vondelpark (Map pp92-3; ☎ 589 89 96; www.stayokay.com/vondelpark; Zandpad 5; dm from €24, d €74; ✗ 🖳) This modern, attractive 536-bed facility – with one section occupying a tall, half-timbered 19th-century school building – has the leafiest location, with views into the Vondelpark.

Flying Pig Uptown Hostel (Map pp92-3; ☎ 400 41 87; www.flyingpig.nl; Vossiusstraat 46; dm from €13; 🖳) The uptown member of the Flying Pig backpacker chain, with almost as much dope, beer and grungy charm as its downtown cousin (see p118).

MIDRANGE
Owl Hotel (Map pp92-3; ☎ 618 94 84; www.owl-hotel .nl; Roemer Visscherstraat 1; s €75-92, d €98-125; 🖳) Some guests love this place so much that they send in owl figurines from all over the world. Staff are warm and welcoming, and the dapper, bright and quiet rooms come with lots of facilities (hairdryers, laptop plug-ins, etc). The buffet breakfast (included in the price) is served in a serene, light-filled room overlooking a gorgeous garden.

Hotel de Filosoof (Map pp86-7; ☎ 683 30 13; www .hotelfilosoof.nl; Anna van den Vondelstraat 6; s/d €111/125) This stately hotel near leafy Vondelpark is owned by two sisters and has 38 rooms themed in honour of such philosophers as Aristotle, Wittgenstein and Spinoza. The furniture can be lush or Zen minimalist, depending on the room's honoree.

Xaviera's Happy House (Map pp86-7; ☎ 673 39 34; www.xavierahollander.com/sleeper; Stadionweg 17; d from €120; 🖳) This small B&B is run by the one and only Xaviera Hollander, author of The Happy Hooker (p45). The two house rooms aren't overly large, but they're colourful and cosy (one has a shared bathroom), while the garden chalet is a fairly simple affair and quite secluded. Xaviera herself is often on hand for a chat and a cup of tea, and can organise all manner of tours and activities in the city, regardless of your desires (within reason of course). She also stages the occasional theatre performance in-house: they range from musical concerts to 'squirter' shows.

TOP END
Hilton Amsterdam (Map pp86-7; ☎ 710 60 00; www .hilton.com; Apollolaan 138-140; r from €202; 🅿 ✗ 🖳) It's an old-school hotel with lots of business guests, but the Hilton was flower-power central in 1969 when John Lennon and Yoko Ono staged their 'bed-in' for world peace here (you can rent the room). Less happily, Herman Brood, the infamous Dutch junkie-artist-musician, committed suicide in 2001 by jumping off the Hilton's roof (he used to frequent the hotel's popular bar carrying a parrot on his head). The building fronts a grassy park with a marina out the back. Rooms are international business standard, and service is crisp and professional. The health club features sauna and Turkish bath.

College Hotel (Map pp86-7; ☎ 571 15 11; www.the steingroup.com/college; Roelof Hartstraat 1; s/d from €175/200; ✗ 🖳) Originally a 19th-century school, this place has now been updated with tremendous style: flat-screen TVs, silk throw pillows, cordless phones, the occasional stained-glass window and exposed beams on the top floor. Continental breakfast costs €17.50.

De Pijp
TOP END
Hotel Okura (Map pp86-7; ☎ 678 71 11; www.okura.nl; Ferdinand Bolstraat 333; s/d from €240/275; ✗ ✗ 🖳 🍷) This is the business traveller's choice, with close proximity to the RAI exhibition centre, private in-room fax lines, wi-fi for computers, and professional staff. Plus, it's got the Netherlands's largest hotel pool, an amazing health club, several fine restaurants (including two with Michelin stars – Yamazato and Ciel Bleu) and wonderfully panoramic views of Amsterdam.

Plantage & Oosterpark
BUDGET
Hotel Rembrandt (Map p95; ☎ 627 27 14; www.hotel rembrandt.nl; Plantage Middenlaan 17; s €73, d from €85; 🖳) The hallways could stand a touch-up, but the Rembrandt shines where it matters. The spotless rooms have TV, phone and coffee maker, and some have hardwood floors and bathtubs. The wood-panelled breakfast room features chandeliers and 17th-century paintings on linen-covered walls.

AMSTERDAM

Hotel Hortus (Map p95; ☎ 625 99 96; www.hotel hortus.com; Plantage Parklaan 8; dm €25, s/d €35/50) Facing the Botanical Garden, this comfy 20-room hotel has small doubles with or without showers (luck of the draw). The lounge will be chock-full of young, happy stoners transfixed by the big-screen TV. Large rooms sleep up to eight people.

MIDRANGE

Hotel Arena (Map pp86-7; ☎ 850 24 00; www.hotel arena.nl; 's Gravesandestraat 51; d/tr from €100/165; 🖳) The Arena, next to lush Oosterpark, has been a chapel, an orphanage and a backpackers' hostel. Now it's a chic 121-room hotel with a stylish restaurant, a café and a well-regarded nightclub, To Night (p129). Rooms are an ode to minimalism, while the large, split-level doubles are sun drenched. Tip: sections A, B, E and F tend to be quieter.

Hotel Fantasia (Map p95; ☎ 623 82 59; www.fantasia -hotel.com; Nieuwe Keizersgracht 16; s/d €67/86; 🖳) This one's perfect for moo-ching around. Pull the udder one. No, really – the owner grew up on a farm and has parlayed that into a workable obsession: this bovine-themed 18th-century house. Bucolic prints and cow motifs gleefully decorate the 19 rooms and breakfast area, complementing the peaceful canalside location.

Eastern Islands
MIDRANGE

Lloyd Hotel (Map pp86-7; ☎ 561 36 36; www.lloydhotel .com; Oostelijke Handelskade 34; d €80-300; 🖳) In 1921 this building was a hotel for migrants, and many of the original fixtures (tiles, cabinetry etc) still exist, now combined with triumphs of more contemporary Dutch design. This combination hotel, cultural centre and local gathering place boasts rooms that span one-star (facilities down the hall) to five-star (plush and huge).

Amstel Botel (Map p95; ☎ 626 42 47; www.amstel botel.com; Oosterdokskade 2-4; s & d with land/water view €87/92, tr with land/water view €117/122; 🖳) This floating hotel is packed with dazed, Europe-in-four-days bus groups and packs of Brit boys/girls celebrating bucks' or hens' nights. The sterile rooms have TV, phone and a tiny bathroom. Breakfast is €10.

Outer Districts
BUDGET

Gaaspercamping (☎ 696 73 26; www.gaaspercamping .nl; Loosdrechtdreef 7, Gaasperdam; camp sites per adult/ under 12/car/caravan €4.75/2.25/4.25/6.25; 🕙 mid-Mar–Dec) Large park/recreation area with café, restaurant, bar, barbecues, supermarket, lake and beach. Take metro 53 from Centraal to Gaasperplas, south of town.

Camping Vliegenbos (Map pp86-7; ☎ 636 88 55; www.vliegenbos.com; Meeuwenlaan 138; camp sites per person €7.60; 🕙 Apr-Sep) Well-equipped camping ground just a few minutes' bus ride from the city centre, with shop, laundry, hot showers, cabins and 25 hectares of woodland. From Centraal Station take bus 32 or 36 to Zamenhofstraat/Merelstraat.

EATING
Amsterdam's culinary scene has hundreds of restaurants and *eetcafés* (pubs serving meals) catering to all tastes.

Utrechtsestraat is a terrific all-rounder, while Haarlemmerstraat has some of the latest hot spots. Try Leidseplein for quantity more than quality. West of Albert Cuypstraat is multicultural heaven with Cambodian, Kurdish and Surinamese cuisines and more.

Medieval Centre
Blauw aan de Wal (Map pp88-9; ☎ 330 22 57; Oudezijds Achterburgwal 99; mains €24-27; 🕙 dinner) Tucked away in a long, often graffiti-covered alley in the middle of the Red Light District, this charming 17th-century herb warehouse (complete with exposed brick and steel weights) is the setting for contemporary French- and Italian-inspired cooking. Service is friendly and knowledgeable. In summer, grab a table in the leafy courtyard that backs onto a monastery.

Lucius (Map pp88-9; ☎ 624 18 31; Spuistraat 247; mains €17.50-28, set menus €35; 🕙 dinner) Simple, delicious and simply delicious, this seafood place is known for fresh ingredients and for not overdoing the sauce and spice. The interior is all fish tanks and tiles, and service is thorough and efficient.

d'Vijff Vlieghen (Map pp88-9; ☎ 530 40 60; www .thefiveflies.com; Spuistraat 294-302; mains €20-28; 🕙 dinner) The second you set foot in this dining complex of five 17th-century canal houses, you know you're in for a treat. Ask to be seated in the Rembrandt Room (with four original etchings) and join splurging business groups being treated to silver service and contemporary Dutch dishes.

Hemelse Modder (Heavenly Mud; Map pp88-9; ☎ 624 32 03; Oude Waal 9; mains €16, set meals from €26; 🕙 dinner) A little hard to locate, but worth it. Extraordinary care goes into the contemporary Dutch dishes – you might find pot-au-feu with chicken or polenta soufflé – and you may even find a sprig of mint in your carafe of water. Desserts are wonderful, including the chocolate mousse.

Nam Kee (Map pp88–9; ☎ 624 34 70; www.namkee .net; Zeedijk 113-116; mains €6-16.50; ☽ lunch & dinner) It won't win any design awards, but Nam Kee is always the most popular Chinese spot in town. There's a new, fancier location at Geldersekade 117 (Map pp88–9).

Supper Club (Map pp88–9; ☎ 638 05 13; www .supperclub.nl; Jonge Roelensteeg 21; 5-course menu €65; ☽ dinner) Enter the theatrical, all-white room, snuggle up on enormous mattresses and snack on platters of contemporary Dutch victuals as DJs spin house music, then head upstairs later to dance. Well, it's a concept, even if the food and service are so-so. They also do this whole thing on a boat trip on the IJ: the Supper Club Cruise leaves from dock 14 behind Centraal Station.

QUICK EATS

Eat Mode (Map pp88–9; ☎ 330 08 06; www .eatmode.nl; Zeedijk 107; mains €4.50-12; ☽ lunch & dinner) Thai, Chinese, Vietnamese and Japanese with casual ambience. Good vegetarian selection plus wi-fi.

Green Planet (Map pp88–9; ☎ 625 82 80; www .greenplanet.nl; Spuistraat 122; sandwiches & salads €6-10, mains €10-16.50; ☽ dinner Tue-Sat) Veggie eatery selling burgers, crostini, wraps, fresh pastries, biscuits and homemade cakes – takeaway comes in biodegradable packaging.

Krua Thai (Map pp92-3; ☎ 622 95 33; Staalstraat 22; mains €6.75-25; ☽ dinner Tue-Sun) Top-shelf (and popular) soups, duck or shrimp curries, and noodle dishes.

Pannenkoekenhuis Upstairs (Map pp88–9; ☎ 626 56 03; Grimburgwal 2; mains €4-10; ☽ lunch & dinner) Climb some of Amsterdam's steepest stairs for flavoursome, filling pancakes – and vintage teapots hanging from the ceiling.

Puccini (Map pp92-3; ☎ 626 54 74; www.puccini.nl; Staalstraat 21; mains €5.30-12.50; ☽ lunch & dinner Tue-Sun) Italian panini rolls and salads with sun-dried ingredients; the handmade chocolate and cake shop next door induces rapture.

Ralph's Asian Wonderfood (Map pp88–9; ☎ 427 62 62; Haarlemmerstraat 32; dishes €6-7; ☽ lunch & dinner) Excellent, fresh Asian-fusion menu.

Vlaams Friteshuis (Map pp92-3; Voetboogstraat 31; fries €2.50) Amsterdam's best-loved fries joint. Remember the words of Vincent Vega, from *Pulp Fiction*: 'You know what they put on French fries in Holland? Mayonnaise. And I don't mean a little bit on the side – they fucken drown 'em in it'. It's true, but Vlaams also offers an arsenal of alternatives, including green peppercorn.

Jordaan & Western Islands

Bordewijk (Map pp8-9; ☎ 624 38 99; Noordermarkt 7; mains €24-29, set menus €37-52; ☽ dinner Tue-Sun) Locals love Bordewijk: they don't come for the sparse interior, but for the super French/Italian cooking. Apparently lamb's testicles were once on the menu, but less adventurous customers needn't worry, and vegetarians are willingly catered for.

Local (Map p91; ☎ 423 40 39; Westerstraat 136; mains €7-19.50; ☽ dinner) Contemporary and cool, with long, tall tables stretching its entire length; you won't be alone. The international mains are grilled on skewers, everything from *yakitori* to beef stroganoff (yes, really), all served with potatoes, salad and appropriate sauces.

Nomads (Map p91; ☎ 344 64 01; www.restaurant nomads.nl; Rozengracht 133; set menu €45; ☽ dinner Tue-Sun) It's like a boudoir: eat your Middle Eastern food while taking it easy on stuffed cushions in a hall festooned with Moroccan curtains and oversized chandeliers. Belly dancers and DJs give it some late in the evening.

Rakang Thai (Map p91; ☎ 627 50 12; Elandsgracht 29; mains €17-21; ☽ dinner) Kooky décor – chairs wrapped in straitjackets, bright art on the walls, neckties in the tables – blends with a relaxed atmosphere and super food. Try the crunchy, spicy duck salad.

QUICK EATS

Café Reibach (Map p91; ☎ 626 77 08; Brouwersgracht 139; mains €2.80-12.50; ☽ breakfast & lunch) Magnificent, fresh-made breakfasts replete with Dutch cheese, pâté, smoked salmon, eggs, coffee and fresh juice.

Duende (Map pp88-9; ☎ 420 66 92; Lindengracht 62; tapas €3-10; ☽ dinner) Tapas; flamenco on Saturday.

Western Canal Belt

our pick Christophe (Map p91; ☎ 625 08 07; www .christophe.nl; Leliegracht 46; mains €31-53; ☽ dinner Tue-Sat) Jean Christophe's subtly swanky French restaurant lives up to its two Michelin stars with its lobster dishes, duck-liver terrine and unusual elegance. The attentive service is also a cut above.

Zuid Zeeland (Map pp92-3; ☎ 624 31 54; Herengracht 413; mains €23-26; ☽ lunch Mon-Fri, dinner nightly) Popular with artists and general Bohemian types, Zuid Zeeland gets props for French-international cuisine. We have it on very good authority that to finish with the port-infused Stilton is divine.

De Belhamel (Map pp88-9; ☎ 622 10 95; Brouwersgracht 60; mains €18-21; ☽ dinner) Belhamel's gorgeous Art

Nouveau interior is a fitting backdrop for excellent French- and Italian-inspired dishes such as silky roast beef. This is a quality spot for a romantic evening, with its canalside tables.

Grekas (Map pp88-9; ☎ 620 35 90; Singel 311; mains €8-10; ⊗ lunch & dinner Wed-Sun) One of the city's best-loved Greek restaurants, with high-quality, generous portions of Greek home cooking: moussaka, roasted artichokes, chicken in lemon sauce.

De Bolhoed (Map p91; ☎ 626 18 03; Prinsengracht 60-62; dishes lunch €3.50-12, dinner €9-15; ⊗ lunch & dinner) Amsterdam's best-known vegetarian restaurant has a prime canalside location. The food is fresh, organic and often Mexican- and Italian-inspired: pancakes, salads, burritos, homemade breads, biological wines, organic beers and cakes.

Koh-I-Noor (Map p91; ☎ 623 31 33; Westermarkt 29; mains €10-19; ⊗ dinner) The interior is gaudy but the Indian food is consistently good, running the gamut from mild to palate-searing for curries, tandoori and biryani dishes.

QUICK EATS

Buffet van Odette & Yvette (Map pp88-9; ☎ 423 60 34; Herengracht 309; mains €3-12; ⊗ breakfast Mon-Sat, lunch daily) Creative, organic soups, sandwiches, pastas and quiches – and gorgeous canal views.

Foodism (Map pp88-9; ☎ 427 51 03; www.foodism .nl; Oude Leliestraat 8; mains €3-10; ⊗ lunch & dinner) All-day breakfasts, healthy filled sandwiches and salads, wild and wicked pasta dishes.

Nielsen (Map p91; ☎ 330 60 06; Berenstraat 19; dishes €4-10, ⊗ breakfast & lunch) Sunny café with a tasty set breakfast: eggs, toast, fruit, juice and coffee (€8). For lunch, a large variety of salads and sandwiches are served.

Pancake Bakery (Map pp88-9; ☎ 625 13 33; Prinsengracht 191; mains €5-12; ⊗ lunch & dinner) Delicious, filling Dutch pancakes – sweet (including chocolate) and savoury (including the 'Egyptian', topped with lamb, sweet peppers and garlic sauce). Also omelettes, soups and desserts.

Small World Catering (Map pp88-9; ☎ 420 27 74; Binnen Oranjestraat 14; sandwiches €5.45-7.50, mains €4-6; ⊗ breakfast, lunch & dinner Tue-Sat, lunch & dinner Sun) Gorgeous prepared vegetables and meat dishes, a variety of quiches and sandwiches, including fresh tuna, tapenade and artichoke hearts.

't Kuyltje (Map pp88-9; ☎ 620 10 45; Gasthuismolensteeg 9; sandwiches €1.75-3.10; ⊗ breakfast & lunch) Little sandwich shop with good pastrami.

Southern Canal Belt

La Rive (Map pp86-7; ☎ 622 60 60; Amstel Intercontinental Hotel, Professor Tulpplein 1; mains €38-58; ⊗ breakfast daily, lunch Mon-Fri, dinner Mon-Sat) Two Michelin stars and a formal dining room with graciously spaced tables and views over the Amstel make La Rive a top-notch option. The French menu changes frequently, but standards include turbot and truffle in potato pasta, and a starter of caviar.

Tempo Doeloe (The Old Days; Map pp92-3; ☎ 625 67 18; www.tempodoeloerestaurant.nl; Utrechtsestraat 75; mains €18-22; ⊗ dinner) Ring a bell to gain entry to this Indonesian restaurant, where the spice levels range from mild to *very* hot. Yet all the subtle flavours remain intact – extraordinary. It does a top-notch version of the classic rijsttafel (rice table; see p60). Reservations are essential.

Segugio (Map pp92-3; ☎ 330 15 03; Utrechtsestraat 96; pastas €15-17, mains €23-27; ⊗ dinner Mon-Sat) This fashionably minimalist storefront with two levels of seating is known for risotto and high-quality ingredients combined with a sure hand. Book ahead – this is one Italian joint that's always busy.

Iguazu (Map pp92-3; ☎ 420 39 10; Prinsengracht 703; mains €14-35; ⊗ lunch & dinner) This Brazilian-Argentinean steakhouse serves cuts so tender they practically dissolve in your mouth, and everything tastes great with *chimichurri* (a spicy sauce), which sits in a small jar on every table. Relax on the canal terrace with your *feijoada* (a stew of rice, beans and various meats) and *caipirinhas* (Brazil's famous cocktail, made with *cachaça* – sugarcane brandy – lime, sugar and ice).

Tujuh Maret (Map pp92-3; ☎ 427 98 65; Utrechtsestraat 73; mains €14-20; ⊗ lunch Mon-Sat, dinner nightly) Well, well, here's a surprise: Tujuh Maret, next door to Tempo Doeloe, serves Indonesian food that's just as good but attitude-free. Grab a wicker chair and tuck into spicy Sulawesi-style dishes such as dried, fried beef or chicken in red pepper sauce. Rijsttafel is laid out according to spice intensity.

Pasta e Basta (Map pp92-3; ☎ 422 22 26; Nieuwe Spiegelstraat 8; set meals €35; ⊗ dinner) An Italian restaurant that's popular with large groups, thanks to its singing waiters, who perform opera, standards and more. Regulars swear by the antipasto buffet and grilled meats. Reserve well in advance.

Sluizer (Map pp92-3; ☎ 622 63 76; Utrechtsestraat 43-45; mains €14-25; ⊗ dinner) This lively Amsterdam institution, with a super-romantic, enclosed terrace, comprises two restaurants: a renowned house of fish at No 45 and a

AN INSIDER'S GUIDE TO AMSTERDAM, PART 3: SEAN CONDON   *Simon Sellars*

Australian Sean Condon is the author of the bittersweet 'non-fiction novel' *My 'Dam Life*, about his time in Amsterdam and his bemused efforts to adapt to the rhythms of Dutch life (the book was saddled with the Orwellian epithet 'Down and Out In Amsterdam' by one reviewer). I prodded Sean to give me his appraisal of this eccentric town.

Do you have a favourite part of Amsterdam? Anywhere to avoid?
My favourite is the Jordaan, because most of my friends live there. I dislike the main red light area behind Warmoesstraat, because it's usually full of loutish drunken tourists who spoil the otherwise lovely, rosy ambience.

Pick an Amsterdam cliché – now debunk it.
There are far fewer Dutch doors than you'd think.

Describe your favourite, and least favourite, 'Amsterdam experience'.
My favourite is riding anywhere, any time, in any weather – on a bike. My least favourite is encountering groups of the aforementioned louts.

Speaking of bikes, can there be anything funnier than a bicyclist giving a ride to a blow-up sex doll?
Yes. Those big, wooden trays on the front of bikes, full of infants, that teachers use to transport kids from one place to another. Hilarious.

What book set in Amsterdam would you recommend for newcomers?
There are few that I know of. There's *Amsterdam*, an excellent and lively history of the city by Geert Mak. Maybe Ian McEwan's *Amsterdam*, but I haven't read it. Some of the scenes early on in Ian Fleming's *Diamonds Are Forever* are set in Amsterdam, and they're cool.

You're a writer – you must have a favourite Amsterdam bar.
Without doubt my favourite is Proeflokaal Fockink (p128), a tiny *jenever* bar founded in the 17th century. It's congenial and a superb place to meet strangers. Every day I miss it and every day my liver thanks me that it's now on the other side of the world.

Where do you like to eat in Amsterdam?
My favourite Amsterdam restaurant is De Reddende Engel, but it's in Antwerp, which should give you some idea of the culinary scene in Amsterdam. There is one place, on Leliegracht, called Christophe (p123) – it's excellent, but boy you'll pay for it. Also the Gouden Real on Prinseneiland used to be good – and it has a great setting, too.

Do you have a favourite local slang or swear word?
Jammer (shame).

Care to reveal Amsterdam's best-kept secret?
No.

What annoys you the most about Amsterdam?
The appalling – and yet very expensive – food served by the rudest wait staff in Europe.

How did living in Amsterdam change you?
It introduced me to the world beyond Australia, and now that I'm back here, I kind of wish it hadn't.

Describe My 'Dam Life for someone who hasn't read it.
Unfortunate cover, great book. A love story about both my wife, Sally, and Amsterdam.

Parisian-style 'meat' establishment at No 43, although both menus are offered in either. Bouillabaisse and spare ribs are the respective house specialities.

Pata Negra (Map pp92-3; ☎ 422 62 50; Utrechtsestraat 142; tapas €4-16; ☺ lunch & dinner) This Spanish eatery is an eyeful of fun, with its alluringly tiled exterior and an equally exuberant crowd inside. Weekends are quite a scene with boisterous groups sharing sangria and tapas plates (try the garlic-fried shrimps and grilled sardines).

QUICK EATS

Maoz (Map pp92-3; ☎ 420 74 35; www.maozveg .com; Muntplein 1; felafel €3.50) Offers felafel pita-bread sandwiches with 'bottomless' salad toppings and sauces. It's common for impecunious Dutch students to linger here for hours on end (possibly days, weeks, months) refilling their pita bread. Also at Centraal Station, Leidsestraat 85,

Ferdinand Bolstraat 67, Eerste van der Helststraat 43 and Oude Brugsteeg.

M Café (Map pp92-3; ☎ 520 78 48; Keizersgracht 455; mains €4-12; ☼ breakfast & lunch) Amazing views are the top draw high above the Keizersgracht in the top-floor gallery of the ritzy Metz & Co department store.

Pasta di Mamma (Map pp92-3; ☎ 664 83 14; Pieter Cornelisz Hooftstraat 52; sandwiches €3-5; ☼ breakfast, lunch & dinner Mon-Sat, lunch & dinner Sun) Great for picnic supplies for Vondelpark. Dozens of antipasti, gorgeous salads and more substantial plates.

Uliveto (Map pp92-3; ☎ 423 00 99; Weteringschans 118; mains €5-8; ☼ breakfast & lunch) Mouth-watering fresh pastas, salads and creamy desserts. Buy takeaway or dine at the large marble table under designer milk urns.

Wagamama (Map pp92-3; ☎ 528 77 78; Max Euweplein 10; mains €8-13; ☼ lunch & dinner) Chicken ramen, Japanese curries and fried noodles or rice.

Old South (Oud Zuid)

Bark (Map pp92-3; ☎ 675 02 10; Van Baerlestraat 120; mains €14.50-22; ☼ lunch Mon-Fri, dinner nightly) Near the Concertgebouw, Bark serves seafood that's suitably genteel and old-school. For starters, choose from a long shellfish menu or try the blinis of smoked oilfish. For mains, the grilled tuna steak with bacon and balsamic sauce is recommended. Some dishes can be a little salty, so let them know if you're averse.

Mansion (Map pp92-3; ☎ 616 66 64; Hobbemastraat 2; mains €12-21; ☼ dinner Tue-Sun) There's no sign out the front, just black lacquered doors. Inside, the gauzy purple curtains and the chandeliers provide the backdrop to Asian fusion specialities such as soft-shell crab with chilli-garlic marinade and lobster in XO sauce. Reservations are essential.

Lalibela (Map pp86-7; ☎ 683 83 32; Eerste Helmersstraat 249; mains €8-12.50; ☼ dinner) This was the Netherlands' first Ethiopian restaurant, and it's still a good 'un. Drink Ethiopian beer from a half-gourd and eat your stews, egg and vegetable dishes with *enjara*, a spongy pancake, instead of utensils. The music's unique, too.

Sama Sebo (Map pp92-3; ☎ 662 81 46; www .samasebo.com; Pieter Cornelisz Hooftstraat 27; rijsttafel per person €27, lunch specials per person €14.50; ☼ lunch & dinner Mon-Sat) Another reliable old-timer, this Indonesian restaurant's got the ambience of a brown café. It's also got a wicked rijsttafel comprising 17 dishes (four to seven at lunch); order individual plates if that's too much.

Waroeng Asje (Map pp92-3; ☎ 616 65 89; Jan Pieter Heijestraat 180; mains €5-12, rijsttafel €28; ☼ lunch Mon-Fri, dinner nightly) This counter-service shop serves rijsttafel, plus the *nasi rames* special (€9) – a heaped plate of roasted meats, on skewers or in spicy stews, with stir-fried or pickled vegetables, and a deep-fried hard-boiled egg.

De Pijp

Bazar Amsterdam (Map pp92-3; ☎ 675 05 44; www .bazaramsterdam.nl; Albert Cuypstraat 182; mains €8-14; ☼ breakfast, lunch & dinner) Like its Rotterdam counterpart (p215), Bazar Amsterdam is a genuine high-flyer. In a glorious former Dutch Reformed Church, the light-filled, Middle Eastern–style décor and tangy, tantalising North African cuisine – mixed grills, kebabs, felafels, pitas, tabouli, Turkish pizza – sees to that.

Mamouche (Map pp92-3; ☎ 673 63 61; Quellijnstraat 104; mains €14.50-22; ☼ dinner Tue-Sun) 'Sexy' is a word that tends to get bandied about when people talk about Mamouche. The case for: the seriously good modern Moroccan food – think couscous, lamb and fish – and the serious minimalism of the décor, all exposed flooring, mottled walls and beamed ceilings. Reservations are essential.

Puyck (Map pp86-7; ☎ 676 76 77; Ceintuurbaan 147; set menus from €38.50; ☼ dinner Mon-Sat) This unpretentious place offers imaginative, sophisticated international cooking such as baby lobster with lettuce, duck breast in Chinese five spice, or a white wine–poached pear, all served with flair. And how about that Thai curry sorbet – your mind is boggling, right?

Nieuw Albina (Map pp92-3; ☎ 379 02 23; Albert Cuypstraat 49; mains €4.50-11.50; ☼ lunch & dinner Wed-Mon) Nieuw Albina's Surinamese food is more polished than that at Albert Cuyp 67 (see below), but the flavours are just as bold. The *moksi meti* (roast mixed meats over rice) is incredible.

QUICK EATS

Albert Cuyp 67 (Map pp92-3; ☎ 671 13 96; Albert Cuypstraat 67; mains €3-9; ☼ lunch & dinner) Surinamese food, and colossal portions of *roti kip* (chicken curry, flaky roti bread, potatoes, egg and cabbage).

Bagels & Beans (Map pp92-3; www.bagelsbeans.nl; Ferdinand Bolstraat 70; bagels from €2.95) Tasty bagels, good coffee, wi-fi access. Also at Keizersgracht 504, Haarlemmerdijk 122, Van Baerlestraat 40, Kinkerstraat 110, Koningsplein 20, Waterlooplein 2, Raadhuisstraat 18 and Zeilstraat 64.

Ralph's Asian Wonderfood (Map pp92-3; ☎ 670 90 07; Eerste van der Helststraat 37; dishes €6-7; ☼ lunch & dinner) Excellent, fresh Asian-fusion menu.

Taart van m'n Tante (Map pp92-3; ☎ 776 46 00; Ferdinand Bolstraat 10; cakes per slice around €4;

10am-6pm) Very popular apple pies, pecan pies, and tarts with lush ingredients such as truffles and marzipan with strawberry liqueur. Savouries include the mozzarella-pesto quiche.

Turkiye (Map pp92-3; Ferdinand Bolstraat 48; mains €6.50-15.50; breakfast, lunch & dinner) Super Turkish food: grilled mains and small plates such as stuffed tomatoes and Turkish pizza (€1 to €3.50). Eat in or take away.

Zen (Map pp92-3; ☎ 627 06 07; Frans Halsstraat 38; mains €7-17; lunch & dinner Tue-Sat) Delicious Japanese food. Try the sushi or *donburi* (beef, chicken or salmon on rice). Takeaway available.

Eastern Islands

11 (Map pp86-7; ☎ 625 59 99; Oosterdokskade 3-5; lunch mains €4-8.50, 4-course menu €30; lunch & dinner) It's got the best views, on the top floor of the former post office tower. For lunch, tuck into sandwiches, pastas and focaccias, or try the changing four-course dinner menu. At night, 11 is variously a cultural centre with lectures on art and the like and a night club.

A Tavola (Map p95; 625 49 94; Kadijksplein 9; mains €12-21; dinner) This authentic Italian restaurant near the Scheepvaartmuseum serves mouth-wateringly tender meats and superb pastas that cry out for a selection from its excellent wine list. Reservations are a must.

Sea Palace (Map p95; ☎ 626 47 77; Oosterdokskade 8; mains €9.60-36, yum-cha courses €13.50-15; lunch & dinner) The three floors at this floating restaurant are always busy with Chinese and non-Chinese, who come not just for great views of the city but also for the super *yum cha*.

DRINKING
Medieval Centre

Lime (Map pp88-9; ☎ 639 30 20; Zeedijk 104) Lime is cool and hip but friendly and laid-back; you won't get the stink-eye in here. The décor comes on like a Stereolab album cover – all dots and loops and browns and oranges – and the cocktails are superb.

Hoppe (Map pp92-3; ☎ 420 44 20; Spuistraat 18-20) This gritty brown café has been luring drinkers for more than 300 years. It has one of Amsterdam's highest beer turnovers – some achievement in a city of hops freaks. In summer the energetic crowd spews from the dark interior out onto the Spui.

Pilsener Club (Map pp88-9; ☎ 623 17 77; Begijnensteeg 4) Also known as Engelse Reet (English Arse), this genuine brown café from 1893 is typical of the holes-in-the-wall around the Spui. Beer is served straight from the kegs via the 'short-

est pipes in Amsterdam' (most places have vats in a cellar or side room with long hoses to the bar) – our Man in the 'Dam says you can taste the difference.

Café de Jaren (Map pp92-3; ☎ 625 57 71; Nieuwe Doelenstraat 20) Watch the Amstel float by from the waterside terrace and balcony of this soaring, bright grand café. The great reading table has loads of foreign publications for whiling away hours over beers or the delectable light lunch of smoked-salmon rolls.

Café Cuba (Map pp88-9; ☎ 627 4919; Nieuwmarkt 3) This place maintains fidelity to Fidel, Che and '50s Cuba, with low lighting, indoor palms, faux faded elegance, rum posters, and cane chairs and tables. Try Papa Hemingway's favourite cocktail, the *caipirinha*, and the ubiquitous *mojito*. The outdoor seating is perched right on the Nieuwmarkt.

Absinthe (Map pp88-9; ☎ 320 6780; www.absinthe .nl; Nieuwezijds Voorburgwal 171) Devoted to the brain-lesioning liquor popularly reputed to have been the cause of Van Gogh's self-mutilation. There's multi-ethnic décor with rather awkward seating arrangements, and the staff can teach you all about their signature drink. You'll leave with your ears intact – it's not as potent as in the old days.

Luxembourg (Map pp92-3; ☎ 620 62 64) This café occupies the best people-watching spot on the Spui. Our advice: grab a newspaper from the reading table, nab a terrace seat in the sun and order the 'Royale' snack platter (bread, cured meats, Dutch cheese and deep-fried croquettes). Inside are parquet floors, a marble bar and an Art Deco stained-glass skylight.

De Drie Fleschjes (Map pp88-9; ☎ 624 84 43; Gravenstraat 18) Behind the Nieuwe Kerk, the distiller Bootz's tasting room dates from 1650. It specialises in liqueurs (although you can also get *jenevers*) – the macaroon one is a treat. Check out the collection of *kalkoentjes*, small bottles with hand-painted portraits of former mayors.

Suite (Map pp88-9; ☎ 344 64 06; www.suite.nu; Sint Nicolaasstraat 43) From the crew behind Supper Club, this sedate 'rest-o-bar' is a rambling suite of rooms: a salon, a lounge room, and a chilled space with embroidered sofas, hassocks and still lifes. Dishes are eclectic small plates, from rib eye in tomato sauce to Vietnamese spring rolls and watermelon soup.

Other options:

Bar Bep (Map pp88-9; ☎ 626 56 49; Nieuwezijds Voorburgwal 260) Olive-green vinyl couches and ruby-red walls – unashamedly kitsch.

AMSTERDAM

De Bekeerde Suster (Map pp88-9; ☎ 423 01 12; Kloveniersburgwal 6-8) The magic ingredients: brew tanks, beautiful hardwood interior, and history (this 16th-century brewery-cloister was once run by nuns).

Proeflokaal Fockink (Map pp88-9; ☎ 639 26 95; www.wynand-fockink.nl; Pijlsteeg 31) This small tasting house (dating from 1679) has scores of *jenevers* and liqueurs – some quite potent.

Jordaan & Western Islands

Café Nol (Map p91; ☎ 624 53 80; Westerstraat 109) Hipsters may cringe, but Café Nol epitomises the old-style Jordaan café with a must-see kitsch interior. It's the sort of place where old-school Jordaanese still sing oompah ballads with drunken abandon. Note: it doesn't open until 9pm.

De Twee Zwaantjes (The Two Swans; Map p91; ☎ 625 27 29; Prinsengracht 114) This small, authentic drinking house is at its hilarious best on weekend nights, when you can join some 100 people belting out torch songs and pop standards. Hours are erratic, so it's best to call first.

Café 't Smalle (Map p91; ☎ 623 96 17; Egelantiersgracht 12) Take your boat and dock right on the pretty terrace – you couldn't wish for a more convivial setting in the daytime or a more romantic one at night. It's equally charming inside – dating back to 1786 as a *jenever* distillery and tasting house, and restored during the 1970s with antique porcelain beer pumps and leadlight windows.

Other options:

Café de Sluyswacht (Map pp88-9; ☎ 625 76 11; Jodenbreestraat 1) Stoners beware: this tiny black building is built on foundations that lean dramatically.

Lokaal 't Loosje (Map pp88-9; ☎ 627 26 35; Nieuwmarkt 32-34) Beautiful etched-glass windows and tile tableaux; a venerable locale.

Western Canal Belt

Het Papeneiland (Papists' Island; Map pp88-9; ☎ 624 19 89; Prinsengracht 2) This popular 1642 gem of a place features Delft-blue tiles and a central stove. The name goes back to the Reformation, when there was a clandestine Catholic church across the canal, allegedly linked to the other side by a once-secret tunnel that's still visible from the top of the stairs.

Café de Vergulde Gaper (Golden Mortar Café; Map pp88-9; ☎ 624 89 75; Prinsenstraat 30) Decorated with old chemists' bottles and vintage posters, this former pharmacy has amiable staff and a terrace that catches the sun (when it chooses to appear). It gets busy late afternoons, with

---

TOP FIVE 'DESIGNER' BARS

- Café Cuba (p127)
- Lime (p127)
- Absinthe (p127)
- Suzy Wong (below)
- Suite (p127)

---

all kinds of people meeting for after-work drinks and big plates of fried snacks or dinner salads.

De Pieper (Map pp92-3; ☎ 626 47 75; Prinsengracht 424) Considered by many to be the king of the brown cafés, De Pieper is small, unassuming and unmistakably old (established 1665). The interior features stained-glass windows, fresh sand on the floors, antique Delft beer mugs hanging from the bar and a working Belgian beer pump (dating from 1875).

Other options:

Gollem (Map pp88-9; ☎ 626 66 45; Raamsteeg 4) Pioneer of Amsterdam 'beer cafés' with 200 brews on offer.

Van Puffelen (Map p91; ☎ 624 62 70; Prinsengracht 377) Popular café-restaurant; lots of nooks and crannies; big, communal.

Southern Canal Belt

Suzy Wong (Map pp92-3; ☎ 626 67 69; Korte Leidsedwarsstraat 45) This bar bustles with Dutch scenesters. It's like a retro-futurist Victorian drawing room, with red velveteen wallpaper and a bamboo garden; a photo of Andy Warhol observes. Fortify yourself here before heading over to Jimmy Woo's nightclub (opposite).

Café de Kroon (Map pp92-3; ☎ 625 20 11; www .dekroon.nl; Rembrandtplein 17) A popular venue, with its high ceilings, velvet chairs and the chance to wave at all the people below on the Rembrandtplein. Climb the two flights and be rewarded with an Art Deco tiled staircase.

Other options:

Eylders (Map pp92-3; ☎ 624 27 04; Korte Leidsedwarsstraat 47) Meeting place for dissident artists during WWII. Exhibits art.

Café Schiller (Map pp92-3; ☎ 624 98 46; Rembrandtplein 26) Has a stylish, Art Deco interior with portraits of Dutch actors and cabaret artists.

Café Américain (Map pp92-3; ☎ 556 32 32; Leidsekade 97) Arguably Amsterdam's most stylish grand café, located in the American Hotel. This Art Deco monument attracts rafts of celebrities to its forecourt tables just off Leidseplein or for a tête-à-tête in the fashionable Nightwatch bar.

Old South (Oud Zuid)

't Blauwe Theehuis (Map pp86-7; ☎ 662 02 54; Vondelpark 5) This functionalist teahouse from 1936 is a wonderful multilevel building serving coffee, cake and alcohol, with a great terrace and balcony.

De Pijp

Bar Ça (Map pp92-3; ☎ 470 41 44; Marie Heinekenplein 30-31) Maybe the hottest café in town, this 'Barcelona in Amsterdam' themed club has brought real life to the area. Take it easy in the posh plush-red and darkwood interior, or spread out onto the terrace.

Eastern Islands

Brouwerij 't IJ (Map pp86-7; ☎ 622 83 25; Funenkade 7) This small brewery produces six regular and several seasonal beers, which can be tasted in the comfortably grungy interior or on the terrace at the foot of the windmill. See p109 for more information.

ENTERTAINMENT

Amsterdam does 'entertainment' better than many cities four times its size: everything from live sex shows to cavernous clubs to intimate bars to smoking dens to cinema to theatre and more. See p80 for some useful websites, or pick up Wednesday's free *Amsterdam Weekly* for tips and tricks galore.

Nightclubs

Jimmy Woo (Map pp92-3; ☎ 626 3150; www.jimmywoo .nl; Korte Leidsedwarsstraat 18) With its uber-stylish, black-lacquered, Oriental décor, Jimmy Woo is as hip as the bony projection of a femur. Plus it has a big focus on hip hop and extracting cash from hip pockets. It's exclusive (no hippies allowed), so good luck getting in; try going with some locals.

Sinners in Heaven (Map pp92-3; ☎ 620 1375; www .sinners.nl; Wagenstraat 3-7) Along with Jimmy Woo, jet-set, celebrity-riddled Sinners heads the A-list of Amsterdam clubs. It serves up hip hop, funk, beats and breaks, and it's possibly harder than Woo to get into: there's always a 'guest list', and by all accounts the door bitch has quite the acid tongue. Try sleeping with a famous footballer for best results.

Winston International (Map pp88-9; ☎ 623 13 80; www.winston.nl; Warmoesstraat 125) Next to the Hotel Winston (p118), it has everything from electronica to spoken word to punk to graffiti art. On Sunday there's Club Vegas, where the

dress code is 'jet set' (sequins, suits, stilettos, bow ties, tiaras) and the music is lounge. Kooky fun.

To Night (Map pp86-7; ☎ 694 74 44; www.hotel arena.nl; 's-Gravesandestraat 51) At the Hotel Arena (p122), each night is different – everything from dance classics to salsa. It's worth a visit just for the magnificent interior; the chapel of this one-time orphanage has been given a solid redo, including the toilets.

Panama (Map pp86-7; ☎ 311 86 86; www.panama .nl; Oostelijke Handelskade 4) This complex has a salsa-tango dance salon, a restaurant and a glam nightclub that programmes Cuban big bands, Brazilian circus acts and a soulful selection of DJ talent.

Other options:

Escape (Map pp92-3; ☎ 622 11 11; www.escape .nl; Rembrandtplein 11) A fixture of Amsterdam nightlife since 1987, it's all lights and video screens, a venue for special parties.

11 (Map pp86-7; ☎ 625 59 99; www.ilove11.nl; Oosterdoksade 3-5) Right by the IJ and at the top of the old post-office building – the only club in town with 360-degree city views.

Exit (Map pp92-3; ☎ 625 87 88; Reguliersdwarsstraat 42) Multistorey nightclub with a selection of theme bars, dance floors and a busy darkroom.

Melkweg (Milky Way; Map pp92-3; ☎ 531 81 81; www .melkweg.nl; Lijnbaansgracht 234A)

Paradiso (Map pp92-3; ☎ 626 45 21; www.paradiso .nl; Weteringschans 6) See p131.

Coffeeshops

Siberië (Map pp88-9; ☎ 623 59 09; Brouwersgracht 111) With its lounge-room feel, canal views and ultra-casual atmosphere, this is an addictive place that draws smokers of all ages for the friendly staff, the wicked weed and the chance to play stoner chess with total strangers. 'Queen takes Bish…that castle thing. Ah, forget it. I resign.'

Barney's (Map pp88-9; ☎ 625 97 61; www.barneys .biz; Haarlemmerstraat 98 & 102) The very popular Barney's, with its trippy biomechanical décor, has beloved all-day breakfasts as well as quality smoke (100% organic).

La Tertulia (Map p91; Prinsengracht 312) A backpackers' favourite, this mother and daughter–run coffeeshop has a greenhouse feel. You can sit outside by the Van Gogh–inspired murals, play some board games or take in those Jurassic-sized crystals by the counter.

Abraxas (Map pp88-9; ☎ 626 57 63; Jonge Roelensteeg 12) Maybe the most beautiful coffeeshop in town. Choose from southwest USA, Middle Eastern and other styles of décor spread over three floors. There are live DJs, extra-friendly staff and Internet usage with a drink purchase.

Grey Area (Map pp88-9; ☎ 420 43 01; www.greyarea.nl; Oude Leliestraat 2) Owned by a couple of laid-back American dudes, this tiny shop introduced the extra-sticky, flavourful 'Double Bubble Gum' weed to the city. The relaxed staff will advise on the lengthy menu.

Other options:

Bulldog (Map pp92-3; ☎ 627 19 08; www.bulldog.nl; Leidseplein 13-17) Amsterdam's most famous coffee-shop chain, with five branches around town.

Greenhouse (Map pp88-9; ☎ 627 17 39; www.greenhouse.org; Oudezijds Voorburgwal 191) Undersea mosaics; psychedelic stained-glass windows; high-quality weed and hash.

Homegrown Fantasy (Map pp88-9; ☎ 627 56 83; Nieuwezijds Voorburgwal 87A) Pleasant staff, hydroponic weed, good tunes, 3m-long glass bongs.

Cinemas

Cinecenter (Map pp92-3; ☎ 623 66 15; Lijnbaansgracht 236) Euro and American art-house fare; last Monday of the month devoted to queer films. The hip bar has white padding.

De Uitkijk (Map pp92-3; ☎ 623 74 60; www.uitkijk.nl; Prinsengracht 452) Amsterdam's oldest surviving cinema (1913), in an old canal house, attracting cineastes who know their Fuller from their Fellini.

Nederlands Filmmuseum (Map pp92-3; ☎ 589 14 00; www.filmmuseum.nl; Vondelpark 3) The esteemed Filmmuseum's programme appeals to a broad audience: shlock-horror, cutting-edge foreign films, docos, Bollywood musicals.

Het Ketelhuis (Map pp86-7; ☎ 684 00 90; www.ketelhuis.nl; Westergasfabriek, Haarlemmerweg 8-10) In the old gas works, an atmospheric platform for art-house films.

Kriterion (Map p95; ☎ 623 17 08; www.kriterion.nl; Roeterstraat 170) Premieres, theme parties, cult movies, classics, kids' flicks and sneaks – all in a former diamond factory.

Movies (Map pp86-7; ☎ 638 60 16; www.themovies.nl; Haarlemmerdijk 161) Arty films, indie US and UK movies, and big studio releases in a beautiful Art Deco cinema.

Tuschinskitheater (Map pp92-3; ☎ 623 15 10; www.pathe.nl/tuschinski; Reguliersbreestraat 26-34) Extensively refurbished, the theatre is a monument to sumptuous Art Deco/Amsterdam School interiors. It screens mainstream blockbusters.

Rialto Cinema (Map pp86-7; ☎ 676 87 00; www.rialtofilm.nl; Ceintuurbaan 338) Great old cinema concentrating on premieres and art-house fare from around the globe.

Live Music
CLASSICAL & CONTEMPORARY

Concertgebouw (Concert Building; Map pp92-3; ☎ 671 83 45; www.concertgebouw.nl; Concertgebouwplein 2-6; ☺ box office 10am-5pm) Each year, this neo-Renaissance centre presents around 650 concerts attracting 840,000 visitors, making it the world's busiest concert hall (with reputedly the best acoustics). Classical musos consider the Concertgebouw a very prestigious gig indeed, as do some rock bands with classical pretensions (such as King Crimson). The venue holds free 'lunch concerts' on Wednesday at 12.30pm between September and June.

Beurs van Berlage (Map pp88-9; ☎ 627 04 66; Damrak 243) This former commodities exchange houses two small concert halls with comfortable seats but underwhelming acoustics. Resident companies, the Netherlands Chamber Orchestra and the Netherlands Philharmonic, play a varied menu of Mozart, Beethoven, Bach, Mahler and Wagner. The building itself is famous for its architecture.

Muziekgebouw aan 't IJ (Map pp86-7; ☎ 788 20 00; www.muziekgebouw.nl; Piet Heinkade 1; ☺ box office noon-7pm Mon-Sat) The Muziekgebouw is home to the long-standing music venues the IJsbreker (which changed its name to that of the new building) and the jazz house Bimhuis (below). The outside may be curiously clad in glass, but the core attraction is the concert halls; the Muziekgebouw has 735 seats, simple maple-slat walls, a flexible stage layout and great acoustics.

Other options:

Bethaniënklooster (Map pp88-9; ☎ 625 00 78; www.bethanienklooster.nl; Barndesteeg 6B) Small former monastery near Nieuwmarkt with a glorious ballroom, perfect for some Stravinsky or Indian sitar.

Conservatorium van Amsterdam (Map pp92-3; ☎ 527 75 50; www.cva.ahk.nl; Van Baerlestraat 27) Students at the Netherlands' largest conservatory of music offer recitals.

Muziektheater (Map pp92-3; ☎ 625 54 55; Waterlooplein 22; ☺ ticket office 10am-6pm Mon-Sat, 11.30am-6pm Sun) Large-scale ballet and opera. Free lunchtime concerts of 20th-century music on Tuesday.

JAZZ & BLUES
Bimhuis (Map pp86-7; ☎ 788 21 50; www.bimhuis.nl; Piet Heinkade 3) Amsterdam's main jazz venue for years, now in stylish new digs in the

Muziekgebouw aan 't IJ (opposite). The venue attracts Dutch and international jazz greats and offers workshops. The intimate auditorium has huge windows giving a view over the city, and a spiffy bar.

Casablanca (Map pp88-9; ☎ 625 56 85; www.casablanca-amsterdam.nl; Zeedijk 26) This jazz café has an illustrious history. Even if its glory days are over, it still books big bands four nights a week and other kinds of jazz the rest of the time. Wednesday to Saturday sees singing and dancing, including karaoke.

Bourbon Street Jazz & Blues Club (Map pp92-3; ☎ 623 34 40; www.bourbonstreet.nl; Leidsekruisstraat 6-8) Catch blues, funk, soul and rock-and-roll performances in this intimate venue filled with local and international performers (Sting's been here, if that kind of thing floats your boat). There are weekly jam sessions and unplugged nights.

Jazz Café Alto (Map pp92-3; ☎ 626 32 49; www.jazz-café-alto.nl; Korte Leidsedwarsstraat 115) A slightly older crowd of jazz lovers toe taps to serious jazz and blues at this small brown café; try to catch tenor saxophonist Hans Dulfer and band.

Maloe Melo (Map p91; ☎ 420 45 92; www.maloemelo.com; Lijnbaansgracht 163) This small venue is home to the city's blues scene, with local and international musicians playing everything from Cajun zydeco and swing to Texas blues and rockabilly.

Other options:

Brasil Music Bar (Map pp92-3; ☎ 626 15 00; www.brasilmusicbar.com; Lange Leidsedwarsstraat 68-70) Live Brazilian and Caribbean music three nights a week, R&B and Brazilian DJs at other times. Hot and steamy.

Cotton Club (Map pp88-9; ☎ 626 61 92; Nieuwmarkt 5) Dark, bustling brown café with live, vibrant jazz every Saturday (5pm to 8pm), plus salsa on Tuesday.

Meander (Map pp92-3; ☎ 625 84 30; www.café meander.nl; Voetboogstraat 3) Live bands often followed up by DJs spinning funk, garage, soul and jazzy beats.

ROCK & POP

Paradiso (Map pp92-3; ☎ 626 45 21; www.paradiso.nl; Weteringschans 6) This large former church has been the city's premier rock venue since the 1960s. Big-name acts like Bright Eyes, Jurassic 5, Wilco and Lucinda have all appeared recently, and its regular dance evenings like Paradisoo and Paradisoul are legendary.

Melkweg (Map pp92-3; Milky Way; ☎ 531 81 81; www.melkweg.nl; Lijnbaansgracht 234A) This former milk factory off Leidseplein has been a top

cultural venue since the 1970s. It's an all-in-one entertainment complex with a café, a multimedia centre and top live music almost every night (everything from Afro-Celtic to thrash), plus nightclubs, a cinema, lounges and art galleries.

Other options (all except Korsakoff are well south of town):

Amsterdam ArenA (☎ 311 13 33; Arena Blvd 11, Bijlmermeer) Stadium rock! Seats 52,000 for mega-acts like the Stones and 'Superman' himself, Mr Jon Bon Jovi.

Heineken Music Hall (☎ 09006874242; Arena Blvd 590, Bijlmermeer) Draws a steady stream of international acts with its high-class acoustics and light shows.

Korsakoff (Map p91; ☎ 625 78 54; www.korsakof famsterdam.nl; Lijnbaansgracht 161) Still grungy after all these years, with lashings of punk, metal and Goth acts.

Pepsi Stage (☎ 09007377478; www.pepsistage.nl; Arena Blvd 584, Bijlmermeer) This 1600-capacity hall stages midleague acts such as Elvis Costello and the Gipsy Kings.

Theatre & Comedy

Stadsschouwburg (Map pp92-3; ☎ 624 23 11; www.stadsschouwburgamsterdam.nl; Leidseplein 26) Amsterdam's most beautiful theatre was built in 1894 and refurbished in the 1990s. It features large-scale productions, operettas, dance and summer English-language productions and performances. Most major festivals also seem to have a presence here.

Amsterdams Marionetten Theater (Map pp88-9; ☎ 620 80 27; www.marionet.demon.nl; Nieuwe Jonkerstraat 8; adult/child from €12/6) In a former blacksmith's shop, this charming, intimate theatre features marionettes performing elaborate productions such as *The Magic Flute*. The skill of the puppeteers is something to see. Call or check the website for show times.

Nachttheater Sugar Factory (Map pp92-3; ☎ 626 5006; www.sugarfactory.nl; Lijnbaansgracht 238) This 'night theatre' showcases theatre, spoken word, exhibitions, poetry readings and live music, after which the space clears and it becomes a bangin' nightclub.

Koninklijk Theater Carré (Map p95; ☎ 09002525255; www.theatercarre.nl; Amstel 115-125) The largest theatre in town offers mainstream international shows, musicals, cabaret, opera, operetta, ballet and circuses. Backstage tours (€8/4 adult/child) are at 11am on Saturday and are also available by reservation; call ☎ 524 94 52.

De Balie (Map pp92-3; ☎ 553 51 51; Kleine Gartmanplantsoen 10) International productions spotlighting multicultural and political issues are the focus here. De Balie also holds short-film festivals and political debates and has new-media facilities and a stylish bar.

Boom Chicago (Map pp92-3; ☎ 423 01 01; www .boomchicago.nl; Leidseplein 12) Now an institution of sorts, Boom Chicago performs English-language stand-up and improvised comedy all year round. You can see shows over dinner and a few drinks – the food here's decent.

Comedy Café Amsterdam (Map pp92-3; ☎ 638 39 71; www.comedycafé.nl; Max Euweplein 43-45) While Boom Chicago is improv, the Comedy Café books in Dutch and international stand-up comics (Sunday is regularly reserved for English-speaking acts).

Other options:

De Kleine Komedie (Map pp92-3; ☎ 624 05 34; www .dekleinekomedie.nl; Amstel 56-58) This internationally renowned theatre, founded in 1786, focuses on concerts, dance, comedy and cabaret, sometimes in English.

Felix Meritis (Map p91; ☎ 623 13 11; www.felix .meritis.nl; Keizersgracht 324) A hub of experimental theatre, music and dance, with a bevy of coproductions between Eastern and Western European artists.

Openluchttheater (Open-Air Theatre; Map pp92-3; ☎ 673 14 99; www.openluchttheater.nl; Vondelpark) From June to August the park's intimate theatre hosts free concerts, from classical to hip – world music, dance and children's performances.

Sport

FOOTBALL

Local club Ajax is the Netherlands' most famous team: they've won the European Cup four times and they launched Johan Cruyff to stellar heights in the '70s. The red-and-white stormers play in the **Amsterdam ArenA** (☎ 311 13 33; Arena Blvd 11, Bijlmermeer) south of town. Matches usually take place on Saturday evening and Sunday afternoon during the season (August to May). The ArenA conducts a one-hour guided **stadium tour** (☎ 311 13 36; adult/child €10/8.50; ☺ 11am-4.30pm daily Apr-Sep, noon-4pm Mon-Sat Oct-Mar, except on game days or during major events) that includes a walk on the hallowed turf and entry to the Ajax museum.

KORFBAL

A cross between netball, volleyball and basketball, this sport elicits giggles from foreigners, but it has a lively local club scene. For information, contact the **Amsterdam Sport Council** (☎ 552 24 90), who can also provide information on other sports in town.

BRILLIANT ORANGE

Here's one of the hottest tips in these pages: if you want the best, the funniest, the most insightful analysis of what makes Amsterdam tick, then read *Brilliant Orange: The Neurotic Genius of Dutch Football* by David Winner, a book about…football. But you don't have to especially like the sport to appreciate *Brilliant Orange*, for Winner's skill lies in setting up a history of modern-day Dutch football as a mirror – as in fact the driving force – of modern-day Dutch society and the Amsterdam we know and love today.

You'll be a believer when you read Winner describe, with humour and intelligence, how the Netherlands' obsession with orderly yet beautiful landscapes, sophisticated built space and innovative architecture is reflected in the fabulously free-flowing yet super-organised Dutch aesthetic of Total Football. According to Winner, this aesthetic was embodied in the great Ajax of Amsterdam side from the 1970s led by talismanic footballer Johan Cruyff, with an entire counterculture, reaching far beyond the game, finding inspiration in Cruyff's progressive attitude, intelligence, rebellion and prophecy.

Dutch football, like Dutch architecture, Dutch art, Dutch tolerance and even Dutch politics, is a trick of perspective: it's all about creating space, or even the illusion of space, out of absolutely nothing. As Winner adroitly demonstrates, nowhere is this more apparent than in 'Magic Centre Amsterdam' itself.

There are numerous illuminating insights, including Ajax's self-image as a de facto 'Jewish' side, and how this compares to Jews in WWII Amsterdam. Winner also dissects the very Dutch footballing tendency to stumble at the final hurdle, usually manifested in losing big-match finals due to too much showing off and arrogance, and he links this to the lingering, stifling influence of Dutch Calvinism.

It's a spectacular book.

SHOPPING

During the 17th century, Amsterdam was the warehouse of the world, stuffed with riches from neighbours and far-off colonies. But even if the Dutch empire has since crumbled, its capital remains a shopper's paradise.

The Damrak and the area around Leidseplein teem with tourist shops, while the busiest shopping streets are the down- to mid-market Nieuwendijk and the more upscale Kalverstraat and Leidsestraat, with department stores and clothing boutiques serving large crowds, especially on Saturday and Sunday. Expensive shops line Pieter Cornelisz Hooftstraat, and there are chic boutiques and cafés in the Negen Straatjes (Nine Alleys) of the western canal belt. Antique and art outlets can be found in the Spiegel Quarter in the southern canal belt, and the Jordaan is full of galleries and quirky shops.

Art & Antiques

Decorativa (Map pp92-3; ☎ 420 50 66; Nieuwe Spiegelstraat 7) Amazing jumble of European antiques, collectables and weird vintage gifts.

EH Ariëns Kappers (Map pp92-3; ☎ 623 53 56; Nieuwe Spiegelstraat 32) Original prints, etchings, engravings, lithographs, 17th- to 19th-century maps, Japanese woodblock prints.

Jaski (Map pp92-3; ☎ 620 39 39; Nieuwe Spiegelstraat 27-29) Large commercial gallery selling paintings, prints, ceramics and sculptures by famous CoBrA artists.

Prestige Art Gallery (Map pp92-3; ☎ 624 01 04; www.prestige-art-amsterdam.com; Reguliersbreestraat 46) Specialises in 17th- to 20th-century oil paintings and bronzes.

Books

For a list of bookshops, see p80 and p104; for book markets, see p134.

Boutiques

Analik (Map p91; ☎ 422 05 61; Hartenstraat 34-36) Amsterdam's pre-eminent fashion designer; stylish, very feminine pieces.

Cora Kemperman (Map pp92-3; ☎ 625 12 84; Leidsestraat 72) Successful Dutch designer specialising in floaty, layered separates and dresses in linen, cotton and wool.

Laundry Industry (Map pp92-3; ☎ 420 25 54; Spui 1) Well-cut, well-designed clothes by leading Dutch design house; soft leather coats, perfectly fitted suits. There's another branch at Magna Plaza (p96).

Razzmatazz (Map p91; ☎ 420 04 83; Wolvenstraat 19) Flamboyant, expensive designer outfits and avant-garde club clothes from labels including Vivienne Westwood, Frankie Morello and Andrew Mackenzie.

Van Ravenstein (Map pp92-3; ☎ 639 00 67; Keizersgracht 359) Upmarket Dutch and Belgian designers such as Dries Van Noten, Ann Demeulemeester, Dirk Bikkembergs, Martin Margiela and Viktor & Rolf.

Department Stores

Try the **Kalvertoren shopping centre** (Map p91; Singel 457) and Magna Plaza (p96) for upmarket fashion, gift and jewellery shops.

De Bijenkorf (Map pp88-9; ☎ 621 80 80; Dam 1) The city's most fashionable department store; quality clothing, toys, household accessories and books.

Hema (Map pp88-9; ☎ 638 99 63; Nieuwendijk 174) Once a Woolworths clone, now has wide-ranging stock including good-value wines and deli foods.

Maison de Bonneterie (Map pp92-3; ☎ 531 34 00; Rokin 140) Exclusive and classic lines of garments for the whole family. Features men's labels such as Ralph Lauren, Tommy Hilfiger and Armani, but lots for women too.

Metz & Co (Map pp92-3; ☎ 520 70 36; Keizersgracht 455) Boutique store with a fine line in luxury furnishings and homewares, upmarket designer clothes, and gifts.

Vroom & Dreesmann (Map pp92-3; ☎ 622 01 71; Kalverstraat 201) Popular for its clothing and cosmetics, but don't expect great flights of fantasy.

PAYMENTS ARE FOREVER

Amsterdam has been a major diamond centre since the 16th century, and about a dozen diamond-cutters still operate in the city today. Of the five offering free guided tours, Gassan Diamonds is probably the best. Caution is advised, for that glint in your eye could lead to a lengthy series of monthly instalments.

Amsterdam Diamond Center (Map pp88-9; ☎ 624 57 87; Rokin 1; 🕙 10.30am-6pm Mon-Wed & Fri-Sun, to 8.30pm Thu)

Coster Diamonds (Map pp92-3; ☎ 305 55 55; Paulus Potterstraat 2-6; 🕙 9am-5pm)

Gassan Diamonds (Map p95; ☎ 622 53 33; Nieuwe Uilenburgerstraat 173-175; 🕙 9am-5pm)

Stoeltie Diamonds (Map pp92-3; ☎ 623 76 01; Wagenstraat 13-17; 🕙 8.30am-5pm)

Van Moppes & Zoon (Map pp92-3; ☎ 676 12 42; Albert Cuypstraat 2-6; 🕙 9am-5pm)

AMSTERDAM MARKETS

Markets mean crowds: beware of pickpockets.

Albert Cuypmarkt (Map pp92-3; Albert Cuypstraat; 🕑 9am-5pm Mon-Sat) General market with food, clothing, hardware and household goods at rock-bottom prices. Wide multicultural mix of wares, vendors and clientele.

Antiques market Amstelveld (Map pp92-3; 🕑 9am-6pm last Fri of month in warmer months); Nieuwmarkt (Map pp88-9; 🕑 9am-5pm Sun May-Sep) You can peruse many genuine articles and loads of books and bric-a-brac. There's also the De Looier antiques market (below).

Bloemenmarkt (Map pp92-3; Singel; 🕑 9am-5pm, closed Sun winter) 'Floating' flower market that's actually on pilings. Traders can advise on import regulations. The market is notorious for pickpockets.

Boerenmarkt (farmers' market) Nieuwmarkt (Map pp88-9; 🕑 10am-3pm Sat); Noordermarkt (Map pp88-9; 🕑 10am-3pm Sat) Home-grown produce, organic foods and picnic provisions.

Book market Oudemanhuispoort (Map pp88-9; 🕑 11am-4pm Mon-Fri); Spui (Map pp92-3; 🕑 8am-6pm Fri) Oudemanhuispoort, the old arcade between Oudezijds Achterburgwal and Kloveniersburgwal (blink and you'll miss it), is the location of a market selling rare and old books plus newer books and art prints. The Spui also hosts a book market one day a week.

De Looier antiques market (Map pp92-3; ☎ 624 90 38; Elandsgracht 109; 🕑 11am-5pm Sat-Thu) Indoor stalls selling jewellery, furniture, art and collectibles.

Lindengracht market (Lindengracht; 🕑 11am-4pm Sat) General market.

Noordermarkt (Map pp88-9; Noorderkerkstraat; 🕑 9am-1pm Mon, 10am-3pm Sat) Antiques, fabrics and secondhand bric-a-brac.

Plant market (Map pp92-3; Amstelveld; 🕑 3-6pm Mon Easter-Christmas) All sorts of plants, pots and vases.

Stamp & coin market (Map pp88-9; Nieuwezijds Voorburgwal 276; 🕑 10am-4pm Wed & Sat) Little streetside market selling stamps, coins and medals.

Waterlooplein flea market (Map pp92-3; Waterlooplein; 🕑 9am-5pm Mon-Fri, 8.30am-5.30pm Sat) Amsterdam's most famous flea market – curios, secondhand clothing, music, electronic gear, hardware, cheap New Age gifts.

Westermarkt (Map p91; Westerstraat; 🕑 9am-1pm Mon) Cheapish clothes and textiles; some real bargains.

Smart Drugs

Remember that taking drugs out of the country is illegal.

Chills & Thrills (Map pp88-9; ☎ 638 00 15; Nieuwendijk 17) Herbal trips, mushrooms, psychoactive cacti, novelty bongs and life-sized alien sculptures. Packed with tourists.

Innerspace (Map pp88-9; ☎ 624 33 38; Spuistraat 108) Known for good service and information, this large shop started as a supplier to large parties.

Magic Mushroom Gallery (Map pp88-9; ☎ 427 57 65; Spuistraat 249) Fresh and dried shrooms, growing kits, herbal ecstasy and smart drinks.

Speciality Shops

Art Multiples (Map pp92-3; ☎ 624 84 19; Keizersgracht 510) Thousands of postcards on unusual topics, including raunchy 3D ones (popular), plus beautiful art posters and museum-shop gifts.

Condomerie het Gulden Vlies (Map pp88-9; ☎ 627 41 74; www.condomerie.nl; Warmoesstraat 141) Hundreds of kooky condoms plus lubricants and saucy gifts.

Droog Design (Map pp92-3; ☎ 523 50 59; www .droogdesign.nl; Staalstraat 7B; 🕑 noon-6pm Tue-Sun) Leading design firm with inventions such as the 85-lamp chandelier, the cow chair and curtains with dress patterns.

Fair Trade Shop (Map pp92-3; ☎ 625 22 45; Heiligeweg 45) Charity shop with quality, stylish goods from developing countries: clothes, gifts, CDs and ceramics. The shop works directly with producers and provides ongoing business training.

Himalaya (Map pp88-9; ☎ 626 08 99; Warmoesstraat 56) A peaceful New Age oasis in the middle of the Red Light District, this is the place to stock up on crystals, ambient CDs and books on the healing arts. More good karma is available in the tea room.

Marañon Hangmatten (Map pp92-3; ☎ 420 71 21; Singel 488) Europe's largest selection of hammocks, made by many producers from indigenous weavers to large manufacturers.

Santa Jet (Map pp88-9; ☎ 427 20 70; Prinsenstraat 7) Mexican shrines, religious icons, *Day of the Dead* paraphernalia, candles and love potions.

Traditional Souvenirs

Galleria d'Arte Rinascimento (Map p91; ☎ 622 75 09; Prinsengracht 170) Royal Delftware, vases, platters, brooches, Christmas ornaments, 19th-century wall tiles and plaques.

Heinen (Map pp92-3; ☎ 627 82 99; Prinsengracht 440) Four floors of Delftware; all the major factories are represented and all budgets are catered for (the 17th-century tulip vases cost thousands).

De Klompenboer (Map pp88-9; ☎ 623 06 32; St Antoniesbreestraat 51) Bruno, the eccentric owner, gets his mum to hand-paint all the wooden shoes. The shop displays samples of miniature wooden shoes and a 700-year-old pair.

GETTING THERE & AWAY

Amsterdam is well connected to the rest of the world. If you're looking for cheap deals, advice or shared rides, you're in the right place.

Air

Most major airlines fly directly to **Schiphol** (Map pp86-7; ☎ 09000141; www.schiphol.nl), 18km south-west of the city centre. For information about getting to and from the Netherlands, including Amsterdam airline offices, see p298.

Boat

Fast Flying Ferries (☎ 639 22 47; adult/child return €7.45/4.35) runs a hydrofoil from pier 7 behind Amsterdam Centraal Station (hourly on the hour, half-hourly during peak times). The 25-minute trip drops you in Velsen, 3km short of IJmuiden, where you can catch Connexxion bus 82 or 83 into IJmuiden. For travellers to the UK and beyond, Scandinavian Seaways sails from IJmuiden to Newcastle (see p303).

Bus

For details of regional buses in the Netherlands, call the **transport information service** (☎ 09009292, per min €0.50). Fares and travel durations are covered under towns in the regional chapters.

Amsterdam has good long-distance bus links with the rest of Europe and North Africa.

Eurolines (Map pp88-9; ☎ 560 87 87; www.eurolines.nl; Rokin 10) tickets can be bought at its office near the Dam, at most travel agencies and at NS Reisburo (Netherlands Railways Travel Bureau) in Centraal Station. Fares are consistently lower than those for the train, and departures are from the **bus station** (☎ 694 56 31) next to Amstelstation.

Busabout (www.busabout.com) tickets can bought through the company's London office – in the UK, call ☎ 020-7950 1661 – or on the coaches themselves. Coaches stop at the Hans Brinker Budget Hotel (p120) on Kerkstraat, smack in the middle of the city.

For further details of Eurolines, Busabout and other coach services, see p301.

Car & Motorcycle

Motorways link Amsterdam to Den Haag and Rotterdam in the south, and to Utrecht and Amersfoort in the southeast. Amsterdam is about 480km from Paris, 840km from Munich, 680km from Berlin and 730km from Copenhagen. The Hoek van Holland ferry port is 80km away; IJmuiden is just up the road along the Noordzeekanaal.

The Dutch automobile association, **ANWB** (Map pp92-3; ☎ 673 08 44; Museumplein 5), provides information and services if you prove membership of your own association.

Train

Amsterdam's main train station is Centraal Station. See p302 for information about international trains.

Destination	Price (€)	Duration (min)	Frequency (per hr)
Den Haag	9.50	50	4
Groningen	26.70	140	2
Haarlem	3.80	15	8
Maastricht	26.70	155	2
Rotterdam	11.20	62	4
Schiphol Airport	3.60	20	6
Utrecht	6.30	35	5

GETTING AROUND
To/From the Airport

A taxi into Amsterdam from Schiphol Airport takes 20 to 45 minutes and costs about €40. Trains to Centraal Station leave every 15 minutes, take 15 to 20 minutes, and cost €3.60/6.20 per single/return. Train-ticket counters are in the central court of Schiphol Plaza; buy your ticket before taking the escalator down to the platforms. Buy a *strippenkaart* here while you're at it (see the boxed text, p307).

Another way to the airport is by **Schiphol Travel Taxi** (☎ 09008876; www.schiphol.nl). This minivan service takes up to eight people from anywhere in the country to the departure terminal, provided you book a day ahead. From central Amsterdam the fare is fixed at €22 per person, one way.

By car, take the A4 freeway to/from the A10 ring road around Amsterdam. A short stretch of A9 connects to the A4 close to Schiphol. The car-hire offices at the airport are in the right corner of the complex, near the central exits of Schiphol Plaza.

PARKING

The airport's short-term parking garages charge €1.90 per half-hour for the first three hours, then €2.70 per hour. The charge is €24 a day for the first three days, €12.50 a day thereafter. The long-term parking area charges a minimum €50 for up to three days and €5 for each day thereafter – a reasonable alternative to parking in the city (see also right).

Bicycle

Amsterdam is an urban cyclist's dream: flat, beautiful and crammed full of dedicated bike paths. Local cyclists have a liberal interpretation of traffic rules, but almost everyone catches on quick. About 80,000 bicycles are stolen each year in Amsterdam alone – it's no surprise that many bikes carry locks worth more than the thing itself.

The Dutch automobile association, **ANWB** (Map pp92-3; ☎ 673 08 44; Museumplein 5), provides cycling maps and information. For details on bicycling laws, tours and more, see p69.

HIRE

Prices listed below are for standard coaster-brake bikes; models with gears cost a bit more. There's also the *bakfiets* (a carrier tricycle that looks like an ice cream vendor's), which is perfect for carting around kids (or drinking buddies). All companies listed here require a passport or ID and a credit-card imprint or cash deposit.

Bike City (Map p91; ☎ 626 37 21; www.bikecity.nl; Bloemgracht 68-70; per day/week €8.50/41) No advertising on the bikes, so you blend in better with the locals.

Holland Rent-a-Bike (Map pp88-9; ☎ 622 32 07; Damrak 247; per day/week €6.50/34.50)

MacBike (www.macbike.nl; per day/week €8.50/29.75); Centraal Station (Map pp88-9; ☎ 624 83 91); Mr Visserplein (Map p95; ☎ 620 09 85; Mr Visserplein 2); Weteringschans (Map pp92-3; ☎ 528 76 88; Weteringschans 2) Bikes come complete with an absolutely ENORMOUS logo. You *will* stand out.

Mike's Bike Tours (Map pp92-3; ☎ 622 79 70; www .mikesbiketours.com; Kerkstraat 134; per half day/full day/additional day €5/7/5)

Boat

FERRIES

There are free ferries from behind Centraal Station to destinations around the IJ, notably Amsterdam Noord (Map pp88–9). Ferries to the eastern docklands cost €1.

CANAL BOAT, BUS & BIKE

The **Canal Bus** (Map pp92-3; ☎ 623 98 86; www .canalbus.nl; day pass per adult/under 13yr €17/11) does several circuits, beginning at its stop near Centraal Station (Map pp88–9) and ending at the Rijksmuseum, between 9.50am and 8pm. The day pass is valid until noon the next day. The same company rents canal bikes (pedal boats) for €9 per person per hour (€7 if more than two people per canal bike). Docks are by Leidseplein and near the Anne Frank Huis.

Every 30 or 45 minutes the **Lovers Museum Boat** (Map pp88-9; ☎ 622 21 81; www.lovers.nl; day pass from €8.50) leaves from the Lovers terminal in front of Centraal Station. There are discounts after 1pm.

Car & Motorcycle

Honestly – why on earth would you drive around Amsterdam when you can either bike it or take advantage of the superb public-transport system? Added to that, parking is far from cheap and there are dire penalties for nonconformists: a wheel clamp and a €91 fine.

Try the **Transferium parking garage** (☎ 400 17 21) at Amsterdam ArenA stadium. Parking costs €5.50 per day including two return metro tickets to the city centre.

Public Transport

When the masses need to move, Amsterdam's public transport – tram, *sneltram* (fast tram), bus and metro – gets them there with startling efficiently. Most tram and bus lines, as well as the metro, converge at Centraal Station.

Amsterdam transport authority **GVB** (Map pp88-9; ☎ 09008011; www.gvb.nl; Stationsplein 10; ⏰ 7am-9pm Mon-Fri, 8am-9pm Sat & Sun) has an information office across the tram tracks from Centraal Station's main entrance. Here you can get tickets, maps and the like. The website has lots of useful information, including details of how to reach key sights.

TICKETS & PASSES

The best deal is the *strippenkaart*: a multifare 'strip ticket' that's valid on all buses, trams and metro routes (see the boxed text, p307).

Taxi

Amsterdam taxis are expensive, even over short journeys. Try **Taxicentrale Amsterdam** (☎ 677 77 77).

Cliché Corner

CHRIS MELLOR

Windmills (p219) near Alkmaar, Noord Holland

Clogs (p34), Amsterdam

RICHARD NEBESKY

Tulip fields near Lisse (p195), Zuid Holland

IZZET KERRIBAR

Gezellig & Festive

Bar, Muziekgebouw aan 't IJ
(p130), Amsterdam

Supporter of the Dutch national football team (p35)

Paradiso nightclub (p131), Amsterdam

Orange Day revellers (p117), Amsterdam

MARTIN MOOS

Café de Sluyswacht (p128), Amsterdam

MARTIN MOOS

Siberië coffeeshop (p129), Amsterdam

MARTIN MOOS

Urban Junky

Steigenberger Kurhaus Hotel (p200), Den Haag,
Zuid Holland

ZAW MIN YU

LEANNE LOGAN

Gaz Union office building,
Groningen City (p245), Groningen

Sightseeing boats (p115) on the Amstel, Amsterdam

FRANS L

AMERENS HEDWICH

Grote of Lebuïnuskerk (p258) and canalside buildings, Deventer, Overijssel

CAROL ANN WILEY

Euromast (p209), Rotterdam, Zuid Holland

Hofje van Staats (p149), Haarlem, Noord Holland

CAROL ANN WILEY

Under a Big Dutch Sky

Holidaymakers, Zandvoort (p152), Noord Holland

Tulip fields and farmhouses near Alkmaar (p159), Noord Holland

Skaters, Kinderdijk (p219), Zuid Holland

FRANS LEMMENS

Cyclist on the frozen Zaan river, Zaanse Schans (p154), Noord Holland

Half-timbered house, Limburg (p278)

JOHN ELK III

Wadlopers (mud-walkers; p251), Friesland

FRANS LEMMENS

Art & the Masters

MARTIN MOOS

Display of Dutch Resistance photographs,
Verzetsmuseum (p108), Amsterdam

Bonnefantenmuseum (p278), Maastricht, Limburg

FRANS LEMMENS

Sign for modern section, Van Gogh Museum (p106), Amsterdam

RICHARD NE

Noord Holland & Flevoland

In this part of the world, there's no denying that Amsterdam rules the roost. But (literally) just outside its borders lies a bountiful region of bucolic sedation sprinkled with heart-warming towns and comely villages that *must* not be overlooked by visitors.

Only 15 minutes west of the capital, graceful Haarlem is Noord Holland's crowning glory, a town of immense charm and 17th-century grandeur. Its pubs are some of the cosiest in the country, and its museums among the most inviting. On its western outskirts are the wide, sandy beaches of Zandvoort and Bloemendaal, and the varied and evocative dunescape of the Kennemerduinen nature reserve.

Moving north, the Gouwzee Bay towns of Edam, Volendam and Marken hold special places in Dutch culture for cheese, traditional customs and defiance of the sea. Easily visited as day trips from Amsterdam, the towns may tempt you to linger overnight to soak up their peaceful ambience once the bus loads have dispersed. Monnickendam, in the heart of the rural Waterland region, is less frequented but has a treasury of 17th-century architecture. Not far north again, the Golden Age ports of Hoorn and Enkhuizen have engaging old centres; the latter is also home to the Zuiderzeemuseum, an open-air extravaganza that is the last remnant of life on the Zuiderzee before the intervention of the Afsluitdijk.

On the way to the Waddenzee island of Texel is Alkmaar, famous for its kitschy but un-forgettable traditional cheese auction. Texel itself is a gem, with generous sand hills built generations ago, long, fine beaches, busy little villages, sheep-swamped *polders*, and a forest or two to add a bit of diversity.

HIGHLIGHTS

- Explore the world-class museums of **Haarlem** (p147) and its charming centre
- Wonder why beautiful **Edam** (p157) isn't flooded with fellow tourists
- Cycle through the high sand dunes, quiet forests, and green pastures of **Texel** (p167)
- Experience the hardy life of Noord Holland's seafaring towns before the Afsluitdijk at Enkhuizen's **Zuiderzeemuseum** (p164)
- Get away with cutting the cheese at Alkmaar's celebrated **cheese market** (p161)

★ Texel Island

Enkhuizen ★

★ Alkmaar

Edam ★

★ Haarlem

NOORD HOLLAND & FLEVOLAND

NOORD HOLLAND & FLEVOLAND

0 ——— 20 km
0 ——— 12 miles

NOORD HOLLAND

History
The peninsula now known as North Holland was part of Friesland until the 12th century, when storm floods created the Zuiderzee and isolated West Friesland. By this time the mercantile counts of Holland ruled the area – or thought they did. One of the early counts, Willem II, became king of the Holy Roman Empire in 1247 but perished in a raid against the West Frisians (his horse fell through the ice). His son, Count Floris V, succeeded in taming his defiant subjects 40 years later (p166).

West Friesland was now owned by the county of Holland, a founding member of the Republic of Seven United Netherlands (1579). Northern Holland played a key role in the long struggle against Spanish domination, and the town of Alkmaar was the first to throw off the yoke. The era of prosperity known as the Golden Age ensued, and North Holland has its fair share of richly ornamented buildings from this period. The fishing and trading ports of Enkhuizen, Medemblik and Edam were at the centre of this boom.

Napoleon invaded Holland in 1795 and split it in two to break its economic power. Even after Holland came under the House of Orange in 1813, a divide remained and the provinces of North and South Holland were established in 1840.

Today North Holland's main business is agriculture.

Getting There & Around
Noord Holland is well served by the national rail service, and where the train ends the bus networks take over. All Connexxion buses in the province cost €2 after 9am and all day on weekends.

Motorways run north–south from Haarlem to Alkmaar (the A9), and from Amsterdam to Den Oever (the A7), which continues on to Friesland via the 30km-long Afsluitdijk. From Enkhuizen there's another fast dyke road, the N302, running across the IJsselmeer to Lelystad in Flevoland. Bike trails lace the province in almost every direction, and you can cover the flat stretch from Amsterdam to Den Helder in two days at a leisurely pace.

HAARLEM
☎ 023 / pop 148,000
Everybody loves Haarlem, and it's not hard to see why. This achingly pretty city of cobble-stone streets, historic buildings, grand churches, even grander museums, cosy bars, top-class restaurants, and antique shops is a sure-fire heart-warmer. It's more than easy to visit as a day trip from Amsterdam, but as a place with so much on offer in such a compact area, you may find yourself turning the tables on the capital and using Haarlem as a base to explore the surrounds.

History
The name Haarlem derives from Haarloheim, meaning a wooded place on high, sandy soil. Its origins date back to the 10th century when the counts of Holland set up a toll post on the Spaarne River. Haarlem quickly became the most important inland port after Amsterdam, but suffered a major setback when the Spanish invaded in 1572. The city surrendered after a seven-month siege but worse was yet to come: upon capitulation virtually the entire population was slaughtered. After the Spanish were finally repelled by Willem van Oranje, Haarlem soared into the prosperity of the Golden Age, attracting painters and artists from throughout Europe.

Orientation
Grote Markt, the main square, is a 500m walk south of the bus and train stations. The centre has a large pedestrianised section, with lots of pubs and restaurants along Zijlstraat, Grote Houtstraat and especially Lange Veerstraat. Grote Kerk van St Bavo, the central landmark, can be seen from anywhere in the city.

Information
GWK exchange office (9am-7pm Mon-Fri, 9am-5pm Sat) In the train station, and close to two ATMs.
Library (☎ 515 76 00; Doelenplein 1; 11am-8pm Mon, Tue & Thu, 10am-4pm Sat) Provides internet terminals that can be tapped for free.
Main post office (Gedempte Oude Gracht 2)
My Beautiful Laundrette (Botermarkt 20; 8.30am-8.30pm) Takes last loads at 7pm.
Tourist office (☎ 09006161600; www.vvvzk.nl; Stationsplein 1; 9.30am-5.30pm Mon-Fri, 10am-4pm Sat Apr-Oct, 9.30am-5pm Mon-Fri, 10am-2pm Sat Nov-Mar) Sells a handy map of the city (€2), along with a useful walking guide (€2). Staff will reserve local accommodation for €5.

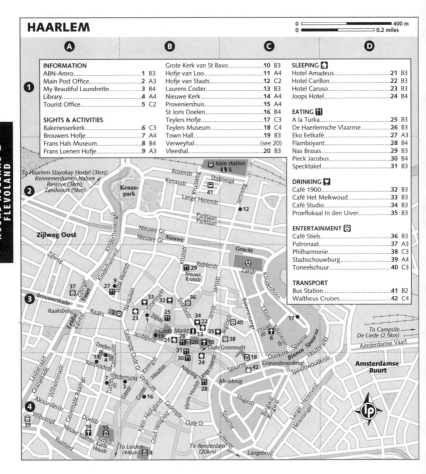

HAARLEM

0 ———— 400 m
0 ———— 0.2 miles

INFORMATION		
ABN-Amro	1	B3
Main Post Office	2	A3
My Beautiful Laundrette	3	B4
Library	4	A4
Tourist Office	5	C2

SIGHTS & ACTIVITIES		
Bakenesserkerk	6	C3
Brouwers Hofje	7	A4
Frans Hals Museum	8	B4
Frans Loenen Hofje	9	A3

Grote Kerk van St Bavo	10	B3
Hofje van Loo	11	A4
Hofje van Staats	12	C2
Laurens Coster	13	B3
Nieuwe Kerk	14	A4
Proveniershuis	15	A4
St Joris Doelen	16	B4
Teylers Hofje	17	C3
Teylers Museum	18	C4
Town Hall	19	B3
Verweyhal	(see 20)	
Vleeshal	20	B3

SLEEPING 🛏		
Hotel Amadeus	21	B3
Hotel Carillon	22	B3
Hotel Caruso	23	B3
Joops Hotel	24	B4

EATING 🍴		
A la Turka	25	B3
De Haerlemsche Vlaamse	26	B3
Eko Eetkafé	27	A3
Flamboyant	28	B4
Nas Brasas	29	B3
Pieck Jacobus	30	B4
Specktakel	31	B3

DRINKING 🍷		
Café 1900	32	B3
Café Het Melkwoud	33	B3
Café Studio	34	B3
Proeflokaal In den Uiver	35	B3

ENTERTAINMENT 🎭		
Café Stiels	36	B3
Patronaat	37	A3
Philharmonie	38	C3
Stadsschouwburg	39	C3
Toneelschuur	40	C3

TRANSPORT		
Bus Station	41	B2
Waltheus Cruises	42	C4

Sights & Activities

Large **Grote Markt**, with its flanks of restaurants and cafés and a clutch of historical buildings, is a good place to start an exploration of Haarlem. At the western end stands the florid, 14th-century **town hall**, which sprouted many extensions including a balcony where judgments from the high court were pronounced. The counts' hall contains 15th-century panel paintings and is normally open during office hours.

At the opposite end looms the **Grote Kerk van St Bavo** (☎ 553 20 40; Oude Groenmarkt 23; adult/child €2/1.25; ☒ 10am-4pm Mon-Sat), the Gothic cathedral with a towering 50m-high steeple. It contains some fine Renaissance artworks, but the star attraction is its stunning Müller organ – one of the most magnificent in the world, stand-

ing 30m high with about 5000 pipes. It was played by Handel and Mozart, the latter when he was just 10. There are tours in English on request. Free organ recitals take place at 3pm on Saturday and also 8.15pm every Tuesday, April to September.

In the centre of Grote Markt stand the 17th-century Vleeshal, a former meat market, and the Verweyhal, an old fish market; both serve as modern art annexes of the Frans Hals Museum. On the square north of the Grote Kerk is a **statue** of Laurens Coster, whom Haarlemmers believe has a claim, along with Gutenberg, to be called the inventor of movable type.

Off Grote Houtstraat to the southwest stands the **Proveniershuis**, the former headquarters of St Joris Doelen (the Civic Guards of St George),

---

HAARLEM'S URBAN OASES

Haarlem is a peaceful city at the rowdiest of times, but even such a serene place needs its fair share of oases. Collectively known as *hofjes* – leafy courtyards enclosed by rows of sweet little homes – these green spaces initially served as monastery gardens in the Middle Ages. Eventually they took on broader roles for hospitals and inns, or as refuges for orphans, widows and the elderly. These private squares also give clues about Dutch social concerns and the origins of the modern welfare state.

Most *hofjes* date from the 15th to the 18th centuries and are open to viewing on weekends only, but you can usually take a discreet peek any time. Ask the tourist office for its walking-guide brochure, *Hofjeswandeling*, which includes the following:

Brouwers Hofje (Tuchthuisstraat 8) Lodging for members of the brewers' guild (1472).

Frans Loenen Hofje (Witte Herenstraat 24) Almshouses built from a merchant's estate (1607).

Hofje van Loo (Barrevoetestraat 7) A women's hospital donated by mayor Sijmon Pieterszoon van Loo (1489); one of the most visible in Haarlem.

Hofje van Staats (Jansweg 39) One of the town's biggest, donated by a Haarlem merchant to poor women of the Reformed Church (1733), and still houses single, elderly women.

St Joris Doelen (Grote Houtstraat 144) A *proveniershuis* given as a donation; almshouse, later a gentlemen's inn (1591).

Teylers Hofje (Koudenhorn 64) Unusually grand affair, built by Pieter Teyler van der Hulst, founder of the Teyler Museum (1787).

The tourist office also runs guided tours, but at €74.50 a pop (up to 25 persons), you'll need either a lot of friends with you or to be completely bonkers for gardens.

---

which started life as an almshouse. Its wonderful old *hofje* (almshouse) is one of Haarlem's prettiest (see above). Around the corner to the west, down charming Korte Houtstraat, is the 17th-century **Nieuwe Kerk** (☯ 10am Sunday); the capricious tower by Lieven de Key is balanced by a rather boxy design by Jacob van Campen.

Northeast of the Teylers Museum stands the striking **Bakenesserkerk** (cnr Vrouwestraat & Bakenesserstraat), a late-15th-century church with a lamp-lit tower of sandstone. The stone was employed here when the Grote Kerk proved too weak to support a heavy steeple – hence the wooden tower of the cathedral we see today. A private firm occupies it but you can still peek inside.

MUSEUMS

The **Frans Hals Museum** (☎ 511 57 75; www.frans halsmuseum.nl; Groot Heiligland 62; adult/child €7/free; ☯ 11am-5pm Mon-Sat, noon-5pm Sun) is a must for anyone interested in the Dutch masters. Kept in an almshouse where Hals spent his final, impoverished years, the collection focuses on the 17th-century Haarlem School, which is regarded as the pinnacle of Dutch mannerist art. Eight group portraits by Hals detailing the companies of the Civic Guard are the museum's pride and joy, revealing the painter's

exceptional attention to mood and psychological tone. Don't miss his two paintings known collectively as the *Regents & the Regentesses of the Old Men's Alms House* (1664). Among other treasures are the curious works by Hals' teacher, Flemish artist Carel van Mander: ceiling-high illustrations of the human anatomy with biblical and mythological allusions. Other highlights include short snippets of the city's history and a peaceful inner *hofje*.

Depending on your tastes, the **Teylers Museum** (☎ 531 90 10; Spaarne 16; adult/child €4.50/1; ☯ 10am-5pm Tue-Sat, noon-5pm Sun) may top Frans Hals. Named after philanthropist-merchant Pieter Teyler van der Hulst, it's the oldest museum in the country (1778) and contains an array of whiz-bang inventions, such as an 18th-century electrostatic machine that conjures up visions of mad scientists. At 4m long and 2m high, this amazing beast once ran on batteries the size of a milk wagon. The eclectic collection also has paintings from the Dutch and French schools and numerous temporary exhibitions. The interiors are as good as the displays: the magnificent, sky-lighted Ovale Zaal (Oval Room) contains natural history specimens in elegant glass cases on two levels. Elsewhere you'll find fossils, ancient relics and mineral crystals.

On Grote Markt, the **Vleeshal** holds contemporary art exhibitions; the **Verweyhal** next door, in a fancy Renaissance building designed by Lieven de Key, houses the Frans Hals Museum's collection of modern art, including works by Dutch impressionists and the CoBrA movement. The museums are known collectively as **De Hallen** (adult/child €5/3.50; 🕑 11am-5pm Mon-Sat, noon-5pm Sun).

Tours

Woltheus Cruises (☎ 535 77 23; Spaarne 11a; adult/child €6.50/3.50) runs canal boat tours in English; 50-minute tours run every hour from noon to 5pm April to October.

Sleeping

The tourist office has a list of B&Bs from €24 per person.

Joops Hotel (☎ 532 20 08; www.joopshotel.com; Oude Groenmarkt 20; r/studio from €85/85; 🖳) The friendly Joops Hotel has 100-plus very individual rooms spread over an entire block near the Grote Kerk. Space isn't an issue and the studios have a kitchenette. Reception is on the ground floor in the Belly & Bolly antique shop, run by a pair of amiable gents.

Hotel Carillon (☎ 531 05 91; www.hotelcarillon.com; Grote Markt 27; s/d from €38/63) Run by a friendly young crew, this small hotel has ageing but completely OK rooms in the shadow of the Grote Kerk. Breakfast can be taken in wicker chairs on the sidewalk café.

Haarlem Stayokay Hostel (☎ 537 37 93; haarlem@ stayokay.com; Jan Gijzenpad 3; dm €26.75; 🖳) This lakeside youth hostel has a 10pm silence rule, but there's no curfew. The super clean rooms are stripped back and basic, but the bar-café has plenty of warmth and character. Laundry and cooking facilities are available. Take bus 2 (direction Haarlem Noord) from the train station (10 minutes).

Hotel Caruso (☎ 542 14 20; www.hotelrestaurant caruso.nl; Zijlstraat 56-58; r from €75) This hotel above the Italian restaurant of the same name is on a quiet pedestrian street in the heart of Haarlem. The no-fuss rooms are large and lightly coloured, and all come with bathroom.

Hotel Amadeus (☎ 532 45 30; www.amadeus-hotel .com; Grote Markt 10; s/d €60/80; 🖳) Amadeus enjoys a brilliant spot nestled in a row of old gabled houses on the main square. Rooms are one step up from bare bones, but they're comfy and have a few mod cons. There's a small café on the first floor.

Campsite De Liede (☎ 533 86 66; Lieoever 68; camp site €12.10, car €3.50) This leafy site 2.5km east of the old centre enjoys a lakeside location and rents canoes and paddle boats. Take bus 2 from the train station (direction Zuidpolder) and alight at Zoete Inval.

Eating

The streets around the Dom and Lange Veerstraat offer a treasure-trove of enticing restaurants. It's a good idea to reserve ahead, although the huge selection means you'll find a table somewhere.

Nas Brasas (☎ 532 88 02; Kruisstraat 13; tapas €4.95; 🕑 lunch & dinner Wed-Sun) Nas Brasas' is a lively tapas restaurant whose convivial, warm atmosphere suits romantic couples and groups alike. The tapas, of which there's a long, long list, are so good that it's almost impossible not to go for a second round.

Eko Eetkafé (☎ 532 65 68; Zijlstraat 39; mains €8-18; 🕑 lunch & dinner) An offshoot of the Eko organic foods association, this obliging little eatery offers fish and vegetarian dishes with a clear conscience. It's a short walk from the town centre but definitely worth the effort.

De Haerlemsche Vlaamse (☎ 532 59 91; Spekstraat 3; frites €1-3; 🕑 lunch & dinner) Practically on the doorstep of the Grote Kerk, this *frites* joint not much bigger than a telephone box is a local institution. Line up for its fries and choose from one of a dozen sauces.

Pieck Jacobus (☎ 532 61 44; Warmoesstraat 18; mains €10-17; 🕑 lunch & dinner) This little *eetcafé* with the big front windows is stripped back and cosy, and offers a variety of delightful dishes, such as kebab sausages or spicy lamb.

Specktakel (☎ 532 38 41; Spekstraat 4; mains €18; 🕑 dinner) This Dutch diner is vying for UN membership judging by its worldly menu of Australian emu fillet to Indian lamb masala. It's another of Haarlem's long, thin diners, and there's streetside seating for sunny days.

Also recommended:

Flamboyant (☎ 542 15 03; Kleine Houtstraat 3; mains €14-20; 🕑 dinner Wed-Mon) Warm and cosy; Haarlem's finest Indonesian restaurant.

A la Turka (☎ 534 11 62; Zijlstraat 95; mains €14-19; 🕑 lunch & dinner Tue-Sun) Hearty Turkish cuisine near the Grote Markt.

Drinking

Haarlem's slew of atmospheric drinking holes are perfect spots to try Jopen Koyt, the local beer. First brewed in 1401, this dark, richly flavoured beer is almost a meal in itself, and you may want to set a limit; its alcohol content is a healthy 8.5%.

Café 1900 (☎ 531 82 83; Barteljorisstraat 10) This authentic brown café is a little gem, with a *fin-de-siècle* interior, long bar perfect for propping up, and pleasantly mixed crowd. Live bands and DJs often feature on weekends.

Café Studio (☎ 531 00 33; Grote Markt 25) Within view of the cathedral is this café/bar, which seems a nice, calm place for a drink in the early evening (inside or on its terrace), but by 10pm it heaves with 20- and 30-somethings looking to make the most of a night out.

Proeflokaal In den Uiver (☎ 532 53 99; Riviervismarkt 13) This quirky old place has shipping knick-knacks and a schooner sailing right over the bar. There's jazz on Thursday and Sunday evenings.

Café het Melkwoud (☎ 531 35 35; Zijlstraat 63) A great place to nurse a beer with crunchy locals behind those ceiling-high windows. You can't miss the sign – a tree shaped like a woman.

Entertainment

To find out what's on, grab a copy of the free local paper *De Haarlemmer* or the listings handout *Luna* at the tourist office or pubs.

CLUBS

Café Stiels (☎ 531 69 40; Smedestraat 21) For jazz and rhythm & blues, bands play on the back stage almost every night of the week from 10pm onwards.

Patronaat (☎ 517 58 58; www.patronaat.nl; Zijlsingel 2) Haarlem's top music and dance club attracts bands with banging tunes. Events in this cavernous venue usually start around 7pm or 9pm unless it's a midnight rave.

THEATRE

Toneelschuur (☎ 517 39 10; www.toneschuur.nl; Lange Begijnestraat 9) This bizarre multilevel stage complex (designed by a Dutch cartoonist, Joost Swarte) has a daring agenda of experimental dance, theatre and art-house cinema, and acts as a production house for up-and-coming directors.

Philharmonie (☎ 512 12 12; www.philharmonie.nu; Lange Begijnestraat 11) Haarlem's venerable concert hall, which features music from every spectrum imaginable (except perhaps Death Metal, but with the Dutch, you never know).

Stadsschouwburg (☎ 512 12 12; Wilsonsplein 23) The city's municipal theatre and sister venue to the Philharmonie, the Stadsschouwburg is currently undergoing major renovation and should be ready – well, sometime in the future is all anyone knew. Check with the tourist office for more information.

Shopping

Monday is market day at Botermarkt and Grote Markt, and again on Saturday at Grote Markt. Friday also sees Botermarkt come alive to a local farmers' market.

Getting There & Away

The city's Art Deco station is served by frequent trains running on the Amsterdam–Rotterdam line.

Destination	Price (€)	Duration (min)	Frequency (per hr)
Alkmaar	5.70	30-50	4
Amsterdam	3.60	15	5-8
Den Haag	7.00	35-40	4-6
Rotterdam	10.10	50	4

Bus 300 links Haarlem train station and Schiphol Airport (45 minutes, six times hourly) between 5am and midnight. Connexxion bus 80 stops at Houtplein, south of the centre, and goes to/from Amsterdam Marnixstraat (40 minutes, two to four times hourly). Bus 81 goes to Zandvoort bus station by way of Overveen (15 minutes, twice hourly). IJmuiden's Dennekoplaan, close to the locks and the beach, can be reached on buses 4 and 75 (40 minutes, four times hourly).

During the tulip season from late March to late May, Connexxion normally runs buses from Haarlem to the Keukenhof bulb fields via Lisse (45 minutes, two to four times hourly). Check with the tourist office (p147) for the most up-to-date information.

Getting Around

The **bus information kiosk** (7.30am-5.30pm Mon-Fri, 9.15am-4.30pm Sat) opposite the train station has plenty of schedules, otherwise check the schedule boards at departure bays. Bus 2 from the train and bus station stops at Zijlstraat, just east of Grote Markt (five minutes).

Regular **taxis** (☎ 515 15 15) are everywhere in Haarlem, and there's a large **bicycle shop** (☎ 531 70 66) for rentals in the train station.

AROUND HAARLEM
Beaches
Just 5km west of Haarlem's peaceful outskirts
lies **Zandvoort**, a popular seaside resort. It's
no great shakes as beach towns go, and drab
apartment blocks line the main drag, but its
proximity to Amsterdam ensures a steady flow
of pleasure-seekers. The main pastime here is
beach bumming, but you can also catch the
occasional sports-car event at the **Circuit Park
Zandvoort** (www.circuit-zandvoort.nl) just to the north
of the resort.

About 3km north of Zandvoort is Haarlem's second beach, **Bloemendaal aan Zee**, an
undeveloped spot with a handful of restaurants and cafés and uninterrupted beaches. It's
frequented by those looking for a semblance
of peace and quiet away from the hustle and
bustle of its bigger neighbour to the south.

The closest accommodation to Bloemendaal is De Lakens (right), but Zandvoort is
bursting at the seams with accommodation.
Haarlem's tourist office (p147) can point you
in the right direction.

Trains link Zandvoort to Amsterdam Centraal Station three times hourly (€4.70, 30
minutes) via Haarlem (€2.10, 10 minutes).

Kennemerduinen Nature Reserve
De Zandwaaier (☎ 023-541 11 23; www.npzk.nl; Zeeweg,
Overveen; ⊙ 10am-5pm Tue-Sun Apr-Oct, noon-5pm Tue-Sun
Nov-Mar), the park's visitors centre, has nature
displays and is a good source of information,
with a range of detailed walking and cycling
maps. At the Koevlak and Parnassia entrances
are car parks, from where paths lead off into
the reserve. The paths snake through hilltop
copses of Corsican firs and valleys of low-lying
thickets; at the western edge you come to a
massive barrier of golden sand that's 1000
years old.

The dunes sprout an extra layer of colour
in spring including desert orchids, the bright
rosettes of the century weed and the white-
blooming grass of Parnassus. Red foxes, fallow
deer and many species of birds are native to
the area; bats slumber in the park's abandoned
bunkers before appearing at dusk.

Among main features, the **Vogelmeer** lake
has a bird observation hut above the south
shore. The artificial lake **'t Wed** teems with
bathers in summer. Lookout points are scattered throughout with evocative names like
Hazenberg (Hare Mountain). At 50m, the
Kopje van Bloemendaal is the highest dune in the

country, just outside the eastern border of the
park, with views of the sea and Amsterdam.

On a sombre note, the WWII cemetery
Erebegraafplaats Bloemendaal (☎ 020-660 1945;
admission free; ⊙ 9am-6pm Apr-Sep, 9am-5pm Oct-Mar)
is the resting place of 372 members of the
Dutch resistance. Its walled compound in the
dunes is isolated from the rest of the park and
accessible only via the main road.

Rough camping is a no-no, but the park-
run site **De Lakens** (☎ 075-647 23 93; www.kdc.nu; camp
sites from €27.10, bungalows per week from €160) enjoys
a sandy, grassy and certainly breezy spot just
a few metres from the beach. There's a lovely
kids' playground, and its wooden bungalows
sleep four. Ticks in the dunes are known to
carry Lyme disease, so insect repellent is a
good idea.

To reach the park, visitors centre and campground, take bus 81 from Haarlem train station
or cycle/drive the N200 towards Bloemendaal
aan Zee.

IJMUIDEN
☎ 0255 / pop 7000
Just 5km up the coast from Haarlem at the
mouth of the Noordzeekanaal (North Sea
Canal) in the port town of IJmuiden is the
huge **North Sea locks**. The largest is the Zuider-
sluis (South Lock), some 400m long and 45m
wide. Few people realise that IJmuiden is also
the largest fishing port in Western Europe,
home to the factory trawlers that plough the
North Atlantic for weeks at a time. The huge
beach is a kite-flyer's delight at low tide, but
unfortunately the view is marred by the steel
mills north of the locks.

Getting There & Around
It's a thrill taking the **hydrofoil** (☎ 020-639 22
47; www.fastflyingferries.ml; adult/child return €8.30/4.85;
⊙ 7am-7pm Mon-Fri, 10am-5.30pm Sat & Sun) from behind Amsterdam Centraal Station (25 minutes, hourly on the hour, half-hourly during
peak times) along the North Sea Canal to
Velsen, 3km short of IJmuiden, where you
catch Connexxion bus 82 or 83 into town. It's a
good idea to take a bicycle (an extra €4 return)
because things are spread out. Cycle from
Velsen along the dyke towards the locks and go
across the 'small' and 'middle' locks to the big
lock on the far side; along the way you'll find
an information centre, **Noordzeekanaal in Zicht**
(North Sea Canal in Pictures; ☎ 51 91 12; Noordersluisweg 120;
⊙ 1-5pm Mon, Wed & Sun).

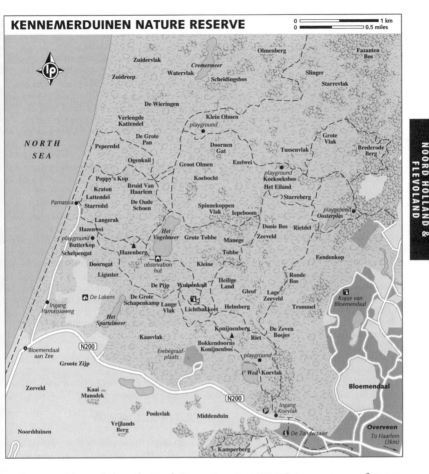

KENNEMERDUINEN NATURE RESERVE

NORTH SEA

If you travel by road along the North Sea Canal, you'll have the surreal experience of passing huge, ocean-going ships that float well above road level.

BEVERWIJK

☎ 0251

Every weekend up to 80,000 visitors flock to the town of Beverwijk to visit the covered **Beverwijkse Bazaar** (☎ 26 26 26; www.beverwijkse bazaar.nl; Montageweg 35; ☺ 8.30am-6pm Sat & Sun), one of Europe's largest ethnic markets. Piled high are Arabian foods and spices, Turkish rugs, garments and hand-crafted ornaments.

The liveliest of the three biggest halls is the **Zwarte Markt** (Black Market; before 9am free, after 9am adult/child €1.50/free), an enormous flea market with a carnival attitude. You can haggle with one of the 3000-plus vendors or just bask in the market chatter, live music and exotic aromas. The admission price includes entry to the **Grand Bazaar**, where the booths are larger and more professional, while the **Oosterse Markt** is free.

Getting There & Away

Parking (free before 9am, €2 on Saturday, €3 on Sunday) becomes a problem after 9.30am. From Amsterdam drive the A9 towards Alkmaar, exit at Beverwijk and follow signs to the bazaar; or take the train to Beverwijk (€4.90, 30 minutes, five times hourly) and then bus 76 (six minutes).

ZAANSE SCHANS

☎ 075

Making a good stab at re-creating a local village from the 17th and 18th centuries is the Zaanse Schans, an open-air museum, some 10km northwest of Amsterdam. It features a grand collection of historic structures from around the country, and there's a plethora of workshops, shops and raised wooden homes, all of which sit on a sweet little tract, complete with canals and tulip gardens. On a sunny day it's a grand day out despite the inevitable crowds. The **visitors centre** (☎ 616 82 18; www .zaanseschans.nl; Schansend 1; ☾ 9am-5pm), at the far end of the village if you're coming by train, hands out the free maps you'll need.

The most striking structures are the six working **windmills** that stand along the riverbanks. One mill sells fat jars of its freshly ground mustard, while the others turn out pigments, oils, meal and sawed wood. All are open for inspection, and it's a treat to clamber about the creaking works while the mills shake in the North Sea breeze.

The cutest shops include an Albert Heijn colonial supermarket, a cheese maker and a popular **clog factory** with exhibits of pointy old footwear. The engaging **pewtersmith** will explain in several languages the story behind dozens of tiny figures while the soft metal sets in the moulds.

Near the visitors centre, the **Zaans Museum** (☎ 616 28 62; adult/child €4.50/2.70; ☾ 9am-5pm) runs temporary exhibitions of historical objects of the Zaan river communities, often with a dramatic or artsy twist such as audiovisual light shows.

When you've finished poking around the village, a **tour boat** (adult/child €5/2.50; ☾ 11am-4pm Tue-Sun Apr-Sep) does 45-minute spins on the river Zaan several times a day.

Getting There & Away

From Amsterdam Centraal Station (€2.80, 20 minutes, four times hourly), take the stop train towards Alkmaar and get off at Koog Zaandijk – it's a well-signposted 400m walk to Zaanse Schans.

ZAANDAM

☎ 075 / pop 25,800

A stone's throw from Zaanse Schans, Zaandam has played home to two famous residents: Russia's Peter the Great and impressionist master Claude Monet. Claude stayed in a nice hotel while Peter preferred a rickety wooden shack, now a shrine and the main reason for visiting this commuter town.

The **Czaar Peterhuisje** (☎ 616 13 90; Krimp 23; adult/child €2/1; ☾ 1-5pm Tue-Sun Apr-Oct, 1-5pm Sat & Sun Nov-Mar) is the gritty abode where Peter spent a week of his life in 1697. The Russian ruler arrived incognito as sailor Peter Mikhailov to garner support for Western forces against the Turks. Despite the hush-hush, news spread and hordes of fans practically besieged the cabin to get a glimpse of his tsarness. Peter eventually slipped away to the wharves to learn shipbuilding and swearing in Dutch, and became adept at both.

Many Russians came here on a pilgrimage in the 19th century to scrawl their graffiti. So great was the PR value that Grand Duchess Anna Paulowna (wife of Dutch King Willem II) commissioned a brick shelter over the house, which finally emerged in Russian orthodox style by the late 1800s. There's a small exhibit about the tsar and his links to the Netherlands, and marble tablets engraved with the monikers of royal visitors. Napoleon stopped by and was apparently delighted.

Getting There & Away

To get there from Amsterdam Centraal, take the train toward Alkmaar and get off at Zaandam (€2.40, 12 minutes, four hourly); from the station, follow the signs.

WATERLAND REGION

☎ 075

Time seems to move more slowly in this rural area about 9km north of Amsterdam, where some farmers still carry scythes, the meadows turn a succulent shade of green and herons stand motionless alongside watery furrows. Despite a large shipping canal nearby, it remains an important bird sanctuary, and picturesque for the mindful visitor.

Broek in Waterland is a precious little burg in the heart of the Waterland region. Some 17th- and 18th-century houses are painted a particular shade of grey, known as *Broeker grijs* after the landscapes painted here by Monet and other masters. The village church was burned by the Spanish in 1573 but restored with a pretty stained-glass window recalling the tragic event. On the lake's edge stands the so-called **Napoleonhuisje**, a white pagoda where the French emperor and the mayor met in 1811.

NOORD HOLLAND & FLEVOLAND

THE WATERLAND TICKET

If you're planning to day trip around the Waterland Region, Monnickendam, Volendam and Marken by bus, consider purchasing a Waterland Ticket (€6). Available from bus drivers, it allows a day's unlimited travel in the area north of Amsterdam (covered by buses 110, 111 and 115) and it's excellent value.

Near the town of Landsmeer, 9km north of Amsterdam, lies the nature reserve and recreational area **Het Twiske**. This is where urbanites go for a calculated dose of nature: well-marked walking trails, playgrounds and artificial but quite decent beaches, especially for families. A full one-third of the area is water and there are several hides for birdwatchers on the lakeshores. Picnic spots are marked throughout for barbecuing. The **visitors centre** (☎ 684 43 38; www.hettwiske.nl; Noorderlaak 1; ☯ 10am-4pm Tue-Fri, noon-4pm Sat & Sun) is next to the canoe rental shop.

Getting There & Away
The best way to experience the Waterland is by bicycle; pick up a rental in Amsterdam (p136) and explore at your leisure. Otherwise pick up a Waterland Ticket (above) and ride the buses.

MONNICKENDAM
☎ 0299 / pop 10,105
Monnickendam, which gained its name from the Benedictines who built a dam here, is a sleepy town that can trace its roots back to 1356. It originally became prosperous by moving goods inland towards Alkmaar but after the fishing industry died, it reinvented itself as a yachting resort, and today the beautiful old trawlers mainly catch pleasure-seekers. History still pervades the narrow lanes around the shipyards and fish smokehouses that have been operating for hundreds of years. Smoked eel remains a local delicacy. Eel is one of the few species still caught in bulk in the IJsselmeer.

Sights
The town's trademark building is the 15th-century **Speeltoren**, an elegant, Italianate clock tower and former town hall. The tower's carillon (glockenspiel) performs only at 11am and noon on Saturday, when the four mechanical knights prance in the open wooden window twice before retiring. If the tone rings true it's because the bells were cast by master bellmaker Peter van de Ghein over 400 years ago.

Inside the clock tower you'll find the **Historisch Museum** (☎ 65 22 03; Noordeinde 4; adult/child €1.50/0.50; ☯ 1-4pm May-Aug, 11am-4pm Mon-Sat & 1-4pm Sun Apr, Sep & Oct), which displays various archaeological finds uncovered during the building of the Afsluitdijk (p175) and retells the history of the Waterlandse Tram that served the Waterland region up until 1956.

The Gothic **Grote Kerk** (☎ 65 06 00; De Zarken; admission free; ☯ 10am-4pm Tue-Sat, 2-4pm Sun-Mon Jun-Aug), on the outskirts of town, is notable for its triple nave, tower galleries and a dazzling oak choir screen dating from the 16th century. It's impossible not to focus on the enormous organ (which is occasionally used for concerts) in the nave, a statement of higher glory and a striking contrast with the spartan interior.

Other stars in the architecture department include the **Waag** (Weigh-house) on the central canal. Built in 1669, this focal point of local economic life was equipped in 1905 with grand Tuscan columns, a common trick of the day to make it look much older and more impressive. **In de Bonten Os** (Coloured Ox; Noordeinde 26) is the only house that's left in its original 17th-century state. In the days before proper glass, the curious vertical shutters at street level were made to let in air and light.

The old harbour along Haringburgwal is famous for its **fish smokehouses**, and you can poke your head inside for a glimpse of the process. A bronze statue of a fisherman curing eels on a spit stands where the central canal meets the harbour.

Activities
As elsewhere on the IJsselmeer, large pleasure boats are the thing in Monnickendam. In July and August you can feel the spray in your face on day trips on an antique clipper. Reserve at **Holland Zeilcharters** (☎ 65 23 51; www.sailing.nl; Het Prooyen 4a; per person from €50, botter rental for up to 8 persons from €360).

The harbour bristles with splendid old *tjalken, botters* and *klippers*, historic boats available for hire (as are skippers if need be). The *botters* can be hired out for a group from around €360 per day. The sky's the limit at the top end, eg three-masted clippers for as long as you (and your wallet) see fit.

Smaller craft can be found at **Bootvloot** (☎ 06-549 42657; Hemmeland beach; ☺ 10am-5.30pm Apr-Oct) where two- to four-person sailboats cost €40/55 per half-day/day, with a €50 deposit. It's a 500m walk through the leafy Hemmeland recreation area northeast of Monnickendam marina – just follow the sign 'Zeilbootverhuur'.

Sleeping & Eating

Hotel Lake Land (☎ 65 37 51; Jachthaven 1; s/d €50/70) Aside from a smattering of B&Bs, Lake Land is all that Monnickendam offers in the way of accommodation. It's situated on the marina with harbour views and a restaurant, and though fairly anonymous is convenient and comfortable.

Camping-Jachthaven Uitdam (☎ 020-403 14 33; www.campinguitdam.nl; Zeedijk 2, Uitdam; camp sites/cabins/bungalows €15/39/66; ☺ Mar-Oct) Tucked away behind a dyke on the IJsselmeer, this well-equipped site has mooring facilities, beach, laundry, snack bar and bicycle rental. Both the basic cabins and bungalows sleep up to four, but the latter has a kitchen and hot and cold running water. Take the dyke road 5km southeast of Monnickendam or bus 111.

De Roef (☎ 65 18 60; Noordeinde 40; mains €15-25; ☺ dinner) The meat cuts like butter at this Western-style steakhouse where Argentine tenderloin or sea bass is prepared over charcoal flames. Half the fun is watching dinner approach your table sizzling atop a red-hot grill.

't Markerveerhuis (☎ 65 57 69; Brugstraat 6; mains €10-15; ☺ lunch & dinner) This is easily the best place to dine on traditional Dutch fare while enjoying the comings and goings in Monnickendam's harbour. Dutch folk music emanates from the stage at weekends.

Stands selling smoked eel and other fruits of the sea are clustered around the old harbour – just follow your nose.

Getting There & Around

Connexxion bus 111 (30 minutes, three to four times an hour) links the centre of Monnickendam to Amsterdam Centraal Station, harbour side, as does bus 115 (twice hourly); the 111 continues on to Marken (12 minutes, hourly). Buses 110 and 114 go north to Volendam (seven minutes) and Edam (10 minutes), but only 114 continues on to Hoorn (30 to 45 minutes, twice hourly).

Ber Koning (☎ 65 12 67; Noordeinde 12) rents out bicycles.

VOLENDAM & MARKEN

☎ 0299 / pop 20,700

Some 22km northeast of Amsterdam lies Volendam, a former fishing port turned tourist trap. It's quaint all right, with its rows of wooden houses and locals who don traditional dress for church and festive events, but the harbour is awash with souvenirs shops and cafés, and on weekends it's even hard to think with all the people swarming about. Best escape the hordes and explore some of the pretty streets behind the harbour for a glimpse of what the old Volendam was really like.

Across Gouwzee Bay lies scenic Marken with a small and determined population. It was an isolated island in the Zuiderzee until 1957 when a causeway linked up with the mainland, effectively turning it into a museum-piece village. It still however manages to exude a fishing-village vibe.

Information

Tourist office (☎ 36 37 47; www.vvv-volendam.nl; Zeestraat 37, Volendam; ☺ 10am-5pm Mon-Sat) Has tonnes of information, including a brochure with a walking tour of Volendam. The old harbour district is about 400m to the southeast.

Sights & Activities

The **Volendams Museum** (☎ 36 92 58; Zeestraat 41, Volendam; adult/child €2/1.25; ☺ 10am-5pm mid-Mar–Oct) is a must for cigar aficionados. Local culture is covered with traditional costumes, prints, paintings of harbour scenes and even a cramped ship's sleeping quarters, but this place is really devoted to lovers of cheap cigars: some 11 million bands are plastered on its walls.

In Marken, the colourful Kerkbuurt is the most authentic area, with tarred or painted houses raised on pilings to escape the Zuiderzee floods. A row of eel-smoking houses here has been converted to the **Marker Museum** (☎ 60 19 04; Kerkbuurt 44, Marken; adult/child €2.50/1.25; ☺ 10am-5pm Mon-Sat, noon-4pm Sun Apr-Oct), which delves into the island's history and includes the re-created interior of a fisherman's home, with a wealth of personal odds and ends.

Sleeping

ourpick Hof Van Marken (☎ 60 13 00; www.hofvan marken.nl; Buurt II, 15, Marken; r from €80) It would be a hard heart that would resist the big beds, fluffy pillows and heavenly duvets at Hof Van

Marken, one of the cosiest hotels around. And it's incredible to think that such a peaceful, rural establishment in the heart of a former fishing village is only 20 minutes from bustling Amsterdam.

Hotel Spaander (☎ 36 35 95; www.spaander.com; Haven 15-19, Volendam; r €105) The town's best hotel has retained much of its atmosphere from the olden days, with traditional carved balconies and cushy rooms that have welcomed the likes of Picasso and Monet. There's an indoor swimming pool too.

Eating

Seafood is the undisputed king in Volendam, and the main street (and harbour) is lined with vendors offering smoked cod, eel and herring.

Hotel Spaander (☎ 36 35 95; Haven 15-19; mains €21-35; ⏰ lunch & dinner) This grand place does a splendid job with all things fishy, be it salmon, stewed eel or bouillabaisse. The waiters fillet your fish right at your table, and the dining area is fantastically quaint, with paintings by renowned artists covering every inch of available wall space.

Old Dutch Restaurant Le Pompadour (☎ 39 98 88; Haven 142; mains €11-28; ⏰ lunch & dinner) Even the name can't take away the old-world flair of a place where faded yellow light falls from Art Deco lamps. There's really only one dish to try in these parts, and this place does it well; smoked eel IJsselmeer style.

Getting There & Around

Connexxion bus 110 runs between Volendam and Amsterdam via Monnickendam (30 minutes) and Edam (12 minutes) every 30 minutes until 1.30am. Bus 111 goes from Amsterdam via Monnickendam to Marken (30 minutes, half-hourly).

The **Marken Express ferry** (adult/child one way €4/3, return €6.50/3.50; ⏰ 10.30am-6pm Mar-Sep) makes the 45-minute crossing from Volendam to Marken every half hour. In Volendam, the ferry leaves from the docks at Havendijkje.

EDAM

☎ 0299 / pop 7400

Once a renowned whaling port – in its 17th-century heyday it had 33 shipyards that built the fleet of legendary admiral Michiel de Ruijter – this scenic little town is another of Noord Holland's hidden gems. With its old shipping warehouses, quiet cobblestone streets, hand-operated drawbridges, and pic-

ture-perfect canals, you'd be hard pressed not to enjoy a stroll around. And it's quite astounding that so many tourists prefer Volendam, only 2km away, unless Edam's cheese market is on, and then they're like flies to, well, cheese.

Information

Tourist office (☎ 31 51 25; www.vvv-edam.nl; Damplein; ⏰ 10am-5pm Mon-Sat Mar-Jun & Sep-Nov, 10am-5pm Mon-Sat & 1-4pm Sun Jul & Aug, 10am-3pm Mon-Sat Dec-Feb) Housed in the splendid 18th-century town hall. Pick up the good English-language booklet for self-guided tours, *A Stroll Through Edam* (€2.50).

Sights & Activities

In the 16th century, Willem van Oranje bestowed on Edam the right to hold a **Kaasmarkt** (Cheese Market; ⏰ 10am-12.30pm Wed Jul & Aug), which was the town's economic anchor right through to the 1920s. At its peak 250,000 rounds of cheese were sold here every year. On the western side of Kaasmarkt stands the old **Kaaswaag** (admission free; ⏰ 10am-5pm Apr-Sep), the cheese weigh-house, which has a display on the town's chief product. The cheese market is smaller than the one in Alkmaar but about as touristy. You can sample and buy some of the cheesy stuff at **Gestam** (☎ 37 15 30; Voorhaven 125; ⏰ 10am-4pm Wed & Fri), or stop in at **Edammer Kaaswinkel** (☎ 37 16 83; cnr Spui & Prinsenstraat) and pick up a round with which to disguise any cheap wine served to guests back home.

The 15th-century **Grote Kerk** (admission free; ⏰ 1-5pm Apr-Sep) has an unfortunate past that stands witness to the vagaries of Dutch weather. The stained-glass windows bearing coats of arms and historical scenes were added after 1602, when the church burned to a crisp after a lightning strike. Its tower can be climbed (admission €2) for views of the surrounds. The taller **Speeltoren**, leaning slightly over Kleine Kerkstraat about 100m further south, is all that remains of the 15th-century Kleine Kerk.

The **Edams Museum** (☎ 37 24 31; Damplein 8; adult/child €3/1; ⏰ 10am-4.30pm Mon-Sat, 1.30-4.30pm Sun) has a so-so collection of old furnishings, porcelain and silverware, spread over three cramped floors. It's best known for its floating cellar, a remarkable pantry that rises and falls with the river's swell to reduce stress on the structure above. The ornate brick structure is Edam's oldest, dating from 1530.

NOORD HOLLAND & FLEVOLAND

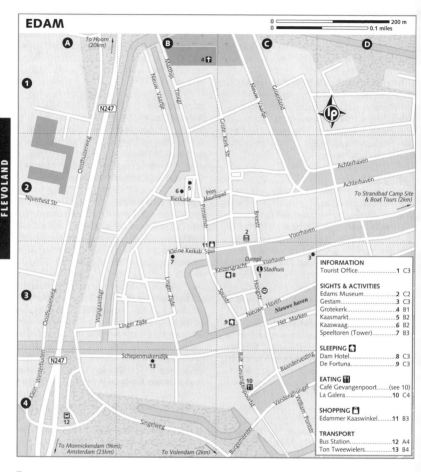

EDAM

INFORMATION
Tourist Office....................1 C3

SIGHTS & ACTIVITIES
Edams Museum.................2 C2
Gestam.............................3 C3
Grotekerk.........................4 B1
Kaasmarkt........................5 B2
Kaaswaag.........................6 B2
Speeltoren (Tower)...........7 B3

SLEEPING
Dam Hotel.........................8 C3
De Fortuna........................9 C3

EATING
Café Gevangenpoort.......(see 10)
La Galera.........................10 C4

SHOPPING
Edammer Kaaswinkel........11 B3

TRANSPORT
Bus Station......................12 A4
Ton Tweewielers...............13 B4

Tours

The tourist office organises 1½-hour **boat tours** (€3; ☺ Jul & Aug) on *tuindersvelts* (small, open-topped boats) in summer, weather permitting. Departure is from the Strandbad Edam camp site (below). You can also rent a boat via the tourist office from about €450 per day.

Sleeping & Eating

In addition to the places reviewed here, the tourist office has a list of private accommodation and farm stays from €20 per person.

Strandbad Edam (☎ 37 19 94; www.campingstrand had nl· 7eevangszeediik 7a: per person/tent €3,10/4,55; ☺ Apr-Sep) This sprawling seaside camp site has a swimming beach, laundry and restaurant. It's usually overrun but remains a convenient

base for boat trips into the IJsselmeer – the docks are right outside the camp site.

La Galera (☎ 37 19 71; Gevangenpoortsteeg 3; mains €6-12; ☺ lunch & dinner) If you're not eating at De Fortuna or the Dam Hotel then La Galera, with its standard pizzas and pasta, will have to suffice.

Café de Gevangenpoort (☎ 37 42 52; Gevangenpoortsteeg 1) Next door to La Galera, this pub has occasional live music and friendly staff.

Getting There & Around

Connexxion bus 110 stops twice an hour at the bus station and continues to Voldendam (five minutes), Monnickendam (25 minutes) and Amsterdam (40 minutes). Bus 114 travels to Hoorn (25 minutes, twice hourly), and 113

STAYING IN STYLE

For such a small town, Edam manages to provide some remarkably good accommodation and eating options.

Dam Hotel (☎ 37 17 66; www.damhotel.nl; Keizersgracht 1; s/d €59.50/110) In the very heart of the city, the boutique Dam Hotel is created with tender loving care. Rooms are individually decorated with genuine and 'new' antiques, but the unbridled theme throughout is Romance. Some rooms are a little on the small side, but this is counterbalanced by huge beds and thoroughly modern bathrooms. Its restaurant (mains around €20; open for lunch and dinner) serves classic French cuisine in silver-service surroundings, and forecourt diners enjoy views of the old town hall.

De Fortuna (☎ 37 16 71; www.fortuna-edam.nl; Spuistraat 3; s/d from €65/90) Another gem, this place might have stood model for an old Dutch painting. Its homy rooms, which overlook one of Edam's many canals, are stuffed with quilts and little perks like coffee and tea facilities. The bathrooms are on the tiny side but they have everything you need. Downstairs in the restaurant (mains €20; open for lunch and dinner), elaborate French dishes are served in a suitably Dutch arena: oil paintings, large bay windows and leather seats buffed shiny over the years. The ever-changing menu features plenty of fish and meat, along with a smattering of wild game, and the wine list would be hard to get through in a week.

---

makes jaunts to Volendam (10 minutes, once or twice an hour). Bicycles can be rented at **Ton Tweewielers** (☎ 37 19 22; Schepenmakersdijk 6).

ALKMAAR

☎ 072 / pop 93,000

If ever there was a cheese town, Alkmaar is it. Come Friday, its picturesque ringed centre is awash with tourists, all eager to catch a glimpse of the city's famous cheese market.

But the city is more than just a purveyor of curdled milk. It holds a special place in Dutch hearts as the first town, in 1573, to repel occupying Spanish troops; locals opened the locks and flooded the area with sea water, forcing the perplexed invaders to retreat. The victory won the town weighing rights, which laid the foundation for its cheese market.

Orientation & Information

The town centre is focused on Waagplein, the main square where the famous cheese market is held. Langestraat is a pedestrianised shopping street with charming restaurants and bars around the Waag and the quay named Bierkade. The pretty, canal-bound centre is 500m southeast of the train station.

Library (☎ 51 5 66 44; Gasthuisstraat 2; internet per hr €1.50; ☺ 11am-9pm Tue-Fri, 11am-3pm Sat) Has rows of internet terminals.

Tourist office (☎ 511 42 84; www.vvvalkmaar.nl; Waagplein 2; ☺ 10am-5.30pm) In the Waaggebouw, the towering old weigh-house. Staff will book accommodation for €2.50.

Sights

Before beginning your exploration of the city, consider purchasing a copy of the *Walking Tour of the Town among the Historic Buildings* booklet (€2) from the tourist office. It covers historical buildings like the Renaissance **town hall** in extensive detail.

Built as a chapel in the 14th century, the **Waaggebouw** was pressed into service as a weigh-house two centuries later. This handsome building houses the tourist office and upstairs, the **Hollands Kaasmuseum** (Dutch Cheese Museum; ☎ 511 42 84; adult/child €2.50/1.50; ☺ 10am-4pm, Mon-Sat Apr-Oct), a reverential display of cheesemaking utensils, photos and a curious stock of paintings by 16th-century female artists.

The **Stedelijk Museum** (Municipal Museum; ☎ 511 07 37; www.stedelijkmuseumalkmaar.nl; Canadaplein 1; adult/child €4.50/free; ☺ 10am-5pm Tue-Fri, 1-5pm Sat & Sun) is overlooked by many visitors who don't get past the cheese market. This is a shame because its collection of oil paintings by Dutch masters, including impressive life-sized portraits of Alkmaar nobles, is alone worth the entry fee. Other works show Alkmaar in post–Golden Age decline; sombre scenes of almswomen caring for the poor recall how the church's role grew as trade declined. The few modern works on display include Charley Toorop's odd oil painting of the Alkmaar cheese market; her cheese bearers with grotesque features remain controversial.

The **Grote Kerk** (admission Jun-Aug €4, Sep-May €2.50; ☺ 10am-5pm Tue-Sun) will remind visitors that Noord Holland has a particularly high concen-

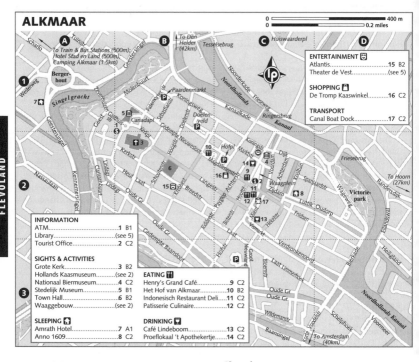

ALKMAAR

ENTERTAINMENT
Atlantis.................................15 B2
Theater de Vest.....................(see 5)

SHOPPING
De Tromp Kaaswinkel............16 C2

TRANSPORT
Canal Boat Dock....................17 C2

INFORMATION
ATM......................................1 B1
Library...............................(see 5)
Tourist Office........................2 C2

SIGHTS & ACTIVITIES
Grote Kerk.............................3 B2
Hollands Kaasmuseum..........(see 2)
Nationaal Biermuseum............4 C2
Stedelijk Museum...................5 B1
Town Hall..............................6 B2
Waaggebouw......................(see 2)

SLEEPING
Amrath Hotel.........................7 A1
Anno 1609.............................8 C2

EATING
Henry's Grand Café................9 C2
Het Hof van Alkmaar.............10 B2
Indonesisch Restaurant Deli...11 C2
Patisserie Culinaire...............12 C2

DRINKING
Café Lindeboom.....................13 C2
Proeflokaal 't Apothekertje.....14 C2

tration of church organs. The most famous one here is the small 'Swallow Organ' in the north ambulatory, one of the country's oldest (1511). The huge beast in the nave was designed by Jacob van Campen, a leading organ-maker in the 16th century. Organ recitals take place from noon to 12.30pm and 1pm to 1.30pm June to August (included in admission) and Wednesday evenings in July and August (€6).

Housed in the attractive old De Boom brewery, the **Nationaal Biermuseum** (☎ 511 38 01; Houttil 1; adult/child €3.50/1.75; ⏰ 10am-4pm Tue-Fri, 1-4pm Sat & Sun Apr-Oct, 1-4pm Tue-Sun Nov-Mar) has a decent collection of beer-making equipment and wax dummies showing how the suds were made. The rare video of Dutch beer commercials since the 1950s will have you in stiches. Choose from 30 beers (eight on draught) in the friendly bar after your tour.

Tours
Departing from Mient near the Waag are 45-minute **tours** (☎ 511 77 50; adult/child €4.70/3.20; ⏰ 11am-5pm Mon-Sat May-Aug) with multilingual commentary. During cheese-market season boats go every 20 minutes from 9.30am.

Sleeping
The tourist office has a list of private rooms from about €20 per person.

ourpick Anno 1609 (☎ 511 61 11; www.anno1609 .nl; Luttik Oudorp 110; d €225) It doesn't get much more romantic than this. The sole suite of this boutique B&B (breakfast is served in the dining room or on the small balcony at the back) extends over an entire floor of a beautifully restored 17th-century granary overlooking one of the city's peaceful canals. The furnishings ooze exclusivity – a freestanding French bath, designer chandeliers, polished parquet and lead-light windows – and it's the soul of discretion: outside there's no hint that this listed monument is even a hotel.

Amrath Hotel (☎ 518 61 86; www.amrathhotelalkmaar .nl; Geestersingel 15; s/d from €105/115; ☒) Only a short walk from the centre is this new hotel, part of the Best Western chain. Its rooms are spacious and thoroughly modern, and the entire outfit is geared to the business crowd. Specials are handed out on a regular basis.

Hotel Stad en Land (☎ 512 39 11; www.stadenland .com; Stationsweg 92; s/d €52.50/75) Close to the train station with slightly dated yet comfy rooms,

---

NOWHERE'S AS CHEESY AS HERE

Cheese is a big thing in the Netherlands; anyone who's breakfasted in a B&B or entered a supermarket can tell you this. But in Noord Holland's Schiereiland, cheese is a very, very serious business.

Alkmaar's traditional **cheese market** (Waagplein; ☺ 10am-noon Fri Apr-Sep) goes back to the 17th century. Every Friday morning around 30,000kg of waxed rounds of Gouda, Edam and Leiden *kaas* (cheese) are ceremoniously stacked on Waagplein, and soon the porters appear in their colourful hats, ready to spring into action. The dealers (looking official in white smocks) insert a hollow rod to extract a cheese sample and go into taste-test mode, sniffing and crumbling to check fat and moisture content. This is one of the few Dutch towns where the old cheese guilds still operate, and the porters' bright green, red and yellow hats denote which company they belong to. Once deals are struck the porters whisk the cheeses on wooden sledges to the old cheese scale in a stride reminiscent of someone hurrying to the toilet. It's primarily for show: nowadays the modern dairy combines have a lock on the cheese trade. Still, as living relics go it's a spectacle not to be missed, and it's fun to see so many people excited about cheese.

Along with its own cheese market, Edam – and the surrounding regions – has a centuries-old reputation as a producer of toothsome cheese. About 8km south of Edam, there are several **cheese farms** that can be visited daily from 8.30am to 6pm (admission free): Irene Hoeve, Jacobs Hoeve (both on Hoogedijk) and Alida Hoeve (on Zaddeweg). Cheese making is a fascinating art, but prepare for a pretty cheesy experience as presenters in traditional duds run through their well-oiled routine before referring you to the shop.

Stad en Land is a good choice for those making a short, overnight visit to Alkmaar. Of the four rooms those at the rear are the quietest and overlook a little pond.

Camping Alkmaar (☎ 511 69 24; www.camping alkmaar.nl; Bergerweg 201; camp site €22, cabins €35) This site lies in a pleasant copse convenient to the ring road, 1km west of the train station. Tent sites are sheltered and wooden cabins sleep two persons. Take bus 160 to Sportpark (10 minutes).

Eating

Alkmaar has a fine variety of restaurants and cafés.

Patisserie Culinaire (☎ 511 29 58; Houttil 13; mains €5-16; ☺ 11am-7pm Mon-Sat) This buzzing artsy café offers freshly made filled baguettes, open sandwiches, quiche and big salads that spill off your plate. It's also the perfect spot to sip a coffee at the sidewalk tables and watch the world go by.

Henry's Grand Café (☎ 511 32 83; Houttil 34; mains €12-20; ☺ lunch & dinner) A convivial place serving soups, salads, sandwiches and set meals including pork or chicken satay, backed up by a good range of beers. Its lunch menu is much easier on the wallet.

Het Hof van Alkmaar (☎ 512 12 12; Hof van Sonoy 1; mains €15-20; ☺ lunch & dinner Tue-Sun) Hof van Alkmaar occupies a former 15th-century nunnery with a rustic dining room overlooking the *hofje*. The menu is full of inventions like Vic-

toria bass in chilli-coconut sauce, but should your palate desire something simpler at lunch, there are chicken satays and sandwiches.

Indonesisch Restaurant Deli (☎ 515 40 82; Mient 8; mains €13-27; ☺ dinner, closed Mon & Tue) This place offers good-value dishes such as nasi goreng as well as elaborate rijsttafels. It's been around for ages, comes highly recommended and has air-con.

Drinking

Proeflokaal 't Apothekertje (☎ 512 41 07; Waagplein 16) Of the bars and brown cafés that hug the north side of Waagplein, this is the most pleasant to grab a relaxing drink in. It's an old-style drinking hole done up like a chemist's shop.

Café Lindeboom (☎ 512 17 43; Verdronkenoord 114) Over by the old fish market is this cosy bar where talkative locals live it up on the (hopefully) sunny canal terrace.

Entertainment

Alkmaar has a lively arts scene – pick up a copy of the monthly *Alkmaar Agenda* (free) from the tourist office to see what's on.

Theater De Vest (☎ 548 99 99; www.theaterdevest.nl; Canadaplein 2) The centre for Alkmaar's highbrow entertainment, De Vest runs the gamut from traditional plays and puppet shows to avant-garde dance. In summer Canadaplein turns into a stage for the performing arts festival Zomer op het plein (Summer on the square).

Atlantis (☎ 511 83 90; www.atlantispodium.nl; Breedstraat 33) Atlantis is *the* downtown music club, always with a fresh and unpredictable programme. Expect anything from a rave one night to a pop quiz the next (entry normally €3 to €10). The Creatif Centrum upstairs offers arts courses, and the Tooncafé, also upstairs, runs exhibitions.

Shopping

De Tromp Kaaswinkel (☎ 511 34 22; Magdalenenstraat 11) There's not much else to buy in Alkmaar except cheese, and this place stocks an excellent range of Dutch and French varieties. You'll be amazed at how much of the yellow stuff can be stored in such a small shop.

Getting There & Away

Trains to/from Alkmaar:

Destination	Price (€)	Duration (min)	Frequency (per hr)
Amsterdam	6.30	30-40	4
Den Helder	6.70	35	2
Enkhuizen	6.70	50	2
Hoorn	4.30	25	2

The station has left-luggage lockers and ATMs.

Getting Around

Connexxion buses 10, 22 and 127 connect the train station to Kanaalkade (five minutes).

There's a **bicycle shop** (☎ 511 79 07) at the train station, but don't bother renting on cheese market day as there're too many people on the streets, and it's likely to be nicked.

BROEK OP LANGEDIJK

☎ 0226

In the town of Broek op Langedijk, about 8km northeast of Alkmaar, the **Museum Broeker Veiling** (Museum Broeker Auction; ☎ 31 38 07; www .broekerveiling.nl; Broek op Langedijk; adult/child €6.25/3.65; ☉ 10am-6pm Mon-Fri, till 9.30pm Thu, 11am-5pm Sat & Sun Jul & Aug, 10am-5pm Mon-Fri, 11am-5pm Sat & Sun Apr-Jun, Sep & Oct) bills itself as the 'oldest sail-through vegetable auction'. Only when you've entered the auction hall – a stunning Art Deco building on the water – does it become clear how this works.

The show begins as barges laden with baskets of produce float in beneath the feet of the auctioneer, who encourages visitors to

bid on the old auction clock. It's entertaining, instructive and above all easy to get carried away, so remember how many tomatoes or bunches of broccoli you can realistically consume.

The museum also runs 45-minute boat tours around the dozens of tiny island plots nearby that once supplied the auction with regular greens. Combination tickets for museum and boat cost adult/child €9.95/5.50.

From Amsterdam, take the A9 to Alkmaar and N25 to Heerhugowaard, exiting for Broek op Langedijk. By train, go to Alkmaar (€6.40, 45 minutes, four times hourly) and change to bus 155 (20 minutes, twice hourly).

HOORN

☎ 0229 / pop 65,500

With a string of museums and a busy harbour, Hoorn attracts both weekend tourists and skippers alike. It was once the capital of West Friesland and, thanks to the presence of the Dutch merchant fleet, a mighty trading city. As a member of the league of Seven Cities, it helped free the country from the Spanish who occupied the town in 1569.

Its most famous son, explorer Willem Schoutens, named South America's storm-lashed tip – Cape Horn – after his home town in 1616.

Orientation & Information

The old quarter begins about 1km southwest of the train station. From the station, walk south along broad Veemarkt to Gedempte Turfhaven, turn right and take the first left into Grote Noord, the pedestrianised shopping street. At the end is the scenic main square, Rode Steen, and the harbour area is a stone's throw further south, down Grote Havensteeg.

Library (Wisselstraat 8; internet per hr €02.80; ☉ 1-8.30pm Mon, Wed & Thu, 1-5pm Tue & Fri, 10am-1pm Sat) Has internet access.

Tourist office (☎ 072-511 42 84; www.vvvhoorn.nl; Veemarkt 4; ☉ 1-6pm Mon, 9.30am-6pm Tue-Fri, 9.30am-5pm Sat) About 250m south of the train station; will book accommodation for a €2.50 fee.

Sights & Activities

Hoorn's heyday as a shipping centre is long gone, but the imposing **statue of Jan Peterszoon Coen**, founder of the Dutch East India Company, still watches over the Rode Steen (Red Stone or Fortress), the square named for the blood that once flowed from the gallows. On the northeastern side of the square it's impossible to overlook the **Waag**, the 17th-century weigh-house that's home to De Waag Café-Restaurant.

On the square also stands the former seat of the **Staten-College** (States' Council), the body that once governed seven towns in North Holland (Alkmaar, Hoorn, Enkhuizen, Medemblik, Edam, Monnickendam and Purmerend). Its wedding-cake façade bears the coat of arms of Oranje-Nassau, the Dutch-German royal dynasty that the Dutch named as rulers when Napoleon left Holland. It now houses the **Westfries Museum** (☎ 28 00 28; www.wfm.nl; Rode Steen; adult/child €3.50/1.50; ☽ 11am-5pm Mon-Fri, 2-5pm Sat & Sun), an absorbing museum with a rich collection of historical paintings – so rich that it was the target of art theft in 2005. Some 20 paintings were stolen, but fortunately the four large group portraits of prominent *schutters* (civic guards) by Jan A Rotius (1624–66) were left in peace. Rotius himself can be seen at the far right in one scene. The rear courtyard has a number of curious stone tablets from local façades.

The **Affiche Museum** (Dutch Poster Museum; ☎ 29 98 46; Grote Oost 2-4; adult/child €3.50/1.75; ☽ 11-5pm Tue-Fri, noon-5pm Sat & Sun) has an extensive collection including every single poster made for the annual Holland Festival since 1948. You'll also find contemporary artwork from big-name designers like Anthon Beeke and Gert Dumbar (of Studio Dumbar fame). It's virtually opposite the old weigh-house.

Housed in two old cheese warehouses, the **Museum of the 20th Century** (☎ 21 40 01; Bierkade 4; adult/child €4/2 ☽ 10am-5pm Tue-Fri, noon-5pm Sat & Sun) is devoted mainly to household goods and modern inventions. Of the few eye-openers there are a 1964 Philips mainframe computer – a clunky bookcase-sized unit with a whole 1KB of memory – and a 30-sq-metre scale *maquette* (model) of Hoorn in 1650, with taped commentary in several languages.

The **Museum Stoomtram** (☎ 21 48 62; www .museumstoomtram.nl; adult/child return €17/12.80; ☽ 11am Tue-Sat mid-Apr–Oct & Mon Jul & Aug, Sat & Sun Nov, Dec & beginning of Apr) isn't a museum in the traditional sense but rather a historic locomotive that puffs an hour between Hoorn station and Medemblik. You can combine the train and boat for a route called the 'Historic Triangle': first from Hoorn to Medemblik by train and then back by boat *and* train via Enkhuizen.

Add a visit to the Zuiderzeemuseum (p164) in Enkhuizen and the whole package costs €28/22.30.

The scenic harbour is lined by stately gabled houses. Overshadowing them all is the massive **Hoofdtoren** (1532), a defensive gate that now hosts a bar and restaurant. The tiny belfry was an afterthought.

Sleeping

Accommodation is not a high point in Hoorn, so you may be better off just spending the day here. The tourist office does however have a list of B&Bs from around €20 per person.

Hotel de Keizerskroon (☎ 21 27 17; www.keizers kroonhoorn.nl; Breed 33; s/d €62.50/75) Very much in the middle of things, this 25-room hotel-restaurant has rooms that are reasonably modern and enticing, and quite brown. Its insulated windows afford a view of the bustling market streets below.

Hotel de Magneet (☎ 21 50 21; hoteldemagneet@ planet.nl; Kleine Oost 5D; s/d from €62/77) This family-run guesthouse lies in a quiet street just east of the old centre, with a bar and restaurant. Rooms are large by Dutch standards, but not particularly exciting and low on atmosphere. The proximity to the coastal paths makes the hotel popular with cyclists' clubs.

Eating

De Waag Café-Restaurant (☎ 21 51 95; Rode Steen 8; mains €16-30; ☽ lunch & dinner) With pride of place on the main square in the stunning Waag building, this restaurant is hard to beat. The international menu is heavily loaded with Dutch staples, and when the sun comes out there's no better place to be than on De Waag's terrace.

Brasserie Bontekoe (☎ 21 93 09; Nieuwendam 1; mains €10-20; ☽ lunch & dinner Wed-Sat) This cosy, terraced brown café enjoys a strategic view of canals and marina. There's an extensive sandwich menu alongside lamb, pork and chicken dishes, and naturally a mystery 'catch of the day' option.

Hendrickje Stoffels (☎ 21 04 17; Oude Doelenkade 3-5; set menu €25-31; ☽ dinner, closed Wed-Thu) With a styled interior, progressive French and fish dishes, and a listing in *Lekker* six years in a row, Hendrickje Stoffels is sure to please.

Vishandel Leen Parlevliet (rolls from €3, meals from €6; ☽ 10am-7pm) Next to the Hoofdtoren at the harbour, this small glass pod sells wonderful seafood rolls and bigger seafood meals. Munch and admire the graceful tall ships moored at the docks.

Open-air markets are held on Wednesday (June to August) and Saturday (year round) along Breed.

Shopping

Delikaas (☎ 21 03 52; Breed 38) This specialist vendor in an ornate colonial-style building is an excellent place to buy cheese, freshly roasted nuts, dried meats and wine.

Getting There & Around

Regular train services to/from Hoorn include the following:

Destination	Price (€)	Duration (min)	Frequency (per hr)
Alkmaar	4.30	25	2
Amsterdam	6.80	40	2
Enkhuizen	3.40	22	2-4

The bus station is right outside Hoorn train station. Connexxion bus 135 goes twice hourly to Den Helder (a one-hour ride) and Leeuwarden (two hours, change buses at Den Oever). Connexxion bus 114 serves Edam (30 minutes, twice hourly).

Hire your two-wheelers at the **bicycle shop** (☎ 21 70 96) at Hoorn train station.

ENKHUIZEN

☎ 0228 / pop 17,000

Enkhuizen may be a small, quaint town in the present day but during the Golden Age its strategic harbour sheltered the Dutch merchant fleet. It slipped into relative obscurity in the late 17th century but now possesses one of the largest fleets on the IJsselmeer – of recreational vessels. For most tourists however Enkhuizen's biggest drawcard is the Zuiderzeemuseum, one of the country's finest.

Orientation

The train station is a terminus on the line to Amsterdam and stands on the southern edge of town. The yacht-filled Buitenhaven (Outer Harbour) and the narrower Oude Haven (Old Harbour) bisect the town east to west; canals ring the old centre. Dijk is the main café-and-restaurant strip, on the northern bank of Oude Haven. About 200m further north, the long, pedestrianised Westerstraat runs parallel and is lined with impressive historic buildings.

Information

Library (☎ 31 24 92; Kwakespad 3; internet per hr €3; 🕑 1.30-9pm Mon & Fri, 1.30-5.30pm Tue-Wed, 10am-noon Thu & Sat) About 500m west along Westerstraat – turn right into the canalside road Kwakespad.

Tourist office (☎ 31 31 64; www.vvenkhuizen.nl; Tussen Twee Havens 1; 🕑 9am-5pm Mon-Sat Apr-Oct, closed Sat Nov-Mar) Just east of the train station; sells ferry tickets in summer and a self-guided tour booklet in English (€1.50).

Sights & Activities

Moving east along Westerstraat you'll spy the remarkable **Westerkerk**, a 15th-century Gothic church with a removable wooden belfry. The ornate choir screen and imposing pulpit are worth a look. Opposite the church is the **Weeshuis**, a 17th-century orphanage with a sugary, curlicued portal.

At the other end of Westerstraat stands the 16th-century **Waag** (weigh-house) on the old cheese market, and nearby the classical **town hall**, modelled after the Amsterdam town hall that once stood on the Dam. You can peek through the windows at the lavish Gobelins and tapestries, but it's closed to the public.

Between the Buitenhaven and the Oude Haven, the **Drommedaris** was built as a defence tower as part of the 16th-cetury town walls. Once a formidable prison, it now serves as an elevated meeting hall. Its clock-tower carillon still tinkles a playful tune on the hour.

The old harbour is chock-a-block with polished schooners, smacks and *tjalks* of a slower era, some of which are available for hire (p287). More modest skippers can hire kayaks, canoes and electric boats at **De Waterspiegel** (☎ 31 74 56; www.dewaterspiegel.com; Olifantsteiger 3; kayaks/canoes/electric boats per hr €5/7/15), mainly for use on the inner canals.

ZUIDERZEEMUSEUM

This very impressive **museum** (☎ 35 11 11; www .zuiderzeemuseum.nl; Buiten & Binnen museums adult/child €11.50/9; Binnenmuseum only €7/6.50, parking €5; 🕑 10am-5pm, Buitenmuseum only Apr-Oct) consists of two parts: the open-air or Buitenmuseum with 130-odd rebuilt dwellings and workshops, and an indoor Binnenmuseum devoted to farming, fishing and shipping. The two parts lie about 300m from each other, but to relieve congestion visitors are encouraged to leave their vehicles at a car park at the edge of town. A ferry (fare included in your ticket) then takes you across the bay to the outdoor displays. Plan a half-day for an unhurried visit to both sections.

The Buitenmuseum is captivating. Opened in 1983, it was carefully assembled from houses, farms and sheds trucked in from around the region to show Zuiderzee life as it was from 1880 to 1932. Every conceivable detail has been thought of, from the fence-top decorations and choice of shrubbery to the entire layout of villages, and the look and feel is certainly authentic. An illustrated guide (in English), included in the ticket price, is an essential companion on your tour of the entire museum.

Inhabitants wear traditional dress, and there are real shops such as a bakery, a chemist and a sweet shop. Workshops run demonstrations throughout the day. Though varying in character, the displays join seamlessly: lime kilns from Akersloot stand a few metres from Zuid-ende and its row of Monnickendam houses, originally built outside the dykes. Don't miss the **Urk quarter**, raised to simulate the island town before the Noordoostpolder was drained. For a special postmark, drop your letters at the old post office from Den Oever. The **Marker Haven** is a copy of the harbour built in 1830 on what was then the island of Marken.

Exit at the rear and walk 300m to reach the Binnenmuseum, which occupies a museum complex adjoining the **Peperhuis**, the former home and warehouse of a Dutch shipping merchant. The displays include a fine ship-ping hall: paintings, prints and other materials relating the rise and fall of the fishing industry, and the construction of the dykes. Here too are cultural artefacts such as regional costumes, porcelain, silver, and jewellery that indicate the extent of Holland's riches at the time.

Sleeping

The tourist office has a list of private rooms from about €18.

Hotel Garni Recuerdos (☎ 56 24 69; www.recuerdos.nl; Westerstraat 217; s/d €60/85) Owned by a warm and welcoming music society patron, this stately manor house is the picture of calm, with three immaculate rooms overlooking a manicured garden. The atmosphere is so friendly even the neighbours chime in with a greeting.

Het Wapen van Enkhuizen (☎ 31 34 34; wapen vanenkhuizen@wanadoo.nl; Breedstraat 59; r €65-79) Close to the Zuiderzeemuseum and harbour is this small hotel, with comfy rooms, a quiet loca-tion, and a restaurant on the ground floor.

Appartement Hotel Driebanen (☎ 31 61 81; www .hoteldriebanen.com; Driebanen 59; s/d from €65/85) Drie-banen is a tranquil canalside guesthouse with an old-fashioned look and feel to it, right down to the host who is big on personal wel-comes, and is a goldmine of local information. Rooms are cheerful and bright.

Camping Enkhuizer Zand (☎ 31 72 89; www .campingenkhuizerzand.nl; Kooizandweg 4; camp sites €21.50; ☒ Apr-Sep) Next to the Zuiderzeemuseum, this popular site is a model of self-sufficiency with an indoor pool, sandy beaches, tennis courts and grocery.

Eating

De Brasserie (☎ 32 28 58; Westerstraat 164; light meals €8-10; ☒ 11am-6pm Tue-Sun) With its own turret, roof-top terrace overlooking a quiet canal, and pavement seating, this chilled teahouse is an excellent choice for coffee and cake in the warmer months. When it's cold, take a pew indoors by a window and watch the Dutch ignore the weather.

Restaurant De Boei (☎ 31 42 80; Havenweg 5; mains around €20; ☒ lunch & dinner Mar-Oct) Occupying a peaceful corner near the harbour, De Boei is a place to head for superfluous amounts of food, but in this case quantity equals quality. Fish of course is a good option in these parts.

Restaurant de Drie Haringhe (☎ 31 86 10; Dijk 28; mains €21-25; ☒ lunch & dinner, closed Tue) This upmar-ket locale excels in Dutch and French-inspired cuisine, and has been receiving rave reviews for years. Though next to a main street, the walled garden is an oasis of calm at mealtimes.

Dikke Mik (☎ 31 64 04; HJ Schimmelstraat 10; mains €10-16; ☒ lunch & dinner) In warm weather the quay fills with aromas of spare ribs, mixed grill, Mexican chicken and a fish stew that'll stick to your ribs; in winter the clientele holes up in the cosy *eetcafé*.

Getting There & Away

Regular train services to/from Enkhuizen:

Destination	Price (€)	Duration (min)	Frequency (per hr)
Alkmaar	6.70	52	2
Amsterdam	9.30	60	2-4
Den Helder	10.50	90	2
Hoorn	3.40	22	2-4

Den Helder connections mean a train change at both Hoorn and Heerhugowaard, which is inconvenient but the fastest option for public transport. The bus station behind Enkhuizen train station serves mainly local destinations. Of the few useful bus links, 150 goes five times daily to Lelystad (35 minutes).

Up to three ferries daily from April to September (and on weekends in October) link Enkhuizen-Spoorhaven to Urk (adult single/return €8/12, child single/return €7/9, 1¾ hours), Stavoren (adult €8.50/11.50, child €5/6.70, 1¼ hours) and Medemblik (adult €8.50/11.50, child €5/6.70, 1¼ hours).

DYKE ROAD

The N302 between Enkhuizen and Lelystad deserves a special mention because it runs along a 32km-long dyke, completed in 1976 as the first step of the reclamation of the Markerwaard (p175). As you get under way you'll pass below a high-tech causeway that connects Enkhuizen harbour with the IJsselmeer, with ships floating surreally over the motorway.

Sights are few along the route, apart from the boats bobbing on the IJsselmeer and a stone monument at the halfway mark in the form of a chain link symbolising the joining of West Friesland with Flevoland.

MEDEMBLIK

☎ 0227 / pop 7900

About 12km northwest of Enkhuizen lies Medemblik, the oldest port on the IJsselmeer, dating back to the 12th century. It's not a pretty town but its busy harbour and medieval fortress are worth a few hours of your time.

Orientation & Information

The castle stands on the eastern side and is signposted from the harbour. The richly decorated façades on Kaasmarkt, Torenstraat, Nieuwstraat and along the Achterom canal are impressive. The old town is only 1km across and thus quickly absorbed.

Tourist office (☎ 54 28 52; www.vvv-medemblik.nl; Kaasmarkt 1; 9am-5pm Mon-Sat) A folksy all-in-one place, with a good stock of maps at the back of the local stationers. Will book accommodation for a €2.50 fee.

Sights & Activities

The rather twee **Kasteel Radboud** (☎ 54 19 60; adult/child €3/2; 10am-5pm Tue-Fri, 2-5pm Sat) at the head of the harbour looks for all the world like a well-fortified mansion rather than the castle it's purported to be. Built by Count Floris V in the 13th century to keep the feisty

natives under his thumb, the fortress served as a prison before a 19th-century restoration by Pierre Cuypers, the designer of Amsterdam's Rijksmuseum. The original floor plan has been preserved and the imposing **Ridderzaal** (Knights' Hall) still looks much as it did in the Middle Ages. The self-guided tour gives details of the castle's long history and the count's undoing.

Ever wondered what drove the industrial revolution? Part of the answer lies at the **Stoommachine Museum** (Steam Engine Museum; ☎ 54 47 32; Oosterdijk 4; adult/child €4.80/2.40; 10am-5pm Tue-Sun Feb-Oct), in the old pump station outside Medemblik. Thirty handsome old steam engines from Holland, England and Germany are fired up for demonstrations in summer months, and kids can stoke small coal-fired models on Wednesdays and weekends.

The **Museum Stoomtram** (p162) departs from the old train station where there's a small display of railway artefacts (free).

Sleeping & Eating

The tourist office has a list of private rooms from €20 to €25 per person, although you're better off making Medemblik a day trip.

Hotel Medemblik (☎ 54 38 44; www.hetwapen vanmedemblik.nu; Oosterhaven 1; s/d from €65/90) Directly opposite the tourist office on one of the town's harbour canals is this slightly dated hotel with friendly staff and adequate rooms. The attached restaurant is one of its best features.

De Driemaster (☎ 54 30 20; Pekelharinghaven 49; mains €12-24; lunch & dinner) Ahh – lovely views of the harbour and IJsselmeer as you relish a braised turbot or launch into a filled croissant. The best spots are canalside for watching the big pleasure boats drift under the drawbridge.

Getting There & Around

The nearest real train station is in Hoorn, from where bus 39 (twice hourly) makes the hour journey to Medemblik. A ferry links Medemblik with Enkhuizen-Spoorhaven (p165).

Ted de Lange (☎ 57 00 93; Vooreiland 1) on the eastern side of town has a huge selection of bicycles for hire.

DEN HELDER

☎ 0223

Before you reach Texel, the only attraction in the unspectacular naval town of Den Helder is the **Marine Museum** (☎ 65 75 34; Hoofdgracht 3;

adult/child €4.50/3.50; 10am-5pm Mon-Fri, noon-5pm Sat & Sun). It's housed in a suitable town in a suitable spot, the former armoury of the Dutch Royal Navy. The display covers naval history mainly after 1815, the year the Netherlands became a kingdom. You can run rampant through several vessels moored on the docks outside, including an ironclad ram ship and a submarine left high and dry (not for the claustrophobic). Note that parents will tire long before their progenies.

See p170 for information on trains to Den Helder. Bus 135 (one hour, hourly) is an alternative to changing trains to reach Hoorn.

TEXEL

☎ 0222 / pop 13,450

About 3km north of the coast of Noord Holland lies Texel (pronounced *tes*-sel), the largest and most visited of the Wadden Islands. It's a remarkably diverse place, with broad white beaches, lush nature reserves, forests and picture-book villages. Now 25km long and 9km wide, it actually consisted of two islands until 1835 when a spit of land to Eyerland Island was pumped dry.

Before the Noordzeekanaal opened in the 19th century, Texel was a main stop for ships en route to Asia, Africa and North America: the first trade mission to the East Indies began and ended here. It was also the scene of a spectacular maritime disaster: on Christmas Day 1593, hurricane-force winds battered a merchant fleet moored off the coast and 44 vessels sank, drowning about a thousand seamen.

Texel relies chiefly on tourism, with the majority of visitors being either Dutch or German. The local wool is highly prized and there are sheep everywhere, lazing, grazing or tippee-toeing along the dykes.

Orientation

Ferries from the mainland dock at 't Horntje on the south side of the isle, from where buses head north to Texel's six main villages. Den Burg, 6km north of 't Horntje, is the island's modest capital and home to the tourist office, while De Koog, another 5km north again, is Texel's tourist mecca with a distinctly tacky streak.

Den Hoorn, only 5km northwest of the ferry terminal, is handy to tulip fields and windswept sand dunes, and Oudeschild, 7km northeast of 't Horntje, has the best harbour facilities on the island. Oosterend, 6km north-

east of Den Burg, is a quiet hamlet with distinctive architecture far from the beaches.

Tiny De Cocksdorp, at the northern end of the island, is a launch pad to the island of Vlieland (p239).

Information

Two handy booklets – *Texel in a Alikruuk* (nutshell) and *Travel Guide Texel* – have accommodation and activity listings, and are available from the tourist office.

ABN-Amro (Parkstraat 20, Den Burg) It's 50m east of the imposing Hervormde Kerk (Dutch Reform Church), and has an ATM. Other banks can be found in De Koog and De Cocksdorp.

Tourist office (☎ 31 47 41; www.texel.net; Emmalaan 66, Den Burg; 9am-5.30pm Mon-Fri, 9am-5pm Sat) Signposted from the ferry terminal; on the southern fringe of town. Has free internet access, plenty of information, and staff book accommodation for a fee.

Sights

DUINEN VAN TEXEL NATIONAL PARK

For many nature lovers this patchwork of varied dunescape running along the entire western coast of the island is the prime reason for visiting Texel. Salt fens and heath alternate with velvety, grass-covered dunes, and you'll find plants endemic to this habitat, such as the dainty marsh orchid or sea buckthorn, a ragged shrub with bright orange berries. Much of the area is bird sanctuary and accessible only on foot.

De Slufter became a brackish wetland after an attempt at land reclamation failed; when a storm breached the dykes in the early 1900s the area was allowed to flood and a unique ecosystem developed. To the south, **De Muy** is renowned for its colony of spoonbills that are monitored with great zeal by local naturalists.

Only a stone's throw from the windswept beach lies the dark, leafy forest of **De Dennen** between Den Hoorn and De Koog. Originally planted as a source of lumber, today it has an enchanting network of walking and biking paths. In springtime the forest floor is carpeted with snowdrops that were first planted here in the 1930s.

ECOMARE

Initially a refuge for sick seals retrieved from the Waddenzee, **Ecomare** (☎ 31 77 41; www.ecomare .nl; Ruyslaan 92, De Koog; adult/child €7.75/4.75; 9am-5pm) has expanded into a nature centre devoted to the preservation and understanding

NOORD HOLLAND & FLEVOLAND

TEXEL ISLAND

0 ————— 6 km
0 ————— 4 miles

TEXEL BUS ROUTES
- - -(28)- - - Route 28: Veerhaven-Klimpstraat
- - -(29)- - - Route 29: Veerhaven-De Witte Hoek

To Vlieland

Duinen Van Texel National Park

Klimpstraat

De Cocksdorp

De Slufter

De Muy

Slufterbosweg

De Koog

Polder Waal En Burg

NORTH SEA

Oosterend

De Staart

N501

De Waal

Waddenzee

Den Burg

De Dennen

N501

Schilderweg

bulk fields

Hoornderw

Oudeschild

Den Hoorn

Duinen Van Texel National Park

Veerhaven

't Hoontje

Hors

To Den Helder (4km)

SIGHTS & ACTIVITIES
Ecomare...**1** A3
Eureka Tropische Tuin.....................**2** C2
Kaasboerderij Wezenspyk...............**3** B4
Luchtvaart & Oorlogsmuseum.........**4** B2
Maritime & Beachcombers Museum...**5** C4
Texelse Bierbrouwerij.......................**6** B3

SLEEPING
De Bremakker...................................**7** B3
Hotel De 14 Sterren.........................**8** B3
Stayokay Hostel Panorama..............**9** B3
Strandhotel Noordzee......................**10** B2

EATING
De Worsteltent...........................(see 8)

TRANSPORT
Ferry Jetty......................................**11** B4

---

of Texel's wildlife. Contained within its walls are displays on Texel's development since the last ice age, islander's interaction with the sea, large aquariums filled with fish from the Wadden and North Seas (including sharks and seaskates), and a national park exposé.

The highlight for young and old, however, is the seals themselves; their playful water ballet lacking in any apparent effort will delight all but the most jaded visitor. Try to catch a feeding at 11am or 3pm. Rescued birds are the other main tenants.

MUSEUMS

Of the six museums on the island, which are covered by the **Texel Museum Combination Card** (adult/child €15/8.50) available from the tourist of-

fice, the **Maritime & Beachcombers Museum** (☎ 31 49 56; Barentszstraat 21, Oudeschild; adult/child €4.50/3.25; 10am-5pm Tue-Sat, noon-5pm Sun) will interest most visitors. Its extraordinary variety of junk recovered from sunken ships is mind-boggling – it's a bit like perusing flotsam from the *Titanic*. In the outdoor section there are demonstrations by rope-makers, fish-smokers and blacksmiths, while the indoor displays cover everything from underwater archaeology to windmill technology.

Next to the airfield, the **Luchtvaart & Oorlogsmuseum** (Aviation Museum; ☎ 31 16 89; adult/child €3/1.85; Tue-Sun 11am-5pm Easter-Oct) revisits the glory days of the island's pint-sized squadron. Artefacts include old aircraft or bits thereof, such as the cockpit of a 1913 Fokker.

OTHER SIGHTS

June is the time to see wild orchids on Texel–a rarity in the country; outside this month, dress lightly and head for the steamy **Eureka Tropische Tuin** (☎ 31 83 64; Schorrenweg 20, Oosterend; adult/child €3.50/2.50; 8.30am-6pm Mon-Fri, 8.30am-5pm Sat). A number of native orchid species can be viewed in all their tender, quivering glory alongside exotic specimens, and a menagerie of tropical birds fill the greenhouse with their colourful plumes.

The isle's only brewery, the **Texelse Bierbrouwerij** (☎ 31 32 29; www.speciaalbier.nl; Schilderweg 214b, Oudeschild; adult/child €6/2.50; 1.30-6pm Wed & Sat) divulges the secrets of its suds including its tasty *Speciaalbier*. The former dairy on the property has a terrace ideal for downing a few.

Kaasboerderijk Wezenspyk (☎ 31 50 90; Hoonndernweg 29), a small cheese farm between Den Hoorn and Den Burg, is the place to scoop up tasty rounds produced from the local cows, sheep and goats.

Activities

Swimming, cycling, walking, boating, relaxing; Texel is an island to enjoy all these. Its pristinely white **beaches**, lining the northwestern shore, are numbered and marked (with a *paal*, or piling) from south to north. Lifeguards are on duty from No 9 southeast of Den Hoorn to No 21 near De Koog in summer. There are two nudist beaches, at No 9 and at No 27 in the north. Swimming is prohibited between Nos 31 and 33 near the lighthouse at De Cocksdorp due to treacherous riptides.

The tourist office sells a useful booklet (in Dutch; €2.50) of **cycle routes** and **hiking trails** that crisscross the island, as well as **horse riding** schools which operate between April and October. The well-marked 80km-long 'Texel Path' takes you through the dunes and over the mud flats before veering inland through the island's villages; the circular local routes along the way make for nice one- to three-hour hikes or bike trips.

Boat trips (leaving from Oudeschild) are conducted by shrimp trawlers such as the **Emmie TX 10** (☎ 31 36 39; Oudeschild; adult/child €8/7; 10.30am & 2pm Mon-Sat). The two-hour trip around the island sails close to an endangered seal colony on the sandbanks. Some shrimp caught on the journey are prepared fresh for passengers. Try your luck or book at the tourist office or directly by phone. Other boats such as **Rival** (☎ 31 34 10; anglers/observers €15/7.50)

do outings for sports fishermen, complete with fishing equipment. If there's a late tide, some boats also go out around 4.30pm.

Catamarans can be hired from **De Eilander** (☎ 0620634413; www.deeilander.nl; Paal 33, De Cocksdorp; catamaran hire for 5hr €112.50; May-Oct) near the Vlieland boat dock. You can board as a passenger for €27.50 per hour – recommended for novices when the North Sea is rough (ie most of the time). Five-hour sailing courses cost €135.

To gather your own beach treasure, board a horse-drawn wagon run by **Jutters Plezier** (☎ 31 62 25; De Cocksdorp; adult/child €7.50/4.25). The 1½-hour trips are more for the journey than the treasure really, and end at the owner's private lair for a round of herbal schnapps. Tours (minimum 15 persons) depart from the lighthouse – check with the tourist office for times.

Tessel Air (☎ 31 14 36; www.paracentrumtexel.nl; Texel Airport) offers pleasure flights over Texel from €30 per person (15-minute flight, minimum two persons), and for a bit more cash they'll explore the other Wadden Islands. To really feel the wind in your face, try a tandem jump (€190 per jump); it includes all the thrill of freefall without the fear of screwing things up.

Festivals & Events

Lammetjes Wandeltrocht (Lamb Walking Route; Easter) Popular walk around the island, attracting plenty of mainland Dutch.

Ronde om Texel (www.roundtexel.com; mid-Jun) The largest catamaran race in the world; spectators line the beaches for hours on end watching boats jive back and forth on the sea.

Sleeping

There are an astounding 46,000 beds on the island, but surprisingly it pays to book ahead, especially in July and August. De Koog has by far the most options, but hamlets such as Den Hoorn or De Cocksdorp are more peaceful and relaxing.

The tourist office has a list of B&Bs from around €25 per person per night; otherwise pick up a copy of *Travel Guide Texel* and strike out on your own. Note that prices drop in the low season (October to April) when island life slips into a lower gear. Texel's 11 main camp sites teem in summer; the tourist office can tell you which ones have vacancies. Many farms also offer rooms and camp sites.

Hotel De 14 Sterren (☎ 32 26 81; www.14sterren.nl; Smitsweg 4, Den Burg; s/d €55/110;) You couldn't wish for a nicer spot than this place, on the edge of De Dennen forest. Each of its 14 rooms is decorated in warm Mediterranean hues, and most have a terrace or balcony with garden views.

't Anker (☎ 31 62 74; t-anker@texel.com; Kikkertstraat 24, De Cocksdorp; d €45) This small, family-run hotel is full of charm and cheer, and has basic yet comfy rooms in quiet De Cocksdorp. Its lush garden is just an appetiser for the Roggesloot nature reserve close by.

Bij Jef (☎ 31 96 23; www.bijjef.nl; Herenstraat 34, Den Hoorn; s/d €72.50/90) The simple yet stylish red rooms here come with a bath tub, well-stocked mini bar, views of the countryside, and a sun drenched balcony (when the sun's out).

Strandhotel Noordzee (☎ 31 73 65; webmaster@ noordzee.nu; Badweg 200; s/d €80/125) This newly built establishment is possibly the only hotel directly on Texel's sandy beaches. Its rooms are fairly standard and lack flair, but they're suitably comfy and the view of the North Sea uninterrupted. There's a restaurant on site and a two-night minimum stay policy.

Stayokay Hostel Panorama (☎ 31 54 41; www .stayokay.com; Haffelderweg 28, Den Burg; dm €25, d €65; ✖) Texel's HI hostel was in the process of moving to the edge of Den Burg at the time of research, but expect to find a brand-spanking new establishment with clean, colourful rooms and a restaurant when it reopens.

Loodman's Welvaren (☎ 31 92 28; www.welvaart texel.nl; Herenstraat 12, Den Hoorn; s/d/ste from €66/83/105) Rooms in this renovated skipper's inn are cheery and spacious with mod cons like mini-bar, phone and TV, and the plush top-floor suite affords a wonderful feeling of privacy. The owner could be a little friendlier, however.

De Bremakker (☎ 31 28 63; www.bremakker.nl; Templierweg 40; camp site €26.50, chalets from €130; ✔ Apr-Oct) This leafy campground is situated between Den Burg and De Koog at the forest's edge, about 1km from the beach. There's a laundry and snack bar, plus sports facilities and almost always an abundance of calm. Its chalets are in excellent condition and sleep up to four persons.

Eating

With over 27,000 sheep roaming the island, lamb naturally gets top billing, but seafood comes a close second.

Vispaleis-Rokerij De Ster (☎ 31 24 41; Heemskerck-straat 13, Oudeschild; snacks €3-6, mains €5-8; ✔ lunch & dinner) There are plenty of fish takeaway joints,

but this is arguably the island's top pick – it cures its own catch behind the harbour dam. Plonk down at a plastic table for an eel or herring sandwich, or its trademark fish soup.

Freya (☎ 32 16 86; Gravenstraat 4, Den Burg; set menu €23.50; ✔ dinner Tue-Sat) This petite restaurant has a reputation for outstanding French and Dutch cuisine, so it's no surprise that reservations are highly recommended. The hosts are warm and welcoming, and while the place bubbles with energy, it has a decidedly romantic air.

Taveerne De Twaalf Balcken (☎ 31 26 81; Weverstraat 20, Den Burg; mains €12-20; ✔ lunch & dinner) The 'Tavern of the 12 Beams' is a locals' haunt that specialises in lamb dishes and cosy ambience. The front section is dark and subdued, perfect for sipping away on one of the many Trappist beers on offer, while the back conservatory is bright and warm, and topped off with a kids' corner.

Rôtisserie Kerckeplein (☎ 31 89 50; Oesterstraat 6, Oosterend; mains €25-35; ✔ dinner Wed-Sun) This cosy Texel-French restaurant has definitely got lamb down to a fine art, with seven choices in this category alone. You can sit in the loft and wash it all down with a dark *Texels Speciaalbier*. In high season it also opens at lunchtime.

Also recommended:

De Worsteltent (☎ 32 26 81; www.14sterren.nl; Smitsweg 4, Den Burg; mains €15-20, ✔ lunch & dinner) This barnhouse restaurant attached to the Hotel de 14 Sterren is a top option for lunch and/or dinner, with an extensive wine list alongside steak, fish and vegetarian dishes.

Bij Jef (☎ 31 96 23; www.bijjef.nl; Herenstraat 34, Den Hoorn; mains around €20; ✔ lunch & dinner) Sumptuous French-influenced cuisine.

Getting There & Away

Trains from Amsterdam to Den Helder (€12, one hour, twice hourly) are met by a bus that whisks you to the awaiting car ferry.

Teso (☎ 36 96 00; www.teso.nl; adult/child/car return €3/1.50/35) runs a ferry service from Den Helder to 't Horntje. The crossing takes 20 minutes and leaves at 30 minutes past the hour from 6.30am to 9.30pm; returning boats leave on the hour between 6am to 9pm. On some summer days there's a service every half-hour – check the timetable to be sure. If you're driving in high season, show up at the docks 15 to 30 minutes before departure as there'll be a queue. Fares for motorcycles and cars are 30% cheaper from Tuesday to Thursday.

Ferry **De Vriendschap** (☎ 31 64 51; www.wadden veer.nl; De Cocksdorp; adult/child return €20/13.50) makes the half-hour crossing from De Cocksdorp to car-free Vlieland (p239), the nearest of the Wadden Islands, at 10.45am on Tuesday, Wednesday, Thursday and Sunday May to September. In July and August it departs daily, and an extra ferry sails at 9.30am. It returns from Vlieland at 5.15pm, and also 4pm July to August.

Getting Around

Connexxion/AOT (☎ 09009292; ☒ 7am-10pm) operates two bus routes on the island throughout the year, and supplements this with another over the summer months; day passes cost €4.50 from the bus driver. Bus 28 links 't Horntje with Den Burg (seven minutes) and De Koog (another 15 minutes) before returning via the Ecomare museum, while bus 29 starts at the ferry jetty and goes to Den Hoorn and Den Burg before snaking its way along the eastern shore to De Cocksdorp via Oudeschild and Oosterend. The summer-only bus 230 zigzags all over the island, taking in Oudeschild, Den Burg, Ecomare and De Koog before finishing up in De Cocksdorp.

The welter of bicycle shops include **Zegel** (☎ 31 21 50; Parkstraat 14, Den Burg), which charges €4/16 for touring bikes per day/week and €6/22.50 for three-speeds. Near the ferry terminal, **Verhuur Heijne** (☎ 31 95 88; Pontweg 2, 't Horntje) charges similar rates.

The **Telekom Taxi** (☎ 32 22 11) takes you between the ferry terminal and any destination on the island for €5 per person. Book at least an hour in advance, or buy a ticket at the Teso counter in Den Helder ferry terminal; taxis wait by the ferry jetty in 't Horntje.

AALSMEER
☎ 0297

A few kilometres southwest of the capital – and not far from the world's largest tulip garden (p195) – in the town of Aalsmeer is the world's biggest **flower auction** (☎ 39 21 85; www .aalsmeer.com; Legmeerdijk 313; adult/child €4.50/2.50; ☒ 7-11am Mon-Fri). On average, 21 million flowers and plants, worth around €6 million, change hands in the period of a day; the romantic rose is the biggest seller by far, surprisingly outselling its nearest competitor, the tulip, almost three to one. The action itself takes place in a staggering arena; at one million square metres in size, it's the largest commercial building in the world.

Bidding usually takes place between 7am and 9.30am, so get there early to catch the spectacle from the viewing gallery. Selling is conducted – surprise! – by Dutch auction, with a huge clock showing the starting price, dropping until someone takes up the offer. There's a self-guided tour of the site with audio boxes at strategic points. Pick your days carefully: Mondays are quiet and Thursdays very, very busy.

Take Connexxion bus 172 from Amsterdam Centraal Station to the Aalsmeer VBA stop (50 minutes, five times hourly).

MUIDEN
☎ 0294 / pop 3400

Only an hour's bike ride southeast of Amsterdam, Muiden is an unhurried historical town renowned for its red-brick castle, the Muiderslot. Life otherwise focuses on the central lock that funnels scores of pleasure boats out into the vast IJsselmeer.

Sights

The town's dominating feature is the **Muiderslot** (Muiden Castle; ☎ 26 13 25; www.muiderslot.nl; Herengracht 1; adult/child €7/5; ☒ 10am-5pm Mon-Fri, noon-6pm Sat & Sun Apr-Oct, noon-6pm Sat & Sun Nov-Mar), a fortress built in 1280 by the ambitious count Floris V, son of Willem II. The castle was one of the first in Holland to be equipped with round towers, a French innovation. The popular Floris was also a champion of the poor and French sympathiser, two factors which were bound to spell trouble; the count was imprisoned in 1296 and murdered while trying to flee.

In the 17th century, historian PC Hooft entertained some of the century's greatest writers, artists and scientists here, a group famously known as the Muiderkring (Muiden Circle). Today it's the most visited castle in the country, with precious furnishings, weapons, and Gobelin hangings designed to re-create Hooft's era. The interior can be seen only on guided tours; tours may be partly improvised in English. Reserve ahead if you want an English-only tour.

Off the coast lies a derelict fort on the island of **Pampus** (☎ 26 23 26; www.pampus.nl; adult/child ferry & guided tour €12/8; ☒ Apr-Oct). This massive 19th-century bunker was a key member of a ring of 42 fortresses built to defend Amsterdam. Rescued from disrepair by Unesco, the facility now receives preservation funds as a World

Heritage site. Ferries to Pampus depart from Muiderslot port at 10.30am, 12.30pm and 2.30pm.

Activities

You won't find a better area on the IJsselmeer for boating and windsurfing. Boat firms at Muiden harbour rent large, often luxurious motor and sailing boats from about €300 to €1300 per week. For smaller craft, the **Watersportcentrum Muiderberg** (☎ 06-223 75489; www .wscmuiderberg.com; ✆ Apr–mid-Oct) rents small sailboats for two to four persons (from €35 per day) as well as windsurf boards and canoes (€5 to €10 per hour) in Muiderberg, 3½km from Muiden. The shop isn't signposted, but seek out the green beach hut and ask for Ben or Jeroen.

Eating & Drinking

Brasserie Muiden (☎ 26 45 07; Herengracht 75; mains €15-20; ✆ lunch & dinner) This centrally located eatery is a step up from most, with a polished interior and outdoor canal-side seating. The menu heavily features seafood, but the likes of ribs and steaks are never very far away.

Café Ome Ko (☎ 0294-261 330; cnr Herengracht & Naardenstraat; ✆ 8am-2am) In warm weather the clientele of this little bar turns the street outside into one big party. When's there's no party on, the café is a perfect spot to watch the comings and goings through the busy lock right outside.

Getting There & Away

Connexxion bus 157 links Muiden with Amsterdam's Amstelstation (20 minutes, twice hourly). Bus 110 links the town with Weesp (15 minutes), Muiderberg (five minutes) and Naarden (15 minutes).

HET GOOI

Along the slow-moving Vecht River southeast of Amsterdam lies Het Gooi, a shady woodland speckled with lakes and heath. In the 17th century, this 'Garden of Amsterdam' was a popular retreat for wealthy merchants, and nature-hungry urbanites still flock to its leafy trails to hike and cycle today. The area's main centre is Hilversum, a one-time commuter town given a fresh start by the Dutch broadcasting industry, which has its headquarters here. The area is roughly bordered by Laren, a well-heeled town a few kilometres to the northeast with a good art museum, Huizen

on the Gooimeer to the north, and Loosdrecht, on the artificial lakes known as the Loosdrechtse Plassen to the east. Huizen and Loosdrecht are popular water-sports centres, while Naarden, on the Gooimeer to the north, has an intriguing fortress.

Naarden

☎ 035 / pop 17,000

Naarden would be just another satellite town to the capital if it wasn't for the magical fortress on its northwest border. This work of art is best seen from the air: a 12-pointed star, with arrowheads at each tip. This defence system, one of the best preserved in the country, was unfortunately built only after the Spanish massacred the inhabitants in the 16th century. The bastions were still staffed by the Dutch army throughout the 1920s, although its strategic importance had already paled before WWI.

INFORMATION

Tourist office (☎ 694 28 36; www.vvvnaarden.nl; Adriaan Dortsmanplein 1B; ✆ 10am-2pm Sat, also 11am-3pm Tue-Fri May–early Jun, 11am-3pm Mon-Fri early Jun–early Sep) In the old barracks; has an English-language leaflet with a self-guided walking tour of the town and accommodation information.

SIGHTS & ACTIVITIES

Most of Naarden's quaint little houses date from 1572, the year the Spaniards razed the place during their colonisation of North Holland. The bloodbath led by Don Frederick of Toledo is commemorated by a stone tablet on the building at Turfpoortstraat 7.

The **Vestingmuseum** (Fortress Museum; ☎ 694 54 59; Westwalstraat 6; adult/child €5/3; ✆ 10.30am-5pm Tue-Fri, noon-5pm Sat & Sun Mar-Oct, noon-5pm Sun Nov-Feb) is a star-shaped fortress thought to be the only one in Europe featuring a buffer of two walls and two moats. You can stroll around on the rolling battlements before descending into the casements for glimpses of a cramped soldier's life.

It's easy to spot the tall tower of the fort's central **Grote Kerk** (☎ 694 98 73; www.grotekerknaarden .nl; Markstraat 13; admission free; ✆ 10.30am-4.30pm Tue-Sat, 2.30-4.30pm Sun-Mon), a Gothic basilica with stunning 16th-century vault paintings of biblical scenes. You can climb the tower (265 steps) for a good view of the leafy Gooi and the Vecht River. Organ concerts (admission €5) are held throughout the year.

The 17th-century Czech educational reformer, Jan Amos Komensky (Comenius), is buried here in the Waalse Kapel. His life and work are related next door at the **Comenius Museum** (☎ 694 30 45; Kloosterstraat 33; adult/child €2.50/1.50; ⊗ noon-5pm Wed-Sun).

The tourist office also organises one-hour **boat tours** (€2) around the moat.

SLEEPING & EATING
Poorters (☎ 694 48 68; www.poorters.nl; Marktstraat 66; s/d €60/70) The sole hotel within the old town walls is splendidly renovated with four simple but atmospheric rooms (only one has private shower and toilet). There's a cosy bar, a restaurant (mains €8 to €18) with canalside dining and regular art exhibitions.

Jachthaven (☎ 695 60 50; Onderwal 4; hut €32) There's no camp site or hostel close to Naarden, but you can book one of the basic *trekkershutten* (hikers' huts) for up to four people at this yacht harbour. They're in a corner of the marina near a leafy recreation area, with hundreds of boats to view and a restaurant on-site. Take bus 110 to Jachthaven (five minutes).

Naarden has a surprising number of top eateries for its size. Some of the better ones:
Beter Broodje (Marktstraat 25; snacks €2-5; ⊗ lunch & dinner) Small, basic fast-food establishment favoured by locals and tourists alike for its quick service and satisfying seafood snacks.

Eetcafé 't Hert (☎ 694 80 55; Cattenhagestraat 12; mains €11-20; ⊗ lunch & dinner) Pleasant pub-café with sunny garden tucked away in one of Naarden's backstreets. Sandwiches, salads and regional specialities served.

Het Arsenaal (☎ 694 91 48; Kooltjesbuurt 1; mains €22-30; ⊗ lunch Mon-Fri, dinner daily) One of the region's strongholds of swank, specialising in French cuisine. The separate brasserie offers more pedestrian fare at lunchtime.

GETTING THERE & AWAY
There are two direct trains hourly between Amsterdam Centraal Station and Naarden-Bussum (€4.10, 20 minutes, twice hourly), and more if you change at Weesp. From the station, bus 110 (five minutes, twice hourly) runs to the fortress, otherwise it's a 20-minute walk. Bus 110 continues on to Muiden (15 minutes) and finally Weesp (30 minutes).

Hilversum
☎ 035 / pop 83,100
Hilversum, a quiet commuter town with a handful of quality museums, is a good launching pad for excursions into the leafy region of Het Gooi. However it's best known to the Dutch as the national broadcasting centre. Commentary from abroad is beamed back here rather than to Den Haag, the seat of the Dutch parliament, or to the nation's capital in Amsterdam – a quirk of Dutch history as the first radio station was founded in Hilversum

ORIENTATION & INFORMATION
The few attractions are in or near the pedestrianised centre, which is immediately west of the train station. Ringed by a street network defined by the old city walls, the centre of Hilversum measures about 1.5km across and is easy to navigate.
Library (☎ 621 29 42; 's Gravelandse Weg 55; ⊗ 1-8pm Mon-Fri, 11am-4pm Sat) A dozen internet terminals that you can use for free.
Tourist office (☎ 629 28 10; www.vvvhilversum.nl; Kerkbrink 6; ⊗ 10am-5pm Mon-Sat) Signposted from the train station; in the heart of town.

SIGHTS & ACTIVITIES
The centre of Hilversum may be marred by modern town planning, but the legacy of Willem Dudok, the architect who shaped the city in the early 20th century, is still plain for everyone to see. Nearly 100 buildings in Hilversum bear Dudok's stamp; the tourist office sells a walking guide to Dudok's buildings in the town.

The beautiful, modernist **Raadhuis** (Town Hall; Dudokpark 1), 700m west of the train station, is the epitome of Dudok's work. The fabulous interior, with its simple, elegant lines that recall Frank Lloyd Wright or the Bauhaus movement, is a must for any architecture fan. The tower, restored in 1996, is stunning in its symmetry and inventive arrangement of horizontal and vertical brick. Inside is the **Dudok Centrum** (☎ 629 2262; adult/child €2/free; ⊗ noon-4.30pm Wed & Fri), which holds regular architecture exhibitions. Tours of both the Raadhuis and Dudok Centrum (adult/child €5/3) take place at 2pm on Sunday.

Directly above the tourist office is the **Museum Hilversum** (☎ 629 28 26; www.museumhilversum.nl; Kerkbrink 6; adult/child €4/2; ⊗ 10am-5pm Mon-Sat, noon-5pm Sun), which is worth checking out if you plan to explore Het Gooi – 'Amsterdam's Back Garden'. Displays include archaeological finds from early Gooi-dwellers and the history of the region, including the town itself.

The **Nederlands Omroepmuseum** (Dutch Broadcast Museum; ☎ 677 34 34; Media Park, Sumatralaan 45) tells the history of Dutch TV and radio going back to 1919. The first broadcasting licence was granted to a Hilversum station, and the Dutch broadcasting industry grew up around it. An interesting aspect is the background about the various political and religious groups now represented on the media landscape, a product of the social 'pillarisation' that moulded 20th-century Dutch life. At the time of research the museum was closed due to substantial renovations; check with the tourist office for up-to-date information.

The tourist office sells a huge range of cycling and hiking maps to the area, including the Wandelroutes and Fietsroutes in 't Gooi en Omstreeken (Hiking Routes and Biking Routes in 't Gooi and Surrounds). If you don't read Dutch, it's no problem as the routes are clearly marked. The cycling series covers 12 paths in the vicinity, all of which are well sign-posted, with distances of 35km to 70km.

SLEEPING & EATING
Hotel de Waag (☎ 624 65 17; www.dewaag.nl; Groest 17; s/d from €45/65) You probably won't spend the night in Hilversum, but if you do this is your best bet. It's a jolly café with an unusually good location in the centre and rooms in fairly good nick. The sidewalk often hums with activity in the early evenings.

Benk (☎ 623 33 61; Kerkbrink 2; mains €14-19; ⌚ lunch & dinner) Occupying a sunny corner of the main square is this modern bar-restaurant. Benk's simple lunch offerings (ie, sandwiches around €5) are a winner with office workers, and its more established dinner menu, heavily laden with meat and seafood, is a fine appetizer for the bar's cocktails.

Not far east of the centre is a conglomeration of three top restaurants, all with outdoor seating:

Zilt & Zo (☎ 628 14 93; Laanstraat 35a; set menu €30; ⌚ dinner) International cuisine of the highest quality, complemented by a worldwide wine list.

De Jonghe Graef van Buuren (☎ 624 54 02; Laanstraat 37; mains around €14; ⌚ dinner) Pub-eatery serving solid fare like deep-fried plaice with chips, but with plenty of care and attention.

Proeverij de Open Keuken (☎ 623 07 77; Laanstraat 31; mains around €15; tapas €4-8) Best visited for its generous choice of tapas and friendly service.

GETTING THERE & AROUND
Direct train services to/from Hilversum include the following:

Destination	Price (€)	Duration (min)	Frequency (per hr)
Amsterdam	4.90	26	1
Naarden-Bussum	1.70	5-8	6
Utrecht	3.40	20	4

Bus 107 goes from the train station to the Raadhuis and Dudok Centrum (five minutes).

Around Hilversum
In Laren, which is 5km northeast of Hilversum, the **Singer Museum** (☎ 539 39 39; www.singerlaren.nl; Oude Drift 1; adult/child €10/free; ⌚ 11am-5pm Tue-Sun) houses a splendid collection of Dutch and foreign paintings, mostly modernist and impressionist works from 1880 to 1950. Not all works are displayed at once, with exhibitions changing several times a year. Take bus 109 from Hilversum train station to Laren Kermisterrein (20 minutes, four hourly).

FLEVOLAND

Flevoland, the Netherlands' 12th and youngest province, is a masterpiece of Dutch hydro-engineering. In the early 1920s, an ambitious scheme went ahead to reclaim more than 1400 sq km of land – an idea mooted as far back as the 17th century. The completion of the Afsluitdijk (opposite) paved the way for the creation of Flevoland. Ringed dykes were erected, allowing water to be pumped out at a snail-like pace. Once part of Overijssel province, the Noordoostpolder was inaugurated in 1942, followed by the Eastern Flevoland (1957) and Southern Flevoland (1968). First residential rights were granted to workers who'd helped in reclamation and to farmers, especially from Zeeland, who lost everything in the great flood of 1953.

The cities that sprang up bring to mind anything but the Golden Age. The main hubs – Almere, Lelystad and Emmeloord – are grindingly dull places, laid out in grid patterns for affordable housing. The star attractions are the Bataviawerf museum at Lelystad, old fishing villages such as Urk and Schokland, and the bird-filled nature reserve of Oostvaardersplassen.

LELYSTAD
☎ 0320 / pop 67,000
With unattractive modern architecture dominating its disjointed sprawl, Lelystad, the capital of Flevoland Province, is a good example

of urban planning gone awry. The main reason for visiting this expanse of steel and concrete is its three museums, which will keep parents and their hangers-on entertained for hours.

Orientation

Most shops and restaurants are in the pedestrianised knot of streets opposite the station; the key museums are a short bus ride west on the IJsselmeer shore. A smattering of tourist leaflets is available at the train station.

Sights

Lelystad's two big sights, the Batavia Museum and Nieuwland Poldermuseum, are next to Bataviastad, a mock fort containing an outlet shopping centre. A combined ticket to both costs €12/5.50 for adults/children, and bus F (10 minutes, four hourly) connects the museums with the train station.

Your first port of call should be the **Bataviawerf Museum** (☎ 26 14 09; Oostvaardersdijk 1-9; adult/child €9/4.50; ☺ 10am-5pm) and its star attraction: a replica of a 17th-century Dutch merchant

frigate, the *Batavia*, which took 10 years to reconstruct. The original was a 17th-century *Titanic* – big, expensive and supposedly unsinkable. True to comparison, the *Batavia*, filled to the brim with cannon and goods for the colonies, went down in 1629 on its maiden voyage off the west coast of Australia. The replica however redeemed its predecessor in 2000 by sailing around the Pacific.

There's ample evidence of the era's wealth on the upper decks, where you'll see carved wooden likenesses of merchant seamen and a gold-leaf lantern above the captain's quarters. Little imagination is required, however, to grasp how punishing a sailor's life could be, especially for those who broke the rules: stealing a loaf of bread might merit a month's confinement in a cramped hole so constructed that it was impossible to either sit or stand upright.

The wooden skeleton alongside belongs to the *Seven Provinces*, a replica of Admiral Michiel de Ruijter's massive flagship that's scheduled for completion in 2015. In a separate building on the northern perimeter, the

---

KEEPING THE RELENTLESS SEA AT BAY

The Netherlands' coastline originally extended as far as the sandy beaches of Texel (p167) and its Frisian Island companions (p238). The relentless sea, however, never seemed to be in agreement with such borders, and by the end of the 13th century storms had washed seawater over flimsy land barriers and pushed it far inland. The end result was the creation of the Zuiderzee (literally South Sea).

The ruling Dutch had for centuries dreamed of draining the Zuiderzee to reclaim the huge tracts of valuable farmland. The seafaring folk of the villages lining the sea were of a different opinion, even though the shallow Zuiderzee constantly flooded their homes and businesses, and often took lives with it. A solution needed to be found, and the only way to tame the waves, it seems, was to block them off.

A huge dyke was proposed as early as the mid-17th century, but it wasn't until the late 19th century, when new engineering techniques were developed, that such a dyke could become reality. Engineer Cornelis Lely, who lent his name to Lelystad, was the first to sketch out a retaining barrier; a major flood in 1916 set the plan in motion, and construction began in 1927. Fishermen worried about their livelihood, and fears that the Wadden Islands would vanish in the rising seas were voiced, and while the former concerns were legitimate, the latter proved unfounded.

In 1932 the Zuiderzee was ceremoniously sealed off by the Afsluitdijk (Barrier Dyke), an impressive dam (30km long and 90m wide) that links the provinces of Noord Holland and Friesland. The water level remained relatively steady, but the fishing industry was effectively killed as the basin gradually filled with fresh water from the river IJssel – the IJsselmeer was born. Vast tracts of land were however created, which were soon turned into arable *polders* (p48). A second barrier between Enkhuizen and Lelystad was completed in 1976 – creating the Markermeer – with the idea of ushering in the next phase of land reclamation, but the plan was shelved to protect the environment.

For more information on this vast human endeavour, spend some time at the Nieuwland Poldermuseum (p176) in Lelystad, which covers in detail the land reclamation.

Netherlands Institute for Maritime Archaeology displays the remains of a 2000-year-old Roman ship found near Utrecht.

Nearly half of the Netherlands was created by massive land reclamation, and **Nieuwland Poldermuseum** (☎ 26 07 99; Oostvaardersdijk 1-13; adult/child €7/3.50; ☒ 10am-5pm Tue-Fri, 11.30am-5pm Sat & Sun, also 10am-5pm Mon Jul & Aug) is the definitive museum on the topic. It's a sure-fire winner with kids, who can build model bridges or dams, and navigate ships through their locks.

No expense has been spared for **Luchtvaart Themapark Aviodrome** (☎ 289 98 40; www.aviodrome .nl; Dakotaweg 11a; adult/child €13.50/11.50; ☒ 10am-5pm Tue-Sun). This huge museum has 70 historic aircraft on display, including a replica of the Wright Brother's 1902 Flyer, Baron von Richthofen's WWI triplane, a Spitfire and a Dakota. You can also play air-traffic controller in a re-created flight tower or watch aviation films in the mega-cinema. It's at Lelystad Airport 4km east of town (bus 148 from the train station).

Sleeping & Eating

Lelystad is neither blessed with good hotels or great restaurants; you're better off visiting the town on a day trip. For a bite to eat while visiting the museums, pop next door to Bataviastad, which has a handful of so-so eateries.

Getting There & Away

Lelystad station is the terminus of trains coming from the south; services include Amsterdam (€8.30, 40 minutes, two hourly) and Utrecht (€10.90, 70 minutes, two hourly).

Flevoland has poor regional bus services. Bus 150 goes from Lelystad station to Enkhuizen via the IJsselmeer dyke road N302 (35 minutes, every two hours). Bus 143 goes east to Kampen in Overijssel (one hour, every half-hour). The Qliner bus 315 goes to Groningen (2¼ hours, hourly).

OOSTVAARDERSPLASSEN NATURE RESERVE

Between Lelystad and Almere lies the marshy realm of Oostvaardersplassen, a 6000-hectare reserve of mostly swampy lake that developed virtually by accident. When Flevoland province opened in 1968 this area was earmarked for an industrial estate, but the planners dawdled and nature stepped in. A virgin landscape of reeds, willows and rough grasslands emerged.

Today it's a bird sanctuary of international repute with a formidable variety of species. Great white egrets, cormorants and spoonbills can be seen nesting, and lucky visitors may also catch a glimpse of endangered species such as the white-tailed eagle. Illustrated boards around the park help to identify what appears in your sights.

You'll also see quirky mammals such as the conic (a docile pony), the horned heck cattle as well as red deer, all of which serve as lawn mowers on the meadows around the perimeter.

Entry into the marsh itself isn't allowed, but the next best thing is a visit to De Kluut observation hut on the northeastern edge of the reserve. The various hiking and bicycle paths begin here, including a 35km route around the entire lake. The Schollevaar observation post near a cormorant colony can only be visited with a park ranger.

The **visitors centre** (☎ 0320-25 45 85; Kitsweg 1; ☒ 10am-5pm Tue-Sun Apr-Oct, 10am-4pm Tue-Sun Nov-Mar), which is currently enjoying a major facelift, has good wildlife exhibits, free hiking maps and vending machines for coffee and cold drinks. If you're looking to stay near the park, **Campground het Oppertje** (☎ 0320-25 36 93; Uilenweg 11, Lelystad; per adult/child/tent €4/2/3.50; ☒ Apr-Sep) is about as close as you're going to get. It's a calm, green waterside site blessed with a constant sea breeze, which is good for windsurfing (you can take lessons here) but not always great for pitching a tent. There is no public transport to the campground.

Getting There & Away

Public transport to the park is nonexistent. To get to the visitors centre by car from Amsterdam, drive the A6 north and take exit No 10 towards Lelystad on the N302 and take a left after 5km onto Buizardweg (also signposted 'Oostvaardersplassen').

URK

☎ 0527 / pop 16,500

This pious village was once a proud little island, home to a sizeable fishing fleet and an important signal post for ships passing into the North Sea. In the 1940s Urk reluctantly joined the mainland when the surrounding Noordoostpolder was pumped dry, and even today some locals pine for the isolation of island life, as tough as it obviously was.

Although now cut off from the North Sea, the town is still a centre of the seafood industry, a holdover from the days when its fleet sailed into the open Zuiderzee. That sweet smell on the air comes from the several fish factories located here.

You'll see dozens of historic fishing boats moored around the harbour, including the brown-sailed *botters* with gleaming wooden hulls and oversized leeboards. At the western end of town, take the coastal walk around the lighthouse for a pinch of local folklore. Just 70m off the shore lies the **Ommelebommelestien**, a slippery rock said to be the birthplace of all native Urkers. Legend also has it that, far from receiving the delivery by stork, dad had to take a rowboat to pick up his newborn.

The supports of the village church, **Kerkje aan de Zee** (Peter Salebienplein), are made entirely out of masts of VOC (Dutch East India Company) ships that brought back exotic goods from the East Indies. Nearby you'll find the **Fishermen's Monument**, a lonely statue of a woman in a billowing dress gazing seaward where her loved ones were lost. Marble tablets around the perimeter list the Urk seafarers who never returned – name, age and ship's ID number – and room has been left for further casualties.

Just below the town's lighthouse is **Restaurant De Kaap** (☎ 68 15 09; www.restaurantdekaap.nl; Wijk 5; mains €10-15), *the* place to sample Urk specialities, such as smoked gurnard, while taking in gorgeous views of the harbour and IJsselmeer. The interior is richly decorated with maritime ornaments; the hotel rooms (singles/doubles €35/60) are comfy and quiet.

Bus 141 runs between Urk and Zwolle several times an hour (1¼ hours). On Sunday there's only a handful of buses, starting in the late afternoon.

SCHOKLAND
☎ 0527

A bleak variation on the island theme, the community of Schokland eked out an existence for hundreds of years on a long, narrow strip of land in the Zuiderzee. By the mid-19th century the clock had run out: fish prices plummeted and vicious storms were literally eroding the island away. The plucky locals hung on, despite the appalling living conditions, prompting Willem III to order their removal in 1859. Schokland was eventually swallowed up by the Noordoostpolder in the 20th century, just like Urk.

Now a Unesco World Heritage site, the **Schokland Museum** (☎ 25 13 96; www.schokland.nl; Middelbuurt 3; adult/child €3.50/2.75; 11am-5pm Tue-Sun Apr-Oct, daily Jul & Aug, Fri-Sun Nov-Mar) affords glimpses into this tortured past. The island's heritage is described in detail with a good historical slide presentation in English. Views from the lower path hint just how big the waves were here, at the prow-shaped barrier constructed from tall wooden pilings. Ironically, since the area was drained the foundations have begun to dry out. Schokland is sinking but, luckily, no longer into the sea.

Be sure to stop by the church, the **Waterstaatkerk**, built to replace the one virtually washed away in the storm of 1825. Here, as in so many Dutch fishing towns, a model ship hangs high above the congregation – the symbol of a union between sea and religious belief.

There's no public transportation to the museum; you can ride a bike the 14km north from Kampen. Turn west off the N50 on the road at Ens and go another 2.5km.

Utrecht

On the surface, there's not much to the tiny, petite province of Utrecht, save for charming Utrecht City itself – its tree-lined canals and medieval quarter hog the limelight, making the province virtually a city-state. Yet, like Doctor Who's Tardis, there's more to discover if you care to poke around. The splendid Kasteel de Haar on the city's doorstep is one of the country's most beautiful castles. Amersfoort, a really pretty walled town in the northeast corner, oozes medieval character. Then there's Oudewater in the southwest, synonymous with witchcraft (Monty Python fans will dig it). Utrecht is also home to palatial mansions to the southeast in Doorn, where a defeated German Kaiser went into exile, and in Amerongen, seat of well-to-do aristocrats since the 13th century.

If you like boating and swimming, what's stopping you from visiting the province's many shallow lakes? For pedal pushers, the countryside is laced with bike paths that can be taken at a relaxed clip.

Yes, Utrecht has come some way since James Boswell whinged in 1763, 'I groaned with the idea of living all winter in so shocking a place'.

UTRECHT

HIGHLIGHTS

- Look out towards Amsterdam, 50km away, from the top of Utrecht's **Domtoren** (p180)
- Make friends with Miffy at Utrecht's **Dick Bruna Huis** (p180)
- Feel the weight of history at the imposing **Kasteel de Haar** (p185)
- Discover the underrated medieval centre at **Amersfoort** (p186)
- Find out if a witch weighs the same as gravy at **Oudewater** (p188)

UTRECHT

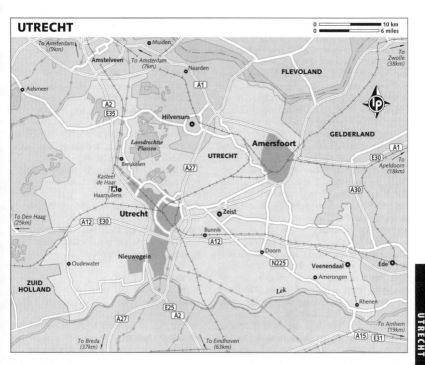

0 ——— 10 km
0 ——— 6 miles

UTRECHT CITY
☎ 030 / pop 282,000

Utrecht is one of the Netherlands' oldest cities (for an outline of its history, see p24) – not that you'd know it when you step off the train and find yourself lost in the maze that is the Hoog Catharijne shopping centre. The Hoog is huge…and it's attached to the station…and it seemingly goes on forever…and ever. Never fear: it's going to be destroyed soon. But fight your way through and you'll emerge starry-eyed into a beautiful, vibrant, old-world city centre, ringed by striking 13th-century canal wharves. The wharves, well below street level, are unique to Utrecht, and the streets along-side brim with shops, restaurants and cafés.

In summer, Utrecht is Festival City, hosting various jazz events (you'll see musicians on every corner) and the Netherlands Film Festival in September. Added to that, the city's student community of 40,000 is the largest in the country, making it one very infectious place.

Orientation

Two canals bisect Utrecht, the Oudegracht and the Nieuwegracht, the old and new canals

from the 11th and 14th centuries. A third canal called the Singel surrounds the old core. Most of the interesting bits lie within 500m of the Dom-toren (Cathedral Tower), although the museum quarter is a pleasant 500m stroll south.

The historic quarters are to the east of the city centre, but reaching the streets from the train station means traversing the Hoog Catharijne; follow the signs marked 'Centrum', then gasp for air when you finally get outside.

Information

Municipal library (☎ 286 18 00; Oudegracht 167; internet per hr €3; 🕑 10am-9pm Mon, 11am-6pm Tue-Fri, 10am-5pm Sat)

Post office (Neude 11)

Tourist office (☎ 09001288732; www.utrecht-city.com; Vinkenburgstraat 19; 🕑 9.30am-6.30pm Mon-Wed & Fri, to 9pm Thu, to 5pm Sat) Get a free map with street index.

Sights

Almost all sights within Utrecht's old town are within 10 minutes' walking distance of each other. In two to three hours you can easily cover the cathedral area and the main canals and have time left over for a museum visit.

DOMTOREN & AROUND

The **Domtoren** (Cathedral Tower; ☎ 233 30 36; www
.domtoren.nl; Domplein; adult/child €7.50/4; ☺ 10am-5pm
Mon-Sat, noon-5pm Sun) is 112m high, with 465 steps
and 50 bells. It's a tough haul to the top but
well worth the exertion, given that the tower
gives unbeatable city views; on a clear day you
can see Amsterdam. The guided tour, in Dutch
and English, is detailed and gives privileged
insight into this beautiful structure.

Finished in the 14th century, the cathedral
and its tower are the most striking medieval
landmarks in a city that once had 40 cathedrals. Appreciate the craft: it took almost
300 years to complete. In 1674 the North
Sea winds reached hurricane force and blew
down the cathedral's nave, leaving the tower
and transept behind.

Back on terra firma, find the row of paving
stones that mark the extents of the nave –
across this extent is the **Domkerk** (Cathedral; 231
04 03; www.domkerk.nl; Achter de Dom 1; ☺ 10am-5pm
Mon-Sat May-Sep, 10am-4pm Mon-Fri Oct-Apr, 11am-3.30pm
Sat, 2-4pm Sun), the surviving chancel of the cathedral, with a few tombs within.

Behind the church is the most charming
component of this ecclesiastical troika: the
Kloostergang, a monastic garden and a peaceful
refuge. A million pigeons and quite a few dope
smokers can't be wrong.

The 19th-century buildings on the western side of Domplein are the **ceremonial buildings** of Utrecht University, surrounding the
old church chapterhouse where the treaty of
Utrecht was signed in 1579. The Treaty formed
a military alliance of the northern provinces.

Walk down Voetiusstraat from behind the
cathedral to **Pieterskerk**, built in 1048 and the
oldest Romanesque church in the Netherlands. Much damage was caused during the
storm in 1674 and again during a dodgy 1965
restoration. Opening hours are sporadic, but
try visiting on Friday or Saturday.

DICK BRUNA HUIS

One of Utrecht's favourite sons, Dick Bruna,
is honoured at the **Dick Bruna Huis** (☎ 236 23 61;
www.dickbrunahuis.nl; Agnietenstraat 2; adult/child under
17yr €8/5; ☺ Tue-Sun 11am-5pm). Bruna is the cre-
ator of beloved cartoon rabbit Miffy, and she
naturally takes pride of place, along with an
extensive overview of Bruna's career: from
the book covers he designed for the family
publishing company to multimedia demonstrations of his technique and philosophy.

Obviously children will get a huge kick out
of it all, but so will adults who appreciate
superlative graphic design.

CANALS

Scene of many a wedding photo, the photo-
genic bend in the Oudegracht is illuminated
by lamplight in the evening; hundreds sit
outside cafés here by day. South of this point
is where the canal is at its most evocative, and
the streets are quieter, stretching 1km to the
southern tip of the old town.

A section of the Singel called the Stads-
buitengracht has its own turn as a lovely canal
on the eastern side of the old quarter, where
it follows many parks built on the site of
the old fortifications. Stroll down beside this
canal and back north through Nieuwegracht,
a peaceful stretch of plush canal houses and
towering, grand old elms.

MUSEUM QUARTER

Utrecht likes its museums, with 14 of them,
some quirkier than a bag of racoons – such
as the one devoted to sewerage.

The pick of the litter by far is the **Museum
het Catharijneconvent** (☎ 231 38 35; www.catharijne
convent.nl; Lange Nieuwstraat 38; adult/child under 17yr
€8.50/5.75; ☺ 10am-5pm Tue-Fri, 11am-5pm Sat & Sun),
with the finest collection of medieval religious
art in the Netherlands – virtually the history
of Christianity, in fact – housed in a Gothic
former convent and an 18th-century canalside house. All but the most jaded art-lover
will marvel at the many beautiful illuminated
manuscripts, carvings and robes. Allow about
1½ hours here to digest it all. Bus 2 from Centraal Station (CS) passes the front entrance.

The **Centraal Museum** (☎ 236 23 62; www.centraal
museum.nl; Nicolaaskerkhof 10; adult/child under 17yr €8/5;
☺ 11am-5pm Tue-Sun) has a wide-ranging collection. It displays applied arts dating back to the
17th century, as well as paintings by some of
the Utrecht School artists and a bit of De Stijl
to boot – including the world's most extensive
Gerrit Rietveld collection, a wet dream for all
minimalists. There's even a 12th-century Viking
longboat that was dug out of the local mud, plus
a sumptuous 17th-century dollhouse.

The **Universiteitsmuseum** (☎ 253 80 08; www
.museum.uu.nl; Lange Nieuwstraat 106; adult/child €4/2;
☺ 11am-5pm Tue-Sun) is a mixed bag – and that's
the 'toof'! There's a re-created late-19th-
century classroom, historic dentistry tools
('Is it safe?') and way too many models of

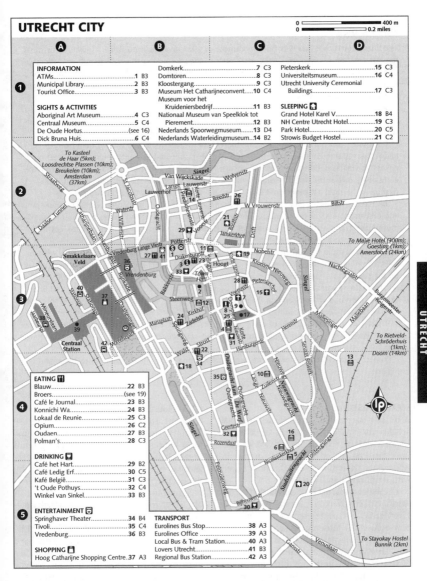

UTRECHT CITY

0 ____ 400 m
0 ____ 0.2 miles

medical maladies. You can find refuge out the back in **De Oude Hortus**, the old botanical garden, along with all the other dentophobes, who'll be quivering amid venerable trees and plants collected by the Dutch during their world exploits. The garden is an oasis of calm, sheltering numerous rare flowers and plants like the ancient *Gingko biloba* tree.

The **Nederlands Spoorwegmuseum** (Dutch Railway Museum; ☎ 230 62 06; www.spoorwegmuseum.nl; Maliebaanstation; adult/child €12.50/9.50; ⏲ 10am-5pm Tue-Sun) features historic locomotives in an old station building; a high-speed minitrain takes kids around the grounds. To get there, take bus 3 from CS to Maliebaan and walk east for about five minutes.

MIFFY & DICK

The illustrator Dick Bruna was born in Utrecht in 1927 and has lived there all his life. His most famous creation is of course Miffy, or Nijntje as she's known in the Netherlands, an adorable cartoon rabbit with dots for eyes and a cross for a mouth that's a clear inspiration for Japan's famous Hello Kitty character. In fact, Utrecht is sometimes besieged by Japanese groupies, eager to catch a glimpse of their 78-year-old Dutch hero.

As an indication of how popular Miffy is, consider the facts: the 120 children's books she stars in have been translated into 40 languages and have sold more than 85 million copies world-wide. Miffy merchandise has generated hundreds of millions of euros worth of sales.

But there's much more to Dick Bruna than Miffy (wonderful as she is). Our man from Utrecht has written and illustrated more than 100 picture books and designed more than 2000 book covers, as well as hundreds of posters, postcards and prints. Today Bruna still rises to go to work early every day at his Utrecht studio and is still every bit as obsessive in his search for perfect design. As he says, 'I'll never do 3-D illustration. I haven't simplified 2-D enough'.

Bruna says he makes pictograms rather than illustrations; that is, pictures with a clear, instant and universal message. He's a master of light and shade, manipulating blocks of colour for maximum impact, but always with a sense of fun and play – even when designing book covers for Susan Sontag or Eldridge Cleaver, hardly the lightest writers around.

From early on in his career, Bruna imposed strict discipline on his art, working with what he calls a 'minimum of means': a specific thickness of lines, a strict division of typographical areas on the page, and a very specific colour palette. Today, any publisher that reproduces Miffy books must adhere to Bruna's colour ideology or else suffer his wrath. It's unsurprising, then, that Bruna says Piet Mondrian influenced him. There's even a Miffy book, *Miffy at the Gallery*, where the little rabbit takes in work by Mondrian and Matisse (another Bruna influence).

These days, a swelling body of opinion is beginning to see beyond the stigma of pop culture and 'children's work' that's applied to Miffy, and see her for what she really is: the ultimate statement of intent by an artist who's clearly Mondrian's equal.

You can learn all of this and more at the Dick Bruna Huis, a worthy shrine to the man and his art.

SMALL MUSEUMS

A bit of a surprise in Utrecht, the **Aboriginal Art Museum** (☎ 238 01 00; www.aamu.nl; Oudegracht 176; adult/child €8/5; ☼ Tue-Fri 10am-5pm, Sat & Sun 11am-5pm), devoted to contemporary Australian Aboriginal art, is sure to delight those bored with Rembrandt and Van Gogh.

The **Museum voor het Kruideniersbedrijf** (Grocery Museum; ☎ 231 66 28; Hoogt 6; admission free; ☼ 12.30-4.30pm Tue-Sat), a charming replica of an old grocery store, isn't a museum per se. It's more like a sweetshop, but what the hey, you'll love it anyway. Upstairs are original cans and packages of yesteryear (the 'museum' bit); downstairs are lovely ladies in old-time aprons selling sweets and tea in decorative containers. As far as souvenirs go, it'll beat your umpteenth clog. Pick up a block of white liquorice candy to add to hot milk – an old Dutch tradition.

The **Nationaal Museum van Speelklok tot Pierement** (National Museum from Musical Clock to Street Organ; ☎ 231 27 89; www.museumspeelklok.nl; Steenweg 6; adult/child €6/4; ☼ 10am-5pm Tue-Sat, noon-5pm Sun) has a colourful collection of musical machines from the 18th century onwards. These are demonstrated with gusto during hourly tours. Most impressive are the street and fairground organs from around Europe, including gargantuan burping contraptions fashioned by the Belgian master organ-builder, Mortier.

Spread throughout the various levels of an old water tower, the **Nederlands Waterleidingmuseum** (Sewer Museum; ☎ 248 72 11; www.waterleidingmuseum.nl; Lauwerhof 29; adult/child €2/1; ☼ 1.30-5pm Tue-Fri & Sun, 11am-4pm Sat) takes a good, hard look at what happens to water before and after humans use it. There's even a big, blown-up photo of a sexy babe bathing (well, it is water-related). The tower itself is ancient and fascinating and provides good views.

RIETVELD-SCHRÖDERHUIS

Just out of the city, the **Rietveld-Schröderhuis** (☎ 236 23 10; www.rietveldschroderhuis.nl; Prins Hendriklaan 50; adult/child €16/8) is a Unesco-protected landmark built in 1924 by Utrecht architect Gerrit

Rietveld. Inside and out, the entire structure conforms to the principles of De Stijl architecture (see p58) – this is the only house in the world that can make this claim. Only six colours are used: red, blue, yellow, white, grey and black. The 'form follows function' concept has been faithfully adhered to, as even the interior walls can be moved to alter the floor plan.

A second building, a **model apartment** (Erasmuslaan 9) from 1931, is also open to the public behind the main house. It's included in the admission to Rietveld-Schröderhuis, and tours of both properties take 90 minutes, starting on the hour. A shuttle bus leaves the Centraal Museum for the house at 11.45am, 12.45pm, 1.45pm and 2.45pm.

Activities

Lovers Utrecht (☎ 272 01 11; adult €7; ☽ 11am-6pm) offers one-hour canal trips that trace a circular route through the old town. The landing is on Oudegracht just south of Lange Viestraat. You can also rent **canal bikes** (paddleboats; per person per hr €6) from in front of the municipal library.

Festivals & Events

Holland Festival Oude Muziek (Holland Festival of Ancient Music; www.oudemuziek.nl) Held in late August, this festival celebrates music from long ago.
Nederlands Film Festival (NFF; www.filmfestival.nl) The Dutch film industry may be tiny, but its output is generally of good quality. Find out for yourself at the NFF each year in late September, culminating in the awarding of the coveted Golden Calf.

Sleeping
BUDGET

Strowis Budget Hostel (☎ 238 02 80; Boothstraat 8; www.strowis.nl; dm from €14, s/d €55; ☐) Run by a cluey group of ex-squatters, this 17th-century building near the city centre has been lovingly restored and converted into a hostel. It's open 24 hours a day and has a cosy bar. It sure beats the antiseptic hospital feel of some hostels.

Stayokay Hostel Bunnik (☎ 656 12 77; www .stayokay.com; Rhijnauwenselaan 14; dm from €23) This charming old mansion overlooks a canal on the fringes of a nature reserve, 5km east of the city centre in Bunnik. There are three dining halls, a traditional bar and a lovely terrace. Take bus 40, 41 or 43 from CS.

MIDRANGE

NH Centre Utrecht Hotel (☎ 231 31 69; www.nh-hotels .com; Janskerkhof 10; s/d €120; ✕) This gorgeous hotel is housed in an atmospheric old building built in 1870. The rooms are very comfortable, with all the conveniences a business traveller would expect, and the views of the old church square are delectable. The suitably elegant Broers restaurant downstairs is an added bonus.

Malie Hotel (☎ 231 64 24; www.maliehotel.nl; Maliestraat 2; s/d from €105/125) Tucked away in a beautiful tree-lined avenue, this elegant and comfortable 19th-century house offers large rooms and old-world charm. There's a nice garden out the back, and all of it away from the city centre for a bit of peace and quiet.

Park Hotel (☎ 251 67 12; Tolsteegsingel 34; s/d €52/65) You'll sleep right in this comfy eight-room guesthouse occupying a canal house. It's not far from Utrecht's buzzing nightlife, and breakfast can be taken in the pretty garden out the back.

TOP END

Grand Hotel Karel V (☎ 233 75 55; Geertebolwerk 1; www.karelv.nl; s/d from €205/225; ⓟ ☒ ☐) The lushest accommodation in Utrecht can be found in this former knights' gathering hall from the 14th century. The service and décor are understated but flawless, and the restaurant is excellent. Note that room prices plummet on the weekend.

Eating

Do as the discerning locals do: avoid the cluster of wharf-side restaurants on the Oudegracht in the dead centre of the old town near the town hall. It's a pretty spot better known for its views than culinary delights. Utrecht's best restaurants lie elsewhere.

RESTAURANTS

Opium (☎ 231 55 15; www.restaurant-opium.nl; Voorstraat 80; mains €15-30; ☽ dinner) This is a hot new place that will rock your socks off. Its Asian fusion cooking matches the gorgeous minimalist interior; think fans, clean angles and plays of light. Tempura of softshell crab in sweet chilli sauce with spring onion and paprika gives you some idea of what's on offer.

Blauw (☎ 234 24 63; Springweg 64; set menu from €19; ☽ dinner) Blauw has worked hard to make Indonesian food trendy in Utrecht – or at least popular. Quality's the key, and the rice table, comprising 14 dishes, is a winner. The décor, a mix of nostalgia, and überhip minimalism packs 'em in, too.

UTRECHT

Goesting (☎ 273 33 46; www.restaurantgoesting.nl; Veeartsenijpad 150; mains €22-35; ✆ dinner) Celebrities and wannabes flock to Goesting to eat fancies such as spit roast, Dutch asparagus, poached tournedos and 'tame duck' in a crypto-minimalist, high-society atmosphere.

Oudaen (☎ 231 18 64; www.oudaen.nl; Oudegracht 99; mains €11-22; ✆ lunch & dinner) The best choice on this popular stretch of the canal. Set in a restored 14th-century banquet hall, it has a varied menu of salads, steaks and succulent seafood such as redfish, grilled tuna and sea bass. Best of all, it brews its own beer, guaranteeing high times under the high ceilings.

our pick **Polman's** (☎ 231 33 68; www.polmanshuis .nl; cnr Jansdam & Keistraat; mains €18-25; ✆ lunch & dinner Mon-Sat) Diners are welcomed in an elegant former ballroom with ceiling frescoes, a hangover from its days as an elite gentlemen's club. The French and Italian menus are honed for the discriminating palate.

Konnichi Wa (☎ 241 63 88; www.konnichiwa.nl; Mariaplaats 9; sushi pieces from €2; ✆ lunch Tue-Sat, dinner) Expect great sushi, *teppanyaki* and tempura. It also serves takeaway.

CAFÉS

Broers (☎ 234 34 06; www.stadscafe-broers.nl; Janskerkhof 9; mains €14-23; ✆ lunch & dinner) This place is a stylish, modern version of a brown café, with good views. It serves basic dishes such as pasta and steak, and there's live music some nights.

Café le Journal (☎ 236 48 39; Neude 32-34; mains €11-22; ✆ lunch & dinner) This classy grand café sits on a very busy square. Unsurprisingly, then, it's a hive of activity in summer.

Lokaal de Reunie (☎ 231 01 00; www.lokaaldereunie .nl; 't Wed 3A; mains €12-30; ✆ lunch & dinner) One of many atmospheric cafés near the cathedral tower, De Reunie is distinguished by its attractive, airy interior.

Drinking

Café het Hart (☎ 231 97 18; www.hethart.com; Voorstraat 10) This is the apex of the A-list of the Utrecht bar scene, with bleeding-edge beats plus stacks of magazines and board games. Try *Trivial Pursuit* with questions in Dutch after a few 9% Belgian beers.

Winkel van Sinkel (☎ 230 30 30; www.dewinkelvan sinkel.nl; Oudegracht 158) This early-19th-century building houses a grand café, a nightclub and a restaurant in a divine interior. It was once the Netherlands' first department store, inspiring this popular Dutch ditty (according to a *Guardian* reader): 'At the big shop of Sinkel's, all things can be bought/Sweeties and shandies, undies for dandies/Needles for knitting, and tablets for shitting'.

Kafé België (☎ 231 26 66; Oudegracht 196) This lively bar is an absolute must for beer-lovers. It stocks examples of most of Benelux's brewers and has a revolving guest-beer policy. It also keeps a large inflatable shark suspended from the ceiling to keep watch over its patrons.

Café Ledig Erf (☎ 231 75 77; Tolsteegbrug 3) This classy pub overlooks a confluence of canals at the southern tip of town. Patrons gather on tables around the oversized chessboards on the terrace, and the place is always packed in warm weather. Inside, the beer list and the bar snacks keep everything groovy. It's a cosy and intimate winner.

't Oude Pothuys (☎ 231 89 70; www.pothuys.nl; Oudegracht 279) Small and dark, this basement pub has nightly music – usually jam sessions with locals trying their hand at rock and jazz, but touring pro bands also feature. The sound system is tops.

Entertainment

Tivoli (☎ 231 14 91; www.tivoli.nl; Oudegracht 245) This former monastery, now a cavernous dance hall with medieval chandeliers, remains highly popular and a fixture on Utrecht's student-oriented music scene, whether it's for old rockers like REM, DJs or big-band jazz.

Vredenburg (☎ 231 45 44; Vredenburgpassage 77) The main performing arts complex, with superb acoustics. A quick flip through its diverse monthly calendar might reveal flamenco, marionette theatre, Ellington or Weber.

Springhaver Theater (☎ 231 37 89; www.springhaver .nl; Springweg 50-52) This Art Deco complex houses intimate cinemas that screen art-house and independent films.

Getting There & Away

Utrecht is a travel hub: train lines and motorways converge on the city from all directions.

BUS

See p301 for details information about international bus services.

TRAIN

Lockers are by platform 4 on the main concourse. Utrecht is the national hub for Dutch rail services, so you'll probably change trains here at some point.

Sample fares and schedules:

Destination	Price (€)	Duration (min)	Frequency (per hr)
Amsterdam	6.30	35	4
Den Helder	16.80	110	2
Groningen	24.50	120	2
Maastricht	23.10	120	2
Rotterdam	8.60	35	2

Getting Around

Local buses and trams leave from underneath the passage linking CS to Hoog Catharijne. Regional buses leave from the adjoining area to the south.

AROUND UTRECHT CITY
Loosdrechtse Plassen

The town of Breukelen is 10km northwest of Utrecht. Although the town in itself is unremarkable, it was actually the inspiration for the New York district of Brooklyn. Breukelen is also the gateway to the **Loosdrechtse Plassen**, a large series of lakes formed from the flooded digs of peat harvesters.

There are all manner of bike paths around the waters and quite a bit of interesting scenery. Parts of the lakes are desolate, while others are surrounded by lovely homes on small islands joined to the road by little bridges.

The best way to visit is by bike from Utrecht. Follow the signs to Breukelen. Otherwise, it's just a short run by train to Breukelen from Utrecht CS (€2.60, 11 minutes, three per hour).

Kasteel de Haar

Feast your senses on one of the most imposing castles in the country, **Kasteel de Haar** (☎ 030-677 85 15; www.kasteeldehaar.nl; Kasteellaan 1; adult/child €8/5; ☉ 10am-5pm), which was restored in a fit of nostalgia little more than a century ago, long after its Gothic turrets ceased to have any defensive purpose. But architect PJ Cuypers (of Rijksmuseum fame) misjudged the weight on the centuries-old foundations; big cracks can be seen above moat level.

What you see now is a spiffed-up version of the fortress as it was believed to look around 1500, but (understandably) equipped with all the creature comforts available in the late 19th century, such as electric lighting and running water. The project was so extensive that the church and the nearby hamlet of **Haarzuilens** be-

came involved. The castle owner, Baron Etienne van Zuylen, spared little expense and had the entire village moved so there'd be adequate space for the park and hunting grounds.

The castle is surrounded by a large English landscaped garden with broad paths, canal-like stretches of pond and statues throughout. The French baroque garden near the entrance bears the stamp of Héléne de Rothschild, the baron's wife and heir of the renowned Rothschild banking family – it was her fortune that paid for the 19th-century restoration.

To get here from Utrecht, take the A2 north to exit 6 (Maarssen) and drive 2km east to Haarzuilens. Alternatively, take bus 127 from Utrecht CS towards Breukelen and get off at Brink, from where it's a 15-minute walk.

AMERSFOORT
☎ 033 / pop 134,904

Beer, wool and tobacco made Amersfoort an exceedingly rich town from the 16th century onwards. Well heeled with a touch of the provincial, the town has many striking merchants' homes that have been lovingly restored. And the egg-shaped old town offers quiet, wonderfully evocative strolls along canals and narrow alleys that still ooze medieval atmosphere.

Many tourists pass Amersfoort by, but drop in if you possibly can. It's a seriously charming place.

Information

Post office (Utrechtseweg 8)
Telstar Telecom (71 Kamp; internet per hr €4.50)
Tourist office (☎ 09001122364; www.amersfoortyour way.nl; Stationsplein 9-11; ☉ 9.30am-5.30pm Mon-Fri, 10am-2pm Sat)

Sights & Activities

Much of Amersfoort's appeal comes from wandering the old centre, which has a couple of attractive little canals and more than 300 pre-18th-century buildings.

MUSEUMS

Mondriaanhuis (☎ 462 01 80; Kortegracht 11; www .mondriaanhuis.nl; admission €3.75; ☉ 10am-5pm Tue-Fri, 1-5pm Sat & Sun) The famous De Stijl artist Piet Mondrian was born in Amersfoort. This small but absorbing museum, in the house where he was born, honours his life and work with a detailed retrospective of prints, reproductions and some originals, as well as music CDs inspired by his art.

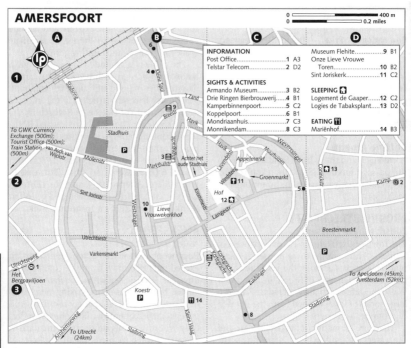

AMERSFOORT

0	400 m
0	0.2 miles

INFORMATION
Post Office..............................1 A3
Telstar Telecom.....................2 D2

SIGHTS & ACTIVITIES
Armando Museum..................3 B2
Drie Ringen Bierbrouwerij.....4 B1
Kamperbinnenpoort..............5 C2
Koppelpoort..........................6 B1
Mondriaanhuis......................7 C3
Monnikendam.......................8 C3

Museum Flehite.....................9 B1
Onze Lieve Vrouwe
   Toren.............................10 B2
Sint Joriskerk......................11 C2

SLEEPING
Logement de Gaaper.......12 C2
Logies de Tabaksplant.....13 D2

EATING
Mariënhof.........................14 B3

Armando Museum (☎ 461 40 88; www.armando
museum.nl; Langegracht 36; admission €3.50; ☺ 11am-5pm
Tue-Fri, Sat noon-5pm) The painter, writer, violin-
ist, and documentary filmmaker Armando
was one of the major artists to emerge from
the postwar era in the Netherlands. His work
is strongly antiwar, derived from his experiences growing up in Amersfoort during
WWII. At this evocative museum, housed in
a former church, you can see examples from
his paintings, drawings, sculptures, writings
and films.

OLD TOWN
Zuidsingel is a fine place to start: the inner ring
on the north side of town along **Muurhuizen** is
quaint and good for walks. **Langestraat** is the
main shopping strip.

Onze Lieve Vrouwe Toren (Lieve Vrouwekerkhof;
adult/child €5/4; ☺ 10am-5pm Tue-Sat Jul & Aug) is
the surviving 15th-century Gothic tower
of the church that used to stand on this
spot. Like so many of the Netherlands'
churches, it was destroyed by tragedy –
in this case a gunpowder explosion in 1787.
The square in front, **Lieve Vrouwekerkhof**, is

Amersfoort's most charming spot. A flower
market is held here on Friday morning.

Amersfoort's surviving old church is the
Sint Joriskerk (Hof 1; admission €1; ☺ 2-4.30pm Mon-Fri
Jul & Aug). It was rebuilt in a sort of Gothic-
cum-aircraft-hangar style in the 16th century
after the original Romanesque church burnt
down (obviously, insuring Dutch churches
has never been a lucrative proposition).

The collections at the **Museum Flehite**
(☎ 461 99 87; Westsingel 50; adult/child €5/3; ☺ 11am-
6pm Tue-Fri, 11am-5pm Sat & Sun) cover local geol-
ogy, history and decorative arts. The building
is attractively set at a junction of canals,
and you enter the museum courtyard over
a bridge.

The town has three surviving gateways,
either to the city roads or over the canals. The
Koppelpoort guards the north and was built
in the 15th century, the **Kamperbinnenpoort** is
at the eastern side and dates from the 13th
century, while the picturesque **Monnikendam**
to the southeast was built in 1430.

Possibly the most fun you will have in
Amersfoort is touring **Drie Ringen Bierbrouwerij**
(☎ 465 65 75; Kleine Spui 18; ☺ 1-7pm Thu-Sat). You

can wander enjoyably around this much-heralded microbrewery and try one of the five beers on tap.

Sleeping

Logies de Tabaksplant (☎ 472 97 97; www.tabaksplant .nl; Coninckstraat 15; s/d from €47/69) This small hotel is just beyond the old town gate of Kamperbin-nenpoort. The rooms are very smart, cheery, full of good vibes and so clean you could eat off the floor. The owner of a tobacco plantation built this heritage-listed building.

Logement de Gaaper (☎ 453 17 95; www.degaaper .nl; Hof 39; s/d from €66/81) It's not at all bad, this one. Home to a pharmacy in the 19th century, this smartly renovated hotel occupies a prime spot on the main square, and all 11 front rooms have great views of Sint Joriskerk. Some of the original structure is visible inside the hotel, but the emphasis is on modern comfort.

Eating

Mariënhof (☎ 463 29 79; www.marienhof.nl; Kleine Haag 2; mains €19-36; ⏰ lunch & dinner Tue-Sat) Enjoy *haute cuisine* and classy service in one of the region's best restaurants. The charismatic dining hall is in an atmospheric former monastery with lavish interiors, courtyard gardens and even a little culinary museum.

Het Bergpaviljoen (☎ 461 50 00; www.bergpaviljoen .nl; Utrechtseweg 180; mains €12-26; ⏰ lunch Mon-Fri, dinner Mon-Sat) When you see the expansive terrace and retro futuristic interior (minimalist and

nostalgic all at once), you know you're backing a winner. The classy international menu will have you enthralled, especially the quail and water cherry with mango chutney, as will the large TV in the dining room that allows you to watch the chefs at work.

Getting There & Around

Sample train fares and schedules:

Destination	Price (€)	Duration (min)	Frequency (per hr)
Amsterdam	7.10	40	4
Apeldoorn	6.80	25	2
Utrecht	3.90	15	4

There's a bicycle shop at the train station.

DOORN

☎ 0343 / pop 10,399

Around 20km southeast of Utrecht lies Doorn, a wealthy little burg with a claim to an oddment in 20th-century Dutch history: **Huis Doorn** (☎ 42 10 20; www.huisdoorn.nl; Langbroek-erweg 10; adult/child €5.50/1; ⏰ 10am-5pm Tue-Sat, 5-5pm Sun 15 Mar–31 Oct, 1-5pm Tue-Sun 1 Nov–14 Mar), a 14th-century castle that was turned into a sort of indefensible mansion during the 1700s. It had numerous owners during its time, but none of them was more infamous than Kaiser Wilhelm II of Germany, who inhabited Huis Doorn in exile from 1920 until his death in 1941.

WITCHERY

During the horrific witch-hunts of the 16th century, close to a million women all over Europe were executed on suspicion of being witches – burnt, drowned or otherwise tortured to death. Weighing was one of the more common methods of determining witchery, as popular belief held that any woman who was too light for the size of her frame was obviously a witch (because hags like that have no soul). A woman who weighed the 'proper' amount was too heavy to ride a broom and thus was not a witch. (Fans of the movie *Monty Python and the Holy Grail* will be familiar with the procedure.) Women who passed the weight test were given a certificate, good for life, proclaiming them to be human.

Women under suspicion were also required to walk over burning coals (if their feet didn't blister, they were witches) or were dropped into the lake – if you sank you were human, if you floated you were a witch. Needless to say, all of this was grossly unfair – if you managed to make it over the coals, your feet would be charred to the stumps. If you sank, you drowned. You win, you lose.

Oudewater emerges with some honour here. No-one was ever proved to be a witch in the town and this is held up as a symbol of the honesty of the locals, as they refused to take bribes to rig the weights. It's also seen as the first stirrings of people power and a turn against the church, which was behind the witch hunts.

There's a fine collection of German art that it seems the Kaiser brought with him from various German palaces. Afterwards, stroll the grounds and ponder the fate of the Kaiser, who had been allowed into exile by the Dutch as long as he remained under 'house arrest' (some house, eh?). Events throughout the year recall his highness: at Christmas you can drop by for gluhwein (mulled wine) and lebkuchen (spiced biscuits).

Bus 50 from Utrecht CS makes the 20km journey to Doorn (50 minutes) every 30 minutes. The castle is right near the bus stop.

AMERONGEN
☎ 0343 / pop 5169

The countryside around the small town of Amerongen on the Nederrijn river is dotted with old wooden tobacco-drying sheds. It's also home to **Kasteel Amerongen** (☎ 45 42 12; www .kasteel-amerongen.nl; Drostestraat 20; ☽ 10am-5pm Tue-Fri, 1-5pm Sat & Sun Apr-Oct), a fortified castle built in the 13th century that took on its present twee appearance in the late 1600s; it was originally owned by Europe's old aristocracy.

OUDEWATER
☎ 0348 / pop 9948

There's only one real reason to visit the sweet little town of Oudewater in the province's southwest: witchcraft. Until the 17th century the **Heksenwaag** (Witches' Weigh-House; ☎ 56 34 00; www.hekenswag.nl; Leeuweringerstraat 2; adult/child €1.50/0.75; ☽ 10am-5pm Tue-Sat, noon-5pm Sun) in the town centre was thought to have the most accurate scales in the land; women came from all over the land to be weighed here, on suspicion of being witches (see the boxed text, p187).

The house has a modest display of witchcraft history in the loft upstairs, and at the end of your visit you'll be invited to step onto the old scale. If you feel light on your feet it's because your *certificaet van weginghe* (weight certificate) makes your weight shrink – an old Dutch pound is 10% heavier than today's unit.

Oudewater is on the route of bus 180, which runs in either direction between Gouda (22 minutes) and Utrecht CS (40 minutes) every 30 minutes.

Zuid Holland & Zeeland

These two provinces are home to some of the strongest imagery – and biggest clichés – associated with the Netherlands. You want dykes? Uh-huh. Windmills? Yeah. Tulips? OK. Well, alright fellas, let's gooooo…

The Keukenhof gardens are a place of pilgrimage for lovers of the lancelike leaves and bell-shaped, varicoloured flower of the tulip, and the Zuid (South) Holland area is great for biking and hiking, with trails and paths everywhere. Meanwhile, the built-up beaches of Noordwijk aan Zee and south to Scheveningen are popular with locals.

Further south, Zeeland (Sea Land) is the dyke-protected province that people often associate with the Netherlands when they're not thinking of tulips, cheese and windmills. Middelburg is the centre, with a serenity belying its proximity to the tragedies that spawned the Delta Project.

Zuid Holland's major cities are the biggest attractions: there's Leiden, with its university culture and old town (and proximity to the bulb fields); Den Haag, with its museums, stately air and kitsch beach; charming, beautiful Delft, the home of Jan Vermeer; and mighty Rotterdam, blessed with an edgy urban vibe, gritty cultural scene, and innovative architecture.

Several smaller places are also worth your time: Gouda is a perfect old canal town, while Dordrecht has its own surprises – for humans and sheep alike. Just east and south of Dordrecht is Biesbosch National Park, a sprawling natural area along the border with Noord Brabant.

ZUID HOLLAND & ZEELAND

HIGHLIGHTS

- Answer the question 'Can you dance to architecture?' in **Rotterdam** (p211)
- Make like Tiny Tim at the **Keukenhof Gardens** (p195)
- Find out if waterfalls flow backwards at Den Haag's **Escher in het Paleis Museum** (p198)
- Look for girls wearing pearl earrings in old-world **Delft** (p204)
- Walk on water at Zeeland's **Delta Project** (p228)

Keukenhof Gardens ★

Den Haag ★ ★ Delft
  ★ Rotterdam

Delta Project ★

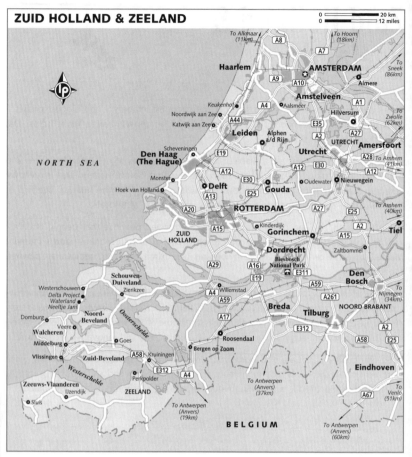

ZUID HOLLAND & ZEELAND

ZUID HOLLAND & ZEELAND

ZUID HOLLAND

Along with Noord (North) Holland and Utrecht, Zuid Holland is part of the Randstad, the economic and population centre of the Netherlands. Two of the nation's most important cities are here: Den Haag, the seat of the royal family and the government; and Rotterdam, Europe's busiest port.

LEIDEN

☎ 071 / pop 118,500

Lovely Leiden is a refreshing, vibrant town, patterned with canals and attractive old buildings. It also has a few claims to fame: it's Rembrandt's birthplace, and it's home to the

Netherlands' oldest university (and 20,000 students), the alma mater of René Descartes.

The university was a gift from Willem the Silent for withstanding two Spanish sieges in 1574. It was a terrible time, ending when the Sea Beggars arrived and repelled the invaders. According to lore, the retreating Spanish legged it so quickly, they abandoned a kettle of *hutspot* (hotchpotch) – today it's still a staple of Dutch menus in restaurants, and in homes.

Decades later, Protestants fleeing persecution elsewhere in the Low Countries, France and England arrived in Leiden to a somewhat warmer welcome. Most notable was the group led by John Robinson, who would sail to America and into history as the pilgrims aboard the *Mayflower*.

Wealth from the linen industry buttressed Leiden's growing prosperity, and during the 17th century the town produced several brilliant artists, most famously Rembrandt van Rijn – better known by his first name alone. Rembrandt was born in Leiden in 1606, and remained here for 26 years before achieving fame in Amsterdam.

Orientation

Old Leiden is a compact town. From Centraal Station a five-minute walk brings you to Beestenmarkt. Haarlemmerstraat and Breestraat are the town's pedestrian arteries, and most sights are within five minutes of either. The town is bisected by many waterways, the most notable being the Oude Rijn and also the Nieuwe Rijn, which meet at Hoogstraat to form a canal simply called the Rijn.

Information

BOOKSHOPS
Joho Company (☎ 516 12 77; www.joho.nl; Stille Rijn 8-9) Travel books, maps, travel gear and supplies, and Internet access.

INTERNET ACCESS
Centrale Bibliotheek (Central Library; ☎ 514 99 43; Nieuwstraat; internet per hr €3; ☺ 10am-6pm)
Ortes Telecom (Steenstraat; internet per hr €3)

POST
Post office (☎ 514 17 88; Breestraat 46; ☺ 9am-6pm Mon-Fri, 10am-1.30pm Sat)

TOURIST INFORMATION
Tourist office (☎ 09002222333; www.leidenpromotie .nl; Stationsweg 2D; ☺ 11am-5.30pm Mon, 9.30am-5.30pm Tue-Fri, 10am-4.30pm Sat)

Sights

Most of the sights are concentrated within Leiden's pretty canal belt and are best experienced on foot.

The **Rijksmuseum van Oudheden** (National Museum of Antiquities; ☎ 516 31 63; www.rmo.nl; Rapenburg 28; adult/under 18yr €7.50/5.50; ☺ 10am-5pm Tue-Fri, noon-5pm Sat & Sun) has a hieroglyph collection, and 94 human and animal mummies. The entrance hall contains the Temple of Taffeh, a gift from Egypt in 1969 for Dutch help in saving ancient monuments when the Aswan High Dam was built.

The 17th-century **Lakenhal** (Cloth Hall; ☎ 516 53 60; www.lakenhal.nl; Oude Singel 28-32; adult/under 18yr €4/free; ☺ 10am-5pm Tue-Sun) houses the Municipal Museum, with an assortment of works by old masters, as well as period rooms and temporary exhibits. The 1st floor has been restored to the way it would have looked when Leiden was at the peak of its cloth trade prosperity.

Leiden's carefully restored windmill, **De Valk** (Falcon; ☎ 516 53 53; http://home.wanadoo.nl /molenmuseum; 2E Binnenvestgracht 1; adult/under 15yr €3/1.70; ☺ 10am-5pm Tue-Sat, 1-5pm Sun), has been carefully restored; its construction and operation highlight the wonders of preindustrial engineering. There are many presentations, including one that laments that local boy Rembrandt, as a miller's son, didn't paint many windmills. The upper levels afford an inspired view of the old town.

Leiden University was an early centre for Dutch medical research, and the **Museum Boerhaave** (National Museum of the History of Science & Medicine; ☎ 521 42 24; www.museumboerhaave.nl; Lange St Agnietenstraat 10; adult/under 19yr €6/3; ☺ 10am-5pm Tue-Sat, noon-5pm Sun) gathers together five centuries of pickled organs, surgical tools and skeletons in its Anatomy Theatre (it's morbid, but just try to look away). The museum is housed in the hospital where the chronically ill Herman Boerhaave taught medicine from his sick-bed until his death in 1738.

A stuffed elephant greets you at **Naturalis – Nationaal Natuurhistorisch Museum** (National Museum of Natural History; ☎ 568 76 00; www.naturalis .nl; Darwinweg 2; adult/child €9/5; ☺ 10am-6pm Tue-Sun). This is a large and well-funded collection of all the usual dead critters, as well as the 1,000,000-year-old Java Man, discovered by Dutch anthropologist Eugène Dubois in 1891. This striking building is 300m west of the train station.

Activities

Rent a canoe or kayak from **Botenverhuur 't Galgewater** (☎ 514 97 90; www.galgewater.nl; Galgewater 44a; per hr €5; ☺ 11am-6pm Oct-May, 11am-10pm Jun-Sep) and explore the canals.

Tours

Rederij Rembrandt (☎ 513 49 38; www.rederij -rembrandt.nl; Beestenmarkt; adult/child €5/3) gives one-hour boat tours of Leiden at various times throughout the year. Check the schedules at the dock or on the website.

There are longer, three-hour cruises of the waterways and lakes around Leiden. Ask the tourist office for details.

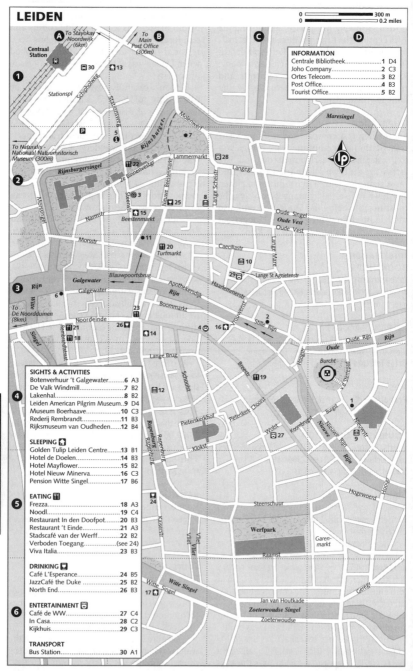

LEIDEN

0 —— 300 m
0 —— 0.2 miles

ZUID HOLLAND & ZEELAND

PILGRIMS' PROGRESS

In 1608 a group of Calvinist Protestants split from the Anglican Church and left persecution in Nottinghamshire, England, for a journey that would span decades and thousands of miles. Travelling first to Amsterdam under the leadership of John Robinson, they encountered theological clashes with local Dutch Protestants.

In Leiden they found a more liberal atmosphere, thanks to the university and some like-minded Calvinists who already lived there. They also found company with refugees who had escaped from persecution elsewhere. However, the group's past was to catch up with them. In 1618 James I of England announced he would assume control over the Calvinists living in Leiden. In addition, the local Dutch were becoming less tolerant of religious splinter groups.

The first group of English left Leiden in 1620 for Delfshaven in what is today Rotterdam, where they bought the *Speedwell* with the intention of sailing to the New World. Unfortunately, the leaky *Speedwell* didn't live up to its name; after several attempts to cross the Atlantic, the group gave up and, against their better judgment, sailed into Southampton in England. After repairs to their ship and a thwarted attempt to restart their journey, the group joined the much more seaworthy *Mayflower* in Dartmouth and sailed, as it were, into history as the Pilgrims.

This legendary voyage was actually just one of many involving the Leiden group. It wasn't until 1630 that most had made their way to the American colonies founded in what is today New England. Some 1000 people made the voyages, including a number of Dutch who were considered oddballs for their unusual beliefs.

In Leiden today, traces of the Pilgrims are elusive. The best place to start is the **Leiden American Pilgrim Museum** (☎ 512 24 13; www.pilgrimhall.org/leidenmuseum.htm; Beschuitsteeg 9; admission €2; 🕑 1-5pm Wed-Sat), a fascinating restoration of a house occupied around 1610 by the soon-to-be Pilgrims. The house itself dates from 1375, but the furnishings are from the Pilgrims' period. Note the tiles on the floor, originals from the 14th century. Pick up a walking-tour brochure, which helps you explore the surviving parts of 17th-century Leiden.

Festivals & Events

Leiden grinds to a halt in early October for **Leidens Ontzet**, commemorating the day the Spanish-caused starvation ended in 1574. The revelry is undiminished even four centuries later, and there is much eating of the ceremonial *hutspot*, herring and white bread. But more than anything, consumption focuses on beer sandwiches (hold the bread) and a drunken time is had by all – especially the night before.

Sleeping

BUDGET

Stayokay Noordwijk (☎ 0252-37 29 20; www.stayokay .com/noordwijk; Langevelderlaan 45; dm from €20) The hostel is next to a popular beach. Take buses 57 or 90 (last bus at 11pm) to Sancta Maria hospital and walk for 10 minutes.

De Noordduinen (☎ 402 52 95; www.tours.nl/noord duinen; Campingweg 1; per camp site from €16.50; 🕑 Apr-Oct) The closest camping ground, 8km to the west. Take buses 31 or 41.

MIDRANGE

Hotel de Doelen (☎ 512 05 27; www.dedoelen.com; Rapenburg 2; s/d with bathroom from €75/95) Some of the Doelen's canalside rooms border on palatial opulence, with all the trimmings, and even the more basic options have bathroom, phone and TV. Rooms come in three flavours: basic, standard and suite.

Hotel Mayflower (☎ 514 26 41; Beestenmarkt 2; www .hotelmayflower.nl; s/d €65/80) These spacious rooms are bright and inviting, with comfy furnishings and lots of trimmings. Apartments are also available.

Hotel Nieuw Minerva (☎ 512 63 58; www.nieuw minerva.nl; Boommarkt 23; s/d €75/100) The Minerva has a traditional look and a quiet canalside location, and its rooms are comfortable and well equipped. If you want a bit more bang for your buck, try the luxury suites, such as the evocatively named 'Room of Roses' and 'Room of Angels'. The décor in these is full-on mock baroque, and it makes a suitable backdrop for canoodling (and anything else).

Pension Witte Singel (☎ 512 45 92; www.pension ws.demon.nl; Witte Singel 80; s/d with shared bathroom €41/62, d with bathroom €76) Fresh, spacious rooms with large windows overlooking most agreeable scenery: the perfectly peaceful Singel canal in the front and a typically Dutch garden out the back.

TOP END

Golden Tulip Leiden Centre (☎ 408 35 00; Schipholweg 3; s/d €150/170; 🔀 🖵 🗙) These large and modern rooms are aimed at business travellers who are happy to trade architectural charm for amenities. You'll get all the charm you can handle out on the town's pretty canalside streets.

Eating

Frezza (Rembrandtstraat 2; tapas from €4; 🕑 dinner Wed-Sun) Frezza is a bit of a Leiden hot spot, finding an audience with its delectable selection of Mediterranean delights, including tapas.

Viva Italia (☎ 514 88 18; Kort Rapenburg 17; mains €16-20; 🕑 lunch & dinner) This classy and fine Italian joint, with its luxurious décor (including white-leather couches, no less) and fine service, dishes up upmarket vittles like veal with rolled-in Parma ham and basil pesto.

Verboden Toegang (☎ 514 33 88; www.verboden toegang.nl; Kaiserstraat 7; mains €13-20; 🕑 dinner) This casual, elegant, wood-panelled restaurant doesn't take itself too seriously (the name means 'access forbidden'). The grub's top-notch, with an emphasis on seafood – try the butterfish in white wine.

Restaurant In Den Doofpot (☎ 512 24 34; www .indendoofpot.nl; Turfmarkt 9; mains €12-45; 🕑 dinner) There's little chance you're going to walk away hungry from this elegant place. It serves twists on Dutch home-style cooking with elaborate French touches and other less bulky options.

Restaurant 't Einde (☎ 512 21 15; Rembrandtstraat 2; mains from €16; 🕑 dinner Tue-Sun) Small and sophisticated, with an excellent menu: exquisite meat, fish, poultry and seafood variations. Not too traditional, not too nouvelle cuisine, the food is mildly progressive and always delicious.

Other options:

Noodl (☎ 513 92 73; www.noodl.nl; Breestraat 88A; dishes €11-16; 🕑 dinner) Vietnamese and good dim sum.

Stadscafé van der Werff (☎ 512 61 20; Stationsweg 7-9; lunch dishes €9-13; 🕑 lunch) Bright, with large windows and the usual café menu.

Drinking

Café L'Esperance (☎ 512 16 00; www.lesperance.nl; Kaiserstraat 1) This is a small, skinny, typically Dutch pub – nostalgic, cheerful, wood panelled, cosy, and pumping in the summer time.

It often has live music, with big and little men belting out big fat tunes to big crowds in a thin space.

JazzCafé the Duke (☎ 566 15 85; Oude Singel 2) No windows, but loads of yellowing, vintage jazz posters on the walls. Their motto is, 'If we don't have it, you don't need it'. It's true: you don't need windows to enjoy this atmospheric den, with its fine live jazz every night, and suitably appreciative crowds.

North End (☎ 512 1541; www.north-end.nl; Noordeinde 55) This superb English-style pub is full of warmth, cosy nooks and character. It comes complete with its very own 'bourbon alley' (not very English, granted, but a welcome selection of booze all the same) and patented beer *strippenkaart* (strip card).

Entertainment
LIVE MUSIC

In Casa (☎ 512 49 38; www.danssalonincasa.nl; Lammermarkt 100) This place is huge and, from the outside, looks as though it has no atmosphere – but appearances can be deceiving. It has live music, a dance floor, comedy and a variety of other events.

Café de WW (☎ 512 59 00; Wolsteeg 6) Live rock is played here to a young crowd in the over-loud, hormonally charged atmosphere on Fridays. On other nights there's a DJ.

CINEMAS

Kijkhuis (☎ 566 15 85; Vrouwenkerksteeg 10) Has an alternative film programme.

Getting There & Away
Centraal Station is bright and modern. It has all the usual conveniences, and the lockers are near platform No 5. Sample fares and schedules:

Destination	Price (€)	Duration (min)	Frequency (per hr)
Amsterdam	7.50	34	6
Den Haag	2.80	10	6
Schiphol Airport	4.50	18	4

Regional and local buses leave from the bus station directly in front of Centraal Station.

Getting Around
Leiden is compact and you'll have a hard time walking for more than 20 minutes in any one direction. The bicycle shop in Centraal Station is around the back.

ZUID HOLLAND & ZEELAND

AROUND LEIDEN
Keukenhof Gardens

Near Lisse, between Haarlem and Leiden, a beautiful enigma unfurls for just two months each year: the blooming of millions of multi-coloured tulip, daffodil and hyacinth bulbs at the **Keukenhof gardens** (☎ 0252-46 55 55; www .keukenhof.nl; Stationsweg 166A, Lisse; adult/child 4-11yr €12.50/5.50; ◷ 8am-7.30pm late Mar-May, cashier to 6pm). The gardens stretch on and on, and there are greenhouses full of more delicate varieties of flowers besides the ephemeral tulips. You'll forgive the presence of thousands of other tourists – little can detract from the rainbow of natural beauty. Wandering about can easily take half a day. From the edges of the gardens, you can see the stark beauty of the commercial bulb fields stretching in all directions.

There are several options for reaching the park – see the boxed text, below, for details.

DEN HAAG (THE HAGUE)
☎ 070 / pop 472,100

Den Haag, officially known as 's-Gravenhage ('the Count's Hedge'), is the Dutch seat of government and home to the royal family. Prior to 1806, Den Haag was the Dutch capi-tal. However, that year, Louis Bonaparte in-stalled his government in Amsterdam. Eight years later, when the French had been ousted, the government returned to Den Haag, but the title of capital remained with Amsterdam.

Den Haag today is a stately, regal place filled with palatial embassies and mansions, green boulevards and parks, prestigious art galleries, a mouthwatering culinary scene, a clutch of tasty museums, and some throb-bing nightlife. Plus it's attached to the seaside suburb of Scheveningen, worth a visit for its lively kitsch and long stretch of beach.

In the 20th century Den Haag became the home of several international legal entities including the UN's International Court of Jus-tice and the Academy of International Law.

Orientation

Den Haag is spread over a fairly large area. Centraal Station is near the heart of town; Hollands Spoor station (HS), on the main line from Amsterdam to Rotterdam and destina-tions further south, is 1km south of the centre. Most streets heading west reach Scheveningen, 4km away, but it's more pleasantly approached at the end of a 15- to 20-minute bike ride that

---

TULIPS – THE BELOVED BULB

Tulips have captured the fancy of the Dutch for centuries. In fact, at times this love has become an absolute mania.

The first stop on any tulip tour is the Keukenhof, the world's largest flower garden, located between the towns of Hillegom and Lisse, south of Haarlem. The 32-hectare park attracts a stag-gering 800,000 people for a mere eight weeks every year. Nature's talents are combined with artificial precision to create a garden where millions of tulips and daffodils bloom, perfectly in place and exactly on time.

The broad stripes of colour are a spectacular feast for the eye. Postcards just don't do justice. The bulbs are left to bloom fully so that they will gain full strength during the growing season, after which over €500 million worth of bulbs are exported worldwide.

To appreciate the blooms you have several options. By train, opt for one of the frequent local (meaning slow) trains between Haarlem and Leiden. These pass through the heart of the fields. By car, cover the same area on the N206 and N208, branching off down tiny side roads as you wish (at the gardens, you'll have to pay a parking fee of around €4). But like so much of the Netherlands, perhaps the best way to see the bulb fields is by bicycle. You can set your course along the smallest roads and get lost in a sea of colour. If you just want to head straight to the gardens, Netherlands Railways sells a ticket (adult/under 11 years €17/9) that combines entrance to the gardens and travel by express bus from Leiden CS (20 minutes).

In Lisse, the **tourist office** (☎ 0252-41 42 62; Grachtweg 53A; ◷ noon-5pm Mon, 9am-5pm Tue-Fri, 9am-4pm Sat) can give you many options for bulb-field touring. Also in Lisse, the small **Museum de Zwarte Tulp** (Museum of the Black Tulip; ☎ 0252-41 79 00; www.museumdezwartetulp.nl; Grachtweg 2A; admission €3; ◷ 1-5pm Tue-Sun) displays everything you might want to know about bulbs, including why there's no such thing as a black tulip.

See p171 for details on the Aalsmeer Flower Auction, the largest of its type in the world.

ZUID HOLLAND & ZEELAND

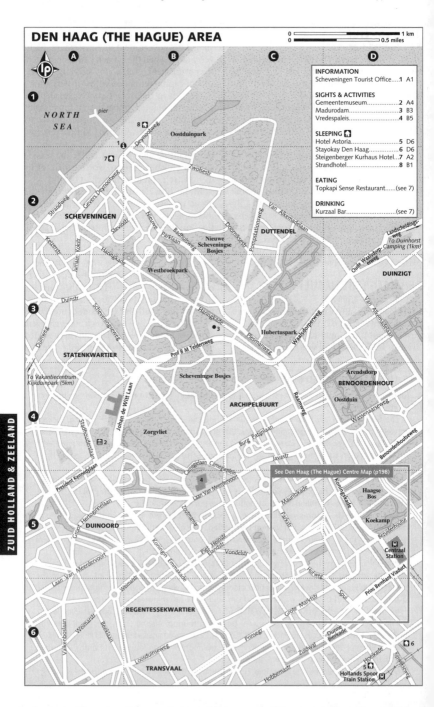

DEN HAAG (THE HAGUE) AREA

0 ——— 1 km
0 ——— 0.5 miles

INFORMATION
Scheveningen Tourist Office.....**1** A1

SIGHTS & ACTIVITIES
Gemeentemuseum...................**2** A4
Madurodam............................**3** B3
Vredespaleis...........................**4** B5

SLEEPING
Hotel Astoria..........................**5** D6
Stayokay Den Haag................**6** D6
Steigenberger Kurhaus Hotel...**7** A2
Strandhotel............................**8** B1

EATING
Topkapi Sense Restaurant......(see 7)

DRINKING
Kurzaal Bar...........................(see 7)

NORTH SEA

pier

Oostduinpark

Zwolsestr

DUTTENDEL

Nieuwe Scheveningse Bosjes

Westbroekpark

DUINZIGT

SCHEVENINGEN

Haringkade

Hubertuspark

STATENKWARTIER

Prof B M Teldersweg

Arendsdorp

BENOORDENHOUT

To Vakantiecentrum
Kijkduinpark (5km)

Scheveningse Bosjes

Oostduin

ARCHIPELBUURT

Zorgvliet

Burg Patijnlaan

Javastr

See Den Haag (The Hague) Centre Map (p198)

Haagse Bos

Koekamp

DUINOORD

Vondelstr

Centraal Station

REGENTESSEKWARTIER

Dunne Bierkade

6

TRANSVAAL

Hollands Spoor
Train Station

5

To Duinhorst Camping (1km)

ZUID HOLLAND & ZEELAND

will take you past the lush homes of some of Den Haag's most well-heeled residents.

Den Haag has no true centre; rather, there are several areas of concentration, including the Binnenhof and the nearby Kerkplein.

Information

BOOKSHOPS

Van Stockum (Map p198; ☎ 365 68 08; www.vanstock um.nl; Venestraat 11) Selection of travel books and magazines.

INTERNET ACCESS

Kado Internet (Map p198; Spui 165; internet per hr €2.75)
Koninklijke Bibliotheek (Royal Library; Map p198; ☎ 314 09 11; Prins Willem-Alexanderhof 5; internet per hr €3; 🕑 9am-6pm Mon & Wed-Fri, 9am-8pm Tue, 9am-1pm Sat)

POST

Post office (Map p198; ☎ 365 38 43; Kerkplein 6; 🕑 9am-6pm Mon-Wed & Fri, 9am-8pm Thu, 9am-4pm Sat)

TOURIST INFORMATION

Tourist office (Map p198; ☎ 09003403505; www.den haag.com; Hofweg 1; 🕑 10am-6pm Mon-Fri, 10am-5pm Sat, noon-5pm Sun)
Scheveningen Tourist Office (Map p196; ☎ 09003403 405; www.scheveningen.nl; Gevers Deynootweg 1134; 🕑 9am-5.30pm Mon-Fri, 10am-5pm Sat, 11am-4pm Sun)

Dangers & Annoyances

The area south of the centre (the Schilders-wijk) near HS can seem far removed from its urbane counterpart to the north. Watch out for pickpockets.

Sights & Activities

Den Haag has no true core, rather a scattering of districts. All are easily reached by public transport or bike.

MAURITSHUIS

The small but grand **Mauritshuis** (Map p198; ☎ 302 34 56; www.mauritshuis.nl; Korte Vijverberg 8; adult/under 18yr incl audiotour €11.50/free; 🕑 10am-5pm Tue-Sat, 11am-5pm Sun) museum houses Dutch and Flemish masterpieces. It includes several of the most famous Vermeers, and a touch of the contemporary with Andy Warhol's *Queen Beatrix of the Netherlands*.

The building was constructed as a mansion in 1640 in classical style; all its dimensions are roughly the same (25m), and the detailing shows exquisite care. In 1822 it was made the home of the royal collection.

The collection is displayed in 16 rooms on two floors – almost every piece is a masterpiece. Even if you're just passing Den Haag on the train, it's worth hopping off to visit.

Highlights include *Girl with a Pearl Earring* by Vermeer and *The Anatomy Lesson of Dr Nicolaes Tulp* by Rembrandt. Note that some paintings are loaned occasionally.

BINNENHOF

Adjoining the Mauritshuis, the Binnenhof (Inner Court; Map p198) is surrounded by parliamentary buildings that have long been at the heart of Dutch politics, though parliament now meets in a modern building on the south side.

The central courtyard looks sterile now but was once used for executions. A highlight of the complex is the 13th-century **Ridderzaal** (Knights' Hall). The Gothic dining hall has been carefully restored.

The North Wing is still home to the Upper Chamber of the Dutch Parliament, in 17th-century splendour. The Lower Chamber used to meet in the ballroom, in the 19th-century wing. It all looks a bit twee and you can see why the politicians were anxious to decamp to the sleek new extension nearby.

The best way to see the Binnenhof's buildings is on a one-hour tour, which leaves from the visitors centre (☎ 364 61 44; 🕑 10am-4pm Mon-Sat). Here you can see a model showing the hotchpotch of buildings that make up the Binnenhof, and you can learn about the turbulent past of the Low Countries, where invaders have flooded in more often than the waters.

After your walk, stroll around the Hofvijver, where the reflections of the Binnenhof and the Mauritshuis have inspired countless snapshots.

DEN HAAG: OLD & NEW

Across the Hofvijver from the Binnenhof, the **Gevangenpoort** (Prison Gate; Map p198; ☎ 346 08 61; www.gevangenpoort.nl; Buitenhof 33; tour adult/child €4/3; 🕑 10am-5pm Tue-Fri, noon-5pm Sat & Sun) is a surviving remnant of the 13th-century city fortifications. It has hourly tours showing how justice was dispensed back then.

Next door, the **Galerij Prins Willem V** (Map p198; ☎ 362 44 44; Buitenhof 35; adult/child €1.50/1; 🕑 11am-4pm Tue-Sun) was the first public museum in the Netherlands when it opened in 1773. It's been restored to its original appearance and the paintings are hung in the manner popular

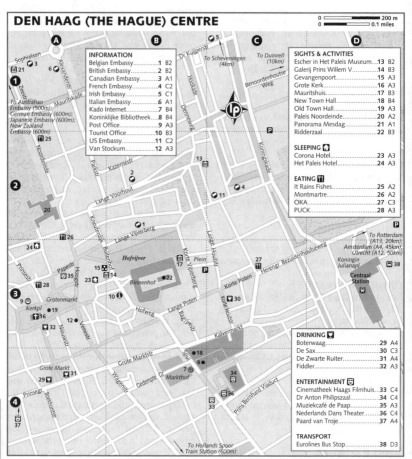

DEN HAAG (THE HAGUE) CENTRE

INFORMATION
Belgian Embassy..............**1** B2
British Embassy..............**2** B2
Canadian Embassy..........**3** A1
French Embassy..............**4** C2
Irish Embassy..................**5** C1
Italian Embassy................**6** A1
Kado Internet..................**7** B4
Koninklijke Bibliotheek.....**8** B4
Post Office.....................**9** A3
Tourist Office.................**10** B3
US Embassy..................**11** C2
Van Stockum...................**12** A3

SIGHTS & ACTIVITIES
Escher in Het Paleis Museum...**13** B2
Galerij Prins Willem V............**14** B3
Gevangenpoort...................**15** A3
Grote Kerk.......................**16** A3
Mauritshuis.....................**17** B3
New Town Hall.................**18** B4
Old Town Hall..................**19** A3
Paleis Noordeinde.............**20** A2
Panorama Mesdag.............**21** A1
Ridderzaal.......................**22** B3

SLEEPING
Corona Hotel....................**23** A3
Het Paleis Hotel................**24** A3

EATING
It Rains Fishes..................**25** A2
Montmartre.....................**26** A2
OKA.............................**27** C3
PUCK...........................**28** A3

DRINKING
Boterwaag......................**29** A4
De Sax..........................**30** C3
De Zwarte Ruiter...............**31** A4
Fiddler..........................**32** A3

ENTERTAINMENT
Cinematheek Haags Filmhuis...**33** C4
Dr Anton Philipszaal...........**34** C4
Muziekcafé de Paap............**35** A3
Nederlands Dans Theater.......**36** C4
Paard van Troje.................**37** A4

TRANSPORT
Eurolines Bus Stop..............**38** D3

in the 18th century; not a skerrick of wall is left bare.

The **Grote Kerk** (Map p198; ☎ 302 86 30; Rond de Grote Kerk 12), dating from 1450, has a fine pulpit that was constructed 100 years later. The neighbouring 1565 **old town hall** (Map p198) is a splendid example of Dutch Renaissance architecture.

The huge **new town hall** (Map p198; Spui 170) is the hotly debated work by US architect Richard Meier. The 'official' nickname of the building is the 'white swan', but locals prefer the 'ice palace'. Even better are the local nicknames for two government buildings nearby; if allowed, take the elevator to the town hall's 11th floor and look at the complex that has two pointed towers at one end and a dome-topped round tower at the other. The local moniker is 'the tits and penis'.

Names are more polite for the king's and queen's official quarters at **Paleis Noordeinde** (Map p198). The Renaissance formality of the structure bespeaks regal digs. It's not open to the public, and the strong gates ensure security in case the populace revolts for having their taxes spent on anatomically suggestive buildings.

ESCHER IN HET PALEIS MUSEUM

The Lange Voorhout Palace was once Queen Emma's residence. Now it's home to the work of Dutch graphic artist MC Escher. **Escher in het Paleis Museum** (Map p198; ☎ 338 11 20; www.escherinhetpaleis.nl; Lange Voorhout; adult/under 15yr €7.50/5;

11am-5pm Tue-Sun) is a permanent exhibition featuring notes, letters, drafts, photos and fully mature works covering Escher's entire career, from his early realism to the later phantasmagoria. There are some imaginative displays, including a virtual reality reconstruction of Escher's impossible buildings and four-dimensional spatial dynamics, and an optical illusion photo booth, where you can take a picture of yourself as if you were actually in an Escher drawing.

GEMEENTEMUSEUM
Admirers of De Stijl, and in particular of Piet Mondrian, mustn't miss the Berlage-designed **Gemeentemuseum** (Map p196; Municipal Museum; ☎ 338 11 20; www.gemeentemuseum.nl; Stadhouderslaan 41; adult/ under 18yr €8/free; ☒ 11am-5pm Tue-Sat). It houses a large collection of works by neoplasticist artists and others from the late 19th century, as well as extensive exhibits of applied arts, costumes and musical instruments.

Mondrian's unfinished *Victory Boogie Woogie* takes pride of place (as it should: the museum paid €30 million for it), and there are also a few Picassos and other works by some of the better-known names of the 20th century. A great repository on a par with many others of similar size in the country, it's also home to a fabulous **Photography Museum**.

PANORAMA MESDAG
Just past the north end of Noordeinde, the **Panorama Mesdag** (Map p198; ☎ 364 45 44; www.panorama-mesdag.nl; Zeestraat 65; adult/child under 13yr €5/2.50; ☒ 10am-5pm Mon-Sat, noon-5pm Sun & holidays) contains the *Panorama* (1881), a huge 360-degree painting of Scheveningen that was painted by Hendrik Willem Mesdag. The panorama is viewed from a constructed dune, with real sand and beach chairs; birdsong and wave sounds are piped through. Mesdag's command of perspective and minute detail was masterly: it's a fully immersive experience.

VREDESPALEIS
The United Nations' International Court of Justice is housed in the **Vredespaleis** (Peace Palace; Map p196; ☎ 302 41 37; Carnegieplein 2; tours adult/child €2.50/1.50; ☒ 10am-4pm Mon-Fri). The grand building was donated by American steel maker Andrew Carnegie for use by the International Court of Arbitration, an early international body whose goal was the prevention of war. Sadly, WWI broke out one year after it opened in 1913.

There are hourly guided tours, but if the courts are in session these tours may be cancelled – check with the tourist office. You need to book ahead (security is strict). Take tram 7 from CS or tram 8 from HS.

MADURODAM
Complete with 1:25 scale versions of Schiphol, Amsterdam, windmills and tulips, Rotterdam harbour, and the Delta dikes, **Madurodam** (Map p196; ☎ 355 39 00; www.madurodam.nl; George Maduroplein 1; adult/child under 11yr €12.50/9; ☒ 9am-8pm) is a miniaturised Netherlands. It's an enlightening example of the Dutch tendency to put their world under a microscope (see p37).

Take tram 1 from CS, or tram 1 or 9 from HS.

SCHEVENINGEN
The long beach at **Scheveningen** (Map p196; www.scheveningen.nl) attracts nine million visitors per year. Crowds can get up close and personal when the weather gets warm, and the shopping strip gets crassly commercial, but the attraction of sea and sand keeps the peace. A palpable frisson of frivolity sweetens the air.

Escape the crowds by heading north along the beach past the end of the tram line. Here the dunes are more pristine and the further you walk or ride, the greater the rewards. You'll also pass a series of WWII bunkers, part of the Nazi Atlantic Wall defence system and an eerie reminder of the Netherlands' place in European history.

Here's another reminder, an oft-repeated story that relates how Dutch resistance fighters during WWII used 'Scheveningen' as a password. It seems that while the Germans could easily learn Dutch, for them the accent required to properly pronounce 'Scheveningen' was impossible to learn. Go on, give it a go: say s'CHay-fuh-ninger.

Tours
The tourist office offers a good bus tour; an 'Architecture Tour' using a specialist guide; and a great range of boat tours. Contact the office for times, as they change with demand.

De Ooievaart (www.ooievaart.nl; adult/3-12yr €8.95/4.95; ☒ departures 11am-4.45pm) also offers boat tours over four different 1½-hour routes, taking in Den Haag's most interesting sights at canal level.

ZUID HOLLAND & ZEELAND

Sleeping

BUDGET

Stayokay Den Haag (Map p196; ☎ 315 78 88; www
.stayokay.com/denhaag; Scheepmakerstraat 27; dm from €21)
This branch of the Stayokay hostel chain has
all the usual facilities including a bar, a restaurant, Internet and games. It's around 15
minutes' walk from Hollands Spoor station.

Duinhorst (☎ 324 22 70; www.duinhorst.nl; Buurtweg
135; camp site per tent €4.65; ☼ Apr-Sep) To get to
this camp site; take bus 28 from HS or bus
29 from CS to the end of the line at Oude
Waalsdorperweg and then walk about 1km
west, or take a taxi.

MIDRANGE

Corona Hotel (Map p198; ☎ 363 79 30; www.corona.nl;
Buitenhof 39-42; r from €74) This pleasant hotel is
across the way from the Binnenhof and has
all the usual facilities and amenities, plus su-
percomfy rooms that come in a range of un-
Dutchlike styles such as 'Colonial English'.

Strandhotel (Map p196; ☎ 354 01 93; www.strandhotel
.demon.nl; Zeekant 111 & Gevers Deynootweg 1344, Scheveningen; s/d from €40/65) It's on the beach, and the rooms
have an unreconstructed 1950s motif. Book
ahead and keep an eye on the weather – prices
soar in summer. Service can be perfunctory.

Hotel Astoria (Map p196; ☎ 384 04 01; Stationsweg
139; s/d €42/55) The rooms are small and a touch
bleak (although they do have private facilities,
which sweetens the deal).

TOP END

ourpick Steigenberger Kurhaus Hotel (Map p196;
☎ 416 26 36; www.kurhaus.nl; Gevers Deynootplein 30,
Scheveningen; r from €275; ✶ ▢ ✗) At the top end
of things and right on the beach. First built in
1885, this sumptuous, elegant building has
been extended and restored several times. The
noted thermal baths are there still, among a
plethora of luxuries that includes a casino.

Het Paleis Hotel (Map p198; ☎ 362 46 21; www
.paleishotel.nl; Molenstraat 26; s/d from €175/185) Near
the Noordeinde and historic Den Haag, its
location is atmospheric enough, and the antique trimmings in the room match all that
superbly. The rooms are well equipped and
very comfortable.

Eating

Den Haag's gastronomic scene is fairly central and very good, with quality matched by
variety. The cobbled streets off Denneweg are
one of the livelier areas.

It Rains Fishes (Map p198; ☎ 365 25 98; www.itrains
fishes.nl; Noordeinde 123; mains €13-24; ☼ lunch & dinner)
It's the 'restaurant on the sunny side of the
street', a multi-award-winning seafood concern serving grilled, fried and poached fish,
mussels and scallops.

PUCK (Pure Unique Californian Kitchen; Map p198; ☎ 427
76 49; www.puckfoodandwines.nl; Prinsestraat 33; mains
€18-25; ☼ lunch & dinner Tue-Sat) The restaurant's
vibrant paint job is apparently a tribute to the
owner's daughter's love of M&Ms, and that
refreshing lack of attitude and formality carries over to the fusion menu. A case in point:
pan-sautéed duck breast over oven-roasted
fries, with Napa cabbage and maple syrup.

Topkapi Sense Restaurant (Map p196; ☎ 358 53
50; www.topkapi-scheveningen.nl; Gevers Deynootplein 36,
Scheveningen; mains €11-22; ☼ lunch & dinner) An 'Ot-
toman' restaurant with cuisine from Greece,
Turkey, Egypt, Syria, Algeria, Morocco… the
couscous with sea bass is a winner, as is the
baked, stuffed zucchini. Ruby-red drapes and
beads combine with low lighting to create a
suitable atmosphere, although the guy in the
corner playing cheesy tunes on his synthetic
organ tempers it.

OKA (Map p198; ☎ 392 01 33; Herengracht 2-6; dishes
€15-25; ☼ lunch & dinner Tue-Sat) This swish, authentic Japanese restaurant serves up delectable
sushi and *teppanyaki*. The hostess, Ms JoJo
Phang, is a bit of a personality – she says she
can arrange on-site bachelor parties, ironing
out all the details in a 'private talk tailored to
that evening's party boy'.

Montmartre (Map p198; ☎ 365 64 54; Molenstraat
4C; snacks €4.30-12.50; ☼ lunch) This brasserie has
décor that's a little bit lacy and a lunch menu
that's very French: understated, yet refined,
with lavish attention to detail. The baguettes
are seriously pleasing, with all kinds of cheeses
and extras like marinated eggplant.

Drinking

Kurzaal Bar (Map p196; ☎ 416 26 36; Steigenberger Kurhaus Hotel, Gevers Deynootplein 30, Scheveningen) Even if
you're not staying at the plush, 19th-century
Kurhaus Hotel, it's worth popping in for a
drink at its bar (but wear your best shoes). The
Kurzaal's on the edge of a stunning dancehall/
restaurant with period trimmings, painted ceiling, frescoes, chandeliers, huge potted plants,
portholes, artworks, and photos of Jacques Brel,
Bing Crosby… The Rolling Stones played their
shortest-ever concert here – just three minutes,
before rioting teenage girls took over.

Boterwaag (Map p198; ☎ 365 96 86; www.september .nl; Grote Markt 8A; ☺ lunch & dinner) This old weigh-house serves as a café-restaurant and provides a distinctive drinking and eating experience, with its high ceilings, large windows, candle fetish, nooks and crannies to hide out in, and great beer list. When we were here, a kooky kid was riding around inside on a unicycle and no-one batted an eyelid.

De Zwarte Ruiter (The Black Rider; Map p198; ☎ 364 95 49; www.september.nl; Grote Markt 27) The Rider faces off with the Boterwaag across the Markt like rival Kings of Cool. With its terrace and Deco mezzanine – light-filled, split-level and cavernous – it's like the interior of an abandoned theatre. This is a classic café, cool bar and casual meeting point all in one.

De Sax (Map p198; ☎ 346 67 55; Korte Houtstraat 14A) This little jazz bar, just off the Plein, is quite the chilled establishment. It has a good vibe, not the least of which is due to the cool music oozing from the sound system. Very dark, very cosy, very friendly.

Fiddler (Map p198; ☎ 365 19 55; www.fiddler.nl; Riviervismarkt 1) This large, split-level, wood-panelled English microbrewery always has a decent crowd snacking on the OK pub food and the Fiddler's own beers: an ale, a pale ale and a stout. In the end, it's probably a bit too cavernous – intimacy's hard to come by. Good location: in the eye of the Grote Kerk.

Entertainment

Nederlands Dans Theater (Map p198; ☎ 880 01 00; www .ndt.nl; Schedeldoekshaven 60) This renowned dance company has gained worldwide fame since its formation in 1959. It was created by a group of dancers frustrated with the ossified creativity of the old Ballet of the Netherlands company. The group has three components: NDT1, the main troupe of 32 dancers; NDT2, a small group of 12 dancers under 21; and NDT3, a group of dancers over 40 who perform more dramatic works.

Paard van Troje (Map p198; ☎ 750 34 34; www.paard .nl; Prinsegracht 12) This emporium has club nights and live music, as well as a café. The pro-gramming's eclectic: everything from booty-shaking drum'n'bass DJs to bowel-destroying sonic maniacs The Hafler Trio.

Muziekcafé de Paap (Map p198; ☎ 365 20 02; www .depaap.nl; Papestraat 32) Den Haag's best place for live music, and just a great, versatile nightspot. It's atmospheric, and has a fab restaurant and bar where you can kick off early. It's a young-ish, cool crowd, but really geared to anyone who's into music.

Other options:

Cinematheek Haags Filmhuis (Map p198; ☎ 365 60 30; www.filmhuisdenhaag.nl; Spui 191) Screens foreign and art movies.

Dr Anton Philipszaal (Map p198; ☎ 360 98 10; www .dapz.ldt.nl; Spui 150) Home to the Residentie Orkest, Den Haag's classical symphony orchestra.

Shopping

There are several good streets for galleries, antiques and interesting boutiques; try Den-neweg, Noordeinde – which also has some great restaurants and bars – and Molenstraat.

Getting There & Away

Den Haag has two main train stations. CS – a terminus – is close to the centre. It has the usual amenities and is a hub for local trams and buses.

HS is about 1km south of the centre and is on the main railway line between Amsterdam and Rotterdam and the south. Thalys high-speed trains to/from Paris stop here, as do many other through-services. HS also has all the usual services.

BUS

Eurolines long-distance buses stop on the east side of CS. Regional buses depart from the bus station above the tracks at CS.

TRAIN

Sample train services:

Destination	Price (€)	Duration (min)	Frequency (per hr)
Amsterdam	9.50	50	4
Leiden	2.80	13	4
Rotterdam	4.10	22	4
Utrecht	9.10	40	4

Getting Around

Most tram routes converge on CS, at the tram and bus station above the tracks. A number of routes also serve HS, including the jack-of-all-trades tram 1, which starts in Scheveningen and runs all the way to Delft, passing the centre of Den Haag and CS along the way. Trams 1, 8 and 9 link Scheveningen with Den Haag; the fare is three strips. The last tram runs in either direction at about 1.30am.

Call **ATC Taxi** (☎ 317 88 77) for a cab. You can hail any available taxi, if you can find one.

The **bicycle shop** (☎ 385 32 35) in CS is under the terminal. The HS **bicycle shop** (☎ 389 08 30) is at the southern end of that station. Both shops rent out bikes.

GOUDA

☎ 0182 / pop 71,797

Gouda's association with cheesy comestibles has made it famous – the town's namesake fermented curd is among the Netherlands' best-known exports. But Gouda, the town, has a bit more to it than that.

Gouda enjoyed economic success and decline in the same manner as the rest of Holland from the 16th century onwards. Its cheese has brought recent wealth, as has the country's largest candle factory, which stays busy supplying all those Dutch brown cafés. The acclaimed 16th-century stained-glass windows in its church are a highlight.

Gouda makes an ideal day trip, easily accessible from any city in Zuid Holland. The compact centre is entirely ringed by canals and is less than five minutes' walk from the station. The large central square, the Markt, is the focus of the town.

Information

Post office (☎ 52 21 00; Westhaven 37; ✆ 7am-5pm Mon-Fri, 7am-1.30pm Sat) South of the Markt.

Tourist office (☎ 090046832888; www.vvvgouda.nl; Markt 27; ✆ 1-5.30pm Mon, 9.30am-5.30pm Tue-Fri, 10am-4pm Sat)

Sights

Most of the notable sights are within 10 minutes' walk of the strangely enormous Markt.

MARKT

The central Markt is one of the largest such squares in the Netherlands. Right in the middle is the mid-15th-century **town hall**. Constructed from shimmering sandstone, this regal Gothic structure bespeaks the wealth Gouda enjoyed from the cloth trade when it was built. The red-and-white shutters provide a fine counterpoint to the carefully maintained stonework.

On the north side of the Markt, you can't miss the **Waag**, a former cheese-weighing house built in 1668. If you have any doubt about its use, check out the reliefs carved into the side showing the cheese being weighed. It houses the **Kaaswaag** (☎ 52 99 96; adult/child €2.50/1;

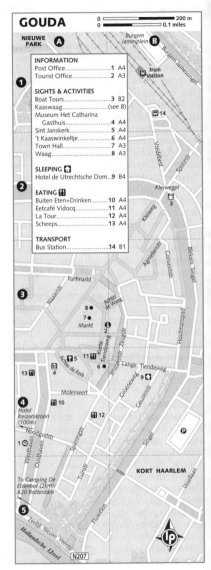

✆ 1-5pm Tue-Sun Apr-Oct), a museum that follows the history of the cheese trade in the Netherlands, especially its history in Gouda.

SINT JANSKERK & AROUND

Just to the south of the Markt is **Sint Janskerk** (☎ 51 26 84; Achter de Kerk; adult/child €2.50/1.75; ✆ 10am-6pm Mon-Sat Mar-Nov, 9am-5pm Dec-Feb). The church itself had chequered beginnings: it burned down with ungodly regularity every 100 years or so from 1361 until the mid-16th century, when what you see today was completed.

Architecturally, Sint Janskerk is an attractive late-Gothic church in need of a better steeple, but its huge windows set it apart, especially those created by Dirck Crabeth, his brother Wouter, and Lambert van Noort from around 1550 to 1570. Their works, which are numbered, include highlights such as window No 6 (John the Baptist; the folks on either side paid for the window) and No 22 (Jesus purifies the temple; note the look on the face of the moneychanger).

To the immediate southwest of the church, near a small canal, the **Museum het Catharina Gasthuis** (☎ 58 84 40; Oosthaven 10; adult/child €2.50/1; ✇ 10am-5pm Mon-Sat, noon-5pm Sun), housed in an old hospital, covers Gouda's history and has a few artworks.

OTHER ATTRACTIONS
Wandering the streets away from the Markt is rewarding, especially Lange Tiendeweg and Zeugstraat with its tiny canal and even tinier bridges. To prove that Gouda cheese really isn't bland, visit **'t Kaaswinkeltje** (☎ 51 42 69; www .kaaswinkeltje.com; Lange Tiendeweg 30). This cheese shop is filled with fabulous smells and it's here that you can sample some of the aged Goudas that the Dutch wisely keep for themselves. The older the cheese, the sharper the flavour, and some of the very old Goudas have a Parmesan-like texture and a rich, smoky taste. With a little mustard smeared on, a hunk of this cheese is great with beer.

Tours
In July and August there are two daily boat trips (€6, three hours) through the canals around Gouda to the nearby Reeuwijk lake district. Contact the tourist office for details.

Festivals & Events
Once upon a time, the Gouda cheese market was the real thing, as the Waag will attest. But the days when more than 1000 dairymen and cheese makers would assemble in the Markt for a raucous day of buying, selling and trading are long past. Now hundreds of tour buses assemble every Thursday morning from June to August for an orgy of buying, selling and very little trading. A few men dress up in traditional costume and go through the motions.

Sleeping
Given that Gouda is such a natural day trip, you might not think of staying here, but you may just appreciate its somnolent charms after dark. The tourist office has a list of a few private rooms it will book for a small fee. These rooms usually cost €20 to €30 per person.

Camping De Elzenhof (☎ 52 44 56; Broekweg 6; camp sites from €10) This camp site is a 45-minute haul from town – you have to detour around canals and waterways and there's no bus. Go south from the centre of Gouda, cross the Julianasluis bridge and follow the signs.

Hotel de Utrechtsche Dom (☎ 52 88 33; www .hotelgouda.nl; Geuzenstraat 6; s/d from €57/75) Neat, clean and on a quiet street, this is a lovely, low-key place to stay, with good amenities. There're a big, spacious breakfast room and hospitable managers – what more could you ask for?

Hotel Keizerskroon (☎ 52 80 96; www.hotel keizerskroon.nl; Keizerstraat 11-13; s/d from €62/72) This one's centrally located, and is homely, cosy, comfortable, warm, welcoming and friendly. Choose from a range of suites, ranging from 'standard' to 'luxury'. Oh, and there's an on-site bar and restaurant.

Eating & Drinking
Buiten Eten+Drinken (☎ 52 48 84; www.buitenetenen drinken.com; Oosthaven 23A; 3-course menu from €26; ✇ dinner Tue-Sun) Buiten has perhaps the best view of Gouda's restaurants, overlooking the pretty canal that rings this town. The global menu delivers, too – French, Asian and Mediterranean palates combining with a good vegetarian selection. Inside, there's a fireplace and seasonal art on the ceilings and walls, and it's all very inviting.

Scheeps (☎ 51 75 72; www.restaurantscheeps.nl; Westhaven 4; mains €17-30; ✇ lunch & dinner) A considered body of local opinion states that Scheeps is Gouda's best restaurant. That may be, considering the fine choice of fish and local specialities on offer (vegetarians haven't been forgotten, either). In summer, dine outside in the lovely garden.

La Tour (☎ 52 47 17; www.la-tour.nl; Spieringstraat 101; mains €17-22; ✇ dinner Tue-Sat) This intimate, relaxed place draws on French and Italian influences for its delectable menu. You could do much worse than sample the furnace-baked cod fish, or indeed the tournedos with Madagascar peppers.

ZUID HOLLAND & ZEELAND

Eetcafé Vidocq (☎ 52 28 19; www.eetcafevidocq .nl; Koster Gijzensteeg 5-8; mains €16-20; ⊗ lunch & dinner) This Gouda classic café has been around for ages. Menu items on offer might include tournedos, cordon bleu rib-eye steak and chilli salmon trout covered with breadcrumbs.

Getting There & Around

Gouda's train station is close to the centre and all you'll need are your feet for local transport. The lockers are in the tunnel under the tracks. Sample fares and schedules:

Destination	Price (€)	Duration (min)	Frequency (per hr)
Amsterdam	9.40	80	2
Den Haag	4.80	19	4
Rotterdam	4.30	19	3
Utrecht	5.30	22	2

The bus station is immediately to the left as you exit the train station on the Centrum side. The one bus of interest here is the 180 to Oudewater (p188).

There are large car parks for your car or motorcycle on the town's periphery. Gouda is near the A12 motorway between Den Haag and Utrecht and the A20 to Rotterdam.

The **bicycle shop** (☎ 51 97 51) is in the train station.

DELFT

☎ 015 / pop 94,486

Ah, lovely Delft: compact, charming, relaxed. It's a very popular tourist destination – day-trippers (and lovers of beauty and refinement) clamour to stroll Delft's narrow, canal-lined streets, gazing at the remarkable old buildings and meditating on the life and career of Golden Age painter Johannes Vermeer. The artist was born in Delft and lived here – *View of Delft*, one of his best-loved works, is an enigmatic, nonrealist vision of the town. Delft is also famous for its 'delftware', the distinctive blue-and-white pottery originally duplicated from Chinese porcelain by 17th-century artisans.

Delft was founded around 1100 and grew rich from weaving and trade in the 13th and 14th centuries. In the 15th century a canal was dug to the Maas River, and the small port there, Delfshaven, was eventually absorbed by Rotterdam.

Orientation

The train station and neighbouring bus station are a 10-minute stroll south of the central Markt.

Information

Boekhandel Huyser (☎ 212 38 20; Choorstraat 12-14) Good travel section and lots of English-language books.

Library (☎ 212 34 50; Kruisstraat 71; internet per hr €3; ⊗ 10am-7pm Mon-Fri, 10am-3pm Sat)

Post office (☎ 212 45 11; Hippolytusbuurt 14; ⊗ 9am-5pm Mon-Fri, 10am-1.30pm Sat)

Tourist office (☎ 09005151555; www.delft.nl; Hippolytusbuurt 4; ⊗ 11am-4pm Mon, 10am-4pm Tue-Fri, 10am-5pm Sat, 10am-4pm Sun) Free internet access.

Sights & Activities

Delft is best seen on foot: almost all the interesting sights lie within a 1km radius of the Markt.

DELFTWARE

The town's ubiquitous blue-and-white china is almost a cliché. Given that the process was first developed in China, it's ironic that the mass of fake delftware sold in tourist shops also comes from China. The real stuff is produced in fairly small quantities at four factories in and around Delft. There are three places where you can actually see the artists at work.

The most central and modest outfit is the **Aardewerkatelier de Candelaer** (☎ 213 18 48; www .candelaer.nl; Kerkstraat 13; ⊗ 9am-5pm Mon-Sat Nov-Feb, 9am-6pm Mon-Sat & 9am-5pm Sun Mar-Oct), just off the Markt. It has five artists, a few of whom work most days. When it's quiet they'll give you a detailed tour of the manufacturing process.

The other two locations, outside the town centre, are basically factories. **De Delftse Pauw** (The Delft Peacock; ☎ 212 49 20; www.delftsepauw.com; Delftweg 133; ⊗ 9am-4.30pm) is the smaller of the two, employing 35 painters who work mainly from home. It has daily tours, but you won't see the painters on weekends. Take tram 1 to Vrijenbanselaan.

Royal Delft (☎ 251 20 30; Rotterdamseweg 196; ⊗ 9.30am-5pm daily Apr-Oct, closed Sun Nov-Mar) is the only original factory operating since the 1650s. Bus 63 from the train station stops nearby at Jaffalaan, or it's a 25-minute walk from the town centre.

The **Museum Lambert van Meerten** (☎ 260 23 58; Oude Delft 199; adult/child €5/4; ⊗ 10am-5pm Tue-Sat, 1-5pm Sun) has a fine collection of porcelain tiles and delftware dating back to the 16th century.

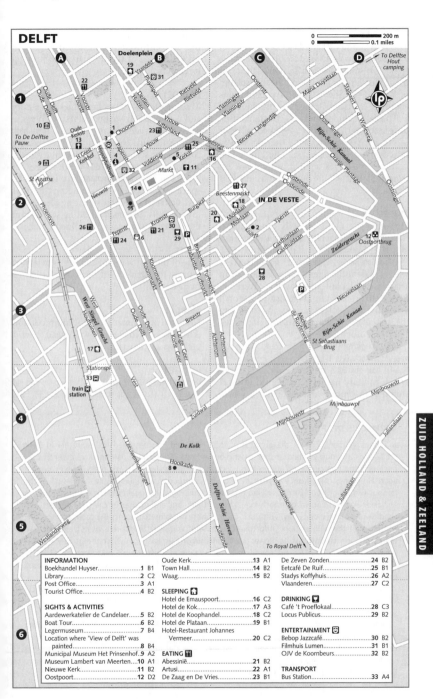

DELFT

INFORMATION		
Boekhandel Huyser	1	B1
Library	2	C2
Post Office	3	A1
Tourist Office	4	B2

SIGHTS & ACTIVITIES		
Aardewerkatelier de Candelaer	5	B2
Boat Tour	6	B2
Legermuseum	7	B4
Location where 'View of Delft' was painted	8	B4
Municipal Museum Het Prinsenhof	9	A2
Museum Lambert van Meerten	10	A1
Nieuwe Kerk	11	B2
Oostpoort	12	D2
Oude Kerk	13	A1
Town Hall	14	B2
Waag	15	B2

SLEEPING 🏠		
Hotel de Emauspoort	16	C2
Hotel de Kok	17	A3
Hotel de Koophandel	18	C2
Hotel de Plataan	19	B1
Hotel-Restaurant Johannes Vermeer	20	C2

EATING 🍴		
Abessinië	21	B2
Artusi	22	A1
De Zaag en De Vries	23	B1
De Zeven Zonden	24	B2
Eetcafé De Ruif	25	B1
Stadys Koffyhuis	26	A2
Vlaanderen	27	C2

DRINKING 🍷		
Café 't Proeflokaal	28	C3
Locus Publicus	29	B2

ENTERTAINMENT 🎭		
Bebop Jazzcafé	30	B2
Filmhuis Lumen	31	B1
OJV de Koornbeurs	32	B2

TRANSPORT		
Bus Station	33	A4

CHURCHES

The 14th-century **Nieuwe Kerk** (☎ 212 30 25; www .nieuwekerk-delft.nl; Markt; adult/child €3/1.50; ☻ 9am-6pm Apr-Oct, 11am-4pm Nov-Apr, closed Sun) houses the crypt of the Dutch royal family and the mausoleum of Willem the Silent. There are exhibitions about the House of Orange and the church.

The fee includes entrance to the Gothic **Oude Kerk** (☎ 212 30 15; www.oudekerk-delft.nl; Heilige Geestkerkhof; ☻ 9am-6pm Apr-Oct, 11am-4pm Nov-Mar, closed Sun) – and vice versa. The latter, 800 years old, is a surreal sight: its tower leans 2m from the vertical. One of the tombs inside is Vermeer's.

MUSEUMS

Opposite the Oude Kerk is the **Municipal Museum het Prinsenhof** (☎ 260 23 58; www.prinsenhof -delft.nl; St Agathaplein 1; adult/child under 16yr €5/4; ☻ 10am-5pm Tue-Sat, 1-5pm Sun), a former convent where Willem the Silent was assassinated in 1584 (the bullet hole in the wall is covered in Perspex to protect it from inquisitive visitors). The museum displays various objects telling the story of the 80-year war with Spain, as well as 17th-century paintings.

The **Legermuseum** (☎ 215 05 00; www.leger museum.nl; Korte Geer 1; adult/child €6/3; ☻ 10am-5pm Mon-Fri, noon-5pm Sat & Sun) has a collection of old Dutch military hardware displayed in a re-stored 17th-century arsenal. There are also exhibits on the modern Dutch army, includ-ing the controversial and disastrous role it played as part of the Bosnian peacekeeping force during the 1990s.

OLD DELFT

Much of the town dates from the 17th century and is remarkably well preserved. Before you leave the crowded Markt, note the **town hall**, with its unusual combination of Renaissance construction surrounding a 13th-century tower. Behind it, the **Waag** is a 1644 weigh-house.

East of here, **Beestenmarkt** is a large open space surrounded by fine buildings. Further east, **Oostpoort** is the sole surviving piece of the town's walls. **Koornmarkt**, leading south from the Waag, is a quiet and tree-lined canal.

Tours

One of the best ways to see Delft is by a boat tour on the canals. Visit the tourist office for more details.

Sleeping

Note that in summer Delft's accommodation is heavily booked. Reserve well ahead, or visit the town as a day trip.

BUDGET

Delftse Hout (☎ 213 00 40; Korftlaan 5; camp sites incl 2 people, car, tent, caravan or motor home from €20) This

---

VERMEER'S DELFT

Johannes Vermeer, one of the greatest of the Dutch old masters, lived his entire life in Delft (1632–75), fathering 11 children and leaving behind just 35 incredible paintings. Vermeer's works have rich and meticulous colouring and he captures light as few other painters have ever man-aged. His scenes come from everyday life in Delft, his interiors capturing simple things such as the famous *Girl with a Pearl Earring*, giving a proto-cinematographic quality to his compositions

Vermeer's best-known exterior work, *View of Delft*, brilliantly captures the play of light and shadow of a partly cloudy day. Visit the location where he painted it, across the canal at Hooikade, southeast of the train station. Unfortunately, none of Vermeer's works remain in Delft. The two works mentioned above can be seen at the Mauritshuis in Den Haag (p197), while arguably his most famous painting, *The Milkmaid*, spends most of its time in Amsterdam's Rijksmuseum (p106).

Vermeer has become a media darling of late. In 2003 the film *Girl with a Pearl Earring* (based on Tracy Chevalier's novel) speculated on his relationship with the eponymous girl.

The following year, a work long thought to be a forgery was finally confirmed as authentic – *Young Woman Seated at the Virginals* was the first Vermeer to be auctioned in more than 80 years, selling to an anonymous buyer for €24 million.

Watch out for the opening of the **Vermeercentrum** (☎ 213 85 88; www.vermeerdelft.nl; Voldersgracht 21; ☻ 10am-5pm Mon-Sat, noon-5pm Sun), which promises to offer 'a fascinating voyage of discovery through the life and work of Johannes Vermeer' – at the time of research, opening day was set for sometime in April 2007. As the publicity bellows, 'Experience life in 17th-century Delft. Experience his studio, and get to know his work'.

camping ground is just northeast of town. Take bus 64 from the station.

MIDRANGE

Hotel de Plataan (☎ 212 60 46; www.hoteldeplataan .nl; Doelenplein 10; s/d €88/99) Delft's finest accommodation is on a delightful square, and features an ace café and a downright dignified breakfast room. Standard rooms are small but elegant. Then there are the wonderfully opulent theme rooms, which come on like a Japanese love hotel: there's the 'Garden of Eden'; the 'Amber', based on Eastern stylings; or the jaw-dropping 'Tamarinde', themed after a desert island.

Hotel De Emauspoort (☎ 219 02 19; www.emaus poort.nl; Vrouwenregt 9-11; s/d €80/90, s/d caravan €75/85) Comfy, old-style rooms, plus two attentively restored gypsy caravans out the back (named 'Pipo de Clown' and 'Mammaloe'). Delightful. Big fat bonus: the bakery-confectionery store next door provides the big fat breakfast.

Other options:

Hotel de Kok (☎ 212 21 25; www.hoteldekok.nl; Houttuinen 15; s/d from €66/80) Simple rooms but very conveniently located, near the train station, with a sweet garden terrace.

Hotel de Koophandel (☎ 214 23 02; www.hotel dekoophandel.nl; Beestenmarkt 30; s/d from €78/91) A little bland, but spotlessly clean.

TOP END

Hotel-Restaurant Johannes Vermeer (☎ 212 64 66; www.hotelvermeer.nl; Molslaan 18; s/d €112/125) This one's an ersatz Vermeer museum, its rooms decorated with Vermeer prints. To be honest, it's a bit tacky, although there are immaculate views of old Delft (canals, churches and street scenes on all sides). The restaurant features rare kettles hanging from the roof and reproductions of all of Vermeer's known works, including a wall-length *Girl with a Pearl Earring* surrounded by exposed brickwork.

Eating

RESTAURANTS

Artusi (☎ 212 03 54; www.restaurant-artusi.nl; Voorstraat 20A; mains €18-22; ☽ dinner Mon-Sat) It's a bar as well as a restaurant, and Italian dishes are the name of the game. It's a stylish place, but not too snobby. Thank God for that. All the usual Italian faves are here, plus ramped up, out-of-left-field goodies like duck udder with olives and balsamic sauce.

Stadys Koffyhuis (☎ 212 46 25; www.stads-koffyhuis .nl; Oude Delft 133; pancakes €7-10) This warm and friendly café has a real ace in the hole: a terrace barge moored out front, where you can take your coffee and eat your delicious sandwiches and pancakes while admiring possibly the best view in Delft – the Oude Kerk, just ahead at the end of the canal.

Other options:

Abessinië (☎ 213 52 60; Kromstraat 21; mains €10-17; ☽ dinner) West African cuisine with starchy tubers, meats and pulses combined with spices, sauces and herbs.

De Zaag en De Vries (☎ 213 70 15; Vrouw Juttenland 17; mains €18; ☽ dinner, closed Mon) Great food in a cheery orange place with a long vegetarian menu.

De Zeven Zonden (The Seven Sins; ☎ 215 86 89; www .dezevenzonden.nl; Oude Delft 78; mains €17; ☽ dinner) Unique, offbeat and cosy – try the kangaroo dish cooked French-provincial style.

CAFÉS

Vlaanderen (☎ 213 33 11; Beestenmarkt 16; mains €18-21; ☽ lunch & dinner) This café-restaurant has a Flemish name but a French-inspired menu. It's good for people-watching, too, with its convivial terrace. Baked and smoked diamond hare gives you an idea of the dishes on offer.

Eetcafé De Ruif (☎ 214 22 06; www.ruif.nl; Kerkstraat 22; mains €12-16; ☽ lunch & dinner) Wonderfully rustic, with a low ceiling, canal views and yummo lunches, like goat-cheese salads and Stellendam shrimps (seafood that's apparently very highly prized round these here parts). At night it's busier, morphing into an exceedingly popular carousing option.

Drinking

Locus Publicus (☎ 213 46 32; Brabantse Turfmarkt 67) With more than 200 beers, it's one of the best beer cafés around. It's also friendly, with good music and warm vibes.

Café 't Proeflokaal (☎ 212 49 22; Gasthuislaan 36-40) Here there are 300 beers to chose from. Service is friendly and attentive.

Entertainment

Bebop Jazzcafé (☎ 213 52 10; Kromstraat 33) Dark and small, with moody music and a great selection of beers.

OJV de Koornbeurs (☎ 212 47 42; www.koornbeurs .nl; Voldersgracht 1) An underground dance floor with alternative tunes.

Filmhuis Lumen (☎ 214 02 26; www.filmhuis-lumen .nl; Doelenplein 5) Screens alternative films.

Getting There & Around

Sample train service fares and schedules:

Destination	Price (€)	Duration (min)	Frequency (per hr)
Amsterdam	10.80	50	2
Den Haag	2.20	8	2
Rotterdam	2.90	13	4

Lockers are in the train station's main concourse and there are all the usual amenities.

Alternatively, bus 129 makes the run to/from Rotterdam every hour along a pretty canal. The ride lasts 30 minutes and takes five strips. Buses depart from the front of the station.

Den Haag is also linked to Delft by tram 1, which takes 30 minutes and costs five strips.

The bicycle shop is in the train station.

ROTTERDAM

☎ 010 / pop 605,000

Rotterdam, the Netherlands' 'second city', was bombed flat during WWII and spent the following decades rebuilding. You won't find the classic Dutch medieval centre here – it was swept away along with the other rubble and detritus of war. In its place is an architectural aesthetic that's unique in Europe, a progressive perpetual-motion approach to construction that's clearly a result of the city's postwar, postmodern 'anything goes' philosophy.

But tradition is strong elsewhere, for Rotterdam is Europe's busiest port (and second in the world) – a lineage as a shipping nexus that dates back to 1572, when Spaniards being pursued by the rebel Sea Beggars were given shelter in the harbour. Rotterdam became a major port during the conflict, and it remains so to this day.

Rotterdam has a crackling energy, with superb nightlife, a multicultural community, a gritty arts scene, and a clutch of excellent museums. It also has a long-standing rivalry with Amsterdam, reflected in most aspects of culture. When local football team, Feyenoord, meets Ajax of Amsterdam, the fur *always* flies. And when Rotterdam unleashed its extreme form of techno, gabber, on the world in the early '90s, one of its most enduring targets was Amsterdam: an early gabber single was memorably titled 'Amsterdam, Waar Lech Dat Dan?' ('Amsterdam, Where the F*** is That?').

Orientation

Rotterdam, split by the Nieuwe Maas shipping channel, is crossed by a series of tunnels and bridges, notably the Erasmusbrug. The centre is on the northern side of the water, and new neighbourhoods are rising to the south. From Centraal Station (CS), a 15-minute walk along the canal-like ponds leads to the waterfront. The commercial centre is to the east and most museums are to the west. The historic neighbourhood of Delfshaven is a further 3km west.

Information

DISCOUNT CARD

The Rotterdam Card offers discounts in hotels and restaurants; it's €22.46/43.11 for 24/72 hours. The card is even available as a watch. Buy it from the tourist office.

INTERNET ACCESS

EasyInternetCafé (Map p212; www.easyeverything.com /map/rot; Stadhuisplein 16-18; internet per hr €3; ☼ 9am-11pm Mon-Sat, 11am-11pm Sun)

LIBRARIES

Centrale Bibliotheek (Map pp210-11; ☎ 281 61 14; Hoogstraat 110; internet per hr €3; ☼ 1-8pm Mon, 10am-8pm Tue-Fri, 10am-5pm Sat) An attraction in itself, with a café, an indoor life-sized chessboard and internet access.

MEDICAL SERVICES

For a doctor, call ☎ 420 11 00.
Erasmus MC (Map pp210-11; ☎ 463 92 22; 's-Gravendijkwal 320) Major teaching hospital.

POST

Post office (Map pp210-11; ☎ 233 02 55; Coolsingel 42; ☼ 9am-6pm Mon-Wed & Fri, to 8.30pm Thu, 9.30am-3pm Sat)

TOURIST INFORMATION

Tourist office (Map p212; ☎ 271 01 28; www.rotterdam .info; Coolsingel 5; ☼ 9am-6pm Mon-Fri, to 5pm Sat & Sun) Free internet access.
Use-It (Map p212; ☎ 240 91 58; www.use-it.nl; Schaatsbaan 41-45; ☼ 9am-6pm Tue-Sun mid-May–mid-Sep, to 5pm Tue-Sat mid-Sep–mid-May) Aimed at young travellers but suitable for anyone who wants information that's more engaging than that from the po-faced official tourist body. Also books accommodation with substantial discounts.

Dangers & Annoyances

Note that the area about 1km west of CS is the scene of many hard-drug deals and accompanying dubious behaviour.

Bike theft, as in any Dutch city with a significant junkie population, is rampant.

Sights & Activities

Rotterdam is easy to navigate, with so many memorable buildings and landmarks with which to orientate yourself. The centre is also a lot smaller than it seems for such a bustling metropolis – you might never need to use the efficient public transport. The best way to see it is by bike, though be alert – both bike theft and car use are higher in Rotterdam than in cities of similar size. Many galleries are concentrated around Museumpark.

MUSEUM BOIJMANS VAN BEUNINGEN

Among Europe's very finest museums, the **Museum Boijmans van Beuningen** (Map pp210-11; ☎ 441 94 00; www.boijmans.nl; Museumpark 18-20; adult/under 18yr €8/free; ☑ 11am-5pm Tue-Sun) has a permanent collection spanning all eras of Dutch and European art, including superb old masters. Among the highlights are *The Marriage at Cana* by Hieronymus Bosch, the *Three Maries at the Open Sepulchre* by Van Eyck, the minutely detailed *Tower of Babel* by Pieter Brueghel the Elder, and *Portrait of Titus* and *Man in a Red Cap* by Rembrandt. Renaissance Italy is well represented; look for *The Wise and Foolish Virgins* by Tintoretto and *Satyr and Nymph* by Titian.

Paintings and sculpture since the mid-19th century are another strength. There are many Monets and other French impressionists; Van Gogh and Gauguin are given space; and there are statues by Degas. The museum rightly prides itself on its collection by a group it calls 'the other surrealists' including Marcel Duchamp, René Magritte and Man Ray. Salvador Dalí gained a special room in the recent expansion and the collection is one of the largest of his work outside Spain and France. All in all, the surrealist wing is utterly absorbing, with ephemera and paraphernalia rubbing against famous works.

Modern modes are not forgotten, and the whole place is nothing if not eclectic: a nude or an old master might be nestled next to a '70s bubble TV – some kind of installation – or a vibrating table.

There's also a good café, a pleasant sculpture garden (featuring Claes Oldenburg's famous *Bent Screw*, among others), a library with more than 125,000 reference books, and wheelchair access/assistance throughout.

Even the traditional 'museum floor plan' is abetted by an innovation the curators call 'The Data Cloud'. It's a three-D interactive multimedia map on the entrance floor that is a brilliant work of design in itself – it allows visitors to find instantly, via a 'holographic projection portal', the location of (and information about) any item in the museum's 120,000 piece collection.

KUNSTHAL

At the south end of Museumpark, the **Kunsthal** (Map pp210-11; ☎ 440 03 00; www.kunsthal.nl; Westzeedijk 341; adult/under 18yr €8.50/3; ☑ 10am-5pm Tue-Sat, 11am-5pm Sun & holidays) hosts around 20 temporary exhibitions (including art and design) each year. As the publicity says, everything from 'elitist to popular' gets an airing.

EUROMAST

At 185m, a shimmy up the **Euromast** (Map pp210-11; ☎ 436 48 11; www.euromast.com; Parkhaven 20; adult/under 11yr €8/5.20; ☑ 9.30am-11pm Apr-Sep, 10am-11pm Oct-Mar) is a must. It offers unparalleled 360-degree views of Rotterdam, with its rotating, glass-walled 'Euroscope' contraption ascending to near the summit. There is a luxury accommodation suite and the Panorama restaurant (p216) near the top. Book an abseiling session (€39.50).

DELFSHAVEN

One of Rotterdam's few districts to survive the war, Delfshaven was once the official seaport for the city of Delft. A reconstructed 18th-century **windmill** overlooks the water at Voorhaven 210. One of the area's claims to fame is that it was where the Pilgrims left Holland for America aboard the *Speedwell*. They could barely keep the leaky boat afloat and, in England, eventually transferred to the *Mayflower* – the rest is history. The **Oude Kerk** on Voorhaven is where the Pilgrims prayed for the last time before leaving on 22 July 1620.

Just south, **De Dubbelde Palmboom** (Map pp210-11; ☎ 476 15 33; www.hmr.rotterdam.nl; Voorhaven 12; adult/child €3/1.50; ☑ 10am-5pm Tue-Sat, 11am-5pm Sun & holidays) is a history museum housing an excellent collection of items relating to Rotterdam's history as a port. Displays are spread throughout the 1826 warehouse, and many have a sociological bent.

Delfshaven is easily reached from the metro stop of the same name by walking 1km east or by taking tram 4, 6 or 9.

ROTTERDAM

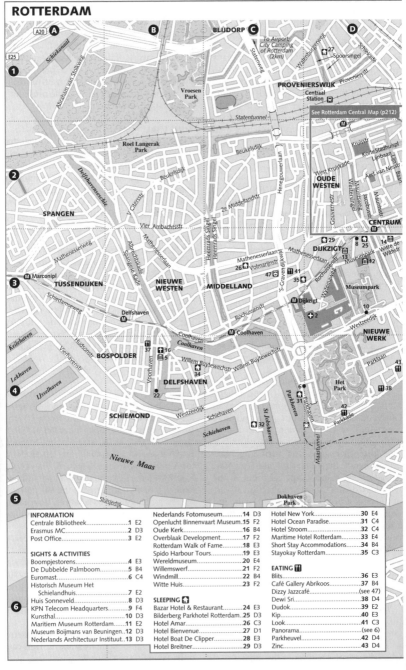

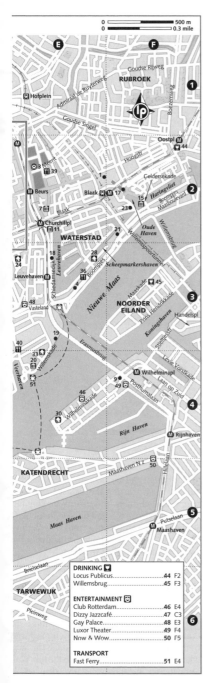

ARCHITECTURE

You won't fail to notice Rotterdam's highest building (152m), right next to Centraal Station: the **Nationale Nederlanden skyscraper**, designed by Abe Bonnema, has two glass-encased office wings that reflect each other and the sky, seemingly disappearing into each other and the elements.

The 800m-long, 1996 **Erasmusbrug**, designed by Ben van Berkel, is near the Leuvehaven metro station. With its spread-eagled struts, it's nicknamed 'The Swan'.

To the south of Erasmusbrug is **KPN Telecom headquarters** (Map pp210–11), built in 2000 and designed by Renzo Piano, who also designed Paris's Pompidou Centre. The building leans to a sharp angle and rests on a long pole.

Retrace your steps and walk northeast alongside the water on Boompjes, where you'll see the three distinctive **Boompjestorens** (Map pp210–11) – apartment blocks, built in 1988. Continue along the water until you see the striking 1998 **Willemswerf** (Map pp210–11), the headquarters of the huge Nedlloyd shipping company. Note the dramatic lines casting shadows on its sleek, white surface.

Another 100m will bring you to Rotterdam's other signature bridge, the **Willemsbrug** (1981), which makes a bold statement with its red pylons. Turn north at Oude Haven on Geldersekade. The regal 12-storey building on the corner is the 1897 **Witte Huis** (White House; Map pp210–11), a rare survivor of the prewar period, giving an idea of the wealth Rotterdam achieved thanks to the shipping industry.

The **Overblaak development** (Map pp210–11), designed by Piet Blom and built from 1978 to 1984, is near Blaak metro station. Marked by its pencil-shaped tower and upended, cube-shaped apartments, it seems plucked straight from the novels of JG Ballard. One apartment, the **Show Cube** (☎ 414 22 85; www.cubehouse.nl; adult/under 12yr €2/1.50; ⏰ 11am-5pm, closed Mon-Thu Jan & Feb), is open to the public. Look for the tiny chess museum in the cube complex, with all kinds of chess pieces on display – everything from ancient Hindu examples to likenesses of Jabba the Hut.

The **Nederlands Architectuur Instituut** (NAI; Map pp210-11; ☎ 440 12 00; www.nai.nl; Museumpark 25; ⏰ 10am-5pm Tue-Sat, 11am-5pm Sun & holidays), with one side surrounded by a moat and the other comprising a sweeping flow of brick along Rochussenstraat, offers an amazingly

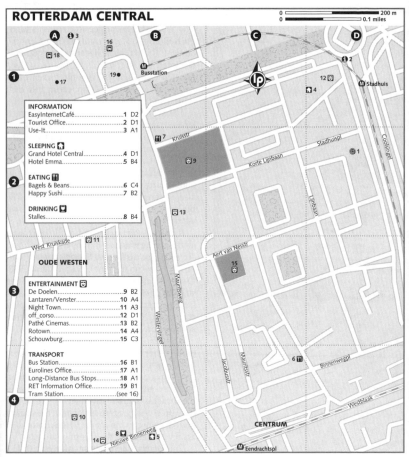

ROTTERDAM CENTRAL

INFORMATION
EasyInternetCafé.............................1 D2
Tourist Office...................................2 D1
Use-It...3 A1

SLEEPING
Grand Hotel Central......................4 D1
Hotel Emma....................................5 B4

EATING
Bagels & Beans...............................6 C4
Happy Sushi....................................7 B2

DRINKING
Stalles..8 B4

OUDE WESTEN

ENTERTAINMENT
De Doelen.......................................9 B2
Lantaren/Venster..........................10 A4
Night Town....................................11 A3
off_corso.......................................12 D1
Pathé Cinemas...............................13 B2
Rotown...14 A4
Schouwburg...................................15 C3

TRANSPORT
Bus Station....................................16 B1
Eurolines Office.............................17 A1
Long-Distance Bus Stops..............18 A1
RET Information Office..................19 B1
Tram Station............................(see 16)

CENTRUM

thorough overview of Dutch architecture. Exhibitions are revelatory, and a recent multimedia presentation devoted to utopian genius Hendrik Wijdeveld was mind-expanding. The NAI is a worthy monument in a city that celebrates built space like no other in the land.

Included in the admission price is a ticket to **Huis Sonneveld** (Map pp210–11; Jongkindstraat25), designed by Brinkman and Van der Vlugt and an outstanding example of the Dutch New Building architectural strain (also known as Dutch functionalism). This 1933 villa has been lovingly restored, with furniture, wallpaper and fixtures present and correct – it is an astonishing experience, almost like virtual reality.

The design and aesthetic seems thoroughly current today; during the '30s it must have seemed the ultimate in futurism, making full use of light and space, and filled with tubular-steel furniture and tech gizmos – including no fewer than 12 telephones, considered the height of modern life at the time.

OTHER SIGHTS
Maritiem Museum Rotterdam (Map pp210–11; ☎ 413 26 80; www.maritiemmuseum.nl; Leuvehaven 1; adult/4–16yr €5/3; ☺ 10am-5pm Tue-Sat & 11am-5pm Sun year-round, 10am-5pm Mon Jul & Aug) is a comprehensive museum that looks at the Netherlands' rich maritime traditions. There's an array of models that any youngster would love to take into the tub, plus more interesting and explanatory displays.

ZUID HOLLAND & ZEELAND

Near here, on Schiedamsedijk, is the **Rotterdam Walk of Fame** (Map pp210-11), featuring handprints from luminaries including Bryan Adams, Bryan Ferry, Dizzy Gillespie, 'Diamond' David Lee Roth, Kamahl, Roxette, Willie Nelson – and even Spandau Ballet (the Netherlands being perhaps the only country in the world that still remembers who they are).

The **Oude Haven** area, near the Blaak train, metro and tram station, preserves the oldest part of the harbour, some of which dates from the 14th century. It's a decent place for a stroll, especially if you take time to look at the large collection of historic boats.

The **Openlucht Binnenvaart Museum** (Map pp210-11; ☎ 411 88 67; Koningsdam 1; admission free; ☼ 8am-8pm) has a collection of historic inland waterway boats that fills much of the basin. You can see the ongoing restoration and can stroll around looking at the boats, even outside the official opening hours.

The city's history is preserved at one of the centre's few surviving 17th-century buildings, at the **Historisch Museum het Schielandhuis** (Map pp210-11; ☎ 217 67 67; www.hmr.rotterdam.nl; Korte Hoogstraat 31; adult/child €3/1.50; ☼ 10am-5pm Tue-Fri, 11am-5pm Sat & Sun). Exhibits focus on everyday life through the ages, such as the (purportedly) oldest surviving wooden shoe. Clogs ahoy!

The **Nederlands Fotomuseum** (Map pp210-11; ☎ 213 20 11; www.nederlandsfotomuseum.nl; Witte de Withstraat 63; adult/child €3.50/2; ☼ 11am-5pm Tue-Sun) is a fabulous photo museum that's also an archive and information centre for photographers. Its activities were recently bolstered by a bequest from one H Weertheim, who wanted to 'further the interests of photography in the Netherlands'. Note that the museum is moving to Wilhelminakade 66 in 2007.

Nearby, the **Wereldmuseum** (World Museum; Map pp210-11; ☎ 270 71 72; www.wereldmuseum.rotterdam.nl; Willemskade 25; adult/child €8/4; ☼ 10am-5pm Tue-Sat) is dedicated to providing a user-friendly repository of multiculturalism for people to use to better understand each other. It's wonderfully apt that it's in a polyglot port like Rotterdam. The building is dominated by a huge sculpture of a stylised woman by artist Nikki de Saint Phalle. Enter through the statue's legs.

On the south side of the Koningshaven, in the middle of an old dock district being reborn as a trendy neighbourhood, there is a solemn reminder of the recent past. A fragment of a **wall** has been preserved here – the wall once surrounded a warehouse that, during WWII,

was the departure point for Jews being sent first to Westerbork and then on to concentration camps.

Walking Tour

Start at the **Maritiem Museum Rotterdam** (**1**; opposite) for a maritime history lesson, before making your way to **Oude Haven** (**2**; left) for real-world aquatic nostalgia.

View the vessels on display at the **Openlucht Binnenvaart Museum** (**3**; left), then cross the **Willemsbrug** (**4**; p211), drinking in the superb views over the river, before emerging on the other side in **Noordereiland (5)**, a residential island that has been styled as the MS *Noordereiland*, a 'ship on the Maas,' by artist Joe Cillen, with its 3000 'sailors' (residents). To the left is **De Brug (6)**, an apartment block with Cillen-constructed starboard lights on the roof (green and red).

Walk towards Noordereiland's eastern tip, where you'll find the ship's **engine room (7)** – an alleyway behind the Aldi supermarket that's been decorated with mechanical sculptures by local artists and kids. Backtrack and walk west along Maaskade, admiring more watery views before stopping in at the maritime-themed pub also named **Willemsbrug** (**8**; p217). Here

---

WALK FACTS

Start Maritiem Museum Rotterdam
Finish Euromast
Duration Three hours

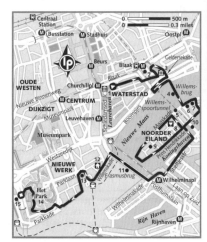

you can have a beer and a sea-dog sing-along with the feisty locals.

Emerging from the cigar smoke, walk through the 'ship's' **cargo holds (9)**, actually the streets and alleys bisecting the island, before making your way across the Koninginnebrug. Look to the left as you cross the water: **De Hef (10)** is a magnificent railway bridge from the 1920s that's been preserved as a National Monument, its drawbridge permanently raised high in the air.

Walk west along Stieltjesstraat, before crossing the incredible **Erasmusbrug (11;** p211). Back on the Maas' northern side, walk west along Willemskade, past the **Maritime Hotel Rotterdam (12;** opposite), where sailors like to sleep, before pausing at **Veerhaven (13)**, a little inlet where numerous boats and yachts are docked. Look back towards the Erasmusbrug and marvel at how the bridge's struts in the background blend in with the sails and masts in the foreground – a thoroughly shiplike bridge for a maritime city *par excellence*.

Continue on down Westerkade, then Parkkade, passing the government boats anchored in the harbour, before walking through the beautiful, and surprisingly green, **Het Park (14)** to the **Euromast (15;** p209). Once there, travel to the summit and look back over the city: from a height of 185m you'll be able to pick out in exact detail the entire route you've just travelled, as well as fully appreciate just how mighty the harbour is.

Tours

There are harbour tours offered daily by **Spido** (☎ 275 99 88; www.spido.nl; Willemsplein 85; adult/child €8.50/5.50; ☺ 9.30am-5pm Jun-Sep, 11am-3.30pm Oct, to 2pm Thu-Sun Nov-Mar). Departures are from the pier at Leuvehoofd near the Erasmusbrug and the Leuvehaven metro stop. Longer trips are possible in the high season.

Rotterdam ByCycle (www.rotterdambycycle.nl) conducts pedal-powered tours (from €15) and also rents out bikes, while **Rotterdam ArchiGuides** (www.rotterdam-archiguides.nl) takes groups on a tour of built space – the city's architectural highlights – via bicycle, bus or shoe leather (group prices only). The tourist office, in association with the Nederlands Architectuur Instituut (p211), also offers Rotterdam architecture tours. For more detailed information, call the NAI or drop into the tourist office.

Festivals & Events

JANUARY–FEBRUARY

International Film Festival Rotterdam (www.film festivalrotterdam.com) From late January to early February. A top-notch selection of independent and experimental films.

JUNE

De Parade (www.deparade.nl) A nationwide inverse-circus tour, where the audiences are in the ring and all manner of music, theatre, film and variety performances go on around them. It hits all the big cities and has an incredibly lively atmosphere. Entry's usually free and performances are on a pay-per-view basis.

Poetry International Festival (www.poetry.nl) Held in late June, hosting top-notch poets from all over the world.

JULY

North Sea Jazz Festival (www.northseajazz.nl) One of the world's most-respected jazz events, drawing some of the best musicians on the planet. Rooms throughout the region will be at a premium as thousands of fans descend on the city from all around. You're best off staying elsewhere and commuting, or booking far in advance. A lot of the acts organise smokin' unofficial jams outside the festival dates, a kind of prefestival minifestival. It's held in mid-July.

Zomer Carnaval (Summer Carnival; www.zomercarnaval .nl) Usually held on the last weekend of July. A carnival-like bash with music, parades, dancing and parties.

Zomerpodium (Summer Stage; www.loederevents.nl /zomer.html) Starting towards the end of July and running into August, Zomerpodium features all manner of outlandish excuses to get crazy in the streets of Rotterdam. There's been a Bollywood Ball, brass band contests, stand-up comedy and more.

AUGUST

FFWD Heineken Dance Parade (www.ffwdheineken danceparade.nl) Turns the centre into one big open-air club with areas for techno, hip-hop, big beat etc. Floats on the backs of trucks drive through town, catering to a crowd of around 350,000 people.

SEPTEMBER

Wereld Havendagen (World Harbour Festival; www .wereldhavendagen.nl) Celebrates the role of the harbour, which directly or indirectly employs over 300,000 people. There are lots of open houses, ship tours and fireworks.

Sleeping

The tourist office makes room reservations, as does Use-It (p208), the latter with substantial – sometimes incredible – discounts. In fact, it's worth checking with Use-It before you do anything sleep-related.

BUDGET

Hotel Amar (Map pp210-11; ☎ 425 57 95; www.amarhotel .nl; Mathenesserlaan 316; s/d €30/50; 🖳) This friendly, small place is in a leafy neighbourhood close to the Museumpark and to good shopping and nightlife. Rooms are simple but comfy, and the ones at the back overlook a large and peaceful garden.

Short Stay Accommodations (Map pp210-11; ☎ 295 35 62; Willem Buytewechstraat 206; d €18; ✂) This great budget apartment setup spans three floors with a couple of different sharing options. The owners are just fine and the place is clean, with laundry facilities and linen included.

Hotel Boat De Clipper (Map pp210-11; ☎ 331 42 44; Scheepmakershaven; B&B from €30; 🖳) This 'botel', docked in Rotterdam's old harbour, is perfect for soaking up the city's maritime atmosphere, even if the quarters are, inevitably, a little cramped.

Other options:

City Camping of Rotterdam (☎ 415 34 40; Kanaalweg 84; camp sites per person/tent €4.95/3.90, 2-person cabins €30) A 20-minute walk northwest from CS, or take bus 33 (direction: Airport).

Stayokay Rotterdam (Map pp210-11; ☎ 436 57 63; www.stayokay.com/rotterdam; Rochussenstraat 107-109; dm from €20.25; 🖳) Typically well-run link in the Stayokay chain; well placed for the museums and with a low-key bar.

MIDRANGE

Hotel New York (Map pp210-11; ☎ 439 05 00; www .hotelnewyork.nl; Koninginnenhoofd 1; d from €98) The city's favourite hotel is housed in the former headquarters of the Holland-America passenger-ship line, and has excellent service and facilities. Often booked far in advance, it's noted for its views, café and boat shuttle that takes guests across the Nieuwe Maas to the centre. The Art Nouveau rooms – with many original and painstakingly restored décor items and fittings –

are divine and come in various configurations, from standard to penthouse.

Maritime Hotel Rotterdam (Map pp210-11; ☎ 411 92 60; www.maritimehotel.nl; Willemskade 13; s/tw from €69/88; 🖳) This hotel ostensibly caters to sea-men ashore from their boats, but all are welcome. The modern facility boasts free internet access, a big breakfast buffet and a cheap bar with pool table. It's a friendly, all-in kind of place.

Grand Hotel Central (Map p212; ☎ 414 07 44; Kruiskade 12; s/d €80/95) If you're into kitsch, you'll like it here: the décor looks like it hasn't been updated for 40 years, yet it's addictively comfy and invitingly atmospheric. You'll feel like kicking back with a Martini while wearing something bright orange and flammable. The rooms are great, service similar.

Hotel Ocean Paradise (Map pp210-11; ☎ 436 17 02; www.oceanparadise.nl; Parkhaven 21; s/d from €58/68) The Ocean Paradise is actually a floating hotel/ Chinese restaurant/Asian supermarket pavilion; it looks like an aquatic temple. Naturally, the rooms have an Oriental theme, and are not too bad, although they get a little hot in summer. It's in a nice part of town, next to the Euromast and surrounding parks and greenery.

Other options:

Hotel Bienvenue (Map pp210-11; ☎ 466 93 94; www .hotelbienvenue.nl; Spoorsingel 24B; s/d from €48/65; 🖳) In a quiet, though central, area; cosy rooms.

Hotel Breitner (Map pp210-11; ☎ 436 02 62; www .hotelbreitner.nl; Breitnerstraat 23; s/d from €68/85; 🖳) Near Museumpark.

Hotel Emma (Map p212; ☎ 436 55 33; www.hotel emma.nl; Nieuwe Binnenweg 6; s/d from €79/99; 🖳) Good locale; comfy rooms.

TOP END

Hotel Stroom (Map pp210-11; ☎ 221 40 60; www.stroom rotterdam.nl; Lloydstraat 1; d from €135) Stroom is the rising star of the Rotto accommodation scene, a brand-new designer hotel that's actually a

MIDDLE EAST MEETS ROTTERDAM

Bazar Hotel & Restaurant (Map pp210-11; ☎ 206 51 51; www.hotelbazar.nl; Witte de Withstraat 16; s/d from €60/75) Bazar is deservedly popular for its Middle Eastern, African and South American–themed rooms: lush, brocaded curtains, exotically tiled bathrooms, comfy beds, and copies of *Tales from the Arabian Nights* scattered about. Breakfast is spectacular: Turkish breads, international cheeses, yogurt, fruit, cold cuts and coffee.

This is an exceptional place to wind down, particularly as its ground-floor bar and restaurant (mains €8 to €13.90, open lunch and dinner) is among the town's best, coming up trumps with similarly stylised Middle Eastern décor and matching menu: dolmades, falafel, mussels, sardines, couscous and kebabs served up in tangy, attention-grabbing combinations.

converted power station. Spiffy design studios come in a range of configurations, such as the 'videostudio' option, a jaw-dropping split-level fancy under a glass roof with a downstairs open bathroom.

Bilderberg Parkhotel Rotterdam (Map pp210-11; ☎ 436 36 11; www.parkhotelrotterdam.nl; Westersingel 70; s/d from €115/165; 🗵 🖳 🗵 **P**) Smack bang amid Rotterdam's most notable sights and attractions, the Parkhotel mainly caters to short stay business travellers year-round – that means bargains and last-minute deals (for leisure travellers) when summer occupancy is well down. Rooms are comfy, clean and have all the mod cons.

Eating

Rotterdam has many wonderful places to eat. The city's (always growing) multicultural population and a steady stream of corporate clientele floating through town on business means that choices are widely varied.

Dudok (Map pp210-11; ☎ 433 31 02; www.dudok.nl; Meent 88; breakfast €1.90-11, lunch €3.30-9.50, dinner €9.90-14.90; 🕑 breakfast, lunch & dinner) This Rotterdam institution, housed in a former insurance office designed by WM Dudok, has a wonderful spacious feel with its high ceilings and big windows. Whether you're here for a meal, a drink or a snack, you must try the scrummy apple pie (€2.90), famous throughout Rotterdam and surrounds. Solo travellers will love the large reading table.

RESTAURANTS

Parkheuvel (Map pp210-11; ☎ 436 05 30; Heuvelaan 21; 3-course menu from €50; 🕑 lunch & dinner Mon-Fri, dinner Sat) Some say it's the Netherlands' best restaurant – as one of only two Dutch fancies with three Michelin stars, it's got a strong claim. The French-international menu is especially fab with seafood – red mullet with balsamic dressing, anyone?

Blits (Map pp210-11; ☎ 282 90 51; www.blits-rotterdam .nl; Boompjes 701; mains €12-25; 🕑 lunch & dinner Tue-Sun) It was only a matter of time. In a city that loves diverse food and cutting-edge architecture, here's a restaurant that combines both: wall-length windows looking out over the Maas, and a classy international menu. Seating arrangements are 'out there': try the bench with pillows or the 'Love Suite', a heart-shaped, rich-red enclosure.

Look (Map pp210-11; ☎ 436 70 00; www.restaurant look.nl; 's-Gravendijkwal; mains €13-20; 🕑 dinner Wed-Sun)

This one's especially recommended for single people, Buffy and Francophiles. Look is a cosy little restaurant that specialises in garlic-based dishes: steamed garlic, fried garlic, garlic soup, garlic vegetables…even garlic dessert, on occasion. It's delicious and you can even be a spoilsport and plump for nongarlic dishes.

Panorama (Map pp210-11; ☎ 436 48 11; www.euro mast.nl; Euromast, Parkhaven 20; mains €11-20; 🕑 lunch & dinner) This brasserie has the best location, in the midsection of the Euromast tower. At 100m it almost doesn't matter about the food, with that kind of view and a design to maximise it (the angled windows impart the odd sensation of eating in mid-air). It's a bonus, then, that the menu is up to scratch: fillet of suckling pig and grilled mackerel were recent offerings.

Kip (Chicken; Map pp210-11; ☎ 436 99 23; www.kip -rotterdam.nl; Van Vollenhovenstraat 25; mains €20-25; 🕑 dinner Tue-Sun) A lovely place that's more elegant than its moniker might imply. It's won a swag of 'Lekkers' (the Dutch restaurant awards) and has crisp, white tablecloths, a dainty dining room, and delicious and immaculately prepared meat, poultry and vegetable concoctions with a haute cuisine feel.

Other options:

Dewi Sri (Map pp210-11; ☎ 436 02 63; www.dewisri.nl; Westerkade 20; mains €15-20; 🕑 lunch & dinner) Great Indonesian food. Also at Grindweg 650 (☎ 422 36 25).

Zinc (Map pp210-11; ☎ 436 65 79; Calandstraat 12A; set menu €25; 🕑 dinner Tue-Sun) Cosy, chic French/Mediterranean bistro using only organic produce.

CAFÉS

Café Gallery Abrikoos (Map pp210-11; ☎ 477 41 40; www.abrikoos.nl; Aelbrechtskolk 51; tapas from €4.75; 🕑 dinner Tue-Sun) This is a bright and cheery tapas bar filled with art and a variety of soups, salads and mains, and wicked Mediterranean mini-meals. Addictive – and a great way to start a long evening.

Dizzy Jazzcafé (Map pp210-11; ☎ 477 30 14; 's-Gravendijkwal 129; mains €10-15; 🕑 lunch & dinner) One of the city's best music bars (opposite) is also a popular restaurant, with a gorgeous garden terrace. Authentic Dutch dishes keep it real, including a dessert called 'Chocolate Slut'.

QUICK EATS

Daily Wok (☎ 411 20 02; www.dailywok.nl; Oude Binnenweg 106C; dishes €4-7; 🕑 lunch & dinner) Wicked noodles – all persuasions and varieties, including vegetarian.

Happy Sushi (Map p212; ☎ 433 47 30; Kruisplein 42; sushi from €1.60; ⏰ lunch & dinner) Sushi on a conveyor belt; you can't go wrong.

Bagels & Beans (Map p212; www.bagelsbeans.nl; Lijnbaan 150; bagels from €2.95; ⏰ 11am-6pm Mon, 9.30am-6pm Tue-Thu, 9.30am-9pm Fri, 9.30am-5pm Sat, noon-5pm Sun) Tasty bagels, good coffee, wi-fi access.

Maoz (www.maozveg.com; Coolsingel 87; felafels €3.50; ⏰ lunch) Felafel pita-bread sandwiches that can be refilled as much as you like with salad toppings and sauces.

Drinking
Stalles (Map p212; ☎ 436 16 55; Nieuwe Binnenweg 11A) This classic brown café is on a great stretch of road near plenty of good shops, cafés and bars. It has an extensive range of single malt whiskys and some reasonable food, including pizza and lasagne.

Locus Publicus (Map pp210-11; ☎ 433 17 61; www.locus-publicus.com; Oostzeedijk 364) With more than 200 beers on its menu, this is an outstanding specialist beer café.

Willemsbrug (Map pp210-11; ☎ 413 58 68; Maaskade 95) This old-time, maritime-themed pub attracts salty sea dogs. It's not for those with weak lungs – the air's blue with cigarette, cigar and pipe smoke (and probably blue with salty language if you understand Dutch well enough). But the staff and clientele are a bit of a laugh – they're liable to turn the cheesy music up full bore and indulge in a woefully off-key sing-along at any time.

Entertainment
CLUBS
Now & Wow (Map pp210-11; ☎ 477 10 74; www.now-wow.com; Maashaven 1) Many believe this to be Rotto's best club. It's an astoundingly popular and cool place, divided in two: 'Now' for mainstream house, and 'Wow' for funky beats. Theme nights with titles like 'Superbimbo' say it all. Watch out for the door bitch: she doesn't like shabby backpackers.

off_corso (Map p212; ☎ 411 38 97; www.off-corso.nl; Kruiskade 22) Then there are others who say that this is where it's at – a varied roster of entertainment and late-night action that sees bleeding-edge local and international DJs mashing up a high-fibre diet of bleeps'n'beats.

Night Town (Map p212; ☎ 436 12 10; www.nighttown.nl; West Kruiskade 26-28) Fencesitters, on the other hand, might come here for a fun-kung-fu-sion urban mash up of jazz, reggae, pop, Latin, funk and house choons: phat beats from the phar side for phreaks and scenesters who like it meaty, beaty, big and bouncy. Restaurant's good, too.

Gay Palace (Map pp210-11; ☎ 414 14 86; www.gay-palace.nl; Schiedamsesingel 139) And here we have Rotterdam's only weekly gay nightclub, with four floors of throbbing gay action – different scenes on each floor – to work you into a lather and get you sweaty.

Club Rotterdam (Map pp210-11; ☎ 290 84 42; www.cáférotterdam.nl; Willhelminakade 699) A popular club-bar-café complex that draws clubbers, groovers, wannabes and hangers-on.

LIVE MUSIC
Rotown (Map p212; ☎ 436 26 69; www.rotown.nl; Nieuwe Binnenweg 19) A smooth bar, a dependable live rock venue, an agreeable restaurant, a popular meeting place. The musical programme features new local talent, established international acts and crossover experiments.

Dizzy Jazzcafé (Map pp210-11; ☎ 477 30 14; www.dizzy.nl; 's-Gravendijkwal 129) Live music Tuesday nights and Sunday afternoons. The evening performances are scorching: everything from hot jazz to fast and funky Brazilian and salsa, with a very lively, sweaty crowd jumping out of their skins.

De Doelen (Map p212; ☎ 217 17 17; www.dedoelen.nl; Schouwburgplein 50) This is where you will find the 'home ground' of the Rotterdam Philharmonic Orchestra, a sumptuous concert centre that dates from 1935 and seats 1300. The orchestra is world class.

COFFEESHOPS
There's a huge number of coffeeshops in Rotterdam, probably the highest concentration outside the capital. Some are dodgy – ask Use-It for a list of reliable faves.

THEATRE
Schouwburg (Map p212; ☎ 411 81 10; www.schouwburg.rotterdam.nl; Schouwburgplein 25) The main cultural centre, the Schouwburg has a rotating calendar of dance, theatre and drama. Note the intriguing light fixtures with red necks out the front.

Luxor Theater (Map pp210-11; ☎ 484 33 33; www.luxortheater.nl; Posthumalaan 1) A major new performance venue, the Luxor features every kind of entertainment you can possibly imagine. Check out its excellent website or pick up one of its abundant programmes around town for more details.

CINEMA

Rotterdam hosts the annual International Film Festival (p214), which has been described as the 'European Sundance'.

De Pleinbioscoop (Lloyd Multiplein; ☺ mid-Aug–Sep) Annual, free, open-air screening season: classics, art-house and blockbusters.

Lantaren/Venster (Map p212; ☎ cashier 277 22 66; Gouvernestraat 133) Great central art-house alternative.

Pathé Cinemas (Map p212; ☎ www.pathe.nl; Schouwburgplein 101) This multiplex has the usual Hollywood selection as well as some lesser lights.

Shopping

Unlike the rest of the country, Rotterdam has gone for Sunday shopping in a big way. Most stores in the centre are open noon to 5pm. The Beurstraverse (known locally as the Koopgoot, or Shopping Ditch) runs from Lijnbaan to Hoogstraat and passes under Coolsingel. Nieuwe Binnenweg is a mix of stylish restaurants, coffee shops, old boozers and stores selling used CDs, vintage clothing and plastic/fluorescent club wear. The Meent has secondhand and retro clothing shops, and West Kruiskade has a welter of ethnic groceries and stores. There's a cluster of great cafés, restaurants and shops on and near the Witte de Withstraat.

Getting There & Away

AIR

See p304 for details of air services to and from Rotterdam.

BUS

Rotterdam is a hub for Eurolines bus services to the rest of Europe. See p301 for details.

BOAT

The **Fast Ferry** (☎ 09002666399; www.fastferry.nl; per passenger one way/return €2.50/3.50, bike €1/2) links Rotterdam with Dordrecht and is a good option for day trips, or in place of the train. The boat leaves from Willemskade at least once an hour during the day, and takes 45 minutes.

CAR & MOTORCYCLE

Rotterdam is well linked by motorways to the rest of the Netherlands and Belgium. Car rental firms at the airport:

Avis (☎ 298 24 24)
Budget (☎ 437 86 22)
Europcar (☎ 437 18 26)
Hertz (☎ 415 82 39)

TRAIN

Rotterdam CS is on the main line from Amsterdam south, and Thalys services between Brussels and Paris stop here. See p308 for details.

Sample fares and schedules:

Destination	Price (€)	Duration (min)	Frequency (per hr)
Amsterdam	12.60	62	4
Den Haag	4.10	15	4
Middelburg	17.60	90	1
Utrecht	8.60	40	2

Getting Around

TO/FROM THE AIRPORT

Bus 33 makes the 15-minute run from the airport to CS every 12 minutes throughout the day. A taxi takes 10 minutes to get to the centre and costs around €20.

BICYCLE

The bicycle shop at CS is underground, off the metro station.

CAR & MOTORCYCLE

Rotterdam has numerous places to park, including along the streets. Look for the blue P signs for large and enclosed garages.

PUBLIC TRANSPORT

Rotterdam's trams, buses and metro are provided by **RET** (☎ 447 69 11; www.ret.nl). Most converge in front of CS, where there is an **information office** (☺ 6am-11pm Mon-Fri, 8am-11pm Sat & Sun) that also sells tickets. There are other information booths in the major metro stations.

Public transport in Rotterdam is easy. For destinations in the centre you won't need to use it, but for Delfshaven and even Oude Haven you might want a lift.

The metro operates two lines, one of which terminates at CS. Beurs/Churchillplein is the interchange station between the lines. Machines to validate tickets are at the station entrances.

Fast and frequent trams cover much of the city. Validate your strip ticket on board. On buses, have the driver validate your strips.

TAXI

For a taxi, call the **Rotterdamse Taxi Centrale** (☎ 462 60 60).

AROUND ROTTERDAM
Kinderdijk

The **Kinderdijk** (Child's Dike; www.kinderdijk.nl) is the best spot in the Netherlands to see windmills. Declared a Unesco World Heritage site in 1997, it has 19 windmills strung out on both sides of canals. These canals were dug behind the tall dykes constructed at the confluence of the Lek river and several tributaries and channels.

This spot has been a focus of Dutch efforts to reclaim land from the water for centuries. It's a starkly beautiful area, with the windmills rising above the empty marshes and waterways. Exacerbating the feeling of having stepped through a ripple in the space–time continuum is the endless structural creaking and groaning of the shiplike mills. It's only once you hear these ghostly sounds that can you really appreciate what delicate skill must have been (and must still be) required to operate a mill, particularly in inclement weather.

Several of the most important types of windmills are here, including hollow post mills and rotating cap mills. The latter are among the highest in the country as they were built to better catch the wind. The mills are kept in operating condition and date from the 18th century.

A visit to Kinderdijk can easily occupy at least half a day. From the bus stop and parking area there are more than 4km of paths along the dykes that run past the windmills. On any Saturday in July and August from 2pm to 5pm, all of the 19 windmills are in operation, an unforgettable sight that was once common but is now impossible to find anywhere else. At other times of the year, one of the mills functions as a **visitors centre** (☎ 078-613 28 00; admission €2; ◷ 9.30am-5.30pm Mon-Sat Apr-Sep).

Take a local train from Rotterdam CS to Rotterdam Lombardijen station, then catch the hourly bus 154. By car, take the N210 12km east from Rotterdam.

BLOWING IN THE WIND

You don't need us to tell you that windmills are a Dutch icon, but did you know that the earliest known windmills appeared in the 13th century, simply built around a tree trunk? The next leap in technology came 100 years later, when a series of gears ensured the mill could be used for all manner of activities, the most important of which was pumping water. Hundreds of these windmills were soon built on dykes throughout Holland and the mass drainage of land began.

The next major advancement in Dutch windmill technology came in the 16th century with the invention of the rotating cap mill. Rather than having to turn the huge body of the mill-top to face the wind, the operators could rotate just the tip, which contained the hub of the sails. This made it possible for mills to be operated by just one person.

Besides pumping water, mills were used for many other industrial purposes, such as sawing wood, making clay for pottery and, most importantly for art lovers, crushing the pigments used by painters.

By the mid-19th century there were over 10,000 windmills operating in all parts of the Netherlands. But the invention of the steam engine soon made them obsolete. By the end of the 20th century there were only 950 operable windmills left, but this number seems to have stabilised and there is great interest in preserving the survivors. The Dutch government runs a three-year school for prospective windmill operators, who must be licensed.

Running one of the mills on a windy day is as complex as being the skipper of a large sailing ship, and anyone who's been inside a mill and listened to the massive timbers creaking will be aware of the similarities. The greatest hazard is a runaway, when the sails begin turning so fast that they can't be slowed down. This frequently ends in catastrophe as the mill remorselessly tears itself apart.

It's sad to see abandoned mills stripped of sails and standing forlorn and denuded, especially since these days you're more likely to see turbine-powered wind farms in the Dutch countryside rather than rows of windmills. However, there are opportunities to see working examples, especially at **Kinderdijk** (above), and at **Zaanse Schans** (p154) in Noord Holland.

Just about every operable windmill in the nation is open to visitors on National Mill Day, usually on the second Saturday of May. Look for windmills flying little blue flags.

DORDRECHT

☎ 078 / pop 118,649

Affable Dordrecht, with its lovely canals and busy port, sits at the confluence of the Oude Maas river and several tributaries and channels. This strategic trading position (precipitating a boom in the wine trade), along with the fact that it is the oldest Dutch city (having been granted a town charter in 1220), ensured that Dordrecht was one of the most powerful Dutch regions until the mid- to late 16th century. Accordingly, in 1572, it was here that town leaders from all over Holland met to declare independence from Spain.

Dordrecht's historical significance – and former affluence – is evidenced in its intact,
charming architecture, a legacy you'll fully appreciate as you wander the oval-shaped old town.

Orientation

The train station is a good 700m walk from the centre, a journey that passes through some less interesting, newer areas. In the old town, most of the sights are on or near the three old canals – the Nieuwehaven, the Wolwevershaven and the Wijnhaven.

Information

The **tourist office** (☎ 632 24 40; www.vvvzhz.nl; Stationsweg 1; ☼ noon-5.30pm Mon, 9am-5.30pm Tue-Fri, 10am-4pm Sat) is near the train station, as is the **post office** (☎ 613 21 11; Johan de Wittstraat 120; ☼ 9am-6pm

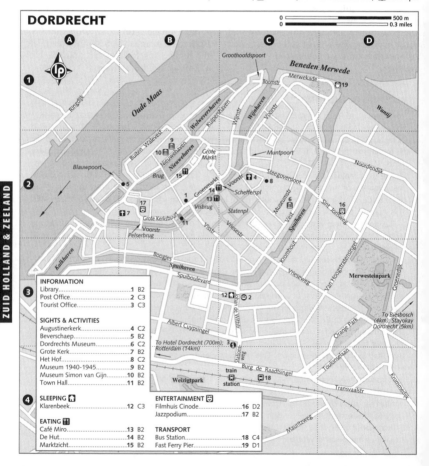

DORDRECHT

0 — 500 m
0 — 0.3 miles

Mon-Fri, 9am-1pm Sat). The **library** (☎ 613 00 77; Groenmarkt 53; internet per hr €2; ☺ noon-8pm Tue-Fri, 10am-1pm Sat) is in a large, modernised building.

Sights & Activities

See Dordrecht on foot: it's eminently suited to it. Begin at the **Visbrug**, the bridge over Wijnhaven that gives fine views of the dignified **town hall**. At the north end of Visbrug, turn right onto Groenmarkt. As you walk northeast you'll pass the oldest houses in town, many from the early 1600s.

At the next square, Scheffersplein, cross diagonally to Voorstraat, the main retail street. The canal runs under this area, which is home to numerous markets.

The **Augustinerkerk**, an old church with a façade dating from 1773, is a little further along on the right. Just past it, watch carefully for a passage leading to **Het Hof**, where the setting alone – especially at night – is moody and evocative. It was here that the states of Holland and Zeeland met in 1572.

Back on Voorstraat, continue north to the next bridge over the canal: Nieuwbrug. Cross over to Wijnstraat and turn right, continuing north. Many of the lopsided houses along here

date from the peak of the wine trade, when the nearby canals were filled with boats bearing the fruits of the fermented grape.

The street ends at an attractive bridge. Pass along the west or left side of the canal to the river – and the **Groothoofdspoort**, once the main gate into town. Walk west along the pavement and view the traffic on the waterways and Oude Maas river.

Circling to the south you'll see the Kuipershaven, the street along the Wolwevershaven, another old canal lined with beautifully restored wine warehouses and filled with many pleasure boats. Watch for artisans at work in their studios in the old buildings. At the tiny bridge, cross over to the north side of the Nieuwehaven. On the right, watch for the **Museum 1940–1945** (☎ 613 01 72; http://museum4045.100free.com/index.htm; Nieuwehaven 28; adult/child €1.50/0.75; ☺ 10am-5pm Tue-Sat, 1-5pm Sun). It has a collection of materials from WWII and shows the privations of the region during the war. Look for the propeller prised from a Lancaster bomber.

Nearby, the **Museum Simon van Gijn** (☎ 613 37 93; http://cms.dordrecht.nl/gijn; Nieuwehaven 29; admission €5; ☺ 11am-5pm Tue-Sun) depicts the life of an

---

A SHEEPISH TOWN

Dordrecht has a long association with squat, hooved and horned mammals. The town's nickname is Ooi-en Ramsgat (Ewe's and Ram's Hole) and the locals are known as Schapenkoppen (Sheepheads), nomenclatures deriving from the 17th century when sheep from elsewhere were heavily taxed.

Legend says that a farmer and his son bought a choice, fat sheep from outside town and then attempted to smuggle it inside the city gates, dressing the bemused beast to look like a small, fat child – with baggy breeches, a voluminous shirt, and a hat with a wide, floppy brim. The two geniuses then grabbed a foreleg each and made the sheep walk, with a noticeable wobble, on its hind legs.

Confronted by a guard at the town gate, they explained away the sheep-child's wobbling gait as 'tiredness' and were through with no problems – until the sheep, who'd had enough, let out a very loud, very unmistakable, 'baaaaa'. Thus the deception was unravelled and the farmer had to pay double the tax.

What this bizarre tale says about the beauty, intelligence or posture of the locals at that time is for you to judge, but, to be fair, Dordrecht wasn't the only 17th-century Dutch town to have had an unnatural attachment to stupidity and livestock (see p262 for the tale of Kampen and the cows).

Actually, Dordrecht was pretty sheepish even in the 16th century: a Man of God at the time decried that 'there are some ten or twelve places in the neighbourhood of Dordrecht…with neither ministers nor services. The inhabitants of these same places daily complain and cry out, "Alas we are like sheep without shepherds, we live without religion and hear nothing of God".'

Even today the town can't escape the past: Dordrecht's football team features a player called – what else? – Olaf Sheep.

Honestly, you couldn't make this stuff up.

18th-century patrician, with vintage knick-knacks, furnishings and tapestries.

Continue southwest to the Engelenburger-brug over the Nieuwehaven's access to the Oude Maas. Take an immediate right onto narrow Engelenburgerkade. At No 18, **Beverschaep** (Beaver & Sheep House) is a 1658 structure that takes its name from the animals supporting a coat of arms over the door.

At the end of the street is **Blauwpoort**, another old trading gate.

GROTE KERK

The massive tower of the 14th- to 15th-century **Grote Kerk** (☎ 614 46 60; www.grotekerk-dordrecht.nl; Langegeldersekade 2; admission church free, tower adult/child €1/0.50; ⏰ 10.30am-4.30pm Apr-Oct, noon-4pm Sun) was originally meant to have been much higher, but it took on a lean during its 150-year-plus construction. You can climb to the top – 275 steps – to enjoy excellent views of the town. Inside, the choir stalls are finely carved and there are several pleasing stained-glass windows.

DORDRECHTS MUSEUM

Away from the old town, the **Dordrechts Museum** (☎ 648 21 48; www.dordrechtsmuseum.nl; Museumstraat 40; adult/child €5/3; ⏰ 11am-5pm Tue-Sun) has works by local artists. Most noteworthy are pieces by Jan van Goyen (1596–1656) and Albert Cuyp (1620–91). Van Goyen was one of the first Dutch painters to capture the interplay of light on landscapes – look for his *View of Dordrecht* – while Cuyp, who lived in Dordrecht his entire life, is known for his many works painted in and around his hometown. These included, in his early career, landscapes featuring, inevitably, the town mascot: sheep.

Sleeping

Hotel choices in Dordrecht are limited. B&Bs might be a better bet – ask the tourist office to set you up. Stayokay Dordrecht, on the edge of Biesbosch National Park, is a combined youth hostel, camping ground and hotel (see opposite).

Hotel Dordrecht (☎ 613 60 11; www.hoteldordrecht .nl; Achterhakkers 72; s/d from €89.50/119) A pleasant option, centrally located, with excellent, spacious rooms that feature four-poster beds with curtains. Some rooms have private balconies. They're nice people, here: they'll even let you use their private golf buggy for free at the Golf Club Crayestein.

Other options:

Klarenbeek (☎ 614 41 33; Johan de Wittstraat 35; s/d €65/75) Near the tourist office.

Bastion Hotel (☎ 651 15 33; Laan der Verenigde Naties 363; d from €78) Business hotel near an industrial estate on the ring road.

Mercure Hotel Dordrecht (☎ 618 44 44; Rijksstraatweg 30; s/d €99/109) Standard business hotel, with all the usual facilities.

Eating

Café Miro (☎ 620 00 17; fax 684 98 50; Voorstraat 256B; tapas from €4) A bright, bold yellow tapas bar that's visually unmissable and named after one of Spain's greatest 20th-century painters. The Latina vibe carries through from the décor to the tapas on offer. The food is great; fresh, tasty and fairly priced. It's definitely a design highlight on the otherwise bland shopping street that is the Voorstraat.

De Hut (☎ 635 20 01; Voorstraat 293; daily special €9; ⏰ lunch & dinner) An innovative fast-food option fusing Dutch and Indonesian styles, meaning hearty ingredients livened up by spicier sauces. Cheap *broodjes* (sandwiches; €2.50 or €4) are fresh, tasty and best accompanied by one of the excellent juices.

Marktzicht (☎ 613 25 84; www.visrestaurant-markt zicht.nl; Varkenmarkt 17-19; mains €20-35; ⏰ dinner Tue-Sat) Well, this is nice! Here you will find most-agreeable, superfresh seafood served in a somewhat old-world, aquatic-themed interior. Angler-fish medallions, bluefin tuna pepper-steaks and scampi burgers were some of the recent delights on offer.

Entertainment

Filmhuis Cinode (☎ 639 79 79; St Jorisweg 76) Serious cinema devoted to offbeat and artistic films.

Jazzpodium (☎ 614 08 15; Grotekerksplein 1; ⏰ 9pm-3am Wed & Fri-Sun) Modern and improvisational jazz and blues.

Getting There & Away

The train station has all the usual services and is right on the main line from Rotterdam south to Belgium. Sample fares and schedules:

Destination	Price (€)	Duration (min)	Frequency (per hr)
Amsterdam	15.10	80	4
Breda	5.10	17	3
Rotterdam	3.70	15	6

Buses leave from the area to your right as you exit the train station. You'll find bus 388 serves Utrecht every hour.

For those with car or motorcycle in tow, the busy E19 south to Belgium and north to Rotterdam and beyond passes close to town.

The **Fast Ferry** (☎ 09002666399; www.fastferry.nl; per passenger one way/return €2.50/3.50, bike €1/2) links Dordrecht with Rotterdam. The boat leaves from Merwekade, which is at stop 12 on the bus 20 route, and takes 45 minutes.

BIESBOSCH NATIONAL PARK

Covering 7100 hectares, Biesbosch National Park encompasses an area on both banks of the Nieuwe Merwede River, east and south of Dordrecht. It's so big that it sprawls across a provincial border; there's a region known as the Brabantse Biesbosch, further east, while the part in this province is the Hollandse Biesbosch. Before 1421 the area was polder land and had a population of over 100,000 living in over 70 villages. However, the huge storm on St Elizabeth's Day (18 November) that year breached the dykes, and floodwaters destroyed all the villages – virtually everyone lost their life.

However, out of this calamity grew both new life and a new lifestyle. The floods created several channels in their wake, including what is today called the Nieuwe Merwede. Linked to the sea, these areas were subject to twice-daily high tides, leading to the growth of tide-loving reed plants, which the descendants of the flood's survivors took to cultivating.

Fast forward to 1970 when the Delta Project (see the boxed text, p228) shut off the tides to the area. The reeds, which had been growing wild during the decades since the collapse of the reed markets, began to die, focusing attention on what is one of the largest expanses of natural space left in the Netherlands.

The park is home to beavers (reintroduced to the Brabant area of the park in 1988) and voles, along with scores of birds. There's an observation point right near the visitors centre where you can observe some that have been fenced off in their own little pond.

Information

The **visitors centre** (☎ 630 53 53; www.biesbosch.org; Baanhoekweg 53; ⏰ 9am-5pm Tue-Sun year-round, 1-5pm Mon May & Jun, 9am-5pm Mon Jul & Aug) is some 7km east of the Dordrecht train station. There are all the usual displays about the park's ecology,

and you can rent kayaks and canoes (from €5 per half an hour) to explore the park and its many channels and streams. There are also numerous trails through the marshlands and along the river.

The centre is also the boarding place for a variety of boat tours of the Biesbosch. The longer cruises are better value, though, because they go to more places, including the **Biesboschmuseum** on the southern shore of the Nieuwe Merwede.

Sleeping

Stayokay Dordrecht (☎ 621 21 67; www.stayokay.com /dordrecht; Baanhoekweg 25; dm from €22.25) This place includes a youth hostel, camping ground and hotel. The hotel, which has a bar and restaurant, is in a modern building right next to the park and is 1km west of the visitors centre. It's a good idea to reserve accommodation here in advance.

Getting There & Away

The Stayokay and the park are easy bike rides from the Dordrecht train station. Otherwise, bus 5 (every 30 minutes) travels to within 2km of Stayokay and 3km of the park.

The easiest option is to get a taxi from Dordrecht station direct to the Stayokay site, then rent a bike there and use it to get around the park/area or into town.

ZEELAND

The province of Zeeland consists of three slivers of land that nestle in the middle of a vast delta through which many of Europe's rivers drain. As you survey the calm, flat landscape, consider that for centuries the plucky Zeelanders have been battling the North Sea waters, and not always with success. In fact the region has suffered two massive waterborne tragedies.

In 1421 the St Elizabeth's Day flood killed over 100,000, irrevocably altering the landscape – and some say the disposition – of the Netherlands and its people.

In 1953, yet another flood laid waste to 2000 lives and 800km of dykes, leaving 500,000 homeless and leading to the Delta Project, an enormous multidecade construction programme that aims to finally ensure the security of these lands. It ranks among the world's greatest engineering feats (see boxed text, p228).

Middelburg is the somnolent historic capital, while the coast along the North Sea is lined with beaches beyond the ever-present dykes. Many people venture to this place of tenuous land and omnipresent water just to see the sheer size of the Delta Project's dykes and barriers.

Getting There & Away

In Zeeland, Middelburg is easily reached by train, but for most other towns you'll need to rely on the many buses. The most important include bus 104, which makes a marathon 2½-hour journey between Rotterdam's Centraal Station and Vlissingen and follows the western edge of the province along the Delta Project. It runs every 30 minutes in both directions.

MIDDELBURG

☎ 0118 / pop 47,000

Pleasant and prosperous Middelburg, Zeeland's sleepy capital, is a friendly, low-key settlement. It's not exactly flush with nightlife, but it's a perfect base for exploring the region.

Although Germany destroyed the town's historic centre in 1940, much has been rebuilt and you can still get a solid feel for what life must have been like hundreds of years ago. The fortifications built by the Sea Beggars in 1595 can still be traced in the pattern of the main canals encircling the old town.

As the main town of the Walcheren peninsula, Middelburg is fairly removed from the rest of the Netherlands – crowds are seldom a

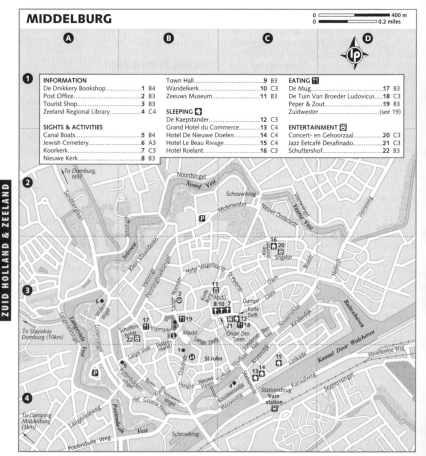

MIDDELBURG

0 — 400 m
0 — 0.2 miles

INFORMATION
De Drvkkery Bookshop...................1 B4
Post Office.......................................2 B3
Tourist Shop....................................3 B3
Zeeland Regional Library................4 C4

SIGHTS & ACTIVITIES
Canal Boats.....................................5 B4
Jewish Cemetery.............................6 A3
Koorkerk..7 C3
Nieuwe Kerk...................................8 B3

Town Hall..9 B3
Wandelkerk...................................10 C3
Zeeuws Museum............................11 B3

SLEEPING
De Kaepstander.............................12 C3
Grand Hotel du Commerce............13 C4
Hotel De Nieuwe Doelen...............14 C4
Hotel Le Beau Rivage....................15 C4
Hotel Roelant................................16 C3

EATING
De Mug..17 B3
De Tuin Van Broeder Ludovicus.....18 C3
Peper & Zout.................................19 B3
Zuidwester..................................(see 19)

ENTERTAINMENT
Concert- en Gehoorzaal................20 C3
Jazz Eetcafé Desafinado................21 B3
Schuttershof..................................22 B3

problem. Note that many of the town's sights are closed in winter.

There's no VVV tourist office, but there is a **tourist shop** (☎ 67 43 00; www.touristshop.nl; Markt 65C; 9.30am-5.30pm Mon-Fri, 9am-5.30pm Sat), and the **Zeeland Regional Library** (☎ 65 40 00; Kousteensedijk 7; internet per hr €3; 5.30-9pm Mon, 10am-9pm Tue-Fri, 10am-1.30pm Sat) has net access. The **post office** (10am-6pm Mon, 9am-6pm Tue-Fri, 9am-12.30pm Sat) is at Lange Noordstraat 48.

For bibliophiles, **De Drvkkery** (☎ 88 68 86; www .de-drvkkery.nl; Markt 51) is one of the country's best bookshops, drawing customers from as far as Belgium and Germany. It has an excellent magazine selection, a café, internet access (€3 per hour), art and photography displays on the walls – and oodles of books.

Orientation

The train station for Middelburg is a five-minute walk from the centre, across two canals. The Markt is the focus of commercial life, but Middelburg's history is concentrated on the medieval Abdij (Abbey).

Sights & Activities

This pretty, airy little town is eminently suitable for walking, with cobblestones and snaking alleyways leading in and away from the town square, which hosts a famous market on Thursdays.

ABDIJ

This huge abbey complex dates from the 12th century and houses the regional government as well as three churches and two museums. Start with the **Historama** (☎ 62 66 55; www.middel burgsekerken.nl; adult/child €2.50/1; 11am-5pm Mon-Sat year-round, noon-5pm Sun Apr-Oct), in the heart of the complex, which portrays the bleaker aspects of cloistered life and covers the history of the abbey.

The three churches are all in a cluster. The **Wandelkerk** dates from the 1600s and holds the tombs of Jan and Cornelis Evertsen, admirals and brothers killed fighting the English in 1666. It encompasses Lange Jan ('Long John'; it has its own locally brewed beer named after it), the 91m tower. Just east is the **Koorkerk**, parts of which date from the 1300s. Just west is **Nieuwe Kerk**, which has a famous organ and dates from the 16th century.

Call ☎ 61 35 96 to check the opening hours and accessibility of the churches. These are subject to more variation than usual while the Zeeuws Museum undergoes its big face-lift. You should still be able to scale the heights of Lange Jan (€2.50), though.

The **Zeeuws Museum** (☎ 62 66 55; www.zeeuws museum.nl) is housed in the former monks' dormitories, and has some of the best first-hand accounts and archival information on the 1953 disaster. However, it's closed for refurbishment until spring 2007.

TOWN HALL

Dominating the Markt, the **town hall** (☎ 67 54 52; admission €2.50; 11am-5pm Mon-Sat year-round, noon-5pm Sun Apr-Oct) grabs the eye. It's staggeringly beautiful, and a pastiche of styles: the Gothic side facing the Markt is from the 1400s; the more-classical portion on Noordstraat dates from the 1600s.

Inside there are several sumptuous ceremonial rooms that boast treasures such as the ubiquitous Belgian tapestries. Visits to the building are by one-hour guided tours only.

OTHER SIGHTS

The area around **Damplein** (east of the Abdij) preserves many 18th-century houses, some of which have recently been turned into interesting shops and cafés.

There is a fairly large old **Jewish Cemetery** on the Walensingel. It has the all-too-common stark memorial to the many Middelburg Jews taken away to their deaths by the Nazis.

Tours

The tourist shop can arrange tours of the canals and guided walking tours of the centre. Inquire within.

Festivals & Events

The Ringrijdendagen (Ring riding days) are held on two separate days, the first in July around the Abbey square, the second in August at the Molenwater. 'Ring riders' charge about with big sticks and in fancy dress on horses towards a target, trying to tilt it.

Sleeping

De Kaepstander (☎ 64 28 48; www.kaepstander.nl; Koorkerkhof 10; s/d with shared bathroom €38.50/65) This place has four rooms featuring B&B-style accommodation, and a downstairs lounge and TV room for all guests. It's cosy and peaceful but, best of all, it's next door to Jazz Eetcafé Desafinado (see p226).

ZUID HOLLAND & ZEELAND

Grand Hotel du Commerce (☎ 63 60 51; www .fletcher.nl; Loskade 1; s/d from €61/71) In a building that would look at home on the Cannes beachfront, this hotel has gaudy red awnings juxtaposed against whitewashed, sun-bleached walls; it's all a bit more faded than the brochures suggest, though. Still, the light-filled rooms are fine, the staff are attentive and the place has all the conveniences. As with all hotels on this road, the front rooms are noisiest.

Hotel Roelant (☎ 62 76 59; www.familiehotelroelant .nl; Koepoortstraat 10; d from €85) Dating from 1530, this building has basic, comfortable rooms with bathroom. It's a small, family-run establishment, a pleasant walk away from the centre on a beautiful old cobbled street. There's a nice garden and an excellent restaurant.

Hotel De Nieuwe Doelen (☎ 61 21 21; www.hotelde nieuwedoelen.nl; Loskade 3-7; s/d from €70/90) This is an older-style hotel with simple, colourful rooms (with private facilities) that are pleasingly decorated, plus the added bonus of lovely staff. There's an enclosed garden, perfect for breakfast in fine weather.

Other options:

Camping Middelburg (☎ 62 53 95; www.camping middelburg.nl; Koninginnelaan 55; camp site per car from €3) Three kilometres from the train station – take bus 56 or 58 and tell the driver where you want to get off.

Hotel Le Beau Rivage (☎ 63 80 60; Loskade 19; s/d from €75/105) Large, quiet rooms – some with sofas. It's the furthest place away from traffic on this road.

Eating

Peper & Zout (Pepper & Salt; ☎ 62 70 58; www.peperen zout.com; Lange Noordstraat 8; mains €12-19; ☼ lunch & dinner) Peper & Zout has a casual yet elegant interior. The menu concentrates on fresh seafood, mainly various kinds of local fish. It's a popular place with a great wine list.

De Mug (The Mosquito; ☎ 61 48 51; www.demug.nl; Vlasmarkt 54-56; mains €16-21; ☼ dinner Tue-Sat) Don't be fooled by the Heineken signs; the beer list is long and boasts many rare Trappist varieties. Also try the Mug Bitter, heavy on the hops. In the kitchen, De Mug has quite a reputation for its trademark dishes prepared with unusual beers. The accommodation (rooms from €30) is clean and comforting.

Other options:

De Tuin Van Broeder Ludovicus (☎ 62 60 11; Lange Delft 2A) A health-food store with an organic bakery, cheese case and more.

Zuidwester (☎ 65 00 40; www.zuidwester.info; Lange Noordstraat 6; mains €10-15; ☼ lunch & dinner Wed-Sat,

dinner Sun & Mon) Latin-tinged, homemade salads and pastas plus organic wines.

Entertainment

Jazz Eetcafé Desafinado (☎ 64 07 67; www.desafinado .nl; Koorkerkstraat 1; mains €13-20; ☼ lunch & dinner) It does exactly what it says on the tin: serves up steaming portions of hot jazz in wood-bound surroundings, with authentic jazz and blues on the stereo, old-time vinyl adorning the walls, and live jazz on Wednesday nights. The food's not too bad, although watch out for those little snail thingies they serve up as nibbles.

Concert- en Gehoorzaal (☎ 61 27 00; Singelstraat 13) This old concert hall, with a plush interior, hosts frequent performances of chamber and other classical music.

Schuttershof (☎ 61 34 82; www.schuttershoftheater.nl; Schuttershofstraat 1) The Schuttershof is a cinema that sometimes has live music.

Getting There & Around

Middelburg is near the end of the train line in Zeeland, and the attractive but austere station has that end-of-line feel. Services are limited: there's a very small newsstand and the lockers are hidden away in the bicycle shop. Sample fares and schedules:

Destination	Price (€)	Duration (min)	Frequency (per hr)
Amsterdam	26.30	150	1
Roosendaal	10.40	45	2
Rotterdam	17.50	60	1

Regional buses, including the 104, stop along Kanaalweg in front of the train station.

The bicycle shop is to the left as you leave the station. A charming cycle route runs along the coastal dykes (see p72).

AROUND MIDDELBURG

The Walcheren peninsula is a very enjoyable place for bicycling: combine journeys to old towns with time at the beach.

Veere

☎ 0118 / pop 1520

Veere is a former fishing village that found a new industry – tourism – when its access to the sea on the Veerse Meer (Veere Lake) was closed as part of the Delta Project. The town now boasts a busy yacht harbour. Much of

Veere dates from the early 16th century – thus, it's an atmospheric place to stroll around.

The **tourist office** (☎ 09002020280; Oudestraat 28; 🕙 10am-4.30pm Mon-Sat Jul & Aug, 1.30-4.30pm Sep-Jun) is in a small building near the Grote Kerk. Staff can advise on boat rentals and bike routes.

SIGHTS & ACTIVITIES

Here, you'll feel like you're in a Vermeer painting: rich Gothic houses abound, a testament to the wealth brought in by the wool trade with the Scots, and at the waterfront, the **Campveerse Toren** was part of the old fortifications. Look for the indications on the side showing the levels of various floods.

The **town hall** on the Markt dates from 1474 but was mostly completed in 1599. Its tower is still stuffed with bells – 48 at last count.

At the south end of town is the 16th-century **Grote Kerk**, another edifice that never matched its designer's intentions – its stump of a steeple (42m) looms ominously.

SLEEPING & EATING

Hotel de Campveerse Toren (☎ 50 12 91; www.campveersetoren.nl; Kade 2; d from €116) A smart place in a historic, castle-shaped building right on the waterfront. It offers really comfortable rooms and particularly fabulous views. Occupancy rises with the thermometer, as do prices.

Hotel 't Waepen van Veere (☎ 50 12 31; www.waepenvanveere.nl; Markt 23-27; d from €75) Veere's other hotel is on the central square, and it's a small place, with just 11 rooms – although all of them are excellent. It also has an elegant restaurant (mains €16 to €26).

GETTING THERE & AWAY

Veere is an easy bike ride from Middelburg (6km). Otherwise, bus 53 makes the 12-minute run every hour (every two hours on Sunday).

Domburg

☎ 0118 / pop 1251

Although Domburg is a fairly low-key seaside town by Dutch standards, in summer it's jam-packed. However, it's the **beach** that's the main event. To escape the urban crowds, head south along the tall dunes. Keep going past the golf course for a good 4km.

The **tourist office** (☎ 58 13 42; www.vvvwnb.nl; Schuitvlotstraat 32; 🕙 9.30am-5pm Mon-Sat, 2-4pm Sun) is near the entrance to town on Roosjesweg.

The staff are experts at ferreting out accommodation.

For information on a 35km bicycle route, the Mantelingen, which begins and ends at Domburg, see p72.

SLEEPING & EATING

The tourist office has myriad additional accommodation options.

Camping Hof Domburg (☎ 58 82 00; info@roompot.nl; Schelpweg 7; camp sites from €10; 🕙 year-round) Located west of the centre; sites accommodating up to five people.

Stayokay Domburg (☎ 58 12 54; www.stayokay.com/domburg; Duinvlietweg 8; dm from €22.25; 🕙 Apr-Oct) A hostel notable for its location in a real castle, complete with moat, 2km east of Domburg and 1km from the beach. Reserve in advance, as the beach is very popular. Bus 53 from Middelburg stops along the N287 near the entrance.

GETTING THERE & AWAY

Bus 52 and 53 link Domburg to Middelburg every hour (every two hours on Sunday). Bus 53 continues south along the beaches.

WATERLAND NEELTJE JANS

Travelling the N57, you can't help but notice the many massive developments of the Delta Project: a succession of huge dykes and dams, designed to avoid a repeat of the many floods. Possibly the most impressive stretch is between Noord Beveland and Schouwen-Duiveland, to the north. The long causeway built atop the massive movable inlets is designed to allow the sea tides in and out of the Oosterschelde. This storm-surge barrier, over 3km long and spanning three inlets and two artificial islands, took 10 years to build, beginning in 1976.

At about the midway point (Haringsvliet), the **Waterland Neeltje Jans** (☎ 111-655 655; www.neeltjejans.nl; winter/summer €11/16; 🕙 10am-5pm), located by the main surge barrier, is a terrific complex that explains the project in minute detail, with working models, and hilarious public-service films from the '70s (complete with bad hair and funky soundtracks). There's also an exhilarating boat trip that takes you out onto the Oosterschelde for a panoramic view of the barriers and beyond.

Several floors deal with the effects of the floods and show how the entire massive project was built. You can also visit one of the nearby complex pylons of the storm-surge barrier and see how the huge movable gate works.

THE DELTA PROJECT

Begun in 1958, the Delta Project consumed billions of guilders, millions of labour hours and untold volumes of concrete and rock before it was completed in 1996. The goal was to avoid a repeat of the catastrophic floods of 1953, when a huge storm surge rushed up the Delta estuaries of Zeeland and broke through inland dykes. This caused a serial failure of dykes throughout the region, and much of the province was flooded.

The original idea was to block up the estuaries and create one vast freshwater network. But by the 1960s this kind of sweeping transformation was unacceptable to the Dutch public, now more environmentally aware. So the Oosterschelde was left open to the sea tides, and 3km of movable barriers were constructed that could be lowered ahead of a possible storm surge. This barrier, between Noord Beveland and Schouwen-Duiveland, is the most dramatic part of the Delta Project and the focus of the Waterland Neeltje Jans, which details the enormous efforts to complete the barrier.

The project raised and strengthened the region's dykes and added a movable barrier at Rotterdam harbour, the last part to be completed. Public opinion later shifted, but large areas of water had already been dammed and made into freshwater lakes. At Veerse Meer (p226) the fishing industry has vanished and been replaced by holidaymakers and sailboats.

The impact of the Delta Project is still being felt. At Biesbosch National Park (p223), the reduction of tides is killing reeds that have grown for centuries. But those who recall the 1953 floods will trade some reeds for their farms any day.

There's an ironic – and ever-tragic – twist to all this. After the 1953 floods, Dutch officials travelled to Louisiana on a fact-finding mission to learn from the levees installed along the Mississippi River. Applying this knowledge directly fed into the actual mechanics of the Delta project.

Fast forward to 2005, and the aftermath of the Hurricane Katrina disaster: this time, Louisiana officials travelled to Zeeland to learn from the Delta Project, similarly in the hope of preventing future catastrophes from ever happening again.

The level of tidal control is truly astounding. Operators are able to balance the mix of fresh water draining out into the sea against the tidal influx of sea water to such an extent that they can affect the rate of corrosion on the hulls of container-ships moored in Rotterdam. This seemingly innocuous feat has saved shipping firms millions of dollars in maintenance and repair costs since the sluice operations started.

Bus 104 stops at the Expo on its run between Rotterdam's Spijkenisse metro station (25 minutes from Rotterdam CS) and Vlissingen. The buses take about an hour from Rotterdam and 30 minutes from Middelburg and run every 30 minutes.

SCHOUWEN-DUIVELAND

The middle 'finger' of the Delta, Schouwen-Duiveland, is a compact island of dunes.

Zierikzee

☎ 0111 / pop 10,313

Zierikzee grew wealthy in the 14th century from trade with the Hanseatic League, but things took a turn for the worse in 1576 when a bunch of Spaniards waded over from the mainland at low tide and captured the town, precipitating a long economic decline.

The **tourist office** (☎ 41 24 50; www.vvvschouwenduiveland.nl; Meelstraat 4; ✆ 10am-5pm Mon-Fri year-round, 10am-1pm Sat Oct-Apr, 10am-3pm Sat May-Sep) can supply you with a list of local rooms for overnight stays; the **post office** (☎ 41 55 55; Poststraat 39; ✆ 9am-5.30pm Mon-Fri, 10am-1pm Sat) offers the usual services, and the **library** (☎ 41 45 48; Haringvlietplein 2; internet per hr €3; ✆ 2-5pm Mon & Wed-Fri, 9.30am-noon Wed & Sat) has internet access.

SIGHTS & ACTIVITIES

The **Maritiem Museum** (☎ 45 44 64; Mol 25; combined ticket with town hall adult/child €4/2; ✆ 10am-5pm Mon-Sat, noon-5pm Sun) is just off Havenpark. It is in the 's-Gravensteen, a sturdy 16th-century prison that still has its bars. Besides the displays on local seafaring, there's a fine garden out the back.

The **town hall** (☎ 45 44 64; Meelstraat 6-8; combined ticket with Maritiem Museum adult/child €4/2; ✆ 10am-5pm Mon-Sat, noon-5pm Sun) has a unique 16th-century wooden tower topped with a statue of Neptune.

At Oude Haven, at the east end of town, the **Noordhavenpoort** and the **Zuidhavenpoort** are old city gates from the 16th and 14th centuries respectively.

GETTING THERE & AWAY

The bus stop is north of the centre, a five-minute walk across the canal along Grachtweg. Bus 132 makes the 30-minute run to Goes at least every 30 minutes. Bus 133 runs to Rotterdam's Zuidplein metro station (the 75-minute ride leaves at least every hour).

Westerschouwen

☎ 0111 / pop 18,000

Sheltered by tall dunes, this small town at the west end of Schouwen-Duiveland adjoins a vast park set among the sands and woods. There are hiking and biking trails for outdoors enthusiasts, and, although busy in summer, you can easily find solitude in some of the more remote parts of the park.

The **tourist office** (☎ 65 15 13; Noordstraat 45A; ⏰ 9am-5pm Mon-Fri, 9am-2pm Sat), in the neighbouring town of Burgh-Haamstede, can help you with camping, private rooms and hotel accommodation.

Bus 133 from Rotterdam via Zierikzee and Bus 134 from Zierikzee both stop right at the sand dunes. Both run every 30 minutes. Bus 104, the Vlissingen–Rotterdam bus, stops about 2km from Westerschouwen in Burgh-Haamstede.

ZEEUWS-VLAANDEREN

Running along the Belgian border south of the Westerschelde, Zeeuws-Vlaanderen is an unremarkable place with numerous farms and a few chemical plants.

The many small villages, such as IJzendijk, all have their 'holy trinity' of the Dutch country skyline: a church steeple, a town hall tower and a windmill.

No part of Zeeuws-Vlaanderen is joined to the rest of the Netherlands by land. Instead, there are two ferry connections. The Vlissingen–Breskens ferry is a link for the Belgian channel ferry ports.

Foot passengers can travel from Brugge in Belgium by bus 2 to Breskens (75 minutes, hourly). From the port in Vlissingen, catch a bus or ferry to points beyond.

The other ferry route, Perkpolder to Kruiningen on Zuid-Beveland, is primarily useful to local motorists. The ferry (€6 per car) runs every 30 minutes in both directions.

Friesland (Fryslân)

For some, Friesland (Fryslân in Frisian) is the crowning glory of the Netherlands. Covering the country's northwestern corner, it has much that attracts visitors to this tiny nation – sandy beaches, flat, green open spaces, water sports galore, and a town or two with a rich historical past.

If this is all you're here to see, then enjoy. But this kind of attitude is only selling Friesland, and the Frisians, short. Scratch the surface and you'll soon discover that the locals, and the landscape, differ subtly from the rest of the country. For starters, there's the language: it's closer to Old English than Dutch, but you'll struggle to understand a word. Then there's the strong sense of self-reliance: even by Dutch standards, the Frisians are an independent, stoic bunch. The land itself is also a curious anomaly: they didn't just have to build dykes to protect their land, they had to build the land itself. North Friesland segues into the Waddenzee so subtly that, aeons ago, it was hard to tell whether you were plodding through watery mud or muddy water.

Far and away the biggest drawcard of Friesland is its four islands. These long slivers of sand and soil attract thousands by the boatload, drawn by the chance to find a pocket of island bliss away from the crowded mainland. Vlieland offers a semblance of civilisation and acres of remote sand dunes, while its neighbour Terschelling is by far the most developed, and yet still manages to pack in kilometres of lonely cycle and walking paths. Ameland is a hybrid of the two, and Schiermonnikoog stands aloof, its serene ambience intact even in the height of tourist season.

HIGHLIGHTS

- Explore the enthralling museums and quiet back streets of **Leeuwarden** (p232)
- Take to the water around **Sneek** (p235) – whether it be fresh, salty, in it, or on it
- Kick back in **Hindeloopen** (p237), a coastal town where you can't help but relax
- Combine a cycling trip through sand dunes and farmland on **Terschelling** (p240) and **Ameland** (p241)
- Find your little piece of island solitude on **Vlieland** (p239) and **Schiermonnikoog** (p242)

FRIESLAND (FRYSLÂN)

FRIESLAND

NORTH
SEA

Schiermonnikoog

Schiermonnikoog ○ Schiermonnikoog National Park

Ameland

Nes

Hollum

Terschelling

Hoorn ○ Oosterend

Holwerd ○

Ferwerd ○ Hogebeintum

Lauwersoog

GRONINGEN

West Terschelling

N358

Dokkum

Oost Vlieland

Vlieland

N393   N357

N356

N361   N355

Leeuwarden

Buitenpost

To Groningen
(4km)

Margrietkanaal

Franeker ○

A31

Harlingen

FRIESLAND

N355

N358

W a d d e n z e e

N31

Texel

Makkum ○

Bolsward ○

A7

N359 N384

E22

N354

Grou ○

E22

Drachten

Sneek

N392

Afsluitdijk

To Den
Helder
(10km)

E22

Workum ○

IJlst

A7

Heerenveen

A7   N380

N381

N354

Hindeloopen ○

Stavoren ○

Sloten ○

Wolvega ○

A32

To
Groningen
(40km)

NOORD
HOLLAND

I J s s e l m e e r

A6

Steenwijk

N371

Weerribben
National Park

To Hoorn (8km);
Amsterdam
(48km)

Enkhuizen

To Amsterdam
(80km)

Giethoorn

To Zwolle
(18km) ○ Meppel

N375

A28

0 ─── 20 km
0 ─── 12 miles

History

Having dredged their home out of the Waddenzee armload by armload, the Frisians are
no strangers to struggling with their natural
environment.

Farming, fishing and nautical know-how
(the building, repair and maintenance of
ships) have been the area's principal activities for centuries, and in the prerepublic era
made Friesland one of the wealthiest regions
in the Netherlands. The Frisians became
integrated further into Dutch society – not
entirely willingly – in 1932 when the Afsluitdijk (Barrier Dyke; p175) opened, closing
the Zuiderzee. This provided better links to
Amsterdam and the south but was devastating
for small fishing villages, who suddenly found

themselves sitting beside a lake. The province
has, however, recently reinvented itself and
is currently enjoying a revival as a domestic
holiday destination.

Language

Frisians speak Frisian, which is actually closer
(in some ways) to German and Old English
than Dutch; there's an old saying that goes 'As
milk is to cheese, are English and Frise'. The
majority of Frisians are, however, perfectly
conversant in mainstream Dutch.

Most people who have lived in the region
for a significant time will speak some Frisian,
although you're more likely to hear Frisian
coming from the mouths of older residents
than younger people's. Don't worry if you

FRIESLAND (FRYSLÂN)

can't make head nor tail of it – even the Dutch have difficulty deciphering Frisian. You'll usually see written examples, such as street signs. You might, for example, see the word 'Snits', which is the Frisian version of Sneek, the region's second city.

A ruling in 2002 officially altered the spelling of the province's name from the Dutch 'Friesland' to 'Fryslân', the local version of the name.

Getting There & Around

The capital, Leeuwarden, is easily reached by train from the south, from where trains can be caught to the coastal towns of the southwest, the port of Harlingen in the west, and Groningen in the east. The rest of the province requires more patience, but can be reached by bus; day passes (€12.80), available on buses, cover the entire region, and after 9am Monday to Friday and all weekend, journeys only cost €1. Cycle paths crisscross Friesland.

By car is also a good way to explore the entire province; the quickest route from Amsterdam is over the Afsluitdijk.

LEEUWARDEN (LJOUWERT)

☎ 058 / pop 90,500

Most tourists to Friesland head directly for the islands, but the majority pass through Leeuwarden, the province's capital. Therefore many see the city only as a transit point, which is a pity, as this laid-back, pretty town is worth an overnight stop, if only to explore its superb trinity of museums. A night here will also allow time to wander its peaceful old streets, and sample some northern hospitality, something easily found in its welcoming bars and clubs.

Orientation

The old town is compact and easily traversed on foot. Much of the commercial life is on or near the network of canals that wind through the centre.

Information

Leeuwarden is dotted with ATMs; for those arriving by train and needing cash, there's a couple located to the right as you exit the station.

Library (☎ 234 77 77; Wirdumerdijk 34; internet per hr €2; 🕑 12.30-5.30pm Mon & Thu, 10am-1pm & 5.30-9pm

LEEUWARDEN

0 ———— 300 m
0 ———— 0.2 miles

INFORMATION
ATMs.....................................1 C3
Library..................................2 C3
Post Office...........................3 B2
Tourist Office......................4 B3
Van der Velde....................5 C2

SIGHTS & ACTIVITIES
Fries Museum.....................6 D2
Mata Hari Statue...............7 C2
Natuurmuseum Fryslân......8 C1
Oldehove.............................9 B2
Princessehof Museum......10 B2
Waag..................................11 C2

SLEEPING 🛏
Eden Oranje Hotel............12 C3
Hotel 't Anker...................13 C2
Stadhouderlijk Hof...........14 C2

EATING 🍴
De Lachende Koe..............15 C2
Humphrey's Deli & Diner..16 C2
Quizin!...............................17 D2
Spijs Lokaal.......................18 C2
Spinoza's............................19 C2

DRINKING 🍷
Cafe De Toeter.................20 C2
Coltrane's.....................(see 19)

ENTERTAINMENT 🎭
Club Noa...........................21 B2
De Harmonie.....................22 B2
Het Filmhuis.....................23 C2
Purple Lounge Club.........24 D2
Repelsteeltje................(see 19)
Tivoli................................25 C2

TRANSPORT
Bicycle Shop.....................26 C3
Bus Station.......................27 B3

Tue & Fri, 10am-5.30pm Wed, 10am-1pm Sat) Overlooks a canal and has a string of internet terminals.

Post office (☎ 213 09 98; Oldehoofsterkerkhof 4; ✆ 7.30am-6pm Mon-Fri, 7.30am-1.30pm Sat)

Tourist office (☎ 234 75 50; www.vvvleeuwarden.nl; Sophialaan 4; ✆ noon-5.30pm Mon, 9.30am-5.30pm Tue-Fri, 10am-3pm Sat) Stocks loads of information on the province, has free internet access, and books accommodation for €1.75 per person.

Van der Velde (☎ 213 23 60; Nieuwestad NZ 57) Bookshop with a smallish but decent selection of English-language and travel books.

Sights

Most of Leeuwarden's sights are concentrated within a leisurely 10-minute walk of Nieuwestad, predominantly on the northern side (Nieuwestad NZ) of the water.

FRIES MUSEUM

This **museum** (☎ 255 55 00; www.friesmuseum.nl; Turfmarkt 11; adult/child €5/2; ✆ 11am-5pm Tue-Sun), Leeuwarden's biggest, is wonderful and concentrates on the history of Friesland from the time when locals began the necessary task of mud-stacking. Spread over two historic buildings, the Kanselarij, a 16th-century courthouse, and the Eysinghaus, a mansion from the late 1700s, it's a place to spend a couple of hours.

The huge collection of silver items – long a local speciality – is spectacular, as are the 19th-century period pieces. There is also a section on the efforts by locals to resist the Nazis, a sorrowful examination of the life of Mata Hari (see the boxed text, p234), a kids' corner to balance things up, and temporary exhibitions of young contemporary artists from across Europe.

PRINCESSEHOF MUSEUM

Pottery lovers will adore the **Princessehof Museum** (☎ 294 89 58; www.princessehof.nl; Grote Kerkstraat 11; adult/child €6/3; ✆ 11am-5pm Tue-Sun), the official museum for ceramics in the Netherlands. Here you'll find the largest collection of tiles on the planet, an unparalleled selection of delftware, and works from around the globe – its Japanese, Chinese and Vietnamese sections are world class. Temporary exhibitions also come and go on a regular basis.

NATUURMUSEUM FRYSLÂN

Even the most brow-beaten parent should let their lovely angels run rampant in the **Natuurmuseum Fryslân** (☎ 233 22 44; www.natuur museumfryslan.nl; Schoenmakersperk 2; adult/child €5/4; ✆ 11am-5pm Tue-Sun), Leeuwarden's revamped children's museum. This well-planned, interactive museum is an engaging experience for all ages, concentrating on Friesland's flora and fauna. Highlights include spooky Captain Severein's collection of curiosities and a virtual bird-flight simulation (strap yourself into the hang-glider harness and away you go), but nothing tops the basement; here you can take in an underwater lake-scene from a fish's perspective, complete with duck bums, boat bottoms and cow snouts.

The museum's café, which occupies the inner courtyard, is topped by a glass roof, making it lovely and warm even on a cold day.

OTHER ATTRACTIONS

Just past the west end of Bagijnestraat, the off-balance **Oldehove** dominates its unfortunate spot on the Oldehoofsterkerkhof parking lot. Things went wrong shortly after the tower was started in 1529 and it started to lean severely when it was only 40m high. While by no means a Leaning Tower of Pisa, it must still be quite worrying for the neighbours. It was closed at the time of writing due to the parking lot overhaul; check with the tourist office for opening times.

The petite **Waag** dominates Waagplein, and is now surrounded by stores. It was the weigh-house for butter and other goods from 1598 to 1884.

Sleeping

Leeuwarden isn't swamped with accommodation options, but there's variety enough to suit everyone's tastes. For B&Bs at around €20 per person, try the tourist office.

Stadhouderlijk Hof (☎ 216 21 80; www.stadhouder lijkhof.nl; Hofplein 29; r €105-285; 🖧) The plain façade of the Stadhouderlijk belies the plush interior of this one-time royal home. Inside, the red-carpeted stairwells lead to basic rooms, which have a semblance of elegance, and sumptuous suites, where those with a decadent streak can satisfy their needs.

Hotel 't Anker (☎ 212 52 16; www.hotelhetanker.nl; Eewal 73; s/d from €26/60) This simple hotel is a fine bet for those just looking for a bed and a clean room to rest their tired tourist bones. It's surprisingly quiet as well, considering the ground floor contains a lively bar, and a string of restaurants and bars are only a quick stroll down the street.

MATA HARI

Had she been born a few decades later, Leeuwarden's own Gertrud Margarete Zelle probably would have been given a TV chat show. Instead, the irrepressible Margarete ended up a martyr to salacious legend.

Margarete was born in 1876. Her wealthy family fell apart in her teens, so she married and moved to Indonesia. By 1902 the marriage was on the rocks and they were back in Leeuwarden. She left her husband and child and moved to Paris, where she changed her name to Mata Hari (Malaysian for 'sun') and began a career as a dancer, achieving fame with her erotic, naked act.

Her affairs and dalliances were legendary. She favoured rich men in uniform, and when WWI broke out she had high-ranking lovers on both sides. Things inevitably became tricky; French officers persuaded her to spy on her German lovers, and German officers managed to do the same. This web of intrigue was not helped by her keen imagination, and mistrust began to rise from both sides.

In 1917, at age 40, she was arrested by the French for spying. There was a dubious trial, during which none of her former 'pals' offered any assistance – probably out of embarrassment – and later that year she was sentenced to death and shot.

Fortunately Margarete/Mata Hari is still – in a manner of speaking – alive and well in Leeuwarden. Her **statue** as a sultry dancer can be found on a bridge over the canal close to her birthplace at Over de Kelders 33, and the Fries Museum has a large and detailed exhibit on her life. The residence where Margarete spent much of her childhood, Grote Kerkstraat 212, currently lies empty awaiting its next incarnation.

De Kleine Wielen (☎ 0511-43 16 60; De Groene Ster 14; camp site €10.50) Centred on a small lake some 6km east of the city off the N355, De Kleine Wielen is a pleasant, green camping ground suitable for families and nature lovers. Bus 10 and 51 pass close to the camp; ask the driver to let you off at De Skieppepoel, from where it's a five-minute walk south.

Eden Oranje Hotel (☎ 212 62 41; infooranjehotel@edenhotelgroup.nl; Stationsweg 4; r €55-125; 🖳) Directly opposite the train station, this business hotel has grand common spaces and comfy, highly functional rooms with a smidgen of charm. Book early to receive substantial discounts.

Eating

ourpick Spinoza's (☎ 212 93 93; Eewal 50-52; mains €10-17; 🕙 lunch & dinner) This large eatery attracts all walks of life with its hearty dishes, convivial atmosphere, and one thing the Dutch love above all – dim lighting. The menu features regional specialities (stews are a particular favourite), plenty of vegetarian options, and a kids' section. The private courtyard is an oasis over summer.

Quizin! (☎ 216 76 70; Over de Kelders 24; mains €13-20; 🕙 dinner Tue-Sat) With its warm browns and reds, attentive staff, and relaxed (but not laid-back) air, Quizin! is a fine place to enjoy an evening meal. Dishes, which loosely fall under the modern European cuisine moniker, are prepared with care by chefs who enjoy a quick chat with their customers.

Spijs Lokaal (☎ 216 22 14; Eewal 54; mains €15-20; 🕙 dinner Mon-Sat) It's easy to see Spijs has nothing to hide; its chefs are on full view from the street, busily preparing what some class as the finest food in Leeuwarden. The modern European fare on the ever-changing menu is often so popular that reservations are highly recommended.

De Lachende Koe (Laughing Cow; ☎ 215 82 45; Groote Hoogstraat 16; mains €10-14; 🕙 dinner Tue-Sun) Covering the ground floor of three connecting houses, The Laughing Cow is an enormous place that amazingly fills up with ease. The atmosphere is more pub- than restaurant-like, but everyone seems to enjoy the hefty servings from the meat-heavy menu, although we're not sure many cows find this particularly amusing.

Humphrey's Deli & Diner (☎ 216 49 63; Nieuwestad NZ 60; mains from €10; 🕙 lunch & dinner Tue-Sat) A chain restaurant with a surprising amount of charm, a small library, filling meals, and all manner of sauces, jams and pickles for purchase.

Drinking

For such a small city, Leeuwarden has an excellent selection of drinking establishments. Two with more energy than most are:

Café De Toeter (☎ 215 79 76; Kleine Hoogstraat 2) A fine place to start the evening; expect a warm welcome, bubbly vibe, chatty locals and a bartender who knows the meaning of good service.

Coltrane's (Eewal 50-52; ☺ Wed-Sun) Below Spinoza's, this is a perfect bar to end the evening in; cavelike, with grungy corners, friendly staff, progressive tunes, and a 25-to-35 crowd.

Entertainment

A concentration of bars, clubs and coffeeshops can be found around Doelesteeg, Kleine Hoogstraat and Grote Hoogstraat. Thursday night is 'students night' where many places offer 10 beers for €10; proving your status as a student doesn't seem a prerequisite to receive such a deal though.

Repelsteeltje (Grote Hoogstraat 44) If ever there was a coffeeshop to calm the fears of those tempted to try pot for the first time, this is it. Next door to Spinoza's and covering three floors of a lovely corner house, Repelsteeltje has the look and feel of a normal coffee house, a chatty owner, regular DJs and a distinct absence of paranoia.

De Harmonie (☎ 233 02 33; www.harmonie.nl; Ruiterskwartier 4) De Harmonie satisfies Leeuwarden's desire for highbrow entertainment by hosting an array of theatre performances, both mainstream and fringe.

Tivoli (☎ 212 38 87; Nieuwestad NZ 85) unspools an interesting line-up of art-house and festival films, as does **Het Filmhuis** (☎ 212 50 60; Ruiterskwartier 6).

Clubs worth checking out for a night's frivolity:

Purple Lounge Club (☎ 216 01 20; www.purplelc.nl; Tweebaksmarkt 49) Club-restaurant with a very purple, very eclectic décor, DJs, live bands and a healthy local following.

Club Noa (www.club-noa.nl; Nieuwstad NZ 63-65) Big, bold, brash club attracting pretty young things with its sexy red interior, *Saturday Night Fever* dance floor and thumping music.

Getting There & Around

Leeuwarden is at the end of the main train line from the south; it's also the hub for local services in Friesland. Lockers can be found on platform eight. Fares and schedules:

Destination	Price (€)	Duration (min)	Frequency (per hr)
Amsterdam	25.70	160	2
Groningen	8.30	50	2
Utrecht	23.50	145	2

Buses are to the left as you exit the train station, and a **bicycle shop** (☎ 213 98 00) is to the right. The latter stays open as late as 2am over the summer months.

AROUND LEEUWARDEN

The N357, which connects Leeuwarden with the Ameland ferry port at Holwerd, 23km north, passes some of the oldest settled parts of Friesland – an excellent route for driving or riding.

At Ferwerd, 6km southwest of Holwerd, watch for a road northeast to **Hogebeintum**, which is 3km off the N357. You'll soon see the highest *terp* (mud mound) in Friesland with a lovely old church perched on top. There are some good displays explaining the ongoing archaeological digs.

SNEEK (SNITS)

☎ 0515 / pop 32,900

'All Frisians know how to sail, and all Frisians know how to fish', so the saying goes. This is certainly true of the residents of Sneek, but then again, they have no choice in the matter; the IJsselmeer is close at hand, as are an abundance of canals and rivers, and the town is the gateway to the Frisian Lakes. If you're seriously interested in improving your sailing technique, there are generations of expertise concentrated around here.

Information

Library (☎ 42 30 23; Wijde Noorderhorne 1; internet per hr €2; ☺ 1.30-8pm Mon & Thu, 10.30am-8pm Tue, 10.30am-5.30pm Wed & Fri, 10.30am-1pm Sat) Has internet access.

Main post office (Martiniplein 15A) In the heart of town.

Tourist office (☎ 41 40 96; www.vvvsneek.nl; Marktstraat 18; ☺ 9.30am-6pm Mon-Fri, 9.30am-5pm Sat) Has long lists of boat rental and charter firms, sailing schools and more, and shares its office with the ANWB.

Sights & Activities

You won't find many conventional sights here in Sneek, given its overwhelming bias towards the water. The **Waterpoort** dates from 1613 and is the former gateway to the old port. Its twin towers are local landmarks. Across from the tourist office, the **town hall** (Marktstraat 15) is an excellent example of the breed. The town's best museum, the **Fries Scheepvaart Museum** (☎ 41 40 57; Kleinzand 14; adult/child €3/1; ☺ 10am-5pm Mon-Sat, noon-5pm Sun), is a maritime museum focusing on local seafaring life.

Sleeping & Eating

The tourist office has lists of local rooms from around €20 to €25 per person.

De Domp Camping (☎ 41 25 59; www.dedomp.nl; Domp 4; camp site €12.50) This lush camp site is about a 20-minute walk from town; follow the signs for the *zwembad* (public swimming pool). It's very well organised and there are some sites for hikers that are well away from the vehicles.

De Wijnberg (☎ 41 24 21; Marktstraat 23; s/d €54/74) Directly opposite the tourist office is this standard hotel, with basic rooms that are spartan and clean, and more expensive varieties with bathtub. The restaurant-pub on the ground floor is often lively and convivial.

Cafe De Draai (☎ 42 28 66; Wijde Noorderhorne 13; mains €10; ⏰ lunch & dinner Mon-Sat). Sneek isn't wallowing in fine restaurants, but there are a few spots along Wijde Noorderhorne which will do, including this cheap and cheerful café, which has a relaxed vibe, a barrel-load of beer varieties, and daily specials.

Getting There & Around

From the train station (which now sports a model train museum), the centre of town is a five-minute walk along Stationstraat. Trains to/from Leeuwarden cost €4 (20 minutes, two per hour).

The friendly staff at **Rijwielhandel Twa Tsjillen** (☎ 41 38 78; Wijde Noorderhorne 8; per day €5) rents bikes.

HARLINGEN (HARNS)

☎ 0517 / pop 15,600

Of all the old Frisian ports, only Harlingen has kept its link to the sea. It still plays an important role for shipping in the area, and is the base for ferries to Terschelling and Vlieland.

Harlingen has also managed to retain a semblance of its architectural history; much of the attractive centre is a preserved zone of pretty 16th- and 18th-century buildings.

Information

Several banks with ATMs can be found on Voorstraat, Harlingen's main street.

Post office (Grote Bredeplaats 6) Two hundred metres from the ferry terminal.

Tourist office (☎ 09005400001; www.vvv-harlingen.nl; Noorderhaven 50; ⏰ 1-5pm Mon, 10am-noon & 1-5pm Tue-Fri, 10am-4pm Sat May-Oct, 10am-noon & 1-5pm Tue-Fri, 10am-2pm Sat Nov-Apr) Offers brochures on the town and its surrounds, and will book accommodation.

Sights & Activities

Harlingen is best enjoyed on foot. Stroll along the canals, especially Noorderhaven, with its many yachts, and Zuiderhaven.

The **Gemeentemuseum het Hannemahuis** (☎ 41 36 58; Voorstraat 56; adult/child €2.50/1; ⏰ 1.30-5pm Tue-Sat Apr-Jun & Oct-Nov, 10am-5pm Tue-Sat, 1.30-5pm Sun Jul-Sep, closed Dec-Mar) is housed in an 18th-century building and includes material on Harlingen's past as a whaling town. Along with farming, whaling was one of the industries that made Friesland one of the most prosperous regions in the Netherlands in the 1700s. Hence the celebration of flensing and flensers – the process of stripping blubber from a whale's carcass, and the lucky chaps who got to do it.

Sleeping

Zeezicht Harlingen (☎ 41 25 36; www.hollandhotels.nl; Zuiderhaven 1; s/d €60/87.50) Zeezicht may be part of a chain, but it's by no means generic. Rooms

---

SNEEK'S WATERSPORTS BONANZA

Sneek is surrounded by water, and any activity associated with it – particularly if it involves wind, of which there is hardly ever a shortage – is big in Sneek.

Several sailing and windsurfing schools, where you can learn from scratch or top up existing skills, operate in the area. One of the largest is **Zeilschool de Friese Meren** (☎ 41 21 41; www .zfm.nl; Eeltjebaasweg 7), which has a range of courses. The tourist office has a long list of various operators and services available.

If you'd just prefer to watch sleek ships skip across the water, then sail into town around the beginning of August to catch **Sneekweek** (www.sneekweek.nl), the largest sailing event on Europe's inland waters. You'll be treated to plenty of racing activity and lots of frivolity.

During the summer months there are **boat cruises** on the local waters. The schedules change by whim, weather and number of operators each season. Most leave from the Oosterkade, at the end of Kleinzand, so either wander over or inquire at the tourist office.

ATYPICAL ACCOMMODATION

For such a small town, Harlingen has some surprisingly unusual places to spend the night.

The **Havenkraan van Harlingen** (Haven; r €299), a crane turned hotel, is the easiest to book. Its one room is well above average and the sunset views from the small lounge will melt the hardest heart. Best of all, though, the crane still functions; you can turn it in any direction you wish.

A little harder to tricky to swing (with a few-months-long waiting list) is the **Reddingsboot Harlingen** (Noorderhaven; r €229). This former life boat – that's still good to go – offers plush (albeit small) rooms with stunning extras such as a classic wooden bathtub. It's also possible to push the boat out, literally – the owners can organise trips romantic and otherwise.

The most sought-after accommodation of all is the **Vuurtoren van Harlingen** (Havenweg 1; r €279). This, Harlingen's former lighthouse, has one stunning room with all manner of luxuries and nonpareil views, and – fortunately – the light no longer works. The catch is a two-year waiting list.

For more information on all three, check the website www.vuurtoren-harlingen.nl. Bookings can be made through the **Workum tourist office** (☎ 0515-54 05 50; bc@friesekust.nl; Noard 5).

---

are in great order, and some have views of the town's harbour, while the downstairs café-bar is comfortable and atmospheric and comes with a warm winter garden.

Eating

Restaurant Noorderpoort (☎ 41 50 43; Noorderhaven 17; mains €17-25; ☿ lunch & dinner) Noorderport occupies a sunny spot on one of the town's canals, and has views of the ferry port. The casual menu mixes Dutch food with French flourishes. Otherwise try the sandwiches at the adjoining café.

Getting There & Away

Harlingen is connected to Leeuwarden (€4.50, 22 minutes) by two trains hourly; most run directly to the harbour, from where it's a short walk to the ferry terminal. For ferry details to Vlieland and Terschelling, see p239 and p241 respectively.

FRANEKER (FRJENTSJER)

☎ 0517 / pop 21,000

About 6km east of Harlingen, the quaint town of Franeker was once a big player in education, until Napoleon closed its university down in 1810. Today its well preserved centre makes for a fine hour's stroll, but Franeker's highlight is its planetarium.

The **Eise Eisinga Planetarium** (☎ 39 30 70; www .planetarium-friesland.nl; Eise Eisingastraat 3; adult/child €3.50/2.75; ☿ 10am-5pm Tue-Sat, 1-5pm Sun year-round, 1-5pm Mon Apr-Oct) is the world's oldest working planetarium. The namesake owner was a tradesman with a serious sideline in cosmic mathematics and astrology, who clearly could

have been a 'somebody' in the astronomical world. Beginning in 1774, he built the planetarium himself to show how the heavens actually worked. It's startling to contemplate how Eisinga could have devised a mechanical timing system built to a viewable working scale that could encompass and illustrate so many different variables of time and motion.

The Harlingen–Leeuwarden train stops in Franeker (from Leeuwarden €3.30, 17 minutes, two hourly), 500m from the centre.

HINDELOOPEN (HYLPEN)

☎ 0514 / pop 1100

Huddled up against the banks of the IJsselmeer, Hindeloopen has been set apart from Friesland for centuries. Until recently, the local women still wore characteristic green and red costumes that were similar to the also characteristic hand-carved furniture.

With its narrow streets, tiny canals, little bridges, long waterfront, and lack of traffic, Hindeloopen makes for a beautiful afternoon escape. In extraordinarily cold winters it is one of the key towns on the route of the Elfstedentocht (see the boxed text, p238) and has a quaint yet reverent museum devoted to the race.

Other coastal towns in the area worth a peek, if you have time, are pretty Makkum and busy Workum; both towns are north of Hindeloopen.

Information

The staff at the **tourist office** (☎ 52 25 50; Nieuwstad 26; ☿ 10.30am-4pm Mon, Wed & Sat) can help with accommodation. For banks and supermarkets, you'll have to go 4km north to Workum.

A DAY AT THE RACES

Skating and the Dutch culture are interwoven and no event better symbolises this than the **Elfstedentocht** (Eleven Cities Race; www.elfstedentocht.nl). Begun officially in 1909, although it had been held for hundreds of years before that, the race is 200km long, starts and finishes in Leeuwarden and passes through 10 Frisian towns (11 including Leeuwarden): Sneek, IJlst, Sloten, Stavoren, Hindeloopen, Workum, Bolsward, Harlingen, Franeker and Dokkum. The record time for completing the race is six hours and 47 minutes, set in 1985.

While it is a marathon, what makes the race a truly special event is that it can only be held in years when it's cold enough for all the canals to freeze totally; this has only happened 15 times since 1909. The last time was in 1997. So how do you schedule such an event? You don't.

Instead, there is a huge Elfstedentocht committee that waits for the mercury to plummet. When it looks as though the canals will be properly frozen, 48 hours' notice is given. All work effectively ends throughout the province as armies of volunteers make preparations for the race, and the thousands of competitors get ready.

On the third day, the race begins at 5.30am. The next few hours are a holiday for the rest of the Netherlands as well, as the population gathers around TVs to watch the live coverage.

Sights & Activities

Hindeloopen is best experienced at a slow pace. If, however, you need a diversion, head for the **Het Eerste Friese Schaatsmuseum** (☎ 52 16 83; www.schaatsmuseum.nl; Kleine Weide 1-3; adult/child €1.50/1.15; ☉ 10am-6pm Mon-Sat, 1-5pm Sun) which focuses on the Elfstedentocht and ice skating in general. The detailed descriptions, pictures and displays of manufacturing techniques and developments in skating technology through the centuries – including clogs with spikes – is quite enthralling, as is the history of the Elfstedentocht.

The race is covered in biographical summaries for each winner of the event, and current record holder and two-time champ Evert van Benthem (in 1985 and '86), a modern-day legend, receives plenty of coverage.

Sleeping & Eating

Camping Hindeloopen (☎ 52 14 52; www.camping hindeloopen.nl; Westerdijk 9; camp site €19.50) To the south of the town behind the protective dyke is this large camping ground, with beach access, windsurfing school, and restaurant on site.

De Stadsboerderij (☎ 52 12 78; info@skutsjearrange menten.nl; Nieuwe Weide 9; s/d €45/70) With comfy rooms in a quiet corner of town, De Stadsboerderij can guarantee a peaceful night's sleep. There's also a restaurant-pub next door, with photos of boats sailing the IJsselmeer at uncomfortable angles.

There's a sprinkling of restaurants and cheap fried-fish places overlooking the town's harbour.

Getting There & Away

The train stop is a pleasant 2.5km walk from town. There is an hourly service to Sneek (€3.70, 18 minutes) and Leeuwarden (€6.70, 40 minutes).

FRISIAN ISLANDS

Friesland's four islands – Vlieland, Terschelling, Ameland and Schiermonnikoog – are collectively known as the Frisian Islands. Despite the fact that they're basically raised banks of sand and mud (with plenty of introduced pine forests to stabilise them), they are a popular target for many city-bound Dutch (and a fair few Germans too) looking to escape the crowds and enjoy a rural beach holiday during the warmer summer months.

Each of the islands has been developed with tourism in mind, and the number of *pensions*, hotels, and rooms and cottages for rent is staggering, considering the islands' size. Despite the development, all have large open spaces where you can get close to the sea grasses or the water itself. Any of the islands makes an interesting trip on its own and there are copious bicycle-rental options near the ferry ports. Paths suitable for hiking and biking circle each of the islands and, away from the built-up areas, you're rewarded with long sandy beaches on the seaward sides.

In summer the islands are very crowded, so don't just show up and expect to find a room; populations routinely multiply by 10 on warm weekends.

Getting There & Away

Almost daily ferries link the islands with the mainland. Island hopping is, however, a bit of a headache, even in the busy summer months. **Rederij Doeksen** (☎ 44 20 02; www.rederij-doeksen.nl) links Vlieland and Terschelling throughout the year, but times change on a frequent basis; it's best to consult the online timetable before making solid plans. Day trips are possible, but you'll have to catch the earliest ferry, although you're better off spending a couple of nights enjoying the island atmosphere.

Vlieland

☎ 0562 / pop 1200

Historically the most isolated of the islands, Vlieland is still ignored by most tourists today. It's a windswept and wild place, with much of its western end at the mercy of sand and sea, but this is part of its charm. The sole town, Oost-Vlieland, is small, and only residents are allowed to bring cars across on the ferry.

INFORMATION

The **tourist office** (☎ 45 11 11; www.vlieland.net; Havenweg 10; internet per hr €6; ☺ 9am-5pm Mon-Fri, 1hr after each ferry arrival Sat & Sun) is as helpful as ever, and has internet access.

SIGHTS & ACTIVITIES

There's not much in the way of human-made attractions on Vlieland, and that's exactly the point: nature is the attraction. Most of the 72 sq km of island lies waiting to be explored by bike or on foot, although its 18km of beaches aren't as much fun to cycle as the untamed interior. Depending on how fit you consider yourself, cycling around Vlieland can be gen-

tle or moderately gruelling; there are many unsealed tracks that confident 'off-roaders' can opt to tackle, opening great new sightseeing possibilities.

For nature hikes and bird-watching walks, consult the tourist office.

SLEEPING & EATING

You will certainly not starve on Vlieland, but the range of eateries on the island is quite small. Sleeping options are another story, although over the summer months, and on sunny weekends, be sure to book ahead.

Camping Stortemelk (☎ 45 12 25; www.stortemelk .nl; Kampweg 1; camp site per person/tent €5.70/4.40) Stortemelk is a typically beachy camp site, with little wind protection but close proximity to sandy beaches and introduced forest. There's a small restaurant, playground and shop on site.

Pension Hotelletje de Veerman (☎ 45 13 78; www .pensiondeveerman.nl; Dorpsstraat 173, Oost-Vlieland; s/d from €40/60) Veerman is very much a homy *pension*, with friendly owners and cosy communal areas. The rooms are basic and filled with mismatching furniture, but they're fine if you're just looking for a bed for the night.

GETTING THERE & AROUND

Regular ferries (return adult/child €20.85/ 10.95, bicycle €10.85) to Vlieland, which leave from Harlingen, take approximately 90 minutes and generally depart at 8.45am, 1.30pm and 7.30pm daily from May to September; in the winter months, there's a 2.30pm sailing Wednesday to Monday, and sometimes an extra one at 9am. A fast service (return adult/child €24.80/14.90), taking around 45

SHIPWRECKED SHOES

Terschelling and its residents are used to all manner of flotsam and jetsam washing up on its northerly beaches, but beachcombers on the morning of 10 February 2006 were treated to an unusual sight, even for these parts – thousands upon thousands of shoes.

The previous night the P&O ship *Mondriaan* was hit by a particularly nasty storm and lost a load of containers overboard. The currents took the booty – which consisted not only of shoes but also briefcases, toys and meat – directly to Terschelling's beaches. Most containers remained sealed, but some had spilled a purported 100,000 pairs of shoes into the North Sea. News soon spread of the veritable goldmine, and locals rushed to find a pair of hiking boots and trainers that would fit (which, when hunting through 200,000 shoes, isn't that easy).

Such a find is a rarity, however – prior to this, the last good opportunity for beachcombing occurred around 15 years ago. But you may still be able to get in on the action; some B&B owners managed to collect dozens of pairs and will sell them to guests (no questions asked, of course) for as little as €5.

FRISIAN ISLANDS

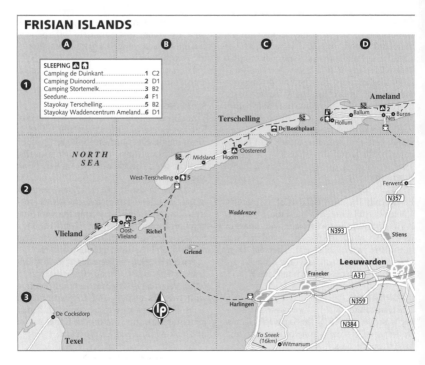

SLEEPING
Camping de Duinkant.....................1	C2
Camping Duinoord...........................2	D1
Camping Stortemelk.......................3	B2
Seedune...4	F1
Stayokay Terschelling....................5	B2
Stayokay Waddencentrum Ameland..6	D1

minutes direct and 90 minutes via Terschelling, also operates from Harlingen; it's very irregular, so check the timetable online before making plans. Ferries also sail to nearby Texel over the summer months; see Texel (p170) for more details.

You can cycle (bike hire around €6) around the island, and there is also a little bus that wanders the few roads of Oost Vlieland.

Terschelling

☎ 0562 / pop 4800

At 110 sq km, Terschelling is the largest of the Frisian Islands; it's also the most visited and commercial. Its small villages, of which West-Terschelling is the largest, are strung out along the southern edge of the island, while its northern coast is all sand dunes and white beaches. The eastern end of the island is a wild and isolated place, and perfect for escaping the crowds.

The smaller villages of Hoorn and Oosterend are east of West-Terschelling and much less commercial, but closer to the very pretty natural parts of the island. Like the other islands, cars are best left on the mainland.

INFORMATION

The **tourist office** (☎ 44 30 00; www.vvv-terschelling.nl; Willem Barentszkade 19A, West-Terschelling; internet per hr €6; 9.30am-5.30pm Mon-Fri, 10am-3pm Sat) is incredibly helpful, with a great range of maps for cycling or walking (around €3.40). They will book hotels and *pensions* for €7.50.

SIGHTS & ACTIVITIES

De Boschplaat, a huge car-free natural reserve at the eastern end of the island, is the highlight of the island. It is the only EU-designated European Natural Monument in the Netherlands.

The **Terschelling Museum 't Behouden Huys** (☎ 44 23 89; www.behouden-huys.nl; Commandeurstraat 30-32; adult/child €3/2; 10am-5pm Mon-Fri, 1-5pm Sat Apr-Oct, also 1-5pm Sun mid-Jun–Sep, closed Oct-Mar) covers the island's maritime past.

FESTIVALS & EVENTS

The annual **Oerol** outdoor performance festival on Terschelling is revered nationwide as a perfect excuse for going offshore. It started years ago with farmers letting their cows run loose one day each year (hence the name *oerol*, which means 'everywhere' or 'all over') –

these days, *everybody* gets into the spirit of things. It's a wild, arty party, piercing the otherwise unflappable northern façade for 10 days towards the end of June.

SLEEPING & EATING

Camping de Duinkant (☎ 44 89 17; camp sites per person/tent €3.20/2.75) This basic camping ground at the eastern end of the main road is just a farmer's field, with no cooking facilities. It is, however, lovely and remote, with nothing but green pastures and sand dunes as neighbours.

Stayokay Terschelling (☎ 44 23 38; terschelling@ stayokay.com; Burg van Heusdenweg 39, West-Terschelling; dm/s/d €25/45/66) Just outside West Terschelling's borders, this suitably standard Stayokay hostel has rooms in good nick, a small restaurant, and a kids' playground.

Hotel Buren (☎ 44 22 26; Mentzstraat 20, West-Terschelling; s/d €50/60) On a quiet street in the heart of West-Terschelling is Buren, a welcoming little B&B. Its rooms are spotless and bright, with personal touches like heart-shaped sinks.

Also recommended:

Zeezicht (☎ 44 22 68; Willem Barentszkade 20, West-Terschelling; mains €12-20; ☺ lunch & dinner) Views

of the sea and harbour, large scale tall-ship models, and plenty of seafood specials.

De Heeren Van Der Schelling (☎ 44 87 80; Oosterend; mains €11-20; ☺ lunch & dinner Thu-Mon) One of the quietest spots on the island in peaceful Oosterend, with a large sun-drenched patio.

GETTING THERE & AROUND

Ferries (return adult/child €20.55/9.85, bicycle €10.85) leave from Harlingen for Terschelling and are operated by **Rederij Doeksen** (☎ 44 20 02; www.rederij-doeksen.nl). The large car ferries take two hours and generally depart at 9.45am and 3pm daily, with an extra couple of services in July and August. The faster hydrofoil service (return adult/child €24.50/13.80) takes around 45 minutes and normally sails at 7.30am, 11.15am and 4.30pm from May to October, and 10am, 4.30pm and 6.20pm November to April.

Hourly buses (day-ticket €5) run the length of the main road; bicycles can be hired for as little as €4.50, and some bicycle rental places will also deliver bikes to the ferry, and transport your luggage to your accommodation.

Ameland
☎ 0519 / pop 3600

If the Frisian Islands were given personalities, Ameland would be the person sitting on the fence. Its four peaceful villages – Buren, Nes, Ballum and Hollum – are less developed than those on Terschelling and Texel, but they provide enough social structure for the majority of tourists. Its large swaths of untouched natural splendour offer places to escape the crowds, but Mother Nature doesn't rule the roost as on Schiermonnikoog or Vlieland.

All in all, Ameland is an island for those looking for a nice balance.

INFORMATION

The island's main **tourist office** (☎ 54 65 46; www .vvv-ameland.nl; Rixt van Doniastraat, Nes; ☺ 9am-12.30pm & 1.30-5.30pm Mon-Fri, 10am-3pm Sat) is seven minutes' walk, or one bus stop, from the ferry terminal. It has plenty of information on the island, including an excellent map (€3.75), and internet access (per hour €3), but doesn't book B&Bs.

SIGHTS & ACTIVITIES

At only 85 sq km in size, Ameland is easily tackled by pedal power. **Bicycle paths** cover the entire island, and include a 27km bicycle path that runs almost the entire length of northern shore just south of protective sand dunes. The eastern third of the island is given over to a combination of wetlands and dunes, with not a settlement in sight; it's by far the best place to take time out for yourself.

Of the villages, the 18th-century former whaling port of **Nes** is the prettiest and most carefully preserved (although all are interesting for a brief stroll), its streets lined with tidy little brick houses. **Hollum**, the most western village, has windswept dunes within easy walk, and is in sight of a famous red and white **lighthouse** (adult/child €3.50/2.50; 10am-5pm & 7-9pm Tue-Sat, 1-5pm & 7-9pm Sun) with expansive views.

SLEEPING & EATING

All four villages have accommodation options, although Nes is the most convenient, being a hop, skip and a jump from the ferry port.

Stayokay Waddencentrum Ameland (55 53 53; ameland@stayokay.com; Oranjeweg 59; dm/s/d €25/45/66) This Stayokay establishment is 200m west of the lighthouse outside Hollum. The atmosphere is decidedly summer-camp, rooms are basic but in great condition, and sand dunes are literally outside the doorstep. Meals, pack lunches and bicycles can also be ordered.

Zeewinde (54 65 00; www.zeewinde.nl; Torenstraat 22, Nes; r from €75) It may be a Best Western, but Zeewinde has just as much character as most hotels on the island. Its brand new rooms are neither large nor small, but do include a kitchenette and bathtub, which is welcome relief after a day on a bike (which can be rented from reception).

Camping Duinoord (54 20 70; Jan van Eijckweg 4; camp site/car €12.40/1.50) This camp site is only 2km north of Nes, right near the beach. It's exposed to the wind and has very few facilities, but shops, restaurants and an expansive playground (ie the beach) are all close by.

Herberg De Zwaan (55 40 02; Zwaneplein 6; mains €16-20; lunch & dinner) De Zwaan is a quaint restaurant in the heart of Hollum and has a menu heavily laden with fish dishes, which is always a good sign for an island eatery. The building dates from 1772, which equates to wood-beam ceilings and plenty of arches.

GETTING THERE & AROUND

Wagenborg (54 61 11; www.wpd.nl; adult/child return €11.25/5.95, bicycle €7.45, car €75.85) operates ferries between Nes and the large ferry port at Hol-

werd on the mainland. The latter has a large parking area for people who sensibly forgo taking cars to the island. The ferries run almost every two hours (45 minutes) all year from 7.30am to 7.30pm, hourly on Friday and Saturday from June to August.

To reach the Holwerd ferry terminal from Leeuwarden, take bus 66 (40 minutes, hourly); a ticket covering this bus, the ferry and a bus ride on the island, can be purchased at the Leeuwarden train station (p235) for €23.10.

Taxis and a small network of public buses that serve the island's four towns meet the ferries. Bicycles can be rented all over the island.

Schiermonnikoog
 0519 / pop 1000

The smallest and most serene of the Frisian Islands, Schiermonnikoog is the place to get away from it all; the feeling of sheer isolation as you move through Schiermonnikoog's 40 sq km, or along the 18km of beaches, can be quite moving. Its name means 'grey monk island', a reference to the 15th-century clerics who once lived here; however all traces of these folk are gone and the island is mostly wild. The Dutch government made Schiermonnikoog a national park in 1989, so the wilderness should remain unfettered.

The island's sole town, Schiermonnikoog, is quiet, even when crowded. Nonresidents are not allowed to bring cars onto the island.

INFORMATION

The **tourist office** (53 12 33; www.vvvschiermonnik oog.nl; Reeweg 5; internet per hr €3; 9am-12.30pm & 1-5.30pm Mon-Fri, to 4.30pm Sat) is in the middle of town and can fill you in on all you need to know about the island.

SIGHTS & ACTIVITIES

The sights and activities on the island revolve around one thing – the great outdoors. The best idea is to grab a map, rent a bike, pack a picnic, and head off in any direction that takes your fancy. You'll come back pleasantly refreshed and ready to face the crowds back on the mainland.

If you require a little more information, head for the national park's **visitors centre** (53 16 41; Torenstreek 20; 10.30am-5.30pm Mon-Sat Apr-Oct, 1.30-5.30pm Sat Nov-Mar) in an old power station in town. It reveals the natural features of the island.

The island is the most popular destination for *wadlopers*, or 'mud-walkers' from the mainland (p251).

SLEEPING & EATING

Schiermonnikoog has very few hotels and B&Bs, but plenty of bungalows and apartments; cafés line the few streets of downtown Schiermonnikoog.

Seedune (☎ 53 13 98; www.schiermonnikoog.net /seedune; Seeduneweg 1; camp site per person/tent €4.10/2.90) Just north of town, this huge camp site (room for 800 tents) is, as expected, sandy, windswept and isolated, which for many will be absolutely perfect.

Pension Lulu (☎ 53 13 06; www.pensionlulu.nl; Langestreek 70; r per person €28.50) Lulu is a quiet, family *pension* with simple, comfortable rooms. Each room has a sink, but the toilet and shower is shared with other guests.

GETTING THERE & AWAY

Wagenborg (☎ 09004554455; www.wpd.nl; adult/child return €11.85/6.55, bicycles €7.45) runs ferries between Schiermonnikoog and the port of Lauwersoog in Groningen province. At least three ferries daily make the 45-minute voyage; the first sails at 6.30am, the last at 5.30pm. A bus meets all incoming ferries, which arrive at the island's port, for the 3km run into the town of Schiermonnikoog.

Bus 163 and bus 50 make the one-hour run to Lauwersoog five times daily from Groningen and Leeuwarden respectively.

Groningen & Drenthe

The provinces of Groningen and Drenthe are far from the tourist trails. Few visitors venture this far north, and if they happen to, choose the islands of Friesland for entertainment instead. This is all well and good, but it's also a shame, for they're missing out on the Netherlands' rural heart, a place where traditions are kept alive, and remnants of prehistoric residents dot the landscape.

Groningen may be the smaller of the two provinces, but it has the most going for it. Its capital, from which the region gained its name, is a delightful city with a cosmopolitan buzz and plenty of youthful energy (mainly due to its substantial student population). Museums, restaurants, bars, theatre, canals, festivals – you name it, the city has it. It's the centre of culture and entertainment in the north and aptly represented by the tourist office's bright orange G-spot logo.

The rest of Groningen province – a rural landscape blessed with a handful of intriguing attractions – is in sleepy contrast. In Pieterburen, even the hardest of hearts will empty their wallets in support of the Zeehondencreche, a refuge for sick seals. The town is also the base for the bizarre pastime of *wadlopen* (mud-walking). Bourtange, on the eastern border to Germany, makes the shortlist for 'Best Fortified Town in the Land'; its hefty defences are just as forbidding now as they were in the 16th century.

Drenthe is an agricultural province, no question. Paddocks of farmland are separated by pockets of woodlands, creating a peaceful environment meant for slow exploration; the only disturbance is the occasional whiff of 'farm' smells. Drenthe's biggest draw is its *hunebedden*, prehistoric rock masses purportedly used as burial chambers, but the likes of Orvelte, a village with one foot firmly planted in the 19th century, will also interest many travellers.

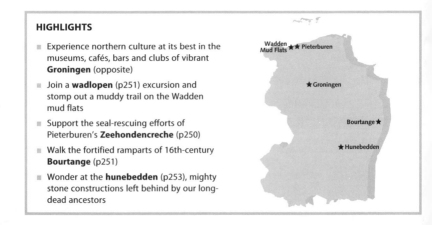

HIGHLIGHTS

- Experience northern culture at its best in the museums, cafés, bars and clubs of vibrant **Groningen** (opposite)
- Join a **wadlopen** (p251) excursion and stomp out a muddy trail on the Wadden mud flats
- Support the seal-rescuing efforts of Pieterburen's **Zeehondencreche** (p250)
- Walk the fortified ramparts of 16th-century **Bourtange** (p251)
- Wonder at the **hunebedden** (p253), mighty stone constructions left behind by our long-dead ancestors

Wadden ★★ Pieterburen
Mud Flats

★ Groningen

Bourtange ★

★ Hunebedden

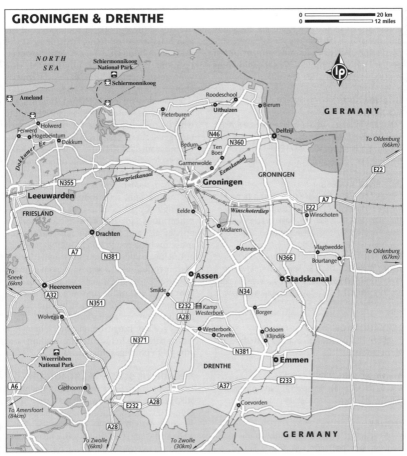

GRONINGEN & DRENTHE

0 — 20 km
0 — 12 miles

GRONINGEN

Like Utrecht, Groningen is a small province named after its primary city. Beyond the buzzing town itself, farmland dominates the landscape in every direction, but among the polders, cows and sheep are a few attributes worth seeking out. If mud, mud and more mud is your thing, then the northern coast will appeal, though the scenery is best near the German border around the fortified town of Bourtange.

GRONINGEN CITY
☎ 050 / pop 177,300
Looking at a map of the Netherlands, Groningen seems a long way from anywhere (we're talking Dutch distances here, not Texan), but looks can be deceiving.

This vibrant, youthful city of the north is very much part of the comings and goings of the country, and has everything you'd expect of a progressive metropolis. Its student population (which has been around since 1614 when the university opened) of 20,000 ensures a healthy and hedonistic nightlife exists alongside the art museums, theatre and classical concerts its more mature, established residents demand. And like everywhere in this waterlogged country, you'll find gabled houses reflected in still canals.

Orientation
The old centre, which can be crossed on foot in 15 minutes, is nicely compact and

entirely ringed by canals. The train station is just across from the Groninger Museum, and around a 10-minute walk from Grote Markt, the main town square. Virulent anticar policies dating from the 1970s mean that the centre is pleasantly free of traffic.

Information

BOOKSHOPS

Scholtens Wristers (☎ 317 25 00; Guldenstraat 20; ⏰ 11am-6pm Mon, 9.30am-6pm Tue, Wed, Fri & Sat, 9.30am-9pm Thu) Large selection of English novels and travel titles on the ground floor.

INTERNET ACCESS

Library (☎ 368 36 83; Oude Boteringestraat 18; per hr €2; ⏰ 1-8pm Mon, 10am-6pm Wed & Fri, 10am-8pm Thu, 11am-4pm Sat, 1-4pm Sun) Main city library with lines of computers offering internet access.

LAUNDRY

Handy Wash (☎ 318 75 87; Schuitendiep 58; wash & dry €7; ⏰ 7.30am-8pm) Small laundry in a row of cafés and bars; perfect for dropping off the washing and grabbing a coffee next door.

LEFT LUGGAGE

Lockers can be found on platform 2b at the train station.

MEDICAL SERVICES

UMCG (☎ 361 61 61; Hanzeplein 1) Teaching hospital with the added bonus of an anatomy museum.

MONEY

ATMs can be found throughout town.
GWK (⏰ 8am-7pm) Currency exchange; in the train station.

POST

Post office (☎ 313 63 75; Munnekeholm 1)

TOURIST INFORMATION

Tourist office (☎ 09002023050; www.vvvgroningen .nl; Grote Markt 25; ⏰ 9am-6pm Mon-Fri, 10am-5pm Sat year-round, 11am-3pm Sun Jul & Aug) Offers advice on a wide range of topics and sells tickets, tours, a handy map (€2) and more.

Sights & Activities

GRONINGER MUSEUM

Arriving by train it's impossible to miss the **Groninger Museum** (☎ 366 65 55; www.groninger -museum.nl; Museumeiland 1; adult/child €8/4; ⏰ 10am-5pm Tue-Sun year-round, noon-5pm Mon Jul & Aug). Occupy-

ing three islands in the middle of the canal in front of the station, the museum is, at the very least, a schizophrenic structure that will draw an opinion from any viewer. However, opinions vary wildly, from a breathtaking venture in form and design, to statements along the lines of 'Why?'

This colourful, oddly shaped museum was the brainchild of architect Alessandro Mendini, who invited three 'guest architects' to each tackle a section. This explains why, to most, the museum has little consistency and appears thrown together at a whim. Inside, things are quite different though; bright, pastel colours add life to the large, square exhibition rooms, and natural light seeps in from all angles.

Originally intended as a permanent exhibition house for historical pieces, modern applied arts and other regional artworks, the museum hit a rough patch in 1998 when its entire lower floor flooded. Fortunately, some of the precious works were saved and now appear well above the water level in the bronze tower. The rest of the museum is devoted to temporary exhibitions, which, like the curatorial direction, are a wonderfully eclectic mix; you'll see anything from classic Golden Age Dutch paintings to futuristic installations and 10m-high photographic portraits.

NOORDELIJK SCHEEPVAARTMUSEUM

Well worth an hour or two, the **Noordelijk Scheepvaartmuseum** (Northern Shipping Museum; ☎ 312 22 02; www.noordelijkscheepvaartmuseum.nl; Brugstraat 24-26; adult/child €3/1.60; ⏰ 10am-5pm Tue-Sat, 1-5pm Sun) is well funded and well organised. The museum is laid out over several floors of buildings that once comprised a 16th-century distillery. Just getting through the labyrinth of 18 rooms is an adventure in itself and guarantees an excellent workout.

Highlights of the museum include an intricately carved replica of the church at Paramaribo – the capital of former Dutch colony Surinam – in a bottle (Room 3), showing just how much time sailors had to kill on long voyages, and detailed models demonstrating just how the many local shipyards operated throughout the centuries (Room 8). After Room 8, there are three rooms devoted to the **Niemeyer Tabaksmuseum** (Niemeyer Tobacco Museum), which is dedicated to the smoking habits of the Dutch through the ages. Unsurprisingly, it looks as though some of the dummies aren't just toking on tobacco.

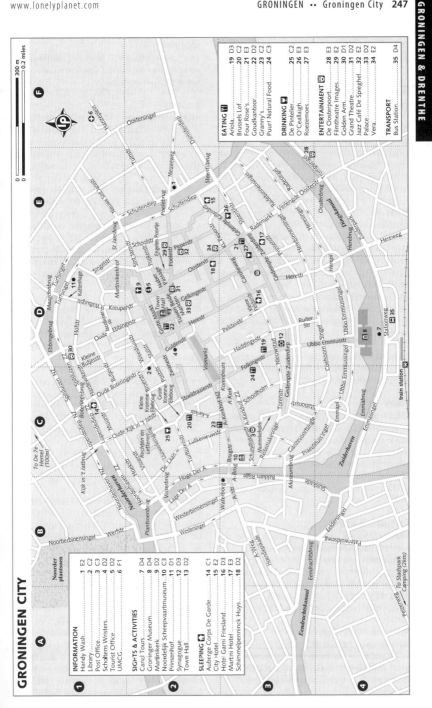

GRONINGEN CITY

INFORMATION
Handy Wash...................................1 E2
Library...2 C2
Post Office....................................3 C3
Schotens Wristers..........................4 D2
Tourist Office...............................5 D2
UMCG..6 F1

SIGHTS & ACTIVITIES
Canal Tours..................................7 D4
Groninger Museum........................8 D4
Martinikerk..................................9 D2
Noordelijk Scheepvaartmuseum...10 C3
Prinsenhof..................................11 D1
Synagogue..................................12 D3
Town Hall...................................13 D2

SLEEPING
Auberge Corps De Garde..............14 C1
City Hotel...................................15 E2
Hote. Garni Friesland...................16 D3
Martni Hotel...............................17 E3
Schimmelpeninck Huys................18 D2

EATING
Ariola..19 D3
Brussels Lof................................20 C2
Four Rose's.................................21 E3
Goudkantoor...............................22 D2
Granny's.....................................23 C3
Puurl Natural Food.......................24 C3

DRINKING
De Pinteller.................................25 C2
O'Ceallaigh.................................26 E3
Rozemoes....................................27 E3

ENTERTAINMENT
De Oosterpoort............................28 E3
Filmtheatre Images......................29 D1
Golden Arm.................................30 D1
Grand Theatre.............................31 D2
Jazz Café De Spieghel..................32 D2
Palace...33 D2
Vera..34 E2

TRANSPORT
Bus Station..................................35 D4

OTHER SIGHTS

The **Grote Markt** is a big, café-ringed square with little charm, but it does feature a few eye-catching buildings. The **town hall**, which dates from 1810, is one of them, but the 16th-century **Martinikerk** (☎ 311 12 77; Grote Markt; ☺ 11am-5pm Apr-Nov, noon-4pm Dec-Mar), at the northern corner of the Grote Markt, steals the show. Its tower, the Martinitoren, is 96m tall and is considered to have one of the most finely balanced profiles in the country. A climb (€3, purchase tickets at tourist office) to the top yields stellar views.

Just southwest of the Grote Markt, **Vismarkt** is a more intimate and attractive square, and not far south of Vismarkt is one of the few working **synagogues** (☎ 312 31 51; Folkingestraat 60; adult/child €1/free) left in the country. It began life a century ago as a mosque (the light arches and minarets are dead giveaways) but now houses a school and temporary exhibition space; its beautifully restored wooden ceiling is one of the interior's highlights. Check Tourist Office for opening times.

If you're exploring the northeastern corner of the city, take a breather at the serene **gardens** (Turfsingel; admission free; ☺ 10am-dusk) of **Prinsenhof**, a 16th-century mansion.

Tours

Canal tours (☎ 312 83 79; www.rondvaartbedrijfkool .nl; adult/child €7.50/5) Tours of the city's largest canals take approximately 60 minutes and leave from in front of the train station anywhere between one and six times daily, depending on the season.

City walks (☎ 0900-2023050; adult €4; ☺ 1pm Mon-Sat) The tourist office operates guided 90-minute walks conducted in Dutch only.

Festivals & Events

Noorderslag (www.eurosonic.nl; mid-Jan) A series of concerts by up-and-coming (they hope) bands.

Noorderzon (www.noorderzon.nl; mid-Aug) Eleven-day art festival featuring everything from theatre and music to children's entertainers and electronic installations.

Bommen Berend (28 Aug) Celebration of the day the city repelled the invading troops of the Bishop of Munster.

Studenten Cabaret Festival (www.gscf.nl; end Oct) Draws performers from around Europe.

Sint Maarten (11 Nov) Locally grown sugar beets are carved into lanterns by kids, not unlike what their US counterparts do to pumpkins two weeks earlier for Halloween.

Sleeping

The tourist office will book accommodation and carries a list of B&Bs and pensions starting at €20 per person.

BUDGET

Hotel Garni Friesland (☎ 312 13 07; ww.hotelfriesland .nl; Kleine Pelsterstraat; s/d €35/50) The Garni is bare bones, but it's in a good location on a street with several cafés and the prices are unbeatable. Service is friendly and amenable, and rooms are spartan yet highly adequate.

Stadspark Camping (☎ 525 16 24; www.stads campings.nl; Campinglaan 4; camp site €18; ☺ mid-Mar–mid-Oct) Stadspark is a spacious, green camp site surrounded by a huge park, yet is within easy shot of the city. Facilities include a shop, restaurant and playground for the kids; from the train station, take bus 4 (direction: Hoogkerk) about 3km west to the Stadspark stop.

MIDRANGE

City Hotel (☎ 588 65 65; www.edenhotelgroup.com; Gedempte Kattendiep 25; r from €75; ☒ ☺) This must be a good hotel – even the cleaners are happy. Rooms are standard business types, but they're a good bet for those requiring a few more creature comforts. Added bonuses include a rooftop deck, free coffee and tea on every floor, free internet and a fine location.

Martini Hotel (☎ 312 99 19; www.martinihotel.nl; Gedempte Zuiderdiep 8; r from €75; ☒ ☺) Like the City Hotel, the Martini is just far enough away from all the noise, yet close enough to provide easy access to the centre. Rooms are bright and airy, though lack character and warmth, but as this is Groningen's largest hotel, there are plenty of them.

Auberge Corps De Garde (☎ 314 54 37; www.corps degarde.nl; Oude Boteringestraat 72-74; r from €121) Originally the town guard's quarters, the Corps De Garde is an attractive listed building, and would be one of the city's finest hotels if its rooms weren't so bland. They are, however, big and well-lit, and the more expensive variety come with a bath.

TOP END

Schimmelpenninck Huys (☎ 318 95 02; www.schim melpenninckhuys.nl; Oosterstraat 53; d from €130; ☒) The Schimmelpenninck is Groningen's *grande dame*, and someone who likes to be draped in finery. The ground floor is occupied by a silver-service restaurant, pristine café, and beautician, while the rest of the building is filled with rooms ranging from simple, stylish standard doubles to suites with antique pieces and chandeliers.

Eating

Groningen may be a student city, but it still has a sizable smorgasbord of fine restaurants; some of our favourites are listed below, but there are plenty more to explore. Those self-catering can head to the organic food market on Tuesday at Vismarkt, and those looking for a quick fix will find Gedempte Zuiderdiep lined with cheap fast-food places and cafés.

Goudkantoor (☎ 589 18 88; Waagplein 1; mains €12-20; ☺ lunch & dinner) To be honest, the quality of the food at Goudkantoor doesn't matter; the architecture of this recently restored historical haunt is sustenance enough. Dating from 1635, the 'Gold Office' is a classic example of 17th century showmanship, with a gold-tinted exterior and graceful interior, complete with striking paintings. Truth be told though, the food (Dutch standards) is quite good.

our pick De 7e Hemel (7th Heaven; ☎ 314 51 41; Zuiderkerkstraat 7; mains €15-18; ☺ dinner Tue-Sat) De 7e Hemel, a short walk north of the centre, prides itself on the quality of what it serves its customers; it even goes as far as to import Scottish mineral water direct from the Glens because of its purity. The menu, a concoction of vegan, vegetarian, fish and meat dishes, is an ever-changing delight, and the cherubs, chandeliers and calming yellow shades all help to create a cosy, romantic air.

Puur! Natural Food (☎ 311 61 75; Folkingestraat 13; meals €3-7; ☺ lunch & dinner Mon-Sat) Puur! is health-food heaven; its bagels, sandwiches, salads and sweets are not only made from organic ingredients, they also taste divine. It's hard to pass over the coffee, tea and freshly squeezed juices on offer too, and everything is either eat-in or takeaway.

Four Rose's (☎ 314 38 87; Oosterstraat 71; mains €10-16; ☺ dinner) With the most authentic Mexican food in the province, and an atmosphere that amazingly suits both families and romantic couples, Four Rose's is an excellent bet for an evening meal. Its cocktails are highly rated too.

Ariola (☎ 318 19 48; Folkingestraat 54; meals from €3.50; ☺ lunch) The head-turning smells wafting from its doorway, and crowds milling inside, speak of only one thing: Ariola is an outstanding little Italian deli. Its *broodjes* (filled bread rolls) are made to order and only topped by the home-made pastas and lasagne.

Brussels Lof (☎ 312 76 03; A-Kerkstraat 24; mains €17-22; ☺ dinner Thu-Mon) This upmarket spot concentrates on seafood and vegetarian creations, and leaves the fancy décor to other establishments. Its mussels receive special mention, but basically anything you try here will be of the highest standard, and the service is professional with a capital 'P'.

Also worth mentioning is **Granny's** (☎ 318 91 117; A-Kerkhof NZ 43; apple tart from €1.60), which has the best apple tart to accompany a great cup of coffee or tea.

Drinking

Groningen's nightlife is centred on Poelestraat and its adjoining streets, although people flock to a multitude of bars scattered throughout the city.

O'Ceallaigh (☎ 314 76 94; Gedempte Kattendiep 13) Respected newspaper *Volkskrant* called O'Ceallaigh 'the best Irish pub in the Netherlands', and they were right; there's regular live music, even more regulars, Guinness and Murphy's on tap, and the atmosphere is thick with smoky and boisterous chatter.

Roezemoes (☎ 314 03 82; Gedempte Zuiderdiep 15) You can tell this gem of a brown café has been around a while; the bullet holes from the 1672 invasion attempt are a dead giveaway. Come evening, expect to find late-night drinking and the occasional blues band.

De Pintelier (☎ 318 51 00; Kleine Kromme Elleboog 9) The selection of beer and *jenevers* (ginlike liqueur) at this cosy bar reads like an encyclopaedia – at last count there were around 30 *jenevers* alongside 10 beers on tap. Its long wooden bar and thicket of tables date from the 1920s.

Entertainment

To find out what's going on around town, check out some of the posters that appear everywhere, or pick up a copy of either the simple and informative *Uit-Loper* (weekly) or meatier *Uit Magazine* (monthly); both are free and in Dutch.

CLUBS

Clubs open and close regularly in Groningen, but the ones listed here are all mainstayers:

Vera (☎ 313 46 81; www.vera-groningen.nl; Oosterstraat 44) The club to see the next big rock act at; U2 played to 30-odd people in the early 1980s here, and Nirvana later gave a performance to a crowd of about 60 people before going supernova. Concerts Thursday to Saturday.

Golden Arm (☎ 313 16 76; www.goldenarm.nl; Hardewikerstraat 7) Huge gay club with four floors of pumping dance music.

Palace (☎ 313 91 00; www.thepalace.nl; Gelkingestraat 1) Standard club attracting a predominantly young crowd with an array of music styles, and huge dance floor.

LIVE MUSIC

De Oosterpoort (☎ 368 03 68; www.de-oosterpoort .nl; Trompsingel) De Oosterpoort is *the* place in Groningen to catch many of the large musical acts passing through town. Jazz and classical concerts are the mainstay of its monthly programme.

Jazz Café De Spieghel (☎ 312 63 00; Peperstraat 11) A perennial favourite with locals – this lively brown café features regular live jazz music, a smooth sultry atmosphere, and a great bar.

THEATRE & CINEMA

Grand Theatre (☎ 314 46 44; www.grand-theatre.nl; Grote Markt 35) This, the city's premiere theatre, offers a thought-provoking array of musical and theatrical performances.

Filmtheatre Images (☎ 312 04 33; Poelestraat 30; tickets €8) With a mix of offbeat films, festival titles and classics, and a chilled café, Images is an excellent place to catch some cinema magic.

Getting There & Away

The 1896 train station, thankfully restored to its original glory, is worth seeing even if you're not catching a train.

Some train fares and schedules:

Destination	Price (€)	Duration (min)	Frequency (per hr)
Amsterdam	26.70	140	2
Leeuwarden	8.30	50	2
Rotterdam	29.60	160	2
Utrecht	24.50	120	2

The bus station is to the right as you exit the train station; the **Arriva bus office** (☼ 7am-11pm) is found opposite the train information office.

Getting Around

Groningen is easily tackled on foot or by bicycle, but if you plan to use the buses, one-day passes (€1) are available from drivers after 9am. Bus 6 connects Grote Markt to the train station, and bicycles can be rented from the **bicycle shop** (☎ 312 41 74) at the train station.

MUSEUM DE BUITENPLAATS

In the little town of Eelde, 5km south of Groningen, is this charming **museum** (☎ 050-309 58 18; www.museumdebuitenplaats.nl; Hoofdweg 76; adult/child Apr-Oct €7/3.30, Nov-Mar €5/2.50; ☼ 11am-5pm Tue-Sun) devoted to figurative art from around Europe. Opened in 1996 by the queen herself, it began as a protest to an apartment block originally planned for the site. The main organic structure, which blends into its natural surroundings, features paintings from some of the Netherlands' more progressive 20th-century artists, such as Wout Muller, Henk Helmantel, Herman Gordijn and Matthijs Röling. Its manicured gardens are peppered with sculptures, and benches aching to be used, and there's also a sun-bathed café. Poetry readings, storytelling and musical concerts are featured over the summer months on the museum's open-air stage.

To get there, take bus 52 (28 minutes, every half-hour) from Groningen.

ZEEHONDENCRECHE PIETERBUREN

Back in 1972 Lenie 't Hart, a resident of the small Groningen coastal town of Pieterburen, began caring for seals in her back yard. Pollution and tourism were taking their toll on the local seal colonies, and it was her way of doing something about it. Her efforts over the years (along with the help of the scientific community and proactive members of maritime industries) have resulted in the **Zeehondencreche** (Seal Creche; ☎ 0595-52 65 26; www.zeehondencreche.nl; Hoofdstraat 94a; admission €2; ☼ 9am-6pm), a centre for the rescue and rehabilitation of sick seals.

The centre normally houses 20 to 30 seals, which can be seen lounging and swimming in various pools. The most popular times to visit are 11am and 4pm when the seals are fed, and if one or more takes your fancy, you can 'adopt' him or her; the website also has details on becoming a donor.

To get to the Zeehondencreche, take the train from Groningen to Warffum (€4.30, 24 minutes, hourly), and then bus 68 (15 minutes, five times a day Monday to Friday) to Pieterburen.

MENKEMABORG

Some 25km northeast of Groningen in the small farming town of Uithuizen is one of the Netherlands' most authentic manor houses, **Menkemaborg** (☎ 0595-43 19 70; Menkemaweg 2; adult/child €4.50/2; ☼ 10am-5pm May-Sep, 10am-noon & 1-4pm

POUNDING MUD

Some folk pay a pretty penny for mud treatments and organised walks; Groningen and Friesland have an activity that combines both. When the tide retreats across the mud flats off the north coast of Groningen, locals and visitors alike attack it with abandon, marching, and inevitably sinking, into the sloppy mess. This mudtastic pastime is known as *wadlopen* (mud-walking), and you'd be a stick-in-the-mud if you didn't give it a try while in the area.

The mud stretches all the way to the Frisian islands offshore, and treks across to the islands are quite popular. Because of the treacherous tides, and the fact that some walkers can become muddled and lose their way, *wadlopen* can only be undertaken on a guided tour. Those who enjoy *wadlopen* say that it is strenuous but enlivening; the unchanging vista of mud and sky has an almost meditative quality, and the sense of achievement on traipsing across the sea bottom with a rising tide hot on your heels brings upon a natural high.

The centre for *wadlopen* is the tiny village of Pieterburen, 22km north of Groningen, where several groups of trained guides are based; **Wadloopcentrum** (☎ 0595-52 83 00; www.wadlopen.org; Hoofdstraat 105) and **Dijkstra's Wadlooptochten** (☎ 0595-52 83 45; www.wadloop-dijkstra.nl; Hoofdstraat 118) are two of the better known. Guided walks, which take place between May and September, range from a short 5km jaunt across the mud flats (€8.50, 2½ hours) to a gruelling, yet exhilarating, 20km pound to Schiermonnikoog (€22.50, five hours); the latter, for some unknown reason, is the most popular. The ferry ride back from the islands is not included in the price and it's essential to book around a month in advance. You'll be told what clothes to bring depending on the time of year, but always take a semblance of balance and plenty of perseverance.

See opposite for public transport details to Pieterburen.

Tue-Sun Oct-Dec & Mar-Apr, closed Jan & Feb). Originally a fortified castle dating back to the 14th century, Menkemaborg received its present gentrified appearance – a moated estate of three houses surrounded by immaculate gardens – early in the 18th century, and it has barely been altered since. Inside, the rooms retain all the pomp and ceremony of 18th-century aristocratic life, complete with carved oak mantelpieces, stately beds and fine china.

Hourly trains run between Uithuizen and Groningen (€5.30, 34 minutes); the train station is a 1km walk west of Menkemaborg.

BOURTANGE
☎ 0599 / pop 1200

Bourtange, a tiny town near the German border, is home to one of the best-preserved fortifications in the country. While rather small and best seen from the air, it is nonetheless a sight to behold, with its flooded moats, stolid defences, and quaint houses protected from all sides. The region around Bourtange is also worth exploring; off the beaten path, it consists of pretty countryside and tree-shaded canals, ideal for tackling by bike.

History
Built in the late 1500s, Bourtange represents the pinnacle of the arms and fortification of

the time. Behind its walls and moats it could withstand months of siege by an invading army. However, by the early 1960s its walls had been mostly breached or levelled and the moats were largely filled in. A road even ran through the present town centre.

In 1964, however, the regional government decided to restore the battlements and the town itself to its 1742 appearance, when the fortifications around the citadel had reached their maximum size. It took three decades, during which time roads were moved and buildings demolished or reconstructed. Archaeologists generally had a party.

The results are impressive and Bourtange is stunningly pretty. The star-shaped rings of walls and canals have been completely rebuilt and the village has been returned to a glossier version of its 18th-century self. It's a cliché, but a visit to Bourtange is truly a step into the past, a time when rogue armies wandered the lands and villagers hid behind defences designed to keep them at bay.

Orientation & Information
From the parking area and tourist office, you pass through two gates and across three drawbridges over the moats before you reach the old town proper. From the town's central square, the Marktplein, cobblestone streets

lead off in all directions; the pentagram-shaped inner fortification can be crossed in a matter of minutes by foot. The town's **tourist office** (☎ 35 46 00; William Lodewijkstraat 33; ☻ 10am-5pm Mon-Fri, 12.30-5pm Sat & Sun) has more than enough information on the town, including detailed displays showing the reconstruction and restoration. Aerial photographs show the remarkable changes between 1965 and the late 1990s. It also sells a handy English-language booklet (€1.50).

Sights & Activities

Inside the walls at the core of the fortification, brick houses make good use of what little space the five bastions afford. **Marktplein** is a good spot to start exploring, with its two restaurants, small craft shops and tree-shaded benches.

Of the old buildings, six have been turned into museums, which open from 10am to 5pm Monday to Friday and from 11am Saturday and Sunday; tickets (adult/child €5.50/3.50), covering entry to all, can be purchased at the tourist office. Two museums – the **Captain's Lodge** and **De Dagen van Roam** – cover the life and times of the militia stationed at Bourtange in the 17th and 18th centuries, while the **Museum de Baracquen** displays artefacts and curios uncovered during the fort's reconstruction. **De Poort** has an excellent model of Bourtange, and the town's **synagogue**, built in 1842, explains the life and times of its Jewish population, and includes a plaque listing the 42 local people taken away to their deaths by the Nazis, a huge number given the town's small size.

However, the best thing to do in Bourtange is traipse up and down its defensive walls. More often than not you'll have whole stretches to yourself, and the view of the small village huddled behind its unbreachable walls is just crying out to be photographed.

Sleeping & Eating

It's possible to stay within the walls, in the original soldiers' (€65) or captains' (€75) quarters. Bookings are taken at the tourist office; the digs aren't particularly plush, but they're warm and comfortable, and breakfast is included.

Albertha Hoeve (☎ 35 47 37; www.alberthahoeve.nl; Vlagtwedderstraat 57; camp sites/d €12.50/47) Just outside the walls, Albertha is one of several small family-run places that has homely rooms and fields for camping. Snacks are also available.

The two small eateries on Marktplein are the only places to eat within the old town: **'t Oal Kroegie** (☎ 35 45 80; Marktplein; snacks €2-6; ☻ 10am-10pm) Provides light meals, sandwiches, pancakes, a few beer varieties, shaded outdoor tables, and friendly service.

's Lands Huys (☎ 35 45 14; Marktplein; mains €14-17; ☻ 10am-10pm) A more cosy option housed in a former officers' inn, with full meals and outdoor seating.

Getting There & Away

Bourtange is not easy to get to without your own wheels. From Groningen, take the hourly train east to Winschoten (€5.70, 33 minutes), then bus 14 south to Vlagtwedde (25 minutes, at least one every hour) and transfer to (mini)bus 72 for Bourtange (12 minutes, 10 daily). With waiting time and transfers, count on the trip taking about two hours – bus 72 only runs before 9am and after 1pm, at half-hour intervals. The return service from Bourtange leaves from the Marktplein at 15 and 45 minutes after the hour, once again before 9am and after 1pm.

If touring by bike, combine Bourtange with visits over a few days to the *hunebedden* (opposite) in Drenthe, some 30km to the west.

DRENTHE

If ever there were a forgotten corner of the Netherlands, this is it. With no sea access or major city to call its own (Emmen, with just over 100,000 people, is its largest), not a national park in sight, and little of the charm the country is so famous for, Drenthe is the Netherlands' black sheep. But that's exactly why this small backwater deserves a little of your time, simply to experience something different in a land where one pretty town follows another and seascape after seascape lines the horizon.

ASSEN

☎ 0592 / pop 60,700

With a close proximity to Groningen, Assen, the capital of Drenthe, will be the first stop on most people's tour of the province. It's a modern, working city with some surprisingly good restaurants, a handful of so-so museums, and a well-informed **tourist office** (☎ 24 37 88; www.vvvdrenthe.nl; Marktstraat 8; ☻ 1-6pm Mon, 9am-6pm Tue-Fri, 9am-5pm Sat) that can book B&Bs in the town.

The **Drents Museum** (☎ 37 77 73; www.drents museum.nl; Brink 1; adult/child €5/3; ⊙ 11am-5pm Tue-Sun), near the centre, has *hunebedden* artefacts and various artworks and furnishings from Drenthe's history. If you've time to kill, or need to booster the energy levels, head to **De Tijd** (Time; ☎ 30 06 42; Beilerstraat 28; mains €12-18), an eccentric restaurant with hearty Dutch portions big enough for two, and an astounding 2346 clocks (thankfully not wound). Take a pew and chat with the owner, whose charm is quite disarming.

The tourist office and museum are 500m from the station by way of Stationsstraat. Frequent trains connect Assen with both Groningen (€4.80, 15 minutes) and Zwolle (€11.60, 40 minutes).

Buses depart from the area to the left as you exit the train station. The **bicycle shop** (☎ 31 04 24) is right next door.

KAMP WESTERBORK

About 10km south of Assen, near the tiny village of Hooghalen, is this, a reminder that the atrocities of the holocaust were not confined to Central and Eastern Europe.

Kamp Westerbork (☎ 0593-59 26 00; www.kamp westerbork.nl; Oosthalen 8, Hooghalen; adult/child €4.50/2.25; ⊙ 10am-5pm Mon-Fri year-round, 1-5pm Sat & Sun Sep-Jun, 11am-5pm Sat & Sun Jul & Aug), ironically, was built by the Dutch government in 1939 to house German Jews *fleeing* the Nazis. When the Germans invaded in May 1940, they found Westerbork ideal for their own ends. At first the camp remained relatively benign, but beginning in 1942 it became a transit point for those being sent to the death camps. More than 107,000 Jews and 250 Roma were shipped through Westerbork. The vast majority never returned.

Today the camp is a memorial to the murdered and a holocaust museum. Most of the buildings are gone, but the remaining monuments are emotionally moving. Consisting mainly of documents and personal effects, the displays are intimate and evocative. Anne Frank was interned here before meeting her own fate at Bergen-Belsen, though undue attention on Westerbork's most famous detainee is thankfully avoided. The camp itself is about 3km from the museum; either walk or take the bus provided (€1.75).

Bus 22 (12 minutes, every 30 minutes Monday to Friday, and 12.14pm, 4.14pm and 8.14pm Saturday and Sunday) from Assen stops in Hooghalen, 2km west of the camp, otherwise take a taxi.

HUNEBEDDEN

People have been enjoying the quiet in Drenthe since as early as 3000 BC, when prehistoric tribes lived here amid the bogs and peat. These early residents began cultivating the land, a pastime still enjoyed by many in the province, and created what is arguably the most interesting aspect of Drenthe today, the *hunebedden*.

Hunebedden, which predate Stonehenge, are prehistoric burial chambers constructed with huge grey stones, some of which weigh up to 25,000kg. It is thought the stones arrived in the Netherlands via glaciers from Sweden some 200,000 years ago, but no one can be certain of the fact. Little is also known about the builders of the *hunebedden*, except that they took burying their dead very seriously, burying people, along with their personal items and tools, under the monolithic stones. Theories as to how the chambers were constructed have been bantered about by the scientific community, but once again, a definitive answer is yet to be found. A total of 54 of these impressive groupings of sombre grey stones can be seen in Drenthe and Groningen.

The **Nationaal Hunebedden Informatiecentrum** (☎ 0599-23 63 74; www.hunebedden.nl; Bron-negerstraat 12; adult/child €4.75/3; ⊙ 10am-5pm Mon-Fri, 11am-5pm Sat & Sun) in Borger, a little town 17km northwest of Emmen, is the centre for the *hunebedden*, and the logical place to start a tour. Here there are many displays relating to the stones as well as excavated artefacts, and the largest *hunebed* is located just outside its doors. Maps of all the sites in Drenthe are also available; most are clumped around the villages of Klijndijk, Odoorn, Annen and Midlaren, which are strung out along N34, a picturesque road linking Emmen and Groningen

It's best to explore the *hunebedden* with your own transport; pick up a map from the Emmen tourist office or Borgor Informatiecentrum and look out for the large brown signs showing a pile of rocks while driving or biking. Bus 300 operates hourly between Emmen and Groningen, stopping at Borger.

ORVELTE
☎ 0593

A foundation governs the tiny village of Orvelte, 17km south of Assen. Its goal, to preserve the feel of a 19th-century Drenthe community, is alive and well here, and visitors are welcome to join them in the past for a day from Easter to the end of October.

No cars are permitted (aside from those of the residents) and owners are forbidden to alter the old buildings in uncharacteristic ways. Residents mainly engage in traditional activities; there's the butcher, the baker… you get the idea. During summer, there are lovely vegetable gardens growing near every house.

The **tourist office** (☎ 32 23 35; www.orvelte.net; 10.30am-5pm Tue-Sun Easter-Jun & Sep-Oct, daily Jul & Aug, closed Nov-Easter) has brochures and maps of the village, and can inform you about what's on when; it can also arrange B&B accommodation in one of the traditional houses (€25 per person).

To get to Orvelte from Assen, take a train to Beilen (€3.20, eight minutes, every half-hour) and change to bus 22 (16 minutes, every 30 minutes Monday to Friday, and 12.14pm, 4.14pm and 8.14pm Saturday and Sunday).

EMMEN
☎ 0591 / pop 108,200

A modern city of industry, Emmen is a useful transportation centre for the *hunebedden*. The **tourist office** (☎ 64 17 92; www.vvvemmen.nl; Hoofdstraat 22; 1-5.30pm Mon, 9.30am-5.30pm Tue-Fri, 10am-4pm Sat) has a good range of bike maps for exploring the *hunebedden*, and the pleasant staff can help with finding accommodation.

The town's zoo, **Noorder Dierenpark** (☎ 85 08 50; www.zoo-emmen.nl; Hoofdstraat 18; adult/child €17/15; 10am-5.30pm) is a short walk from the train station. It's noted for its apes and African animals displayed in a 'natural' setting. Of course, few areas of the savanna have weather like this.

Emmen is at the end of the train line from Zwolle (€11.20, 55 minutes, every half-hour); for information on buses between Emmen, Groningen and Borger, see the boxed text, p253. The station has lockers and is 600m from the tourist office. Buses leave from in front of the station. The station has a **bicycle shop** (☎ 61 37 31).

Overijssel & Gelderland

Although the 'forgotten' provinces of Overijssel and Gelderland can't boast blockbuster cities like Amsterdam, Rotterdam or Maastricht, they make up for it with reserves of natural beauty – forest, rivers, lakes, national parks – and abundant history. That's not to say that there aren't major attractions: the Hoge Veluwe National Park, containing the Kröller-Müller Museum (with probably the world's finest Van Gogh collection), should be near the top of any Dutch itinerary. Generally, though, the region's pleasures are small and concentrated, adding up to a compelling whole. If you're looking to escape the Randstad's hectic urban sprawl, then you could do a lot worse than take time out here.

Zwolle, Deventer and Kampen, in Overijssel, are delightful, atmospheric towns, filled with many inspiring examples of historical architecture; all three were key member towns of the Hanseatic League. Then there's the Weerribben National Park, a remarkable area of wetlands.

Nijmegen, in Gelderland, is an underrated destination. But with its waterfront culture, excellent cafés and an annual march that now takes the form of a week-long party, it's full of bounce. On the other side of history, it was here and near Arnhem where attempts to liberate the occupied Netherlands went horribly awry for the Allies in 1944; there are many WWII memorials and locations to explore.

HIGHLIGHTS

- Lose yourself in the amazing **Hoge Veluwe National Park** (p269)
- Have an art attack at the **Kröller-Müller Museum** (p269)
- Spook yourself in the otherworldly ambience of the **Weerribben** (p256), Overijssel's strange wetlands
- Have a fine old time in **Nijmegen** (p263), with its busy waterways
- Remember the past at Gelderland's **war cemeteries and memorials** (p267)

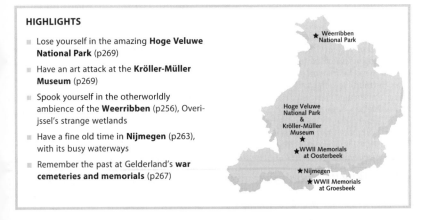

★ Weerribben National Park

Hoge Veluwe National Park & Kröller-Müller Museum ★

★ WWII Memorials at Oosterbeek

★ Nijmegen

★ WWII Memorials at Groesbeek

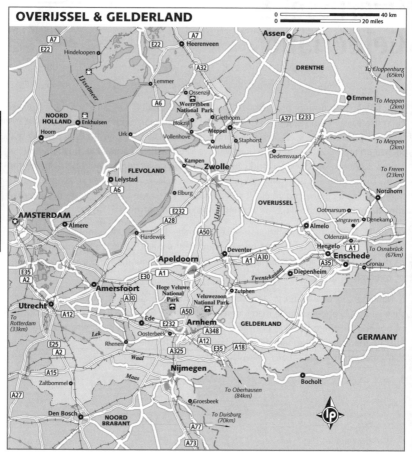

OVERIJSSEL & GELDERLAND

OVERIJSSEL

Overijssel means 'beyond the IJssel', after the river forming much of the province's western border. The province is hilly in the east near Germany and flat and soggy in the west along the former coastline, now landlocked by Flevoland's Noordoostpolder.

You might like to anchor yourself in Deventer to explore Overijssel, though Zwolle is the capital. Giethoorn in the north is pretty as well, but be aware of swollen summer crowds.

WEERRIBBEN NATIONAL PARK

A serene and occasionally eerie landscape of watery striations, **Weerribben National Park** is 3500 hectares of marshy land. This entire area was worked by peat and reed harvesters, among the hardest imaginable jobs. The long, water-filled stripes across the landscape are the result of peat removal: as one line of peat was dug, it was laid on the adjoining land to dry.

Reed harvesting was no easier, and still goes on; you can see huge piles at many points in the park. Generations of harvesters lived out here with little contact with the outside world. Even now, their descendants live on some of the farms in the surrounding countryside in Ossenzijl and Blokzijl. Weerribben is also an amazing natural landscape and an important stop for migratory birds in Europe.

As you ride along one of the isolated bike paths or row the channels, you might get the sense you're on another planet. A chief factor in creating this illusion is the sound of the Weerribben: as you move through the sea of reeds, you'll hear the calls, clucks, coos and splashes of numerous birds, fish, frogs, otters and eels.

The park's **visitors centre** (☎ 0561-47 72 72; 🕙 10am-5pm Tue-Fri, noon-4pm Sat & Sun) is in Ossenzijl, a tiny village on the northern edge of the park. Pick up dozens of maps of different cycling and walking routes, as well as advice on boat and canoe rental.

To reach Ossenzijl, take bus 81 from Steenwijk, a stop on the train line from Leeuwarden

WEERRIBBEN NATIONAL PARK

to Zwolle. The bus takes 25 minutes and runs every two hours on weekdays and just a few times on weekends.

DEVENTER

☎ 0570 / pop 95,614

Deventer was already a bustling mercantile port as far back as AD 800, and it maintained its prosperous trading ties for centuries, evidence of which you'll see everywhere in its sumptuously detailed old buildings. In fact, so rich is the detail that the WWII film *A Bridge Too Far*, which was essentially about Arnhem's role in the war, was filmed here (Arnhem, of course, having being levelled by the war).

Information

Library (☎ 64 99 62; Brink 70; internet access per hr €3; ☯ 11am-10.30pm Tue & Thu, 11am-5.30pm Wed & Fri, 11am-4pm Sat)

Post office (☎ 67 63 58; Diepenveenseweg 1; ☯ 9am-6pm Mon-Fri, 9am-12.30pm Sat)

Tourist office (☎ 69 14 10; www.vvvdeventer.nl; Keizerstraat 22; ☯ 9.30am-6pm Mon-Fri, 9.30am-5pm Sat)

Sights

The **Brink** is the main square and Deventer's commercial heart. The town's famous **Waag**, the 1528 weigh-house in the middle of the square, was restored in 2003. Look for the cauldron on the north side – a gruesome and well-supported legend tells of a 16th-century clerk boiled alive in it, after he was discovered substituting cheap metals for precious ones in the local money supply.

There's a small **museum** (☎ 69 37 80; admission €3; ☯ 10am-5pm Tue-Sat) inside the Waag, with historical displays and a selection of traditional costumery.

The **Grote of Lebuïnuskerk** (☯ 1am-5pm Mon-Sat; admission €2.50) is the city's main church. It stands on a site where other churches were razed by flames and other catastrophes time and again, before the present Gothic structure was built between 1450 and 1530.

Deventer is so well preserved that most streets will have something to see. On **Assenstraat** and **Polstraat** there are wall carvings and window decorations created over several centuries. Assenstraat 67–79 is more contemporary, while **Walstraat 20** shows a woman

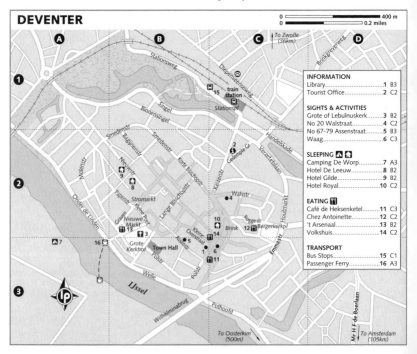

DEVENTER

0 ————— 400 m
0 ————— 0.2 miles

To Zwolle (36km)

INFORMATION	
Library	1 B3
Tourist Office	2 C2

SIGHTS & ACTIVITIES	
Grote of Lebuïnuskerk	3 B2
No 20 Walstraat	4 C2
No 67-79 Assenstraat	5 B3
Waag	6 C3

SLEEPING	
Camping De Worp	7 A3
Hotel De Leeuw	8 B2
Hotel Gilde	9 B2
Hotel Royal	10 C2

EATING	
Café de Heksenketel	11 C3
Chez Antoinette	12 C2
't Arsenaal	13 B2
Volkshuis	14 C2

TRANSPORT	
Bus Stops	15 C1
Passenger Ferry	16 A3

To Oosterkm (500m)

To Amsterdam (105km)

OVERIJSSEL & GELDERLAND

THE HANSEATIC LEAGUE

Although it was primarily composed of northern German cities such as Lübeck and Hamburg, the Hanseatic League also included seven Dutch cities along the IJssel: Hasselt, Zwolle, Kampen, Hattem, Deventer, Zutphen and Doesburg. The powerful trading community was initially organised in the mid-13th century, its member towns quickly growing rich off the proceeds of importing and exporting goods including grain, ore, honey, textiles, timbers and flax. The league was not a government as such, but it would defend its ships from attack and it entered into monopolistic trading agreements with other groups, such as the Swedes. The fact that the trading community achieved its powerful trading position through such means as bribery, boycotts and general fiscal ruthlessness shouldn't sound particularly unusual to business students today. League members did work hard to prevent war among their partners for the simple reason that conflict was bad for business.

It's ironic that the League's demise in the 15th century was mostly attributable to the Dutch. Amsterdam's traders recognised a good thing and essentially beat the League at its own game, out-muscling it in market after market.

climbing down the wall while hanging by a sheet.

Activities

The banks of the IJssel river are a scenic place for **biking**. Riding 36km north to Zwolle is a fine option, while a good 32km round trip follows the river north to Olst, where you can take a ferry across and return along the other side to Deventer. You can do the same thing going south to Zutphen, a 47km trip.

Sleeping

Hotel Gilde (☎ 64 18 46; Nieuwstraat 41; s/d from €90/120) This charming building, once a 17th-century convent, has been restored to its former architectural glory. With all that weight of history on the trimmings and frills, you just know that this is the swishest place in Deventer (despite the austerity of its former tenants).

Hotel de Leeuw (☎ 61 02 90; http://members.home.nl/deleeuw; Nieuwstraat 25; s/d from €71/85) This lovely building with well-designed yet simple rooms, dates back to 1645. It's on a popular shopping street no more than 10 minutes from the heart of Deventer. The hotel has reduced rates for longer stays.

Other options:

Camping De Worp (☎ 61 36 01; Worp 12; sites from €11; May-Sep) Right across the IJssel from the centre of town, about two minutes north of the passenger ferry.

Hotel Royal (☎ 61 18 80; www.royal-deventer.nl; Brink 94; s/d €60/70) Basic but spotless rooms.

Eating

't Arsenaal (☎ 61 64 95; www.restaurantsarsenaal.nl; Nieuwe Markt 33-34; dinner €13-29; lunch & dinner) This stylish restaurant, next to the Lebuïnuskerk, really comes into its own in summer, when the courtyard and alleyway, in the shadow of the old church, makes for a grand and dramatic setting. The menu is classic French with modern twinges, and is typified by filets of fish served with octopus pasta.

Volkshuis (☎ 60 02 54; Kleine Overstraat 97a; dinner €12-16; lunch & dinner) Run by and supporting people with disabilities, Volkshuis uses its own produce to create simple food with quality organic ingredients, including appealing vegetarian options such as chilli 'non' carne.

Café de Heksenketel (☎ 61 34 12; Brink 62; mains €13; lunch & dinner) The menu here offers typical Dutch restaurant fare, like schnitzel with fries and salad. You'll need to eat something solid to go with one of the beers from their excellent selection.

Chez Antoinette (☎ 61 66 30; Roggestraat 10-12; mains €16-22; dinner Tue-Sun) The popular Portuguese and Latin-influenced food here goes all out to impress, with local seafood, beef and poultry stocks, and Iberian seasonings like saffron, chilli, tomatoes, garlic and olive oil.

Shopping

The local speciality is Deventer *koek*, a mildly spiced gingerbread made with honey. It's widely available.

Getting There & Around

Deventer sits at the junction of two train lines; service is good in all directions. There are lockers in the main concourse.

Destination	Price (€)	Duration (min)	Frequency (per hr)
Amsterdam	14.70	75	1
Apeldoorn	3	12	2
Arnhem	7.10	36	2
Enschede	9.30	43	2
Nijmegen	9.70	51	2
Zwolle	5.20	24	2

The bus area is located to the right as you leave the train station.

The bicycle shop is in the train station. There is parking around the town's periphery, but the best place to park is the free lot on the west bank of the IJssel. To get there, take the free passenger ferry. The voyage takes less than five minutes and operates most of the day and night. The pier on the town side is near Vispoort.

ZWOLLE
☎ 038 / 110,027

Zwolle, the capital of Overijssel, is a compact town that can easily occupy a day of exploration – longer in summer, when a seemingly endless schedule of small festivals and the weekend market keep things bubbling. In the 14th and 15th centuries, Zwolle garnered wealth as the main trading port for the Hanseatic League and became a cultural centre of some repute. While those days are long gone, you can still step back in time, courtesy of the moat and ancient fortifications that surround the town.

Naturally, there's a **tourist office** (☎ 0900-1122375; www.vvvzwolle.nl; Grote Kerkplein 14; ⏰ 1-5pm Mon, 10am-5pm Tue-Fri, 10am-4pm Sat) and a **post office** (☎ 421 78 21; Nieuwe Markt 1A; ⏰ 9am-6pm Mon-Fri, 9am-2pm Sat).

Sights & Activities

People from Zwolle say they know they're home when they see the Onze Lieve Vrouwetoren (also known as the Peperbus, or Peppermill), the huge former church that dominates the skyline as you approach town.

The **Stedelijk Museum Zwolle** (☎ 421 46 50; www.museumzwolle.nl; Melkmarkt 41; adult/child €4/2; ⏰ 10am-5pm Tue-Sat, 1-5pm Sun) has a fine collection of items, including a wealth of Hanseatic material. It also hosts about 25 special exhibitions a year, ranging from high-art painting retrospectives to contemporary photography and multimedia.

The **Grote Kerk** is grand, but it was grander before the usual series of disasters knocked down the tower – accursedly, it's been struck (and destroyed) by lightning an astonishing three times. The 15th-century **Sassenpoort**, situated at the corner of Sassenstraat and Wilhelminasingel, is one of the remaining town gates.

Ecodrome (☎ 421 50 50; Willemsvaart 19; adult/child under 12 €9.95/8.5o; ⏰ 10am-5pm Apr-Oct, 10am-5pm Wed, Sat & Sun Nov-Apr) is a science-based, interactive multimedia education centre housed in futuristic-looking buildings. Well suited to travellers with kids in tow, it's a 1km walk turning right from the station.

The tourist office can help to organise canal tours.

Sleeping

Accommodation is tight here. Try the tourist office's booking service; there are some excellent B&Bs run by friendly locals, starting at around €20 to €25.

Bilderberg Grand Hotel Wientjes (☎ 425 42 54; www.grandhotelwientjes.nl; Stationsweg 7; s from €93) This stately establishment is a grand, sumptuous business hotel, with all the usual facilities and service to match. Creature comforts are a big deal here, with deluxe and executive rooms at the top of the range.

City Hotel (☎ 421 81 82; www.hotelzwolle.com; Rode Torenplein 10-11; s/d €55/70) An unaffected, down-to-earth place, well located with good, basic rooms. As one of the few central options, it's worth phoning ahead.

Eating

De Librije (☎ 21 20 83; www.librije.com; Broerenkerkplein 13; 3-course meals from €45; ⏰ lunch & dinner) With three Michelin stars (just one of two restaurants in the country so decorated), you don't need us to tell you the grub scrubs up. As the name suggests, the experience takes place inside the wonderful ambience of a 500-year-old monastery library. The food is contemporary French with Dutch infusions.

Other options:

Baiyok (☎ 22 98 82; www.baiyok.nl; Diezerpoortenplas 3; mains from €12; ⏰ dinner Wed-Sun) Good Thai food, Zwolle's only such restaurant.

La Stalla (☎ 421 25 83; Kamperstraat 7-9; mains from €15; ⏰ lunch & dinner Tue-Sat, dinner Sun) Dutch take on Italian cuisine.

Peppermill American Restaurant (☎ 423 08 06; www.thepeppermill.nl; Melkmarkt 56; mains €16-29;

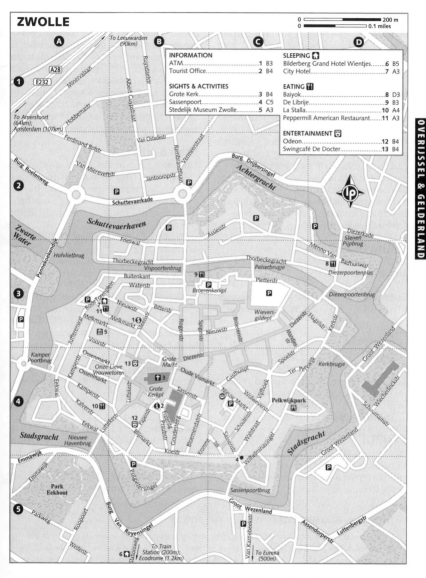

ZWOLLE

INFORMATION
ATM.....................................**1** B3
Tourist Office.....................**2** B4

SIGHTS & ACTIVITIES
Grote Kerk.........................**3** B4
Sassenpoort.......................**4** C5
Stedelijk Museum Zwolle....**5** A3

SLEEPING
Bilderberg Grand Hotel Wientjes.......**6** B5
City Hotel...........................**7** A3

EATING
Baiyok................................**8** D3
De Librije...........................**9** B3
La Stalla............................**10** A4
Peppermill American Restaurant......**11** A3

ENTERTAINMENT
Odeon...............................**12** B4
Swingcafé De Docter...........**13** B4

OVERIJSSEL & GELDERLAND

---

dinner Tue-Sun) Classy North American cuisine, including Mexican and Cajun.

Entertainment

Swingcafé De Docter (☎ 421 52 35; www.dedocter.nl; Voorstraat 3) A great place, dark and musty, the swingcafé hosts live rock bands a few nights per week, and has inviting open frontage

and ample supplies of Hertog Jan, a great Brabant pilsener.

Eureka (☎ 422 29 03; www.eureka-zwolle.nl; Assendorperplein 9) This magical space is a community arts centre-cum-venue-cum-café. People of every age, disposition or species roam its creaky floors, and the mood is warm and inclusive.

Odeon (☎ 428 82 80; www.schouwburg-odeon.nl; Blijmarkt 25) This grand building is a multi-purpose entertainment venue hosting everything from theatre and dance to live rock and electronica nights.

Shopping

The market occupies most of the former Melkmarkt, Oude Vismarkt and the star-shaped centre in general on Friday and Saturday. Fish, fresh fruit and vegetables, clothes – anything goes. There's also cheap cheese and bread, a great way to stock up for a picnic. Pelkwijkpark or the area just south of Kerkbrugje are good areas for this activity.

In summer, market day is often augmented by alfresco music – anything from blues to Germanic 'oompah' stylings.

Getting There & Around

Zwolle is a transfer point for trains and has good connections.

Destination	Price (€)	Duration (min)	Frequency (per hr)
Deventer	5.20	24	2
Groningen	15.10	60	2
Leeuwarden	13.70	60	2

Local buses leave from the right as you exit the station. Intercity services are 100m further over in the same direction.

The **bicycle shop** is to the left of the station.

KAMPEN

☎ 038 / pop 48,964

Picturesque Kampen, another lovely Hanseatic city, is a perfect day trip: 15km west of Zwolle, about 20 minutes by bicycle. Its surrounding parklands are pretty and its historic centre is one of the country's best preserved, boasting no less than 500 medieval monuments: houses, gates and towers. It's difficult to get lost in Kampen, as it's small and laid out in a linear fashion, parallel to the IJssel.

Plan your day with the help of the **tourist office** (☎ 331 35 00; www.vvvkampen.nl; Oudestraat 151; ☺ 9am-5.30pm Mon-Fri, 9am-4pm Sat), which can also organise private rooms (about €30).

Sights & Activities

The major sights lie along Oudestraat.

The **Nieuwe Toren** is immediately obvious: it's the 17th-century tower with the incredible lean. There's a little statue of a cow here, linked to a rather ludicrous old story (see the boxed text, below).

The **Oude Raadhuis** (Old Town Hall; ☎ 339 2999; Oudestraat 133) was – surprise, surprise – badly damaged by fire and rebuilt in 1543.

The **Bovenkerk** (☎ 331 6453; Koornmarkt 28) features an organ with over 3000 pipes, while the **Gotische Huis** (Gothic House; Ousestraat 158) is a 15th-century merchant's house that's worth a look, not least for its housing of the **Stedelijk Museum** (admission €3; ☺ 11am-12.30pm & 1.30-5pm Tue-Sat, plus 1-5pm Sun Jun-Sep) and a collection of local, historical relics.

Two 15th-century **city gates** survive along the gorgeous park on Kampen's west side.

Sleeping

The town has but two places to lay your hat, the **Hotel Van Dijk** (☎ 331 49 25; fax 331 65 08; IJsselkade 30-3; r from €60) and the **Hotel-Restaurant 't Haasje** (☎ 331 38 26; Flevoweg 90). Both, naturally, are often full.

Camping Seveningen (☎ 331 48 91; Frieseweg 7; camp sites €11; ☺ Apr-Oct), on a pretty waterside location,

---

THE GRASS IS ALWAYS GREENER...UP THE TOWER

Once upon a time, a local farmer mistook moss growing atop Nieuwe Toren for grass and wondered aloud if he could get his cows up there to graze. So what he did was, he hoisted one of his cows up to the top via a dodgy system of pulleys and ropes. The cheering townspeople below saw the cow's tongue protruding from its mouth and assumed it was indeed having a good old feed. And there was much rejoicing. Unfortunately, the poor animal was actually choking to death, a ridiculous episode that made Kampen the butt of Dutch jokes for many, many years.

Credit, though, to the town: it has turned stupidity into a virtue, and these days, on a summer's morning in July, the incident is celebrated as Kampen Cow Day, with the ceremonial hoisting of a stuffed cow up the tower, accompanied by live music, where the bovine symbol remains for weeks.

The dates for Cow Day vary, so contact the tourist office for confirmation.

is an alternative. From the train station, walk
northwest along the river for 20 minutes.

Getting There & Around

Trains make the run between Zwolle and
Kampen (€2.80, 10 minutes, two per hour).
There's a small phalanx of bus stands behind
the train station.

NORTHERN OVERIJSSEL

Before the Noordoostpolder was created,
the Northern Overijssel region was on the
Zuiderzee. Today the former coastal villages
are landlocked, but maintain their links to
the water through the spider web of canals
that crisscross this marshy area. It's a difficult
area to get around without a car or a bike and
a set of energetic legs, as buses are infrequent
and involve inconvenient connections. Still,
it's worth the effort to explore as you'll take
in great scenery and feel a bit detached from
the rest of the Netherlands.

The region is home to **Giethoorn** (☎ 0521), a
town with no streets, only canals, walking paths
and bike trails (inevitably it's tagged the 'Dutch
Venice') – contrary to most Dutch geography,
Giethoorn is built on water crossed by a few bits
of land, and farmers even used to move their
cows around in rowboats filled with hay. This
is a sentimental place for the Dutch as it was the
setting for *Fanfare*, a popular, funny 1958 film
about the local folk, which was one of the first
films to dissect the Dutch psyche.

The entire area is a joy to pedal through.
At any time there are countless opportunities
for boat rides, although joining a cow will be
tougher these days: recently, Giethoorn has
been discovered in a big way, appearing in
summer to be populated entirely by camper
vans along the ample canalside space.

Giethoorn's **tourist office** (☎ 0900-5674637; www
.vvvgiethoorn.nl; Beulakerweg 114A; ☾ 9am-6pm Mon-Sat,
9am-5pm Sun May-Sep; 9am-5pm Mon-Fri Oct-Apr) is on the
main road and will sort your accommodation –
there are scores of camping grounds, rooms
and cabins for rent. The town itself, five minutes away, has banks and other services.

Bus 70 serves Giethoorn on its route between Steenwijk (18 minutes) and Zwolle
(one hour). Service is hourly on weekdays
and shocking on weekends.

It's difficult to get around Giethoorn without a boat, a bike or a combination thereof.
A few of the canalside service stations run
bike-hire services.

GELDERLAND

The lush province of Gelderland features a
genuine attraction in the form of Hoge Veluwe National Park, with its superb modern
art museum and beautiful forestry. There
are other, excellent cultural repositories in
Apeldoorn and Arnhem, and the latter of
course was the setting for Operation Market
Garden, immortalised in the WWII actioner,
A Bridge Too Far.

NIJMEGEN

☎ 024 / pop 159,556

Primarily a trading and manufacturing town,
Nijmegen survived many invasions right up
until WWII: the Roman Empire conquered
it in AD 70, promptly burning it down, an
ominous taste of things to come.

In February 1944, as a marshalling point
for German forces, Nijmegen was bombed
heavily by the Americans; later that year, the
town was devastated by the 'Operation Market
Garden' fiasco (see p267).

The postwar years have seen many rebuilding schemes of varying success, but
Nijmegen has always bounced back, for it has

ANIMAL ATTRACTION

There is a surfeit of zoological parks in
Gelderland and near the borders of neighbouring provinces.

Harderwijk's aquatic megapark, the **Dolfinarium** (☎ 0341-46 74 67; www.dolfinarium
.nl; Strandboulevard Oost 1, Hardewijk; adult/child
€23/19.50; ☾ 10am-5pm, 10am-6pm Jul & Aug),
features its namesake alongside stingrays,
seals and other aquatic life.

Apeldoorn's **Apenheul** (☎ 055-357 57 57;
www.apenheul.nl; JC Wilslaan 21-31; adult/child
€15/12; ☾ 9.30am-5pm, to 6pm Jul & Aug) is
home to primates that will have the nerve
to come and sit on your shoulder – if you
have no food, they will attempt to snatch
anything small and shiny. Make sure your
Prince Albert is well hidden.

Arnhem's **Burgers' Zoo** (☎ 442 45 34;
www.burgerszoo.nl; Antoon van Hooffplein 1;
adult/child €16/14; ☾ 9am-7pm or sunset) tries
to recreate the natural environments of its
many animals. The creatures mostly don't
buy this ruse, given the climate.

OVERIJSSEL & GELDERLAND

OVERIJSSEL & GELDERLAND

NIJMEGEN

```
0          500 m
0          0.3 miles
```

INFORMATION		SLEEPING		DRINKING	
Library..........................1 C3		Hotel Apollo.....................10 B3		De Blauwe Hand..............(see 8)	
Post Office......................2 C3		Hotel Atlanta....................11 C3		De Hemel........................(see 4)	
Tourist Office...................3 B4		Hotel Courage..................(see 6)			
		Mercure Nijmegen Centre......12 A4		ENTERTAINMENT	
SIGHTS & ACTIVITIES				Concertgebouw de Vereeniging...15 B4	
Commanderie van St Jan......4 C2		EATING		Lux Filmcentrum...............16 C3	
Museum Het Valkhof............5 C3		Circus.............................13 C3		Schouwburg....................17 B3	
Nationaal Fietsmuseum Velorama..6 C2		De Schat.........................14 C2			
Sint Nicolaaskapel..............7 C3		De Waagh........................(see 9)		TRANSPORT	
Sint Stevenskerk................8 B3				Boat Tours......................18 C2	
Waag.............................9 C3					

To Arnhem
(17km)

Waal

Waal

Benedenstad

Beurtse Weg

Waalhaven

Waalkade

Oude Haven

Lage Markt

Waalbrug

Vluchthaven

Ooyse Schependom

Nonnenstr

Waalkade

Voorstadslaan

Lange Hezelstr

Kronenburgersingel

Doddendaal

Grotestr

Smidstr

Hezelstr

Burchtstr

Valkhof

Keizer Traianuspl

't Meertje

T Mariënburg

Kronenburgerpark

Bloemerstr

Molenstr

Grote Markt

Broerstr

Hunnerpark

Marikenstr

Ziekerstr

Hertogstr

Krayenhofflaan

train station

Tunnelweg

Tunnelweg

Nassausingel

Walstr

Van Welderenstr

Oranjesingel

Sint Canisiussingel

Van Schaeck Mathonsingel

Keizer Karelpl

Bijleveldsingel

Daalse Weg

Berg en Dalseweg

Koninginnelaan

Van Oldenbarneveltstr

Waldeck-Pyrmontsingel

Prins Bernhard Str

Van Demerbroekstr

Sint Annastr

Graafseweg

Groenestr

Spoorstr

Groesbeekse Weg

Wolfskuil

Altrade

Bottendaal

To St Anna B&B
(500m);
Doornroosje
(1km)

To Camping
Maikenshof (2km)

history on its side: there's a rivalry between it and Maastricht for the title of 'oldest city in the Netherlands', although these days it's archaeologically accepted that Nijmegen is older.

Nijmegen also has a bustling waterfront culture on the Waal, Western Europe's busiest expanse of river.

Information

Library (☎ 327 49 11; Mariënburg 29; internet per hr €4; ☺ 2-6pm Mon-Wed, 2-8pm Fri, 10am-2pm Sat)
Post office (☎ 323 90 92; Van Schevichavenstraat 1; ☺ 8am-6pm Mon-Fri, 8am-1pm Sat)
Tourist office (☎ 0900-1122344; www.vvvnijmegen.nl; Keizer Karelplein 2; ☺ 9.30am-5.30pm Mon-Fri, 9.30am-5pm Sat)

Sights & Activities

The **Museum het Valkhof** (☎ 360 88 05; www.museumhetvalkhof.nl; Kelfkensbos 59; adult/child €6/3; ☺ 10am-5pm Tue-Fri; 2-5pm Sat & Sun) is housed in a striking building, the heaving, 16-sided St Nicolaaskapel – originally a replica of Charlemagne's palace at Aachen – that has been remodelled and reworked in a multitude of styles (depending on who held power in Nijmegen) during its 950-year life-span. The museum's collections cover regional history and art and there's a first-rate section of Roman artefacts.

The **Nationaal Fietsmuseum Velorama** (National Cycling Museum; ☎ 322 58 51; www.velorama.nl; Waalkade 107; adult/child €4.60/2.80; ☺ 10am-5pm Mon-Fri, 11am-5pm Sun & public holidays) is a small but interesting museum with over 250 bikes: everything from

19th-century wooden contraptions to hand-propelled bikes, to an entire room devoted to penny-farthings, plus more modern – and sane – machines. It's a must-see for anyone who's marvelled at the remarkable Dutch affinity with two-wheelers.

A few important bits of the old town either survived the war or have been reconstructed. The **Waag** (weigh-house) on Grote Markt was built in 1612 and has a lovely interior (see p266), while **Sint Stevenskerk** (☎ 360 47 10; tower climb €1; ☼ 1-4pm Sat & Sun) is the large 14th-century church.

Commanderie van St Jan, near Grote Markt on Franseplaats, was a 12th-century hospital for the knights of St John. It has a very different use today: it's a brewery (p266).

Even allowing for the usual air of frivolity commonly associated with such watery zones, strolling along the **Waalkade**, Nijmegen's waterfront, is delightful – especially if you're into boats and shipping. This stretch of river, Europe's busiest, sees a large barge or ferry plying past Nijmegen every few minutes. Sometimes it's busier than the traffic on the road. Walk or ride a bike along the **Waalbrug** for breath-stealing sunset views of the old town, the water and the boats chugging below.

Cruises on the Waal depart from the waterfront along Waalkade. Some go all the way to Rotterdam. There are various companies; make inquiries at the tourist office for best results.

Festivals & Events

Nijmegen's big event is the **Internationale Wandelvierdaagse** (www.4daagse.nl), a four-day, 120km- to 200km-long march held in mid-July every year. It has a long history: the first one was held in 1909. Thousands walk it, even though the shortest or easiest route is a minimum of 30km a day. Many suffer debilitating blisters, while thousands more endure debilitating hangovers, as the Wandelvierdaagse is the city's excuse for a week-long party. Competitors set off in a different direction (north, south, east, west) each day, and there are varying route classifications according to gender and age.

Note: Two walkers died on the first day of the 2006 event, causing the Wandelvierdaagse to be cancelled. The future of the event is now very much in flux. Check the website for updates.

Sleeping

St Anna B&B (☎ 350 18 08; www.sintanna.nl; St Annastraat 208; s/d from €58/70) Perhaps Nijmegen's most charming accommodation; St Anna's owners also run a travel agency specialising in New Zealand, which explains the sheep motif. It also explains why one of the rooms has pictures of kiwi fruit on the walls and on the bedding. There are numerous comforts here as well as a wonderfully warm welcome.

Hotel Atlanta (☎ 360 30 00; www.atlanta-hotel.nl; Grote Markt 38-40; s/d €57.50/83.50) This place is a great-value option with comfy room. It's also home to a popular café on the Grote Markt. Beware, though – the central location gets quite noisy at night.

our pick **Hotel Courage** (☎ 360 49 70; www.hotelcourage.nl; Waalkade 108-112; s/d from €75/98) Restored old-style hotel with a superb location right on the waterfront – in the shadow of the Waalbrug –plus a nice restaurant and bar and very cosy rooms. Choose from tiered pricing packages: more cash for river views, less for park views.

Mercure Nijmegen Centre (☎ 323 88 88; www.accorhotels.com; Stationsplein 29; r from €85; ☐ ✗) Not bad, but you know, it's a large chain hotel aimed at business travellers, so design features are not a high priority. Having said that, rooms are super comfortable, well-appointed (aesthetically bland, of course) and spotlessly clean. Other options:

Camping Maikenshof (☎ 684 16 51; Oude Kleefsbaan 134; campsites from €12) Take bus 6 from the train station east for 6km (direction: Beek) to the last stop in Berg en Dal.

Hotel Apollo (☎ 322 35 94; www.apollo-hotel-nijmegen.nl; Hamerstraat 14; s/d €75/98) Basic, friendly place; spartan but comfortable rooms.

Eating

Circus (☎ 360 66 56; www.restauranthetcircus.nl; Kelfkensbos 21; mains €14-26; ☼ dinner) This is a more stylish restaurant than its free-wheeling moniker implies – no tiger or elephant on the menu, although it is meaty Dutch fare, even if that most un-Dutch of animals, the kangaroo, sometimes makes a cameo appearance.

De Schat (☎ 322 40 60; www.deschat.nl; Waalkade 1; ☼ lunch & dinner) A nice place along the Waalkade, with white-linen tables heaving with fresh seafood in Dutch variations. There's a great *fruits-de-mer* (seafood) selection, too, eminently fitting for the location.

OVERIJSSEL & GELDERLAND

De Waagh (☎ 323 07 57; www.de-waagh.nl; Grote Markt 26; ✇ lunch & dinner) This is an atmospheric place in which to eat, being as it is the town's 1612 former weigh-house. The interior has been restored to a rich, sumptuous Burgundian ideal. The food's perhaps not as thrilling, although it is hearty: trip out on the sea bream with acid cabbage.

Drinking
De Blauwe Hand (Blue Hand; ☎ 360 61 67; Achter de Hoofdwacht 3) The best bar in Nijmegen is also its oldest, an ancient survivor that derives its name from its 17th-century customers: workers at a nearby dye shop. The Blue Hand is the perfect little Dutch bar, friendly and inviting, as evidenced by its motto: 'A frosty mug of rich beer gives you warmth, joy and sweet pleasure'.

De Hemel (Heaven; ☎ 360 61 67; www.brouwerijde hemel.nl; Franseplaats 1; ✇ 12-8pm Tue-Sun) The building housing this brewery and distillery, the ancient Commanderie van St Jan (p265), is worth a visit on its own. But the goods also pass muster. Of the beers, there's Luna, a 5% lager; Helse Engel (Hell's Angels), weighing in at a whopping 8%; and Nieuw Ligt, which is anything but, being heavy in taste, body and colour – it'll knock you sideways with its 10% alcohol quotient. Of the liqueurs, try the beer brandy and the beer gin (both 40%), and the cinnamon liqueur (20%). There's also beer vinegar, beer mustard, beer bread and beer chocolate, and all of this and more is available in their shop.

Entertainment
CLASSICAL MUSIC
Nijmegen boasts two large, formal performance venues.
Concertgebouw de Vereeniging (Oranjesingel 11A; ☎ schedule & ticket info, both venues 322 11 00)
Schouwburg (Keizer Karelplein 32)

LIVE MUSIC
Doornroosje (☎ 355 98 87; www.doornroosje.nl; Groene-woudseweg 322) Long-running, eclectic multipurpose venue, with live comedy and music ranging from electronica and house to indie-rock and world music. It's got its own gym, with a 10% discount on membership just for flashing their monthly guide.

CINEMA
Lux Filmcentrum (☎ 381 68 55; www.lux-nijmegen.nl; Mariënburg 38-39; admission €6-7, 5-film card €25)

Getting There & Around
The train station is large and modern with many services. Lockers are near the ticket windows.

Destination	Price (€)	Duration (min)	Frequency (per hr)
Amsterdam	16.20	90	2
Arnhem	4.60	12	5
Den Bosch	8.00	30	4

Regional and local buses depart from the area in front of the station.

The bicycle shop is underground in front of the station.

ARNHEM
☎ 026 / pop 142,162
With its centre all but levelled during WWII, Arnhem today is a nondescript, though prosperous township with several museums and attractions around its northern outskirts. Plus it's a desirable launch pad for Hoge Veluwe National Park. Another fact from the war years: Audrey Hepburn attended Arnhem Conservatory from 1939 to 1945.

The **tourist office** (☎ 370 02 26; www.vvvarnhem .nl; Willemsplein 8; ✇ 9am-6pm Mon-Fri, 9am-1pm Sat) is a 10-minute walk east of the train station.

Sights & Activities
Southeast of the Korenmarkt, is the **John Frost-brug**, a replica of the infamous 'bridge too far' (opposite). It's not much to look at, but its symbolic value is immense.

The **Museum voor Moderne Kunst** (☎ 351 24 31; www.mmkarnhem.nl; Utrechtseweg 87; €6; ✇ 10am-5pm Tue-Fri, 11am-5pm Sat & Sun) has a commanding spot overlooking the Rijn (Rhine), and its modern art collection represents Arnhem's determination to look forward. Most of the collection is by Dutch artists and the progressive curatorial policy is that at least half of the works on display at any time must be by women.

Here's a change of pace: the **Nederlands Open-luchtmuseum** (☎ 357 61 11; www.openluchtmuseum.nl; Schelmseweg 89; adult/child €12.90/9; ✇ 10am-5pm Apr-Oct) is an open-air museum of Dutch heritage with a collection of buildings and artefacts from all provinces, everything from farmhouses and old trams to working windmills. Volunteers in authentic costume demonstrate traditional skills including weaving, smithing and farming.

A BRIDGE TOO FAR: OPERATION MARKET GARDEN

The battle they called Operation Market Garden was devised by British General Bernard Montgomery to end WWII in Europe by Christmas. Despite advisers warning that the entire operation was likely to fail, Montgomery pushed on. He had often groused that the Americans under General George Patton were getting all the headlines in their charge across France. The plan was for British forces in Belgium to make a huge push along a narrow corridor to Arnhem in the Netherlands, where they would cut off large numbers of German troops from being able to return to Germany, thereby allowing the British to dash east to Berlin and end the war.

Everything went wrong. The British paratroops were only given two days' rations and the forces from the south had to cross 14 bridges, all of which had to remain traversable and lightly defended for the plan to work. The southern forces encountered some of the German army's most hardened troops and the bridges weren't all completely intact. This, in effect, stranded the Arnhem paratroops. They held out there and in neighbouring Oosterbeek for eight days without food or reinforcements. The survivors, a mere 2163, retreated under darkness. Over 17,000 other British troops were killed.

The results of the debacle were devastating for the Dutch: Arnhem and other towns were levelled and hundreds of civilians killed. The Dutch resistance, thinking that liberation was at hand, came out of hiding to fight the Germans. But without the anticipated Allied forces supporting them, hundreds were captured and killed.

Finally Montgomery abandoned the country. The winter of 1944–45 came to be known as the 'winter of hunger', with starvation rife as no food could be imported from Allied-held Belgium.

Most of the Netherlands was still occupied when the war ended in Europe in May 1945.

Sleeping

Hotel Parkzicht (☎ 442 06 98; Apeldoornsestraat 16; s/d from €37.50/70) This convenient place is 10 minutes – downhill – from the station and has basic, decent rooms including triples and quads. It's okay to bring your pets to this laidback place (dogs are welcome in the Hoge Veluwe, but not necessarily at every hotel).

Hotel Old Dutch (☎ 442 07 92; www.old-dutch.nl; Stationsplein 8; s/d from €73.50/97) Conveniently located for transport connections, it's across the road from the main train station with comfortable, pretty rooms and a homey, friendly feel. In fact, it's the best all-round option within walking distance of Arnhem's commercial centre.

Stayokay Arnhem (☎ 442 01 14; www.stayokay .com/arnhem; Diepenbrocklaan 27; d €22.50) Inconvenient to the town centre, at 2km north of town, but perfectly situated for seeing a lot of the sights on Arnhem's outskirts, especially by bike. Take bus 3 (direction: Alteveer) and get off at Rijnstate Ziekenhuis (hospital).

Getting There & Around

Buses and public transport leave from in front of the station, although the renovation sporadically affects this.

Destination	Price (€)	Duration (min)	Frequency (per hr)
Amsterdam	13.80	70	2
Deventer	7.10	36	2
Nijmegen	3.60	12	5

The bicycle shop is to the right as you exit the station.

AROUND ARNHEM
WWII Cemeteries
OOSTERBEEK

An old suburb 5km west of Arnhem, Oosterbeek was the scene of heavy combat during Operation Market Garden.

The **Airborne Museum Hartenstein** (☎ 333 77 10; www.airbornemuseum.org; Utrechtsweg 232; adult/child & veteran €4.80/3.80; ☯ 11am-5pm Mon-Sat, 12-5pm Sun) is inside a mansion used by the British as HQ during the battle. Take trolleybus 1 serving both Oosterbeek and Arnhem train stations.

The **Oosterbeek War Cemetery** is 200m northeast of Oosterbeek train station (follow the signs). Over 1700 Allied (mostly British and Free Polish) troops are buried here.

The tourist offices in Nijmegen and Arnhem can both provide more specific information on how to visit any or all of these monuments to the Allied war fallen.

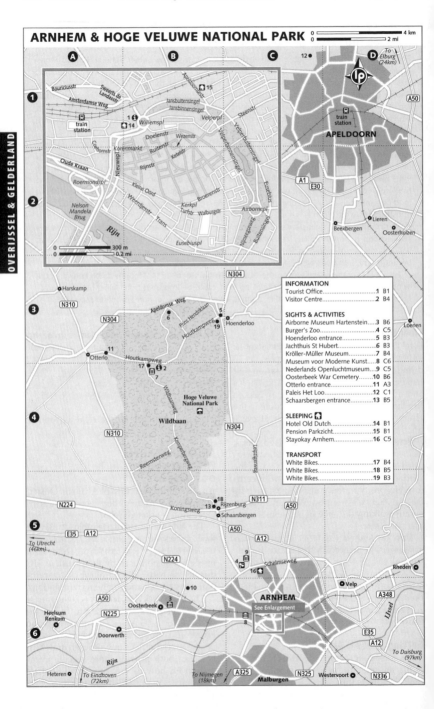

ARNHEM & HOGE VELUWE NATIONAL PARK

INFORMATION
Tourist Office.............................**1** B1
Visitor Centre.............................**2** B4

SIGHTS & ACTIVITIES
Airborne Museum Hartenstein.....**3** B6
Burger's Zoo.............................**4** C5
Hoenderloo entrance.................**5** B3
Jachthuis St Hubert...................**6** B3
Kröller-Müller Museum...............**7** B4
Museum voor Moderne Kunst.....**8** C6
Nederlands Openluchtmuseum.....**9** C5
Oosterbeek War Cemetery.........**10** B6
Otterlo entrance.......................**11** A3
Paleis Het Loo.........................**12** C1
Schaarsbergen entrance............**13** B5

SLEEPING
Hotel Old Dutch.......................**14** B1
Pension Parkzicht......................**15** B1
Stayokay Arnhem......................**16** C5

TRANSPORT
White Bikes.............................**17** B4
White Bikes.............................**18** B5
White Bikes.............................**19** B3

GROESBEEK

The small town of Groesbeek, just inside Gelderland's southern border, 10km south of Nijmegen, is home to the **National Liberation Museum 1944–45** (☎ 397 44 04; www.bevrijdings museum.nl; Wylerbaan 4; adult/child €8/4; ☒ 10am-5pm Mon-Sat, noon-5pm Sun). The museum aims to show the causes, events and outcomes of the Allied efforts leading to the liberation of the Netherlands. Using interactive displays and historical artefacts, visitors can 'relive' the strategic decisions and tactical actions of the various campaigns and battle locations. The ambitious museum also attempts to define for younger visitors what the ideals of democracy, freedom and human rights mean, and why people die fighting to protect them.

Nearby, the **Groesbeek Canadian War Cemetery** is a mausoleum dedicated to the soldiers who fell here during Operation Market Garden. Of the 2610 Commonwealth soldiers commemorated, 2331 are Canadian. There is a memorial listing by name 1000 soldiers whose graves' whereabouts are unknown.

In the tiny township of Jonkerbos (a short distance from Nijmegen), **Jonkerbos War Cemetery** is the final resting place of mainly British servicemen.

HOGE VELUWE NATIONAL PARK

This **park** (☎ 0318-59 10 41; www.hogeveluwe.nl; adult/child €6/3, park & museum €12/6; ☒ 9am-6pm Nov-Mar, 8am-8pm Apr, 8am-9pm May & Aug, 8am-10pm Jun & Jul, 9am-8pm Sep, 9am-7pm Oct), the largest in the Netherlands, would be a fantastic place to visit for its marshlands, forests and sand dunes alone, but its brilliant museum makes it unmissable.

The park was purchased by Anton and Helene Kröller-Müller, a wealthy German-Dutch couple, in 1914. He wanted hunting grounds, she wanted a museum site. They got both. It was given to the state in 1930, and in 1938 a museum opened for Helene's remarkable art collection. A visit to the park can fill an entire day, and even if you don't have a bike, you can borrow one of the park's hundreds of famous, free white bicycles.

The ticket booths at each of the three entrances at Hoenderloo, Otterlo and Schaarsbergen have basic information and highly useful park maps (€3.50). In the heart of the park, the main visitors centre is an attraction itself. It has displays on the flora and fauna, including one showing the gruesome results

when a deer has a bad day and a crow has a good day.

Roads through the park are limited. There are many bike paths and 42km of hiking trails, with three routes signposted. The most interesting area is the **Wildbaan**, south of the Kröller-Müller Museum. At the north edge, **Jachthuis St Hubert** is the baronial hunting lodge that Anton had built. Named after the patron saint of hunting (but not the hunted), you can tour its woodsy interior.

Cars are not admitted after 8pm.

Kröller-Müller Museum

About 10km into the park (an hour by cycle) and among the best museums in the land, the **Kröller-Müller Museum** (☎ 0318-59 12 41; www.kmm.nl; Houtkampweg 6; adult/child €12/6; ☒ 10am-5pm Tue-Sun) has works by Picasso, Gris, Renoir, Sisley and Manet. Good enough, but it's the Van Gogh collection that elevates it to world class, a stunning collection of 278 of the artist's work that rivals the collection in the eponymous Amsterdam museum.

There's also a sculpture garden featuring works by Rodin, Moore and more.

Getting There & Around

There is a bus service from the train stations in Arnhem and Apeldoorn. From Arnhem, take bus 2 (direction: Deelevy OC) to the Schaarsbergen entrance and on to the Kröller-Müller Museum. The first bus leaves at 10.10am (April to October) and there are three more through the day (one per hour in July and August). From Apeldoorn, bus 110 leaves the station every hour from 8.42am to 4.42pm.

There is car parking at the visitors centre, museum and lodge. By bike, the park is easily reached from any direction. You can also wait and use a free white bicycle, available at the entrance.

APELDOORN

The rather featureless town of Apeldoorn has one class attraction: the **Paleis het Loo** (☎ 055-577 24 00; www.paleishetloo.nl; Koninklijk Park 1; adult/child €9/3; ☒ 10am-5pm Tue-Sun), built in 1685 for William III; Queen Wilhelmina lived here until 1962. Now it's a magnificent museum celebrating the history of the royal House of Oranje-Nassau. View the royal bedchambers, regal paintings, royal furniture, silverware, the lavish dining room dating from 1686, the vintage car fleet, the immense gardens with their maze of hedgerows and pathways…

ELBURG

☎ 0525 / pop 22,022

Gorgeous Elburg has a sculpted, cobbled 16th-century splendour. Compact and gridlike, its centre can be easily explored on foot. One highlight is the old harbour. Continue all the way down Jufferenstraat, through the old gate at the end of Vischpoortstraat and into the harbour itself, where a small flotilla of pleasure and fishing boats can take you on a boat tour. There's also an enjoyable market in good weather, where you can help yourself to cheap snacks or local crafts.

Visit the **tourist office** (☎ 68 15 20; www.vvvelburg .nl; Ledige Stede 31; ☉ 9am-5pm Mon-Fri year-round, 10am-4pm Sat May-Aug) for more information.

There's just one hotel, the **Elburg** (☎ 68 38 77; www.hotelelburg.nl; Smedestraat 5-7; s/d €58.50/89.50).

Getting There & Around

Take bus 100, 200, 184 or 144 from Zwolle train station on any weekday. Bus 100 is the only one that runs on weekends. The service runs every 30 minutes, and will deposit you about 100 metres from the beginning of Jufferenstraat, the main drag.

Noord Brabant & Limburg

The Dutch southeast belies most clichés about the Netherlands: tulips, windmills and dykes are scarce. Noord Brabant is primarily a land of agriculture and industry peppered with a few pleasant towns, including Den Bosch. It's also home to the Netherlands' most popular tourist draw, De Efteling theme park, and the biggest street fair in Benelux, the Tilburgse Kermis.

Meanwhile, Limburg is home to beautiful Maastricht, contender for the title of Finest Dutch City, as well as – drum roll – hills. It also hosts Europe's biggest art sale, the European Fine Art Foundation show.

Neither province has its roots in the asceticism of the north, a fact made obvious during *carnaval*, when the streets fill with fireworks, bands and impromptu parties. And both provinces' proximity to Belgium and all those indulgent Catholic monasteries – most of which doubled as excellent microbreweries – mean there are many chances to imbibe.

In fact, the Dutch call the southeastern lifestyle *bourgondisch*: like the epicurean inhabitants of Burgundy in France, people in these parts love to eat and drink heartily.

NOORD BRABANT & LIMBURG

HIGHLIGHTS

- Thrill to the rarefied vibe in **Maastricht** (p278), a world apart from the north.
- Scare yourself silly in the tunnels at **Sint Pietersberg** (p280).
- Take it easy in laid-back **Den Bosch** (p272).
- Admire European modern art at Eindhoven's **Stedelijk Van Abbemuseum** (p274).
- Do the day-trip thing in lovely **Breda** (p275).

★ Den Bosch
★ Breda
★ Eindhoven
Maastricht & Sint Pietersberg ★ Tunnels

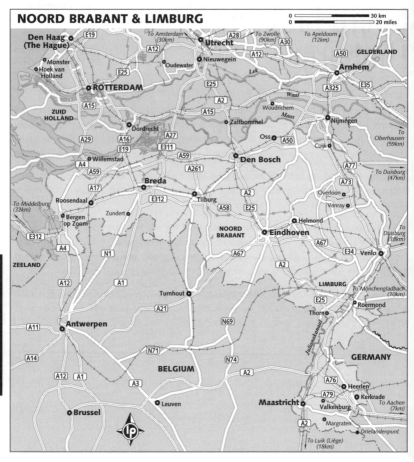

NOORD BRABANT & LIMBURG

NOORD BRABANT

The Netherlands' largest province spans the bottom of the country from the waterlogged west to the elevated east. The towns here have mostly transformed from wealthy medieval fiefdoms to laid-back shopping, student and tourism precincts. Den Bosch is the main city and, along with Breda, is an interesting place to spend the day.

Despite its size, Noord Brabant won't hold you up. It's primarily a land of agriculture and industry, peppered with a few towns pleasant and engaging enough to use as way stations on your pilgrimage to Limburg or beyond.

DEN BOSCH ('S-HERTOGENBOSCH)
☎ 073 / pop 134,000

This sweet old town has a top-notch church, a good museum, outstanding cafés and restaurants, and atmospheric streets that make for plenty of enjoyable strolling. The official name of the town is 's-Hertogenbosch (Duke's Forest), but locals call it Den Bosch (den boss). It's the birthplace of the well-known 15th-century painter Hieronymous Bosch, who took his surname from the town.

Orientation
The town's pedestrianised centre is based around the Markt, 600m east of the train station.

Information
Bosch Medicentrum (☎ 699 20 00; Nieuwstraat 34) Regional hospital.
Library (☎ 612 30 33; Hinthamerstraat 72; internet per hr €3; ☻ noon-4pm Mon, Tue-Sat 11am-8pm)
Post office (Kerkstraat 67; ☻ 9am-6pm Mon-Fri, 9am-2pm Sat)
Tourist office (☎ 09001122334; www.regio-vvv.nl; Markt 77; ☻ 1-6pm Mon, 9.30am-6pm Tue-Fri, 9am-5pm Sat)

Sights & Activities
The main attraction is **Sint Janskathedraal** (☎ 613 03 14; www.sint-jan.nl; Choorstraat 1; admission free; ☻ 10am-4.30pm Mon-Sat, 1-4.30pm Sun), one of the finest churches in the Netherlands. It took from 1336 to 1550 to complete, and there's an interesting contrast between the red-brick tower and the ornate stone buttresses. The interior is also of interest, with late-Gothic stained-glass windows, an impressive statue of the Madonna, and an amazing organ case from the 17th century.

Unfortunately, Protestants destroyed the cathedral's paintings in 1566. Thankfully, two by Bosch remain.

Take the opportunity to climb the 73m **tower** (admission €3.50), with its carillon and great views.

The **Stadhuis** (town hall) was given its classical baroque appearance in 1670. There's a statue of Hieronymus Bosch at the front of the building.

The **Noordbrabants Museum** (☎ 687 78 77; www.noordbrabantsmuseum.nl; Verwersstraat 41; adult/child €6.50/3.50; ☻ 10am-5pm Tue-Fri, noon-5pm Sat), in the 18th-century former governor's residence, features a sculpture garden and exhibits about Brabant life and art, including drawings and other work by Bosch.

Boat tours leave from the canal by Sint Janssingel. Check the tourist office for times.

Sleeping
Hotel Terminus (☎ 613 06 66; fax 613 07 26; Boschveldweg 15; s/d €31/60) As its name suggests, it's close to the station. The simple, brightly coloured rooms are decent enough, plus there's an appealing bar (well, the owners call it a 'folk pub') and regular live folk music.

Hotel Euro (☎ 613 77 77; www.eurohotel-denbosch .com; Kerkstraat 56; s/d from €65/85) This business hotel

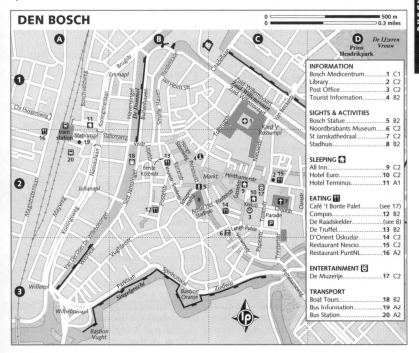

DEN BOSCH

0 ——————— 500 m
0 ——————— 0.3 miles

INFORMATION	
Bosch Medicentrum............1	C1
Library..............................2	C2
Post Office........................3	C2
Tourist Information............4	B2

SIGHTS & ACTIVITIES	
Bosch Statue.....................5	B2
Noordbrabants Museum.....6	C2
St Janskathedraal..............7	C2
Stadhuis............................8	B2

SLEEPING	
All Inn..............................9	C2
Hotel Euro.......................10	C2
Hotel Terminus.................11	A1

EATING	
Café 't Bonte Palet...........(see 17)	
Compas...........................12	B2
De Raadskelder.................(see 8)	
De Truffel........................13	B2
D'Orient Üskudar.............14	C2
Restaurant Nescio............15	C2
Restaurant PuntNL............16	A2

ENTERTAINMENT	
De Muzerije.....................17	C2

TRANSPORT	
Boat Tours.......................18	B2
Bus Information................19	A2
Bus Station......................20	A2

NOORD BRABANT & LIMBURG

is part of a chain, but it's still got a certain degree of warmth, even if the rooms are draped in chintzy corporate pastels. The location is central and next to a warren of great cafés and eating houses.

All Inn (☎ 613 40 57; Gasselstraat 1; s/d from €35/50; Ⓧ closed Aug & carnaval) On the lovably shabby but clean side. Note: midnight curfew.

Eating & Drinking

Try the local speciality, a heart-failure calorie-fest known as the *Bossche bol* (Den Bosch ball). It's a chocolate-coated cake the size of a softball, filled with sweetened cream.

De Truffel (☎ 614 27 42; www.detruffel.com; Kruisstraat 37; mains €10-25; Ⓧ dinner) Located in a restored warehouse, De Truffel serves top-notch Mediterranean food in a relaxed atmosphere. Try this: whole roasted trout with browned almonds and a stuffed potato. Now that's attention to detail you don't see everywhere.

Restaurant Nescio (☎ 610 09 00; www.nescio -restaurant.nl; Hinthamerstraat 80; dishes from €4; Ⓧ dinner) Nescio only serves appetisers, the idea being to emphasise taste via concentrated, small portions, as well as the notion that to sample several experiences is preferable than one main one. Try fancies such as the 'preserved Oriental duck bolts' or ask the chef for a 'wild card': be sure to tell him your boundaries (no bulls' penises, for example) and let him surprise you.

Compas (☎ 614 20 20; Postelstraat 79; mains €12-18; Ⓧ lunch & dinner) Perched on a little square a few streets behind the Markt, this is a very charming and classy little option. Expect Mediterranean food with an oh-so-delectable flourish and sense of panache.

Restaurant puntNL (☎ 623 44 55; www.restaurant puntnl.nl; Magistratenlaan 100; mains €7-15; Ⓧ lunch Tue-Sun) If this relaxed place was any more Dutch, it'd rust. Try local favourites such as roasted aubergine with sugary *stroop* (syrup), grated radish, chopped chives and giant shrimp – just the kind of taste clash that is favoured here. Wash it down with *jenever* (Dutch gin) or elderberry juice and you'll be wearing clogs in no time.

Café 't Bonte Palet (☎ 613 25 32; Hinthamerstraat 97) Talk about quirky: the front window of this little hole-in-the-wall bar is stuffed with all kinds of trinkets including miniature carillons, toy cars, tiny theatrical sets, and the crowning glory: an Asterix triptych. There's sometimes live music.

Other options:

De Raadskelder (☎ 613 69 19; Markt 1A; Ⓧ Tue-Sat 10.30am-5pm, dinner Sun 5.30-10.30pm) A 16th-century Gothic cellar kitchen/restaurant right under the town hall. The ambience is nothing short of inspirational.

D' Orient Üskudar (☎ 614 20 20; Verwersstraat 3; mains €8-15; Ⓧ dinner) Great Turkish food; lots of goats cheese throughout.

Entertainment

De Muzerije (☎ 614 10 84; Hinthamerstraat 74) This all-in-one venue features different kinds of theatre, dance and film.

Getting There & Around

The train station is new and brimming with services, including a good grocery store aimed at travellers. Lockers are on the concourse over the tracks. Sample fares and schedules:

Destination	Price (€)	Duration (min)	Frequency (per hr)
Amsterdam	12.70	60	2
Maastricht	18.00	90	1
Nijmegen	6.80	30	4
Utrecht	7.50	30	4

Buses leave from the area to the right as you exit the station.

A bicycle shop is located below the station.

EINDHOVEN

☎ 040 / pop 209,286

A mere village in 1900, Eindhoven grew exponentially thanks to Philips, founded here in 1891. During the 1990s the electronics giant found it was having trouble recruiting employees to work in its home town; it solved the problem by moving to Amsterdam, although its research and engineering arms remain here. That sums up the fortunes of this huge industrial town: while it's not the most thrilling place, it's not without merits.

Electronics aside, Eindhoven is best known for its football team, PSV, who routinely dominate the national league.

There's a **tourist office** (☎ 297 91 00; www .vvveindhoven.nl; Stationsplein 17; Ⓧ 10am-5.30pm Mon, 9am-5.30pm Tue-Thu, 9am-6.30pm Fri, 10am-5pm Sat) next to the train station.

Eindhoven's main attraction is the excellent **Stedelijk Van Abbemuseum** (☎ 275 52 75; www .vanabbemuseum.nl; Bilderdijklaan 10; adult/child under 12 €8.50/free; Ⓧ 11am-5pm Tue, Wed & Fri-Sun, until 9pm

Thu). With a wonderful, first-rate collection of 20th-century paintings – including works by Picasso, Chagall and Kandinsky – it almost, but not quite, matches the greatness of the Stedelijk Museum in Amsterdam or the Boijmans van Beuningen in Rotterdam.

There's a unique nightlife district, **Het Stratumseind**, where more than 30 cafés, bars and restaurants within a single stretch of street make it one of the most concentrated such areas in the country. There are many options, and obviously bar-hopping is easy to do.

Eindhoven Airport (www.eindhovenairport.nl) is 6km west of the centre, and aimed at business travellers.

The train station is at a junction of lines to Amsterdam, Maastricht and Rotterdam.

Sample fares and schedules:

Destination	Price (€)	Duration (min)	Frequency (per hr)
Amsterdam	16.70	90	2
Maastricht	14.10	80	2
Rotterdam	15.30	70	2

TILBURG
☎ 013 / pop 198,000

With one of the highest ratios of students in the Netherlands (almost 15% of the population), you'd expect a more progressive vibe. But Tilburg, a former textile town, is in flux, now that the mills have closed due to foreign competition, and its centre bears the scars of unfortunate 1960s urban renewal schemes (think East Berlin).

People generally make a beeline to Tilburg in the middle of July, when the **Tilburgse Kermis** (Tilburg Fair; www.tilburgsekermis.com) takes place for close to two weeks. Basically an enormous street party, it's a massive celebration of street fair and street fare. Rides, beer, bad music, sugary treats, stalls offering stuffed prizes for games of 'skill'… It's the biggest fair in Benelux, and for that reason alone it's remarkable.

DE EFTELING
Near Tilburg, in the unassuming town of Kaatsheuvel, is **De Efteling** (☎ 0416-288 111; www.efteling .nl; Europalaan 1, Kaatsheuvel; admission €26; ☒ 10am-6pm Apr-Oct, until 9pm 10 Jul-27 Aug), the biggest domestic tourist attraction in the Netherlands. This 'Dutch Disneyland' pulls more than three million visitors annually, proving its 40-year history as a family favourite is undiminished

by the emergence of newer competitors such as Flevoland's Six Flags.

All the usual suspects are here: huge, scary rides, walk-through entertainment with animatronic robot models, scenes from popular stories and fairy tales, live shows performed by 'talent', sticky hands, crying kids…

There's on-site accommodation – the website provides full details.

To get to De Efteling, take bus 136 or 137 from Tilburg or Den Bosch train station.

BREDA
☎ 076 / pop 167,908

Lovely Breda has a wealth of attractions: interesting streets, flower-filled parks and a stunning main church. Its present peace belies its turbulent past, where its proximity to the Belgian border meant it has been overrun by invading armies many times.

The town centre is 500m south of the station through the large, leafy park, the Valkenberg.

There are two **tourist offices** (www.vvvbreda.nl; Grote Markt ☎ 09005222444; Grote Markt 38; ☒ 10.30am-5.30pm Wed-Fri, 10.30am-5pm Sat; Willemstraat ☎ 09005222444; Willemstraat 17; ☒ 1-6pm Mon, 9am-6pm Tue-Fri, 9am-5pm Sat) and a **post office** (☎ 522 55 20; Willemstraat 30; ☒ 9am-6pm Mon-Fri, 10am-1.30pm Sat) further down from the Willemstraat tourist office.

Sights & Activities
The **Valkenberg** (Falcon Mountain) is the huge park between the station and the centre. Hunting falcons were trained here for royalty. On the south side is the 12th-century **Begijnhof**, a home that sheltered unmarried women. Breda has wonderfully preserved examples of these homes, which were found throughout the Netherlands.

The **Breda castle** is worth a quick look (though note that you can't go inside); approach from the south and you'll also see the **Spanjaardsgat** (Spanish gate), a reminder of just one of the various incursions the town has endured.

The **Grote Kerk** (admission €2; ☒ 10am-5pm Mon-Sat, 1-5pm Sun) recently emerged from years of restoration, its now-gleaming white stones free of grime. This beautiful Gothic church was built between the 15th and 17th centuries.

Festivals & Events
The **Bloemencorso** (www.bloemencorsozundert.nl) is a huge annual parade of gorgeously decorated,

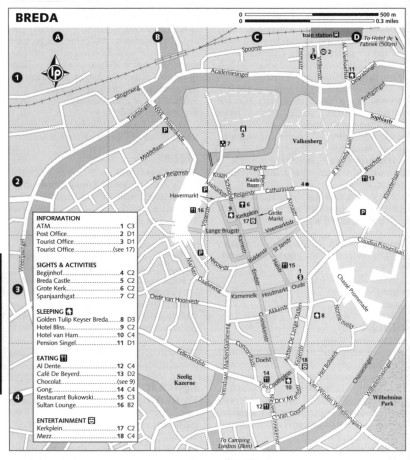

BREDA

0   500 m
0   0.3 miles

INFORMATION
ATM..1 C3
Post Office.....................................2 D1
Tourist Office................................3 D1
Tourist Office........................(see 17)

SIGHTS & ACTIVITIES
Begijnhof..4 C2
Breda Castle...................................5 C2
Grote Kerk.....................................6 C2
Spanjaardsgat................................7 C2

SLEEPING 🏠
Golden Tulip Keyser Breda......8 D3
Hotel Bliss.....................................9 D1
Hotel van Ham............................10 C4
Pension Singel.............................11 D1

EATING 🍴
Al Dente.......................................12 C4
Café De Beyerd...........................13 D2
Chocolat.................................(see 9)
Gong...14 C4
Restaurant Bukowski..................15 C3
Sultan Lounge..............................16 B2

ENTERTAINMENT 🎭
Kerkplein......................................17 C2
Mezz...18 C4

multicoloured floats – each one of them constructed entirely from flowers – that passes through the streets of Zundert, 20km southwest of Breda. It takes place in early September.

Sleeping
BUDGET

Camping Liesbos (☎ 514 35 14; www.camping-liesbos.nl; Liesdreef 40; sites €8; ✆ Apr-Oct) If you're a camper, this place is your best bet. Take bus 10 or 111 (direction: Etten-Leur) to the Boswachterij Liesbos stop.

Pension Singel (☎ 521 62 71; pensionsingel@planet.nl; Delpratsingel 14; per person €25) Simple but charming singles and doubles. It's a short walk from the station.

MIDRANGE

Hotel Bliss (☎ 533 59 80; www.blisshotel.nl; Torenstraat 9; ste from €112.50) This funky new designer hotel is head and shoulders above the rest of the Breda competition. The spacious, comfortable suites are filled with the kind of interior-design touches that will make you feel like a mover and shaker: interesting art; angles and planes; retro-futurism bisected with industrial chic; bold reds mixed with deep browns.

Golden Tulip Keyser Breda (☎ 520 51 73; www.hotel keyser.nl; Keizerstraat 5; r from €79) Although it's part of a chain, the Golden Tulip Keyser Breda (say *that* 10 times fast after a few ales) sets itself apart by its attentive staff – its strongest asset. Rooms are standard business-hotel types, with all the trimmings. Prices plunge on weekends.

Hotel van Ham (☎ 521 52 29; hotel.van.ham@hetnet
.nl; Van Coothplein 23; s/d €45/65) John and Sylvia
van Hooydonk are the proud proprietors of
this charming hotel, which is also home to a
delightful café-restaurant. It's in a building
that's been a prominent meeting point for
more than 100 years. The rooms are OK, but
the bar is grand.

Hotel de Fabriek (☎ 581 00 08; Speelhuislaan 150;
s/d €65/80) This is a laid-back, quiet place with
comfortable rooms.

Eating
Sultan Lounge (☎ 520 30 50; www.sultanlounge.nl; Haven
10; mains €11-18; ☯ dinner) OK, you know what
to expect with a name like this. An 'Arabian
Nights' feel spread over two floors is reflected
in the décor and the attitude: the ground
floor has tables and chairs, upstairs has cushions and a lounge. Eat your Middle Eastern
kebabs, tapas, *tajines* (slow cooked stews),
dolmades and spiced, stuffed aubergines on
either level.

Chocolat (☎ 533 59 75; Torenstraat 9; mains €15-30;
☯ lunch & dinner) Part of the Hotel Bliss complex (opposite), Chocolat is as classy as the
accommodation, with its Frenchified menu
delivering the goods: hares, truffles and croquettes feature prominently, as does veal and
fine wine.

Restaurant Bukowski (☎ 529 75 55; www.restaurant
bukowski.nl; Halstraat 21A; mains €16-22; ☯ lunch & dinner)
Bukowski's slick *haute cuisine* is a real treat,
presented in an informal, though elegant setting. The duck breast, pan fried and served with
a vegetable purée of beets, artichoke and carrots
plus honey-thyme sauce, is a clear winner.

Café De Beyerd (☎ 521 42 65; www.beyerd.nl;
Boschstraat 26; ☯ lunch & dinner Thu-Tue) The Beyerd
is a highly regarded beer café, with more
than 122 brews. It's also the perfect place to
try some *bitterballen* (small crumbed, deep-
fried pureed meatballs) or other typical beer-
accompanying snacks.

Other options:

Al Dente (☎ 520 43 33; Nieuwe Ginnekenstraat 20; mains
€11-18; ☯ lunch Mon-Fri, dinner Mon-Sat) Excellent
Italian fare.

Gong (☎ 521 66 96; www.restaurantgong.nl; Van
Coothplein 24; mains €16-20; ☯ dinner) Great Asian and
Pacific Rim fusion cuisine.

Entertainment
There's a concentration of places around the
Havermarkt, mostly of varying quality.

Mezz (☎ 515 66 77; www.mezz.nl; Keizerstraat 101)
This armadillo-shaped nightclub has a great
bar and cool staff to match its eclectic programme – everything from drum 'n' bass
nights to Latin swing and rock.

Kerkplein (www.kerkpleinbreda.nl) A bangin' club,
located right behind the Grote Kerk on Kerkplein, that stays open well into the morning.

Getting There & Around
The train station has all the usual services.
Some fares and schedules:

Destination	Price (€)	Duration (min)	Frequency (per hr)
Amsterdam	18	110	4
Den Bosch	6.80	33	2
Roosendaal	5	17	2
Rotterdam	8.50	32	3

Buses leave from the area to the right as you
exit the station.

A bicycle shop is right next to the station.
For information on a 52km bicycle route,
the Baronie Route, which begins and ends at
Breda, see p73.

SLOT LOEVESTEIN
Near the tiny, beautiful little walled town of
Woudrichem you'll find the 14th-century
castle, **Slot Loevestein** (☎ 0183-44 71 71; www.slotloeve
stein.nl; Loevestein 1; adult/child €6.30/4.80; ☯ 10am-
5pm Mon-Fri, 1-5pm Sat & Sun May-Sep; 1-5pm Sat, Sun &
Wed Oct-Apr). The ancient keep is wonderfully
evocative, perhaps more so for the difficulty
involved in getting there. It's been a prison,
residence and toll castle, though more recently
it has hosted a varied calendar of cultural
events (check the website). It's best accessed
by the ferry from Woudrichem, which stops
right out front.

WEST NOORD BRABANT
Near the border with Zeeland, Noord Brabant
more closely resembles its soggy neighbour:
canals and rivers crisscross the land, and everything is absolutely flat.

Roosendaal is a major rail junction for lines
north to Rotterdam, south to Belgium, east to
Breda and west to Zeeland.

Bergen op Zoom was plundered at various times
by the Spanish, French and even the British. The
results are a hodgepodge of buildings and styles.
It's an unremarkable place except for one week

a year. If you want to see the aftermath of a real party, show up on the Wednesday after Shrove Tuesday. Bergen op Zoom's *carnaval* is the most raucous west of Maastricht, drawing revellers from throughout Europe who basically go on a four-day bender.

LIMBURG

This long and narrow province at times barely seems part of the Netherlands, especially so in the hilly south. There are all sorts of amusing notices on the A2 motorway into Maastricht warning drivers of impending 'steep grades' that would be considered mere humps in other countries.

MAASTRICHT

☎ 043 / pop 121,573

Make no bones about it: Maastricht is utterly beautiful. The Crown Jewel of the south – maybe even the entire country – it's about as far from windmills, clogs and tulips as you'd want. Much of the Netherlands has a 'samey' feel to it, but here there are Spanish and Roman ruins, cosmopolitan food, French and Belgian twists in the architecture, a shrugging off of the shackles of Dutch restraint. Even the landscape's different: there are actually hilly streets and what passes for mountains ringing the centre. Unsurprisingly, many locals see themselves as a sophisticated breed apart from the north; by the same token, earthy northerners see posh Maastricht as having an identity crisis – are these people Dutch or what?

Spanning both banks of the Maas river, with a host of pavement cafés and lovely old cobblestone streets, Maastricht is renowned for world-class dining and an elegant atmosphere that's exquisitely addictive. Hemmed in between Belgium and Germany, it has a pan-European flavour: the average citizen bounces easily between Dutch, English, French, German and Flemish (maybe more). Appropriately, the city hosted two key moments in the history of the EU: on 10 December 1991, the 12 members of the then European Community met to sign the treaty for economic, monetary and political union; they reconvened the following February to sign the treaty creating the EU.

No Netherlands itinerary is complete without visiting Maastricht. If you're heading this way by rail or road to Belgium, you'd be doing yourself a disservice to bypass this wonderful town.

Orientation

The centre of Maastricht is quite compact, bisected by the Maas river. The area on the east side is known as Wyck, and to the south of here is Céramique. It's about 750m from the train station to the Vrijthof, the cultural heart.

Information

BOOKSHOPS

Plantage Boekhandel (☎ 321 08 25; Nieuwstraat 9) Good selection of travel and English-language books.

INTERNET ACCESS

Centre Céramique (☎ 350 56 00; Ave Céramique 50; free internet; ⏰ 10.30am-8.30pm Tue & Thu, 10.30am-5pm Wed & Fri, 10am-5pm Sat, 1-5pm Sun) Contains the library, as well as earthenware displays and a scale model of Maastricht.

MEDICAL SERVICES

Academisch Ziekenhuis Maastricht (☎ 387 65 43; P Debyelaan 25) A huge academic hospital just east of the MECC exposition centre.

POST

Post office (☎ 329 91 99; Statenstraat 4; ⏰ 9am-6pm Mon-Fri, 9am-1.30pm Sat) There's another post office at Stationsstraat 60.

TOURIST INFORMATION

Tourist office (☎ 325 21 21; www.vvvmaastricht.nl; Kleine Staat 1; ⏰ 9am-6pm Mon-Fri, 9am-5pm Sat, 11am-3pm Sun)

Sights & Activities

Maastricht's many delights are scattered along both banks of the Maas, but it's always a pleasant stroll from one side to the other. There's so much historical information to digest around the Vrijthof while strolling the beautiful streets winding through and around it. There are also some great museums and remnants of the medieval city in the Wyck district.

BONNEFANTENMUSEUM

The **Bonnefantenmuseum** (☎ 329 01 90; www.bonne fantenmuseum.nl; Ave Céramique 250; adult/child under 12yr €7/3.50; ⏰ 11am-5pm Tue-Sun) features a 28m tower that's now a local landmark. Designed by Aldo Rossi, the museum opened in 1995, and is well laid-out with collections divided

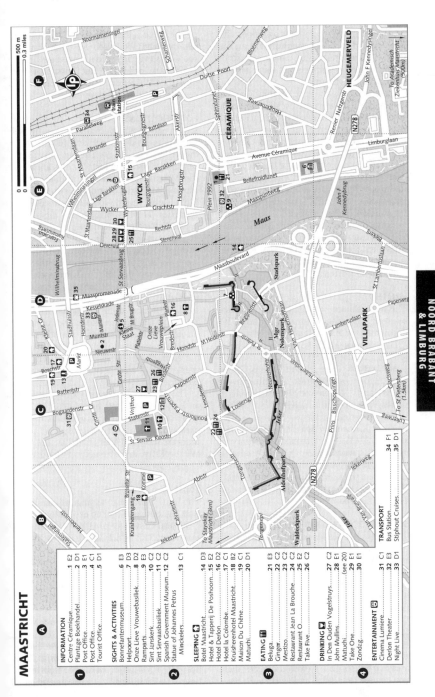

MAASTRICHT

NOORD BRABANT & LIMBURG

into departments, each on its own floor: Old Masters and medieval sculpture are on one floor, contemporary art by Limburg artists on the next. A dramatic sweep of stairs beckons visitors to both floors.

Space is devoted to special exhibitions and shows, of which there are usually four annually, two following classical/historical themes, two on more contemporary material. It also espouses an ongoing commitment to solo exhibitions by young and emerging artists, and is the patron of the major biannual Vincent Van Gogh Award for Contemporary Art in Europe. Temporary exhibitions are revelatory, such as the recent 'Travellin' Light' show, focusing on Dadaist lineages.

From 2006 until 2008, while Amsterdam's Rijksmuseum is undergoing renovation, the Bonnefantenmuseum will display Rijksmuseum classics from the southern Netherlands, Antwerp and Bruges.

VRIJTHOF
The large square of Vrijthof is surrounded by lively cafés and cultural institutions. It's dominated by **Sint Servaasbasiliek** (admission €2; ⊗ 10am-5pm Apr-Oct, Sun Nov-Mar), a pastiche of architecture dating from 1000.

Sint Janskerk is a small 17th-century Gothic church, one of the most beautiful in the Netherlands. A remarkable red colour, it photographs beautifully. Climb to the top (€1.15) for gorgeous views.

The 16th-century **Spanish Government Museum** (☎ 321 13 27; www.museumspaansgouvernement .nl; Vrijthof 18; admission €2.50; ⊗ 1-5pm Wed-Sun) is where Philip II outlawed his former lieutenant Willem the Silent at the start of the Eighty Years' War. The exhibits feature statues and 17th-century paintings.

STREETS, SQUARES & BRIDGES
The best way to see Maastricht is to just stroll. Streets not to miss include those south and east of Vrijthof: you'll be rewarded with a medieval labyrinth punctuated by interesting shops and cafés.

Onze Lieve Vrouweplein is an intimate café-filled square named after its church, the **Onze Lieve Vrouwebasiliek** (treasury adult/child €2/1; ⊗ 10am-5pm), which has parts dating from before 1000 and may well be built on the foundations of a Roman cathedral. There is a separate treasury area that houses gaudy jewels and riches; these you can see for a small and worthwhile fee.

The statue at the north end of the **Markt** is of **Johannes Petrus Minckelers**, who holds a flaming rod – he's the chap who invented gas light.

The busy pedestrian **Sint Servaasbrug** dates from the 13th-century and links Maastricht's centre with the Wyck district.

FORTIFICATIONS
At the end of Sint Bernardusstraat, the **Helpoort** is the oldest surviving town gate in the Netherlands (1229). The remains of 13th-century **ramparts** and fortifications are across the Maas in the new Céramique district. Much of Maastricht is riddled with defensive tunnels dug into the soft sandstone over the centuries. The best place to see the tunnels is **Sint Pietersberg**, a Roman fort 2km south of Helpoort. This is a really beautiful area, pastoral and peaceful – the fort is an arresting sight peeking over the charming hillside – and it's a very relaxing walk from town. If you must, take bus 29, which goes past the fort from Vrijthof.

The Romans built the **Northern Corridor System Tunnels** (see the boxed text, opposite) throughout the hills over a period of 2000 years; at one stage, the tunnels extended under the Netherlands–Belgium border. Thirteen species of bats have been found living below the surface.

The tourist office leads spooky, thrilling, and educational **cave tours** (☎ 321 78 78; €3; ⊗ 3.30pm daily Jul-Aug & school holidays) – this experience is highly recommended. Although tours are supposed to be conducted in Dutch, ask for Kitty, an extremely knowledgeable, English-speaking guide.

Tours
The tourist office can arrange all manner of walking tours and cycling expeditions.

Stiphout Cruises (☎ 351 53 00; Maaspromenade 27; adult/child €6/3.75; ⊗ daily Apr-Oct, Sat & Sun Nov-Dec) runs boat cruises on the Maas. On certain days there are day-long round-trip cruises to Liege in Belgium (adult/child €18.95/11.25), although you can get a one-way ticket.

Festivals & Events
Three events stand out from the busy Maastricht calendar:
Carnaval Celebrated with greater vigour in Maastricht than anywhere else in Europe save Venice (Italy) and Sitges (Spain). The orgy of partying and carousing begins the Friday before Shrove Tuesday and lasts until the last person

GOING UNDERGROUND

The Romans developed the Sint Pietersberg tunnels by quarrying soft marlstone at a painstaking rate of just four blocks per day, creating an underground system that provided refuge during the numerous occasions when Maastricht found itself under attack. During WWII, for example, the tunnels housed a well, a storeroom, a chapel, a kitchen and a bakery – even a pen for livestock.

The component called the Northern Corridor System Tunnels is an amazing feat of pre-industrial engineering: at one stage there were 20,000 separate passages, adding up to a length of 200km and stretching past the Belgian border – until the French blew up a large chunk of it, thinking they were under the Roman fort of Sint Pietersberg. Instead, the French army only succeeded in entombing hundreds of their own men. There are prehistoric fossils of fish and other creatures down here, a reminder of an inland sea that once held sway.

Walking through the tunnels is an eerie experience and you'll feel a deep chill, not only from fear of ghosts but also because it's extremely cold and dark, perfect for growing mushrooms – which some people do. People hiding down here during sieges would often die of exposure.

One of the most fascinating aspects of the tunnels is the graffiti from throughout the ages. You can see generations of drawings on the walls, everything from ancient Roman stick figures to wartime depictions of movie stars like Bette Davis, to '70s hippy nudes (the tunnels were barred from general access from the '80s on, before Dutch rappers could lay down some murals).

The VVV guides like to play little tricks, asking your permission first to ensure you won't completely freak out. A favourite is to take your gas light away from you – the guide then walks around a bend until they and all available light completely disappears into a black hole. You are then left in the stillest, thickest, heaviest darkness imaginable – a blackness you can literally feel. You are then asked to make your way to the guide, using your sense of touch to follow the curves of the wall.

As our favourite guide, Kitty, loves to relate, this little game can make grown men cry. When a Swedish, all-male TV crew filming a documentary on the tunnels took up the dare, Kitty took away all the lights and disappeared around a corner, asking them to feel their way around the bend. But they couldn't do it and all three broke down in tears.

'But once you were mighty Vikings' Kitty admonished, 'and now you cry like babies.'

collapses sometime on Wednesday. *Everything* stops for *carnaval*.

Preuvenemint As befitting its culinary reputation, each year Maastricht hosts this foodie festival, which takes over the Vrijthof for four days, with 40 stands featuring the best food and wine from all over the region. It's called the largest 'open-air restaurant in the world'.

European Fine Art Foundation Show (TEFAF; www .tefaf.com) Europe's largest annual art show is held in late March at the cavernous MECC exposition centre, just south of Céramique. More than 200 exhibitors converge on Maastricht offering masterpieces to those with a few million euros to spare. The event is open to the public.

Sleeping

Maastricht is a popular weekend destination throughout the year, so reservations are a must. The tourist office has a list of private rooms travellers can book.

BUDGET

Stayokay Maastricht (☎ 346 67 77; www.stayokay .com/maastricht; Dousbergweg 4; dm from €24; 🖳) On the perimeter of a nature reserve, a 3km walk from the town centre. Take bus 11 (Monday to Friday) or 8 or 18 (Saturday and Sunday) from Maastricht station to the Dousberg stop.

MIDRANGE

Matuchi (☎ 354 06 92; Kleine Gracht 34; s/d €50/65) These rooms, above the supersmooth bar of the same name (p282), are elegant, minimal and stylish, and surprisingly large for the price range. All include flat-screen TVs for your supine pleasure.

Maison Du Chêne (☎ 321 35 23; www.maastrichthotel .com; Boschstraat 104; s/d from €40/58) In an elegant 1855 building, the Maison's rooms are very clean and the brasserie on the ground floor is class and a half. Beware: it's right on the Markt, which can make for a noisy Friday or Saturday night. Ask for rooms at the back.

Hotel la Colombe (☎ 321 57 74; www.hotellacolombe .nl; Markt 30; s/d €61/80) Also on the Markt, in a simple, white building, la Colombe has rooms that are equally unadorned, but all have a TV and bath. This unassuming but friendly hotel has a decent café.

Botel Maastricht (☎ 321 90 23; Maasboulevard 95; s/d €37/58; 🖳) Two barges lashed together make up the Botel, the smaller vessel acting as an exemplary deck for beer drinking when the sun's out. Inside, rooms are narrow and portholed for that sea-dog feel, but comfy enough. There's a beaut little shipshape bar inside.

Hotel & Tapperij De Poshoorn (☎ 321 73 34; www .poshoorn.nl; Stationsstraat 47; s/d €57.50/70) This is a good, simple place with a great café.

TOP END

our pick **Kruisherenhotel Maastricht** (☎ 329 20 20; www.chateauhotels.nl; Kruiserengang 19-23; s/d from €85/145; 🖳) This stunning option is housed inside the former Crutched Friar monastery complex that dates from 1483. The publicity calls it a 'designer hotel', but the past hasn't been overwhelmed. Where there are modern touches, like moulded furniture and padded walls, they accent the historical surrounds. The rooms feature flat-screen TVs and wall-length paintings. Sumptuous.

Hotel Derlon (☎ 321 67 70; www.derlon.com; Onze Lieve Vrouweplein 6; r from €155; 🖳) The sleekly luxurious and smartly suave Derlon boasts slimline and slyly singular rooms and enthusiastic staff, and the breakfast room in the basement is built around Roman ruins. A pampering and luxurious experience.

Eating

Maastricht has four restaurants with Michelin stars – this is a very classy dining scene. To put this into perspective, Amsterdam, with four times the population, has six such establishments.

RESTAURANTS

Beluga (☎ 321 33 64; www.restbeluga.com; Plein 1992; ☺ lunch Tue-Fri, dinner Tue-Sat) With two Michelin stars, Beluga leads the pack. This sleek, angular, elegant designer restaurant not far from the Maas features excellent service and Frenchified cuisine that never fails to impress with its attention to detail. A recent menu sample included lightly steamed sole with pan-fried langoustines and *pommes à la tsarine* filled with caviar, butter asparagus and a sour cream and black pepper sauce.

Restaurant O (☎ 325 97 47; www.restaurant-o.nl; Rechtstraat 76; mains €18-21; ☺ lunch & dinner) This (mainly) seafood restaurant wins us over with

striking, stylish decor, and ever-present, ever-tasty aquatic meals. Lobster soup with mussels and shrimps, anyone? Pan-roasted moonfish? There's even a separate *fruits-de-mer* (seafood) menu – grand! Fresh and delightful.

Ginger (☎ 326 00 22; Tongersestraat 7; mains €10-20; ☺ lunch & dinner) Super-smooth and healthy Asian noodle soups come to Maastricht. And Ginger's the place to get them. Fabulous, fresh ingredients in a serene and wonderful contemporary setting.

Restaurant Jean La Brouche (☎ 321 46 09; Tongersestraat 9; 3-course menu €28; ☺ dinner Mon-Sat) This is classic cuisine in a quiet, lovely part of town. Think white tablecloths and cutlery with a bit of heft to it. If you're a fan of old-style French cooking, give this place a whirl.

Mestizo (☎ 327 08 74; www.mestizo.nl; Bredestraat 18; mains €12-19; ☺ lunch & dinner) Need a break from French and Dutch cuisine? Try Mestizo, a very inspired Latin restaurant serving up terrific Spanish and Mexican food. Now, exactly who among us can resist marinated lamb steaks roasted with garlic and chilli? Well, vegetarians, obviously – but there's a reasonable selection for them, too.

CAFÉS

Take Five (☎ 321 09 71; Bredestraat 14; lunch €6; ☺ lunch & dinner) Situated on a quiet street parallel to the cramped terraces of heaving Platielstraat, Take Five combines fusion cooking with a stark interior, chill-out music and engaging staff. Expect live jazz on many nights.

Drinking

Take One (☎ 321 64 23; www.takeonebiercafé.nl; Rechtstraat 28) Cramped and narrow from the outside, this 1930s tavern is manages to stock well over 100 beers from the most obscure parts of the Benelux region. It's run by a husband-and-wife team who also organise beer tastings and refer to their customers as 'victims'. Relax, though, they'll willingly help you select the brew most appropriate to your tastes. Some of these beers have a huge kick, attaining 10% alcohol volume in some cases. Take One also stocks what's termed the 'world's bitterest beer' – indeed, sucking lemons is milder but less pleasurable.

Matuchi (☎ 354 06 92; Kleine Gracht 34) This venue bills itself as an 'Orient Style Lab', but it's a bit more than that: there's a dash of *A Clockwork Orange* in the interior design, mixed with *de rigueur* Arabian themes. All in all, a hot joint in which to have a cool drink.

Zondag (☎ 321 93 00; www.cafézondag.nl; Wyckerbrugstraat 42) Here the cool is a bit more standard: the interior is a little more old-fashioned, though still jaw-achingly hip. Chow down on light lunches, tapas and other bar snacks, as well as musical accompaniment such as live Latin music or breakbeat DJs.

John Mullins (☎ 350 01 41; www.johnmullins.nl; Wyckerbrugstraat 50) This superfriendly Irish pub features a very popular but challenging quiz night on Tuesdays. Sample questions might include this: 'What was the first to feature seat belts: cars or planes?' The collective groans can be heard for streets around.

In Den Ouden Vogelstruys (☎ 321 48 88; www.vogelstruys.nl; Vrijthof 15) On the main drag, this antique bar is a little bit naughty and a little bit nice. The entrance has big, old, heavy red curtains, and inside there are photos of big, old, heavy men on the wall, big, old, heavy light fittings, and big, old, heavy Trappist beer.

Entertainment
Night Live (☎ 09002020158; Kesselskade 43) A nightclub in an old church that opens after midnight at weekends; eclectic musical policy.

Derlon Theater (☎ 350 50 50; Plein 1992) Near the new library, Derlon has drama and music. The café has fine river views from the terrace.

Cinema Lumiere (☎ 321 40 80; Bogaardenstraat 40B) Offbeat and classic films are screened on a regular basis at this cinema.

Getting There & Away
Maastricht Airport is a small facility served by KLM subsidiaries, which have flights to London and connecting flights to Schiphol. It is 10km north of the centre – see p304 for more information.

Sample train fares and schedules:

Destination	Price (€)	Duration (min)	Frequency (per hr)
Amsterdam	26.70	155	1
Rotterdam	25.70	140	2
Utrecht	23.10	120	1

There is an hourly international service to Liege, from where you can catch trains to Brussels, Paris and Cologne.

The bus station is to the right as you exit the train station. Eurolines has one bus a day

to/from Brussels. Interliner has hourly buses to/from Aachen.

Getting Around
There is car and motorcycle parking in massive underground lots by the river.

A bicycle shop is in a separate building to the left as you exit the station.

AROUND MAASTRICHT
The hills and forests of southern Limburg make for excellent hiking and biking. The **Drielandenpunt** (the convergence of the Netherlands, Belgium and Germany) is on the highest hill in the country (323m), in Vaals, 26km southeast of Maastricht. It's an excellent driving or biking destination.

Valkenburg
☎ 043 / pop 18,000
This small town in the hills east of Maastricht has possibly the most overcommercialised centre in the Netherlands, attracting hordes of tour buses. But away from the town are excellent trails and cycle paths through the nearby forests.

The **tourist office** (☎ 09009798; www.vvvzuidlimburg.nl; Walramplein 5) has a huge selection of maps of the area and can assist with bicycle hire. You might start at the over-restored **castle** (admission €6; ☺ 10am-5pm Apr-Oct) above town from where trails radiate out through the countryside.

ASP Adventure (☎ 604 06 75; www.aspadventure.nl) gives 90-minute guided tours (€22, minimum 10 people) of the networks of caves that riddle the soft sandstone of the hills. There are many options, including riding bikes underground.

Valkenburg is easily reached from Maastricht by train (€2.50, 12 minutes, two per hour).

Netherlands American Cemetery & Memorial
In Margraten, 10km southeast of Maastricht, the **Netherlands American Cemetery & Memorial** (☺ sunrise-sunset) is dedicated to US soldiers who died in 'Operation Market Garden' and the general Allied push to liberate the Dutch. It's a sombre memorial with row after row of silent white crosses – a stark but necessary testament to the futility of war.

The bus service to the cemetery runs from Maastricht's train station.

NORTH LIMBURG

Clinging to the Maas river, the northern half of Limburg, barely 30km across at its widest point, is a no-nonsense place of industry and agriculture. **Venlo**, the major town, has a small historic quarter near the train station. Venlo along with **Thorn** and **Roermond** are worth a quick look if you are changing trains for the hourly service to Cologne.

Nationaal Oorlogs- en Verzetsmuseum

Overloon, a tiny town on the border with Noord Brabant, was the scene of fierce battles between the Americans, British and the Germans as part of 'Operation Market Garden' in 1944. The heart of the battlefield is now the site of the sober **Nationaal Oorlogs- en Verzetsmuseum** (National War & Resistance Museum; ☎ 0478-64 18 20; www.oorlogsmuseum-overloon.nl; Museumpark 1; adult/child €6.50/5; ☺ 10am-5pm), a thoughtful place that examines the role of the Netherlands in WWII.

To reach the museum take the hourly train to Venray from either Roermond (€7.20, 40 minutes) or Nijmegen (€6.20, 25 minutes). Then call a *treintaxi* (see p309) and buy your ticket (€4.10) from the ticket machine. The museum is 7km from the station. Make arrangements with the driver for your return.

Directory

CONTENTS

ACCOMMODATION

The country's wealth of home stays, hotels and hostels provide any traveller – whether they be backpacker or five-star aficionado – with plenty of choice. Hotels and B&Bs are the mainstay of accommodation in the country,

BOOK ACCOMMODATION ONLINE

For more accommodation reviews and recommendations by Lonely Planet authors, check out the online booking service at www.lonelyplanet.com. You'll find the true, insider lowdown on the best places to stay. Reviews are thorough and independent. Best of all, you can book online.

and, while most are fairly standard and highly functional, a few gems fly the boutique flag or are simply bizarre (p237).

Note that a good part of the country suffers from the 'Amsterdam effect': because transport is so efficient and the city is so popular, many visitors stay in the capital even if they're travelling further afield.

B&Bs

Bed-and-breakfasts are an excellent way to meet the friendly locals face to face, and to see the weird, the wacky and the wonderful interior designs of the Dutch first-hand. Unfortunately, they're not abundant in cities, but the countryside is awash with them. Local tourist offices keep a list of B&Bs on file, where costs usually range from €18 to €25 per person.

Camping

The Dutch are avid campers, even within their own country. Campgrounds tend to be self-contained communities complete with shops, cafés, playgrounds and swimming pools. Lists of sites with ratings (one to five stars) are available from the ANWB (the Dutch automobile organisation) and tourist offices. If you plan to do a lot of camping, pick up a copy of ANWB's yearly *Campinggids* (€9.50); it's in Dutch, but the listings are easy to follow.

A camp site, which costs anything between €10 and €20, covers two people and a small tent; a car is an extra €1.50 to €6. Caravans are popular – every one in 15 residents owns one – so there are oodles of hook-ups.

Simple bungalows or *trekkershutten* (hiker huts; from €32) are another option. A typical hiker hut has four bunks, cooking facilities and electricity, but you'll need to bring your own sleeping bags, dishes and utensils. Consult www.trekkershutten.nl.

Rough camping is illegal. To get away from it all, seek out *natuurkampeerterreinen* (nature campgrounds) attached to farms. You'll enjoy a simpler and less crowded existence than at the major campgrounds. Reserve through tourist offices or check information online at www.natuurkampeerterreinen.nl.

DIRECTORY

Hostels

The Dutch youth-hostel association **Stayokay** (☎ 020-551 31 55; www.stayokay.com; Postbus 9191, 1006 AD Amsterdam) still uses the Hostelling International (HI) logo, but the hostels themselves go under the name Stayokay. Most offer a good variety of rooms. As facilities have improved over the years to cater to groups and families, so prices have increased.

A youth-hostel card costs €15 at the hostels, or nonmembers can pay an extra €2.50 per night and thus become a member after six nights. HI members get discounts on international travel and pay less commission on money exchange at GWK offices. Members and nonmembers have the same privileges, and there are no age limits.

Apart from the usual dormitories there are rooms for one to eight people, depending on the hostel. Nightly rates normally range from €20 to €25 per person for dorm beds. Be sure to book ahead, especially in high season.

Hotels

The Dutch rating system goes up to five stars; accommodation with less than one star can call itself a pension or guesthouse but not a hotel. The stars aren't very helpful because they measure the amenities and the number of rooms but not the quality of the rooms themselves. Hotels tend to be small, with less than 20 rooms.

Many establishments have steep stairs but no lifts, which can pose problems for the mobility-impaired. Having said that, most top-end and a few midrange hotels do have lifts.

Many tourist offices can book hotel rooms virtually anywhere in the country for a small fee (usually a few euros). GWK currency-exchange offices take hotel reservations, charging a small fee and 10% of the room charge in advance. The **Netherlands Reservation Centre** (☎ 0299-68 91 44; www.hotelres.nl; Plantsoengracht 2, 1441 DE Purmerend) accepts bookings from abroad. You can generally save money by booking directly with the hotel, but many won't take credit cards and may insist on a down payment.

Prices vary, but in cities you should expect to pay under €50 for a double room in a budget hotel, up to €125 in a midrange hotel and from €125 for the top end. Prices in Amsterdam tend to be higher: under €70 for a budget double, €70 to €150 for a midrange double and upwards from €150 for a top-end double.

Last but not least, when booking for two people, make clear whether you want two single (twin) beds or a double bed.

Rental Accommodation

Special rules apply to rental accommodation to combat a perpetual housing shortage. Rents under €564 per month require a housing permit, but you aren't likely to get one swiftly, so expect to pay substantially more – say, €900 for a smallish two-bedroom flat in a not-grotty area of Amsterdam. Rents vary quite a bit in the big cities, with Amsterdam and Den Haag at the top and Rotterdam somewhere near the bottom of the scale. Most Dutch residents usually find a place through the so-called housing corporations after waiting a couple of years.

Some lucky folks find places in the classifieds of the daily *Telegraaf* (Wednesday), *Volkskrant* or *Parool* (Saturday), or through the twice-weekly *ViaVia*. All the papers have websites with rental ads in Dutch; scan under 'Te huur' or 'Huurwoningen'. The **Expatica** (www.expatica.com/holland) website has ads and a handy 'Where to live in (city)' section, and **Craigs List** (www.craigslist.com), a worldwide classified ads website, has a small but effective Amsterdam presence. If a flat sounds good, pick up the phone right then and there because it may be gone in a matter of hours. Be aware that some people try to let out their rent-subsidised flats to foreigners at inflated prices, which is illegal.

If time is of the essence, try the following agents:

Amsterdam Apartment (☎ 020-668 26 54; www .amsterdamapartment.nl; Oude Nieuwstraat 1, Amsterdam)

Apartment Services (☎ 020-672 18 40; www .apartmentservices.nl; Waalstraat 58, Amsterdam)

IDA Housing (☎ 020-624 83 01; www.idahousing.com; Den Texstraat 30, Amsterdam)

ACTIVITIES

The most popular outdoor activities are linked to the defining characteristics of the Dutch landscape: flat land and water. There is no shortage of sports clubs and special-interest groups for your favourite pastime, as the Dutch have a penchant for organisation.

Boating

It seems as though everyone in the Netherlands is the proud owner of a boat; stroll by the canals and lakes and you'll see all manner of water craft, some impossibly wacky, often decades old, lovingly maintained and enjoyed in weather fair or fearful. Small canoes and sailboats can be hired on lakes throughout the country – the likes of Loosdrechtse Plassen in Utrecht province (p185) or Sneek (p235) in Friesland make particularly good bases for such an activity.

Sailing on a traditional boat is an unforgettable experience. Named for its ruddy sails, the 'brown fleet' of restored flat-bottomed vessels is a familiar sight on the vast IJsselmeer at weekends. The cheapest rental option are *botters*, old fishing boats with long, narrow leeboards and sleeping berths for up to eight passengers. Larger groups can go for converted freight barges known as *tjalks* (smacks), ancient pilot boats or massive clippers. You'll also find motorboats for gliding through the country canals.

The **Netherlands Board of Tourism** (www.holland .com) will match you up with boat-rental firms depending on your location and budget and the type of boat you want. On the website, follow the 'boat rental' link under 'Search'. Local tourist offices will also have a list of boat rentals. The **Royal Dutch Watersports Association** (☎ 030-656 65 50; www.watersportverbond.nl; Daltonlaan 400, 3584 BK Utrecht) provides advice on boating rules and hundreds of links to relevant websites. ANWB stocks maps of the Netherlands' most popular waterways.

The following companies have typical rates, bearing in mind that everything is negotiable (after all, bargaining is a Dutch tradition):

Flevo Sailing (☎ 0320-26 03 24; www.flevosailing.nl; Oostvaardersdijk 59c, Lelystad) Has a fleet of four- to eight-passenger sailing yachts for rent.

Holiday Boatin Yachtcharter (☎ 0515-41 37 81; Eeltjebaasweg 3, Sneek) Rents motorboats for puttering about on Friesland's myriad lakes and canals.

Holland Zeilcharters (see p155).

Hollands Glorie (☎ 0294-27 15 61; www.hollands glorie.nl; Ossenmarkt 6, Muiden) Has *tjalks* for rent from a day to a week. Boats depart from harbours around the country, including Amsterdam, Edam, Hoorn, Medemblik and Muiden.

Top of Holland Yacht Charter (www.topofholland .com) Represents companies in Friesland, the IJsselmeer region and Zuid Holland, renting out everything from small sailboats to large cabin cruisers.

Cycling

Cycling is a way of life in the Netherlands. The country offers easy cycling terrain with many designated paths, including loads of off-road routes through pastures and woodland. The infrastructure gives priority to bikes over other forms of transportation, and car drivers often yield to cyclists even when the latter are pushing their luck. For more on traffic rules and specific bike routes, see p69.

Skating

The Netherlands is practically tailor-made for in-line skating. City parks are breeding grounds for the latest flashy manoeuvres on half-pipes, but the popularity of skating is such that day trips have been mapped throughout the country. The Achterhoek region (the eastern part of Gelderland) combines quiet conditions with a nice variety of landscapes; the Graafschap area in the northwest has seven signposted skating routes with a total length of 200km. The list of places to skate is endless – any dyke top can be perfect for a spin. See the **iSkate** (www.iskate.nl) website for details of events, hot skating spots and night skates, though the **Skatebond Nederland** (Dutch Skating Club; www.skatebond.nl) is more authoritative.

Ice skating was part of the Dutch psyche long before scarfed figures appeared in Golden Age winterscapes. The first skates were made from cow shanks and ribs, had hand-drilled holes and were tied to the feet. When canals and ponds freeze over, everyone takes to the ice, and you can join them with a pair of hockey skates (the best thing for beginners) bought either secondhand or from a department store. The famous Elfstedentocht (Eleven Cities Race, p238) takes place in Friesland every seven years on average, and even Crown Prince Willem-Alexander took part in 1986, to be greeted by Queen Beatrix at the finish line. Not surprisingly, the Dutch have had plenty of ice-skating champions.

Walking

The Dutch are avid walkers and hikers – in almost any weather and surroundings. The International Nijmegen Four Days' March (Internationale Wandelvierdaagse; p265) is the world's largest walking event and attracts more than 40,000 enthusiasts every July.

For salt breezes you might head for the coasts of Friesland, Zeeland or the coastal towns along the IJsselmeer. National parks such as Hoge Veluwe, Weerribben and Biesbosch offer a varied backdrop ranging from bogs to dunes to forest. The pretty, undulating knolls of Limburg can be a welcome change after the flatlands in the rest of the country. Thinly populated provinces such as Drenthe are ideal for untroubled treks through quiet farmland.

Nederlandse Wandelsportbond (Netherlands Hiking Club; ☎ 030-231 94 58; www.nwb-wandelen.nl; Pieterskerkhof 22, Utrecht) is a goldmine of information about the nicest paths and events. Branches of the ANWB motoring club, tourist offices and bookshops have more brochures than you can shake a walking stick at.

Windsurfing & Kite-Surfing

Abundant water and near-constant breezes make a perfect combination for windsurfing. Most developed beaches along the coast of the North Sea, the IJsselmeer and the Wadden Islands have places that rent windsurfing boards (look for *surfplanken*). In winter the frozen lakes become racecourses for ice-surfing, with breakneck speeds of 100km per hour or more. Websites such as **Windlords** (www.windlords.com/nl) list the most popular locations to windsurf around the country. You can also inquire at any tourist office.

Wherever there's windsurfing, kite-surfing won't be far away. Harder to master but arguably more exhilarating, this relatively new pastime is catching on quickly with lovers of wind and water. If you're interested in giving it a try or want to hone your skills while on holiday, check out www.kitesurf.pagina.nl; it's in Dutch, but the lists of Dutch kite-surfing websites are easy to navigate.

BUSINESS HOURS

As a general rule, opening hours occur as follows:

Banks Open 9.30am to 4pm Monday to Friday.

Bars Open 11am to 1am, although some stay open longer at weekends and others won't open for service till the late afternoon.

Businesses Hours are 8.30am to 5pm Monday to Friday.

Nightclubs Hours vary across the country, but in general clubs open 10pm to 4am Friday and Saturday; some also open on Wednesday, Thursday and Sunday.

Post offices Open 9am to 6pm Monday to Friday.

Restaurants Open 10am or 11am to 11pm, with a break in the afternoon from 3pm to 6pm.

Shops Open noon to 6pm Monday, and 8.30am or 9am to 6pm Tuesday to Saturday. Most towns have *koopavond* (evening shopping), when stores open till 9pm on Thursday or Friday. Bigger supermarkets in cities stay open until 8pm.

Most museums are closed on Monday. Government offices, private institutions and monuments keep limited opening hours; these hours are mentioned in this book where possible.

In the city centres an increasing number of shops are open from noon to 5pm on Sunday, especially on the first weekend of the month. Shops in Rotterdam and Den Haag are open every Sunday afternoon.

CHILDREN

Lonely Planet's *Travel with Children* by Cathy Lanigan is worth reading if you're unsure about travelling with kids. Much of her advice is valid in the Netherlands, where there is a lot to keep them occupied. Attitudes to children are very positive, and Dutch children tend to be spontaneous and confident, thanks to a relaxed approach to parenting.

Practicalities

Some hotels have a no-children policy – check when you book. Most restaurants have high chairs and children's menus. Facilities for changing nappies, however, are limited to the big department stores, major museums and train stations, and you'll pay to use them. Breast-feeding is generally OK in public if done discreetly. Kids are allowed in pubs but aren't supposed to drink until they're 16.

Children aged under four travel free on trains if they don't take up a seat. There's a Railrunner fare (€2) for kids aged four to 11.

Sights & Activities

Zaanse Schans (p154) near Amsterdam is a great afternoon out, with its re-created windmill village, traditional Dutch houses, cheese farm and craft centre. Further north, the island of Texel has the Ecomare (p167), with oodles of birds and seals and strokeable fish.

A child's fantasies can run wild at De Efteling amusement park (p275), especially in the maze or Fairy Tale Forest. Animal parks abound and the good-natured frolics at the Dolfinarium will keep smiles on little faces all day long (see the boxed text, p263). The Apenheul will show the little ones what it means to really monkey about (see the boxed text, p263).

For more ideas, see p21.

CLIMATE

In general the Netherlands has a maritime climate of cool winters and mild summers. Wind and rain are year-round factors; March is the driest month, July and August the wettest (and hottest), and wind invariably comes from the southwest, although it always seems to be head-on when you're cycling.

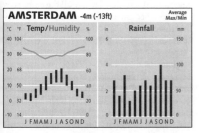

For more detailed climate information, see p12.

COURSES
Language

Dutch is a close relative of English, but that doesn't make it easy to learn. Standard courses take months, and intensive courses last several weeks. Make inquiries well in advance.

Well-reputed schools include:

Amsterdam Summer University (☎ 020-620 02 25; www.amsu.edu; Keizersgracht 324, 1016 EZ Amsterdam) Conducts all of its courses and workshops in English (apart from its Dutch language training).

British Language Training Centre (☎ 020-622 36 34; www.bltc.nl; Nieuwezijds Voorburgwal 328E, 1012 RW Amsterdam) Offers both Dutch and English courses.

Tropeninstituut (Royal Institute for the Tropics; ☎ 020-568 87 11; www.kit.nl; Mauritskade 63, 1092 AD Amsterdam) Intensive language courses aimed specifically at foreigners moving to the Netherlands.

Volksuniversiteit Amsterdam (☎ 020-626 16 26; www.volksuniversiteitamsterdam.nl; Rapenburgerstraat 73, 1011 VK Amsterdam) A range of well-regarded day and evening courses.

CUSTOMS

EU nationals can bring virtually anything they like, provided it's for personal use and they paid local tax in an EU country. Visitors from non-EU countries can import the following goods tax-free:

Alcohol Up to 1L of spirits or 2L of sparkling wine or fortified wine, such as sherry or port; 2L of non-sparkling wine.

Coffee Up to 500g of coffee or 200g of coffee extracts or coffee essences.

Perfume Up to 50g of perfume and 0.25L of eau de toilette.

Tea Up to 100g of tea or 40g of tea extracts or tea essences.

Tobacco Up to 200 cigarettes or 250g of tobacco (rolling or pipe tobacco) or 100 cigarillos or 50 cigars.

Bringing meat or meat products, flowers, fruit, plants and protected species to the Netherlands is illegal. Tobacco and alcohol may only be imported by people aged 17 and over.

DANGERS & ANNOYANCES

Much of the Netherlands is utterly safe, but caution is advised in the larger cities. Amsterdam and Rotterdam require a modicum of big-city street sense but nothing you wouldn't normally do at home.

Cars with foreign registration are popular targets for smash-and-grab theft. Don't leave things in the car: remove registration and ID papers and the radio/stereo if possible.

If something is stolen, get a police report for insurance purposes but don't expect the police to retrieve your property or to apprehend the thief – put the matter down to experience.

Mosquitoes can be a pain in summer. They breed in stagnant parts of the canals and in water under houses. In parts of the country near lakes or canals people sleep under netting.

Bicycles can be quite a challenge to pedestrians. Remember when crossing the street to look for speeding bikes as well as cars; straying into a bike lane without looking both ways is a no-no.

Intensive urban development means there's often little grass for dog dirt, and you may spend more time watching the pavement than the sights.

Scams

Big cities breed scams. Take special care in the train stations: someone might help you put your bags into a luggage locker, lock the door and hand you the key. When you return you find the key fits a different locker and your stuff is gone. If something feels wrong about a stranger who approaches you, chances are your instincts are right. Thieves sometimes pose as police (see p82).

DISCOUNT CARDS

Teachers, professional artists, museum conservators and certain categories of students may get discounts at a few museums or even be admitted free – it can depend on the person behind the counter. Bring proof of affiliation such as the International Teacher Identity Card (ITIC). People over 65 (60 for the partner) receive discounts on public transport, museum entry fees, concerts and more. You could try flashing your home-country senior card, but you might have to show your passport too. Other discount cards:

Cultureel Jongeren Paspoort (Cultural Youth Passport, CJP; www.cjp.nl; €12.50) Purchase from tourist offices. Provides people aged under 27 with big discounts to museums and cultural events around the country.

Hostelling International Card Useful at the official youth hostels (called Stayokay in the Netherlands); provides a €2.50 per night discount.

I Amsterdam Card (www.iamsterdamcard.com; 24/48/72hr €33/43/53) Available at tourist offices and some large hotels in Amsterdam. Gives free public transport, free entry to most museums, and discounts on some attractions and restaurants.

International Student Identity Card (ISIC; www.isic .org) Will get some admission discounts and might pay for itself through discounted air and ferry tickets. The same applies to hostel cards.

Museumkaart (www.museumkaart.nl; over/under 26yr €29.95/17.45) Gives free access to over 400 museums across the country.

EMBASSIES & CONSULATES
Dutch Embassies & Consulates

Diplomatic representation abroad:

Australia (☎ 02-6220 9400; www.netherlands.org.au; 120 Empire Circuit, Yarralumla, ACT 2600)

Belgium (☎ 02-679 17 11; www.nederlandse ambassade.be; Herrmann-Debroux 48, 1160 Brussels)

Canada (☎ 613-237-5030; www.netherlandsembassy .ca; 350 Albert St, Ste 2020, Ottawa, Ontario K1R 1A4)

France (☎ 01 40 62 33 00; www.amb-pays-bas.fr; 7-9 Rue Eblé, 75007 Paris)

Germany (☎ 030-20 95 60; www.niederlandeweb.de; Klosterstrasse 50, 10179 Berlin)

Ireland (☎ 01-269 3444; www.mfa.nl/dub-en; 160 Merrion Rd, Dublin 4)

Italy (☎ 06-367671; www.mfa.nl/rom-nl; Via della Camilluccia, 701-703, 00135 Rome)

Japan (☎ 03-5401 0411; www.oranda.or.jp; Shibakoen, 3-6-3 Minato-ku, 105-0011 Tokyo)

New Zealand (☎ 04-471 6390; www.netherlands embassy.co.nz; Investment House, cnr Ballance & Featherston Sts, Wellington)

UK (☎ 020-7590 3200; www.netherlands-embassy.org .uk; 38 Hyde Park Gate, London SW7 5DP)

USA (☎ 202-244-5300; www.netherlands-embassy.org; 4200 Linnean Ave NW, Washington DC 20008)

Embassies & Consulates in the Netherlands

Amsterdam is the country's capital but, confusingly, Den Haag (The Hague) is the seat of government – so that's where all the embassies are. Several countries also maintain consulates in Amsterdam.

Australia (☎ 070-310 82 00; www.australian-embassy.nl; Carnegielaan 4, Den Haag)

Belgium (Map p198; ☎ 070-312 34 56; www.diplomatie .be/thehague; Alexanderveld 97, Den Haag)

Canada (Map p198; ☎ 070-311 16 00; www.dfait-maeci .gc.ca/canadaeuropa/netherlands; Sophialaan 7, Den Haag)

France embassy (Map p198; ☎ 070-312 58 00; www .ambafrance.nl; Smidsplein 1, Den Haag); consulate

(Map pp92-3; ☎ 020-530 69 69; www.consulfrance
-amsterdam.org; Vijzelgracht 2, Amsterdam)
Germany embassy (☎ 070-342 06 00; www.duitse
-ambassade.nl; Groot Hertoginnelaan 18-20, Den Haag);
consulate (Map pp92-3; ☎ 020-574 77 00; Honthorststraat
36-38, Amsterdam)
Ireland (Map p198; ☎ 070-363 09 93; Dr Kuijperstraat
9, Den Haag)
Italy embassy (Map p198; ☎ 070-302 10 30; www.italy
.nl; Alexanderstraat 12, Den Haag); consulate (Map pp92-3;
☎ 020-550 20 50; Vijzelstraat 79, Amsterdam)
Japan (☎ 070-346 95 44; www.nl.emb-japan.go.jp;
Tobias Asserlaan 2, Den Haag)
New Zealand (☎ 070-346 93 24; www.nzembassy.com;
Carnegielaan10-IV, Den Haag)
UK embassy (Map p198; ☎ 070-427 04 27; www.britain
.nl; Lange Voorhout 10, Den Haag); consulate (Map pp86-7;
☎ 020-676 43 43; Koningslaan 44, Amsterdam)
USA embassy (Map p198; ☎ 070-310 22 09; www
.usembassy.nl; Lange Voorhout 102, Den Haag); consulate
(Map pp92-3; ☎ 020-575 53 09; Museumplein 19,
Amsterdam)

FESTIVALS & EVENTS

Following are the cream of the largest and
most important events in the country – they
may well be reason for a special trip. More
goings-on are listed in destination chapters.

February/March

Carnaval Weekend before Shrove Tuesday. Celebrations
with gusto that would do Rio or New Orleans proud, mostly
in the Catholic provinces of Noord Brabant, Gelderland and
Limburg. Maastricht's party means days of uninhibited
drinking, dancing and street music.

March

Tefaf Maastricht Art & Antique Show (☎ 041-164
50 90; www.tefaf.com) For 10 days in the first half of
March. Europe's largest art show is your chance to pick up
a Monet, or at least do some serious browsing.

April

Koninginnedag (Queen's Day) On 30 April. Marked
throughout the country with wearing of orange, drinking, and
flea-market activity. Processions, dances and live music.
Amsterdam Fantastic Film Festival (www.afff.nl)
European and international fantasy, horror and science-
fiction movies.

May

Herdenkingsdag & Bevrijdingsdag (Remembrance
Day & Liberation Day) On 4 and 5 May. The fallen from
WWII are honoured in an Amsterdam ceremony, followed
by live music, debate and a market the next day.

Nationale Molendag (National Mill Day) Second
Saturday. Nearly every working windmill in the country
(there are more than 600 in total) throws open its doors to
visitors. Look for the sweet blue pennants.

June

Holland Festival (www.hollandfestival.nl) Virtually all
month. The country's biggest extravaganza for theatre,
dance, film and pop music, with a justified claim to
cutting-edge innovation.
De Parade (www.deparade.nl) Mid-June to August.
Nationwide inverse-circus tour, where the audience is
in the ring while all manner of music, theatre, film and
variety performances go on around them.

July

North Sea Jazz Festival (www.northseajazz.nl) Mid-
July, in Rotterdam. World's largest jazz festival; attracts big
names from around the planet, and even bigger crowds.
Dance Valley (www.dancevalley.nl) Mid-July. This
outdoor dance technothon draws over 100 DJs and bands
performing to fields of 40,000 or more.

August

Gay Pride Canal Parade First Saturday. The only water-
borne gay parade in the world, with lots of pride showing
on the outlandish floats.
FFWD Dance Parade (www.ffwdheinekendanceparade
.nl) Downtown Rotterdam lets down its hair in a big
way and turns into one big open-air techno club in early
August.
Uitmarkt (www.uitmarkt.nl) Three days in late August.
The reopening of Amsterdam's cultural season with free
concerts and information booths around the big museums
and Leidseplein.
Lowlands (www.lowlands.nl) Mid-August, in Bidding-
huizen (Flevoland). Alternative music and cultural mega-
bash, with campgrounds for the masses.

November

Sinterklaas Intocht Mid-November. Every year the
Dutch Santa Claus arrives 'from Spain' with his staff and
Black Pete helpers at a different port.

December

Sinterklaas On 5 December. Families exchange small gifts
ahead of religious celebrations for Christmas.

FOOD

Prices tend to be high by European standards.
As a general rule, snacks and light takeaway
items cost about €3 to €8, while a three-course
sit-down meal at a midpriced restaurant will
run from €18 to €30 including a beer or a
glass of wine; the bill rises to €40 to €60 at

the swish top-end places with Michelin stars. Tourist centres such as Amsterdam tend to be expensive and you may get much better value for money out in the provinces. Ethnic eateries, particularly with Surinamese and Chinese-Indonesian menus, are a reliable stand-by for cheap and tasty food.

See p59 for more details.

GAY & LESBIAN TRAVELLERS

The best national source of information is **COC** (☎ 020-623 45 96; www.coc.nl; Rozenstraat 8, 1016 NX Amsterdam). It has branches throughout the country that are happy to offer advice to newcomers.

Partisan estimates put the proportion of gay and lesbian people in Amsterdam at 20% to 30%. This is probably an exaggeration, but Amsterdam is certainly one of the gay capitals of Europe. Mainstream attitudes have always been reasonably tolerant, but it wasn't until the early 1970s that the age of consent for gay sex was lowered to 16. The last decade has seen considerable progress: it's now illegal to discriminate against job-seekers on the basis of sexual orientation. A landmark move came in 2001, when the Netherlands became the first country to legalise same-sex marriage.

The government has long subsidised COC, one of the world's largest (and the world's first) organisations for gay and lesbian rights. Now trade unions research the lot of homosexual employees, the police advertise in the gay media for applicants, and homosexuals are admitted to the armed forces on an equal footing.

Amsterdam's well-developed scene isn't typical of the country as a whole. The further one gets from the capital, the more often gay and lesbian bars and clubs operate behind dark windows. Rotterdam is an exception, as are the university towns with large, albeit transient, gay and lesbian populations.

HOLIDAYS
Public Holidays

People take public holidays seriously. Most museums adopt Sunday hours on the days below (except Christmas and New Year) even if they fall on a day when the place would otherwise be closed. Many people treat Remembrance Day (4 May) as a day off.

Carnaval is celebrated with vigour in the Catholic south. Huge lager-fed parties are thrown in the run-up to Shrove Tuesday and little work gets done.

The holidays:

Nieuwjaarsdag New Year's Day; parties and fireworks galore
Goede Vrijdag Good Friday
Eerste Paasdag Easter Sunday
Tweede Paasdag Easter Monday
Koninginnedag 30 April. Queen's Day
Bevrijdingsdag 5 May; Liberation Day – this isn't a universal holiday: government workers have the day off, but almost everyone else has to work
Hemelvaartsdag Ascension Day; 40th day after Easter Sunday
Eerste Pinksterdag Whit Sunday (Pentecost); 50th day after Easter Sunday
Tweede Pinksterdag Whit Monday; 50th day after Easter Monday
Eerste Kerstdag 25 December; Christmas Day
Tweede Kerstdag 26 December; Boxing Day

School Holidays

School holidays are staggered across three regions (north, central and south) to relieve congestion on the roads. Generally the holidays are scheduled as follows:

Spring holiday Two weeks in mid-February, also known as 'crocus' holiday
May holiday First week of the month
Summer holiday July, August and sometimes the first few days of September
Autumn holiday Second half of October
Christmas holiday Two weeks through the first full week of January

INSURANCE

Seriously consider taking out travel insurance. Medical or dental costs might already be covered through reciprocal health-care arrangements, but you'll still need cover for theft or loss, and for unexpected changes to travel arrangements (ticket cancellation etc). Check what's already covered by your local insurance policies or credit-card issue.

See also the Insurance sections of the Health chapter (p311) and the Transport chapter (p306).

INTERNET ACCESS

If you pack a laptop, note that Dutch phones have a cord with a four-prong plug. Adapters are available at the airport and retail outlets. Most phones also have a modular RJ-11 plug on the other end, so you can always plug right into your modem. Major internet service providers such as AOL, AT&T and Earthlink have access numbers in the Netherlands.

You'll need to keep three pieces of information handy: your incoming (POP or IMAP) mail server name, your account name and your password. Wi-fi is another option, but you'll generally need to be signed up with a Dutch provider, which isn't cheap.

Otherwise internet cafés are the easiest way to check mail while travelling; they're everywhere and often have long opening hours. Some libraries, tourist offices and hotels also provide internet terminals. Expect to pay anything from €1.50 to €6 per hour.

LEGAL MATTERS

The Dutch police (*politie*) are a pretty relaxed lot and helpful to travellers. You're unlikely to incite their ire unless you do something instinctively wrong – like chucking litter or smoking a joint under their noses.

Officers can hold you up to six hours for questioning and another six if they can't establish your identity. If the matter's serious, you can be detained for 24 hours. You won't have the right to a phone call, but they'll notify your embassy or consulate. Relax – you're presumed innocent until proven guilty.

Anyone over 14 years of age is required by law to carry ID. Foreigners should carry their passport or a photocopy of the relevant data pages; a driving licence isn't sufficient.

Drugs

Contrary to what you may have heard, marijuana is illegal. The confusion arises because the authorities distinguish between 'soft' drugs (eg cannabis) and addictive 'hard' drugs such as heroin, crack or cocaine. Possession of soft drugs up to 5g is tolerated, but larger amounts make you a 'dealer' and subject to prosecution. However, if you're caught with, say, 10g, you'll probably only receive a fine.

The key term is *gedogen*. This wonderful word means that officials condemn the action but look the other way if common sense dictates. Hard drugs are treated as a serious

---

> **LEGAL AGE**
>
> **Voting and driving:** 18
> **Consent:** 12 (but 16 if the parents object)
> **Homosexual marriage:** 18
> **Drinking:** 16

---

crime, but under the unique Dutch drug policy the authorities tend to treat genuine, registered addicts as medical cases rather than hardened criminals.

These tolerant policies attract many drug tourists; drugs are cheaper, more readily available and generally of better quality in the Netherlands than elsewhere. The country has become a major exporter of high-grade marijuana (grown locally) and is the European centre for the production of ecstasy. Much of Europe's cocaine passes through Rotterdam harbour.

For more about soft drugs, see the boxed text, p44.

Prostitution

Prostitution is legal in the Netherlands – based on the view that its practitioners are victims rather than criminals. The industry is protected by law, and prostitutes pay tax and even have their own lobby. Health checks are performed regularly to screen for disease, and some prostitutes qualify for pensions and insurance. Much of this open policy stems from a desire to undermine the role of pimps and the underworld in the sex industry. That hasn't always helped the plight of prostitutes, many of them immigrants from the Third World and Eastern Europe.

In Amsterdam's Red Light District you have little to fear as the streets are well-policed, but the back alleys are more dubious. This also goes for other Dutch cities such as Rotterdam and Den Haag. Even towns such as Leiden and Groningen have red-light areas plopped down amid otherwise quiet streets.

MAPS

The maps in this book will probably suffice. Lonely Planet's handy *Amsterdam City Map* is plastic-coated for the elements and has a street index that covers the most popular parts of the city.

Otherwise the best road maps of the Netherlands are those produced by Michelin and the Dutch automobile association ANWB.

> **WARNING**
>
> Never, ever buy drugs on the street: you'll get ripped off or mugged.
>
> Don't light up in view of the police, or in an establishment without checking that it's OK to do so. The Dutch detest tourists who think they can just smoke dope anywhere.

DIRECTORY

The ANWB also puts out provincial maps detailing cycling paths and picturesque road routes. You'll find a wide variety of maps for sale at any tourist office, as well as at bookstores and newsstands.

MONEY

Like other members of the EU, the Netherlands currency is the euro, which is divided into 100 cents. There are coins for one, two, five, 10, 20 and 50 cents, and €1 and €2. Notes come in denominations of €5, €10, €20, €50, €100, €200 and €500. The one- and two-cent coins are still in circulation but are unofficially being phased out; most, if not all, shops now round up or down to the nearest five cents.

The Quick Reference page just inside the front cover lists exchange rates, while the Getting Started chapter (p12) has a rundown of costs.

ATMs

Automated teller machines can be found outside most banks and at airports and most train stations. Credit cards such as Visa and MasterCard/Eurocard are widely accepted, as well as cash cards that access the Cirrus network. Be aware that, if you're limited to a maximum withdrawal per day, the 'day' will coincide with that in your home country. Also note that using an ATM can be the cheapest way to exchange your money from home – but check with your home bank for service charges before you leave.

Cash

Cash is still common and nothing beats it for convenience – or risk of theft or loss. Plan to pay cash for most daily expenses. However, staff at upmarket hotels might cast a furtive glance if you pay a huge bill with small-denomination notes rather than a credit card, and car-rental agencies will probably refuse to do business if you only have cash. Keep the equivalent of about US$100 separate from the rest of your money as an emergency stash.

Credit Cards

All major international cards are recognised, and you will find that most hotels, restaurants and major stores accept them. But always check first to avoid, as they say, disappointment. Shops often levy a 5% surcharge (or more) on credit cards to offset the commissions charged by card providers.

To withdraw money at a bank counter instead of from an ATM, go to a GWK branch (see Moneychangers, below). You'll need to show your passport.

Report lost or stolen cards to the following 24-hour numbers:

American Express (☎ 020-504 80 00, 020-504 86 66)
Diners Club (☎ 08000334)
Eurocard and MasterCard (☎ 030-283 55 55)
Visa (☎ 08000223110)

International Transfers

Transferring money from your home bank will be easier if you've authorised somebody back home to access your account. In the Netherlands, find a large bank and ask for the international division. A commission is charged on telegraphic transfers, which can take up to a week but usually less if you're well prepared; by mail, allow two weeks.

The GWK (see Moneychangers, below) is an agent for Western Union and money is transferred within 15 minutes of lodgement at the other end. The person lodging the transfer pays a commission that varies from country to country. Money can also be transferred via American Express and Thomas Cook at their Amsterdam offices.

Moneychangers

Generally your best bet for exchanging money is to use **GWK** (☎ 09000566; www.gwk.nl) – note that calls to this number cost €0.25 per minute. Offices are in almost every medium-sized and larger train station as well as at the borders on major highways. Many locations, such as those at Amsterdam's Centraal Station and at Schiphol Airport, are open 24 hours. Banks and the Postbank (at post offices) are also good options; they stick to official exchange rates and charge a sensible commission.

Avoid the private exchange booths dotted around tourist areas. They're convenient and open late hours, but rates or commissions are lousy, though competition is fierce and you may do OK if you hunt around.

Tipping

Tipping is not essential as restaurants, hotels, bars etc include a service charge on their bills. A little extra is always welcomed though, and it's an excellent way to compliment the service (if you feel it needs complimenting). The tip can be anything from rounding up to the nearest euro, to 10% of the bill.

Travellers Cheques

Travellers cheques (including eurocheques) are on the way out in the Netherlands – you'll be very hard pressed to find a bank who will change them for you. If you insist on carrying cheques, take American Express or Thomas Cook: their offices don't charge commission. GWK offices (see Moneychangers, opposite) still exchange cheques.

Shops, restaurants and hotels always prefer cash; a few might accept travellers cheques, but their rates will be anybody's guess.

POST

Poste restante is best handled in Amsterdam. Unless you're sending mail within the post office's local region, the slot to use in the rectangular red letter boxes is Overige Postcodes (Other Postal Codes).

For queries about postal services, ring ☎ 058-233 33 33 or consult www.tpgpost.nl.

Postal Rates

Within the country, letters up to 20g and postcards cost €0.39. Letters up to 20g and postcards within Europe cost €0.69 (air mail, known as 'priority') or €0.65 (standard); beyond Europe they are €0.85 or €0.80.

Standard mail (also available within Europe for parcels and printed matter) is not much cheaper than priority and takes about twice as long to reach the destination.

SHOPPING

The Netherlands isn't a shopper's haven; there's not a lot in the country that you won't find back home, aside from dope, pornography, round after round of cheese, rare flower bulbs and even rarer types of *jenever* (Dutch gin). Even the majority of the ubiquitous Delftware – blue-and-white porcelain stocked in every single souvenir shop – is made in China. Clogs, on the other hand, are one item you normally won't find outside the Netherlands, but they're available in almost every town across the country.

However, Amsterdam is a diamond in the rough, so to speak. For centuries it has been a centre for a girl's best friend, and while prices aren't necessarily cheaper here than elsewhere, diamond quality is high and prices are at least competitive.

The capital is also filled with speciality shops. You might be able to find banana-flavoured condoms and Mexican shrines

back home, but not an entire shop devoted to them.

Dutch bicycles may also catch the eye of shoppers. Prices are generally comparable to those in other European countries, but the variety – from lazy cruisers and kiddie carriers to stream-lined, space-age speedsters – is quite astounding and very tempting, considering how easy it is to transport your new transport on trains and planes.

SOLO TRAVELLERS

The Dutch are uninhibited when it comes to striking up conversations with complete strangers, whether at the next table in a restaurant or in a supermarket queue, and before you know it you'll find yourself in a conversation.

Booking into a group activity such as a walking tour or boat trip is a good recipe for making contacts. Young travellers also hook up with like-minded people at youth hostels or budget hotels. Nightclubs in cities such as Amsterdam and Rotterdam draw a large, fun-loving contingent of foreigners, and many also make their way to beach parties in places like Bloemendaal or Scheveningen. Single women should try to join forces before hitting the clubs – that's what the Dutch do.

TELEPHONE

The Dutch phone network is efficient and prices are reasonable by European standards. Most public phones accept credit cards as well as various phonecards. Phone booths are scattered around towns and you can always call from a post office.

For national directory inquiries, call ☎ 118 (€1.09 per call) or ☎ 09008008 for a human operator (€1.30 per call). International directory inquiries can be reached on ☎ 09008418 (€0.90 per minute). To place a *collect gesprek* (collect call) ring ☎ 08000101 (€0.25 per minute).

Mobile Phones

The Netherlands uses GSM 900/1800, which is compatible with the rest of Europe and Australia but not with the North American GSM 1900 (though some North Americans have dual- or triple-band phones that do work here). Check with your service provider about using your phone in the Netherlands, and beware of calls being routed internationally, which becomes *very* expensive.

Prepaid mobile phones are available at mobile shops from €40. Packages with prepaid SIM cards are an excellent option – KPN, Telfort, Orange, T-Mobile and Vodaphone offer cards from €10 with €5 worth of calls. Make sure your phone is unlocked before purchasing such a card.

Phone Codes

The international access code is 0. Area codes for the Dutch cities covered in this book are given at the start of each city's section. The country code for the Netherlands is ☎ 31.

Many information services use phone numbers beginning with ☎ 0800 (free) or ☎ 0900 (which cost between €0.10 and €0.70 per minute depending on the number).

Numbers beginning with ☎ 06 are mobile or pager numbers.

Phonecards

Most public telephones are cardphones and there's no shortage of prepaid cards to fill them. Various cards are available at post offices, train station counters, tourist and GWK offices, supermarkets, and tobacco shops for €5, €10 and €20. Other cards are available at call centres, internet shops and street vendors, but be sure of their authenticity before handing over cash – readers have reported dodgy cards that eat your money in a matter of minutes.

KPN's cards are the most common, but railway stations only have Telfort phone booths that require a Telfort card (available at GWK offices or ticket counters), although there should be KPN booths close by.

The official, KPN-Telecom public phone boxes charge €0.10 per 20 seconds for national calls. Phones in cafés, supermarkets and hotel lobbies often charge more. Ringing a mobile number costs €0.55 per minute from a public phone.

TIME

The Netherlands is on Central European time, GMT/UTC plus one hour. Noon in Amsterdam is 11am in London, 6am in New York, 3am in San Francisco, 6am in Toronto, 9pm in Sydney and 11pm in Auckland, and then there's daylight-saving time. Clocks are put forward one hour at 2am on the last Sunday in March and back again at 3am on the last Sunday in October.

When telling the time, beware that Dutch uses half to indicate 'half before' the hour. If you say 'half eight' (8.30 in many forms of English), a Dutch person will take this to mean 7.30. Dutch also uses constructions such as *tien voor half acht* (ten to half eight – 7.20) and *kwart over acht* (quarter past eight – 8.15).

TOURIST INFORMATION

Within the Netherlands, tourist information is supplied by the **VVV** (Vereniging voor Vreemdelingenverkeer, Netherlands Tourism Board; www.vvv.nl), which has offices throughout the country. Although each tourist office is locally run, they all have a huge amount of information that covers not just their area but the rest of the country as well. However, most VVV publications cost money and there are commissions for services (eg €3 to €15 to find a room, €2 to €3 on theatre tickets). The **VVV information line** (☎ 09004004040; ⏱ 9am-5pm Mon-Fri) costs €0.55 per minute. People ringing from abroad should try ☎ 020-551 25 25 (no extra charge). See the individual city listings for details of local services as well as opening hours.

The Dutch automobile association **ANWB** (☎ 08000503; www.anwb.nl; ⏱ 10am-6pm Mon-Sat) has free or discounted maps and brochures. It provides a wide range of useful information and assistance if you're travelling with any type of vehicle (car, bicycle, motorcycle, yacht etc). In many cities the VVV and ANWB share offices. You'll probably have to show proof of membership of your home automobile club. Its offices are open until 9pm during *koopavond* (evening shopping), which is on Thursday or Friday night, depending on the city.

TRAVELLERS WITH DISABILITIES

Travellers with mobility problems will find the Netherlands fairly well equipped despite the limitations of some older buildings. A large number of government offices and museums have lifts or ramps; many hotels, however, are in old buildings where steep, narrow stairs are the only option. Restaurants tend to be on the ground floor, though they sometimes include a few steps up or down.

Train and other public transport stations have lifts, and most train stations and public buildings have toilets for the disabled. The trains themselves have wheelchair access in most instances, and people with a disability get discounts on public transport. For those with impaired vision, train timetables are published in Braille and banknotes have raised shapes on the corners for identification. **Netherlands Railways** (☎ 030-235 78 22) has an information line with details of all its services for travellers with disabilities. The Dutch national organisation for the disabled is **ANGO** (Algemene Nederlandse Gehandicapten Organisatie, Dutch Society for the Disabled; ☎ 033-465 43 43; www.ango.nl; Koningin Wilhelminalaan 17, 3818 HM Amersfoort); the blind and deaf can contact **LED** (Landelijk Expertisecentrum Doofblindheid, Association for the Deaf & Blind; ☎ 030-267 92 88; www.doofblind.nl; Vrieslantlaan 3A, 3526 AA Utrecht).

VISAS

Tourists from nearly 60 countries – including Australia, Canada, Israel, Japan, South Korea, New Zealand, Singapore, the USA and most of Europe – need only a valid passport to visit the Netherlands for up to three months. EU nationals can enter for three months with just their national identity card.

Nationals of most other countries need a so-called Schengen visa, named after the Schengen Agreement that abolished passport controls between the EU member states (except the UK and Ireland) plus Norway and Iceland. A visa for any of these countries is valid for 90 days within a period of six months. Some countries may impose restrictions on some nationalities.

Schengen visas are issued by Dutch embassies or consulates and can be valid for anything from a few days to two months. You'll need a passport valid until at least three months after your visit, and you must be able to prove that you have sufficient funds for your stay. Fees vary depending on your nationality, but expect to pay around €35. Tourist visas can be extended for another three months maximum, but you'll need a good reason and the extension will only be valid for the Netherlands, not the Schengen area.

Visa extensions are handled by the **Immigratie en Naturalisatiedienst** (Immigration & Naturalisation Service; ☎ 020-889 3045, 09001234561; www.ind .nl); call it about visa extensions for anywhere in the country (the 0900 number costs €0.10 per minute). Study visas must be applied for via your college or university in the Netherlands. For information about working visas, see right.

WOMEN TRAVELLERS

There's little street harassment in Dutch cities, where most women will feel safe. Amsterdam is probably as secure as it gets in the major cities of Europe. Just take care in the Red Light District, where it's best to walk with a friend to minimise unwelcome attention.

The feminist movement is less politicised than elsewhere and certainly more laid-back. Efforts focus on practical solutions such as cultural centres, bicycle repair shops run by and for women, or support systems to help women set up businesses.

Most women's organisations are based in Amsterdam, among them **Rutgershuis Amsterdam** (☎ 020-624 54 26; Sarphatistraat 618), a clinic offering information and help with sexual problems and birth control, including the morning-after pill. Elsewhere, look under Vrouwenhuis (Women's House) in the phone directory.

WORK

All-important work permits must be applied for by your employer in the Netherlands; in general, the employer must prove that the position cannot be filled by someone from within the EU before offering it to a non-EU citizen. Nationals from many countries must apply for a Temporary Entry Permit (Machtiging tot Voorlopig Verblijf, or MVV). Citizens of EU countries as well as Australia, Canada, Iceland, Japan, Monaco, New Zealand, Norway, Switzerland and the USA are exempt.

You'll need to apply for temporary residence before an employer can ask for your work permit. The process should take five weeks; contact the Dutch embassy or consulate in your home country.

In the Netherlands residence permits are issued by the **Immigratie en Naturalisatiedienst** (Immigration & Naturalisation Service; ☎ 020-889 30 45; www.ind.nl; Postbus 30125, 2500 GC Den Haag). For details of work permits, contact the **CWI** (Centrum voor Werk en Inkomen, Employment Services Authority; ☎ 079-371 29 03; www.cwinet.nl; Postbus 883, 2700 AW Zoetermeer). The CWI also runs www.werk.nl, which features up-to-date job offers.

Transport

The Netherlands is an extraordinarily simple place to reach. Amsterdam's Schiphol Airport has copious air links worldwide, including many on low-cost European airlines, and the links on high-speed trains are especially good from France, Belgium and Germany. Other land options are user-friendly and the border crossings are nearly invisible thanks to the EU. There are also several ferry links with the UK and Scandinavia.

What's more, once you get to the Netherlands the transport stays hassle-free. Most journeys by rail, car or bus are so short that you can reach most regional destinations before your next meal. And with a country as flat as this, getting around by bicycle is a dream.

THINGS CHANGE...

The information in this chapter is particularly vulnerable to change. Check directly with the airline or a travel agent to make sure you understand how a fare (and ticket you may buy) works and be aware of the security requirements for international travel. Shop carefully. The details given in this chapter should be regarded as pointers and are not a substitute for your own careful, up-to-date research.

GETTING THERE & AWAY

ENTERING THE COUNTRY
Passport
In principle all passengers with passports are allowed entry to the Netherlands, although those coming from 'suspected terrorist centres' may be detained for questioning.

AIR
Airports & Airlines
Conveniently near Amsterdam, **Schiphol Airport** (code AMS; ☎ 020-794 08 00; www.schiphol.nl) is the Netherlands' main international airport and the third busiest in Europe. It is the seat of Dutch passenger carrier KLM, and dozens of other airlines have direct flights and connections to all continents. **Rotterdam Airport** (code RTM; ☎ 010-446 34 44; www.rotterdam-airport.nl) is much smaller but has handy links to the UK, Germany and Mediterranean destinations.

Eindhoven, Groningen and Maastricht act as feeder airports to Amsterdam, catering to business travellers and holiday charters to sunny climes. From **Eindhoven** (code EIN; ☎ 040-291 98 18; www.eindhovenairport.com), Ryanair serves London, Dublin, Milan and a handful of Mediterranean cities, while KLM flies to/from London and Paris.

AIRLINES FLYING TO & FROM THE NETHERLANDS
Unless otherwise stated, dial ☎ 020 before calling the numbers below.

Aer Lingus (code EI; ☎ 517 47 47; www.aerlingus.com; Folkstoneweg 28, Schiphol)

Air Canada (code AC; ☎ 346 95 39; www.aircanada.ca; Evert van de Beekstraat 5, Schiphol)

Air France (code AF; ☎ 654 57 20; www.airfrance.nl; Evert van der Beekstraat 7; Schiphol)

Alitalia (code AZ; ☎ 676 44 79; www.alitalia.com; Evert van de Beekstraat 9, Schiphol)

Austrian (code OS; ☎ 09002658920; www.aua.com; Evert van de Beekstraat 37, Schiphol)

British Airways (code BA; ☎ 346 95 59; www.british airways.com)

British Midland (code BD; ☎ 346 92 11; www.flybmi .com; Vertrekpassage 1, Schiphol)

CLIMATE CHANGE & TRAVEL

Climate change is a serious threat to the ecosystems that humans rely upon, and air travel is the fastest-growing contributor to the problem. Lonely Planet regards travel, overall, as a global benefit, but believes we all have a responsibility to limit our personal impact on global warming.

Flying & climate change

Pretty much every form of motorized travel generates CO2 (the main cause of human-induced climate change) but planes are far and away the worst offenders, not just because of the sheer distances they allow us to travel, but because they release greenhouse gases high into the atmosphere. The statistics are frightening: two people taking a return flight between Europe and the US will contribute as much to climate change as an average household's gas and electricity consumption over a whole year.

Carbon offset schemes

Climatecare.org and other websites use 'carbon calculators' that allow travellers to offset the level of greenhouse gases they are responsible for with financial contributions to sustainable travel schemes that reduce global warming – including projects in India, Honduras, Kazakhstan and Uganda.

Lonely Planet, together with Rough Guides and other concerned partners in the travel industry, supports the carbon offset scheme run by climatecare.org. Lonely Planet offsets all of its staff and author travel.

For more information check out our website: www.lonelyplanet.com.

Cathay Pacific (code CX; ☎ 653 20 10; www.cathay pacific.nl; Evert van der Beekstraat 18, Schiphol)

China Airlines (code CI; ☎ 646 10 01; www.china-air lines.com; De Boelelaan 7, Amsterdam)

Continental Airlines (code CO; ☎ 346 93 81; www .continental.com; Schiphol Blvd 275, Schiphol)

Delta Air Lines (code DL; ☎ 201 35 36; www.delta.com; Evert van der Beekstraat 7, Schiphol)

El Al (code LY; ☎ 644 01 01; www.elal.com; Prof Bavincklaan 5, Amstelveen)

EasyJet (code U2; ☎ 023-568 48 80; www.easyjet.com; Antareslaan 35, Hoofddorp)

Japan Airlines (code JL; ☎ 305 00 75; www.jal-europe .com; Jozef Israelskade 48E, Amsterdam)

Jet2.com (code LS; ☎ 09002021067; www.jet2.com)

KLM (code KL; ☎ 474 77 47; www.klm.nl; Amsterdamse-weg 55, Amstelveen)

Lufthansa (code LH; ☎ 09001234777; www.lufthansa .nl; Vertrekpassage 1, Schiphol)

Malaysia Airlines (code MH; ☎ 521 62 62; www .malaysiaairlines.com; Weteringschans 24/A, Amsterdam)

Northwest Airlines (code NW; ☎ 474 77 47; www .nwa.com; Amsterdamseweg 55, Amstelveen)

Ryanair (code FL; ☎ 09002022184; www.ryanair.com; Vertrekpassage 1, Schiphol)

Singapore Airlines (code SQ; ☎ 548 88 88; www .singaporeair.com; Evert van de Beekstraat 26, Schiphol)

Transavia (code HV; ☎ 09000737; www.transavia .com)

United Airlines (code UA; ☎ 201 37 08; www.united airlines.nl; Vertrekpassage 246, Schiphol)

Tickets

Within Europe there are plenty of no-frills airlines connecting Amsterdam's Schiphol Airport to other cities, and more often than not their bargain flights can be found online rather than through a travel agent. For long-haul flights the opposite is true – agents are a valuable source for tracking down cheaper flights between continents. Stable travel agents, such as **STA Travel** (www.statravel.com) and **Trailfinders** (www.trailfinders .com), offer good prices to many destinations.

Below is a short list of sites that sell air tickets to/from Schiphol Airport:

Ebookers (www.ebookers.com) Offers separate web gateways for many European countries and bargains on flights and hotels.

Expedia (www.expedia.com, www.expedia.co.uk) Lists major airline flights from the US and UK; the earlier you book the better.

Flight Centre (www.flightcentre.com) Respected operator handling direct flights, with sites for Australia, New Zealand, the UK, the US and Canada.

Last Minute (www.lastminute.com) One of the better sites for last-minute deals, including hotels.

Opodo (www.opodo.co.uk) UK-based company with excellent deals for European destinations.

Orbitz (www.orbitz.com) Cheap deals when flying from the US.
Price Line (www.priceline.com) Name-your-own-price US site.
Skyscanner (www.skyscanner.net) Collates cheap no-frills airline fares for many destinations around the world.
Travelocity (www.travelocity.com) US site that allows you to search fares (in US dollars) to/from practically anywhere.
Vliegtarieven (www.vliegtarieven.nl) Dutch site with hotel and car-rental deals alongside flights.
WaarheenWaarvoor (www.waarheenwaarvoor.nl) Dutch site offering flight-price comparisons and last-minute deals.

Africa

KLM has numerous services to Africa, including daily flights to Johannesburg, Dar es Salaam and Nairobi. Kenya Airways also offers daily links to the country's capital. From Johannesburg, low-season return fares to Amsterdam can start at around R5480 (€645) but can be considerably higher if not booked well in advance.

Rennies Travel (www.renniestravel.com) and **STA Travel** (www.statravel.co.za) have offices throughout Southern Africa. Check their websites for branch locations.

Asia

The major Asian airlines, such as Singapore Airlines, Cathay Pacific, Japan Airlines and Malaysia Airlines, have flights into Amsterdam. KLM links Jakarta with the capital. Although most flights are via another European capital, there are some direct links to Amsterdam. It's a good idea to shop around as there are often some good deals on offer. From Bangkok, return fares to Amsterdam are around US$1500. Return fares from Singapore start at US$850; expect to pay from US$1250 from Hong Kong and US$1100 from Tokyo for a return fare.

STA Travel (Bangkok ☎ 0662-236 0262; www.statravel.co.th; Hong Kong ☎ 852-2736 1618; www.statravel.com.hk; Singapore ☎ 65-6737 7188; www.statravel.com.sg; Tokyo ☎ 03-5391 2922; www.statravel.co.jp) is always a good bet in Asia.

Australia

Flights from Australia to Amsterdam generally go via a Southeast Asian capital such as Kuala Lumpur, Bangkok or Singapore, and occasionally another European city. Expect to pay around A$2000 return in low season,

but shop around as there are often good deals on offer.

Quite a few travel offices specialise in discount air tickets. Some travel agents, particularly smaller ones, advertise cheap air fares in the travel sections of weekend newspapers, such as the *Age* in Melbourne and the *Sydney Morning Herald* in Sydney.

Contact **STA Travel** (☎ 03-9207 5900; www.statravel.com.au) for the location of branches. **Flight Centre** (☎ 133 133; www.flightcentre.com.au) has offices throughout Australia. For online bookings, try www.travel.com.au.

Canada

Air Canada, among others, serves Amsterdam from Toronto. Fares vary from C$400 in winter to C$700 in summer.

Canadian discount air ticket sellers are also known as consolidators. The *Globe & Mail*, *Toronto Star*, *Montreal Gazette* and *Vancouver Sun* carry travel agents' ads and are good places to look for cheap fares.

Travel CUTS (☎ 1866-246-9762; www.travelcuts.com) is Canada's national student travel agency and has offices in all major cities.

Continental Europe

Amsterdam is well connected to almost all other European cities. KLM and the major airlines of each country all serve each other. You should be able to find return fares from the major hub airports such as Copenhagen, Frankfurt, Paris and Madrid for €100 to €200.

Generally, there is not much variation in airfare prices for departures from the main European cities. All the major airlines are usually offering some sort of deal, and travel agents generally have a number of promotions on offer, so shop around.

Across Europe dozens of travel agencies have ties with **STA Travel** (www.statravel.com), where cheap tickets can be purchased and STA-issued tickets can be altered (usually for a US$25 fee).

Recommended are the following travel agents:

Airstop (☎ 070 233 188; www.airstop.be) Belgium.
CTS Viaggi (☎ 06 462 04 31; www.cts.it) Italy.
Just Travel (☎ 089-747 3330; www.justtravel.de) Germany.
Nouvelles Frontières (☎ 0825 000 747; www.nouvelles-frontieres.fr) France.
OTU Voyages (☎ 0820 817 817; www.otu.fr) France.

STA Travel (☎ 01803100040; www.statravel.de) Germany.
Viaggi Wasteels (☎ 06 446 66 79) Italy.
Voyageurs du Monde (☎ 01 42 86 16 00; www.vdm
.com) France.

New Zealand
Reaching Amsterdam from Auckland means
you have a choice of transiting though Los
Angeles or via a Southeast Asian city, and
usually one other European city. Low season
return fares start from around US$2000.

Both **Flight Centre** (☎ 0800243544; www.flight
centre.co.nz) and **STA Travel** (☎ 0508782872; www.sta
travel.co.nz) have branches throughout the country.
For on-line bookings try www.travel.co.nz.

UK & Ireland
KLM, British Airways and British Midland
fly to the Netherlands from the UK. Budget
airlines EasyJet, Ryanair and Jet2.com do too,
and have made big inroads into the business
of the mainstream carriers. Watch for special
fares that can be as low as UK£1 for a single
(plus tax), although €40 to €60 is more likely
in peak periods.

Ticket discounters, or bucket shops as
they're known in the UK, can sometimes offer
big savings. Discount air travel is big business in London, and advertisements for many
travel agents appear in the travel pages of the
weekend broadsheets, such as the *Independent*
on Saturday and the *Sunday Times*. Also look
out for free magazines such as TNT.

Popular travel agencies include **STA Travel**
(☎ 08701630026; www.statravel.co.uk), with offices
throughout the UK. It sells tickets to all travellers but caters especially to young people
and students. Other recommended agencies
include **Trailfinders** (☎ 0845-050 5940; www.trail
finders.com) and **Travelbag** (☎ 08706070620; www
.travelbag.co.uk).

From Ireland, fares run from about €150
in low season for return flights from Dublin
to Amsterdam, but can cost twice that (and
sometimes more) in high season. Travelling
via London may save money. **USIT** (☎ 01-602
1904; www.usitnow.ie) has branches in Ireland and
Northern Ireland specialising in student and
independent travel.

USA
Continental Airlines, Delta Air Lines,
Northwest Airlines and United Airlines all
have nonstop services to Amsterdam from
cities in the US. Fares vary by season, from a
low of US$300/500 from the east coast/west
coast in winter to a high of US$700/900 in
summer.

Discount travel agents in the USA are
known as consolidators (although you
probably won't see a sign on the door saying 'Consolidator'). The *New York Times*,
the *Los Angeles Times*, the *Chicago Tribune*
and the *San Francisco Chronicle* all produce
Sunday travel sections in which you will find
consolidators' ads.

STA Travel (☎ 1-800-781-4040; www.statravel.com)
is one of the biggest travel agents in the US,
with offices in most states.

LAND
Bicycle
In a land where the humble bicycle is king,
bringing your own bike into the Netherlands
will cause no problems.

By air, it's possible to first take your bicycle
apart and protect it with a bike bag or box before handing it over to the baggage handlers,
but it's much easier simply to wheel your
bike to the check-in desk, where it should be
treated as a piece of baggage. You may have
to remove the pedals and turn the handlebars
sideways so that it takes up less space in the
aircraft's hold; check all this with the airline
well in advance, preferably before you pay
for your ticket.

Your bike can also travel with you on the
Eurostar and Thalys high-speed trains from
Belgium, France and the UK, provided you
can disassemble the bike and fit it into a stow-
age bag that will fit into the normal luggage-
storage racks on board.

If you want to bring your own bike, consider the risk of theft in Amsterdam – rental
might be the wiser option in the capital.

Bus
Amsterdam and Rotterdam, and a few of
Holland's smaller cities such as Den Haag
and Utrecht, are well connected to the rest
of Europe and North Africa by long-distance
bus. See p302 for information on buses to and
from Germany and p303 for details on buses
to and from the UK.

The most extensive European bus network
is maintained by **Eurolines** (www.eurolines.com),
a consortium of coach operators. It offers a
variety of passes with prices that vary by time
of year, but if you book well ahead bargains
can be had.

TRANSPORT

Car & Motorcycle

For details about car ferries from England, see opposite.

Drivers of cars and riders of motorbikes will need the vehicle's registration papers, third-party insurance and an international driving permit in addition to their domestic licence. It's a good idea to also have complete insurance coverage – be sure to ask for a Green Card from your insurer.

The ANWB (p296) provides a wide range of information, maps, advice and services if you can show a letter of introduction or membership card from your own automobile association.

Traffic flows freely among EU countries, so border posts are largely a thing of the past. Customs officials still make spot checks, however, if a particular vehicle draws their attention.

Hitching

Hitching is never entirely safe anywhere in the world and we don't recommend it. Travellers who decide to hitch should understand that they are taking a small but potentially serious risk.

Many Dutch students have a government-issued pass allowing free public transport. Consequently, the number of hitchhikers has dropped dramatically and car drivers are no longer used to the phenomenon. Hitchers have reported long waits.

On Channel crossings from the UK, the car fares on the Harwich–Hoek van Holland ferry as well as the shuttle through the Channel Tunnel include passengers, so you can hitch to the continent at no cost to the driver (though the driver will still be responsible if you do something illegal).

Looking for a ride out of the country? Try the notice boards at universities, public libraries and youth hostels. **Bugride** (http://europe .bugride.com) is a good meeting place for European drivers and potential passengers.

Belgium & Germany

BICYCLE

Long-distance cyclists can choose from a variety of safe, easy, specially designated routes to get to the Netherlands from Belgium and Germany. The bicycle paths are called *landelijke fietsroutes* (LF) and retain that label in northern Belgium. The LF2 route runs 340km from Brussels via Ghent to Amsterdam; the

LF4 stretches 300km from Enschede near the German border to Den Haag.

Beware that mopeds also use bike paths and might be travelling well above their 40km/h speed limit (30km/h in built-up areas). Only competition cyclists and poseurs tend to wear bicycle helmets, but that shouldn't stop you from protecting your own cranium.

Repair shops are as common as *frites* vendors in the Netherlands – most train stations even have a bicycle shop with a resident mechanic.

For select cycling routes, see p69.

BUS

Aside from Eurolines (see p301), **Gullivers Reisen** (☎ 030-3110 2110; www.gullivers.de) links Berlin (one way/return from €29/58, nine hours, once daily), Hamburg (from €19/38, eight hours, once daily) and Hanover (from €19/38, 5½ hours, once daily) with Amsterdam. Sleeper coach beds are available for another €10 – a wise investment.

CAR & MOTORCYCLE

The main entry points from Belgium are the E22 (Antwerp–Breda) and the E25 (Liege–Maastricht). From Germany there are loads of border crossings, but the chief arteries are the E40 (Cologne–Maastricht), the E35 (Düsseldorf–Arnhem) and the A1 (Hanover–Amsterdam).

TRAIN

The Netherlands has good train links to Germany and Belgium and on to France. All Eurail, Inter-Rail, Europass and Flexipass tickets are valid on the Dutch national train service, **Nederlandse Spoorwegen** (NS; www.ns.nl). See p308 for more about trains within the country.

Major Dutch train stations have international ticket offices, and in peak periods it's wise to reserve seats in advance. You can also buy tickets for local trains to Belgium and Germany at the normal ticket counters.

For international train information, ring the Teleservice NS Internationaal on ☎ 09009296 (calls cost €0.35 per minute) or consult the website, www.nsinternational.nl. If you book ahead, NS charges a €3.50 reservation fee per ticket.

From Amsterdam, two main trains travel south. The first, an Intercity (IC), passes through Den Haag and Rotterdam and on to Antwerp (€28, 2¼ hours, hourly), Bruges (€39.40, 3½ hours, hourly), Brussels (€33.40, three hours, hourly) and Luxembourg City (€63.60, 6¼ hours, every one to two hours).

The second train, the high-speed Thalys, runs six times a day between Amsterdam and Antwerp (€28, 2¼ hours), Brussels (€33.40, 2½ hours) and Paris (€97.50, 4¼ hours). Those under 26 receive a 50% discount, and seniors with a Rail Europe Senior (RES) card are entitled to 25% off travel. Only a handful of tickets are set aside for such discounts, so it is essential to book ahead.

The German ICE high-speed service runs six times a day between Amsterdam and Cologne (€49.20, 2½ hours) and on to Frankfurt (€107, four hours); there's a surcharge of €2 and €19 respectively. Cologne is also available for €58.50. There's also a night train between Amsterdam and Munich (from €79) – expect fat surcharges for the sleeper berths. The IC to Berlin (€92.20, six hours, three daily) passes through Hanover.

Weekend return tickets are much cheaper than during the week. A weekend return Amsterdam–Brussels (departure Friday to Sunday, return by Monday) is 40% cheaper than a regular ticket.

UK
BICYCLE
Most cross-Channel ferries don't charge foot passengers extra to take a bicycle. You can also bring your two-wheeler on the Eurostar (right).

BUS
Eurolines (see p301) runs a regular coach service to Amsterdam via Rotterdam and Den Haag or Utrecht from London's Victoria coach station (from UK£30 for adults, 12 hours). Coaches have onboard toilets, reclining seats and air-con.

Busabout (☎ 020-7950 1661; www.busabout.com) is a UK-based budget alternative to Eurolines. It runs coaches on circuits in Continental Europe; its Northern Loop circuit (UK£275) passes through Amsterdam and eventually links up with its western and southern routes in Paris and Munich respectively. Tickets are valid from May to October.

CAR & MOTORCYCLE
Ferries take cars and motorcycles to the Netherlands from several ports in the UK (for

details, see below). Le Shuttle express trains will take vehicles from the UK to France, from where you can drive to the Netherlands (see below).

TRAIN
Rail Europe (☎ 08708371371; www.raileurope.co.uk) will get you from London to Amsterdam on the highly civilised Eurostar service from Waterloo Station through the Channel Tunnel to Brussels, with an onward Thalys connection from there. The quickest connection will take around 6½ hours and starts from UK£90 return in 2nd class with special deals. A bicycle costs UK£20 one way unless it is in a bike bag, in which case it is classed as hand luggage.

Eurotunnel (☎ 08705353535; www.eurotunnel.com) runs a 'drive-on, drive off' shuttle linking Folkstone, UK, to Calais, France, on a 35-minute journey via the Channel Tunnel. One-way journeys for cars/motorcycles cost from UK£49/24 with advance reservations.

The **Dutch Flyer** (☎ 08705455455; www.dutchflyer.co.uk) is one of the cheapest ways to reach the Netherlands from the UK. Trains from London (Liverpool Street Station), Cambridge and Norwich connect with ferries sailing from Harwich to Hoek van Holland, where a further train travels on to Amsterdam. The journey takes around 9½ hours and costs as little as UK£25 one way.

SEA
UK
FERRY
Several companies operate car/passenger ferries between the Netherlands and the UK. Most travel agents have details of the following services but might not always know the finer points. For information on train-ferry-train services, see above. Reservations are essential for motorists in high season, although motorcycles can often be squeezed in.

Stenaline (☎ 08705707070; www.stenaline.co.uk) sails between Harwich and Hoek van Holland. The fast HSS ferries take only three hours 40 minutes and depart in each direction twice a day. Overnight ferries take 6¼ hours (one daily), as do normal day ferries (one daily). Foot passengers pay upwards of UK£40 return. Fares for a car with up to five people range from UK£300 to UK£350 return depending on the season and the day of the week. A motorcycle and driver cost UK£110/UK£200 in low/high season. Options such as

TRANSPORT

reclining chairs and cabins cost extra and are compulsory on night crossings.

P&O North Sea Ferries (☎ 08705202020; www.po ferries.com) operates an overnight ferry every evening (11 hours) between Hull and Europoort (near Rotterdam). Return fares start at UK£112 for a foot passenger (for two persons travelling together it's only UK£133), UK£238 for a car with up to four people, and UK£198 for a motorcycle and rider. Prices here include berths in an inside cabin, and luxury cabins are available.

DFDS Scandinavian Seaways (☎ 08702520524; www .dfds.co.uk) sails between Newcastle and IJmuiden (p152), which is close to Amsterdam; the 15-hour sailings depart every day. The earlier you book, the lower your fare: single fares start at UK£19 for a foot passenger in an economy berth with private facilities, plus UK£41 for a car. The fare for a motorcycle and rider is UK£49 one way. Bear in mind that prices go up in high season.

Most ferries don't charge for a bike and have no shortage of storage space.

GETTING AROUND

The Netherlands is more than easy to get around. If you are sticking to the major cities and sights, you won't need a car as the train and bus system blankets the country. Or you can do as the Dutch do and provide your power on a bike.

An excellent online information source, covering everything from bus and train connections to city metro lines, is www.9292ov.nl. It's in Dutch but quite easy to follow.

AIR

With a country as small as the Netherlands (the longest train journey, between Groningen and Maastricht, takes 4¼ hours), there is no need to fly anywhere. There is however the occasional flight from Amsterdam Schiphol to Eindhoven, and a number of daily flights between Amsterdam and Maastricht. They're chiefly used by business passengers transferring to international flights at Schiphol, and flights are quite expensive.

BICYCLE

The Netherlands is extremely bike-friendly and a *fiets* (bicycle) is the way to go; once you're in the country you can pedal almost everywhere on 20,000km of dedicated bicycle paths. Everything is wonderfully flat, but that also means powerful wind.

The ANWB (see p296) publishes cycling maps for each province, and tourist offices always have numerous routes and suggestions. Major roads have separate bike lanes, and, except for motorways, there's virtually nowhere bicycles can't go. That said, in places such as the Delta region and along the coast you'll often need muscles to combat the North Sea headwinds.

Over 100 stations throughout the country have bicycle facilities for hire, protected parking, repair and sales. Details are noted throughout this book.

Bicycles are prohibited on trains during the weekday rush hours (6.30am to 9am and 4.30pm to 6pm), except for the Hoek van Holland boat train. There are no restrictions on holidays, at weekends or during July and August.

You may bring your bicycle onto any train as long as there is room; a day pass for bikes (€6) is valid in the entire country regardless of the distance involved. There are no fees for collapsible bikes so long as they can be considered hand luggage. Some trains such as the single-level Intercity carriages have very limited space. However, on popular stretches there's often a special bicycle carriage that increases capacity. If your planned train has no room for your bike, you'll have to wait for the next train.

For more information about cycling, see p69.

Hire

Although about 85% of the population owns bikes, and there are more bikes than people, bikes are also abundantly available for hire. In most cases you'll need to show your passport and leave an imprint of your credit card or a deposit (around €25 to €100). Private operators and train station hire shops (called Rijwiel) charge €4 to €7 per day, and €25 to €35 per week; rental in Amsterdam is around 30% higher.

Purchase

Your basic used bicycle (no gears, with coaster brakes, maybe a bit rickety) can be bought for around €50 to €75 from bicycle shops or the classified ads. Count on paying €100 or more for a reliable two-wheeler with gears. Stolen bikes are available on the street for as little as €15, but it's highly illegal and the cash usually goes straight into a junkie's arm. Good new models start at around €200 on sale, but top-of-the-line brands can cost €1000 or more.

BOAT
Ferry
Ferries connect the mainland with the five Frisian Islands. See the Friesland (p230) and Noord Holland (p145) chapters for details. Other ferries span the Westerschelde in the south of Zeeland, providing a link between the southwestern expanse of the country and Belgium. These are popular with people using the Zeebrugge ferry terminal and run frequently year-round. There is also a frequent ferry service on the IJsselmeer linking Enkhuizen with Stavoren and Urk. You'll also find a few small river ferries providing crossings on remote stretches of the IJssel and other rivers.

Hire
Renting a boat is a popular way to tour the many rivers, lakes and inland seas. Boats come in all shapes and sizes from canoes to motor boats to small sailing boats to large and historic former cargo sloops. Prices run the gamut and there are hundreds of rental firms throughout the country. See p287 for more details.

BUS
Buses are used for regional transport rather than for long distances, which are better travelled by train. They provide a vital service, especially in parts of the north and east, where trains are less frequent or nonexistent. The national *strippenkaart* (p307) is used on most regional buses. The fares are zone-based, but figure on roughly one strip for every five minutes of riding.

There is only one class of travel and passes exist for regions within provinces; drivers are well informed on such deals and can sell them on the spot. Reservations aren't possible – and definitely not necessary – on either regional or municipal lines, most of which run quite frequently. For details about regional buses around the country, consult www.9292ov.nl or call the transport information service on ☎ 09009292 (calls cost €0.70 per minute).

CAR & MOTORCYCLE
Dutch freeways are extensive but prone to congestion. Those around Amsterdam, the A4 south to Belgium and the A2 southeast to Maastricht are especially likely to be jammed at rush hours and during busy travel periods; a total length of 350km or more isn't unheard of during the holiday season.

Smaller roads are usually well maintained, but the campaign to discourage car use throws up obstacles – you may find the road narrows to a single lane in sections, or an assortment of speed-bumps and other 'traffic-calming schemes'.

Automobile Associations
For motoring information, contact the **ANWB** (☎ 070-314 71 47; Wassenaarseweg 220, Den Haag); its headquarters are in Den, but most big towns and cities have an office.

Driving Licence
You'll need to show a valid driving licence when hiring a car in the Netherlands. Visitors from outside the EU should also consider an international driving permit (IDP). Car-rental firms will rarely ask for one, but the police might do so if they pull you up. An IDP can be obtained for a small fee from your local automobile association – bring along a valid licence and a passport photo – and is valid for one year together with your original licence.

Fuel
Like much of Western Europe, petrol is very expensive and fluctuates on a regular basis. At the time of research it was about €1.40 per litre (about US$6.50 per gallon). Gasoline (petrol) is *benzine* in Dutch, while unleaded fuel is *loodvrij*. Leaded fuel is no longer sold in the Netherlands. Liquid petroleum gas can be purchased at petrol stations displaying LPG signs.

Petrol isn't noticeably more or less expensive outside of towns. Cheaper fuel is generally available from cut-rate chains such as Tango or TinQ – just ask the locals.

Hire
The Netherlands is well covered for car hire. However, outside Amsterdam the car-hire companies can be in inconvenient locations if you're arriving by train. You can look for local car-rental firms in telephone directories under the heading Autoverhuur. You must be at least 23 years of age to hire a car in the Netherlands.

www.lonelyplanet.com

ROAD DISTANCES (KM)

	Amsterdam	Apeldoorn	Arnhem	Breda	Den Bosch	Den Haag	Dordrecht	Eindhoven	Enschede	Groningen	Haarlem	Leeuwarden	Leiden	Maastricht	Nijmegen	Rotterdam	Tilburg	Utrecht
Amsterdam	---																	
Apeldoorn	86	---																
Arnhem	99	27	---															
Breda	101	141	111	---														
Den Bosch	88	91	64	48	---													
Den Haag	55	133	118	72	102	---												
Dordrecht	98	133	102	30	65	45	---											
Eindhoven	121	109	82	57	32	134	92	---										
Enschede	161	75	98	212	162	224	200	180	---									
Groningen	203	147	172	260	236	252	248	254	148	---								
Haarlem	19	117	114	121	103	51	94	136	184	204	---							
Leeuwarden	139	133	158	248	222	188	234	240	163	62	148	---						
Leiden	45	125	110	87	99	17	60	132	192	242	42	178	---					
Maastricht	213	201	167	146	124	223	181	86	274	348	228	334	239	---				
Nijmegen	122	63	18	101	44	135	98	62	134	208	135	194	131	148	---			
Rotterdam	73	128	118	51	81	21	24	113	195	251	70	206	36	202	114	---		
Tilburg	114	115	88	25	25	102	60	34	186	260	129	246	117	123	68	81	---	
Utrecht	37	72	64	73	55	62	61	88	139	195	54	181	54	180	85	57	81	---

Some car-hire firms levy a small surcharge (€10 or so) for drivers under 25. Most will ask either for a deposit or a credit-card imprint as a guarantee of payment.

Insurance

Collision damage waiver (CDW), an insurance policy which limits your financial liability for damage, is highly recommended when hiring a car. If you don't take out this insurance, you'll be liable for damages up to the full value of the vehicle.

If you rely on your credit card for cover, take time to review the terms and conditions. In the event of an accident you may be required to pay for repairs out of your own pocket and reclaim the sum from the credit-card company later, a procedure that can be fraught with problems.

BIG BROTHER IS WATCHING

More than 800 unmanned radar cameras (known as *flitspalen*) watch over Dutch motorways.

Note that at most car-rental firms, CDW does not cover the first €500 to €1000 of damages incurred, but an excess cover package, for around €10 to €20 per day, is normally available to cover this amount.

Road Rules

As in the rest of Continental Europe, traffic travels on the right. The minimum driving age is 18 for vehicles and 16 for motorcycles. Seat belts are required for everyone in a vehicle, and children under 12 must ride in the back if there's room.

The standard European road rules and traffic signs apply. Trams always have the right of way. If you are trying to turn right, bikes have priority. One grey area is at roundabouts: in principle, approaching vehicles have right of way, but in practice they yield to vehicles already travelling on the circle.

Speed limits are 50km/h in built-up areas, 80km/h in the country, 100km/h on major through-roads and 120km/h on freeways (sometimes 100km/h, clearly marked). The blood-alcohol limit is 0.05%, or 0.02% for those who got their licence after 30 March 2002.

HITCHING

For information on hitching in the Nether-lands, see p302.

LOCAL TRANSPORT
Bicycle

Any Dutch town you visit is liable to be blan-keted with bicycle paths. They're either on the streets or in the form of smooth off-road routes. In many cases the fastest way to get around is by bike.

Bus, Tram & Metro

Buses and trams operate in most cities, and Amsterdam and Rotterdam have the added bonus of metro networks.

One fare system covers the entire country, and comes in the form of the handy strip-penkaart (strip card), the Netherlands' uni-versal tool of travel. It's available from tobacco shops, post offices, train-station counters, many bookshops and newsagencies, and can be bought in denominations of two (€1.60), three (€2.40), 15 (€6.70) and 45 (€19.80) strips. Bus and tram drivers only sell two- and three-strip cards, so you're better off hunting down the larger, more economical strip cards.

To validate your journey just jump on a tram, bus or metro and stamp off a number of strips depending on how many zones you plan to cross. The ticket is then valid on all buses, trams, metro systems and city trains for an hour or longer depending on the number of strips you've stamped. In most towns you punch two strips (one for the journey and one for the zone), with an additional strip for each additional zone.

In the central areas of cities and towns, you usually will only need to stamp two strips – the minimum fee (see the boxed text, right). When riding on trams and metros it's up to you to stamp your card, as fare dodgers can be fined on the spot. The machines are usually located on board trams and at the entrance to metro platforms.

The buses are more conventional, with drivers stamping the strips as you get on. More than one person can use a *strippenkaart*, and children and pensioners get reductions. Note that if you get caught without a properly stamped strip, playing the ignorant foreigner (the 'doofus' strategy) will guarantee that you get fined €30.

Note that plans are afoot to phase out the *strippenkaart* by the end of 2007, to be re-

---

STRIPP TEASE

Some well-meaning travellers are tempted to punch every single field on a *strip-penkaart*. But remember, passengers on Dutch public transport need to validate their tickets only once per trip regardless of how many people travel on the same ticket. You're travelling alone within one zone – say, central Amsterdam? The canal belt and surrounding districts are one zone but require *two* strips; fold the ticket and punch the second available strip. You're with a friend? Punch the second and fourth strip. And so on. Journeys to another zone take three strips per person; when in doubt consult the transport maps at bus/tram stops or ask the driver.

---

placed by chip cards. At the time of research information was thin on the ground, but the cards will work like debit cards; money can be loaded onto them and then the cards can be used to validate travel on buses, trams and metros. For more information, consult a tour-ist office or train station ticketing office.

Taxi

Usually booked by phone – officially you're not supposed to wave them down on the street – taxis also hover outside train stations and hotels and cost roughly €12 for 5km. Even short trips in town can get expensive quickly. *Treintaxis* (see p309), which operate from many train stations, are a cheaper and more practical bet.

TOURS

Several companies offer tours of the Neth-erlands aboard luxury riverboats. Aimed at older and well-heeled travellers, these tours are more like cruises than actual sightseeing tours.

Cycletours Holland (☎ 020-521 84 90; www.cycletours .com; Buiksloterweg 7A, Amsterdam) Conducts short tours of up to a week by bicycle and canal barge. Tours aver-age eight days and cost around €640 (cabin with shared shower and toilet).

Hat Tours (☎ 0299-690 771; www.hat-tours.com; Venediën 26-I, 1441 AK Purmerend) Offers similar tours to Cycletours Holland and appeals to cyclists and nature lovers.

Holland River Line (☎ 026-445 80 08; www.holland riverline.nl; Teldersstraat 9, 68 42 CT Arnhem) Cruise in

style with one of the biggest operators, with lazy trips along Dutch rivers into Belgium and Germany.
Lowlands Travel (☎ 06-2334 2046; www.lowlands travel.nl; Korvelplein 176, 5025 JX Tilburg) Down-to-earth nature- and culture-oriented holidays, lasting from three days to a week for groups of two to eight people, mostly outdoorsy types aged 20 to 40.

TRAIN

Dutch trains are efficient, fast and comfortable – most of the time. Trains are frequent and serve domestic destinations at regular intervals, sometimes five or six times an hour. Short-term visitors may be fortunate, but overall the network has been plagued by poor punctuality in recent years. Rush-hour periods around the Randstad seem to notch up the most delays. The situation may be improving, if only because **NS** (☎ national inquiries 09009292, international inquiries 09009296; www .ns.nl) has little choice: its profitability is linked to its on-time rates. Some rural lines have been hived off to combination train-and-bus operators who coordinate schedules across the region.

Many stations across the country have electronic left-luggage lockers, which cost around €4 for 24 hours. The majority, inconveniently, are bank-card operated; Amsterdam's Centraal Station lockers are still coin operated, however.

Classes

The longest train journey in the Netherlands (Maastricht–Groningen) takes about 4½ hours, but the majority of trips are far shorter. Trains have 1st-class sections, but these are often little different from the 2nd-class areas and, given the short journeys, not worth the extra cost.

Trains can be an all-stops *stoptrein*, a faster *sneltrein* (fast train, indicated with an S) or an even faster Intercity (IC). Intercity Express (ICE) trains travel between Amsterdam and Cologne and only stop in Utrecht and Arnhem; they're quite fast (a 10-minute saving to Arnhem), but you pay a €2 supplement at the counter or ticket machine, or €4 on board the train.

TRAVELLING DOGS

Dog owners can travel with Fido all day long on Dutch trains using a *dagkaart hond* (doggie day pass), which costs €3.

The high-speed Thalys only stops at Amsterdam, Schiphol, Den Haag and Rotterdam before going on to Antwerp, Brussels and Paris (or Luxembourg). It requires a special ticket, available at the international ticket counters.

Reservations

For national trains, simply turn up at the station: you'll rarely have to wait more than an hour for a train to anywhere. Services along the major routes stop around midnight (often much earlier on minor routes), but there are night trains once an hour in both directions along the Utrecht–Amsterdam–Schiphol–Leiden–Den Haag–Delft–Rotterdam route. *Intercityboekje* (€2) is a handy small booklet listing the schedules of all IC trains, with an excellent map of the entire system.

In stations, schedules are posted by route. Figure out where you're going and look up the schedule and track numbers. One annoyance: trip duration and arrival time information aren't included on the station schedules, so you'll have to ask staff.

For train and ticketing information hotlines and the NS website, see left.

Train Passes

There are several train passes for people living both inside and outside the Netherlands. These can all be purchased in Europe or in the Netherlands, with the exception of the Holland Rail Pass; generally, you'll need to show your passport. The websites www.inter national-rail.com, www.raileurope.co.uk and www.raileurope.com offer online purchases.

The Voordeelurenabonnement (Off-Peak Discount Pass) is a great way to save money if you're going to be seeing the country by train. It costs €55, is valid for one year and provides a 40% discount on train travel on weekdays after 9am, as well as at weekends and on public holidays. The discount also applies to up to three people travelling with you on the same trip. The card is available at train-station counters.

The Eurodomino Pass allows three to eight days' unlimited travel during a one-month period in one of 25 European and North African countries. For the Netherlands, the three-day pass costs UK£43/32 adult/under 26 in 2nd class and about 50% more in 1st class. The five-day version runs UK£69/53 adult/under 26 and roughly two-thirds more for 1st class.

TRAIN COSTS

Train travel in the Netherlands is cheaper than in the UK but far more expensive than in Eastern Europe. Tickets cost the same during the day as in the evening and can be bought at windows or ticketing machines, although most tickets purchased at windows incur a €0.50 fee. Buying a ticket on board costs the normal fare price, *plus* €35 regardless of the destination.

Buying tickets from vending machines is fast and fairly straightforward when using the newer touch-screen variety – instructions are in a number of languages. The older machines, which use codes to choose destinations, require a bit more thinking, but you should find it easy after a couple of tries. First, check your destination on the alphabetical list of place names and enter the relevant code into the machine. Then you must choose 1st or 2nd class, *zonder/met korting* (without/with discount – this refers to a discount card such as the Voordeel-Urenkaart, discussed below) and *vandaag geldig/zonder datum* (valid today/without date). The machine will then indicate how much it wants to be fed – most are coin only, but more and more accept ATM and credit cards. However, it's best to carry plenty of loose change rather than rack up hefty bank fees back home from using the machines. If you choose a ticket without date you can travel on another day, but you'll have to stamp the ticket in one of the yellow punch gadgets near the platforms.

Tickets and discount cards:

- *Enkele reis* (one-way) – single one-way ticket; with a valid ticket you can break your journey along the direct route.

- *Dagretour* (day return) – normal day return; 10% to 15% cheaper than two one-ways

- *Weekendretour* (weekend return) – costs the same as a normal return and is valid from 7pm Friday to 4am Monday.

- *Dagkaart* (day pass) – costs €39.90/65 for 2nd/1st class and allows unlimited train travel throughout the country. Only good value if you're planning extensive train travel on any one day.

- *OV-dagkaart* (public transport day pass) – €5; bought in conjunction with the *dagkaart* (above), it allows use of trams, buses and metros for one day.

- *Railrunner* – €2; day pass for children aged four to 11.

Note that for delays in excess of half an hour – irrespective of the cause – you're entitled to a refund. Delays of 30 to 60 minutes warrant a 50% refund and delays of an hour or more a 100% refund.

Another option is the Holland Rail Pass, which allows you unlimited travel for any three (1st/2nd class UK£73/49) or five (1st/2nd class UK£118/79) days within one month. There are no reductions for youths or seniors.

If your trip will encompass all three Low Countries then the Benelux Pass is useful, as it covers Belgium and Luxembourg in addition to the Netherlands. The pass is good for any five days in one month and includes a substantial Eurostar discount if you are travelling from the UK. In 2nd class it costs UK£129/97 adult/under 26. A 1st-class version costs UK£193 (there's no age discount).

An Inter-Rail Pass is good for people who can show they have lived in Europe for at least six months. A 2nd-class pass covering the Netherlands, Belgium, Luxembourg and France costs UK£215/145 adult/under 26 for 16 days' unlimited travel.

Outside Europe the Eurailpass is heavily marketed. Good for 18 countries, it's more than overkill if you're just visiting the Netherlands or even the Benelux region. A 15-day pass costs US$394 for those under 26 in 2nd class (the only class available); adults pay US$605 in 1st class (again, the only option). You can buy these at travel agents or **Europe Rail** (www.europerail.com), an international sales arm of the French railways.

Treintaxi

More than 100 train stations offer an excellent *treintaxi* (train taxi) service that takes you to/from the station within a limited area. The cost per person per ride is €4.20 at a train-station counter or ticketing machine, or €5 direct from the driver. The service operates daily from 7am (from 8am Sunday and public holidays) till the last train. There's usually a special call box outside near the normal taxi rank.

These are special taxis and it's a shared service – the driver determines the route and the ride might take a bit longer than with a normal taxi, but the price is certainly right.

Ask the counter operator or taxi driver for a pamphlet listing all participating stations and the relevant phone numbers for bookings. There's also a central information number; call ☎ 09008734682 (calls cost €0.35 per minute).

The *treintaxi* service is handy for reaching places far from stations that don't have frequent bus services. Unfortunately, some major stations (Amsterdam CS, Den Haag CS or HS, Rotterdam CS) are excluded.

TRANSPORT

Health

CONTENTS

Travel health depends on your predeparture preparations, your daily health care while travelling and how you handle any medical problem that does develop. For the Netherlands, peace of mind is the first thing to pack, as health care and medical facilities are generally excellent.

BEFORE YOU GO

Prevention is the key to staying healthy while abroad. A little planning before departure, particularly for pre-existing illnesses, will save trouble later: see your dentist before a long trip; carry a spare pair of contact lenses and glasses; and take your optical prescription with you. Bring medications in their original, clearly labelled, containers. A signed and dated letter from your physician describing your medical conditions and medications, including generic names, is also a good idea. If carrying syringes or needles, be sure to have a physician's letter documenting their medical necessity.

INSURANCE

If you're an EU citizen, a European Health Insurance Card (EHIC), available from health centres or, in the UK, post offices, covers you for most medical care. It will not cover you for nonemergencies or emergency repatriation.

Citizens from other countries should find out if there is a reciprocal arrangement for free medical care between their country and the Netherlands. If you do need health insurance, make sure you get a policy that covers you for the worst possible scenario, such as an accident requiring an emergency flight home. Find out in advance if your insurance plan will make payments directly to providers or reimburse you later for overseas health expenditures.

RECOMMENDED VACCINATIONS

No jabs are required to travel to the Netherlands. The World Health Organization (WHO) recommends that all travellers should be covered for diphtheria, tetanus, measles, mumps, rubella and polio, as well as hepatitis B, regardless of their destination. Since most vaccines don't produce immunity until at least two weeks after they're given, visit a physician at least six weeks before departure.

ONLINE RESOURCES

The WHO's publication *International Travel and Health* is revised annually and is available online at www.who.int/ith/. Other useful websites include www.mdtravelhealth.com (travel-health recommendations for every country, updated daily), www.fitfortravel.nhs .uk (general travel advice for the layman), www.ageconcern.org.uk (advice on travel for the elderly) and www.mariestopes.org .uk (information on women's health and contraception).

NATIONAL HEALTH WEBSITES

It's usually a good idea to consult your government's travel-health website before departure, if one is available:

Australia (www.smartraveller.gov.au)
Canada (www.phac-aspc.gc.ca/tmp-pmv/index .html)
United Kingdom (www.dh.gov.uk/PolicyAnd GuidanceHealthAdviceForTravellers/fs/en)
United States (www.cdc.gov/travel/)

FURTHER READING

Health Advice for Travellers (currently called the 'T6' leaflet) is an annually updated leaflet produced by the UK Department of Health and available free in post offices. It contains some general information, legally required and recommended vaccines for different countries, reciprocal health agreements and an E111 application form. Lonely Planet's *Travel with Children* includes advice on travel health for younger children. Other recommended references include *Traveller's Health* by Dr Richard Dawood (published by Oxford University Press) and *The Traveller's Good Health Guide* by Ted Lankester (published by Sheldon Press).

IN TRANSIT

DEEP VEIN THROMBOSIS

Blood clots may form in the legs during plane flights, chiefly because of prolonged immobility. The longer the flight, the greater the risk. The chief symptom of deep vein thrombosis (DVT) is swelling or pain of the foot, ankle or calf, usually – but not always – on just one side. When a blood clot travels to the lungs it may cause chest pain and breathing difficulties. Travellers with any of these symptoms should immediately seek medical attention.

To prevent the development of DVT on long flights you should walk about the cabin, contract the leg muscles while sitting, drink plenty of fluids, and avoid alcohol and tobacco.

JET LAG & MOTION SICKNESS

To avoid jet lag (which is common when crossing more than five time zones), try drinking plenty of nonalchoholic fluids and eating light meals. Upon arrival, get exposure to natural sunlight and readjust your schedule (for meals, sleep and so on) to the time zone you're in as soon as possible.

Antihistamines such as dimenhydrinate (Dramamine) and meclizine (Antivert, Bonine) are usually the first choice for treating motion sickness. A herbal alternative is ginger.

IN THE NETHERLANDS

AVAILABILITY & COST OF HEALTH CARE

Good health care is readily available. For minor self-limiting illnesses an *apotheek* (pharmacy) can give valuable advice and sell over-the-counter medication. It can also advise when more specialised help is required and point you in the right direction. The standard of dental care is usually good; however, it is sensible to have a dental checkup before a long trip.

ENVIRONMENTAL HAZARDS
Heat Exhaustion & Heat Stroke

Heat exhaustion (yes, it can happen, even in the Netherlands!) occurs following excessive fluid loss with inadequate replacement of fluids and salt. Symptoms include headache, dizziness and tiredness. Dehydration is already happening by the time you feel thirsty – aim to drink sufficient water to produce pale, diluted urine. To treat heat exhaustion, replace fluids with water and/or fruit juice, and cool the body with cold water and fans. Treat salt loss with salty fluids such as soup or bouillon, or add a little more table salt to foods than usual.

Heat stroke is much more serious, resulting in irrational and hyperactive behaviour and eventually loss of consciousness and death. Rapid cooling by spraying the body with water and fanning is ideal. Emergency fluid and electrolyte replacement by intravenous drip is recommended.

Insect Bites & Stings

Mosquitoes are found in most parts of Europe and are well represented in the Netherlands. They may not carry malaria but can cause irritation and infected bites. Use a DEET-based insect repellent.

Bees and wasps only cause real problems for those with a severe allergy (anaphylaxis.) If you have a severe allergy to bee or wasp stings, carry an Epipen or similar adrenaline injection.

Bed bugs lead to very itchy lumpy bites. Spraying the mattress with crawling insect killer after changing bedding will get rid of them.

Scabies are tiny mites that live in the skin, particularly between the fingers. They cause an intensely itchy rash. Scabies is easily treated with lotion from a pharmacy; other members of the household also need treating to avoid spreading scabies between asymptomatic carriers.

LYME DISEASE

Ticks can carry a serious bacterial infection called Lyme disease. A bite from an infected tick may produce a red welt and a 'bull's eye' around the spot within a day or two. Mild flu-like symptoms (headache, nausea etc) may follow or may not, but antibiotics are needed to avoid the next stage of the illness – pain in the joints, fatigue and fever. If left untreated, Lyme disease can cause mental and muscular deterioration.

The most risky places in the Netherlands are the wooded areas of Friesland, Groningen and Drenthe, Hoge Veluwe National Park, parts of Zeeland and on the Wadden Islands. The best prevention is to wear clothing that covers your arms and legs when walking in grassy or wooded areas, apply insect repellent containing DEET and check your body for ticks after outdoor activities.

If a tick has attached itself to you, use tweezers to pull it straight out – do not twist it. Do not touch the tick with a hot object such as a cigarette because this can cause the tick to regurgitate noxious saliva into the wound. Do not rub oil or petroleum jelly on it.

TRAVELLING WITH CHILDREN

All travellers with children should know how to treat minor ailments and when to seek medical treatment. Make sure the children are up to date with routine vaccinations, and discuss possible travel vaccines well before departure, as some vaccines are not suitable for children under a year old.

Remember to avoid contaminated food and water. If your child is vomiting or has diarrhoea, lost fluid and salts must be replaced. It may be helpful to take along rehydration powders for reconstituting with boiled water.

Children should be encouraged to avoid and mistrust any dogs or other mammals because of the risk of rabies and other diseases. Any bite, scratch or lick from a warm-blooded, furry animal should immediately be thoroughly cleaned. If there is any possibility that the animal is infected with rabies, immediate medical assistance should be sought.

WOMEN'S HEALTH

Emotional stress, exhaustion and travelling through different time zones can all contribute to an upset in the menstrual pattern. If using oral contraceptives, remember that some antibiotics, diarrhoea and vomiting can stop the pill from working and lead to the risk of pregnancy – remember to take condoms with you just in case. Time zones, gastrointestinal upsets and antibiotics do not affect injectable contraception.

Travelling during pregnancy is usually possible, but there are important things to consider. Always seek a medical checkup before planning your trip. The most risky times for travel are during the first 12 weeks of pregnancy and after 30 weeks. Illness during pregnancy can be more severe, so take special care to avoid contaminated food and water and insect and animal bites. A general rule is to only use vaccines, like other medications, if the risk of infection is substantial. Remember that the baby could be in serious danger if you were to contract infections such as typhoid or hepatitis. Some vaccines are best avoided; for example, those that contain live organisms. However, there is very little evidence that damage has been caused to an unborn child when vaccines have been given to a woman very early in pregnancy before the pregnancy was suspected. Take written records of the pregnancy with you. Ensure your insurance policy covers pregnancy delivery and postnatal care. Always consult your doctor before you travel.

SEXUAL HEALTH

Emergency contraception is most effective if taken within 24 hours after unprotected sex.

When buying condoms, look for a European CE mark, which means they have been rigorously tested, and then keep them in a cool, dry place or they may crack and perish. Condoms are widely available from pharmacies and vending machines in many restaurants and nightclubs.

The **Rutgers Foundation** (www.rutgersnissogroep.nl) manages seven regional centres in the Netherlands that provide a range of sexual and reproductive health-care services. Emergency contraception can be obtained at short notice. Contact the telephone helpline at ☎ 030-231 34 31. The Amsterdam centre, the **Rutgershuis** (☎ 020-624 54 26; www.acsg.nl; Sarphatistraat 618), is open for walk-in visitors.

Language

Almost every Dutch person from age five onwards seems to speak English, often very well and better than you'll ever learn Dutch, so why bother? That's a good question because you'll rarely get the opportunity to practise: your Dutch acquaintances will launch into English, probably because they relish the opportunity to practise their language skills. Nevertheless, a few words in Dutch show goodwill, which is always appreciated, and you might even get to understand a bit more of what's going on around you. The phrase *Spreekt u Engels?* (Do you speak English?) before launching into English is best used with older people. The young, thanks to years of English in school, as well as exposure to vast amounts of English-language media (movies are usually subtitled rather than dubbed), will likely look at you like you've gone around the bend if you ask about their English skills.

The people of the northern Friesland province speak their own language. Although Frisian is actually the nearest relative to English, you won't be able to make much sense of it, and you'll have to go to a small-town shop or a farm to really hear it anyway. It's not the dominant language in the province, but most of the locals know some as a sign of cultural pride.

Most English speakers use the term 'Dutch' to describe the language spoken in the Netherlands and 'Flemish' for that spoken in the northern half of Belgium. Both are in fact the same language, called Netherlandic *(Nederlands)* or simply Dutch. The differences between Dutch and Flemish *(Vlaams)* are similar in degree to those between British and North American English.

Dutch nouns come in one of three genders: masculine, feminine (both with *de* for 'the') and neuter (with *het* for 'the'). Where English uses 'a' or 'an', Dutch uses *een*, regardless of gender.

There's also a polite and an informal version of the English 'you'. The polite form is *u* (pronounced with the lips pursed and rounded), the informal is *je*. As a general rule, people who are older than you should be addressed as *u*.

For useful information that will help when ordering food and dining out, including Dutch words and phrases, see p64. For more extensive coverage of Dutch than we have space for here, get a copy of Lonely Planet's *Western Europe Phrasebook*.

PRONUNCIATION

Note that the following lists describe the pronunciation of the letters used in our guides to pronunciation, not written Dutch.

Vowels

a	as the 'u' in 'run'
e	as in 'bet'
i	as in 'hit'
o	as in 'pot'
u	pronounced with pursed, rounded lips, as in the French *tu*
ə	a neutral vowel, as the 'a' in 'ago'
aa	as the 'a' in 'father'
ee	as in 'eel'
oa	as in 'boat'
oo	as in 'zoo'
ow	as in 'cow'
ay	as in 'say'
əy	similar to the sound of 'er-y' in 'her year' (with no 'r' sound) or, if you're familiar with it, as the 'eui' in the French *fauteuil*
eu	similar the 'er' in 'her', but with no 'r' sound

WHAT'S IN A NAME?

Dutch, like German, strings words together, which can baffle a foreigner trying to decipher (let alone remember) street names. *Eerste Goudsbloemdwarsstraat* (First Marigold Cross Street) is a good example! Chopping a seemingly endless name into its separate components might help a bit. The following terms appear frequently in street names and on signs:

baan – path, way
binnen – inside, inner
bloem – flower
brug – bridge
buiten – outside, outer
dijk – dyke
dwars – transverse
eiland – island
gracht – canal
groot – great, large, big
haven – harbour
hoek – corner
huis – house
kade – quay
kapel – chapel
kerk – church
klein – minor, small
laan – avenue
markt – market

molen – (wind)mill
nieuw – new
noord – north
oost – east
oud – old
plein – square
poort – city gate, gate
sloot – ditch
sluis – sluice, lock
steeg – alley
straat – street
toren – tower
veld – field
(burg)wal – (fortified) embankment
weg – road
west – west
wijk – district
zuid – south

Consonants

Most consonants in the pronunciation guides are similar to their English counterparts (**b**, **d**, **f**, **g**, **h**, **k**, **l**, **m**, **n**, **p**, **s**, **t**, **v**, **w**, **z**). A few trickier sounds are listed below:

ch as in 'chip'
g as in 'go'
kh as the 'ch' in the Scottish *loch*; it's like a hiss produced by tightening the tongue against top of the throat
ng as in 'ring'
r trilled, either with the tongue forward or held back restricting the flow of air in the throat
y as in 'yes'
zh as the 's' in 'pleasure'

ACCOMMODATION

I'm looking for a ... *Ik ben op zoek naar een ...* ik ben op zook naar ən ...
  camping ground *camping* kem·ping
  guesthouse *pension* pen·syon
  hotel *hotel* ho·tel
  youth hostel *jeugdherberg* yeukht·her·berkh

Where is a cheap hotel?
Waar is een goedkoop hotel?
waar is ən khoot·koap ho·tel

What is the address?
Wat is het adres?
wat is hət a·dres

Could you write the address, please?
Kunt u het adres opschrijven alstublieft?
kunt u hət a·dres op·skhray·vən als·tu·bleeft

Do you have any rooms available?
Heeft u een kamer vrij?
hayft u ən kaa·mər vray

I'd like (a) ... *Ik wil graag een ...* ik wil khraakh ən ...
  bed *bed* bet
  single room *eenpersoons-kamer* ayn·pər·soans·kaa·mər
  double room *tweepersoons-kamer* tway·pər·soans·kaa·mər
  room with two beds *kamer met twee bedden* kaa·mər met tway be·dən
  room with a bathroom *kamer met badkamer* kaa·mər met bat·kaa·mər
  to share a dorm *bed op een slaapzaal* bet op ən slaap·zaal

How much is it ...? *Hoeveel is het ...?* hoo·vayl is hət ...?
  per night *per nacht* pər nakht
  per person *per persoon* pər per·soan

Is breakfast included?
Is ontbijt inbegrepen? is ont·bayt in·bə·khray·pən

MAKING A RESERVATION

(for phone or written requests)

To ...	*Tot ...*
From ...	*Van ...*
Date	*Datum*
I'd like to book ...	*Ik wil ... reserveren.* (see the list under 'Accommodation' for bed and room options)
in the name of ...	*op naam van ...*
for the night/s of ...	*voor de nacht(en) van ...*
credit card	*kredietkaart*
number	*nummer*
expiry date	*vervaldag*
Please confirm availability and price.	*Gelieve de prijs en beschikbaarheid te bevestigen.*

May I see the room?
Mag ik de kamer zien?   makh ik də *kaa*·mər zeen
Where is the bathroom?
Waar is de badkamer?   waar is də *bat*·kaa·mər
I'm leaving today.
Ik vertrek vandaag.   ik vər·*trek* van·*daakh*
We're leaving today.
Wij vertrekken vandaag.   way vər·*tre*·kən van·*daakh*

CONVERSATION & ESSENTIALS

Hello.
Dag/Hallo.   dakh/ha·*loa*
Goodbye.
Dag.   dakh
Yes.
Ja.   yaa
No.
Nee.   nay
Please.
Alstublieft. (pol)   als·tu·*bleeft*
Alsjeblieft. (inf)   a·shə·*bleeft*
Thank you (very much).
Dank u (wel). (pol)   *dangk* u (wel)
Dank je (wel). (inf)   *dangk* yə (wel)
Thanks.
Bedankt. (pol or inf)   bə·*dangt*
That's fine/You're welcome.
Graag gedaan.   khraakh khə·*daan*
Excuse me.
Pardon.   par·*don*
or *Excuseer mij.*   eks·ku·*zayr* may
I'm sorry.
Sorry/Excuses.   so·ree/eks·ku·*zəs*

How are you?
Hoe gaat het met   hoo khaat hət met u/yow
u/jou? (pol/inf)
I'm fine, thanks.
Goed, bedankt.   khoot, bə·*dangt*
See you soon.
Tot ziens.   tot zeens
What's your name?
Hoe heet u? (pol)   hoo hayt u
Hoe heet je? (inf)   hoo hayt yə
My name is ...
Ik heet ...   ik hayt ...
Where are you from?
Waar komt u   waar komt u
vandaan? (pol)   van·*daan*
Waar kom je   waar kom yə
vandaan? (inf)   van·*daan*
I'm from ...
Ik kom uit ...   ik kom əyt ...
I (don't) like.
Ik hou (niet) van ...   ik how (neet) van ...
Just a minute.
Een moment.   ən mo·*ment*

DIRECTIONS

Where is ...?
Waar is ...?   waar is ...
How do I get to ...?
Hoe kom ik bij ...?   hoo kom ik bay ...
(Go) straight ahead.
(Ga) rechtdoor.   (khaa) rekht·*doar*
(Turn) left.
(Ga) naar links.   (khaa) naar lings
(Turn) right.
(Ga) naar rechts.   (khaa) naar rekhs
at the corner
op de hoek   op də hook
at the traffic lights
bij de verkeerslichten   bay də vər·*kayrs*·likh·tən

SIGNS

Ingang	Entrance
Uitgang	Exit
Informatie/Inlichtingen	Information
Open	Open
Gesloten	Closed
Verboden/Niet Toegelaten	Prohibited
Kamers Vrij	Rooms Available
Vol	Full/No Vacancies
Politiebureau	Police Station
WCs/Toiletten	Toilets
Heren	Men
Dames	Women

What street/road is this?
Welke straat/weg is dit? wel·kə straat/wekh is dit?

behind	achter	akh·tər
in front of	voor	vor
far (from)	ver (van)	ver (van)
near (to)	dichtbij	dikht·bay
opposite	tegenover	tay·khən·oa·vər

beach	strand	strant
bridge	brug	brukh
castle	kasteel	kas·tayl
cathedral	kathedraal	ka·tay·draal
island	eiland	ay·lant
main square	stadsplein	stats·playn
market	markt	markt
old city	oude stad	ow·də stat
palace	paleis	pa·lays
ruins	ruines	rwee·nəs
sea	zee	zay
square	plein	playn
tower	toren	toa·rən

EMERGENCIES

Help!
Help! help
There's been an accident.
Er is een ongeluk ər is ən on·khə·luk
gebeurd. khə·beurt
I'm lost.
Ik ben de weg kwijt. ik ben də wekh kwayt
Go away!
Ga weg! kha wekh

Call ...!	Haal ...	haal ...
a doctor	een doktor	ən dok·tər
the police	de politie	də po·leet·see

HEALTH

I need a doctor.	Ik heb een dokter nodig.	ik hep ən dok·tər noa·dikh
Where is the hospital?	Waar is het ziekenhuis?	waar is hət zee·kən·həys
I'm ill.	Ik ben ziek.	ik ben zeek
It hurts here.	Het doet hier pijn.	hət doot heer payn

I'm ...	Ik ben ...	ik ben ...
asthmatic	asthmatisch	ast·maa·tis
diabetic	suikerziek	səy·kər·zeek

I have epilepsy.
Ik heb epilepsie. ik hep ay·pee·lep·see

I'm allergic to ...	Ik ben allergisch voor...	ik ben a·ler·khis voar ...
antibiotics	antibiotica	an·tee·bee·o·tee·ka
aspirin	aspirine	as·pee·ree·nə
penicillin	penicilline	pay·nee·see·lee·nə
bees	bijen	bay·ən
nuts	noten	noa·tən

antiseptic	ontsmettings-middel	ont·sme·tings·mi·dəl
aspirin	aspirine	as·pee·ree·nə
condoms	condooms	kon·doams
constipation	verstopping	vər·sto·ping
contraceptive	anticonceptie-middel	an·tee·kon·sep·see·mi·dəl
diarrhoea	diarree	dee·a·ray
medicine	geneesmiddel/ medicijn	khə·nays·mi·dəl/ may·dee·sayn
sunscreen	zonnebrandolie	zo·nə·brant·oa·lee
tampons	tampons	tam·pons
nausea	misselijkheid	mi·sə·lək·hayt

LANGUAGE DIFFICULTIES
Do you speak English?
Spreekt u Engels? spraykt u eng·əls
Does anyone here speak English?
Spreekt er hier iemand Engels? spraykt ər heer ee·mant eng·əls
How do you say ... in Dutch?
Hoe zeg je ... in het Nederlands? hoo zekh yə ... in hət nay·dər·lants
What does ... mean?
Wat betekent ...? wat bə·tay·kənt ...
I (don't) understand.
Ik begrijp het (niet). ik bə·khrayp hət (neet)
Please write it down.
Schrijf het alstublieft op. skhrayf hət als·tu·bleeft op
Can you show me (on the map)?
Kunt u het mij tonen (op de kaart)? kunt u hət may toa·nən (op də kaart)

NUMBERS
0	nul	nul
1	één	ayn
2	twee	tway
3	drie	dree
4	vier	veer
5	vijf	vayf
6	zes	zes
7	zeven	zay·vən
8	acht	akht
9	negen	nay·khən
10	tien	teen
11	elf	elf

12	twaalf	twaalf
13	dertien	der·teen
14	veertien	vayr·teen
15	vijftien	vayf·teen
16	zestien	zes·teen
17	zeventien	zay·vən·teen
18	achttien	akh·teen
19	negentien	nay·khən·teen
20	twintig	twin·təkh
21	eenentwintig	ayn·en·twin·təkh
22	tweeëntwintig	tway·en·twin·təkh
30	dertig	der·təkh
40	veertig	vayr·təkh
50	vijftig	vayf·təkh
60	zestig	zes·təkh
70	zeventig	zay·vən·təkh
80	tachtig	takh·təkh
90	negentig	nay·khən·təkh
100	honderd	hon·dərt
1000	duizend	dəy·zənt
2000	tweeduizend	twee·dəy·zənt

PAPERWORK

name	naam	naam
nationality	nationaliteit	na·syo·na·lee·tayt
date of birth	geboortedatum	khə·boar·tə·daa·təm
place of birth	geboorteplaats	khə·boar·tə·plaats
sex (gender)	geslacht	khə·slakht
passport	paspoort	pas·poart
visa	visum	vee·zum

SHOPPING & SERVICES

I'd like to buy ...
Ik wil graag ... kopen.   ik wil khraakh ... koa·pən
How much is it?
Hoeveel is het?   hoo·vayl is hət?
I don't like it.
Ik vind het niet leuk.   ik vint hət neet leuk
May I look at it?
Mag ik het zien?   makh ik hət zeen
Can I try it (on)?
Kan ik het eens proberen?   kan ik hət ayns pro·bay·rən
I'm just looking.
Ik kijk alleen maar.   ik kayk a·layn maar
It's cheap.
Het is goedkoop.   hət is khoot·koap
It's too expensive (for me).
Het is (mij) te duur.   hət is (may) tə dur
I'll take it.
Ik neem het.   ik naym hət

Do you accept ...?	*Accepteert u ...*	ak·sep·tayrt u ...
credit cards	*kredietkaarten*	kray·deet·kaar·tən
travellers cheques	*reischeques*	rays·sheks

more	meer	mayr
less	minder	min·dər
smaller	kleiner	klay·nər
bigger	groter	khroa·tər

I'm looking for ...	*Ik ben op zoek naar ...*	ik ben op zook naar ...
the bank	de bank	də bangk
a bookshop	een boekenwinkel	ən boo·kən·win·kəl
the chemist/ pharmacy	de drogist/ apotheek	də dro·khist a·po·tayk
the city centre	het stadscentrum	hət stat·sen·trum
a clothing store	een kledingzaak	ən klay·ding·zaak
the church	de kerk	də kerk
the ... embassy	de ... ambassade	də ... am·ba·saa·də
the exchange office	het wisselkantoor	hət wi·səl·kan·toar
a laundry	een wasserette	ən wa·sə·re·tə
the market	de markt	də markt
the museum	het museum	hət mu·say·əm
the newsagency	de kranten- winkel	də kran·tən· wing·kəl
the post office	het postkantoor	hət post·kan·toar
a public toilet	een openbaar toilet	ən oa·pən·baar twa·let
the stationers	de kantoorboek- handel	də kan·toar·book· han·dəl
a supermarket	een supermarkt	ən su·pər·mart
the tourist office	de VVV	də vay·vay·vay

What time does it open/close?
Hoe laat opent/ sluit het?   hoo laat oa·pənt/ sləyt hət

I want to change ...	*Ik wil ... wisselen.*	ik wil ... wi·sə·lən
money	geld	khelt
travellers cheques	reischeques	rays·sheks

TIME & DATES

What time is it?
Hoe laat is het?   hoo laat is hət
It's (8 o'clock).
Het is (acht uur).   hət is (akht ur)

in the morning	's morgens	smor·ghəns
in the afternoon	's middags	smi·dakhs
in the evening	's avonds	saa·vonts
When?	Wanneer?	wa·nayr
today	vandaag	van·daakh
tomorrow	morgen	mor·khən
yesterday	gisteren	khis·tə·rən

Monday	*maandag*	*maan·*dakh
Tuesday	*dinsdag*	*dins·*dakh
Wednesday	*woensdag*	*woons·*dakh
Thursday	*donderdag*	*don·dər·*dakh
Friday	*vrijdag*	*vray·*dakh
Saturday	*zaterdag*	*zaa·tər·*dakh
Sunday	*zondag*	*zon·*dakh

January	*januari*	*ya·*nu·aa·ree
February	*februari*	*fay·*bru·aa·ree
March	*maart*	maart
April	*april*	a·*pril*
May	*mei*	may
June	*juni*	*yu·*nee
July	*juli*	*yu·*lee
August	*augustus*	ow·*gus·*tus
September	*september*	sep·*tem·*bər
October	*oktober*	ok·*to·*bər
November	*november*	no·*vem·*bər
December	*december*	day·*sem·*bər

TRANSPORT
Public Transport
What time does the ... leave?
Hoe laat vertrekt ...?   hoo laat vər·*trekt* ...
What time does the ... arrive?
Hoe laat komt ... aan?   hoo laat komt ... aan

boat	*de boot*	də boat
bus	*de bus*	də bus
plane	*het vliegtuig*	hət *fleekh·*təykh
train	*de trein*	də trayn
tram	*de tram*	də trem

Where is ...?	*Waar is ...?*	waar is ...
the airport	*de luchthaven*	də *lukht·*haa·vən
the bus stop	*de bushalte*	də *bus·*hal·tə
the metro station	*het metro- station*	hət *may·*tro· sta·*syon*
the train station	*het (trein)- station*	hət (trayn) sta·*syon*
the tram stop	*de tramhalte*	də *trem·*hal·tə

I'd like ... ticket.	*Ik wil graag ...*	ik wil khraakh ...
a one-way	*een enkele reis*	ən *eng·*kə·lə rays
a return	*een retourticket*	ən rə·*toor·*ti·ket
a 1st-class	*eerste klas*	*ayr·*stə klas
a 2nd-class	*tweede klas*	*tway·*də klas

I want to go to ...
Ik wil naar ... gaan.   ik wil naar ... khaan
The train has been cancelled/delayed.
De trein is afgelast/   də trayn is af·khə·*last/*
vertraagd.   vər·*traakht*

the first	*de eerste*	də *ayr·*stə
the last	*de laatste*	də *laat·*stə

platform	*spoor/perron*	spoar/pe·*ron*
number	*nummer*	*nu·*mər
ticket office	*loket*	*loa·*ket
timetable	*dienstregeling*	*deenst·*ray·khə·ling

Private Transport
I'd like to hire a/an ...	*Ik wil graag een ... huren.*	ik wil khraakh ən ... *hu·*rən
bicycle	*fiets*	feets
car	*auto*	*ow·*to
motorbike	*motorfiets*	*mo·*tər·feets

ROAD SIGNS

Afrit/Uitrit	Exit (from freeway)
Eenrichtingsverkeer	One Way
Gevaar	Danger
Ingang	Entrance
Omleiding	Detour
Oprit	Entrance (to freeway)
Tol	Toll
Uitgang	Exit
Verboden Toegang	No Entry
Verboden in te Halen/ Inhaalverbod	No Overtaking
Verboden te Parkeren/ Parkeerverbod	No Parking
Vertragen	Slow Down
Voorrang Verlenen	Give Way
Vrij Houden	Keep Clear

Is this the road to ...?
Is dit de weg naar ...?   is dit də wekh naar ...
Where's a service station?
Waar is er een   waar is ər ən
benzinestation?   ben·*zee·*nə·sta·syon
Please fill it up.
Vol alstublieft.   vol als·tu·*bleeft*
I'd like (30) litres.
Ik wil graag (dertig) liter.   ik wil khraakh (*der·*tikh) *lee·*tər

diesel		
diesel	*dee·*zəl	

leaded petrol
gelode benzine   khə·*lo·*də ben·*zee·*nə
unleaded petrol
loodvrije benzine   loat·*vray·*ə ben·*zee·*nə
(How long) Can I park here?
(Hoe lang) Kan ik hier   (hoo lang) kan ik heer
parkeren?   par·*kay·*rən
Where do I pay?
Waar kan ik betalen?   waar kan ik be·*taa·*lən
I need a mechanic.
Ik heb een mecanicien   ik hep een may·ka·nee·*sye*
nodig.   *noa·*dikh

The car/motorbike has broken down (at ...).

Ik heb auto/motorfiets   ik heb *ow*·to/*moa*·tər·feets
  pech (in ...)   pekh (in ...)

The car/motorbike won't start.

De auto/motorfiets   də *ow*·to/*moa*·tər·feets
  wil niet starten.   wil neet *star*·tən

I have a flat tyre.

Ik heb een lekke band.   ik heb ən *le*·kə bant

I've run out of petrol.

Ik zit zonder benzine.   ik zit *zon*·dər ben·*zee*·nə

I've had an accident.

Ik heb een ongeluk gehad.   ik hep ən *on*·khə·luk khə·*hat*

TRAVEL WITH CHILDREN

I need (a/an) ...   *Ik heb ... nodig.*   ik hep ... *noa*·dikh
Do you have   *Heeft u ...?*   hayft u ...
(a/an) ...?
  car baby seat   *een autozitje*   ən *ow*·to·zi·chə
    voor de baby   voar də *bay*·bee
  child-minding   *een oppasdienst*   ən op·pas·*deenst*
   service

children's menu   *een kindermenu*   ən *kin*·dər·mə·nu
(disposable)   *(wegwerp-)*   (wekh·werp·)
  nappies/diapers   *luiers*   *ləy*·ərs
formula (milk)   *melkpoeder (voor*   *melk*·poo·dər (voar
   zuigflessen)   *zəykh*·fle·sən)
(English-   *een babysit (die*   ən *bay*·bee·sit (dee
  speaking)   *Engels spreekt)*   *eng*·əls spraykt)
  babysitter
highchair   *een kinderstoel*   ən *kin*·der·stool
potty   *een potje*   ən *po*·chə
stroller   *een wandel-*   ən *wan*·dəl·
   wagen   waa·khən

Is there a baby change room?

Kan ik hier ergens   kan ik heer *er*·khəns
  de baby verschonen?   də *bay*·bee vər·*skhoa*·nən

Do you mind if I breastfeed here?

Stoort het u als ik   stoart hət u als ik
  hier de borst geef?   heer də *borst* gayf

Are children allowed?

Zijn kinderen toegelaten?   zayn *kin*·də·rən *too*·khə·la·tən

Also available from Lonely Planet:
Europe Phrasebook

Glossary

See the boxed text, p315, for a list of terms commonly encountered in street names and sights.

abdij – abbey
apotheek – chemist/pharmacy

bad – bath, pool
benzine – petrol/gasoline
bevrijding – liberation
bibliotheek – library
bos – woods or forest
botter – type of 19th-century fishing boat
broodje – bread roll (with filling)
bruin café – brown café; traditional drinking establishment
buurt – neighbourhood

café – pub, bar; also known as *kroeg*
coffeeshop – cafe authorised to sell cannabis

dagschotel – daily special in Dutch restaurants
drop – salted or sweet liquorice

eetcafé – cafés serving meals

fierljeppen – pole-jumping over canals (Frisian; see also *polstokspringen*)
fiets – bicycle
fietsenstalling – secure bicycle storage
fietspad – bicycle path

gasthuis – hospital, hospice
gemeente – municipal, municipality
gezellig – convivial, cosy
GVB – Gemeentevervoerbedrijf (Amsterdam municipal transport authority)
GWK – Grenswisselkantoren; official currency-exchange offices

hal – hall, entrance hall
haven – port
herberg – hostel
hervormd – reformed (as in church)
hof – courtyard
hofje – almshouse or series of buildings around a small courtyard, also known as Begijnhof
hoofd – main

jacht – yacht
jenever – Dutch gin; also *genever*

kaas – cheese
kantoor – office
koffiehuis – espresso bar (as distinct from a *coffeeshop*)
klompen – clogs
klooster – cloister, religious house
koningin – queen
koninklijk – royal
korfbal – a cross between netball, volleyball and basketball
kunst – art
kwartier – quarter

loodvrij – unleaded petrol/gasoline

markt – town square
meer – lake
molen – windmill

NS – Nederlandse Spoorwegen; national railway company

paleis – palace
polder – area of drained land
polstokspringen – pole-jumping over canals (Frisian: *fierljeppen*)
postbus – post office box

raam – window
Randstad – literally `rim-city'; the urban agglomeration including Amsterdam, Utrecht, Rotterdam and Den Haag
Rijk(s-) – the State

scheepvaart – shipping
schilder – artist, painter
schouwburg – theatre
sluis – lock (for boats/ships)
spoor – platform (in train station)
stadhouder – chief magistrate
stadhuis – city hall
stedelijk – civic, municipal
stichting – foundation, institute
strand – beach
strippenkaart – punchable multiticket used on all public transport

terp – mound of packed mud in Friesland that served as a refuge during floods (plural *terpen*)

treintaxi – taxi for train passengers
tuin – garden
tulp – tulip
turf – peat

verzet – resistance
Vlaams – Flemish
VVV – tourist information office

waag – old weigh-house
wadlopen – mud-walking
weeshuis – orphanage
werf – wharf, shipyard
winkel – shop

zaal – hall
zee – sea
ziekenhuis – hospital

Behind the Scenes

THIS BOOK

This 3rd edition of *The Netherlands* was written by Neal Bedford and Simon Sellars. The 2nd edition was written by Jeremy Gray and Reuben Acciano, and the 1st edition was the work of Ryan Ver Berkmoes and Jeremy Gray. This guidebook was commissioned in Lonely Planet's London office and produced by the following:

Commissioning Editor Judith Bamber
Coordinating Editor Sarah Bailey
Coordinating Cartographer Sophie Reed
Coordinating Layout Designer Tamsin Wilson
Managing Editor Bruce Evans
Managing Cartographer Adrian Persoglia
Assisting Editors John Hinman, Shawn Low, Joanne Newell, Phillip Tang
Assisting Cartographer Andrew Smith
Proofreader Roy Garner
Cover Designer Wendy Wright
Project Managers Eoin Dunlevy, Craig Kilburn
Language Content Coordinator Quentin Frayne

Thanks to Csanad Csutoros, Hunor Csutoros, Sally Darmody, Mark Griffiths, Erin McManus, Wayne Murphy, Trent Paton, Celia Wood

THANKS
NEAL BEDFORD

A well-earned thanks first goes to my coauthor, Simon, for his good cheer, sharp wit and company during my days in Amsterdam. The Dutch folk, as always, were kind, helpful and refreshingly straightforward, and I thank them for that. My work was made lighter by an army of knowledge-able tourist-office staff (particular gratitude goes to the Texel and Amsterdam tourist offices), bus and train station assistants, restaurant and bar owners, barflies, coffeeshop proprietors, museum workers, B&B owners – the list is almost endless. For allowing me to drag them through an epic Queen's Day weekend, and for lending their eyes, ears, stomachs and lungs in the name of research, special thanks (and a few of Holland's best) go to Nik (aka Space Boy) and John (aka Mr Jack). Last, but most certainly not least, *bussi* to Tiffany for her unwavering support and love, and some memorable days discovering the north.

SIMON SELLARS

Thank you to Justine for the whole bit. Especial thanks to the Buglet. At Lonely Planet many thanks to Neal Bedford – the perfect partner in crime. Also, thank you to Judith Bamber, my London connection; Sarah Bailey, the consummate professional; the brothers Csutoros, Csanad and Hunor; and Sophie Reed (congratulations on the new addition, Sophie).

OUR READERS

Many thanks to the travellers who used the last edition and wrote to us with helpful hints, useful advice and interesting anecdotes:

A Jack Alessil, Philip Altbach, Coreena Arriola, Nick Atchison **B** Kaitlin Beare, Becky Blake, Regina Blanco, Margaret Bletsoe, Karin Bos, John Bosch, Deborah Burnett, Eleanor Butler, Richard Butler **C** Michelle Cahalone, Chris Card, Lisa Card, Grace Catao, Deborah Celley, Michael Chambers, Matt Colonell, Rita Colonell **D** Michael Dawson, Fokke de

THE LONELY PLANET STORY

The story begins with a classic travel adventure: Tony and Maureen Wheeler's 1972 journey across Europe and Asia to Australia. There was no useful information about the overland trail then, so Tony and Maureen published the first Lonely Planet guidebook to meet a growing need.

From a kitchen table, Lonely Planet has grown to become the largest independent travel publisher in the world, with offices in Melbourne (Australia), Oakland (USA) and London (UK). Today Lonely Planet guidebooks cover the globe. There is an ever-growing list of books and information in a variety of media. Some things haven't changed. The main aim is still to make it possible for adventurous travellers to get out there – to explore and better understand the world.

At Lonely Planet we believe travellers can make a positive contribution to the countries they visit – if they respect their host communities and spend their money wisely. Every year 5% of company profit is donated to charities around the world.

SEND US YOUR FEEDBACK

We love to hear from travellers – your comments keep us on our toes and help make our books better. Our well-travelled team reads every word on what you loved or loathed about this book. Although we cannot reply individually to postal submissions, we always guarantee that your feedback goes straight to the appropriate authors, in time for the next edition. Each person who sends us information is thanked in the next edition – and the most useful submissions are rewarded with a free book. See the Behind the Scenes section.

To send us your updates – and find out about Lonely Planet events, newsletters and travel news – visit our award-winning website: **www.lonelyplanet.com/feedback**.

Note: We may edit, reproduce and incorporate your comments in Lonely Planet products such as guidebooks, websites and digital products, so let us know if you don't want your comments reproduced or your name acknowledged. For a copy of our privacy policy, go to www.lonelyplanet.com/privacy.

Jong, Rop de Poorter, Sandra Dekker, Bryon Dudley **E** Dagmar Ernst **F** Terri Festa **G** Bernadette Gabris, Patch Garcia, Planet Glassberg, Marci Goldberg, Anne Goldgar, Lynne Grabar **H** Bas Halmans, Barbara Hejjas, Susan Herman, Darren Hopkinson, Annemarie Hosper **I** Nina Innocenti **J** R Jacques **K** Russell Kallen, Maureen Kelly, Raymond Kisch, Anatoliy Kurmanaev **L** Carol Lawless, Shireen Liew, Foh Lin Lim **M** Kirsty Mackenzie, Lis Maurer, Debra McBride, Ned Mcevoy, Alastair McInnes, Edward Mcsheehy, John Miller, Joshua Mirwis, Jane Mooney, Janet Moore, Jill Moore **N** Stephen Nau, Lauren Norwood, Zachary Nowak **O** Eric Ogden

P Johan Pabon, Lance Patford, Anton Pauw, Lizzy Pike **R** Nancy Roberts, Daniel Rodríguez, Andrew Roper, Emily Rosenberg, Leon Ruyters **S** Andrew Saunders, Ton Schlaman, Jeremy Secomb, Alice Seet, Raymond Smith, Benny Snepvangers, Philipe Souren, Bonnie Spoales, Susen Sprenger, Michael Staff, Stefanie Stanisz, Jennifer Steers, Bill and Ann Stoughton **T** Christian Taal, David Thomas, Anne Timonen **V** Jeroen van der Weegen, Erwin van Engelen, Francis van Haeften, Christiaan van Oorshot, Saskia Vanloenen, Marc Vila **W** Adrian Wakenshaw, David Williams, Andrea Willis, Alethea Wood

Index

INDEX

000 Map pages
000 Photograph pages

INDEX

INDEX

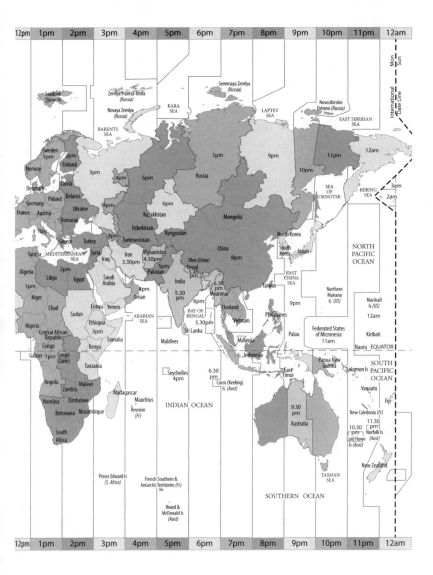

MAP LEGEND

ROUTES

Tollway	Mall/Steps
Freeway	Tunnel
Primary	Pedestrian Overpass
Secondary	Walking Tour
Tertiary	Walking Tour Detour
Lane	Walking Trail
Under Construction	Walking Path
Unsealed Road	Track
One-Way Street	

TRANSPORT

Ferry	Rail
Metro	Rail (Underground)
Bus Route	Tram

HYDROGRAPHY

River, Creek	Canal
Intermittent River	Water
Swamp	Lake (Dry)

BOUNDARIES

International	Regional, Suburb
State, Provincial	Ancient Wall
Marine Park	Cliff

AREA FEATURES

Airport	Land
Area of Interest	Mall
Beach, Desert	Market
Building	Park
Campus	Reservation
Cemetery, Christian	Rocks
Cemetery, Other	Sports
Forest	Urban

POPULATION

CAPITAL (NATIONAL)	CAPITAL (STATE)
Large City	Medium City
Small City	Town, Village

SYMBOLS

Sights/Activities
- Beach
- Castle, Fortress
- Christian
- Monument
- Museum, Gallery
- Point of Interest
- Pool
- Pub/Bar
- Ruin
- Zoo, Bird Sanctuary

Eating
- Eating

Drinking
- Drinking
- Café

Entertainment
- Entertainment

Shopping
- Shopping

Sleeping
- Sleeping
- Camping

Transport
- Airport, Airfield
- Border Crossing
- Bus Station
- Cycling, Bicycle Path
- General Transport
- Parking Area
- Petrol Station
- Taxi Rank

Information
- Bank, ATM
- Embassy/Consulate
- Hospital, Medical
- Information
- Internet Facilities
- Police Station
- Post Office, GPO
- Telephone
- Toilets

Geographic
- Lighthouse
- Lookout
- Mountain, Volcano
- National Park
- Pass, Canyon
- Picnic Area
- River Flow
- Shelter, Hut

LONELY PLANET OFFICES

Australia
Head Office
Locked Bag 1, Footscray, Victoria 3011
☎ 03 8379 8000, fax 03 8379 8111
talk2us@lonelyplanet.com.au

USA
150 Linden St, Oakland, CA 94607
☎ 510 893 8555, toll free 800 275 8555
fax 510 893 8572
info@lonelyplanet.com

UK
72–82 Rosebery Ave,
Clerkenwell, London EC1R 4RW
☎ 020 7841 9000, fax 020 7841 9001
go@lonelyplanet.co.uk

Published by Lonely Planet Publications Pty Ltd
ABN 36 005 607 983

© Lonely Planet Publications Pty Ltd 2007

© photographers as indicated 2007

Cover photograph: Women wearing traditional clogs, Alkmaar cheese market, Noord Holland: Stuart Dee/Getty Images. Many of the images in this guide are available for licensing from Lonely Planet Images: www.lonelyplanetimages.com.

Printed through The Bookmaker International Ltd
Printed in China